THE PENGUIN CLASSICS
FOUNDER EDITOR (1944–64): E. V. RIEU
Editor: Betty Radice

Few facts are known about the life of HERODOTUS, although his personality is reflected clearly in his writing. He was born between 490 and 480 B.C. at Halicarnassus on the south-west coast of Asia Minor. As a young man he travelled widely – in Egypt, in Africa, and in other parts of the Greek world. He knew Athens well, and is said to have given a public reading of part of his History there in 446 and to have been awarded ten talents. Herodotus has been called by Cicero and others 'the Father of History'. In later life he became a citizen of Thuria in Italy, where he expanded and revised his History. He died in 425 B.C.

AUBREY DE SÉLINCOURT, scholar and translator, translated Livy's *The Early History of Rome* (Books I–IV) and *The War with Hannibal* (Books XXI–XXX), *The Histories* of Herodotus and *The Life of Alexander the Great* by Arrian, all for the Penguin Classics. He was born in 1896 and educated at Rugby, and University College, Oxford. A schoolmaster of genius for twenty-six years, he retired in 1947 to the Isle of Wight where he lived until his death in 1962.

A. R. BURN was born in 1902, and educated at Uppingham School and Christ Church, Oxford. His publications include *The World of Hesiod* (1936), *The Lyric Age of Greece* (1960), *Persia and the Greeks* (1962), and the *Pelican History of Greece* (1966). A. R. Burn was Reader in Ancient History at Glasgow University until his retirement in 1969.

HERODOTUS
THE HISTORIES

Translated by Aubrey de Sélincourt

Revised, with an introduction
and notes by A. R. Burn

PENGUIN BOOKS

Penguin Books Ltd, Harmondsworth, Middlesex, England
Penguin Books, 625 Madison Avenue, New York, New York 10022, U.S.A.
Penguin Books Australia Ltd, Ringwood, Victoria, Australia
Penguin Books Canada Ltd, 41 Steelcase Road West, Markham, Ontario, Canada
Penguin Books (N.Z.) Ltd, 182–190 Wairau Road, Auckland 10, New Zealand

—

This translation was first published 1954
Reprinted 1955, 1959, 1960, 1961, 1963, 1964
Reprinted with an index, 1965, 1966, 1968, 1971
Revised edition with new introducton, 1972
Reprinted 1973, 1974, 1975, 1976 (twice)

—

Copyright © the Estate of Aubrey de Sélincourt, 1954
Copyright © A. R. Burn, 1972

—

Made and printed in Great Britain
by Richard Clay (The Chaucer Press) Ltd,
Bungay, Suffolk
Set in Monotype Bembo

CONTENTS

INTRODUCTION

I. HERODOTUS IN HIS OWN WORDS

HERODOTUS OF HALICARNASSUS: RESEARCHES. These words, visible when the papyrus was rolled up, served the purpose of those on our book-covers. 'Research', or 'inquiry', a word often used in the text, is in Greek *historia*; and its specialized meaning of *history* was born there. Herodotus goes on, in the manner of an expansive early-modern title-page, to state his purpose: 'that the great deeds of men may not be forgotten . . . whether Greeks or foreigners: and especially, the causes of the war between them'.

The book itself contains the chief information that we have about its author. His culminating story of the great invasion of 480–479 B.C. comes from men with whom he had talked; he never claims to remember any incident in it personally; and in agreement with this, later Greeks dated his birth in 484. He often has occasion to refer to later events; and the four latest, all in the last four books, refer to the first years of the Peloponnesian War, 431–430 (VI, 91; VII, 133 and 233; IX, 73). Perhaps soon after that, then, Herodotus died.

Halicarnassus lies on a rocky bay on the southern Aegean coast of Asia Minor. To be born there and then, or about then, was to be born under the great and, when opposed, ruthless, but not ignoble, Persian Empire. Childhood there may have helped to foster the breadth of vision with which Herodotus surveys the great conflict from both sides. It may even have facilitated his travels within the Empire: to Egypt after the rebellion of 459–454, when he saw the bones of those killed in the initial Egyptian victory still lying in the sand of what is now the Canal Zone (II, 12); thence to Tyre (II, 49) and very likely from there to Babylon, by way of the Euphrates with its round cargo-

boats (I, 194). A reminiscence of Babylonia when he was in Egypt
(II, 150) may imply a second Egyptian trip. He implies that he has
talked with many Egyptians, as well as Persians (I, 1 and elsewhere),
Babylonians and others; though he does not seem to have learned any
language but his own, and his excursions into foreign etymology (e.g
in I, 139; VI, 98) are disastrous. And he remains Halicarnassian enough,
though he may never have lived there after early youth, to take pride
in the stories of his city's queen Artemisia, who commanded her own
ships under Xerxes and, we are assured (no doubt from local patriotic
legend) stood high in his confidence (VIII, 68, 87 f., 98, 103 ff.).

His other great foreign travels, to the Black Sea and far up some of
its rivers[1] (IV, 18–117), are not dated by reference to any event; but in
IV, 76, he quotes information from 'Tymnes, the agent' (in the important Greek colony of Olbia, near modern Odessa?) 'of Ariapeithes'. Ariapeithes, mentioned as well-known, was the son and successor
of Idanthyrsos, the king of the Scythian nomads, who fought the
Persians about 512; and since Ariapeithes was murdered by a neighbouring king, presumably not in extreme old age, he is not likely to
have reigned much after, say, 460. These travels, perhaps with Greek
trading vessels, may then have taken place when Herodotus was still
young and living, as we shall see, at Samos.

For Samos he shows affection and partiality (see especially III, 39–62);
but more particularly, in the Greek world, he fell under the spell of
Periclean Athens. He knows the topography of the city well (VI, 137;
VIII, 52–5). Some odd passages in Sophocles' extant plays even seem
as if borrowed from his history.[2] He has many stories of the great
Athenian Alcmeonid family, to which Pericles' mother belonged;
defends them (more vigorously than convincingly) against charges of
collaboration with Persia or with the Peisistratid despotism; and in

1. E.g. (IV, 52 and 81) to the place called Sacred Ways, Exampaeus – some
have suggested a German name Hexenpfad – where he speaks of seeing a
huge bronze vessel; we are reminded of the now famous Vix Crater, at the
source of the Seine.

2. *Antigone* (produced in spring, 441) 950 ff.; cf. Herodotus, III, 119, where
likewise a woman prefers her unreplaceable brother to a replaceable son or
husband; *Oedipus at Colonus*, 337 ff. on 'customs of Egypt' (cf. Herodotus,
II, 35); less certainly, the Oedipodean dream, in *King Oedipus*, 981 (cf. Herodotus, VI, 107).

particular, traces the descent of Pericles himself (VI, 131). His praise of democracy, as responsible for the vigour of Athens (V, 78), is his most explicit statement of a political preference; and in inter-state politics he no less explicitly takes sides on a controversial issue, when he states a view which, he says, 'I know will be unpopular', that Athenian resolution saved Greece from Persian conquest. It is reasonable to infer that, like many other intellectuals of his time, he had migrated to the imperial city, and was known to its leading men.

Such are the inferences that we can, without straining, draw from Herodotus' book. More certainly it reveals, without any selfconciousness, a personality of great charm and a Shakespearean width of interest in humanity. The man who collected all that information and could not bear to let it die with him was a great lover of his kind; and the man who traversed those distances, largely on foot, sometimes riding, certainly in a great variety of engineless wooden boats, was also tough. How he financed his travels he does not reveal. Very likely he traded, as did another wise man, according to the Aristotelian *Athenian Constitution* – Solon. Certainly a man so rich in stories of foreign parts would never have lacked, in the ancient or indeed the modern Near East, for spontaneous hospitality. Everywhere he went, he fell into conversation, seeking out when necessary the most promising sources of information, such as the priests, whom he repeatedly mentions, in Egypt. It has been doubted whether a casual stranger would have penetrated further than Egyptian vergers and tourist-guides; but when the stranger was Herodotus, we may take leave to doubt the doubters. How he communicated, since, as we saw, he does not appear to have been a linguist, is another mystery; but he obviously did, though sometimes imperfectly, as when he understood the Persian god Mithra to be feminine (I, 131). It looks rather as if, with the rise in Greek prestige consequent on the repulse of Xerxes, and with the ubiquity of Greek traders and other travellers, which he mentions in Egypt, there was always someone who could make do in Greek, as there is nowadays in English. Certainly this would be true all round the Mediterranean; and when he quotes, for instance, 'the Cretans' and 'the Carians', *tout court*, for their different accounts of Carian origins (I, 171), and remembers the explicit and dogmatic versions of history that one may still pick up in modern Greek boats and taverns –

we may suspect that Herodotus picked up a good deal in the same way. He certainly did not understand the wide difference between popular tradition and history that would satisfy a modern western professor; nor yet how often, even in dealing with a recent incident, an eye-witness account may be contradicted by another eye-witness account. Thucydides, half a generation younger, and so just the right age to learn from his great predecessor, did understand, and is rather hard on Herodotus on the strength of it; but one has to make one's mistakes in order to make progress. Herodotus was a great pioneer; and if what 'the Carians' and 'the Cretans' said about Carian origins – or what he understood Egyptian priests to be telling him about *their* history – cannot both be the whole truth, *the fact that these stories were current* is, after all, itself a *historical* fact. The strange facts that Herodotus reports at second hand, about the customs of barbarian tribes, from north Africa to south Russia and Afghanistan, used also, in early modern times, to be among the features that caused him to be called the father of lies rather than of history; but since, during the nineteenth century, prac-tically all of them have been found to be paralleled in widely different parts of the world, these too have been realized to be significant facts about man in society. The Father of History is also the father of com-parative anthropology. Moreover the charm of his story, which is the charm of its author, produced the effect that, even when later classical authors or early moderns censured him as over-credulous or even an outright liar, they never stopped reading him; nor did the ancient world permit his work to be lost. That charm never fails. One thinks of him as 'old Herodotus'; but that is only because he tells us things. In fact, if he was born *c.* 484 and died soon after 430, he never reached sixty; and the great travels were a young man's adventures. He is 'old' (not only ancient) as our beloved and entertaining travelling com-panion. Everybody who reads his book feels to him as a friend.

2. THE BIOGRAPHICAL TRADITION ABOUT HERODOTUS

That we can thus know Herodotus from his own work is just as well; for the biographical tradition about him is weak. As with many great men of antiquity, no one bothered to write about him while everyone remembered him; and after that, it was too late. Still, there is something; though, as will be seen, we have to use it with reserve.

Our only information on his family comes actually from a book compiled much nearer our own times than his; a Byzantine dictionary of proper names and rare words, bearing the name of Suidas, or, as some scholars think, rather a title, *Suda*, 'the Stronghold'. This mentions events as late as the eleventh century A.D.; but even so, it was compiled before the major losses of ancient literature that had survived so far, in the devastations of Constantinople by the Fourth Crusade in 1204 and the Turks in 1453. Its entry, *Herodotus*, describes him as of a prominent family in Halicarnassus, and going into exile at Samos 'because of the despot Lygdamis' (son of Pisindelis, son of the queen Artemisia). Another entry, *Panyassis* (a Carian name), describes this man, an epic poet, as a relative of Herodotus and as being put to death by the tyrant. Later, we are told, Herodotus returned to Halicarnassus and took part in expelling the dynasts, but, finding himself unpopular (a thing which might happen to anyone in the course of Greek politics – but why in this case we are not told), left and took part in the colonization of Thuria in south Italy (a city founded by Athens, but admitting colonists from all Greece, in 443, soon after the peace between Athens and Sparta of 445). All this may well be true; but reserve is necessary. 'Suidas' warns us, for instance, that Panyassis' relationship to Herodotus and the names of his parents were variously given by different writers; and Suidas himself assures us that it was in Samos that the historian learned his Ionic dialect. This is wrong; for two inscriptions from Halicarnassus, of this very period, show that that city, though reckoned a settlement of Dorians from the Peloponnese, used Ionic even in official documents. Carian names, including Panyassis as that of two different people, also appear beside Greek names, even in the same families; in short, the city was a mixed community; Herodotus himself tells us that it was excluded, after a quarrel, from the religious meetings and games of the neighbouring Dorian cities (I, 144); though it was among the many eastward-trading cities which united for worship and local government at the treaty-port of Naucratis in Egypt before the Persian conquest (II, 178). The light shed upon Herodotus' Greco-Asian background is of much interest.

The more important of the two inscriptions[1] shows Lygdamis the dynast taking part, together with a town-meeting of the citizens (so his power is not unlimited), to agree on a resolution forbidding legal claims to real property by persons other than the occupiers after the lapse of eighteen months; a measure which makes sense, as an attempt to reach a permanent settlement after some troubles in which property will have changed hands in a revolutionary manner. We cannot date it exactly; but it is consistent with the possibility that when Herodotus was a young man, a faction, including members of his family, attempted unsuccessfully to liberate the city from its pro-Persian dynasty. Then, before 454, liberation is successfully accomplished, and takes the city into alliance with Athens; Halicarnassus appears in the first Tribute-List of Athens' Delian League, without the name of Lygdamis; whereas some other Carian dynasts are named in those lists.

After his eastern travels and, we may suppose, some writing, some public readings of his work at festival gatherings (a regular method of 'publication' in the ancient world), some fame, and some residence at Athens, comes the migration to Thuria (often, though less correctly, called by the name of its people, Thurii). Many writers, including Aristotle, quote the name on his 'title-page' as 'Herodotus the Thurian'; but it is 'the Halicarnassian' in all our manuscripts. That he took part in this Athenian-backed enterprise (a re-foundation of luxurious Sybaris, destroyed by its sister-city Croton under the 'puritan' Pythagoreans sixty-six years before) is intelligible as the result of a great disappointment. In 451, Athens had reversed her policy, in force since the time of the wise Solon, of easy naturalization. Immigrants had no doubt been pouring in, since Athens became an imperial city; and the Demos was no longer willing to share and dilute its privileges. Thenceforth it required an 'act of Parliament', a vote of a well-attended meeting of the Assembly, confirmed at another, to make a foreigner a citizen. It became a rare honour; and Herodotus' friends were unable to win it for him. At Thuria, now in his forties, with the leisure which landed property will have given him, he probably did much writing-up of his travel-notes and historical material collected earlier. But then – another sorrow – feelings towards Athens at Thuria cooled. Athens'

1. It is No. 32 in the *Selection of Greek Historical Inscriptions*, ed. Meiggs and Lewis (O.U.P., 1969); No. 25 in the earlier edition, ed. Tod (1933).

western imperial dreams, at least after about 435, became too obvious; and presently the Thurians disclaimed any 'special connection'. The sections on Greek Italy and Sicily in the *History* are relatively slight, and there are few western geographical touches – though one, in IV, 99, shows him very clearly writing for a western audience. (He refers to south-east Italy for a parallel, while explaining the peculiarities of the Crimea and its relation to the mainland.) Herodotus is generally thought to have returned to Athens, on account of the allusions, mentioned above, to events of the years 431–430 – events not of great importance, though of interest in relation to Herodotus' main history, but such as he would be much more likely to hear of if on the spot.

The allusions, as we saw, end about 430; the second year of the great war, and the first (out of four in all) of the great plague. Herodotus may, as Mr Enoch Powell suggested, have died of it, and at Athens. No ancient writer says so; but in view of the scantiness of the whole tradition, absence of evidence is no negative proof. But another Byzantine, Stephanus, who compiled a geographical gazetteer containing some literary allusions, says of Thuria that there was a tomb in the market-place – where only a very distinguished citizen would be buried – with his epitaph:

> Herodotus the son of Lyxes here
> Lies; in Ionic history without peer;
> A Dorian born, who fled from slander's brand
> And made in Thuria his new native land.

It could be a fake, much later, when the Thurians had had time to realize that he *was* much their most famous citizen – possibly even transhuming the bones from some other grave bearing the name Herodotus; for that name, 'Gift of Hera', the queen of the gods, was a common one. It could also, like scores of pseudo-epitaphs in the *Greek Anthology*, be purely literary composition, known to Stephanus or a predecessor from his reading. But it may also be genuine. Herodotus may have fled to escape the plague at Athens (wherefore no more allusions to events there) and died still a property-owner in the colony.

Bearing in mind, then, that practically every detail is uncertain, we may hazard the following biography:

484: Herodotus born in Halicarnassus.

As a boy, listens to men who had sailed under Artemisia, to Carians who had fought against and under Persia; perhaps to Scylax of Caryanda (IV, 44).

c. 464? Uprising against Artemisia's grandson Lygdamis, who recovers control; death of Herodotus' kinsman Panyassis; Herodotus flees to Samos.

? Voyage to the Black Sea.

Before 454: takes part in liberating Halicarnassus.

After 454: travels in Egypt, thence to Tyre, perhaps down Euphrates to Babylon. Finds himself unpopular in Halicarnassus (probably for political reasons); migrates to Athens; but the law of 451 prevents him from becoming an Athenian citizen. Perhaps declaims parts of his work at Athens and at Olympia.

443 (or after): joins the colony at Thuria.

431–30: revisits Athens.

? Dies in Thuria; later honoured with a mausoleum in the market-place.

There is a good deal more in the tradition about Herodotus; but it concerns his book rather than his life and movements. The recensions of Bishop Eusebius' great chronological work date his public readings at Athens c. 446–5, probably enough; and Plutarch quotes a fourth-century Athenian historian as saying that the Athenians voted him ten talents – 60,000 drachmas or good day-wages, a fortune – for his tributes to them, on the proposal of Anytos. But if this is the Anytos famous for the prosecution of Socrates in 399 – the only well-known man of his name – he would have been much too young. It looks as if Diyllos, Plutarch's source, had been researching in archives, on stone or in the public record-office, as men were beginning to do in that century, and had found a decree rewarding *a* Herodotus, but not ours – probably for political services, when Athens was recovering after the Peloponnesian War. The chronological impossibility could easily escape the notice of a researcher, because of the lack of any such convenient dating system as we have in our B.C. and A.D. Plutarch goes on to allege that Herodotus was hostile to Thebes (which he is) because the Thebans had refused him permission to open a school there; and Dio the Golden-Tongued (Dio Chrysostom), a popular lecturer under the Roman empire, even says that he rewrote his account of the Corinthians' behaviour at Salamis (VIII, 94), making it sound worse, because the Corinthians had refused to pay him. This at least is a silly slander; for Herodotus there quotes the Athenian story that the Corinthians fled, only to add that other Greeks, as well as the Corinthians, denied it. Since he wrote the story of the war under strong Athenian influence (see below, pp. 31 f.), it is to his credit that he could, at least occasionally, doubt what his friends told him.

Plutarch's allegation of bias, with much more to the same effect, comes in an essay On the Malignity (better, Meanness) of Herodotus, in which, amid much tedious declamation, he does quote some contemporary poetry and early prose writing which, at a few points, usefully corrects or supplements him. It has been doubted whether the essay is really by Plutarch, because, in the famous Lives, Plutarch uses Herodotus without apparent misgiving. But this is unnecessary. Plutarch wrote the Lives late in life, after the bulk of his miscellaneous work, and had had time to come round to a more balanced view. The fact about this earlier essay is that Plutarch disliked Herodotus at first sight, especially because of his account of the behaviour of Boeotian Thebes (Plutarch was a Boeotian), and generally because he failed to justify the later 'vulgate' legend of the Great War, which Plutarch had absorbed at school; a fairly revolting product of patriotic classroom history, which turned it into a straight black-and-white struggle of Goodies and Baddies. Herodotus' Greeks – even those who fought the battles – are, as the reader will see, far from perfect, and his Persians far from all black; which makes him, for Plutarch, pro-barbarian or pro-Persian, but for us testifies to his sincere attempt at honesty and fairness.

Herodotus inevitably does have his biases; but to discuss them, and his sources, and how far he was at the mercy of his sources; in short how we should criticize and how far we may believe him, will come better after a general survey of the work and its plan, including a detailed table of its contents.

3. THE LIFE WORK

Herodotus' great life-work, as we have it, is carefully and elaborately planned. Starting with Greece and its relations with the east in the generation of Cyrus, the founder of Persian power, it builds up steadily through sixty-six years to the great invasion of 480, which Greeks at once recognized as an axial point in their history. It is still recognized (though its importance *can* be exaggerated) as a vital point in the history of western civilization. It is important to grasp the plan; for the forest of Herodotus' knowledge contains so many fascinating trees that it is easy to lose sight of the wood.

Herodotus knew that the best works of literary art *have* a plan. He knew it from Homer, whose *Iliad* and *Odyssey* both start, as Roman Horace said, by plunging us *in medias res*. They get through their main narratives in a few weeks, while telling us all that the poet thinks worthwhile about earlier events at suitable points. Lesser poets, the authors of sequels to the *Iliad* and (conspicuously) of the *Cyprian Verses*, a prelude to it, had failed to grasp the importance of this. They went back to chronicle form, starting at the beginning and losing unity of structure as the story rolls on. (Herodotus, we may notice, did not believe that the *Cypria* could be by the great man (II, 117); whereas the uncritical in his day ascribed to 'Homer' the entire epic corpus.)

Like Homer, he faced – and solved – a problem. He knew, and wanted to tell, an enormous number of things: 'that the doings of men may not be forgotten'. About Egypt, about Babylonia (which he calls Assyria; meaning the whole of the late Assyrian empire); about the northern nomads, about lake-dwellers in Europe; about the sexual and other practices of north-African and Caucasian barbarians, about warriors from the Sudan with war-paint and stone arrow-heads and central Asians who still fought with bronze. Other men had already written detailed geographical works with history thrown in; notably Hecataeus of Miletus, writer and statesman (see below, p. 24); but Herodotus reckoned he could do better than that. As Homer gets his story started and then introduces, in Book II, his List of the Contingents, so Herodotus would tell his story of two generations, four Persian reigns, introducing and taking in the history of other peoples as they came into the story; pretty well everyone came in sooner or later. As he says in IV, 30 (p.280 of this edition), 'Digressions are part of my plan'. Some of the digressions are certainly enormous; the largest, Book II, being a whole geography, social anthropology and history of Egypt, inserted between the Persian kings decision to conquer that country and the conquest itself.

The division into books, it must be noted, is not Herodotus' own; it was made for convenience, probably by the librarians of Alexandria after 280 B.C., perhaps originally into eight; but V and VI, which form a single section and have no break between them, were found inconveniently large for a roll. Before 99 B.C. someone had had the idea of attaching to the nine books the names of the Muses, which appear in our manuscripts. The divisions are usually sensible and often at obvious points, though between VII and VIII a better point would have been before VII, 201, giving books of more even size and avoiding a division between Thermopylae and the contemporary naval operations.

4. THE PLAN OF THE WORK

Herodotus deliberately introduces digressions, 'that notable achievements may not be forgotten'; but never loses sight of his theme: Greece and the East, 'and especially the causes of their conflict'. Peoples are introduced in detail, as they come into the story; and from time to time Herodotus points a moral. This may be shown by a table of contents, citing some of the chief digressions. The introductory part requires the most detailed treatment. The division into Books, it will be remembered, is not Herodotus' own.

Part I: The Rise of the Persian Empire (to c. 510 B.C.): Books I to V, 27

I, 1–5: The Subject: East *versus* West. 6–94: LYDIA TO THE PERSIAN CONQUEST (28–45: *a moral*: What is happiness? Croesus' pride and nemesis. 56–68: *The Greeks*: Ethnology; Athens (59 ff.), Sparta (65 ff.) in Cyrus' time). 95–216: CYRUS AND ASIA (95–106: Assyria and the Medes. 107–130: the Cyrus legend. 131–40: *The Persians*: religion and customs. 141–76: The Asian Greeks and their neighbours; Persian conquest. 177–200: Babylon; Persian conquest. 201–16: the Caspian and beyond; Cyrus' failure and death.)

II to III, 66: CAMBYSES AND EGYPT. Book II, Egypt: 2–34, geography and anthropology; 99–182, history; Book III, 1–15, Persian conquest. 16–38: *Cambyses' failures* beyond Egypt, atrocities and madness; *a moral*: Law is King (38). 39–60: contemporary Greece, especially Samos; *a moral*: Polycrates' greatness and nemesis. 61 ff.: the Magian conspiracy and death of Cambyses.

III, 67, to V, 27: DARIUS; THE EMPIRE, THE MEDITERRANEAN AND EUROPE (67–79: conspiracy of the Seven Persians. 80–82: *dialogue on government*. 83 ff.: King Darius. 89–97: *the Satrapies and their tribute*. 98–117: marvels of distant lands). 120–49: DARIUS AND THE WEST (120 ff.: end of Polycrates. 126 ff.: Darius recovers Asia Minor. 134 ff.: reconnaissance in the Mediterranean. 139 ff.: capture of Samos. 150 ff.: revolt of Babylon).

IV, 1–143: SCYTHIA (1–82, geography and ethnology; 83 ff., *Darius' failure*). 145–205: North Africa (145–67: the Greeks in Cyrenaica. 168–99: tribes of north-west Africa; 200–205: Persian conquest of Cyrenaica).

V, 1–27: Ethnology of the Balkans and beyond; Persian conquest of north Aegean coast and suppression of Greek revolt in the Straits region. A short period of peace (28, 1).

Part II: Greece and the Persian Wars: Books V (28) to IX. (500–479 B.C.)

V, 28, to VI, 42: THE IONIAN REVOLT: its origins, suppression and settlement (28 ff.: Persian failure at Naxos; 38–51: Sparta, and 55–96: Athens, taken up from Book I; between them, 52–4: Persia's Royal Road).

VI, 43 ff.: RENEWED PERSIAN ADVANCE INTO EUROPE and (48) formal demand for submission of the Greek states. 49–93: Sparta, Athens and Aegina. 94–120: seaborne invasion and Battle of *Marathon*. 121–40: Factions at Athens; tales of the Alcmaeonidae (taken up from Books I and V, above) and their rivals, the family of Miltiades (taken up from VI, 34–41, 103–4).

[Conspicuous absence of any treatment of Greek history between 489 and 481]

VII to IX: THE GREAT INVASION OF XERXES

VII, 1–18: the decision (1, revolt of Egypt; 4, death of Darius; 7, Egypt subdued; 10, a warning on the *envy of heaven*). 19–25: preparations. 26–138: the advance into Europe (49–50, the problem of harbours and supplies; 60–99, *the army and fleet*). 138–71: not all Greece unites (153–68, *Sicily and Carthage*). 172–4: Thessaly lost.

VII, 175, to VIII, 26: THERMOPYLAE AND ARTEMISIUM (VII, 188 ff., VIII 12 f., storm damage to the Persian fleet). VIII, 27–99: advance to Athens; battle of *Salamis* (43–8, 72–3, ethnology of the allied Greeks). 100–144: withdrawal of Xerxes and of the fleet; Mardonius stays in Greece; diplomacy (winter 480–479).

IX: The operations of 479 (1–89); Mardonius reoccupies Athens; campaign and battle of *Plataea*. 90–122: battle of *Mycale* and new revolt in Ionia (107–16, Persian demoralization and atrocities; 122, a concluding moral).

5. HOW WAS IT COMPOSED?

Endless and not very profitable discussion has gone on as to the order in which the different sections of this life-work were composed, and whether Herodotus meant to continue further. The book does have a plan, as our summary shows; and if the ending is by modern standards rather abrupt, rather quiet, that is in accordance with Greek practice in the great works which our author knew, from the *Iliad* and *Odyssey* to Attic tragedy. Planning is evident in the way in which, for instance, the Athenian and Spartan history in Book V picks up the thread from Book I, and in many promises to give further information later on a topic briefly mentioned, most of which are faithfully and efficiently carried out. There are in fact just three famous unfulfilled promises:

I, 106, on how the Medes took Nineveh;

I, 184, to give an account of 'many kings of Babylon ... in the Assyrian story' – a 'story' (*logoi*, plural) of which he has actually given us only a short section (I, 192–200) on Babylonian manners and customs;

VII, 213, relatively unimportant, on the murder of the betrayer of Thermopylae in a private feud.

Now this last *could* have come in a further book on the operations of 478 in northern Greece and the Bosphorus, including the disgrace of both the victors of 479, Leotychides and Pausanias, which he mentions (VI, 72; VIII, 3) – but *without* any such promises. This is probably significant.

The loss of the 'Assyrian *story*' on the other hand is a great pity. Our author and traveller must have had many interesting things to say, and (surely?) notes; though Myres believed that he took no notes, even in Egypt, but relied on his memory.[1] Powell believes that he suppressed the Assyrian history, as being simply too long, and such as to unbalance the narrative;[2] but this surely is not like our author as he reveals himself, with his concern that what he knew about 'the great deeds of men' should 'not be forgotten'. On the other hand, there are traces of Herodotus the artist confronting problems of balance and of where best to fit things in; e.g., his Libyan *logoi* (IV, 145 to end) make an awkward break where they are, between the Scythian story and its immediate sequel – including even the rewards for good service on the Danube (V, 1–27); and they *could* have been brought in, if not in the middle of the Egyptian story, where reference is actually made to them (II, 161), then after the conquest of Egypt, when, in III, 13 and 17–19, Cambyses' western designs and the surrender of Greek Cyrenaica are mentioned. Why not there? Presumably from a feeling that the huge Egyptian digression ought not to be made any longer; whereas by putting the Cyrenian and Libyan *logoi* after Scythia Herodotus provided *two* blocks of digression, on an ancient civilization and on the outer barbarian world, of evenly balanced length. We may be loth to believe that he did not intend to push in the promised Assyrian *logoi* somewhere, in connection with either Cyrus' or Darius' capture of Babylon; but if he did intend to, he was overtaken by death before he had done it, and whatever notes he left failed to make a deep enough impression on his heirs (whoever they were) to survive.

As to the order of composition, such a life-work – huge indeed, when we remember that it had all to be written with reed pens, papy-

1. *Herodotus, Father of History* (O.U.P., 1953), p. 153, citing the phrase 'as I well remember' from II, 125; but this does not prove his point.
2. *The History of Herodotus* (C.U.P., 1939), pp. 19 ff., after de Sanctis in *Riv. fil. cl.* (1926).

rus paper and ink of lamp-black; materials which we should find intolerably awkward – clearly must have taken shape over many years; and the rearrangement of sections, so long as the sheets were not yet gummed together to make a roll (the equivalent of our paging and binding), would be relatively easy. There have been many theories on the subject, among which may be mentioned that of R.W. Macan in his voluminous, elegantly written, sometimes a little facile *Commentary* on Books VII to IX (O.U.P., 1908), heartily approved by J.B. Bury in *The Ancient Greek Historians* (Harvard lectures, in the same year). This is that the books on the invasion of Xerxes, with their elaborate and balanced speeches, leisurely account of the huge 'build-up'. and catalogue of the forces (in much the same relative position as that in the *Iliad*) were originally written as a free-standing work, revised, with addition of the references to later incidents, later. This would account for the weak and unsatisfactory treatment of relevant Greek history between Marathon and 481: the renewal of war between Athens and Aegina after the fall of Cleomenes, the rise of Themistocles and building of the great Athenian navy, all of which are either reserved for a 'flash-back' in VII, 144, or placed (almost certainly *mis*placed) before Marathon (see note on the plan of the work, above); as also to the ways in which men, peoples and incidents previously mentioned are formally introduced, often less well than they now are in earlier books: e.g. the Greeks, VIII, 43–4, cf. I, 56–8; Sophanes, IX, 75, cf. VI, 92. However, this theory is so far from having convinced Powell, for one, that he (*op. cit.*), with a detailed analysis of Herodotus' cross-references, fulfilled promises, and some passages which, Powell argues, are untrue or inappropriate where they stand, concludes that the historian began by intending a straight history of Persia, and changed only late in life to the plan of a pro-Athenian history of the invasion and what led up to it. That intelligent men after detailed study can reach such diametrically opposite conclusions is enough to convince the present writer that the evidence is simply insufficient for proof; though he personally inclines to the Macan–Bury view. The interested reader can derive much amusement from making his own detailed study of the text with an eye to these problems; though it is unlikely, after so much debate, that any more conclusive results are to be expected.

6. HERODOTUS' SOURCES

On the face of it, Herodotus collected nearly all his material orally; from men who had taken part in the war (chiefly as young soldiers; for the Greek generals were not young men, and were mostly dead before he came to Athens); from Athenian and Spartan family traditions, from priests and other men at Delphi or in Egypt who knew the stories about their monuments and dedications. Many monuments also bore inscriptions, which he could read if they were in Greek. He quotes, for instance, those at Thermopylae, showing incidentally that he was not the first to number Xerxes' army in millions, and is deceived by some forgeries at Thebes (V, 19ff.), ostensibly dating from the age of Oedipus (in which case they would have had to be in Mycenean). He says nothing about the great historical inscriptions of Darius at Behistun and elsewhere, and Darius' grim Median war, with which they deal in detail, has dropped out of sight, like the 'Assyrian story', except for one bare reference (I, 130). But – and it is one of the best pieces of evidence of his competence – he records correctly six of the seven names of the conspirators against the Magian king; and for the seventh, he gives a rather similar name (Aspathines, III, 70, for Ardomanes), and a name moreover which does appear on another of Darius' inscriptions (at Naksh-i-Rustem) as that of his 'quiver-bearer'. The error could even be a slip of memory by his Persian informant – perhaps Zopyrus, the son of the marshal Megabyzus, whose desertion to Athens is mentioned at the end of Book III. Whatever we are to make of the detailed story of the conspiracy, or of the speeches in conference at the beginning of VII, or, *a fortiori*, of what the queen (prompted by Democedes, from whom the story no doubt comes) said to Darius in bed (III, 134), it is evident that Herodotus did have serious Persian sources, and made good use of them.

But there had also been Greek prose-writers, both geographical and historical, before Herodotus; and it is a serious question, what use he made of *them*. German scholars, who invented the term 'source-criticism' and the method itself – a valuable method, if used with discretion – have sometimes pursued it to a point described by a great British scholar as amounting to the denial that any famous ancient historian ever did any work for himself; his apparent merits are always due to a great predecessor, whose importance or even existence has been unsuspected, until detected by the acumen of the writer of the thesis.[1] Herodotus has suffered much from strivers after originality;[2] but the question posed is a real one.

Prose literature in Greek begins in Ionia in the sixth century B.C.; the idea that 'simple speech', as Greeks called prose, could *be* literature being introduced like so many starting-points for Greek art and thought, no doubt from the east, where prose (including the Hebrew chronicles in their original form) had long existed. Dionysius of Halicarnassus, a good literary critic of the age of Augustus, gives the best list of Herodotus' lost predecessors and junior contemporaries – seven of the former and four of the latter, adding that there were 'many others'.[3] They wrote, he says, accounts of their own or other cities and peoples, Greek or foreign, publishing temple or civic records [laws, treaties, perhaps honorary decrees praising distinguished services?], along with traditions of the foundations of their cities, and popular legends, sometimes, he says, 'melodramatic and naive', all in a simple unadorned style, not without its charm. They sound, in short, not a little like Herodotus himself, who, his countryman says, in essentially the same genre but with larger plans and greater art, surpassed them all.

Here indeed is ample scope for playing the game of attributing as much as possible of Herodotus to predecessors; a game which should be all the easier for the fact that the surviving 'fragments' of most of

1. A. W. Gomme, in the Introduction to his *Commentary on Thucydides*, Vol. I (with reference to Plutarch). I use the word thesis advisedly; since the excesses of *Quellenkritik* are mainly due to the Ph.D. system, which makes a high salary depend on producing *original* work. In a field as well-trodden as that of classical literature, to require a young scholar to be original is as inhumane as requiring him to be a humorist, or a poet; a truly original theory has a high probability of being a perverse theory, and a branch of study that has not been well worked over is likely to be one that is not worth much attention. (This does not apply to archaeology, the chief growing-point of modern classical studies, nor, of course, to modern history or the natural sciences; though the danger exists in any study.)

2. For a summary of Herodotean scholarship through 150 years, see Myres, *op. cit.*, pp. 20–31.

3. In his *Essay on Thucydides*, §5; translated and discussed in Lionel Pearson's *Early Ionian Historians* (*O.U.P.*, 1939), pp. 3 ff.

these authors (i.e. quotations – sometimes as short as one rare word in a dictionary, or a place-name in a gazetteer) are scanty in the extreme. But putting a name to the 'great unknown', whom some scholars have been so anxious to detect behind Herodotus, proves not so easy after all. There is just one prose author whom he names – four times: Hecataeus of Miletus, traveller, geographer, and a senior statesman at the time of the Ionian revolt of 499–494, named with respect for his strategic acumen, but as a writer only to criticize him. To him we shall return. Plutarch *On the Meanness of Herodotus* twice quotes another of Dionysius' writers, Charon of Lampsacus, on the capture of Pactyas (Hdt. I, 158 ff.) and on the Eretrian aid to the Ionian revolt (V, 99); but both quotations seem to indicate a work of such brevity that it cannot have been a major source. With Plutarch's learning and animosity, if Herodotus had really had a major literary source it is strange that Plutarch does not mention him. Modern research is thrown back upon a certain Dionysius of Miletus, said by the eleventh-century Suidas (see p. 11) to have been a contemporary of Hecataeus and to have written a Persian history among other works. He is taken seriously even by Bury (*op. cit.*, pp. 22–34) and Myres (pp. 24, 72). But he is not among those named by Dionysius of Halicarnassus, nor indeed by anyone before the Byzantine era. Unlike any of the Halicarnassian's eleven he is not represented by a single quotation, except by one Byzantine annotator of Herodotus, who cites him for a variant (and inferior) spelling of the Persian name Patizeithes (Hdt. III, 61). On the whole, it seems most likely that his alleged work was a forgery (it would be far from being the only one produced in the age after Alexander) produced perhaps for amusement and perhaps also in the hope of selling it as a rarity to one of the great libraries. Pearson (*op. cit.*, p. 27) considers his very existence a matter of doubt.

No: the case for considering Herodotus to have owed much to any earlier historian, except perhaps Hecataeus, is ill-supported; and if he had been the kind of man to take pleasure in disguising his indebtedness, what is really surprising is that no one else appears to have taken pleasure in unmasking him. Later Greeks censure him for credulity; Plutarch, for failure to tell the edifying, patriotic story *and* for plagiarism; but no one names any other name. And it is not as if Herodotus was averse to naming writers; of poets, he names Homer (soundly doubting his authorship of parts of the epic cycle), Hesiod, Archilochus, Solon, Alcaeus, Sappho, Anacreon, Phrynichus the predecessor of Aeschylus and Aeschylus himself, Simonides and Pindar (for references, see Index); and he detects as forgeries the religious poems which claimed to be older than Homer (II, 53). If he had had good prose sources for the Persian wars, he would presumably have named them, if only when criticizing, as he names Hecataeus.

This is not to deny that he can ever have used *any* other prose authors. A possibility is his contemporary, according to Dionysius, Hellanicus of Lesbos, who may have invented the estimated 39-year average generation of the Spartan kings that gives the traditional dates: Heracles 1260 B.C., fall of Troy 1182 (Thucydides' round eighty years before the Dorian invasion, 1104 – sixteen generations before Xerxes' invasion – gives the 'vulgate' 1184). We notice that in Herodotus four reigns = 156 years both in Media (I, 106, 130) and among the ancestors of Croesus (I, 14–25); but Herodotus himself was not much interested in detailed chronology. An apparently obvious candidate as a source on Lydia is Xanthus, another contemporary according to Dionysius, and a Lydian himself; but he is quite definitely 'out'; for we have considerable extracts on Lydian history, drawn *probably* from him, in the works of Nicolaus of Damascus, court historian to Herod the Great; and they are quite different from Herodotus, and good enough (giving an *a priori* more convincing story of Gyges' conspiracy, for instance) for Herodotus to have used if he had known them.

Among sources that Herodotus may have used on Lydia is, curiously enough, drama: very oddly to our ideas; but apart from a tendency to rationalize, not systematically, the miraculous or otherwise supernatural, he never shows any sense of the profound difference between what is told and what happened. Stories for him do not seem to be more or less right, only right or wrong, and accordingly, drama was no less acceptable as a source than other poetry. It must have struck many readers how the story of Atys and the Boar (I, 34 ff.), with the vegetation-god of Asia Minor made into a son of the most famous Lydian king, conforms to the type of an Attic drama, culminating in Messenger's Speech and Funeral Procession; and in 1950 there was published an actual fragment, in a papyrus from Egypt, of such another drama on Lydian 'history': a short page of iambic dialogue from an account of the conspiracy of Gyges, conforming closely to Herodotus' story in I, 8 ff.[1] The possibility cannot be overlooked that a later tragedian dramatized Herodotus; but it seems less likely that a playwright would have followed so closely a text that was widely circulated than that Herodotus followed the story of an early tragedy, which probably was not.

Herodotus, then, used literary sources when available; he used everything that came to hand; but there is no satisfactory evidence of the existence of any significant prose source, except Hecataeus.

Hecataeus is named by Herodotus in II, 143, with a laugh at him for claiming to have a god for his sixteenth ancestor; in V, 36 and 125, as an elder statesman, giving excellent advice to the leaders of the Ionian revolt, which however was not taken; and in VI, 137, to quote (not definitely adopt) a complaint that he handled unfairly the story of Athenian dealings with the non-Greek Pelasgians in Attica (showing incidentally how seriously such quasi-historical myths were still taken). But how much did Herodotus *use* Hecataeus *without* naming him?

Unfortunately there is much doubt here too. Porphyry, a Pythagorean of the third century of our era,[2] said that Herodotus paraphrased much of Hecataeus on Egypt, citing specifically the sections on crocodile-hunting, the hippopotamus and the phoenix (II, 70, 71, 73); and he may well have him in mind when he mocks at geographers, unnamed, for their views of a perfectly circular earth surrounded by the stream of Ocean (as in Homer) and divided into continents of equal size. These are views attributed by other writers to Hecataeus, as may be seen in his fragments (numerous, though many are only placenames in Stephanus' gazetteer) in the collections of F. Jacoby or (older, not quite so complete, but easier to use) K. Müller. But some, including the great Dutch scholar Cobet and the learned Oxford co-author of a good commentary on Herodotus, Joseph Wells,[3] have believed that the later writers' quotations from 'Hecataeus' were themselves from a

1. E. Lobel in *Proc. Brit. Academy*, XXXV; D. L. Page, *A New Chapter in the History of Greek Tragedy* (C.U.P., 1951).

2. Quoted by Eusebius, *Preparation of the Gospel*, X, 3.

3. How and Wells, *Commentary* (O.U.P., 1912); Introduction (by Wells), which I have used in these pages, pp. 25 ff. A new Oxford commentary, destined to succeed this, is reported in preparation. Wells' views are argued more fully in the *Journal of Hellenic Studies*, XXIX.

forgery – as Callimachus, the Alexandrian poet and librarian, already suspected. There certainly were such forgeries (cf. above, p. 24); there is even a work extant under the name of Scylax of Caryanda, the explorer of 'an Indian river flowing east', with crocodiles in it, named in Hdt. IV, 44; it is quite certainly of the fourth century B.C., and (curiously) deals with the Mediterranean. If 'Hecataeus' was a forgery, the paraphrasing will simply have been the other way round.

On the whole the present writer, though he would be glad to spare Herodotus' reputation, inclines to believe that the Hecataeus fragments are genuine,[1] and therefore that Herodotus did use him extensively, in passages where he is not named. The ancients, it may be said in extenuation, did not share our rather pedantic views on plagiarism, i.e. on the sacredness of the exact form of words, or our more humane views on the duty of giving credit to our sources. But at the same time, we need not suspect Herodotus of using Hecataeus whenever he criticizes 'uncritical Greek views', even on Egypt. A good example of a 'silly Greek story' for which Hecataeus was not to blame is that in II, 45, on how the Egyptians, really totally averse to human sacrifice, tried with disastrous results to sacrifice Heracles; for this story (popular enough to be depicted more than once in extant Greek vase-painting) finds its best representation on a famous Caeretan *hydria*, painted when Hecataeus must have been very young. Here, *if* Herodotus used his predecessor, he will have been using Hecataeus' own correction of a 'silly story'; for Hecataeus' work is said to have opened with the majestic statement: 'I write what to me seems probable; for the tales told by the Greeks are both various and absurd.'

Here was, then, probably, a great predecessor, and Herodotus *may* have owed much to him. What must still be stressed is that there is no *other* for whom the evidence is comparable, and that Hecataeus him-

1. One reason is that the place-names in Stephanus show a much more extensive knowledge of the western Mediterranean than Herodotus has. Herodotus had not travelled there, partly for purely personal reasons; but also, it seems that Greek knowledge of the western shores, on which Hecataeus probably drew through sea-captains' accounts, had shrunk, through the development of Carthaginian and Etruscan hostility, provoked by Greek piracy, as we read in Hdt. I, 166. The lists of place-names, of which further knowledge had in many cases been lost, do not look like the remains of material that would interest a forger or his prospective readers.

self certainly did not cover the invasion of Xerxes. In the words of
Professor Momigliano:

We cannot say how much [Herodotus] owed to earlier writers. But
we know enough about [his] alleged predecessors – Cadmus of Miletus, Hecataeus, Dionysius of Miletus, Charon of Lampsacus, Xanthus
of Sardes – to state confidently that they did not do the work for him.
There was no Herodotus before Herodotus.[1]

7. WHAT CAN WE BELIEVE?

We have considered the evidence, never as ample as we could wish,
for Herodotus' life and travels, the composition of his work, the
sources available to him, and the question of his indebtedness to
earlier *historical* literary sources. It is time finally, since his is a work of
history, to consider the question of credibility; and for an *introducer* of
readers to such a work to come off the fence and speak in the first
person. He must not try to dictate views; which means that he must
not conceal the existence of views which he does not hold; but he
should suggest principles for the critical reader, especially the questions
which the reader should have always at the threshold of consciousness,
and be ready to ask when the moment occurs.

The question of the credibility of Herodotus breaks up into three:

(i) What were his sources?

(ii) Is he honest?

(iii) When we have very little other evidence, how far and by
what methods can we criticize Herodotus out of Herodotus' own
story, with any hope of getting closer to what really happened?

We have dealt briefly with (i), though it must reappear when we
come to (iii). (ii): 'Is he honest?' is not only a vital question, but one
to which answers, since scholars are to be found on both sides, are evidently subjective and personal. Ancient references to him continually
call him a 'liar'; apparently to confess to believing Herodotus, by and
large, was to invite being considered naïve; and as Thucydides, the
first of his critics, remarks in a different context (III, 82), the average

1. A. Momigliano, 'The Place of Herodotus in the History of Historio-
graphy', in *History*, XLIII (1958), p. 2.

middling-dishonest man would rather be suspected of dishonesty it-self – so long as it is *cute* dishonesty – than of that. But what was it that was disbelieved? Apparently his evidence, given as unqualified, direct statement, about remote times and places; the imaginary Persian speeches, or items from bazaar story-tellers, of which the most elab-orate is 'Rhampsinitus and the Thieves' (II, 121). That this sort of stuff should be served up as *history* perhaps really angered some of his earlier successors; whereas we can afford to laugh at it. Never having imag-ined that anyone would suspect *us* of taking this Arabian Nights story for history, we are grateful to Herodotus for preserving, not a history of the Pharaohs, but the *fact* that this and other stories were told.

'Liar', then, he was called for inviting other people to believe such stories – or the stories of gold-getting at the ends of the earth, either by Arimaspians from gryphons or by Indians from ants 'bigger than foxes'; which was unfair on any showing, considering that he expressly mentions his disbelief in one-eyed men (III, 116). He does, it is true, recount as fact the gold-digging-ant story (III, 102–5), and a remark-ably tall story it is, including the statement that some of the ants were in the Persian king's menagerie. Here he really has been imprudent in repeating such an extravagance, whether from somebody else's book or from an oral source, without his repeated disclaimer, 'It is my prin-ciple, that I ought to repeat what is said; but I am *not* bound always to believe it' (VII, 152, cf. II, 123, etc.); but clearly he could not be saying it all the time. It should be noted, too, that the words used of him are not always as rude as 'liar', to us, would suggest; Cicero's 'fabulosus' might better be translated 'story-teller', reminding us of Thucydides' announcement that *he*, for a change, is not going to indulge in such publicity-hunting (I, 22); and if the explicit word *pseustes* is often used, it might be noted that to this day in Greek *psemmata*, 'lies', is often less rude than it sounds to us, meaning rather 'Nonsense!' than 'That is said with intention to deceive.' We really ought to be grate-ful to Herodotus for his inclusiveness; for on two famous occasions statements which he explicitly says he disbelieves are important evi-dence for other men's real geographical information; i.e. in II, 22, that the Nile flood is caused by the melting of snow between two moun-tains in the far south ('How *could* there be snow in the hottest part of the world?'); and IV, 42, where Pharaoh Necoh's Phoenicians, who sailed round Africa, 'reported, what I cannot believe though somebody else may, that when sailing westward they had the sun on their right.'

Where his veracity, rather than his credulity, is in question is over what he says he has seen, and the extent of his travels; and here we have to notice that he tells us what he has *not* seen and where he has *not* been, too. Of Babylon he says that he was there, but did not see the great golden statue of Bel – it had been carried off by Xerxes (I, 183); but on central Asia, which follows directly, he *emphasizes* that his information is hearsay ('It is said' or 'They say', three times at the beginning of the section (I, 201 f.). This does not prevent him from giving a correct account of the Caspian as an inland sea, in contrast to later geographers, including Ptolemy, who thought it opened to the ocean in the north. In Egypt he says 'I went and saw for myself as far as Elephantine' [near Assuan] 'but further information is from hearsay' (II, 29). He went, that is, exactly as far as the Persian frontier-post (II, 30). In Scythia, he claims to have seen the huge bronze bowl at Exampaeus, far up the Dnieper (IV, 81); but for remoter regions, he again emphasizes 'hearsay' (IV, 16) and 'report' (23). In view of all this, it really seems to be wanton scepticism to deny that he went where he says he did. He only claims to have gone where a Greek merchant could go without undue difficulty – though it was a notable feat to go to all these places; and if he had spent his life sitting at home in Halicarnassus and plagiarizing Hecataeus, it is curious that he does *not* follow him to some of the places which he mentions in the west. Likewise over 'marvels', when giving a vivid description of the phoenix, he carefully tells us 'I myself have not seen this bird, except in a picture' (II, 73); a refreshing contrast to Ctesias, one of his fiercest assailants, who says of the 'man-eater' (*martichora*, a good Iranian word – the beast might be the Indian tiger), (a) that he had seen one, sent as a gift to the king of Persia when Ctesias was court physician, and (b) that it had a face like a man, two rows of teeth in each jaw, and shot darts out of the end of its tail.

The last influential writer in English who stigmatized Herodotus as a liar and tried to prove that he had not seen what he says he had, was A. H. Sayce, in his three-volume commentary on Books I to III (1883), of which Macan's much more friendly commentaries on the later books are a continuation. But after two generations of general belief in his honesty, that belief is seriously challenged in a commentary, as yet unpublished, on Books VII to IX by a young American scholar, O. Kemball Armayor.[1] I disagree with practically every word of Dr Armayor's conclusions; but this is a work of genuine learning. It will be interesting to see whether it proves to represent a more general 'swing of the pendulum'; and it is always good that prevailing views should be challenged and made to defend themselves.

Being human, Herodotus is always liable to error. He makes the god Mitra (Mithras) feminine (I, 131); we may reasonably doubt whether the walls of Babylon were 300 feet high (I, 178); and if he saw an inscription on the side of the Great Pyramid (it is not there now, and the sides of pyramids were not a place for inscriptions, at least official ones), it certainly did not record the expenditure on onions and garlic for the workers (II, 125). Here, on the most charitable view, he may be suspected both of having forgotten exactly where the inscription was (perhaps on a temple wall nearby?) and of being misinformed by a guide – perhaps having his leg pulled. His mis-statements on details in Egypt are too many to note here; reference must be made to the commentaries. But the progress of Egyptology has, on the whole, contributed to a favourable view of his efforts. Experts say that he gives a reasonably accurate account of embalming, for instance (II, 86 ff.); and the great Egyptologist E. Erman reckoned his to be a reasonably good tourist's account of the country generally. No one would go to him for an account of Egyptian history; what we may demand of him – and reasonably criticize him when he fails to give it – is a picture of Egypt in Greek times, and a glimpse of what Egyptians said about their past; just as we do not go to Herodotus for the information that the Caspian is an inland sea or that the sun appears to the north in South Africa, but are interested in what he reveals of the state of geographical knowledge.

When we come to his recent Greek history, on the other hand, and especially that of the great invasion, we have the right to hope for the truth and to apply our criticism on that basis. We get a good impression of his honesty from the frank manner in which he declares his Athenian sympathies, in expressing the opinion that Athens saved Greece, however unpopular it may be to say so (cf. above, p. 9). So

1. Oxford Ph.D. thesis, 1969, which I had the honour to read as an examiner

we know where to look for his bias; and this is just as well, for it, and still more the fact that his informants were predominantly Athenian, has palpably affected his presentation of the story. Within Athens, moreover, his informants were largely of the Alcmeonid faction, that of Pericles' mother's family and their allies. This we infer from his vehement defence of their political past (above, p. 8) – in the course of which, incidentally, when he says that they were in exile 'the whole time' under the Peisistratids (VI, 123), it appears (on the reasonable interpretation of a later inscription as a fragment of an archon-list, complete for 527–522 B.C.).[1] that those informants had kept from him the fact that the famous Cleisthenes had held the chief magistracy, reserved for 'reliable people', under Hippias in 525–524! This is in accordance with the somewhat hostile picture of Themistocles, architect of victory, it could not be denied, but 'always enriching himself' (VIII, 112, cf. VIII, 5) even during the war; a trait of which Thucydides in his character-sketch (I, 138) says nothing. So too at Sparta, Herodotus has received the 'establishment's' hostile story of Cleomenes, a great king who broke the power of Argos and had the breadth of mind to make common cause with democratic Athens, which had once humiliated him, for the good of Greece and against Sparta's Dorian ally Aegina (VI, 75 ff., 61 ff., V, 70 ff.); and we can detect an error of fact when Herodotus says that he reigned 'no long time' (V, 48), if, as appears from Thucydides (III, 68), his commendation of Plataea to Athenian protection took place in 519. This would give him a reign of about thirty years, ended by violence after he had incurred the bitter enmity of the Spartan establishment by trying to build up personal power for himself (VI, 74 f.).

Most conspicuously of all, the prejudice of Athenian informants stands out in the treatment of cities for the parts they played in 480; and it is the prejudice of Athenian informants after Athens' quarrel with Sparta and reversal of alliances, after 464. Athens from then on was friendly to Argos and to the quarrelsome lords of Thessaly; and this accounts for the gentleness of the treatment handed out to these powers, both of which had joined the Persians, 'or as good as' (VIII, 73). Thebes, on the other hand, which had also joined the invader under compulsion, gets the full vials of wrath, and even its contingent sent

1. Now conveniently available in Meiggs and Lewis, *op. cit.*, No. 6.

to Thermopylae is slandered; for Thebes was Athens' enemy both then and later. The Phocians, who had not at all a bad war-record (a contingent at Thermopylae, and some guerilla warfare from Parnassus even after the harrying of their lowlands), get the wantonly catty comment that this was only from hatred of the Thessalians; if the Thessalians had resisted the Persians, no doubt the Phocians would have joined them (VIII, 30). The reason is that, whereas Thessaly was in alliance with Athens during all the time that Herodotus was writing, Phocis, after being in the same camp from 457 to 447, had gone back to that of Sparta.

But it is the treatment of cities that were on the patriotic side throughout that shows Herodotus most disastrously misled by his Athenian friends. Aegina, he knew, had won high praise for good work at Salamis; but he describes them as slow to give Apollo his share of their prize of valour (VIII, 122), an Aeginetan as proposing the mutilation of Mardonius' body and, absurdly, the island's wealth as 'originating' from the purchase of golden ornaments looted on the field of Plataea by Sparta's helots, who thought they were bronze (IX, 78–80).

Corinth is the most conspicuous victim of this unfairness; and Plutarch's *Meanness of Herodotus*, quoting some contemporary poetry, is at its best in this controversy. Corinth's admiral Adeimantus – whose son Aristeus was a determined enemy of imperial Athens, finally caught by the Athenians and put to death (VII, 137; cf. Thuc. I, 60; II, 67) – was described on his epitaph as 'he who by his counsels saved all Greece', and gave his daughter names of pride, such as 'Sea-Victory', Nausinice; he was proud of his services, and Corinth was proud of him; his son was a daring general and the leading Corinthian of his time. But throughout Herodotus' story of the naval campaign he is depicted as a coward, a fool, and corrupt (VIII, 5, etc.). At Salamis, the Athenians said that the Corinthians hoisted sail and fled, Adeimantus leading; but here at least our historian shows good faith, and that he does not deliberately sacrifice truth to Athenian prejudice: 'The Corinthians deny this and say that they were among the foremost in the battle; and the other Greeks support their version'(VIII, 94).[1] Herodo-

1. I have suggested a theory elsewhere (*Persia and the Greeks 458–61*) as to how the *canard* arose.

tus here saves his reputation for honesty. He cannot be acquitted of blame for failing to get other opinions on other points too; but since Athens and Corinth (old friends, VI, 89) were at war and on terms of great bitterness from 461 to 445, and probably soon after the peace of 445 Herodotus will have sailed to Thuria, one can see how the failure happened.

The first principle of critical reading of Herodotus on the Persian Wars is therefore that one must look out for the bias of his sources, whom he rarely names. (We notice that he does name them twice for cases of what he regards as supernormal foresight, VIII, 65 and IX, 16, as he also quotes from oracles, often of Bacis, the Greek Cagliostro, which, he was evidently confident, dated from before the war; VIII, 20, 77, 96; IX, 43.) A second is that the possibilities of error over a 'public' fact, such as that an army moved from A to B, are slight, whereas the reasons for moves or for immobility (e.g. the days of waiting before Marathon, VI, 110), even if discussed in councils of war, would not be known to the men in the ranks, with whom Herodotus talked some thirty years later. That he believes he knows so well what was said in councils of war, both Greek and Persian, probably reflects a strong oral 'saga' tradition, which it did not occur to him or anyone else to doubt. To this day, Greeks are often ready to repeat their own popular versions of anything from recent history to classical mythology, and, when they do, are confident about them – no uneducated Greek, one might say, ever admits 'I do not know' – and, like other people, are very loth to change their minds when once made up. Another and an unbeautiful characteristic of such oral tradition is that, once they have taken sides, Athenians against Corinthians or nowadays against an opposite political faction, they are unwilling to admit that these enemies, even if former allies, ever did anything good at all; and Herodotus' account of the Corinthians in Xerxes' invasion (except for Mycale, IX, 105) is very much of this kind.

I will end with one example.

A narrative which lends itself to critical reading on these lines is that of the last major episode in Greece, the operations at Plataea. These are less easy to study on the spot than Thermopylae or Salamis, because they took place in small-featured country, at the foot of the great slope of Cithaeron and among the headwaters of the Oeroe in their

small, geologically recent gullies. Herodotus is careful to give landmarks: a temple of Demeter, round whose 'churchyard' the fiercest
fighting took place (IX, 65, 69), and a chapel of the hero Androcrates;
and difficulties in following his story are due largely to the fact that
these have disappeared. But the old spite against Athens' and Sparta's
allies, nearly all of them later Athens' enemies, appears vividly in the
accounts of the movements of the centre (half the whole army) on the
night before the battle. At IX, 51, half the army is to move back to the
hill-foot of Cithaeron to cover the food-convoys against Persian cavalry when they come down; and when in IX, 52 they do move to the
Temple of Hera before Plataea, *this is what they have done*, though
Herodotus does not say so. We must remember, though he does not,
that 18,000 armoured men plus light-armed servants could not be 'at
a point'; they would extend for a good two miles – from Plataea to
the Oak Heads pass. The whole army cannot, moreover, have been ordered to occupy the 'Island' between the headwaters of the Oeroe
(*ib.*), because there is not room for them there. There *is* just about room
for the Athenians, who may well have been ordered there; ordered to
close up on the Spartans (55, 60), so that the Spartans might have the
support of their archers, which would have been very useful if the
Athenians had managed to complete their movement. As it was, the
Spartans did the essential thing, destroying the native Persian division,
almost without help.

But it is the account of what the allies 'at the Temple of Hera' did
that highlights, above all, the effect on the narrative of that same old
spite. We are informed (69) that they advanced in two bodies: the
Corinthians and others 'straight for the Demeter Temple', where the
Spartans were fighting, and 'the men of Megara, Phlious and others'
(i.e. probably from Megara *to* Phlious in the old order of battle, cf. §29;
some 7,300 men) 'into the low ground', i.e. west of the 'Island' where
the Athenians had been brought to bay; where they were caught
on the move by Theban cavalry and suffered severely. But we are
assured (*ib.*) that they 'heard news that the battle had happened'
only when it was won, and 'missed the battle'. This is incredible; for
the Heraeum, probably at the far (left) end of their line, was in full
view from Pausanias' command post on the right, some two miles
away (61), and not one mile from where the Athenians were fighting,

between the streams, in the 'Island'. The Athenian soldiers, heavily engaged in front, doubtless did not *see* the move; but only spite can account for their insistence that the Megarians and others died 'to no purpose' (70) and that the Corinthians and other Peloponnesians of the right centre division had no casualties at all. Their burial mounds were there to see; but Herodotus insists that they were sham cenotaphs, that of Aegina, for instance, set up ten years later by the Plataean who was Aegina's 'official friend', to disguise their shame. They may not have had many killed; but probably some, to make up the figures in Herodotus (759, of the Spartans, Tegeans, one Athenian regiment and the unfortunate left division) to Plutarch's total (in his *Aristides*) of 1,360. (Probably far more were wounded, in their unarmoured arms and legs.)

Herodotus' story is thus unconvincing as it stands; and we are, for once, not entirely without *earlier* evidence; for Plutarch in his attack on Herodotus (§42) quotes an elegiac poem on the battle (*not* commissioned specially by Corinth), by the contemporary Simonides, in which the Corinthians rated at least a mention as 'holding the centre'. He did not agree that they 'missed the battle'.

So much by way of example of how Herodotus can, on occasion, be shown up out of his own mouth as having been misled by his sources. Thucydides, a trained soldier, would not have been so misled. But Herodotus, to his credit, himself gives us the means of criticizing him, not only by naïveté but by honesty and thoroughness, including a visit to the battlefield, where he noted its landmarks; and of these, at least the early site of Plataea (which gives us the Hera-Temple) can be identified. Many books have been written on Herodotus and on his theme; we have cited some. But with that, let the reader make his acquaintance in his own text. Even in translation, he makes good reading.

8. A NOTE ON DRACHMAS AND TALENTS

The Athenian unit of currency in the time of Herodotus was the silver drachma (or 'handful') of six obols ('spits'); the terms have come down from the days of iron currency-bars. The coin, on what was called the Euboean standard, was about the weight of a Swiss silver franc; those of other cities could be different, e.g. Aegina's was heavier. On its silver content, older books such as Bury's *History* (1899) used to value the drachma at twenty-five to the pound sterling; but this took no account of its purchasing power – and that, too, in a world with so much less to purchase, and with many people still living mainly on their own produce – and since 1914 and still more since 1950, with depreciating currencies, has become meaningless. In this edition, therefore, translations into £ have been abandoned, and the following note will indicate what the purchasing power of a drachma was.

A drachma was the top day-wage for heavy or skilled manual work, or for a man-at-arms or oarsman; if money was short, the latter in particular might get only half that amount. Higher pay was rare. Pheidias the sculptor, at the top of his profession, was paid 2 drachmas by the state in the time of Pericles, as were, later, when prices were higher, the most popular flute-girls for an evening's entertainment. Jurymen in Pericles' time were paid one obol; ration-money, which attracted chiefly elderly citizens, getting past heavier work. The tiny silver obol could be changed into nine 'coppers'.

Larger sums were reckoned in *minae* of 100 drachmas and talents of 60 *minae*. 200 drachmas are twice mentioned by Herodotus as a standard ransom for a prisoner of war (V, 77; VI, 79), and the same sum later in the century would buy a good slave. At 1 drachma per man per day, 1 talent would pay the crew of a trireme for a month. A fine of 50 talents (VI, 136) was a crippling burden on a great estate; and the annual revenue of the Persian empire is given in III, 95 as 14,560 Euboean talents, or 87,360,000 Athenian top day-wages.

Pōgōn, Troezenia, 1970   A. R. BURN

HERODOTUS

THE HISTORIES

BOOK ONE

HERODOTUS of Halicarnassus, his *Researches* are here set down to preserve the memory of the past by putting on record the astonishing achievements both of our own and of other peoples; and more particularly, to show how they came into conflict.

Learned Persians put the responsibility for the quarrel on the Phoenicians. These people came originally from the so called Red Sea[1]; and as soon as they had penetrated to the Mediterranean and settled in the country where they are to-day, they took to making long trading voyages. Loaded with Egyptian and Assyrian goods, they called at various places along the coast, including Argos, in those days the most important place in the land, now called Hellas.

Here in Argos they displayed their wares, and five or six days later when they were nearly sold out, a number of women came down to the beach to see the fair. Amongst these was the king's daughter, whom Greek and Persian writers agree in calling Io, daughter of Inachus. These women were standing about near the vessel's stern, buying what they fancied, when suddenly the Phoenician sailors passed the word along and made a rush at them. The greater number got away; but Io and some others were caught and bundled aboard the ship, which cleared at once and made off for Egypt.

This, according to the Persian account (the Greeks have a different story), was how Io came to Egypt; and this was the first in a series of provocative acts.

Later on some Greeks, whose name the Persians fail to record – they were probably Cretans – put into the Phoenician port of Tyre and

1. Red Sea: the Greeks used this expression for all parts of the southern (our Indian) Ocean. Here the Persian Gulf is meant, and the reference is to (real) ancient influences from Mesopotamia. Cf. p. 132 n.

carried off the king's daughter Europa, thus giving them tit for tat.

For the next outrage it was the Greeks again who were responsible. They sailed in an armed merchantman to Aea in Colchis on the river Phasis, and, not content with the regular business which had brought them there, they abducted the king's daughter Medea. The king sent to Greece demanding reparations and his daughter's return; but the only answer he got was that the Greeks had no intention of offering reparation, having received none themselves for the abduction of Io from Argos.

The accounts go on to say that some forty or fifty years afterwards Paris, the son of Priam, was inspired by these stories to steal a wife for himself out of Greece, being confident that he would not have to pay for the venture any more than the Greeks had done. And that was how he came to carry off Helen.

The first idea of the Greeks after the rape was to send a demand for satisfaction and for Helen's return. The demand was met by a reference to the seizure of Medea and the injustice of expecting satisfaction from people to whom they themselves had refused it, not to mention the fact that they had kept the girl.

Thus far there had been nothing worse than woman-stealing on both sides; but for what happened next the Greeks, they say, were seriously to blame; for it was the Greeks who were, in a military sense, the aggressors. Abducting young women, in their opinion, is not, indeed, a lawful act; but it is stupid after the event to make a fuss about it. The only sensible thing is to take no notice; for it is obvious that no young woman allows herself to be abducted if she does not wish to be. The Asiatics, according to the Persians, took the seizure of the women lightly enough, but not so the Greeks: the Greeks, merely on account of a girl from Sparta, raised a big army, invaded Asia and destroyed the empire of Priam. From that root sprang their belief in the perpetual enmity of the Grecian world towards them – Asia with its various foreign-speaking peoples belonging to the Persians, Europe and the Greek states being, in their opinion, quite separate and distinct from them.

Such then is the Persian story. In their view it was the capture of Troy that first made them enemies of the Greeks.

As to Io, the Phoenicians do not accept the Persians' account; they deny that they took her to Egypt by force. On the contrary, the girl while she was still in Argos went to bed with the ship's captain, found herself pregnant, and, ashamed to face her parents, sailed away voluntarily to escape exposure.

So much for what Persians and Phoenicians say; and I have no intention of passing judgement on its truth or falsity. I prefer to rely on my own knowledge, and to point out who it was in actual fact that first injured the Greeks; then I will proceed with my history, telling the story as I go along of small cities no less than of great. For most of those which were great once are small to-day; and those which used to be small were great in my own time. Knowing, therefore, that human prosperity never abides long in the same place, I shall pay attention to both alike.

Croesus of Lydia, son of Alyattes, was king of all the peoples to the west of the river Halys, which runs northward into the Black Sea and forms the boundary between Cappadocia and Paphlagonia. He was the first foreigner so far as we know to come into direct contact with the Greeks, both in the way of conquest and alliance, forcing tribute from Ionians, Aeolians, and Asiatic Dorians, and forming a pact of friendship with the Lacedaemonians. Before Croesus' time all the Greeks had been free; for the earlier Cimmerian attack on Ionia was not a conquest, but a mere plundering raid.

The sovereignty of Lydia, which had belonged to the Heraclids, passed into the family of Croesus – the Mermnadae – in the following way. Candaules, king of Sardis (the Greeks call him Myrsilus), was descended from Alcaeus, son of Heracles. His father was Myrsus, and he was the last of the Heraclids to reign at Sardis, the first being Agron, son of Ninus, grandson of Belus, and great-grandson of Alcaeus. Before the time of Agron, the reigning house had been of the family of Lydus, son of Atys: hence the name 'Lydians', the people being previously known as Maeonians. These princes turned over the management of affairs to the Heraclids, the descendants of Heracles and a slave-girl belonging to Iardanus; the Heraclids later had their power confirmed by an oracle. They reigned for twenty-two generations, a period in all of five hundred and five years, son succeeding father right down the line to Candaules, son of Myrsus.

Now Candaules conceived a passion for his own wife, and thought she was the most beautiful woman on earth. So, having in his body-guard a fellow he particularly liked whose name was Gyges, son of Dascylus, Candaules not only discussed his most important business with him, but even used to make him listen to eulogies of his wife's beauty.

One day the king (who was doomed to a bad end) said to Gyges: 'It appears you don't believe me when I tell you how lovely my wife is. Well, a man always believes his eyes better than his ears; so do as I tell you – contrive to see her naked.'

Gyges gave a cry of horror. 'Master,' he said, 'what an improper suggestion! Do you tell me to look at the queen when she has no clothes on? No, no: "off with her skirt, off with her shame" – you know what they say of women. Let us learn from experience. Right and wrong were distinguished long ago – and I'll tell you one thing that is right: a man should mind his own business. I do not doubt that your wife is the most beautiful of women; so for goodness' sake do not ask me to behave like a criminal.'

Thus he did his utmost to decline the king's invitation, because he was afraid of what might happen if he accepted it.

The king, however, told him not to distress himself. 'There is nothing to be afraid of,' he said, 'either from me or my wife. I am not laying a trap for you; and as for her, I promise she will do you no harm. I'll manage so that she doesn't even know that you have seen her. Look: I will hide you behind the open door of our bedroom. My wife will follow me in to bed. Near the door there's a chair – she will put her clothes on it as she takes them off, one by one. You will be able to watch her with perfect ease. Then, while she's walking away from the chair towards the bed with her back to you, slip away through the door – and mind she doesn't catch you.'

Gyges, since he was unable to avoid it, consented, and when bed-time came Candaules brought him to the room. Presently the queen arrived, and Gyges watched her walk in and put her clothes on the chair. Then, just as she had turned her back and was going to bed, he slipped softly out of the room. But the queen saw him.

At once she realized what her husband had done. But she did not betray the shame she felt by screaming, or even let it appear that she had noticed anything. Instead she silently resolved to have her revenge. For with the Lydians, as with most barbarian races, it is thought highly indecent even for a man to be seen naked.

For the moment she kept her mouth shut and did nothing; but at dawn the next morning she sent for Gyges after preparing the most trustworthy of her servants for what was to come. There was nothing unusual in his being asked to attend upon the queen; so Gyges answered the summons without any suspicion that she knew what had occurred on the previous night.[1]

'Gyges,' she said, as soon as he presented himself, 'there are two courses open to you, and you may take your choice between them. Kill Candaules and seize the throne, with me as your wife; or die yourself on the spot, so that never again may your blind obedience to the king tempt you to see what you have no right to see. One of you must die; either my husband, the author of this wicked plot; or you, who have outraged propriety by seeing me naked.'

For a time Gyges was too much astonished to speak. At last he found words and begged the queen not to force him to make so difficult a choice. But it was no good; he soon saw that he really was faced with the alternatives, either of murdering his master, or of being murdered himself. He made his choice – to live.

'Tell me,' he said, 'since you drive me against my will to kill the king, how shall we set on him?'

'We will attack him when he is asleep,' was the answer; 'and on the very spot where he showed me to you naked.'

All was made ready for the attempt. The queen would not let Gyges go or give him any chance of escaping the dilemma: either Candaules or he must die. Night came, and he followed her into the bedroom. She put a knife into his hand, and hid him behind the same door as before. Then, when Candaules was asleep, he crept from behind the door and struck.

Thus Gyges usurped the throne and married the queen. This is the Gyges whom Archilochus of Paros mentions as a comtemporary in his Satires.

1. See Introduction, p. 26.

Later he had his power confirmed by an oracle from Delphi. The Lydians, indignant at the murder of Candaules, were prepared to fight; however, they managed to agree with the supporters of Gyges that he should continue to reign if the oracle declared that he was really the king; if on the other hand the oracle should declare against him, he should restore the throne to the Heraclids.

The answer of the oracle was in favour of Gyges, so his royal power was established. Nevertheless the Priestess of the Shrine added that the Heraclids would have their revenge on Gyges in the fifth generation: a prophecy to which neither the Lydians nor their kings paid any attention, until it was actually fulfilled.

This was the way in which the Mermnadae got rid of the Heraclids and assumed sovereign power. Gyges, as soon as he had made himself supreme, sent a number of presents to the shrine at Delphi; indeed, most of the silver there came from him, and in addition he presented a vast number of vessels of gold of various kinds, the most noteworthy being six golden mixing-bowls. These bowls weigh in all nearly 2500 lb. and stand in the Corinthian treasury – though to speak strictly it should not be called the public treasury of the Corinthians, but the treasury of Cypselus, son of Eëtion.

Gyges was the first foreigner we know of, after King Midas of Phrygia, son of Gordias, to dedicate offerings at Delphi. Midas presented the royal throne from which he used to give judgement; it stands with Gyges' bowls, and is well worth seeing.

The Delphians call all this silver and gold which Gyges sent the Gygean Treasure, after the name of the donor.

Once established in power, Gyges sent a military expedition against Miletus and Smyrna and captured Colophon. That, however, being his only act of any importance during a reign of thirty-eight years, I will pass on without further comment and mention his son Ardys who succeeded him.

Ardys took Priene and attacked Miletus; and during his reign the Cimmerians, driven from their homes by nomadic Scythian tribes, came to Asia and captured Sardis, except for its citadel.

Next on the throne after Ardys, who reigned forty-nine years, was his son Sadyattes, who reigned twelve years and was succeeded by Alyattes. Alyattes made war on the Medes under Cyaxares, grandson of Deioces, expelled the Cimmerians from Asia, captured Smyrna, a city which had been founded by people from Colophon, and attacked Clazomenae – where he did not succeed as he hoped, but met with disaster.

Furthermore – to continue the tale of what was most memorable during his reign – Alyattes carried on the war which he had taken over from his father, against the Milesians. His custom each year was to invade Milesian territory when the crops were ripe, marching in to the music of pipes, harps, and treble and tenor oboes. On arrival he never destroyed or burned the houses in the country, or pulled their doors off, but left them unmolested. He would merely destroy the trees and crops, and then retire. The reason for this was the Milesian command of the sea, which made it useless for his army to attempt a regular siege; and he refrained from demolishing houses in order that the Milesians, having somewhere to live, might continue to work the land and sow their seed, with the result that he himself would have something to plunder each time he invaded their country.

He employed this strategy for eleven consecutive years, during which the Milesians suffered two serious defeats, one in the neighbourhood of Limeneium in their own country, the other in the plain of the Maeander.

For six out of the eleven years Sadyattes, son of Ardys, who began the invasion of Milesia and was the originator of the war, was still on the throne of Lydia; for the five which followed Alyattes, who, as I have already mentioned, inherited it from his father, carried it on with all possible energy.

The Milesians received no help from any of the Ionians except the men of Chios, who fought by their side in payment of a debt of honour, the Milesians having previously assisted them right through their war against the Erythraeans.

In the twelfth year of the fighting, the burning of the crops was the cause of an accident. No sooner had the fire taken hold, than the wind drove the flames on to the temple of Athene at Assesus, which was set alight and burnt down. Nobody bothered much about this at the moment; but on the army's return to Sardis, Alyattes fell ill. For a considerable time he got no better; so either on somebody's advice, or because he thought it the sensible thing to do, he sent to Delphi to inquire of the god about his health. When the messengers arrived, the Priestess of Apollo refused to give an answer until the Lydians had rebuilt Athene's temple, which they had burnt down at Assesus. I know this at first hand, for I heard it from some Delphians; the Milesians, however, have something to add to the story. They say that Periander, son of Cypselus, who was a very close friend of Thrasybulus, king of Miletus at that time, got to know of what the Delphic Priestess had said to Alyattes' messengers, and had thereupon sent to tell Thrasybulus all about it, knowing that to be forewarned is to be forearmed.

Now Alyattes, as soon as he received the message from Delphi, sent a herald to Miletus in the hope of concluding a truce until the temple could be rebuilt. Off went the herald – and Thrasybulus, meanwhile, thought of a clever plan. On the strength of the information he had received, he had made a good guess at the line Alyattes was likely to take; so he had all the grain in the city, both from his own and from private stores, collected in the public square, and issued an order that everyone in the town, on a given signal, was to start drinking and revelling. His object was to get the messenger from Sardis to tell Alyattes about the enormous quantity of grain he had seen poured recklessly out in the street, and how the townspeople were enjoying themselves.

This is just what happened. The messenger, having seen the merrymaking and delivered his master's message to Thrasybulus, returned to Sardis, and, so far as my information goes, peace was concluded for no other reason than because Alyattes, expecting to find the Milesians reduced to extremities by famine, was told by the herald on his return to Sardis that this was not so: that the Milesians, in fact, were by no means hungry, but very much the reverse.

By the terms of the peace the two peoples afterwards became friends and allies; Alyattes built two temples for Athene at Assesus instead of one, and recovered his health.

This, then, is the story of Alyattes and his war with Thrasybulus and the Milesians.

Periander, who told Thrasybulus about the oracle, was the son of Cypselus, the despot of Corinth. The Corinthians tell of an extraordinary thing that occurred during his life, and the Lesbians confirm the truth of it. It concerns Arion of Methymna, the most distinguished musician of that date, and the man who first, so far as we know, composed and named the dithyramb, and trained choirs to perform it in Corinth. The tale is, that Arion rode on a dolphin's back to Taenarum. Most of his time Arion had spent with Periander, till he felt a longing to sail to Italy and Sicily. This he did; and after making a great deal of money in those countries, he decided to return to Corinth. He sailed from Tarentum in a Corinthian vessel, because he had more confidence in Corinthians than in anyone else. The crew, however, when the ship was at sea, hatched a plot to throw him overboard and steal his money. He got wind of their intention, and begged them to take his money, but spare his life. To no purpose, however; for the sailors told him either to kill himself if he wanted to be buried ashore, or to jump overboard at once.

Arion, seeing they had made up their minds, as a last resource begged permission to stand on the after-deck, dressed in his singing robes, and give them a song; the song over, he promised to kill himself. Delighted at the prospect of hearing a song from the world's most famous singer, the sailors all made their way forward from the stern and assembled amidships. Arion put on his full professional costume, took up his lute and, standing on the after-deck, played and sang a lively tune. Then he leapt into the sea, just as he was, with all his clothes on.

The ship continued her voyage to Corinth, but a dolphin picked up Arion and carried him on its back to Taenarum. Here Arion landed, and made his way in his singing costume to Corinth, where he told the whole story. Periander was not too ready to believe it; so he put Arion under strict supervision, keeping the ship's crew meanwhile carefully in mind. On their return he sent for them, and asked if they had anything to tell him about Arion. 'Oh yes,' they answered, 'we left him safe and sound at Tarentum in Italy.' But no sooner were the words out of their mouths than Arion himself appeared, just as he was when he jumped overboard. This was an unpleasant shock for the sailors. The lie was detected, and further denial useless.

That is the story as the Corinthians and Lesbians tell it. There is, moreover, at Taenarum to-day an offering of Arion's in the temple, a small bronze figure of a man on a dolphin.

After bringing the war with Miletus to an end, Alyattes died, having reigned for fifty-seven years. He was the second of his family to send a present to Delphi, for in return for the recovery of his health he gave a large silver bowl, and a salver of welded iron – the most remarkable of all the offerings at Delphi. It was the work of Glaucus of Chios, the inventor of the art of welding.

Alyattes was succeeded by his son Croesus, a man of thirty-five. The first Greek city that Croesus attacked was Ephesus. The Ephesians, when he laid siege to them, ran a rope from their walls to the temple of Artemis, putting the town, by means of this link, under the goddess' protection. The distance between the temple and the old town which was then under siege is just under a mile. Having started with the Ephesians, Croesus subsequently attacked all the Ionian and Aeolian cities in turn on various pretexts, substantial or trivial, according to what ground of complaint he could find against them. He forced all the Asiatic Greeks to pay him tribute, and then turned his attention to ship-building in order to attack the islanders. However, when everything was ready to begin building, something happened which persuaded him to desist. A certain Bias, of Priene – or some say it was Pittacus a Mytilenaean – came to Sardis, and in answer to Croesus' request for news from Greece, told him that the islanders were raising ten thousand horse to attack him in Sardis.

Croesus took the remark literally, and exclaimed: 'What? The islanders mean to attack the Lydians with cavalry? I only wish they would!'

'Sire,' the man replied, 'I think you are longing to catch the islanders on horseback on the continent. Indeed, you are perfectly justified. But they know your intention of building a fleet to attack them – and what do you think they want more than a chance of catching the Lydians at sea? It would give them their revenge for their brothers on the mainland, whom you have enslaved.'

This way of putting the matter tickled Croesus' fancy. Moreover, it seemed so much to the point, that he abandoned the ideal of building a fleet, and formed a treaty of friendship with the Ionian islanders.

In the course of time Croesus subdued all the peoples west of the river Halys, except the Cilicians and Lycians. The rest he kept in subjection – Lydians, Phrygians, Mysians, Mariandynians, Chalybians,

Paphlagonians, Thracians (both Thynian and Bithynian), Carians, Ionians, Dorians, Aeolians, and Pamphylians.

When all these nations had been added to the Lydian empire, and Sardis was at the height of her wealth and prosperity, all the great Greek teachers of that epoch, one after another, paid visits to the capital. Much the most distinguished of them was Solon the Athenian, the man who at the request of his countrymen had made a code of laws for Athens. He was on his travels at the time, intending to be away ten years, in order to avoid the necessity of repealing any of the laws he had made. That, at any rate, was the real reason of his absence, though he gave it out that what he wanted was just to see the world. The Athenians could not alter any of Solon's laws without him, because they had solemnly sworn to give them a ten years' trial.

For this reason, then – and also no doubt for the pleasure of foreign travel – Solon left home and, after a visit to the court of Amasis in Egypt, went to Sardis to see Croesus.

Croesus entertained him hospitably in the palace, and three or four days after his arrival instructed some servants to take him on a tour of the royal treasuries and point out the richness and magnificence of everything. When Solon had made as thorough an inspection as opportunity allowed, Croesus said: 'Well, my Athenian friend, I have heard a great deal about your wisdom, and how widely you have travelled in the pursuit of knowledge. I cannot resist my desire to ask you a question: who is the happiest man you have ever seen?'

The point of the question was that Croesus supposed himself to be the happiest of men. Solon, however, refused to flatter, and answered in strict accordance with his view of the truth. 'An Athenian,' he said, 'called Tellus.'

Croesus was taken aback. 'And what,' he asked sharply, 'is your reason for this choice?'

'There are two good reasons,' said Solon, 'first, his city was prosperous, and he had fine sons, and lived to see children born to each of them, and all these children surviving: secondly, he had wealth enough by our standards; and he had a glorious death. In a battle with the neighbouring town of Eleusis, he fought for his countrymen, routed the enemy, and died like a soldier; and the Athenians paid him the high honour of a public funeral on the spot where he fell.'

All these details about the happiness of Tellus, Solon doubtless intended as a moral lesson for the king; Croesus, however, thinking he
would at least be awarded second prize, asked who was the next
happiest person whom Solon had seen.

'Two young men of Argos,' was the reply; 'Cleobis and Biton.
They had enough to live on comfortably; and their physical strength
is proved not merely by their success in athletics, but much more by
the following incident. The Argives were celebrating the festival of
Hera, and it was most important that the mother of the two young
men should drive to the temple in her ox-cart; but it so happened that
the oxen were late in coming back from the fields. Her two sons
therefore, as there was no time to lose, harnessed themselves to the cart
and dragged it along, with their mother inside, for a distance of nearly
six miles, until they reached the temple. After this exploit, which was
witnessed by the assembled crowd, they had a most enviable death –
a heaven-sent proof of how much better it is to be dead than alive.
Men kept crowding round them and congratulating them on their
strength, and women kept telling the mother how lucky she was to
have such sons, when, in sheer pleasure at this public recognition of
her sons' act, she prayed the goddess Hera, before whose shrine she
stood, to grant Cleobis and Biton, who had brought her such honour,
the greatest blessing that can fall to mortal man.

'After her prayer came the ceremonies of sacrifice and feasting; and
the two lads, when all was over, fell asleep in the temple – and that
was the end of them, for they never woke again.

'The Argives had statues made of them, which they sent to Delphi,
as a mark of their particular respect.'

Croesus was vexed with Solon for giving the second prize for
happiness to the two young Argives, and snapped out: 'That's all
very well, my Athenian friend; but what of my own happiness? Is it
so utterly contemptible that you won't even compare me with mere
common folk like those you have mentioned?'

'My lord,' replied Solon, 'I know God is envious of human prosperity and likes to trouble us; and you question me about the lot of
man. Listen then: as the years lengthen out, there is much both to see
and to suffer which one would wish otherwise. Take seventy years
as the span of a man's life: those seventy years contain 25,200 days,

without counting intercalary months. Add a month every other year, to make the seasons come round with proper regularity, and you will have thirty-five additional months, which will make 1,050 additional days. Thus the total of days for your seventy years is 26,250, and not a single one of them is like the next in what it brings. You can see from that, Croesus, what a chancy thing life is. You are very rich, and you rule a numerous people; but the question you asked me I will not answer, until I know that you have died happily. Great wealth can make a man no happier than moderate means, unless he has the luck to continue in prosperity to the end. Many very rich men have been unfortunate, and many with a modest competence have had good luck. The former are better off than the latter in two respects only, whereas the poor but lucky man has the advantage in many ways; for though the rich have the means to satisfy their appetites and to bear calamities, and the poor have not, the poor, if they are lucky, are more likely to keep clear of trouble, and will have besides the blessings of a sound body, health, freedom from trouble, fine children, and good looks.

'Now if a man thus favoured dies as he has lived, he will be just the one you are looking for: the only sort of person who deserves to be called happy. But mark this: until he is dead, keep the word "happy" in reserve. Till then, he is not happy, but only lucky.

'Nobody of course can have all these advantages, any more than a country can produce everything it needs: whatever it has, it is bound to lack something. The best country is the one which has most. It is the same with people: no man is ever self-sufficient – there is sure to be something missing. But whoever has the greatest number of the good things I have mentioned, and keeps them to the end, and dies a peaceful death, that man, my lord Croesus, deserves in my opinion to be called happy.

'Look to the end, no matter what it is you are considering. Often enough God gives a man a glimpse of happiness, and then utterly ruins him.'

These sentiments were not of the sort to give Croesus any pleasure; he let Solon go with cold indifference, firmly convinced that he was a fool. For what could be more stupid than to keep telling him to look at the 'end' of everything, without any regard to present prosperity?

After Solon's departure nemesis fell upon Croesus, presumably because God was angry with him for supposing himself the happiest of men. It began with a dream he had about a disaster to one of his sons: a dream which came true. He had two sons: one with a physical disability, being deaf and dumb; the other, named Atys, as fine a young man as one can fancy. Croesus dreamt that Atys would be killed by a blow from an iron weapon. He woke from the dream in horror, and lost no time in getting his son a wife, and seeing to it that he no longer took the field with the Lydian soldiers, whom he used to command. He also removed all the weapons – javelins, spears and so on – from the men's rooms, and had them piled up in the women's quarters, because he was afraid that some blade hanging on the wall might fall on Atys' head.[1]

The arrangements for the wedding were well in hand, when there came to Sardis an unfortunate stranger who had been guilty of man-slaughter. He was a Phrygian, and related to the Phrygian royal house. This man presented himself at the palace and begged Croesus to cleanse him from blood-guilt according to the laws of the country (the ceremony is much the same in Lydia as in Greece): and Croesus did as he asked. When the formalities were over, Croesus, wishing to know who he was and where he came from, said: 'What is your name, stranger, and what part of Phrygia have you come from, to take refuge with me? What man or woman did you kill?'

'Sire,' the stranger replied, 'I am the son of Gordias, and Midas was my grandfather. My name is Adrastus. I killed my brother by accident, and here I am driven from home by my father and stripped of all I possessed.'

'Your family and mine,' said Croesus, 'are friends. You have come to a friendly house. If you stay in my dominions, you shall have all you need. The best thing for you will be not to take your misfortune too much to heart.' Adrastus, therefore, took up his residence in the palace.

Now it happened just at this time that Mount Olympus in Mysia was infested by a monstrous boar. This tremendous creature used to issue from his mountain lair and play havoc with the crops, and many times the Mysians had taken the field against him, but to no purpose.

1. On pp. 26–9, See Introduction, p. 25.

The unfortunate hunters received more damage than they were able to inflict. As a last resource the Mysians sent to Croesus.

'Sire,' the messengers said, 'a huge beast of a boar has appeared amongst us, and is doing fearful damage. We want to catch him, but we can't. Please, my lord, send us your son with a party of young men, and some dogs, so that we can get rid of the brute.'

Croesus had not forgotten his dream, and in answer to this request forbade any further mention of his son.

'I could not send him,' he said; 'he is just married, and that keeps him busy. But I will certainly send picked men, with a complete hunting outfit, and I will urge them to do all they can to help rid you of the animal.'

This answer satisfied the Mysians; but at that moment Atys, who had heard of their request, entered the room. The young man, finding that Croesus persisted in his refusal to let him join the hunting party, said to his father: 'Once honour demanded that I should win fame as a huntsman and fighter; but now, father, though you cannot accuse me of cowardice or lack of spirit, you won't let me take part in either of these admirable pursuits. Think what a figure I must cut when I walk between here and the place of assembly! What will people take me for? What must my young wife think of me? That she hasn't married much of a husband, I fear! Now, father, either let me join this hunt, or give me an intelligible reason why what you're doing is good for me.'

'My son,' said Croesus, 'of course you are not a coward or anything unpleasant of that kind. That is not the reason for what I'm doing. The fact is, I dreamt that you had not long to live – that you would be killed by an iron weapon. It was that dream that made me hasten your wedding; and the same thing makes me refuse to let you join in this enterprise. As long as I live, I am determined to protect you, and to rob death of his prize. You are my only son, for I do not count that wretched cripple, your brother.'

'No one can blame you, father,' Atys replied, 'for taking care of me after a dream like that. Nevertheless there is something which you have failed to observe, and it is only right that I should point it out to you. You dreamt that I should be killed by an iron weapon. Very well: has a boar got hands? Can a boar hold this weapon you fear so much? Had you dreamt that I should be killed by a boar's tusk or anything of that sort, your precautions would be justified. But you didn't: it was a weapon which was to kill me. Let me go, then. It is only to hunt an animal, not to fight against me.'

'My boy,' said Croesus, 'I own myself beaten. You interpret the dream better than I did. I cannot but change my mind, and allow you to join the expedition.'

The king then sent for Adrastus the Phrygian, and said to him: 'Through no fault of your own, Adrastus, you came to me in great distress and with an ugly stain on your character. I gave you ritual purification, welcomed you to my house, and have spared no expense to entertain you. Now I expect a fair return for my generosity: take charge of my son on this boar-hunt; protect him from footpads and cut-throats on the road. In any case it is your duty to go where you can distinguish yourself: your family honour demands it, and you are a stalwart fellow besides.'

'Sire,' Adrastus answered, 'under ordinary circumstances I should have taken no part in this adventure. A man under a cloud has no business to associate with those who are luckier than himself. Indeed I have no heart for it, and there are many reasons to prevent my going. But your wishes make all the difference. It is my duty to gratify you in return for your kindness: so I am ready to do as you ask. So far as it lies in my power to protect your son, you may count on his returning safe and sound.'

When Adrastus had given his answer, the party set out, men, dogs, and all. They made their way to Olympus and kept their eyes open for the boar. As soon as they spotted him, they surrounded him and let fly with spears – and then it was that the stranger – Adrastus, the very man whom Croesus had cleansed from the stain of blood – aimed at the boar, missed him, and struck the king's son. Croesus' dream had come true.

A messenger hurried off to Sardis, and Croesus was told of the encounter with the boar and the death of his son. The shock of the news was dreadful; and the horror of it was increased by the fact that the weapon had been thrown by the very man whom the king had cleansed from the guilt of blood. In the violence of his grief Croesus prayed to Zeus, calling on him as God of Purification to witness what he had suffered at the hands of his guest; he invoked him again under his title of Protector of the Hearth, because he had unwittingly entertained his son's murderer in his own house; and yet again as God of Friendship, because the man he had sent to guard his son had turned out to be his bitterest enemy.

Before long the Lydians arrived with the body, followed by the unlucky killer. He took his stand in front of the corpse, and stretching out his hands in an attitude of submission begged the king to cut his throat there and then upon the dead body of his son.

'My former trouble,' he said, 'was bad enough. But now that I have ruined the man who absolved me of my guilt, I cannot bear to live.'

In spite of his grief Croesus was moved to pity by these words.

'Friend,' he said, 'as you condemn yourself to death, there is nothing more I can require of you. Justice is satisfied. This calamity is not your fault; you never meant to strike the blow, though strike it you did. Some God is to blame – some God who long ago warned me of what was to happen.'

Croesus buried his son with all proper ceremony; and as soon as everything was quiet after the funeral, Adrastus – the son of Gordias, the grandson of Midas: the man who had killed his brother and ruined the host who gave him purification – convinced that he was the unluckiest of all the men he had ever known, stabbed himself and fell dead upon the tomb.

For two years Croesus grieved for the death of his son, until the news from Persia put an end to his mourning: Cyrus, son of Cambyses, had destroyed the empire of Astyages, and the power of Persia was steadily increasing. This gave Croesus food for thought, and he wondered if he might be able to check Persian expansion before it had gone too far. With this purpose in view he at once prepared to try his luck with the oracles, and sent to Delphi, to Abae in Phocis, to Dodona, to the oracles of Amphiaraus and Trophonius, and to Branchidae in Milesia. These were the Greek ones which he consulted, but, not content with them, he sent also to the oracle of Ammon in Libya. His object was to test the knowledge of the oracles, so that if they should prove to be in possession of the truth he might send a second time and ask if he should undertake a campaign against Persia.

The Lydians whom Croesus sent to make the test were given the following orders: on the hundredth day, reckoning from the day on which they left Sardis, they were to consult the oracles, and inquire what Croesus, son of Alyattes and king of Lydia, was doing at that moment. The answer of each oracle was to be taken down in writing and brought back to Sardis. No one has recorded the answer of any of the oracles except that of Delphi; here, however, immediately the Lydians entered the shrine for their consultation, and almost before the question they had been told to ask was out of their mouths, the Priestess gave them, in hexameter verse, the following reply:

> I count the grains of sand on the beach and measure the sea;
> I understand the speech of the dumb and hear the voiceless.
> The smell has come to my sense of a hard-shelled tortoise
> Boiling and bubbling with lamb's flesh in a bronze pot:
> The cauldron underneath is of bronze, and of bronze the lid.

The Lydians took down the Priestess' answer and returned with it to Sardis.

When the other messengers came back with the answers they had received, Croesus opened all the rolls and read what they contained. None had the least effect upon him except the one which contained the answer from Delphi. But no sooner had this one been read to him than he accepted it with profound reverence, declaring that the oracle at Delphi was the only genuine one in the world, because it had succeeded in finding out what he had been doing. And indeed it had; for after sending off the messengers, Croesus had thought of something which no one would be likely to guess, and with his own hands, keeping carefully to the prearranged date, had cut up a tortoise and a lamb and boiled them together in a bronze cauldron with a bronze lid.

So much for the answer from Delphi. As to the oracle of Amphiaraus, there is no record of what answer the Lydians received when they had performed the customary rites in the temple; all I can say is, that Croesus believed this oracle too to be in possession of the truth.

Croesus now attempted to win the favour of the Delphian Apollo by a magnificent sacrifice. Of every kind of appropriate animal he slaughtered three thousand; he burnt in a huge pile a number of precious objects – couches overlaid with gold or silver, golden cups,

tunics, and other richly coloured garments – in the hope of binding
the god more closely to his interest; and he issued a command that
every Lydian was also to offer a sacrifice according to his means. After
this ceremony he melted down an enormous quantity of gold into one
hundred and seventeen ingots about eighteen inches long, nine inches
wide, and three inches thick; four of the ingots were of refined gold
weighing approximately a hundred and forty-two pounds each: the
rest were alloyed and weighed about a hundred and fourteen pounds.
He also caused the image of a lion to be made of refined gold, in
weight some five hundred and seventy pounds. This statue, when the
temple at Delphi was burnt down, fell from the gold bricks which
formed its base and lies to-day in the Corinthian treasury. It lost about
two hundred pounds weight in the fire, and now weighs only three
hundred and seventy pounds.

This was by no means all that Croesus sent to Delphi; there were
also two huge mixing-bowls, one of gold which was placed on the
right-hand side of the entrance to the temple, the other of silver, on
the left. These also were moved at the time of the fire, and the golden
one, which weighs nearly a quarter of a ton, now stands in the treasury
of the Clazomenians, and the silver one, which holds over five
thousand gallons, is in the corner of the ante-chapel. Its capacity is
known because the Delphians use it for mixing wine at the festival
called Theophania. It is a most remarkable piece of work, and I should
say the Delphians are right in ascribing it to Theodorus of Samos. In
addition Croesus sent four silver casks, which are in the Corinthian
treasury, and two sprinklers for lustral water, one of gold, the other
of silver; the former has the name of the Lacedaemonians engraved
upon it, and they claim to have presented it. But this is not true:
Croesus presented it along with all the rest, and some Delphian (I
know his name but will not mention it) cut the inscription to please
the Lacedaemonians. I admit that the boy through whose hand the
water runs is a Lacedaemonian gift, but not either of the two sprinklers. There were many other gifts of no great importance, including
round silver basins; but I must not forget to mention a figure of a
woman, in gold, four and a half feet high, said by the Delphians to
represent the woman who baked Croesus' bread. Lastly, he sent his
own wife's necklaces and girdles. These, then, were the offerings

which Croesus sent to Delphi; to the shrine of Amphiaraus, the story of whose valour and misfortune he knew, he sent a shield of solid gold and a spear, also of solid gold throughout, both shaft and head; the shield and spear were still at Thebes in my own day, in the temple of Ismenian Apollo.

The Lydians who were to bring the presents to the temples were instructed by Croesus to ask the oracles if he should undertake the campaign against Persia, and if he should strengthen his army by some alliance. On their arrival, therefore, they offered the gifts with proper ceremony and put their question in the following words: 'Croesus, King of Lydia and other nations, in the belief that these are the only true oracles in the world, has given you gifts such as your power of divination deserves, and now asks you if he should march against Persia and if it would be wise to seek an alliance.' To this question both oracles returned a similar answer; they foretold that if Croesus attacked the Persians, he would destroy a great empire, and they advised him to find out which of the Greek states was the most powerful, and to come to an understanding with it.

Croesus was overjoyed when he learnt the answer which the oracles had given, and was fully confident of destroying the power of Cyrus. To express his satisfaction he sent a further present to Delphi of two gold staters for every man, having first inquired how many men there were. The Delphians in return granted in perpetuity to Croesus and the people of Lydia the right of citizenship for any who wished, together with exemption from dues, front seats at state functions and priority in consulting the oracle.

When Croesus had given the Delphians their presents, he consulted the oracle a third time, for one true answer had made him greedy for more. On this occasion he asked if his reign would be a long one. The Priestess answered:

> When comes the day that a mule shall sit on the Median throne,
> Then, tender-footed Lydian, by pebbly Hermus
> Run and abide not, nor think it shame to be a coward.

This reply gave Croesus more pleasure than anything he had yet heard; for he did not suppose that a mule was likely to become king of the Medes, and that meant that he and his line would remain in power for ever. He then turned his attention to finding out which of the Greek states was the most powerful, with a view to forming an alliance. His inquiries revealed that the Lacedaemonians were the most eminent of the Dorian peoples and the Athenians of the Ionian. These two, one originally Pelasgian the other Hellenic, were the most powerful of the Greek peoples. The Ionians are an indigenous race, but the Dorians on the contrary have been constantly on the move; their home in Deucalion's reign was Phthiotis and in the reign of Dorus son of Hellen the country known as Histiaeotis in the neighbourhood of Ossa and Olympus; driven from there by the Cadmeians they settled in Pindus and were known as Macedonians; thence they migrated to Dryopis, and finally to the Peloponnese, where they got their present name of Dorians. Of the Pelasgian language I cannot speak with certainty, but that it was not Greek may be inferred from the language of those of Pelasgian race now living in Creston above the Tyrrhenians, who were neighbours of the people now known as Dorians when their home was in the country which we call Thessaliotis; also from the language of the Pelasgian peoples who settled at Placia and Scylace on the Hellespont and were fellow countrymen of the Athenians, and of the other Pelasgian towns which have since changed their names. Granted, then, that these are a fair sample of the Pelasgian race, one may conclude that the Athenians, being themselves Pelasgian, changed their language when they were absorbed into the Greek family of nations. In Creston and Placia the same language is spoken, but it is not the language of the surrounding country: which indicates that these people did not change their language when they changed their home. I believe myself that the Greek peoples have always spoken the same language, but they were weak after their separation from the Pelasgians of whom they were a branch, and have since grown from small beginnings to their present numbers by the addition of various foreign elements, amongst which were the Pelasgians themselves. I do not think that the Pelasgians, a non-Greek people, ever became very numerous or powerful.

Athens, he learned, had been split by faction and was now under the dictatorship of Pisistratus the son of Hippocrates. An extraordinary thing had occurred when Hippocrates, who held no public office, was present at the festival of Olympia: he had slaughtered the animals for his sacrifice, when the cauldrons with the flesh and water in them boiled over, though no fire had been lighted. Chilon the Lacedaemonian chanced to be passing, and seeing this ominous sight advised Hippocrates not to marry and have children, or, if he was married already, to divorce his wife, or again, if he had a son, to disown him. Hippocrates refused to take Chilon's advice, and some time later Pisistratus, of whom I was speaking, was born. When there was strife in Attica between the coastal villages under the leadership of Megacles, son of Alcmaeon, and the inland settlements under Lycurgus, Pisistratus with a view to seizing power for himself organized a third party. He collected adherents and coming forward as the nominal champion of the hillmen,[1] he devised the following ruse: he cut himself and his mules about the body and then drove his cart into the market square, and pretended that he had escaped from his enemies who tried to kill him as he was driving out of town. Then, relying on the reputation he had won during his command of the expedition against Megara, during which the capture of Nisaea was not the least of his distinguished services, he asked the people to give him a guard. The Athenians, who were taken in by the trick, consented, and told off a number of men for his bodyguard, who followed him armed with clubs instead of spears. With their assistance Pisistratus captured the Acropolis, and from that moment found himself master of Athens. He was no revolutionary, but governed the country in an orderly and excellent manner, without changing the laws or disturbing the existing magistracies.

Not long afterwards the two parties under Megacles and Lycurgus agreed to combine, and drove Pisistratus out, so that in this first phase of his dictatorship he lost his power before it had really taken root. His rivals, however, falling foul of one another once again, Megacles found himself so harassed that he made overtures to Pisistratus and promised to restore him to power if he would consent to marry his daughter. Pisistratus agreed to the terms which Megacles proposed, and then, to bring about his return to power, they devised between them what seems to me the silliest trick which history has to record. The Greeks have never been simpletons; for centuries past they have been distinguished from other nations by superior wits; and of all

1. The poorest section of the community.

Greeks the Athenians are allowed to be the most intelligent: yet it was at the Athenians' expense that this ridiculous trick was played. In the village of Paeania there was a handsome woman called Phye, nearly six feet tall, whom they fitted out in a suit of armour and mounted in a chariot; then, after getting her to pose in the most striking attitude, they drove into Athens, where messengers who had preceded them were already, according to their instructions, talking to the people and urging them to welcome Pisistratus back, because the goddess Athene herself had shown him extraordinary honour and was bringing him home to her own Acropolis. They spread this nonsense all over the town, and it was not long before rumour reached the outlying villages that Athene was bringing Pisistratus back, and both villagers and townsfolk, convinced that the woman Phye was indeed the goddess, offered her their prayers and received Pisistratus with open arms.

After the recovery of his power in this way Pisistratus married Megacles' daughter, as he had agreed to do; but because of a story that Megacles' family, the Alcmaeonids, had a curse upon it, and because he already had grown-up sons of his own, he did not want children from his new wife, and to prevent her from having any refused normal intercourse and lay with her in an unnatural way. For a time his wife said nothing about this insult, but later – perhaps in answer to a question – she told her mother, and her mother told Megacles, who was so angry at the slight upon himself and his daughter, that he made up his quarrel with his political enemies. This new threat determined Pisistratus to get right out of the country. He went to Eretria and there discussed the situation with his sons. The view of Hippias that an attempt should be made to recover his lost position proved the most acceptable, and they began to collect contributions from the towns which were in any way favourable to their cause. Many towns gave large sums of money, but the contribution from Thebes was by far the most handsome. Time passed; they were joined by Argive mercenaries from the Peloponnese; a certain Lygdamis from Naxos freely offered his enthusiastic support, contributing both money and men; and at last – to cut the story short – everything was ready for the march on Athens. More than ten years had passed, when they left Eretria and returned.

The first place in Attica which they took was Marathon. Here they were joined in camp by their supporters in the town, and others who preferred dictatorship to democracy trickled in from the villages to swell their force. While Pisistratus had been collecting supplies, and even after he occupied Marathon, the Athenians ignored him; but the news that he was marching against Athens soon brought them into the field in full force against the returning exiles, and they were met by Pisistratus on his way from Marathon at the temple of Athene Pallenis, where the two armies halted and faced one another. Here it providentially occurred that Amphilytus, the soothsayer from Acarnia, accosted Pisistratus and made a prophecy to him in verse;

> The net is cast and the meshes of it are spread wide;
> In the moonlit night the tunnies will come darting through the sea.

Pisistratus understood the meaning of this inspired utterance and, declaring that he accepted the oracle, gave the order to advance. Just at this time the Athenians in the city were taking their lunch, while others were following the meal by a game of dice or a siesta, so that the attack of Pisistratus' army met with no resistance. The Athenians fled, and Pisistratus by a clever stratagem prevented any subsequent rally and ensured that they should remain scattered: he told his son to ride on in advance, and they, each time they overtook a group of fugitives, spoke to them according to Pisistratus' instructions, urging every man to keep his spirits up and go home. The Athenians did as they were bidden, and thus for the third time Pisistratus made himself master of the city.

He now proceeded to establish his power on a firm basis. He hired bodyguards, raised revenue from various sources, partly in Attica, partly from property on the river Strymon, took as hostages and sent for safe keeping to Naxos (which he had captured and turned over to Lygdamis) the sons of those Athenians who had remained in the city and not immediately fled; and, finally, 'cleansed' the island of Delos. The object of this was to obey the injunctions of an oracle, and the method he adopted was to dig up all the dead bodies which were buried within sight of the temple and re-inter them in another part of the island.

Thus it was that Pisistratus won undisputed power in Athens. A number of the Athenians had been killed in the fighting, and others, including the Alcmaeonidae, had fled the country.

The condition of Athens at the time when Croesus made his inquiry was such as I have described. He then proceeded to get information about Sparta. Here he found that the Lacedaemonians after a period of depression had been successful in their struggle with Tegea, which during the joint reign of Leon and Agasides had been the only town to hold out against their victorious arms. At an earlier date they had been the worst governed people in Greece, both in their internal and external relations – for they would have no dealings of any kind with strangers. How the change to good government came about I will now relate. Lycurgus, a distinguished Spartan, visited the Delphic oracle, and no sooner had he entered the shrine than he was greeted with these words:

> Hither to my rich temple have you come, Lycurgus,
> Dear to Zeus and to all gods that dwell in Olympus.
> I know not whether to declare you human or divine –
> Yet I incline to believe, Lycurgus, that you are a god.

There is a story that the Priestess also revealed to him the system of government which obtains at Sparta to-day, but the Lacedaemonians themselves say that Lycurgus brought it from Crete after he became guardian of his nephew Leobotas, king of Sparta, and acted as his regent; for it is a fact that as soon as he received this appointment he made fundamental changes in the laws, and took good care that the new ones should not be broken. Later he reorganized the army, introducing the system of messes and the new tactical divisions of squadrons and companies, in addition to the new civil offices of Ephor and Elder. By these changes Spartan government was put upon a sound basis, and when Lycurgus died a temple was built in his honour, and he is still regarded with profound reverence.

Thanks to a good soil and a numerous population the Lacedaemonians soon shot up and flourished like a sturdy tree. No longer content to let things be, they took it into their heads that they were better men than the Arcadians, and consulted the oracle at Delphi with a view to the conquest of the whole of their country. This was the answer they received:

Arcady? Great is the thing you ask. I will not grant it.
In Arcady are many men, acorn–eaters,
And they will keep you out. Yet, for I am not grudging,
I will give you Tegea to dance in with stamping feet
And her fair plain to measure out with the line.

The Lacedaemonians failed to perceive the ambiguity of this oracle, and decided to leave the rest of Arcadia alone and march against Tegea: and so confident were they of reducing the men of Tegea to slavery, that they took the chains with them. But they lost the battle, and those who were taken prisoner were forced to wear on their own legs the chains they had brought, and to 'measure out with the line' the plain of Tegea as labourers. In my own lifetime the fetters they were bound with were still preserved in Tegea, hanging up round the temple of Athene Alea.

In this former war with Tegea the Spartans had continually the worst of it, but by the time of Croesus, under their kings Anaxandrides and Ariston, they had got the upper hand. This is the story of their success: after a long series of reverses in the war they sent to Delphi and asked of which god they should beg favour in order to ensure their conquest of Tegea, and the Priestess promised them victory if they brought home the bones of Orestes, Agamemnon's son. Unable to find the tomb of Orestes, they sent again to inquire where the body lay, and the messengers received this answer:

In Arcady lies Tegea in the level plain,
Where under strong constraint two winds are blowing;
Smiting is there and counter-smiting, and woe on woe;
This earth, the giver of life, holds Agamemnon's son.
Bring him home, and you will prevail over Tegea.

This oracle brought them no nearer than the previous one to finding the body. They searched everywhere; but all in vain until Lichas, who was one of the Spartan special agents called 'Agathoergi', or 'good-service men', solved the riddle. The Agathoergi are the five eldest men who quit the cavalry each year, and it is their duty to spend the subsequent year in active employment on whatever service the state may require of them. Lichas, as I have said, was one of them, and he it was who, by the aid of luck and his own wits, found the body in Tegea. Taking advantage of the better relations which existed at this time between the two towns, he went to Tegea and entered a forge where he watched some iron being hammered out, a process which caused him great surprise. The smith, seeing his astonishment, paused in his work and said: 'Well, my friend, your surprise at seeing me work in iron would be nothing to what you'd have felt, if you had seen what I saw. I wanted to make a well in the yard here, and as I was digging I came on a huge coffin – ten feet long! I couldn't believe that men were ever bigger than they are to-day, so I opened it – and there was the corpse, as big as the coffin! I measured it, and then shovelled the earth back.' Lichas turned over in his mind the smith's account of his discovery, and came to the conclusion that the oracle was fulfilled and that this was the body of Orestes. He found the explanation of the 'winds' in the smith's two pairs of bellows; the 'smiting and counter-smiting' were the hammer and anvil, and the 'woe on woe' the beaten iron – the inference being drawn from the fact that the discovery of iron was a bad thing for mankind. Confident that he had solved the puzzle, he returned to Sparta and told the whole story. The Spartans pretended that he had committed some crime, charged him with it and drove him out of the country; whereupon he went back to Tegea, told the smith what had happened to him, took from him a lease of the courtyard, as he refused to sell it, and having persuaded him took up his quarters there. Then he dug up the grave, collected the bones and took them away to Sparta; and ever since that day the Lacedaemonians in any trial of strength had by far the better of it. They had now subdued the greater part of the Peloponnese.

Now when Croesus had gathered all this information, he sent messengers to Sparta with presents, to ask for an alliance. They were instructed what words to use, so on their arrival they said that they came from Croesus, king of Lydia and other nations, with the following message: 'Men of Lacedaemon, I the King have been advised by the oracle to make the Greek my friend, and because I am told that you are the most eminent of the Greeks, I am obeying the oracle in asking for your help. I wish to be your friend and ally, without deceit or underhand dealing.'

Now the Lacedaemonians, who had themselves heard about the oracle, were very glad that the Lydians had come with this proposal from Croesus, and made a pact of friendship and alliance with him. This was partly in gratitude for a favour which Croesus had done them on a former occasion, when they had sent to Sardis to buy gold for a statue of Apollo (the one which now stands in the Laconian town of Thornax) and Croesus had given it to them as a free gift. For this reason, then, and also because Croesus had chosen them out of all the Greeks to be his friends, the Lacedaemonians consented to give him their help. Not only, moreover, were they ready to serve when he should call upon them, but wishing to make Croesus some return for his presents they had a bronze bowl made, large enough to hold two thousand five hundred gallons and covered with small figures round the outside of the rim. They meant to take this bowl to Croesus, but for one reason or another it never reached Sardis. The Lacedaemonians say that off Samos the islanders got wind of its presence and sailed out in their warships and stole it. But the Samians deny the theft: according to them, the Lacedaemonians who were taking the bowl to Sardis were too late, and when they heard that the city had fallen and Croesus was a prisoner, they sold it in Samos to some men who placed it as an offering in the temple of Hera. And indeed if they did sell it, it is not unlikely that on their return to Sparta they would pretend to have been robbed. So much for the story of the bowl.

Croesus, who had failed to grasp the true meaning of the oracle, now prepared an expedition against Cappadocia, sure of success in bringing down the power of Cyrus and the Persians. But while the preparations were going on, he received a piece of advice from a Lydian named Sandanis, who was already known for his good sense, and by the opinion he then expressed greatly increased his reputation amongst the Lydians. 'My lord,' he said, 'you are preparing to fight against men who dress in leather – both breeches and everything else. So rough is their country that they eat as much as they have, never as much as they want. They drink no wine but only water. They have no good things at all, not even figs for dessert. Now if you conquer this people, what will you get from them, seeing they have nothing for you to take? And if they conquer you, think how many good things you will lose; for once they taste the luxuries of Lydia they will hold on to them so tightly that nothing will make them let go.

I am thankful myself that the gods have never put it into the Persians' heads to attack the Lydians.'

Croesus did not take this advice – though Sandanis was right: the Persians before their conquest of Lydia had no luxuries of any kind.

The Cappadocians are known by the Greeks as Syrians. Before the rise of Persian power they were subject to the Medes, but at this period to Cyrus. The boundary between the Median and Lydian empires was the river Halys, which flows from a mountain region in Armenia through Cilician territory, and then, passing between the Matieni and Phrygians, turns northward and forms the boundary between the Cappadocians to the east and the Paphlagonians to the west. The Halys is thus the boundary of nearly the whole of southern Asia Minor from the Mediterranean in the neighbourhood of Cyprus to the Black Sea. This is where the neck of the peninsula lies, and it is five days' journey across for a man travelling light.[1]

Croesus had a craving to extend his territories, but there were two other reasons for his attack on Cappadocia: namely his trust in the oracle and his desire to punish Cyrus for his treatment of Astyages. Astyages, son of Cyaxares and king of Media, was Croesus' brother-in-law, and had been dethroned by Cyrus, son of Cambyses. I will now relate how this relationship arose. A number of nomad Scythians, driven out in a quarrel, emigrated to Media, which was at that time ruled by Cyaxares, son of Phraortes and grandson of Deioces. Cyaxares at first respected their dependence and treated them kindly, and even valued them so far as to make them guardians of some boys, whom they were to teach their language and the use of the bow. Now as time went on it so happened that the Scythians, who were continually out hunting and continually bringing in game, one day came home empty-handed. Cyaxares (who was, as he showed, a quick-tempered man) received them with insult and abuse. The Scythians, in revenge for treatment which they considered undeserved, decided to kill one of their young pupils, chop him up, dress the pieces in the ordinary way like meat, serve them to Cyaxares as a dish of game, and then make the best of their escape to the court of Alyattes in Sardis. This they actually did. Cyaxares and the guests at his table ate some of the meat, and the Scythians escaped to Sardis and

1. A great underestimate.

threw themselves on the mercy of Alyattes. Cyaxares demanded that they should be given up; but when Alyattes refused, war subsequently broke out between the two countries and continued for five years, during which both Lydians and Medes won a number of victories. One battle was fought at night. But then, after five years of indecisive warfare, a battle took place in which the armies had already engaged when day was suddenly turned into night. This change from daylight to darkness had been foretold to the Ionians by Thales of Miletus, who fixed the date for it in the year in which it did, in fact, take place. Both Lydians and Medes broke off the engagement when they saw this darkening of the day: they were more anxious than they had been to conclude peace, and a reconciliation was brought about by Syennesis of Cilicia and Labynetus of Babylon, who were the men responsible both for the pact to keep the peace and for the exchange of marriages between the two kingdoms. They persuaded Alyattes to give his daughter Aryenis to Astyages, son of Cyaxares – knowing that treaties seldom remain intact without powerful sanctions. These nations have the same form of oath as the Greeks, but for additional confirmation they make a shallow cut in their arms and lick each other's blood.

Astyages was Cyrus' maternal grandfather and had been attacked and defeated by him for a reason which I will explain later on. My point at the moment is that Croesus blamed Cyrus for his action, and therefore sent to ask the oracles about his invasion of Persia, and, when the ambiguous answer arrived, interpreted it in his own favour and began the war. When he reached the Halys, he crossed it by the existing bridge; that, at any rate, is my own belief in spite of the common Greek story that it was Thales of Miletus who contrived the crossing. This tale supposes that the bridge had not yet been built, and that while Croesus was wondering how his men were to get across, Thales, who was in camp with them, made the river flow on both sides of the army instead of only on the left. He managed this feat by digging a deep crescent-shaped channel, from a spot a little above the camp and thence round to the rear of it, for the purpose of diverting some of the water from the original bed, into which it would flow again once it had passed the camp. In this way the river was split in two, so that both parts at once became fordable. Some say that the original river-bed was completely dried up; but I do not believe this – for had it been so, how would they have crossed on their return journey?

When the army was over the river and had reached the district called Pteria in Cappadocia (Pteria is the strongest place hereabouts and lies more or less in a line with Sinope on the Black Sea), Croesus encamped and began to devastate the crops on the Syrians' land. He captured the town, enslaved the inhabitants, and took all the neighbouring settlements, driving the innocent Syrians from house and home.

Cyrus meanwhile had collected his army and was on his way to meet him, increasing his forces as he went by levying troops from all the peoples that lay on his route. Before starting he had sent representatives to the Ionians in an attempt to detach them from Croesus, but without success. He marched none the less to Pteria, and when he had pitched camp in the face of Croesus' army, there was a trial of strength between them. After a sharp struggle in which both sides lost heavily, night fell and the battle was broken off without a decision.

Croesus laid the blame for his lack of success upon the size of his army, which in that engagement was much smaller than the army of Cyrus; so when on the next day Cyrus did not advance to the attack, he marched back to Sardis with the intention of calling upon the Egyptians to assist him according to the pact which he had concluded with King Amasis before the treaty of alliance with Sparta; he meant also to summon the Babylonians (for with them too, under their king, Labynetus, he had perviously formed an alliance), and, lastly, to call upon the Lacedaemonians to join him on a definite date. Thus, with all these reinforcements added to his own army, he proposed to wait until winter was over, and attack the Persians in the following spring.

With this purpose in mind, Croesus, as soon as he reached home, sent instructions to his allies to send troops to Sardis after an interval of four months. All the mercenary troops which had been engaged with the Persians and had returned with him, he disbanded and sent home, for he did not for a moment suppose that Cyrus after so close a fight would venture to advance on Sardis. While he was thinking

these arrangements over, he was surprised by an unusual occurrence:
snakes swarmed into the suburbs of the town, and on their appearance
the horses in the meadows stopped grazing and came and ate them.
Croesus, quite rightly, took this extraordinary sight as an omen, and
at once sent to Telmessus where there were men who interpreted such
things. His messenger did indeed learn the significance of the omen
from the men of Telmessus, but they never told Croesus what it
was – for before their ship made Sardis on the return voyage, Croesus
had been taken prisoner. This interpretation was that Croesus must
expect the coming of a foreign army, which would subdue the people
whose home was in Sardis; for the snakes (so they explained it) sprang
from the soil, but horses were beasts of war and not native to the
country. The men of Telmessus who gave this answer had not yet
had the news from Sardis, though Croesus was already a prisoner.

When Croesus started for home after the battle in Pteria, Cyrus
was sure that he would disband his army as soon as he arrived; so
after consideration he found that his best course was to press on to
Sardis with all speed before the Lydian forces had time to muster
again. This was no sooner determined than done. Indeed he was his
own messenger – for so swift was his advance into Lydia that Croesus
had no news that he was on the way. This unexpected turn of events
put Croesus into a very difficult position; however, he made an
attempt to resist the invader. (In those days, by the way, there were
no stouter or more courageous fighters in Asia than the Lydians. They
were cavalrymen, excellent horsemen, and their weapon was the
long spear.)

The armies met on the level ground in front of Sardis; it is a broad
expanse, bare of trees, and watered by the Hyllus and other streams
which join another and larger one called the Hermus. The Hermus
has its source in the mountains sacred to the Phrygian Cybele, and
flows into the sea near the town of Phocaea. When Cyrus saw the
Lydians take up battle positions on this plain, his fear of their cavalry
led him to adopt a suggestion of Harpagus, one of the Medes; this
was to get together all the camels (they were used as pack-animals to
carry equipment and stores), unload them and mount men armed as
cavalrymen on their backs. He then ordered them to advance as the
first line of attack against the cavalry of Croesus, with the infantry

following and his own cavalry bringing up the rear. Having made his dispositions, he reminded his troops of their duty to kill without mercy every Lydian they met – except Croesus. Croesus was on no account to be killed, even if he tried to resist capture.

The reason for confronting the Lydian cavalry with camels was the instinctive fear which they inspire in horses. No horse can endure the sight or smell of a camel. This is the fact upon which the stratagem was based, and its object was to render useless Croesus' cavalry, the very arm in which the Lydians expected to distinguish themselves. The ruse succeeded, for when the battle began, the horses turned tail the moment they smelt and saw the camels – and Croesus' chief ground of confidence was cut from under him. The Lydians, however, did not play the coward; seeing what had happened they leapt from the saddle and engaged the Persians on foot. Both sides suffered heavy losses, but finally the Lydians, forced to retire, were driven within the city walls, where they were besieged by the Persians.

Thus the siege of Sardis began, and Croesus, in the belief that it would last a long time, sent a second appeal for help to his allies. The first messenger had been sent to ask for reinforcements to be at Sardis after four months, but these, now that Croesus was already beleaguered, were to beg for immediate assistance. All the states which were in treaty with Cyrus were applied to, but the most urgent request was to Sparta.

It happened that just at this time the Spartans were engaged in a quarrel with Argos over Thyreae, a place in Argive territory which the Spartans had cut off and occupied. (The country to the west as far as Malea once belonged to the Argives, including Cythera and the other islands in that neighbourhood.) The Argives marched to recover their stolen property, and agreed in conference with the Spartans that three hundred picked men a side should fight it out, and that Thyreae should belong to the victors; the rest of the two armies were to go home without staying to watch the fight, lest either side, seeing its champions getting the worst of it, might be tempted to intervene. On these terms they parted, leaving behind the men chosen to represent them, and the battle began. So closely was it contested that of the six hundred men only three were left alive – two Argives, Alcenor and Chromios, and one Spartan, Othryades –

and even these would have been killed had not darkness put an end to the fighting. The two Argives claimed the victory and hurried back to Argos; but the Spartan Othryades remained under arms and, having stripped the bodies of the Argive dead, carried their equipment to his own camp.

Both parties met again on the following day, when they had heard the result of the battle. For a while both Argives and Spartans maintained that they had won, the former because they had the greater number of survivors, the latter because the two Argives had run away, whereas their own man had remained on the battlefield and stripped the bodies of the dead. The argument ended in blows, and a fresh battle began, in which after severe losses on both sides the Spartans were victorious. From that day the Argives, who were previously compelled by custom to wear their hair long, began to cut it short, and made it an offence against religion for any man to grow his hair, and for any women to wear gold, until Thyreae was recovered. The Spartans also adopted a new custom, but in precisely the opposite sense: they used not to grow their hair long, but from that time they began to do so. It is said that Othryades, the sole survivor of the three hundred, was ashamed to return to Sparta after the death of his companions, and killed himself at Thyreae.

It was in the midst of these troubles that the messenger arrived at Sparta to ask for help in raising the siege of Sardis, and the Spartans in spite of their difficulties were eager to render assistance, when they heard what he had to say. But by the time their preparations were complete and their ships ready to sail, a second message brought the news that the city had fallen and that Croesus was a prisoner. They were much distressed to hear of his misfortune, but they could do no more.

This was how Sardis was taken. On the fourteenth day of the siege Cyrus sent officers to ride round his lines and tell the troops that he promised a reward for the first man to scale the wall. Following this an attempt was made in force, but it failed and was abandoned; then a Mardian called Hyroeades resolved to try at a point in the fortifications which was unguarded, because a successful attack there had never been supposed possible. It was a section of the central stronghold so precipitous as to be almost inaccessible. In old days the

Telmessians had pronounced that Sardis would never be taken if Meles, who was king at that time, carried round the walls the lion which his concubine had borne him. So far as the rest of the fortifications were concerned, where they were open to attack, Meles took their advice and had the lion carried round; but this one point he neglected, thinking that the sheer drop was sufficient defence. It is on the side of the city which faces Tmolus.

On the previous day Hyroeades the Mardian had seen one of the Lydians fetch a helmet, which had rolled down this precipitous slope, and the sight of the man climbing down had set him thinking. He had then made the ascent himself, and other Persians followed; after them a great many more climbed up, and Sardis was taken and sacked.

What happened to Croesus remains to be told. I have already mentioned his son who was dumb, but in other ways a fine enough young man. In the time of his prosperity – now gone   Croesus had done everything he could for the boy, not even omitting to ask advice from the Delphic oracle. The Priestess had replied:

> O Lydian lord of many nations, foolish Croesus,
> Wish not to hear the longed-for voice within your palace,
> Even your son's voice: better for you were it otherwise;
> For his first word will he speak on a day of sorrow.

When the city was stormed, a Persian soldier was about to cut Croesus down, not knowing who he was. Croesus saw him coming; but because in his misery he did not care if he lived or died, he made no effort to defend himself. But this dumb son, seeing the danger, was so terrified by the fearful thing that was about to happen that he broke into speech, and cried: 'Do not kill Croesus, fellow!' Those were the first words he ever uttered – and he retained the power of speech for the rest of his life.

In this way Sardis was captured by the Persians and Croesus taken prisoner, after a reign of fourteen years and a siege of fourteen days. The oracle was fulfilled; Croesus had destroyed a mighty empire – his own.

The Persians brought their prisoner into the presence of the king, and Cyrus chained Croesus and placed him with fourteen Lydian boys on a great pyre that he had built; perhaps he intended them as a choice offering to some god of his, or perhaps he had made a vow and wished to fulfil it; or it may be that he had heard that Croesus was a godfearing man, and set him on the pyre to see if any divine power would save him from being burnt alive. But whatever the reason, that was what he did; and Croesus, for all his misery, as he stood on the pyre, remembered with what divine truth Solon had declared that no man could be called happy until he was dead. Till then Croesus had not uttered a sound; but when he remembered, he sighed bitterly and three times, in anguish of spirit, pronounced Solon's name.

Cyrus heard the name and told his interpreters to ask who Solon was; but for a while Croesus refused to answer the question and kept silent; at last, however, he was forced to speak. 'He was a man,' he said, 'who ought to have talked with every king in the world. I would give a fortune to have had it so.' Not understanding what he meant, they renewed their questions and pressed him so urgently to explain, that he could no longer refuse. He then related how Solon the Athenian once came to Sardis, and made light of the splendour which he saw there, and how everything he said had proved true, and not only for him but for all men and especially for those who imagine themselves fortunate – had in his own case proved all too true.

While Croesus was speaking, the fire had been lit and was already burning round the edges. The interpreters told Cyrus what Croesus had said, and the story touched him. He himself was a mortal man, and was burning alive another who had once been as prosperous as he. The thought of that, and the fear of retribution, and the realization of the instability of human things, made him change his mind and give orders that the flames should at once be put out, and Croesus and the boys brought down from the pyre. But the fire had got a hold, and the attempt to extinguish it failed. The Lydians say that when Croesus understood that Cyrus had changed his mind, and saw everyone vainly trying to master the fire, he called loudly upon Apollo with tears to come and save him from his misery, if any of his gifts had been pleasant to him. It was a clear and windless day; but suddenly in answer to Croesus' prayer clouds gathered and a storm broke with such violent rain that the flames were put out.

This was proof enough for Cyrus that Croesus was a good man whom the gods loved; so he brought him down from the pyre and said, 'Tell me, Croesus, who was it who persuaded you to march against my country and be my enemy rather than my friend?'

'My lord,' Croesus replied, 'the luck was yours when I did it, and the loss was mine. The god of the Greeks encouraged me to fight you: the blame is his. No one is fool enough to choose war instead of peace – in peace sons bury fathers, but in war fathers bury sons. It must have been heaven's will that this should happen.'

Cyrus had his chains taken off and invited him to sit by his side. He made much of him and looked at him with wonder, as did everyone who was near enough to see.

For a while Croesus was deep in his thoughts and did not speak. Then he turned, and seeing that the Persians were sacking the town, said: 'Should I tell you, my lord, what I have in my mind, or must I now keep silent?' Cyrus replied that he might say what he pleased without fear, so Croesus put another question: 'What is it,' he asked, 'that all those men of yours are so intent upon doing?'

'They are plundering your city and carrying off your treasures.'

'Not my city or my treasures,' Croesus answered. 'Nothing there any longer belongs to me. It is you they are robbing.'

Cyrus thought this carefully over; then he sent away all the company that was present, and asked Croesus what advice he saw fit to give him in the matter.

'Since the gods have made me your slave,' Croesus said, 'I think it my duty, if I have advice worth giving you, not to withhold it. The Persians are violent men; and they are poor. They are ransacking the town, and if you let them get possession of all that wealth you may be sure that whichever of them gets the most will rebel against you. So do what I advise – if you like the advice: put men from your guard on watch at every gate, and when anyone brings out anything of value, let the sentries take it and say that a tenth part of the spoil must be given to Zeus. If you do that, they will not hate you, as they certainly would if you confiscated the things by mere authority. They will admit that it is an act of justice, and be willing to give up what they have got.'

Cyrus was delighted with this advice, which he thought was excellent. With many compliments to Croesus he gave orders to the guard to put the proposal into practice. Then turning to Croesus, 'I

see,' he said, 'that though you are a king you are ready to do me good
service in word and deed. I should like to make you some return: ask,
therefore, for whatever you wish, and it shall immediately be yours.'

'Master,' Croesus answered, 'you will please me best if you let me
send these chains to the god of the Greeks, whom I most honoured,
and ask if he is accustomed to cheat his benefactors.' Cyrus asked the
reason for this request, whereupon Croesus repeated the whole story
of what he had hoped to accomplish and of the answers of the oracles,
and dwelt at length upon the rich gifts he had sent and on how his
belief in the prophecies had emboldened him to invade Persia. Then
he ended by repeating his request for permission to reproach Apollo
for his deceit. Cyrus laughed, and told Croesus he should have what
he wanted, and anything else he might ask for, no matter when.
Croesus, therefore, sent to Delphi, and instructed his messengers to
lay the chains on the threshold of the temple; then, pointing to the
chains, they were to ask the god if, when such things were the fruits
of war, he was not ashamed to have encouraged Croesus by his
oracles to invade Persia in the confident hope of destroying the power
of Cyrus. And they were also to ask if it was the habit of Greek gods
to be ungrateful.

It is said that when the Lydian messengers reached Delphi and asked
the questions they had been told to ask, the Priestess replied that not
God himself could escape destiny. As for Croesus, he had expiated
in the fifth generation the crime of his ancestor, who was a soldier
in the bodyguard of the Heraclids, and, tempted by a woman's
treachery, had murdered his master and stolen his office, to which he
had no claim. The God of Prophecy was eager that the fall of Sardis
might occur in the time of Croesus' sons rather than in his own, but
he had been unable to divert the course of destiny. Nevertheless what
little the Fates allowed, he had obtained for Croesus' advantage: he
had postponed the capture of Sardis for three years, so Croesus must
realize that he had enjoyed three years of freedom more than was
appointed for him. Secondly, the god had saved him when he was on
the pyre. As to the oracle, Croesus had no right to find fault with it:
the god had declared that if he attacked the Persians he would bring
down a mighty empire. After an answer like that, the wise thing
would have been to send again to inquire which empire was meant,

Cyrus' or his own. But as he misinterpreted what was said and made no second inquiry, he must admit the fault to have been his own. Moreover, the last time he consulted the oracle he failed also to understand what Apollo said about the mule. The mule was Cyrus, who was the child of parents of different races – a nobler mother and a baser father. His mother was a Mede and daughter of Astyages, king of Media; but his father was a Persian, subject to the Medes, and had married his queen to whom he was in every way inferior.

When the Lydians returned to Sardis with the Priestess' answer and reported it to Croesus, he admitted that the god was innocent and he had only himself to blame.

Such are the facts about the reign of Croesus and the first conquest of Ionia. I must add that Croesus sent many offerings to Greek shrines in addition to those I have already mentioned: for instance a tripod of gold (now at Thebes in Boeotia) which he dedicated to Ismenian Apollo, the golden cows and most of the columns at Ephesus, and a large golden shield in the Pronaea at Delphi. All these were in existence in my own day, and there were others which have since disappeared. There were others, again, at Branchidae, near Miletus, similar in weight and kind, so far as my information goes, to those at Delphi.

Everything which Croesus sent to Delphi and to the shrine of Amphiaraus came from his own treasure and what he had inherited from his father; but the other gifts were originally the property of an enemy, who had opposed him before his reign began and supported the claim of Pantaleon to the throne. Pantaleon was Croesus' brother, a son of Alyattes by a different woman – Croesus' mother being a Carian, Pantaleon's an Ionian. Croesus obtained the succession by his father's gift, and this fellow, who had plotted against him, he put to death by dragging him on a carding-comb; his property, which he had already vowed to confiscate, he then sent as offerings to the various shrines in the way I have already described.

I will now leave the subject of Croesus' dedicatory offerings, and go on to say a word about Lydia. The country, unlike some others, has few natural features of much consequence for a historian to describe, except the gold dust which is washed down from Tmolus; it can show, however, the greatest work of human hands in the world, apart from the Egyptian and Babylonian: I mean the tomb of Croesus' father Alyattes.[1] The base of this monument is built of huge stone blocks; the rest of it is a mound of earth. It was raised by the joint labour of the tradesmen, craftsmen, and prostitutes, and on the top of it there survived to my own day five stone pillars with inscriptions cut in them to show the amount of work done by each class. Calculation revealed that the prostitutes' share was the largest. Working-class girls in Lydia prostitute themselves without exception to collect money for their dowries, and continue the practice until they marry. They choose their own husbands. The circumference of the tomb is nearly three-quarters of a mile, and its breadth about four hundred yards. Near it is a large lake, the lake of Gyges, said by the Lydians to be never dry. Apart from the fact that they prostitute their daughters, the Lydian way of life is not unlike our own. The Lydians were the first people we know of to use a gold and silver coinage and to introduce retail trade, and they also claim to have invented the games which are now commonly played both by themselves and by the Greeks. These games are supposed to have been invented at the time when they sent a colony to settle in Tyrrhenia, and the story is that in the reign of Atys, the son of Manes, the whole of Lydia suffered from a severe famine. For a time the people lingered on as patiently as they could, but later, when there was no improvement, they began to look for something to alleviate their misery. Various expedients were devised: for instance, the invention of dice, knucklebones, and ball-games. In fact they claim to have invented all games of this sort except draughts. The way they used these inventions to help them endure their hunger was to eat and play on alternate days – one day playing so continuously that they had no time to think of food, and eating on the next without playing at all. They managed to live like this for eighteen years. There was still no remission of their suffering – indeed it grew worse; so the King divided the population into two groups and determined by drawing lots which should emigrate and which should remain at home. He appointed himself to rule the section whose lot determined that they should remain, and his son Tyrrhenus to command the emigrants. The lots were drawn, and one section went down to the coast at Smyrna, where they built

1. Recently excavated by American and Turkish archaeologists.

vessels, put aboard all their household effects and sailed in search of a livelihood elsewhere. They passed many countries and finally reached Umbria in the north of Italy, where they settled and still live to this day. Here they changed their name from Lydians to Tyrrhenians, after the king's son Tyrrhenus, who was their leader.

So far I have described the subjugation of Lydia by the Persians. The course of my story now leads me to Cyrus: who was this man who destroyed the empire of Croesus, and how did the Persians win their predominant position in Asia? I could, if I wished, give three versions of Cyrus' history, all different from what follows; but I propose to base my account on those Persian authorities who seem to tell the simple truth about him without trying to exaggerate his exploits.

The Assyrians had been masters of upper Asia over a period of five hundred and twenty years, when the Medes set the example of revolt from their authority. They took arms in the cause of liberty and fought with such gallantry that they shook off the Assyrian yoke and became a free people. Their lead was followed by the other nations within the Assyrian empire, until every people in that part of the continent had won its independence. But it was not to last, and they became once more subject to autocratic government. The change was brought about by Deioces, a Median, son of Phraortes, who was a man of great ability and ambitious for power. The Medes had established themselves in small settlements, and Deioces, who was already a man of mark in his own village, now entered wholeheartedly into the task of distinguishing himself for just dealing. In this he had a purpose; for throughout the country at that time there was no sort of organized government whatever, and he was well aware that there could be no compromise between right and wrong. The result was that the men of his own village, seeing his habit of fair dealing, chose him to arbitrate their disputes. Bent upon getting all power into his own hands, he performed this office with perfect integrity and thus won no small praise from the men of his village. His reputation for being the only man to settle a dispute according to strict justice spread to the other villages, where corrupt processes of law were causing much distress, so that once the news of Deioces' integrity got abroad, everyone was glad to submit cases to his judgement, until in the end he became the only person they would turn to. As the knowledge of his impartiality

spread, so the number of his clients increased, and he himself realized
the supremacy of his position. He then announced that he had had
enough of it – he would no longer sit in the chair of judgement; he
would hear no more suits. It was contrary to his interest to spend all
his time settling his neighbours' quarrels to the neglect of his own
affairs. The result was that robbery increased and the contempt of law
throughout the country was worse than ever. The Medes discussed
the situation at a general meeting, at which (I presume) the friends of
Deioces did most of the talking. 'We cannot,' they said, 'continue to
live in this country under the present intolerable conditions. Let us
appoint one of our number to rule us so that we can get on with our
work under orderly government, and not lose our homes altogether
in the present chaos.' The argument prevailed and the assembly was
persuaded to set up a monarchy. The next step was to propose candi-
dates for the royal office, and as during the debate Deioces and his
admirable qualities were on everybody's lips, he was the man they
agreed to appoint.

Deioces' first act was to command his subjects to build a palace
worthy of a king, and to grant him the protection of a private guard.
The Medes complied; they built a large and well-defended palace on
a site he himself indicated, and allowed him to select a bodyguard
without restriction of choice.

Once firmly on the throne, Deioces put pressure on the Medes to
build a single great city to which, as the capital of the country, all
other towns were to be held of secondary importance. Again they
complied, and the city now known as Ecbatana was built, a place of
great size and strength fortified by concentric walls, these so planned
that each successive circle was higher than the one below it by the
height of the battlements. The fact that it was built on a hill helped to
bring about this effect, but still more was done by deliberate contrivance. The circles are seven in number, and the innermost contains
the royal palace and treasury. The circuit of the outer wall is much
the same in extent as at Athens. The battlements of the five outer
rings are painted in different colours, the first white, the second
black, the third crimson, the fourth blue, the fifth orange; the battlements of the two inner rings are plated with silver and gold respectively. These fortifications were to protect the king and his palace;

the people had to build their houses outside the circuit of the walls.

When the work of building was complete, Deioces introduced for the first time the ceremonial of royalty: admission to the king's presence was forbidden, and all communication had to be through messengers. Nobody was allowed to see the king, and it was an offence for anyone to laugh or spit in the royal presence. This solemn ceremonial was designed as a safeguard against his contemporaries, men as good as himself in birth and personal quality, with whom he had been brought up in earlier years. There was a risk that if they saw him habitually, it might lead to jealousy and resentment, and plots would follow; but if nobody saw him, the legend would grow that he was a being of a different order from mere men.

Once his sovereign power was firmly established, he continued his strict administration of justice. All suits were conveyed to him in the form of written documents, which he would send back after recording upon them his decisions. In addition to this there were other practices he introduced: if he heard of any act of arrogance or ostentation, he would send for the offender and punish him as the offence deserved, and his spies were busy watching and listening in every corner of his dominions.

The achievement of Deioces, who reigned for fifty-three years, was to unite under his rule the people of Media – Busae, Parataceni, Struchates, Arizanti, Budii, Magi; beyond these he did not extend his empire. His son Phraortes, however, who succeeded to the throne on his father's death, was not content to be king only of Media; he carried his military operations further afield, and the first country he attacked and brought into subjection was Persia. By the combination of these two powerful peoples he proceeded to the systematic conquest of Asia, and finally attacked the Assyrians – the Assyrians of Nineveh, that is, who were formerly masters of all Asia, but at that time stood alone because of the desertion of their allies. However, they were still powerful and prosperous, and in the campaign against them Phraortes and most of his army were killed. Phraortes reigned for twenty-two years and was succeeded by his son Cyaxares, grandson of Deioces. This prince had a far greater military reputation than his father or grandfather. It was he who first organized the Asiatic armies by dividing them into separate units – spearmen, archers, and cavalry. Previously the different arms had all been mixed up in a mob. It was Cyaxares who fought the battle with the Lydians on the occasion when the day was darkened, and it was he who united all Asia beyond the Halys under his rule.

The first act of his reign was to march against Nineveh at the head of all his subject nations, with the object of destroying the town and avenging his father. He fought a successful battle agianst the Assyrians, but while he was besieging the town he was attacked by a large Scythian army under the command of King Madyas, son of Proto-thyes. The Scythians had entered Asia in pursuit of the Cimmerians whom they had expelled from Europe, a fact which explains their presence in Median territory at this time. From the sea of Azov to the Phasis and the Colchians is a thirty days' journey for a quick traveller; but it is not far from Colchis to Media, and to reach it one has to pass through the country of only one intervening people, the Saspires. The Scythians, however, did not enter Media by this way, but took the much longer upper, or northern, route, keeping the Caucasus mountains on their right. A battle was fought, in which the Medes were defeated and lost their power in Asia, which was taken over in its entirety by the Scythians.

The Scythians next turned their attention to Egypt, but were met in Palestine by Psammetichus the Egyptian king, who by earnest entreaties supported by bribery managed to prevent their further advance. They withdrew by way of Ascalon in Syria. The bulk of the army passed the town without doing any damage, but a small number of men got left behind and robbed the temple of Aphrodite Urania – the most ancient, I am told, of all the temples of this goddess. The one in Cyprus the Cyprians themselves admit was derived from it, and the one in Cythera was built by the Phoenicians, who belong to this part of Syria. The Scythians who robbed the temple at Ascalon were punished by the goddess with the infliction of what is called the 'female disease', and their descendants still suffer from it. This is the reason the Scythians give for this mysterious complaint, and travellers to the country can see what it is like. The Scythians call those who suffer from it 'Enarees'.

During the twenty-eight years of Scythian supremacy in Asia, violence and neglect of law led to absolute chaos. Apart from tribute arbitrarily imposed and forcibly exacted, they behaved like mere robbers, riding up and down the country and seizing people's property. At last Cyaxares and the Medes invited the greater number of them to a banquet, at which they made them drunk and murdered them, and in this way recovered their former power and dominion. They captured Nineveh (the story of the capture I will relate in another place[1]) and subdued the Assyrians, all except the territory belonging to Babylon. Then Cyaxares died, after a reign – including the period of Scythian domination – of forty years. He was succeeded by his son Astyages.

Astyages had a daughter called Mandane, and he dreamed one night that she made water in such enormous quantities that it filled his city and swamped the whole of Asia. He told his dream to the Magi, whose business it was to interpret such things, and was much alarmed by what they said it meant. Consequently when Mandane was old enough to marry, he did not give her to some Mede of suitable rank, but was induced by his fear of the dream's significance to marry her to a Persian named Cambyses, a man he knew to be of good family and quiet habits – though he considered him much below a Mede even of middle rank.

Before Mandane and Cambyses had been married a year, Astyages had another dream. This time it was that a vine grew from his daughter's private parts and spread over Asia. As before, he told the interpreters about this dream, and then sent for his daughter, who was now pregnant. When she arrived, he kept her under strict watch, intending to make away with her child; for the fact was that the Magi had interpreted the dream to mean that his daughter's son would usurp his throne. To guard against this, Astyages, when Cyrus was born, sent for his kinsman Harpagus, the steward of his property, whom he trusted more than anyone, and said to him: 'I have some instructions for you, Harpagus, and mind you pay attention to them, whatever they may be. My safety depends upon you. If you neglect it and prefer to serve others, the day will come when you will be caught in your own trap. Get hold of Mandane's child – take it home and kill it. Then bury it how you please.'

1. An unfulfilled promise; cf. Introduction, p. 19.

'Sire,' Harpagus replied, 'you have never had cause to find fault with me yet, and I will take care not to offend you in the future. If this is your will, it is for me to do my duty and obey.'

The baby was dressed in grave-clothes and handed over to Harpagus, who wept as he took it home. On his arrival, he told his wife everything that Astyages had said, and she asked him what he intended to do. 'Not,' Harpagus replied, 'what Astyages has ordered. He can rage and rave as much as he likes – even worse than he does now; but I will not consent to do what he wants. Never will I take a hand in so brutal a murder. There are many reasons why I will not do it – he is related to me by blood, and Astyages is old and has no son. Suppose, when he dies, Mandane – whose child I am to be the instrument of murdering – should succeed to the throne: shouldn't I be in the utmost peril? For my own safety's sake the baby must be killed. But one of Astyages' servants must do it, not one of mine.'

He promptly sent a messenger to one of the king's herdsmen, who he knew had a stretch of pasture amongst mountains ranged by wild beasts, and therefore most suitable to the purpose in hand. The fellow's name was Mitradates, and he lived with another of the king's slaves, a woman whose name in Greek would be Cyno, or Bitch: (the Median form of it was Spaco – 'spaca' being the Median for bitch). The foothills of the mountains where Mitradates pastured his oxen, lie to the north of Ecbatana in the direction of the Black Sea. Everywhere else Media is flat, but here, south of the country of the Saspires, it is very high, mountainous, and thickly wooded.

The herdsman made haste to answer the summons, and Harpagus said to him: 'The king's orders are that you must expose this infant in the wildest spot you know of amongst the hills, where it may soonest die. I am to tell you, moreover, that if you disobey and find some means of saving the child, the king will have you put to death in a way not pleasant to think of. I am commanded to see for myself that the child has been exposed.'

Mitradates picked up the baby and, returning by the way he had come, took it back to the shack where he lived. Fate had decreed that his wife, who had been daily expecting a child of her own, was on that very day brought to bed, while her husband was away in the city. Each had been worrying about the other, he in anxiety over his wife's confinement, and she because Harpagus had sent for her husband. What, she wondered, could be the meaning of that? In her fear she had hardly expected ever to see him again, so the instant he returned she asked him, before he could speak, why Harpagus had sent such an urgent message.

'My dear,' he said, 'I am sorry to say our masters in town are in trouble. I would give much not to have heard or seen what I saw there to-day. Why, in Harpagus' house there was nothing but sobs and tears – a most extraordinary thing. I went in, and no sooner was I inside than I saw a baby kicking and howling; it had lovely clothes on, too; all gold and bright colours. When Harpagus saw me, he told me to carry it off at once to the wildest spot in the mountains and leave it there. According to him it was the king's orders that I should do this – and he said he'd do dreadful things to me if I disobeyed. Of course I picked up the child and went off with it. It might have belonged to one of the servants, for all I knew; though I *was* surprised at the gold and the grand clothes, and all those tears that nobody in the house was trying to hide – but I should never have guessed whose it really was, if the servant who put it into my arms, and showed me the way out of town, had not told me the whole story as we went along. Well, what do you think? it's the child of Mandane, the king's daughter, and Cambyses the son of Cyrus, and the king has given orders to make away with it. Look – here it is!'

As he said this, the herdsman uncovered the baby and showed it to his wife, who, seeing that it was a fine strong child, burst out crying, and put her arms round her husband's knees, imploring him to do anything rather than expose it. The man replied that he had no choice in the matter – for Harpagus would send people to see that it was done; and if he disobeyed, he would be put to death by torture. His wife therefore, seeing that her entreaties were in vain and that she could not dissuade her husband from exposing the baby, said that if the sight of the dead body was really necessary in order to prove that the deed was done, she had a suggestion to make.

'My own child,' she said, 'was born to-day – and it was born dead. Take the body and expose it, and let us bring up Mandane's son as our own. If we do this, no one will find out that you have disobeyed your masters. Moreover, we shall have managed pretty well for ourselves too: our dead baby will have a royal burial, and this live one will not be killed.'

Mitradates was pleased with his wife's proposal, and at once proceeded to act upon it. He took Mandane's child, which he had intended to kill, from the box in which he had brought it, stripped it of its fine clothes, and gave it to his wife, next he dressed his own dead child in the princely robes and put it in the box in place of the other. Then he took it to a lonely spot amongst the hills, and left it there.

When the child had lain there for two days, Mitradates went into town on the following morning, leaving one of his assistants on guard. Going to Harpagus' house, he said that he was ready to show him the child's corpse. Harpagus dispatched some trusty members of his guard, and through them obtained the proof he wanted, and had the herdsman's child buried. And so came about that the herdsman's wife, when her own son was buried, brought up the child that was one day to be Cyrus, though she, of course, did not call him by that name.

When the boy was ten years old, his identity was revealed in the way I will now relate. He and some other boys were playing the game of 'Kings' in the street of the village, where Mitradates kept his oxen, and it so happened that Cyrus – the supposed son of the herdsman – was the one whom the boys picked as their king. In the course of their game, he was giving his subjects their various tasks – some to build houses, others to be his bodyguard, one to be the 'king's eye', and another his messenger – when one of the players, who happened to be the son of a distinguished Mede called Artembares, refused to do what King Cyrus commanded, and Cyrus ordered his arrest. The other boys accordingly seized him, and Cyrus beat him savagely with a whip. Furious at this indignity the boy, as soon as he was released, ran home to his father's house in the city and bitterly complained of his rough handling – saying, of course, that it was the son of Astyages' herdsman who had beaten him. He did not say it was Cyrus, because that was not yet his name. Artembares was very angry. He took his boy to Astyages, and reported the monstrous treatment he had received, showing the weals on his shoulders and complaining of the insult offered them both by a cowman's brat, a mere slave of the king. Seeing his raw shoulders, Astyages, when he had heard the story, was willing for the sake of the father's rank to give the boy his due; so he sent for the herdsman and his son. They came, and Astyages, fixing his eyes upon Cyrus, said: 'Had you – the son of a slave – the impudence to handle in this outrageous manner a boy whose father is my most distinguished subject?'

'Master,' Cyrus replied, 'there was nothing wrong in what I did to him. We boys in the village – and he was with us – were playing our game, and they made me king, because they thought I was the best man to hold the office. The others obeyed my orders, but *he* did not; he took no notice of me – until he was punished. That is what happened; and if I deserve to suffer for it, I am ready.'

Almost before he finished speaking, Astyages had guessed who he was, for that was not the answer of a slave; moreover, the cast of the boy's features seemed to resemble his own, and he was just of an age to fit the date of the exposure. Deeply troubled, for a long time Astyages did not speak; at last he recovered himself and, wishing for an opportunity to examine the herdsman privately, told Artembares that he would deal with the matter so as to leave neither him nor his son any cause for complaint; then he dismissed Artembares and told his servants to take Cyrus into another room. When the two were left alone, Astyages asked the herdsman how the child had come into his possession, and the name of the man who had given it him.

'The child is my own,' answered the herdsman, 'and its mother is still my wife.'

Saying he was a fool if he wanted to have the truth dragged out of him, Astyages signed to his guards, who sezied Mitradates and were about to take him off to the torture, when he revealed what had actually happened.

He told the whole story truthfully from the beginning and ended by begging the king for mercy. Once he had got the truth from him, Astyages put the herdsman out of his mind and transferred his wrath to Harpagus, whom he ordered his guard to summon. As soon as he appeared, Astyages said: 'Harpagus, when I gave you my daughter's child, how did you kill it?' Harpagus, seeing that the herdsman was in the palace, made no attempt to lie, for he knew that if he did he would be caught and refuted. 'My lord,' he said, 'when I took the

child, I considered how best I might fulfil your wishes and at the
same time, without offending you, avoid the guilt of killing with my
own hands your daughter's child – your own grandchild. What I did
was to employ this herdsman: I gave the child to him, and told him
it was your orders that it should be killed. And that was the truth: it
was indeed what you commanded. I gave him, moreover, careful
instructions, telling him to expose it in a lonely place amongst the
hills, and to keep watch there until it was dead. And I threatened him
with all sorts of punishments if he should disobey. He carried out my
orders, and when the child died, I sent the most trustworthy eunuchs
I possess to witness for me that it was dead, and to have it buried.
That, sire, is the fact of the matter, and that is how the child was made
away with.'

Harpagus' tale was a straightforward one, and Astyages, concealing his anger, first repeated to him the herdsman's account of the
affair, and then, when he had gone over the whole story, ended by
saying that all was well and the child was still alive; he had been
greatly distressed, he added, by what had been done to it, and
seriously concerned at the hatred he could not have failed to arouse
in his daughter. 'And now,' he said, 'since things have taken this
lucky turn, I want you to send your own son to visit the young new-
comer; and come to dinner with me yourself, as I intend to celebrate
my grandson's deliverance by a sacrifice to the gods to whom such
rites belong.'

Harpagus bowed low when he heard what the king said, and went
home much pleased with his invitation to dinner on so happy an
occasion: it was a great thing, he thought, to have come off so lightly.
As soon as he reached home, he sent his son – his only son, a boy of
about thirteen years old – to Astyages' palace, with instructions to
do whatever the king should command. Then in high glee he told
his wife everything that had occurred.

When Harpagus' son arrived at the palace, Astyages had him
butchered, cut up into joints and cooked, roasting some, boiling the
rest, and having the whole properly prepared for the table. Dinner-
time came and the guests assembled, with Harpagus amongst them.
Dishes of mutton were placed in front of Astyages and of everybody
else – except Harpagus. To Harpagus was served the flesh of his son:

all of it, except the head, the hands, and the feet, which had been put separately on a platter covered with a lid.

When Harpagus thought he had eaten as much as he wanted, Astyages asked him if he had enjoyed his dinner. He answered that he had enjoyed it very much indeed, whereupon those whose business it was to do so brought in the boy's head, hands, and feet in the covered dish, stood by Harpagus's chair and told him to lift the lid and take what he fancied. Harpagus removed the cover and saw the fragments of his son's body. As he kept control of himself and did not lose his head at the dreadful sight, Astyages asked him if he knew what animal it was whose flesh he had eaten. 'I know, my lord,' was Harpagus' reply; 'and for my part – may the king's will be done.' He said no other word, but took up what remained of the flesh and went home, intending, I suppose, to bury all of it together. And that was how Harpagus was punished.

Astyages now turned his attention to Cyrus, and summoning the Magi who had previously interpreted his dream, asked them again what they judged its meaning to be. They answered just as before, saying that the boy was certainly destined to be king, had he grown to manhood instead of meeting a too early death. 'The boy is not dead,' Astyages answered; 'he is alive and safe; and when he was living in the country, the village boys chose him as their king. He did to perfection everything that real kings do: he gave his play fellows their tasks as guards, sentries, messengers, and ruled them all. Tell me now – what do you think this signifies?'

'If he is alive,' said the Magi, 'and has already been a king by no contrivance of your own, then you may feel confident about him and need not lose heart. He has been king once and will never be so again. Even our regular prophecies are sometimes fulfilled in apparently small incidents, and as for dreams – they often work out in something quite trivial.'

'That is very much my own opinion,' Astyages answered. 'My dream has been filled by the mere fact that the boy had been called king, and he is no longer a danger to me. Nevertheless I wish you to consider the position carefully, and give me your advice on what is likely to be the safest course for my family and yourselves.'

'Sire,' the Magi answered, 'for us too it is of the greatest moment that your rule should prosper. This boy is a Persian and a foreigner, and if the power passes into his hands, we, who are Medes and of a different race, will be despised and enslaved by the Persians; but you are our countryman, and with you on the throne we have our share of power and the positions of honour which you grant us. That is quite enough to ensure our deepest concern for you and your empire. If we saw danger in the present situation, we should tell you without reserve; but now that your dream has had this trifling conclusion, we feel quite comfortable and advise you not to be any more anxious than we are ourselves. We suggest, however, that you should send the boy to his parents in Persia, where he will be out of your sight.'

Astyages was much pleased by the Magi's advice. He called Cyrus and said to him: 'I did you a wrong, my boy, because of a dream which was not fulfilled; but your own fortune saved you. Be off now to Persia – I will give you an escort on your way – and good luck to you. You will find a father and mother there of a different sort from Mitradates the herdsman and his wife.'

So Cyrus was dismissed, and on his return to Cambyses' palace was received by his parents. When they found he was the son who they were sure had died long before, they greeted him with delight and asked how he had escaped death. Cyrus replied that it was only on the way thither that he had learnt his own history; previously he had known nothing and had made the mistake of supposing that he was the son of Astyages' herdsman. In the course of the journey, however, he had heard the whole truth from his guides, and he described how he had been brought up by Cyno the herdsman's wife. He was full of her praises, and through his story her name was continually on his tongue. The name Cyno – 'Bitch' – suggested to his parents a way of creating a legend amongst the Persians about the miraculous preservation of their son; so they put it about that a bitch had found him abandoned in the mountains and had suckled him. That was the origin of this well-known tale.

When Cyrus grew up to be the bravest and most popular young man in Persia, Harpagus, who was burning for revenge upon Astyages, began to pay him court and send him presents. His own position, he thought, was inadequate to justify hopes of punishing the king without assistance; so when he saw Cyrus, who had suffered injuries not unlike his own, coming to maturity, he exerted himself to win his support. He had already paved the way to his design by severally persuading the great Median nobles that it would be to their advantage, in view of the harshness of Astyages' rule, to dethrone him in favour of Cyrus. This done by way of preparation, Harpagus wished to inform Cyrus of his purpose; but, as Cyrus lived in Persia and the roads were guarded, there was only one way he could think of to get a message through to him: this was by slitting open a hare, without pulling the fur off, and inserting into its belly a slip of paper on which he had written what he wanted to say. He then sewed up the hare, gave it to a trusted servant, together with a net to make him look like a huntsman, and sent him off to Persia with orders to present the hare to Cyrus, and tell him by word of mouth to cut it open with his own hands, and to let no one be present while he did so. The orders were obeyed. Cyrus received the hare, cut it open, found the letter inside and read it. 'Son of Cambyses,' it ran, 'since the gods watch over you – for without them you would never have been so fortunate – punish Astyages, your would-be murderer. Had he achieved his purpose, you would have died; to the gods, and to me, you owe your deliverance. Doubtless you have long known what was done to you, and how Astyages punished me for giving you to the cowherd instead of killing you. Do now as I advise, and you will become master of the whole realm of Astyages. Persuade the Persians to revolt, and march against the Medes. It makes no odds whether I or any other Mede of distinction is appointed by the king to take command against you: you will succeed in either case, for the Median nobility will be the first to desert him and join you in the attempt to pull him down. All our preparations are made. Do what I advise, and do it quickly.'

The letter set Cyrus thinking of the means by which he could most effectively persuade the Persians to revolt, and his deliberations led him to adopt the following plan, which he found best suited to his purpose. He wrote on a roll of parchment that Astyages had appointed him to command the Persian army; then he summoned an assembly of the Persians, opened the roll in their presence and read out what he had written. 'And now,' he added, 'I have an order for you: every man is to appear on parade with a billhook.' The Persian nation contains a number of tribes, and the ones which Cyrus assembled and persuaded to revolt were the Pasargadae, Maraphii, and Maspii, upon which all the other tribes are dependent. Of these the Pasargadae are the most distinguished; they contain the clan of the Achaemenidae from which spring the Perseid kings. Other tribes are the Panthialaei, Derusiaei, Germanii, all of which are attached to the soil, the remainder – Dai, Mardi, Dropici, Sagartii – being nomadic.

The order was obeyed. All the men assembled with their billhooks, and Cyrus' next command was that before the day was out they should clear a certain piece of rough land full of thorn bushes, about eighteen or twenty furlongs square. This too was done, whereupon Cyrus issued the further order that they should present themselves again on the following day, after having taken a bath. Meanwhile Cyrus collected and slaughtered all his father's goats, sheep, and oxen in preparation for entertaining the whole Persian army at a banquet, together with the best wine and bread he could procure. The next day the guests assembled, and were told to sit down on the grass and enjoy themselves. After the meal Cyrus asked them which they preferred – yesterday's work or to-day's amusement; and they repled that it was indeed a far cry from the previous day's misery to their present pleasures. This was the answer which Cyrus wanted; he seized upon it at once and proceeded to lay bare what he had in mind. 'Men of Persia,' he said, 'listen to me: obey my orders, and you will be able to enjoy a thousand pleasures as good as this without ever turning your hands to menial labour; but, if you disobey, yesterday's task will be the pattern of innumerable others you will be forced to perform. Take my advice and win your freedom. I am the man destined to undertake your liberation, and it is my belief that you are a match for the Medes in war as in everything else. It is the truth I tell you. Do not delay, but fling off the yoke of Astyages at once.'

The Persians had long resented their subjection to the Medes. At last they had found a leader, and welcomed with enthusiasm the prospect of liberty.

When news of these events reached Astyages, he summoned Cyrus to appear before him; but Cyrus' answer was to send the messenger back with the threat that he would be there a good deal sooner than

Astyages liked. Astyages thereupon armed the Medes to a man, and so far lost his wits as to appoint Harpagus to command them – having apparently forgotten how he had treated him. The result was that when they took the field and engaged the Persian army, a few who were not in the plot did their duty, but of the remainder some deserted to the Persians and the greater number deliberately shirked fighting and took to their heels. When Astyages learnt of the disgraceful collapse of the Median army, he swore that even so Cyrus should not get away with it so easily; then, having first impaled the Magi who had advised him to let Cyrus go, he armed all Medes, both under and over military age, who had been left in the city, led them out to battle and was defeated. His men were killed and he himself was taken alive.

After the capture of Astyages, Harpagus came and jeered at him, the most bitter of his insults being a reference to the supper at which the king had regaled him with his son's flesh, followed by the question of what it felt like to be a slave instead of a king. Astyages looked at him and countered the question by another: did Harpagus, he asked, claim responsibility for what Cyrus had done? Harpagus replied that he most certainly did, for it was he who wrote the letter urging Cyrus to revolt.

'Then,' said Astyages, 'you are not only the wickedest but the most stupid of men: you are stupid, because when you might have been king yourself (if you really were responsible for what has happened) you gave another man the power; and you are wicked, because merely on account of that supper you have brought the Medes into slavery. If you had to hand the throne over to somebody else rather than keep it to yourself, it would have been more proper to give so fine a prize to a Mede than to a Persian; but as things are, the innocent Medes have become slaves instead of masters, and the Persians masters of the Medes though they were once their slaves.'

Astyages had reigned for thirty-five years before he was deposed in the manner I have described. Because of his harsh rule the Medes, who had been masters of Asia beyond the Halys for a hundred and twenty-eight years except for the period of Scythian domination, were forced to bow before the power of Persia. At a later period they regretted their submission and revolted from Darius, but were defeated and again reduced. On the present occasion the Persians under Cyrus rose against the Medes and from then onwards were masters of Asia.

Cyrus treated Astyages with great consideration and kept him at his court until he died.

That, then, is the story of the birth and upbringing of Cyrus, and of how he seized the throne. I have already related his subsequent success in resisting the aggression of Croesus, a victory which gave him control of the whole of Asia.

The following are certain Persian customs which I can describe from personal knowledge. The erection of statues, temples, and altars is not an accepted practice amongst them, and anyone who does such a thing is considered a fool, because, presumably, the Persian religion is not anthropomorphic like the Greek. Zeus, in their system, is the whole circle of the heavens, and they sacrifice to him from the tops of mountains. They also worship the sun, moon, and earth, fire, water, and winds, which are their only original deities: it was later that they learned from the Assyrians and Arabians the cult of Uranian Aphrodite. The Assyrian name for Aphrodite is Mylitta, the Arabian Alilat, the Persian Mitra.[1]

As for ceremonial, when they offer sacrifice to the deities I mentioned, they erect no altar and kindle no fire; the libation, the flute-music, the garlands, the sprinkled meal – all these things, familiar to us, they have no use for; but before a ceremony a man sticks a spray of leaves, usually myrtle leaves, into his headdress, takes his victim to some open place and invokes the deity to whom he wishes to sacrifice. The actual worshipper is not permitted to pray for any personal or private blessing, but only for the king and for the general good of the community, of which he is himself a part. When he has cut up the animal and cooked it, he makes a little heap of the softest green-stuff he can find, preferably clover, and lays all the meat upon it. This done, a Magus (a member of this caste is always present at sacrifices) utters an incantation over it in a form of words which is supposed to recount the Birth of the Gods. Then after a short interval the worshipper removes the flesh and does what he pleases with it.

Of all days in the year a Persian most distinguishes his birthday, and celebrates it with a dinner of special magnificence. A rich Persian on

1. A blunder; see Introduction p. 31.

his birthday will have an ox or a horse or a camel or a donkey baked whole in the oven and served up at table, and the poor some smaller beast. The main dishes at their meals are few, but they have many sorts of dessert, the various courses being served separately. It is this custom that has made them say that the Greeks leave the table hungry, because we never have anything worth mentioning after the first course: they think that if we did, we should go on eating. They are very fond of wine, and no one is allowed to vomit or relieve himself in the presence of another person.

If an important decision is to be made, they discuss the question when they are drunk, and the following day the master of the house where the discussion was held submits their decision for reconsideration when they are sober. If they still approve it, it is adopted; if not, it is abandoned. Conversely, any decision they make when they are sober, is reconsidered afterwards when they are drunk.

When Persians meet in the streets one can always tell by their mode of greeting whether or not they are of the same rank; for they so not speak but kiss – their equals upon the mouth, those somewhat superior on the cheeks. A man of greatly inferior rank prostrates himself in profound reverence. After their own nation they hold their nearest neighbours most in honour, then the nearest but one – and so on, their respect decreasing as the distance grows, and the most remote being the most despised. Themselves they consider in every way superior to everyone else in the world, and allow other nations a share of good qualities decreasing according to distance, the furthest off being in their view the worst. By a similar sort of principle the Medes extended their system of administration and government during the period of their dominance: the various nations governed each other, the Medes being the supreme authority and concerning themselves specially with their nearest neighbours; these in their turn ruling *their* neighbours, who were responsible for the next, and so on.

No race is so ready to adopt foreign ways as the Persian; for instance, they wear the Median costume because they think it handsomer than their own, and their soldiers wear the Egyptian corselet. Pleasures, too, of all sorts they are quick to indulge in when they get to know about them – a notable instance is pederasty, which they learned from the Greeks. Every man has a number of wives, and a much greater number of concubines. After prowess in fighting, the chief proof of manliness is to be the father of a large family of boys. Those who have most sons receive an annual present from the king – on the principle that there is strength in numbers. The period of a boy's education is between the ages of five and twenty, and they are taught three things only: to ride, to use the bow, and to speak the truth. Before the age of five a boy lives with the women and never sees his father, the object being to spare the father distress if the child should die in the early stages of its upbringing. In my view this is a sound practice. I admire also the custom which forbids even the king himself to put a man to death for a single offence, and any Persian under similar circumstances to punish a servant by an irreparable injury. Their way is to balance faults against services, and then, if the faults are greater and more numerous, anger may take its course. They declare that no man has ever yet killed his father or mother; in the cases where this has apparently happened, they are quite certain that inquiry would reveal that the son was either a changeling or born out of wedlock, for they insist that it is most improbable that the actual parent should be killed by his child. What they are forbidden to do, they are forbidden also to mention. They consider telling lies more disgraceful than anything else, and, next to that, owing money. There are many reasons for their horror of debt, but the chief is their conviction that a man who owes money is bound also to tell lies. Sufferers from the scab or from leprosy are isolated and forbidden the city. They say these diseases are punishments for offending the sun, and they expel any stranger who catches them: many Persians drive away even white doves, as if they, too, were guilty of the same offence. They have a profound reverence for rivers: they will never pollute a river with urine or spittle, or even wash their hands in one, or allow anyone else to do so. There is one other peculiarity which one notices about them, though they themselves are unaware of it: all their names, which express magnificence or physical qualities, end in the letter S (the Dorian 'san'). Inquiry will prove this in every case without exception.[1]

All this I am able to state definitely from personal knowledge. There is another practice, however, concerning the burial of the dead,

1. It is only true of the Greek renderings of Persian names.

which is not spoken of openly and is something of a mystery: it is that a male Persian is never buried until the body has been torn by a bird or a dog. I know for certain that the Magi have this custom, for they are quite open about it. The Persians in general, however, cover a body with wax and then bury it. The Magi are a peculiar caste, quite different from the Egyptian priests and indeed from any other sort of person. The Egyptian priests make it an article of religion to kill no living creature except for sacrifice, but the Magi not only kill anything, except dogs and men, with their own hands but make a special point of doing so; ants, snakes, animals, birds – no matter what, they kill them indiscriminately. Well, it is an ancient custom, so let them keep it.

I will now resume the thread of my story. The Ionians and Aeolians immediately after the Persian conquest of Lydia sent representatives to Cyrus at Sardis, to try to obtain from him the same terms as they had had under Croesus, their former master. Cyrus replied to their request by the story of the fluteplayer who saw some fish in the sea and played his flute to them in the hope that they would come ashore. When they refused to do so, he took a net, netted a large catch, and hauled them in. Seeing the fish jumping about, he said to them: 'It is too late to dance now: you might have danced to my music – but you would not.' The point of the story was, that when Cyrus had sent to the Ionians to ask them to revolt from Croesus, they had been unwilling to do so, though they were ready enough to offer their allegiance now that everything was settled in his favour. Cyrus was angry with them – and hence his reply.

When the news reached the various cities, the Ionians began to erect defences and held meetings at the Panionium. The meetings were attended by all except the Milesians, who were the only ones to have obtained the same terms from Cyrus as from Croesus. The others came to a common agreement to apply for help to Sparta.

These Ionians to whom the Panionium belongs had the good fortune to establish their settlements in a region which enjoys a better climate than any other we know of. It does not resemble what is found either further north, where there is an excess of cold and wet, or further south, where the weather is both too hot and too dry. There are four different dialects of the Ionic language, distributed as follows: the most southerly of the Ionian towns is Miletus, with Myrus to the north of it, and then Priene, these three being in Caria and speaking the same dialect. Ephesus, Colophon, Lebedus, Teos, Clazomenae, and Phocaea are in Lydia, and share a common dialect quite distinct from what is spoken at the places previously mentioned. There are three other Ionian settlements, two being the islands of Samos and Chios and one, Erythrae, a mainland town. The two latter use the same dialect, Samos a peculiar one of its own.

The Milesians were in no danger from Cyrus, because of the treaty they had made with him; and of the other Ionians the islanders had nothing to fear, because the Phoenicians were not yet subject to Persia and Persia herself was not a sea power.

The reason for the separation of Miletus from the other Ionian towns was simply the general weakness of the Hellenic peoples at that date, and particularly of the Ionians, who of all the Greek races had least power and influence.[1] There was no Ionian settlement of any consequence except Athens. The nation as a whole, including Athens and with the exception only of the twelve cities previously mentioned, took a dislike to the very name 'Ionian' and refused to admit to it – and even to-day I believe that most of them are ashamed of it. The twelve cities, on the contrary, were proud of it and marked their pride by building a temple for their own use which they called the Panionium, and by excluding from it all the other Ionians – though in point of fact only Smyrna ever applied for admission. Something similar can be seen in the case of the Dorian Pentapolis (or Hexapolis as it used to be), where the Dorians are careful to exclude their neighbours from the use of their temple, the Triopium, and even went so far as to put a ban upon some of their own body who failed to observe the proprieties in regard to it. It used to be customary at the Games of the Triopian Apollo to give bronze tripods as prizes, and the winners were not allowed to take them away, but were required to dedicate them on the spot to the god. This ancient custom was openly defied by a Halicarnassian called Agasicles, who, after winning his tripod, took it home and fastened it up on the wall of his house. In punish-

1. An example of Herodotus' curious prejudice against the Ionians of Asia.

ment for this offence the five cities of Lindus, Ialyssus, Camirus, Cos, and Cnidus excluded Halicarnassus (which was the sixth) from the temple privileges. The reason why the Ionians chose the number twelve for their Asiatic settlements and refused to increase it, is, I fancy, the fact that they were divided into twelve states when they lived in the Peloponnese, just as the Achaeans, who drove them out, are to-day. Of the Achaean cities, that nearest Sicyon is Pallene; then comes Aegira, then Aegae on the Crathis, a stream which is never dry and gave its name to the Italian Crathis; then Bura and Helice (where the Ionians took refuge after their defeat by the Achaeans); then Aegium, Rhypes, Patres, Phares, and Olenus (on the large river Pirus); then Dyme and Tritaeës. Of these only the last lies inland. Those, then, are the twelve divisions of what is now Achaea but used to be Ionia: and that is the reason, as I have said, why the Ionians founded twelve settlements in Asia. It is quite absurd to pretend that they are any more Ionian, or of purer blood, than the Ionians generally; for a large section of them were actually Abantians from Euboea, who are not Ionians at all, even in name, to say nothing of the admixture of Minyae from Orchomenus and of Cadmeians, Dryopes, Phocians from various towns in Phocis, Molossians, Arcadian Pelasgi, Dorians from Epidaurus, and many others. Even those who started from the Government House in Athens and believe themselves to be of the purest Ionian blood, took no women with them but married Carian girls, whose parents they had killed. The fact that these women were forced into marriage after the murder of their fathers, husbands, and sons was the origin of the law, established by oath and passed down to their female descendants, forbidding them to sit at table with their husbands or to address them by name. It was at Miletus that this took place.

As to government, some of them took kings of Lycian nationality, descended from Glaucus the son of Hippolochus, others men of the Caucones from Pylus, descended from Codrus the son of Melanthus; and others, again, were ruled by men from both these families. But since these Ionians set more store by the name that the others, they may as well pass for the pure-bred ones. In point of fact, the name applies to all who originate from Athens and keep the festival of the Apaturia: all the Ionians, that is, except the men of Ephesus and Colophon, who, because of some murder or other, are the only ones to be excluded from it.

The Panionium is a consecrated spot on the north side of Mycale, chosen by common consent of the Ionians and dedicated to Poseidon, who was previously worshipped at Helice. Mycale itself is a promontory of the mainland running out in a westerly direction towards Samos, and it is here that the Ionians gathered from their various cities to keep the festival called the Panionia. The names of festivals, not only amongst the Ionians but amongst all the Greeks, end, like the Persian proper names, in the same letter.

Those I have mentioned, then, are the twelve towns of the Ionians; the Aeolic towns are Cyme (also known as Phriconis), Larissa, Neon Tichus, Temnus, Cilla, Notium, Aegiroessa, Pitane, Aegaeae, Myrina, and Grynea. These are the eleven ancient towns of the Aeolians. Originally, indeed, they had twelve on the mainland, as the Ionians did, but one of them – Smyrna – the Ionians took from them. The soil of Aeolis is better than that of Ionia, but the climate is not so good.

The Aeolians lost Smyrna by treachery. They had received into the town some men from Colophon, who had been defeated by the rival faction and expelled; the fugitives watched their chance and, when the people of Smyrna were celebrating a festival of Dionysus outside the walls, shut the gates and got possession of the towns. The Aeolians of the other states came to their help, and terms were agreed to whereby the Ionians should surrender all moveable property but keep possession of the town. The people of Smyrna were then distributed amongst the other eleven Aeolian towns, where they were given civic rights. These, then, are the Aeolian settlements on the mainland, excluding those about Mt Ida which are not part of the confederacy. Of the island settlements, Lesbos has five (the sixth, Arisba, was taken by the Methymnaeans, their kinsmen, and the inhabitants enslaved), Tenedos one, and the so-called Hundred Isles one more. The Aeolians of Lesbos and Tenedos, like the Ionian islanders, had at this time nothing to fear. The other Aeolians came to a general agreement to follow the Ionians in whatever course they should take.

When the Aeolian and Ionian envoys reached Sparta (no time had been lost in the business) they chose Pythermus, a Phocaean, as their spokesman. In order to draw as large an audience as possible, he dressed himself in purple clothes and came forward to make a long speech asking for Spartan aid. The speech was a failure. The Spartans refused to help the Ionians, and the envoys left. Nevertheless, in spite of their rejection of the Ionian request, the Spartans dispatched a fifty-oared galley to the Asiatic coast, in order, I suppose, to watch Cyrus and what was going on in Ionia. The vessel put in at Phocaea, and the most distinguished of the men on board, a man called Lacrines, was sent to Sardis to forbid Cyrus, on behalf of the Lacedaemonians, to harm any Greek city or they would take action. The story goes that when Cyrus heard what the herald said, he asked some Greeks who happened to be with him who the Lacedaemonians were, and what were their numbers that they dared to send him such a command. On being informed, he gave the following answer to the Spartan herald: 'I have never yet been afraid of men who have a special meeting place in the centre of their city, where they swear this and that and cheat each other. Such people, if I have anything to do with it, will not have merely the troubles of Ionia to chatter about, but their own.' This was intended by Cyrus as a criticism of the Greeks generally, because they have markets for buying and selling, unlike the Persians who never buy in open market, and indeed have not a single market-place in the whole country. After this Cyrus left Tabalus, a Persian, as governor of Sardis, entrusted to a Lydian named Pactyes the task of collecting and conveying the treasure belonging to Croesus and the other Lydians, and himself started eastwards on his march to Ecbatana, taking Croesus with him. He did not think the Ionians important enough to constitute a primary objective, for his mind was on Babylon and the Bactrians and the Sacae and the Egyptians, against whom he intended to lead an expedition in person. Some other commander would suffice to tackle the Ionians.

As soon as Cyrus had gone, Pactyes induced the Lydians to rise against their Persian governor, and going down to the coast was enabled by his possession of the Sardian gold to hire soldiers and persuade the men from the coastal districts to support him. He then marched against Sardis and laid siege to Tabalus, who was shut up in the inner fortress of the city. Cyrus, when the news reached him on the road, asked Croesus what he thought would be the end of it all.

'For I don't suppose,' he said, 'that the Lydians will stop being a nuisance to me – and to themselves too for that matter. I am not at all sure that the best thing would not be to make slaves of them. As things are, I seem to have acted like a man who kills a father and spares the sons; for you, who were more than a father to the Lydians, are now my prisoner, and to the Lydians themselves I have made a present of Sardis – and then feel surprised because they are not loyal to me.'

When Croesus heard him give this expression to his thoughts, he was afraid Sardis might be laid in ruins; so he replied: 'My lord, your argument is reasonable enough; nevertheless I beg you not to indulge your anger without restraint, or destroy an ancient city which is not responsible for the present situation any more than for what happened previously. The previous offence was my own: I was the guilty one, and I am paying the penalty for it; this time the villain is Pactyes, in whose charge you put Sardis. So it is Pactyes you should punish. As for the Lydians, forgive them – but at the same time, if you want to keep them loyal and to prevent any danger from them in future, I suggest you put a veto upon their possession of arms. Make them wear tunics under their cloaks, and high boots, and tell them to teach their sons to play the zither and harp, and to start shopkeeping. If you do that, my lord, you will soon see them turn into women instead of men, and there will not be any more danger of their rebelling against you.'

Croesus gave this advice, because it seemed to him preferable from the Lydians' point of view to being sold into slavery. Moreover, he was aware that he would never induce Cyrus to change his mind, unless the suggestion he made was something worth listening to; and he was afraid that the Lydians, if they escaped the immediate danger, might nevertheless at some future date risk a rebellion against Persia and so come to grief. The proposal pleased Cyrus, and he promised to accept it; then, saying he was no longer angry, he sent for Mazares, a Mede, and ordered him to make a proclamation to the Lydians along the lines suggested by Croesus, and to sell into slavery everybody who had joined in the Lydian attack on Sardis. Pactyes himself was at all costs to be taken alive and brought before him. Then, having given his orders, Cyrus continued his journey towards Persian territory.

Pactyes, when he learnt that an army was on his tracks and already near, took fright and fled to Cyme, and Mazares the Mede marched to Sardis with a detachment of Cyrus' troops. Finding Pactyes and his supporters gone, the first thing he did was to compel the Lydians to carry out Cyrus' orders – as a result of which they altered from that moment their whole way of life; he then sent a demand to Cyme that Pactyes should be surrendered, and the men of the town decided to take the advice of the oracle at Branchidae as to whether they should obey. Branchidae is in Milesian territory close to the harbour of Panormus, and the oracle there, frequently consulted by the Ionians and Aeolians, is a very ancient one. The messengers from Cyme were instructed to ask how to deal with Pactyes in the way most likely to win the favour of the god, and the answer they received was that he must be given up to the Persians. The messengers returned home to report, and the citizens of Cyme were prepared in consequence to give up the wanted man. But just as they were about to do so, one of their number, a man of repute called Aristodicus, son of Heracleides, stopped them, because, as he said, he had his doubts about the oracle's answer and thought the messengers had not reported it correctly. The result of this was that another party, of which Aristodicus himself was a member, left for Branchidae to repeat the question about Pactyes. On their arrival Aristodicus, as spokesman, put to the oracle this question: 'Lord Apollo, Pactyes the Lydian has fled to us for safety, to escape violent death at the hands of the Persians, who are now demanding that we should hand him over. It is a wicked thing to betray a suppliant, and in spite of our fear of Persian power we have not dared to do it until we receive from you clear instructions upon how we should act.' The answer to this second question was the same as before: namely that Pactyes must be handed over to the Persians.

Aristodicus, however, who had expected this answer, was not yet satisfied. He went all round the outside of the temple, and took from their nests the sparrows and other birds which had built there; and the story goes that while he was doing it he heard a voice from the innermost shrine, saying: 'Impious wretch, how dare you do this wicked thing? Would you destroy those who have come to my temple for protection?' Aristodicus, by no means at a loss, replied:

'Lord Apollo, do you protect your suppliants, yet tell the men of Cyme to abandon theirs?' 'Yes,' answered the god; 'I do indeed, that you may suffer the sooner for the sacrilege, and never come here again to consult my oracle about handing over suppliants.'

This answer put the people of Cyme in a dilemma. They did not want to come to grief as a result of surrendering their suppliant, any more than to be besieged by the Persians as a result of keeping him – so they sent him to Mytilene, and the Mytilenaeans, on receiving a demand from Mazares, were about to give him up in return for a sum of money (how much I cannot say definitely, for it was never paid), when the people of Cyme, hearing of these negotiations, sent a boat to Lesbos and took Pactyes off to Chios. It was here that he was dragged by the Chians from the temple of Athene the Guardian and surrendered to the Persians. They were paid by getting in exchange the district of Atarneus, a tract of land in Mysia opposite Lesbos. So the Persians got hold of Pactyes and kept him under guard, meaning to bring him before Cyrus.

For a considerable time after this no Chian would use barley meal from Atarneus to sprinkle on a sacrifice, or make any cake from the grain grown there; in fact they put a ban upon all the produce of the district so far as religious purposes were concerned.

After Pactyes had been given up by the Chians, Mazares began a campaign against the men who had taken part in besieging Tabalus. He sold the inhabitants of Priene into slavery, overran and plundered the district of Magnesia and the plain of the Maeander. Then he fell ill and died. The command was taken over by Harpagus, another Mede – the same man who was given the abominable supper by the Median King Astyages, and helped to put Cyrus on the throne. On his appointment by Cyrus to the command, he marched into Ionia and set about taking the towns by means of earthworks. His method was to force the defenders inside their fortifications, raise a mound of earth close up against the wall, and so get an entrance and carry the town. The first Ionian town he attacked was Phocaea.

The Phocaeans were the first Greeks to make long sea voyages; it was they who showed the way to the Adriatic, Tyrrhenia, Iberia, and Tartessus. They used to sail not in deep, broad-beamed merchant vessels but in fifty-oared galleys. When they went to Tartessus they made themselves agreeable to Arganthonius, the King, who had ruled the place for eighty years, and lived to be a hundred and twenty. Indeed, this person took such a fancy to them that he asked them to quit Ionia permanently and settle wherever they liked on his own land; the Phocaeans, however, refused the offer, whereupon the king, hearing that the Median power was on the increase in their part of the world, gave them money to build a wall round their town. And he must have given a great deal, for the wall at Phocaea is of pretty considerable extent, and constructed of large stone blocks well fitted together.

Harpagus, then, brought his troops to Phocaea, whose defences were built in the way I have described, and began a siege, proclaiming to the Phocaeans that he would be satisfied if they consented to pull down a single tower in the fortifications and sacrifice one house. The Phocaeans, however, indignant at the thought of slavery, asked for one day in which to consider the proposal before answering; stipulating at the same time that Harpagus should withdraw his forces during their deliberations. This Harpagus consented to do, though he said he was perfectly aware of their intention. So the troops were withdrawn, and the Phocaeans at once launched their galleys, put aboard their women and children and moveable property, including the statues and other sacred objects from their temples – everything, in fact, except paintings, and images made of bronze or marble – and sailed for Chios. So the Persians on their return took possession of an empty town.

The Phocaeans made an offer for the islands known as the Oenussae, but the Chians, who were afraid that they might be turned into a new centre of trade to the exclusion of their own island, refused to sell; so the Phocaeans prepared to sail to Corsica, where twenty years previously on the advice of an oracle they had founded a city called Alalia. At the time Arganthonius was already dead. But before starting on the voyage, they returned to Phocaea and killed the Persian garrison left there by Harpagus. Then they tried to secure unity for their expedition by laying fearful curses upon any man who should fail to accompany it. They also dropped a lump of iron into the sea and swore never to return to Phocaea until it floated up again. But at the very beginning of the voyage to Corsica more than half of them were seized with such passionate longing to see their city and their old homes once more, that they broke their oath and sailed back to Phocaea. The others kept their oath, and continuing the voyage from the Oenussae, arrived safely in Corsica. For five years they lived at Alalia with the former settlers and built temples in the town; but during that period they caused so much annoyance to their neighbours by plunder and pillage, that the Tyrrhenians and Carthaginians agreed to attack them with a fleet of sixty ships apiece. The Phocaeans manned their own vessels, also sixty in number, and sailed to meet them in the Sardinian sea, as it is called. In the engagement which followed the Phocaeans won; but it was a Cadmeian[1] sort of victory with more loss than gain, for forty of their vessels were destroyed and the remaining twenty had their rams so badly bent as to render them unfit for service. The survivors returned to Alalia, took aboard their women and children and such of their property as there was room for, and sailed from Corsica to Rhegium. The Carthaginians and Tyrrhenians drew lots for the possession of the prisoners from the ships which were sunk. Of the Tyrrhenians, the people of Agylla got by far the largest number, and they took them all ashore and stoned them to death. The result of this outrage was that when any living thing – sheep, ox, or man – subsequently passed the place where the Phocaeans had lain, its body became twisted and crippled by a paralytic stroke. Wishing to expiate the crime of the murder, the men of Agylla sent to Delphi, and were told by the Priestess to begin the custom, which they still observe to-day, of honouring the dead men with a grand funeral ceremony and the holding of athletic and equestrian contests.

Such was the fate of this section of the Phocaeans. Those who went off to Rhegium made it the base from which they afterwards sent men to found a new city in Oenotria. It is known to-day as Elea.[2] It was founded on the advice of a man of Posidonia, who suggested that when the oracle said 'Cyrnus' – or Corsica – it meant not the island but the hero of that name, whose worship they were to institute.

1. Cadmus at Thebes sowed the Dragon's Teeth; a crop of armed men sprang up, who fought until only five survived.
2. Latin Uelia; also spelt by the Greeks, who did not have the W-sound, 'Hüéle', which is in fact Herodotus' spelling here.

So much for the Ionian city of Phocaea. The story of Teos was not very different, for the Teians, when Harpagus took their city by means of his mound, also took to their ships and escaped by sea to Thrace. There they founded Abdera, a place where Timesius of Clazomenae had previously tried to settle but without success, as he was driven out by the Thracians. He is honoured to-day as a demigod by the Teians of Abdera.

The men of Phocaea and Teos were the only Ionians who preferred voluntary exile to the prospect of slavery; the others remained where they were. All of them, except the Milesians, fought Harpagus as the Phocaeans and Teians had done, but in spite of invidual acts of great courage in defence of their homes they were defeated; their towns were taken, and they were forced to submit to their new masters. The Milesians, as I have already mentioned, had already come to terms with Cyrus, so the war did not affect them.

In this way Ionia was once more reduced to subjection; and after the defeat of the mainland towns by Harpagus, the islanders took fright and surrendered to Cyrus.

In spite of their defeat the Ionians continued the practice of meeting at the Panionium, and I am told that it was at one of these meetings that a man of Priene, called Bias, made a most admirable suggestion which, had they taken it, might have made them the most prosperous people in the Greek world. The proposal was that all the Ionians should unite and sail for Sardinia and settle together in a single community; there, living in the biggest island in the world, they would escape subjection, rule over their neighbours and be rich and happy. If, on the other hand, they stayed in Ionia, there was little chance, so far as he could see, of ever regaining their freedom. This proposal was made by Bias after the Ionian defeat; but there was another, hardly less excellent, which had been made before it by Thales of Miletus, a Phoenician by remote descent: this was that the Ionians should set up a common centre of government at Teos, as that place occupied a central position; the other cities would continue as going concerns, but subject to the central government, in the relationship of outlying districts to the mother city. Such were the two proposals.

After the subjugation of Ionia, Harpagus attacked the Carians,

Caunians, and Lycians, taking with him both Ionians and Aeolians in his army. The Carians, now a mainland people, were originally islanders. Long ago, when they inhabited the islands, they were known as Leleges and were subjects of Minos; but as far as I have been able to gather information on the subject, they never paid tribute in money but manned his ships whenever he had need of them; and in this way, because Minos had great military success and extended his conquests over a wide area, they became in his day by far the most famous of all nations. The Greeks are indebted to them for three inventions: fitting crests on helmets, putting devices on shields, and making shields with handles. Hitherto everyone who used a shield had managed it, not by a handle, but by means of a leather thong slung round the neck and left shoulder. Long after this period the Carians were driven from the islands by the Dorians and Ionians, and settled on the mainland: that, at any rate, is the account the Cretans give – though the Carians themselves deny it, and claim to have been mainlanders from the first and never to have been known by any other name than their present one. In support of the claim to be aboriginals, they point to an ancient temple of the Carian Zeus at Mylasa, the use of which is shared by Mysians and Lydians as brother races of the Carians – Lydus and Mysus, according to them, having been the brothers of Car. These people, then, have the use of the temple; but others, even those which speak the same dialect as the Carians, are excluded from it.

The Caunians I believe myself to be of native stock, though by their own account they came originally from Crete. As to dialect they have come to resemble the Carians – or the Carians them, for I cannot say definitely which way round it should be; but in their way of life they are very different from the Carians, and indeed from everybody else; for they think it the finest thing in the world for men, women, or children to organize large drinking parties of friends of similar age. Again, having decided on one occasion to reject certain foreign cults which had been established amongst them, and to worship only their own ancestral gods, all but the boys put on their armour and went as far as the boundary of Calynda, striking the air with their spears and saying they were driving out the foreign gods.

The Lycians came originally from Crete, which in ancient times was occupied entirely by non-Greek peoples. The two sons of Europa, Sarpedon and Minos, fought for the throne, and the victorious Minos expelled Sarpedon and his party. The exiles sailed for Asia and landed on Milyan territory, Milyas being the ancient name of the country where the Lycians live to-day, though it was occupied then by the Solymi. During the rule of Sarpedon, the Lycians were known as the Termilae, the name they had brought with them from Crete – and which is still in use amongst their neighbours; but after Lycus, son of Pandion, had been driven from Athens by *his* brother Aegeus, and had taken refuge with Sarpedon amongst the Termilae, in the course of time they adopted his name and came to be called Lycians. In their manners they resemble in some ways the Cretans, in others the Carians, but in one of their customs, that of taking the mother's name instead of the father's, they are unique. Ask a Lycian who he is, and he will tell you his own name and his mother's, then his grandmother's and great-grandmother's and so on. And if a free woman has a child by a slave, the child is considered legitimate, whereas the children of a free man, however distinguished he may be, and a foreign wife or mistress have no citizen rights at all.

The Carians were subdued by Harpagus, and neither they nor any of the Greeks who lived in this country managed to distinguish themselves. Amongst the latter were the Cnidians, colonists from Lacedaemon, who occupy a district on the coast, called Triopium, adjoining the peninsula of Bybassus. All but a narrow neck is surrounded by water, the Ceramic gulf lying to the northward and the sea off Syme and Rhodes to the southward. The neck of the peninsula is about half a mile across, and while Harpagus was conquering Ionia, the Cnidians began to dig through it, with the intention of turning their country into an island. The isthmus they were trying to cut lies just where the Cnidian territory ends on the mainland side, so it is all contained within the peninsula. A large number of men turned to, but it was observed that the workmen got hurt by splinters of stone in various places about the body, especially the eyes, more often than might have been expected. Indeed, there was something so unnatural about it, that they sent to Delphi to ask what it was that was hindering the work. Their own account is that the Priestess gave them the following answer in iambic verse:

> Do not fence off the isthmus; do not dig.
> Zeus would have made an island, had he willed it.

Having received their answer, the Cnidians stopped digging, and surrendered without a struggle on the approach of Harpagus and his army.

Inland, east of Halicarnassus, there were the men of Pedasus. These people used to get warning of any impending disaster to them and their neighbours by the priestess of Athene growing a long beard, a thing which has actually happened on three occasions. They were the only Carians who resisted Harpagus for any length of time, and they did in fact cause him a good deal of trouble by holding out behind the defences they erected on Mount Lida. But the place was ultimately taken.

The fate of the Lycians of Xanthus makes a different story. When Harpagus advanced into the plain of Xanthus, they met him in battle, though greatly outnumbered, and fought with much gallantry; at length. however, they were defeated and forced to retire within their walls, whereupon they collected their women, children, slaves, and other property and shut them up in the citadel, set fire to it and burnt it to the ground. Then having sworn to do or die, they marched out to meet the enemy and were killed to a man. Most of the Lycians who now claim to be Xanthians are foreign immigrants, except eighty families who happened on that occasion to be away from home, and consequently survived. The people of Caunus followed in most respects the example of the Lycians, and their town fell into Harpagus' hands in much the same way as Xanthus did.

While Harpagus was turning upside-down the lower, or western, part of Asia, Cyrus was engaged with the north and east, bringing into subjection every nation without exception. Most of his minor conquests I will say nothing about, but mention only those of his campaigns which gave him the greatest trouble and are in themselves the most interesting.

Having subdued the rest of the continent, he turned his attention to Assyria, a country remarkable for the number of great cities it contained, and especially for the most powerful and renowned of them all – Babylon, to which the seat of government was transferred after the fall of Nineveh. Babylon lies in a wide plain, a vast city in the form of a square with sides nearly fourteen miles long and a circuit of some fifty-six miles, and in addition to its enormous size it surpasses in splendour any city of the known world. It is surrounded by a broad deep moat full of water, and within the moat there is a wall fifty cubits wide and two hundred high (the royal cubit is three inches longer than the ordinary cubit). And now I must describe how the soil dug out to make the moat was used, and the method of building the wall. While the digging was going on, the earth that was shovelled out was formed into bricks, which were baked in ovens as soon as a sufficient number were made; then using hot bitumen for mortar the workmen began by revetting with brick each side of the moat, and then went on to erect the actual wall. In both cases they laid rush-mats between every thirty courses of brick. On the top of the wall they constructed, along each edge, a row of one-roomed buildings facing inwards with enough space between for a four-horse chariot to pass. There are a hundred gates in the circuit of the wall, all of bronze with bronze uprights and lintels.

Eight days' journey from Babylon there is a city called Is on a smallish river of the same name, a tributary of the Euphrates, and in this river lumps of bitumen are found in great quantity. This was the source of supply for the bitumen used in building the wall of Babylon. The Euphrates, a broad, deep, swift river which rises in Armenia and flows into the Persian Gulf, runs through the middle of the city and divides it in two. The wall is brought right down to the water on both sides, and at an angle to it there is another wall on each bank, built of baked bricks without mortar, running through the town. There are a great many houses of three and four storeys. The main streets and the side streets which lead to the river are all dead straight, and for every one of the side streets or alleys there was a bronze gate in the river wall by which the water could be reached.

The great wall I have described is the chief armour of the city; but there is a second one within it, hardly less strong though smaller. There is a fortress in the middle of each half of the city: in one the royal palace surrounded by a wall of great strength, in the other the temple of Bel, the Babylonian Zeus. The temple is a square building, two furlongs each way, with bronze gates, and was still in existence in my time; it has a solid central tower, one furlong square, with a second erected on top of it and then a third, and so on up to eight. All eight towers can be climbed by a spiral way running round the out- side, and about half-way up there are seats for those who make the ascent to rest on. On the summit of the topmost tower stands a great temple with a fine large couch in it, richly covered, and a golden table beside it. The shrine contains no image and no one spends the night there except (if we may believe the Chaldaeans who are the priests of Bel) one Assyrian woman, all alone, whoever it may be that the god has chosen. The Chaldaeans also say – though I do not believe them – that the god enters the temple in person and takes his rest upon the bed. There is a similar story told by the Egyptians at Thebes, where a woman always passes the night in the temple of the Theban Zeus and is forbidden, so they say, like the woman in the temple at Babylon, to have any intercourse with men; and there is yet another instance in the Lycian town of Patara, where the priestess who delivers the oracles when required (for there is not always an oracle there) is shut up in the temple during the night.

In the temple of Babylon there is a second shrine lower down, in which is a great sitting figure of Bel, all of gold on a golden throne, supported on a base of gold, with a golden table standing beside it. I was told by the Chaldaeans that, to make all this, more than twenty-two tons of gold were used. Outside the temple is a golden altar, and there is another one, not of gold, but of great size, on which full-grown sheep are sacrificed. (The golden altar is reserved for the sacri-fice of sucklings only.) On the larger altar the Chaldaeans also offer something like two and a half tons of frankincense every year at the festival of Bel. In the time of Cyrus there was also in this sacred build-ing a solid golden statue of a man some fifteen feet high – I have this on the authority of the Chaldaeans, though I never saw it myself. Darius the son of Hystaspes had designs upon it, but he never carried it off because his courage failed him; Xerxes, however, did take it and killed the priest who tried to prevent the sacrilege. In addition to the adornments I have described there are also many private offerings in the temple.

There have been many kings of Babylon who helped to fortify the city and adorn its temples, and I will tell their story in my History of Assyria.[1] There were also two queens, the earlier, Semiramis, preceding the later by five generations. It was Semiramis who was responsible for certain remarkable embankments in the plain outside the city, built to control the river which until then used to flood the whole countryside. The later of the two queens, Nitocris, was a woman of greater intelligence than Semiramis, and not only left as a memorial of her reign the works which I will presently describe, but also, having her eye on the great and expanding power of the Medes and the many cities, including Nineveh itself, which had fallen before them, took every possible measure to increase her security. For instance, she changed the course of the Euphrates, which flows through Babylon. Its course was originally straight, but by cutting channels higher upstream she made it wind about with so many twists and turns that now it actually passes a certain Assyrian village called Ardericca three separate times, so that anyone to-day who travels from the Mediterranean to Babylon and comes down the Euphrates finds himself three times over at Ardericca, on three different days. In addition to this she constructed embankments on both sides of the river of remarkable strength and height, and a long way above the city, close beside the river, dug a basin for a lake some forty-seven miles in circumference. The depth of the basin was governed by the point at which the workmen came to water as they dug down. The soil from the excavation was used for the embankments. When the basin was finished, the queen had stone brought to the place and built up the edge of it the whole way round. The purpose both of the excavation and of the diversion of the river was to cause the frequent bends to reduce the speed of the current, and to prevent a direct voyage downstream to the city. A boat would be faced with a devious course, and at the end of her trip she would have to make the tedious circuit of the lake. Moreover, these works lay in the neighbourhood of the approaches to Assyria and on the direct route to Media, and the intention of the queen was to discourage the Medes from mixing with the peoples of Babylon and thus getting to know what was going on there. Besides these defences

1. The second unfulfilled promise. See Introduction p. 19.

she was responsible for another undertaking of a less important kind: the city, as I have said, being divided in two by the river, it was necessary under its previous rulers for anyone who wanted to get from one half to the other to cross over by boat and no doubt this was a tiresome business. Nitocris, however, when she was having the basin dug for the lake, had the foresight to make that work a means of getting rid of the inconvenience as well as of leaving yet another monument of her reign. She ordered long stone blocks to be cut, and when they were ready and the excavation complete, she diverted the river into the basin; and while the basin was filling and the original bed of the stream was drying up, she built with burnt brick, on the same pattern as the wall, an embankment on each side of the river where it flowed through the city, and also along the descent to the water's edge from the gates at the end of the side streets; then, as near as possible to the centre of the city, she built a bridge over the river with the blocks of stone which she had had prepared, using iron and lead to bind the blocks together. Between the piers of the bridge she had squared baulks of timber laid down for the inhabitants to cross by – but only during daylight, for every night the timber was removed to prevent people from going over in the dark and robbing each other. Finally when the basin had been filled and the bridge finished, the river was brought back into its original bed, with the result that the basin had been made to serve the queen's purpose, and the people of the town had their bridge into the bargain.

This same princess was also the perpetrator of a grim practical joke. She had a tomb made for herself over one of the main gateways of the city, right high up above the actual entrance, and caused the following inscription to be cut on it: 'If any king of Babylon hereafter is short of money, let him open my tomb and take as much as he likes. But this must be done only in case of need. Whoever opens my tomb under any other circumstances will get no good of it.' The tomb remained undisturbed till the reign of Darius, who resented being unable to use one of the city gates – for he never did use the one under the tomb because, had he done so, he would have had to drive directly under the corpse; moreover, he thought it was absurd, when treasure was lying there asking to be taken, not to take it. So he opened the tomb. He found, however, not a penny inside – but only the body of the queen and another inscription, which read: 'If you had not been insatiably greedy and eager to get money by the most despicable means, you would never have opened the tomb of the dead.' So much, then, for the tradition about the character of Nitocris.

The expedition of Cyrus was directed against her son, who, like his father, was called Labynetus and was king of Assyria. When the Persian king goes to war, he is always well provided not only with victuals from home and his own cattle, but also with water from the Choaspes, a river which flows past Susa. No Persian king ever drinks the water of any other stream, and a supply of it ready boiled for use is brought along in silver jars carried in a long train of four-wheeled mule waggons wherever the king goes.

On his march to Babylon Cyrus came to the river Gyndes which rises in the Matienian mountains, runs through the country of the Dardanes and then joins the Tigris which passes the city of Opis and flows into the Persian Gulf. Cyrus was preparing to cross this river, for which boats were needed, when one of his sacred white horses, a high-spirited creature, entered the water and attempted to swim across but was swept under by the rapid current and carried away. Cyrus was so furious with the river for daring to do such a thing, that he swore he would punish it by making it so weak that even a woman could get over in future without difficulty and without wetting her knees. He held up his march against Babylon, divided his army into two parts, marked out on each side of the river a hundred and eighty channels running off from it in various directions, and ordered his men to set to work and dig. Having a vast number of hands employed, he managed to finish the job, but only at the cost of the whole summer wasted. Then, having punished the Gyndes by splitting it into three hundred and sixty separate channels, Cyrus, at the beginning of the following spring, resumed his march to Babylon.

The Babylonians had taken the field and were awaiting his approach. When he arrived near the city they attacked him, but were defeated and forced to retire inside their defences; they already knew of Cyrus' restless ambition and had watched his successive acts of aggression against one nation after another, and as they had taken the precaution of accumulating in Babylon a stock of provisions sufficient to last many years, they were able to regard the prospect of a siege with indifference. The siege dragged on, no progress was made, and Cyrus was beginning to despair of success. Then somebody suggested or he himself thought up the following plan: he stationed part of his force at the point where the Euphrates flows into the city and another contingent at the opposite end where it flows out, with orders to both to force an entrance along the river-bed as soon as they saw that the water was shallow enough. Then, taking with him all his non-combatant troops, he withdrew to the spot where Nitocris had excavated the lake, and proceeded to repeat the operation which the queen had previously performed: by means of a cutting he diverted the river into the lake (which was then a marsh) and in this way so greatly reduced the depth of water in the actual bed of the river that it became fordable, and the Persian army, which had been left at Babylon for the purpose, entered the river, now only deep enough to reach about the middle of a man's thigh, and, making their way along it, got into the town. If the Babylonians had learnt what Cyrus was doing or had seen it for themselves in time, they could have let the Persians enter and then, by shutting all the gates which led to the waterside and manning the walls on either side of the river, they could have caught them in a trap and wiped them out. But as it was they were taken by surprise. The Babylonians themselves say that owing to the great size of the city the outskirts were captured without the people in the centre knowing anything about it; there was a festival going on, and they continued to dance and enjoy themselves, until they learned the news the hard way. That, then, is the story of the first capture of Babylon.

I will give several indications of the wealth and resources of Babylon, but the following is a specially striking one. Apart from normal tribute, the whole Persian empire is divided into regions for the purpose of furnishing supplies for the king and his army, and for four months out of the twelve the supplies come from Babylonian territory, the whole of the rest of Asia being responsible for the remaining eight. This shows that the resources of Assyria are a third part of the resources of Asia as a whole. It will be seen that the governorship (or satrapy, as the Persians call it) of Assyria is by far the most coveted of all their provincial posts, when one realizes that Tritantaechmes the son of Artabazus, who held it from the king, received an *artaba* of silver every day – the artaba is a Persian dry measure of about five bushels, exceeding the Attic *medimnus* by three *choinikes*, or about five pints. He also had as his personal property, in addition to war horses, eight hundred stallions and sixteen thousand mares, twenty for each stallion, and so many Indian dogs that four large villages in the plain were exempted from other charges on condition of supplying them with food. This will give an idea of the wealth of the governor of Babylon.

The rainfall of Assyria is slight and provides enough moisture only to burst the seed and start the root growing, but to swell the grain and bring it to maturity artificial irrigation is used, not, as in Egypt, by the natural flooding of the river, but by hand-worked swipes.[1] Like Egypt, the whole country is intersected by dykes; the largest of them has to be crossed in boats and runs in a south-easterly direction from the Euphrates until it joins another river, the Tigris, on which Nineveh was built. As a grain-bearing country Assyria is the richest in the world. No attempt is made there to grow figs, grapes, or olives or any other fruit trees, but so great is the fertility of the grain fields that they normally produce crops of two-hundredfold, and in an exceptional year as much as three-hundredfold. The blades of wheat and barley are at least three inches wide. As for millet and sesame, I will not say to what an astonishing size they grow, though I know well enough; but I also know that people who have not been to Babylonia have refused to believe even what I have said already about its fertility. The only oil these people use is made from sesame; date-palms grow everywhere, mostly of the fruit-bearing kind, and the fruit supplies them with food, wine, and honey. The method of cultivation is the same as for figs, particularly in regard to the practice of taking the fruit of what the Greeks call the 'male' palm and tying it into the 'female' or date-bearing tree, to allow the gall-fly to enter the fruit and ripen it and prevent it from dropping off. For it is a fact that the male palms have the gall-fly in their fruit, like wild figs.

I will next describe the thing which surprised me most of all in this

1. No doubt the *shadouf*, still used in the Near East: a fifteen-foot beam, pivoting on a three-foot support, and with a dipper at one end and a counter-weight at the other.

country, after Babylon itself: I mean the boats which ply down the Euphrates to the city. These boats are circular in shape and made of hide; they build them in Armenia to the northward of Assyria, where they cut withies to make the frames and then stretch skins taut on the under side for the body of the craft; they are not fined-off or tapered in any way at bow or stern, but quite round like a shield. The men fill them with straw, put the cargo on board – mostly wine in palm-wood casks – and let the current take them downstream. They are controlled by two men; each has a paddle which he works standing up, one in front drawing his paddle towards him, the other behind giving it a backward thrust. The boats vary a great deal in size; some are very big, the biggest of all having a capacity of some fourteen tons. Every boat carries a live donkey – the larger ones several – and when they reach Babylon and the cargoes have been offered for sale, the boats are broken up, the frames and straw sold and the hides loaded on the donkeys' backs for the return journey overland to Armenia. It is quite impossible to paddle the boats up-stream because of the strength of the current, and that is why they are constructed of hide instead of wood. Back in Armenia with their donkeys, the men build another lot of boats to the same design.

The dress of the Babylonians consists of a linen tunic reaching to the feet with a woollen one over it, and a short white cloak on top; they have their own fashion in shoes, which resemble the slippers one sees in Boeotia. They grow their hair long, wear turbans, and perfume themselves all over; everyone owns a seal and a walking-stick specially made for him, with a device carved on the top of it, an apple or rose or lily or eagle or something of the sort; for it is not the custom to have a stick without some such ornament. I will say no more about dress and so forth, but will go on to describe some of their practices. The most ingenious in my opinion is a custom which, I understand, they share with the Eneti in Illyria. In every village once a year all the girls of marriageable age used to be collected together in one place, while the men stood round them in a circle; an auctioneer then called each one in turn to stand up and offered her for sale, beginning with the best-looking and going on to the second best as soon as the first had been sold for a good price. Marriage was the object of the transaction. The rich men who wanted wives bid against each other for the prettiest girls, while the humbler folk, who had no use for good looks in a wife, were actually paid to take the ugly ones, for when the auctioneer had got through all the pretty girls he would call upon the plainest, or even perhaps a crippled one, to stand up, and then ask who was willing to take the least money to marry her – and she was knocked down to whoever accepted the smallest sum. The money came from the sale of the beauties, who in this way provided dowries for their ugly or misshapen sisters. It was illegal for a man to marry his daughter to anyone he happened to fancy, and no one could take home a girl he had bought without first finding a backer to guarantee his intention of marrying her. In cases of disagreement between husband and wife the law allowed the return of the purchase money. Anyone who wished could come even from a different village to buy a wife.

This admirable practice has now fallen into disuse and they have of late years hit upon another scheme, namely the prostitution of all girls of the lower classes to provide some relief from the poverty which followed upon the conquest with its attendant hardship and general ruin.

Next in ingenuity to the old marriage custom is their treatment of disease. They have no doctors, but bring their invalids out into the street, where anyone who comes along offers the sufferer advice on his complaint, either from personal experience or observation of a similar complaint in others. Anyone will stop by the sick man's side and suggest remedies which he has himself proved successful in whatever the trouble may be, or which he has known to succeed with other people. Nobody is allowed to pass a sick person in silence; but everyone must ask him what is the matter. They bury their dead in honey, and their dirges for the dead are like the Egyptian ones. When a Babylonian has had intercourse with his wife, he sits over incense to fumigate himself, with his wife opposite doing the same, and at daybreak they both wash. Before they have washed they will not touch any household utensils. In this they resemble the Arabians.

There is one custom amongst these people which is wholly shameful: every woman who is a native of the country must once in her life go and sit in the temple of Aphrodite and there give herself to a strange man. Many of the rich women, who are too proud to mix with the rest, drive to the temple in covered carriages with a whole host of servants following behind, and there wait; most, however, sit in the precinct of the temple with a band of plaited string round their heads – and a great crowd they are, what with some sitting there, others arriving, others going away – and through them all gangways are marked off running in every direction for the men to pass along and make their choice. Once a woman has taken her seat she is not allowed to go home until a man has thrown a silver coin into her lap and taken her outside to lie with her. As he throws the coin, the man has to say, 'In the name of the goddess Mylitta' – that being the Assyrian name for Aphrodite. The value of the coin is of no consequence; once thrown it becomes sacred, and the law forbids that it should ever be refused. The woman has no privilege of choice – she must go with the first man who throws her the money. When she has lain with him, her duty to the goddess is discharged and she may go home, after which it will be impossible to seduce her by any offer, however large. Tall, handsome women soon manage to get home again, but the ugly ones stay a long time before they can fulfil the condition which the law demands, some of them, indeed, as much as three or four years. There is a custom similar to this in parts of Cyprus.

In addition to the general practices I have mentioned, there is one which is peculiar to three of their clans: these people live entirely on fish which they catch and dry in the sun and then pound in a mortar; the smooth powder is then bolted through muslin and eaten either kneaded into cakes or baked like a sort of bread, according to taste.

After the conquest of Assyria, Cyrus' next desire was to subdue the Massagetae, whose country lies far to the eastward beyond the Araxes, opposite the Issedones; they are reputed to be a numerous and warlike people and some suppose them to be of Scythian nationality. The Araxes is said by some to be bigger than the Danube, by others to be not so big. It is also said to have a number of islands in it as large as Lesbos, where men live during summer on various kinds of roots which they dig up, and for their winter supplies pick as it ripens and put into store any sort of tree-fruit which they have found to be suitable for food. They have also discovered another tree whose fruit has a very odd property: for when they have parties and sit round a fire, they throw some of it into the flames, and as it burns it smokes like incense, and the smell of it makes them drunk just as wine does us; and they get more and more intoxicated as more fruit is thrown on until they jump up and start dancing and singing. Such at least are the reports on how these people live.

Like the Gyndes, which Cyrus divided into three hundred and sixty channels, the river Araxes rises in the country of the Matieni. It has forty mouths, all but one issuing into swamp and marshland, where men are said to live who eat raw fish and dress in seal-skins; by the remaining mouth it flows clear into the Caspian Sea. The Caspian is a sea in itself and has no connexion with the sea elsewhere, unlike the Mediterranean which the Greeks use, and what is called the Atlantic beyond the Pillars of Hercules, and the Indian Ocean, all of which are in reality parts of a single sea. The Caspian, however, is quite separate; in length it is a fifteen days' voyage, using the oars, and it is eight days' voyage across in its broadest part. Along the west of it stretches the chain of the Caucasus, the longest and loftiest of all mountain ranges, inhabited by many different tribes, most of whom live off wild fruits. It is also said that there are trees here of which the leaves when crushed and mixed with water produce a dye with which the natives paint figures on their clothes, and the dye is so permanent that the designs never wash out but last as long as the material does, as if they had been woven into it when it was first made; and that these people copulate in the open like animals.

On the west, then, the Caspian is bounded by the Caucasus; eastwards lies an immense tract of flat country over which the eye wanders till it is lost in the distance. The greater part of this region is occupied by the Massagetae, whom Cyrus wished to attack. There were many things which roused his ambition and gave him courage to undertake this new war, the two most important being the legend of his superhuman origin and the success of all his previous campaigns; for it was a fact that till then it had been impossible for any nation to escape, once he had marched against it.

At this time Tomyris was queen of the Massagetae, her husband having died. Cyrus sent to her and pretended to sue for her hand in marriage; but he was met with a refusal, for the queen was well aware that he was wooing not herself but her dominions. Cyrus, therefore, having failed to achieve his object by cunning, turned to open force, and advancing to the Araxes began his assault upon the Massagetae by bridging the river for his men to cross and constructing upper-works on the ferry boats. While these works were still in hand, Tomyris sent him a message: 'King of the Medes,' it ran, 'I advise you to abandon this enterprise, for you cannot know if in the end it will do you any good. Rule your own people, and try to bear the sight of me ruling mine. But of course you will refuse my advice, as the last thing you wish for is to live in peace. Listen then – if you are so bent upon trying your strength against the Massagetae, give up the laborious task of building that bridge, and let my army withdraw three days' march from the river, and then come over yourself. Or, if you prefer it, retire the same distance yourselves, and let us meet you on your side of the river.'

When he heard the queen's message, Cyrus called a meeting of his chief officers and laid the question before them, to get their opinions on which course to adopt. Every one of them voted to let Tomyris and her army cross to their side. There was, however, one dissentient – Croesus the Lydian, who had attended the meeting of Persian officers and put forward a quite different view. 'My lord,' he said, 'I have already told you that since God has made me your servant I will do all I can to avert any danger which I see threatening your house; and I have learnt much from my own cruel misfortunes. Doubtless, if you think that you and your men are immortal, there is little point in my telling you my opinion; but if you recognize the fact that both you and the troops under your command are merely human, then the first thing I would tell you is that human life is like a revolving wheel and never allows the same man to continue long in prosperity. My view of the question you are discussing is the opposite of what the others have expressed. In my opinion, if we allow the enemy to come over to this side of the river, the danger will be that in the event of defeat you may lose not only the battle but your whole empire as well; for obviously the Massagetae, if they are victorious, are not likely to run away home again: on the contrary, they will advance into your dominions. If on the other hand the fight goes in your favour, the victory will be less decisive than it might have been, had you crossed into their territory and followed it up by a pursuit of the beaten enemy. As you see, I balance what the Massagetae will do by what I am sure you will do yourself: namely that, in the event of victory, you will drive straight against the kingdom of Tomyris. And, apart from what I have already said, it would surely be an intolerable disgrace for Cyrus son of Cambyses to give ground before a woman. Here, then, is my advice: cross the river, advance to the limit of the enemies' withdrawal, and then try to get the better of them by a piece of strategy. I have heard that these people have no experience of such luxuries as the Persians enjoy and know nothing about the pleasures of life. Let us take advantage of this fact and set out a banquet in our camp on the most generous scale, with a great many sheep slaughtered and dressed, all sorts of other dishes, and bowls of strong wine in liberal quantities. Then when the banquet is all prepared, let us march back to the river, leaving only a detachment of inferior troops behind. Unless I am very much mistaken, when our enemies see all those good things, they will set to work upon them – and that will be our chance to distinguish ourselves by a bold stroke.'

When Cyrus had heard these two conflicting opinions, he changed his mind in favour of Croesus, and sent a message to Tomyris to the effect that she should withdraw her troops, as he intended to cross the river himself. This she did according to her previous offer; and Cyrus, putting Croesus under the protection of his son Cambyses, whom he had named as his successor, with many injunctions to treat him with kindness and respect should the expedition end in disaster, sent the two back home to Persia and himself crossed the river with his army.

On the night after the crossing of the Araxes, when Cyrus was lying asleep in the country of the Massagetae, he dreamed that he saw the eldest son of Hystaspes with a pair of wings on his shoulders, with one of which he cast a shadow upon Asia and with the other upon Europe. The eldest son of Hystaspes and grandson of Arsames – Hystaspes belonged to the Achaemenid family – was Darius, a young man of about twenty at that time, who had been left behind in Persia as not yet old enough for campaigning. When Cyrus awoke, he thought over his dream and came to the conclusion that it was a serious matter; so he sent for Hystaspes and took him aside to speak to him. 'Hystaspes,' he said, 'I have discovered that your son is plotting against me and my throne, and I will tell you the source of my information, which admits of no doubt whatever. When I was asleep last night – and the gods, remember, watch over me and always warn me of approaching danger – I saw your eldest son with a pair of wings on his shoulders, shadowing Asia with one of them and Europe with the other. One cannot possibly get away from the fact that this dream means that he is plotting against me. You, therefore, must at once return to Persia and see to it that you can produce the young man for examination when I come home victorious after this war.'

Though Cyrus was so sure of Darius' treachery, the real meaning of the dream was not as he supposed: rather it was sent by God to warn him of his death then and there, and of the ultimate succession of Darius to the throne.

Hystaspes, when he heard about the dream, said, 'Heaven forbid, my lord, that any Persian alive should plot against you. If any does, may he die on the spot! Why – you found the Persians slaves and have made them free men; you found them subjects and have made them kings. If a dream has told you that my son is planning treason, I make you a present of him to do with as you please.' And having given his answer, he crossed the Araxes and returned to Persia, to keep a watch on his son Darius in accordance with Cyrus' orders.

Cyrus now advanced a day's march from the river and proceeded to do what Croesus had proposed; then, leaving behind the feeblest portion of his men, he marched back again with his army thus purged. A detachment of the Massagetae, one-third of their whole force, fell upon the Persians who had been left behind and killed them all, in spite of an attempt to resist; then, after this victory, they saw the splendid meal all ready laid out for them. At once they took their seats and began to regale themselves, and ate and drank so much that they went to sleep. This was the Persians' opportunity: they fell upon them, killed many, and took an even greater number of prisoners, amongst whom was Spargapises, the son of Tomyris the queen and general of the army.

When news of the defeat of her army and the capture of her son got through to the queen, she sent a message to Cyrus in the following terms: 'Glutton as you are for blood, you have no cause to be proud of this day's work, which has no smack of soldierly courage. Your weapon was the fruit of the vine, with which you fill yourselves till you are so mad that, as the liquor goes down, shameful words float up on the fumes of it – that is the poison you treacherously used to get my son into your clutches. Now listen to me and I will advise you for your good: give me back my son and get out of my country with your forces intact, and be content with your triumph over a third part of the Massagetae. If you refuse, I swear by the sun our master to give you more blood than you can drink, for all your gluttony.'

To this threat Cyrus paid not the least attention. The queen's son Spargapises, when he was sober again and able to realize his position, begged Cyrus to have his fetters removed. The request was granted, and, as soon as he had the use of his hands, he killed himself. The queen, on hearing that Cyrus ignored her terms, engaged him in the field with all the forces she possessed. The battle which followed I judge to have been more violent than any other fought between foreign nations. According to the information I have, the engagement began by the two armies coming to a halt within range of each other and exchanging shots with bows and arrows until their arrows were used up; after which there was a long period of close fighting with spears and daggers, neither side being willing to retreat. Finally, however, the Massagetae got the upper hand, the greater part of the Persian army was destroyed where it stood, and Cyrus himself was killed. He had been on the throne for twenty-nine years.

After the battle Tomyris ordered a search to be made amongst the Persian dead for the body of Cyrus; and when it was found she pushed his head into a skin which she had filled with human blood, and cried out as she committed this outrage: 'Though I have conquered you and live, yet you have ruined me by treacherously taking my son. See now – I fulfil my threat: you have your fill of blood.' There are many accounts of Cyrus' death; I have given the one which I think most likely to be true.

In their dress and way of living the Massagetae are like the Scythians. Some ride, some do not – for they use both infantry and cavalry. They have archers and spearmen and are accustomed to carry the 'sagaris', or bill. The only metals they use are gold and bronze:

bronze for spearheads, arrow-points, and bill, and gold for headgear, belts, and girdles. Similarly they give their horses bronze breastplates, and use gold about the bridle, bit, and cheek-pieces. Silver and iron are unknown to them, none being found in the country, though it produces bronze and gold in unlimited quantity. As to their customs: every man has a wife, but all wives are used promiscuously. The Greeks believe this to be a Scythian custom; but it is not – it belongs to the Massagetae. If a man wants a woman, all he does is to hang up his quiver in front of her waggon and then enjoy her without misgiving. They have one way only of determining the appropriate time to die, namely this: when a man is very old, all his relatives give a party and include him in a general sacrifice of cattle; then they boil the flesh and eat it. This they consider to be the best sort of death. Those who die of disease are not eaten but buried, and it is held a misfortune not to have lived long enough to be sacrificed. They have no agriculture, but live on meat and fish, of which there is an abundant supply in the Araxes. They are milk-drinkers. The only god they worship is the sun, to which they sacrifice horses: the idea behind this is to offer the swiftest animal to the swiftest of the gods.

BOOK TWO

CYRUS was succeeded by his son Cambyses, whose mother was Pharnaspes' daughter Cassandane. Cassandane had died while Cyrus was still alive, and he not only bitterly lamented her loss but issued a proclamation that all his subjects should go into mourning for her.

Cambyses, the son of Cyrus and of this princess, on the ground that he had inherited his father's dominion over the Ionians and Aeolians, included them amongst his other subjects in the army he was preparing for an expedition against Egypt.

The Egyptians before the reign of Psammetichus used to think that of all races in the world they were the most ancient; Psammetichus, however, when he came to the throne, took it into his head to settle this question of priority, and ever since his time the Egyptians have believed that the Phrygians surpass them in antiquity and that they themselves come second. Psammetichus, finding that mere inquiry failed to reveal which was the original race of mankind, devised an ingenious method of determining the matter. He took at random, from an ordinary family, two newly born infants and gave them to a shepherd to be brought up amongst his flocks, under strict orders that no one should utter a word in their presence. They were to be kept by themselves in a lonely cottage, and the shepherd was to bring in goats from time to time, to see that the babies had enough milk to drink, and to look after them in any other way that was necessary. All these arrangements were made by Psammetichus because he wished to find out what word the children would first utter, once they had grown out of their meaningless baby-talk. The plan succeeded; two years later the shepherd, who during that time had done everything he had been told to do, happened one day to open the door of the cottage and go in, when both children, running up to him with hands outstretched, pronounced the word 'becos'. The first time this occurred the shepherd made no mention of it; but later, when he found that every time he visited the children to attend to their needs the same word was constantly repeated by them, he informed his master. Psammetichus ordered the children to be brought to him, and when he himself heard them say 'becos' he determined to find out to what language the word belonged. His inquiries revealed that it was the Phrygian for 'bread', and in consideration of this the Egyptians yielded their claims and admitted the superior antiquity of the Phrygians. That this was what really happened I myself learnt from the priests of Hephaestus[1] at Memphis – though the Greeks have various improbable versions of the story, such as that Psammetichus had the children brought up by women whose tongues he had cut out. The version of the priests, however, is the one I have given. There were other things, too, which I learnt at Memphis in conversation with the priests of Hephaestus, and I actually went to Thebes and Heliopolis for the express purpose of finding out if the priests in those cities would agree in what they told me with the priests at Memphis. It is at Heliopolis that the most learned of the Egyptians are said to be found. I am not anxious to repeat what I was told about the Egyptian religion, apart from the mere names of their deities, for I do not think that any one nation knows much more about such things than any other; whatever I shall mention on the subject will be due simply to the exigencies of my story. As to practical matters, they all agreed in saying that the Egyptians by their study of astronomy discovered the solar year and were the first to divide it into twelve parts – and in my opinion their method of calculation is better than the Greek; for the Greeks, to make the seasons work out properly, intercalate a whole month every other year, while the Egyptians make the year consist of twelve months of thirty days each and every year intercalate five additional days, and so complete the regular circle of the seasons. They also told me that the Egyptians first brought into use the names of the twelve gods, which the Greeks took over from them, and were the first to assign altars and images and temples to the gods, and to carve figures in stone. They proved the truth of most of these asser-

1. Ptah.

tions, and went on to tell me that the first man to rule Egypt was
Min, in whose time the whole country, except the district around
Thebes, was marsh, none of the land below Lake Moeris – seven
days' voyage up river from the sea – then showing above the water.
I have little doubt that they were right in this; for it is clear to any intelligent observer, even if he has no previous information on the
subject, that the Egypt to which we sail nowadays is, as it were, the
gift of the river and has come only recently into the possession of its
inhabitants. The same is true of the country above the lake for the
distance of a three days' voyage: the priests said nothing to me about
it, but it is, in fact, precisely the same type of country.

The following is a general description of the physical features of
Egypt. If you take a cast of the lead a day's sail off-shore, you will get
eleven fathoms, muddy bottom – which shows how far out the silt
from the river extends. The length of the Egyptian coastline (defining
Egypt, as we usually do, from the gulf of Plinthine to Lake Serbonis
which lies along the base of Mt Casius) is sixty *schoeni* – the *schoenus*
being an Egyptian measure equivalent to sixty *stades*.[1] The people
there who own very little land measure it by fathoms; those not so
poor, by *stades*, or furlongs; those with much land in *parasangs*, and
those with vast estates in *schoeni*. The *parasang* is equal to thirty *stades*,
the *schoenus*, as I have said, to sixty. Thus the coastline of Egypt is
3600 *stades* in length.[2] From the coast inland as far as Heliopolis – just
about the same distance as along the road from the altar of the Twelve
Gods in Athens to the temple of Olympian Zeus at Pisa – the country
is broad and flat, with much swamp and mud. In point of fact these
two distances – from Heliopolis to the sea, and from Athens to Pisa –
are not exactly the same, but very nearly: careful reckoning would
show that they differ by only fifteen *stades*. The latter is fifteen short
of the fifteen hundred: the former just the round number – fifteen
hundred precisely. Southward of Heliopolis the country narrows. It
is confined on the one side by the range of the Arabian mountains
which run north and south and then continue without a break in the
direction of the Arabian Gulf. In these mountains are the quarries
where the stone was cut for the pyramids at Memphis. This is the

1. About seven miles.
2. About 420 miles.

point where the range changes its direction and bends away towards the Arabian Gulf. I learnt that its greatest length from east to west is a two months' journey, and that towards its eastern limit frankincense is produced. On the Libyan side of Egypt there is another range of hills where the pyramids stand; these hills are rocky and covered with sand, and run in a southerly direction like the Arabian range before it bends eastward. Above Heliopolis, then, for a distance of four days' voyage up the river Egypt is narrow, and the extent of territory, for so important a country, is meagre enough. Between the two mountain ranges – the Libyan and Arabian – it is a level plain, in its narrowest part, so far as I could judge, not more than about two hundred furlongs across. South of this the country broadens again.

From Heliopolis to Thebes is a nine days' voyage up the Nile, a distance of eighty-one *schoeni* or 4860 *stades*.[1] Putting together the various measurements I have given, one finds that the Egyptian coastline is, as I have said, about 420 miles in length, and the distance from the sea inland to Thebes about 714 miles. It is another 210 miles from Thebes to Elephantine.

My own observation bears out the statement made to me by the priests that the greater part of the country I have described has been built up by silt from the Nile. I formed the opinion that the whole region above Memphis between the two ranges of hills was originally a gulf of the sea, and resembles (if I may compare small things with great) the country around Troy, Teuthrania, Ephesus and the plain of the Maeander – not that any of the rivers which have caused the alluvial deposits in those neighbourhoods are comparable in size to any one of the five mouths of the Nile. There are other rivers too I could mention, much smaller than the Nile, which have effected important changes in the coastline: for instance, the Achelous which flows through Acarnania and has already joined to the mainland half the islands of the Echinades group.

In Arabia not far from Egypt there is a very long narrow gulf running up from the Red Sea[2] (as it is called). It is only half a day's voyage across in its narrowest part, but its length from its extreme

1. 552 miles.
2. i.e. Indian Ocean. See note on p. 41. The 'long narrow gulf' is thus our Red Sea.

limit to the open sea is a voyage of forty days for a vessel under oars. It is tidal. Now it is my belief that Egypt itself was originally some such arm of the sea – there were two gulfs, that is, one running from the Mediterranean southwards towards Ethiopia, and the other northwards from the Indian Ocean towards Syria, and the two almost met at their extreme ends, leaving only a small stretch of country between them. Suppose, now, that the Nile should change its course and flow into this gulf – the Red Sea – what is to prevent it from being silted up by the stream within, say, twenty thousand years? Personally I think even ten thousand would be enough. That being so, surely in the vast stretch of time which has passed before I was born, a much bigger gulf than this could have been turned into dry land by the silt brought down by the Nile – for the Nile is a great river and does, in fact, work great changes. So I not only believe the people who gave me this account of Egypt, but my own conclusions strongly support what they said. I have observed for myself that Egypt at the Nile Delta projects into the sea beyond the coast on either side; I have seen shells on the hills and noticed how salt exudes from the soil to such an extent that it affects even the pyramids; I have noticed, too, that the only hill where there is sand is the hill above Memphis, and – a further point – that the soil of Egypt does not resemble that of the neighbouring country of Arabia, or of Libya, or even of Syria (the Mediterranean coast of Arabia is inhabited by Syrians), but is black and friable as one would expect of an alluvial soil formed of the silt brought down by the river from Ethiopia. The soil of Libya is, as we know, reddish and sandy, while in Arabia and Syria it has a larger proportion of stone and clay. I had from the priests another striking piece of evidence about the origin of the country: namely that in the reign of Moeris the whole area below Memphis used to be flooded when the river rose only twelve feet – and when I got that information Moeris had been dead for less than nine hundred years. To-day, however, the river never floods unless it rises at least twenty-three and a half, or twenty-four, feet. It seems to me therefore that, if the land continues to increase at the same rate in height and extent, the Egyptians who live below Lake Moeris in the Delta and thereabouts will, if the Nile fails to flood, suffer permanently the same fate as they said would some day overtake the Greeks;

for when they learned that all Greece is watered by rain and not, as Egypt is, by the flooding of rivers, they remarked that the day would come when the Greeks would be sadly disappointed and starve – in other words, if God sees fit to send no rain but afflicts us with a drought, we shall all die from famine because we have no source of water other than the rain which God chooses to grant us. All this is only too true – but let me point out in answer how the case stands with the Egyptians themselves: if, as I said before, the land below Memphis (for this is the part which is always rising) continues to increase in height at the same rate as in the past, is it not obvious that when the river can no longer flood the fields – and there is no chance of rain either – the people who live there will have to go hungry? As things are at present these people get their harvests with less labour than anyone else in the world, the rest of the Egyptians included; they have no need to work with plough or hoe, or to use any other of the ordinary methods of cultivating their land; they merely wait for the river of its own accord to flood their fields; then, when the water has receded, each farmer sows his plot, turns pigs into it to tread in the seed, and then waits for the harvest. Pigs are used also for threshing, after which the grain is put into store.

The Ionians maintain that Egypt proper is confined to the Nile Delta, a stretch of country running along the coast from what is known as Perseus' Watchtower to the Pelusian Salt-pans – a distance of forty *schoeni* – and inland as far as Cercasorus, where the Nile divides into the two branches which enter the sea at Pelusium and Canopus. The rest of what is usually called Egypt belongs, according to this view, either to Libya or Arabia. If, therefore, we accept it, we are forced to the conclusion that there was a time when the Egyptians had no country at all; for I am convinced – and the Egyptians themselves admit the fact – that the Delta is alluvial land and has only recently (if I may so put it) appeared above water. If, then, they once had no place to live in, why did they make such a business of the theory that they are the oldest race in the world? Surely there was no need whatever to experiment with those two children to find out what word they would utter first. But the fact is, I do not believe that the Egyptians came into being at the same period as the Delta (as the Ionians call it); on the contrary, they have existed ever since men appeared upon the earth, and as the Delta increased with the passage of time, many of them moved down into the new territory and many remained where they originally were. The name of Egypt was in ancient times given to Thebes, the whole circumference of whose territory is only 6120 furlongs. If, then, my judgement is correct, the Ionians are mistaken in their opinions about Egypt; if, on the other hand, the Ionians are right, I am ready to prove that neither they nor the rest of the Greeks know how to count: for they hold that the world consists of three parts – Asia, Europe, and Libya – whereas it is obvious that they should add a fourth, namely the Egyptian Delta, since they do not include it in either Asia or Libya. According to their theory the Nile is the boundary between Asia and Libya; but the Nile splits at the apex of the Delta and flows round it, thus making it a separate tract of land lying between the two.

About the Ionians' opinion I have said enough; here now is my own: Egypt, I consider, is the whole extent of territory inhabited by Egyptians, just as Cilicia is the country occupied by Cilicians or Assyria the country occupied by Assyrians. The only true boundary between Asia and Libya is formed by the frontiers of Egypt. By the usual Greek reckoning we should have to suppose that Egypt, all the way from the Cataracts and Elephantine, is cut in two, one half belonging to Libya and the other to Asia; for the Nile divides, flowing from the Cataracts to the sea right through the middle of the country – as far as Cercasorus in a single stream, and below that city splitting into three branches, of which one trends eastward and is known as the mouth of Pelusium, and another trends westward and is called the mouth of Canopus. There remains the third branch which, coming down from the southward to the tip of the Delta, flows straight on and cuts it in two on its course to the sea. This branch, issuing at what is called the mouth of Sebennytus, is neither the least in volume, nor the least famous of the three. In addition to these there are two other mouths, the Saitic and Mendesian, which split off from the Sebennytic and so run into the sea. The Bolbitine and Bucolic mouths are not natural branches but excavated channels.

The opinion I have expressed about the extent of Egypt is supported by an oracle delivered from the shrine of Ammon which came to my notice after I had formed my own conclusions. The people of Marea and Apis, on the Libyan frontier, took a dislike to certain religious observances, especially the prohibition against eating the flesh of cows; accordingly, they sent to the shrine of Ammon and said they were in no way bound by Egyptian custom as they considered themselves not to be Egyptians at all, but Libyans; they lived outside the Delta, had nothing in common with Egypt, and wished to be allowed to eat what they pleased. The oracle, however, refused their request, and declared that all the country irrigated by the Nile was Egypt and all the people who lived below Elephantine and drank the Nile's water were Egyptians. Now when the Nile overflows, it floods not only the Delta but parts of the territory on either side supposed to be Libyan and Arabian respectively, to a distance of two days' journey – in some places more, in some less.

About why the Nile behaves precisely as it does I could get no information from the priests or anyone else. What I particularly wished to know was why the water begins to rise at the summer solstice, continues to do so for a hundred days, and then falls again at the end of that period, so that it remains low throughout the winter until the summer solstice comes round again in the following year. Nobody in Egypt could give me any explanation of this, in spite of my constant attempts to find out what was the peculiar property which made the Nile behave in the opposite way to other rivers, and why – another point on which I hoped for information – it was the only river to cause no breezes.

Certain Greeks, hoping to advertise how clever they are, have tried to account for the flooding of the Nile in three different ways. Two of the explanations are not worth dwelling upon, beyond a bare mention of what they are: one is that the summer north winds cause the water to rise by checking the flow of the current towards the sea. In fact, however, these winds on many occasions have failed to blow, yet the Nile has risen as usual; moreover, if these winds were responsible for the rise, the other rivers which happen to run against them would certainly be affected in the same way as the Nile – and to a greater extent, in that they are smaller and have a less powerful current. There are many such rivers in Syria and Libya, but none of them are affected in the same way as the Nile. The second explanation is less rational, being somewhat, if I may so put it, of a legendary character: it is that the Nile exhibits its remarkable characteristics because it flows from the Ocean, the stream of which encircles the world. The third theory is much the most plausible, but at the same time furthest from the truth; according to this, the water of the Nile comes from melting snow,[1] but as it flows from Libya through Ethiopia into Egypt, that is, from a very hot into a cooler climate, how could it possibly originate in snow? Obviously, this view is as worthless as the other two. Anyone who can use his wits about such matters will find plenty of arguments to prove how unlikely it is that snow is the cause of the flooding of the river: the strongest is provided by the winds, which blow hot from those regions; secondly rain and frost are unknown there – and after snow rain is bound to fall within five days. So that if there were snow in that part of the world, there would necessarily be rain too; thirdly, the natives are black because of the hot climate. Again, kites and swallows remain throughout the year, and cranes migrate thither in winter to escape the cold weather of Scythia. But if there were any snow, however little, in the region through which the Nile flows and in which it rises, none of these things could possibly be; for they are contrary to reason. As to the writer who mentions the Ocean in this connexion, his account is a mere fairy-tale depending upon an unknown quantity and cannot therefore be disproved by argument. I know myself of no river called Ocean, and can only suppose that Homer or some earlier poet invented the name and introduced it into poetry. If, after criticizing these theories, I must express an opinion myself about a matter so obscure as the reason why the Nile floods in summer, I would say (to put the whole thing in the fewest words) that during winter the sun is driven out of his course by storms towards the upper parts of Libya. It stands to reason that the country nearest to, and most directly under, the sun should be most short of water, and that the streams which feed the rivers in that neighbourhood should most readily dry up.

But let me explain in somewhat greater detail my view of what happens when the sun passes across the upper regions of Libya. The atmosphere there is always clear, and there are no cold winds to tem-

1. See Introduction, p. 29.

per the heat; and the result of this is that the sun, as it passes over, has the same effect as it normally has elsewhere in summer on its passage through the mid-heaven: namely, it draws the water towards itself and then thrusts it into those parts of the country still further inland, where it comes under the influence of the winds which scatter and disperse it in vapour – so naturally the winds (the south and south-west) which blow from this region, are the most rainy. It seems to me, moreover, that not all the moisture drawn each year from the Nile is dispersed but that a certain amount is retained, as it were, in the neighbourhood of the sun. When the rough winter weather is over the sun resumes its normal course in mid-heaven, and from then on exercises an equal attraction upon all rivers. In winter, then, all rivers but the Nile run in flood, because a great deal of rainwater is added to their volume – the rain cutting watercourses all over the country – but in summer, when the attraction of the sun's heat is added to the lack of rain, their volume is diminished. The Nile, on the other hand, behaves in the opposite way, and for an obvious reason: being subject to evaporation by the sun and having no rain to swell it, it is the only river which is much lower in winter than in summer – for in summer it is subject to the same force of solar attraction as other rivers, but in winter it is the only one to feel it. These, then, are my reasons for thinking that the sun is the cause of this phenomenon, as also, I believe, of the dryness of the atmosphere in Egypt; the sun parching whatever lies in its path – so that in the upper parts of Libya it is always summer. Suppose for a moment the relative positions of north and south were changed – suppose, that is, the north wind and the south wind each, so to speak, usurped that part of the heavens which now belongs to the other: if such a thing occurred, the sun, when driven from its normal course by the northerly gales of winter, would pass over the north of Europe instead of – as now – over the south of Libya, and I have no doubt that during its passage across Europe its effect upon the Danube would be precisely the same as its present effect upon the Nile. I mentioned the fact that no breeze blows from the Nile; I would suggest, in explanation of this, that the usual thing is for winds to originate in a cold region, not in a hot one.

Well, these things have been as they are since the beginning of time, and there is no changing them; so I will pass to another subject. Concerning the sources of the Nile, nobody I have spoken with, Egyptian, Libyan, or Greek, professed to have any knowledge, except the scribe who kept the register of the treasures of Athene in the Egyptian city of Sais. But even this person's account, though he pretended to exact knowledge, seemed to me hardly serious. He told me that between Syene, near Thebes, and Elephantine there were two mountains of conical shape called Crophi and Mophi; and that the springs of the Nile, which were of fathomless depth, flowed out from between them. Half of the water flowed northwards towards Egypt and half southwards towards Ethiopia. The fact that the springs were bottomless he said had been proved by the Egyptian king Psammetichus, who had a rope made many thousands of fathoms long which he let down into the water without finding the bottom. I think myself that if there is any truth in this story of the scribe's, it indicates the presence of powerful whirlpools and eddies in the water, caused by its impact upon the mountains, and it was these eddies which prevented the sounding-line from reaching the bottom.

On this subject I could get no further information from anybody. As far as Elephantine I speak as an eye-witness, but further south from hearsay. The most I could learn was that beyond Elephantine the country rises steeply; and in that part of the river boats have to be hauled along by ropes – one rope on each side – much as one drags an ox. If the rope parts, the boat is gone in a moment, carried away by the force of the stream. These conditions last over a four days' journey, the river all the time winding greatly, like the Maeander, and the distance to be covered amounting to twelve *schoeni*. After this one reaches a level plain, where the river is divided by an island named Tachompso. South of Elephantine the country is inhabited by Ethiopians who also possess half of Tachompso, the other half being occupied by Egyptians. Beyond the island is a great lake, and round its shores live nomadic tribes of Ethiopians. After crossing the lake one comes again to the stream of the Nile, which flows into it. At this point one must land and travel along the bank fo the river for forty days, because sharp rocks, some showing above water and many just awash, make the river impracticable for boats. After the forty days' journey on land one takes another boat and in twelve days reaches a big city named Meroe, said to be the capital city of the Ethiopians. The inhabitants worship Zeus and Dionysus alone of the gods, holding them in great honour. There is an oracle of Zeus there, and they make war according to its pronouncements, taking from it both the occasion and the object of their various expeditions. Continuing upstream for the same length of time as it takes to travel from Elephantine to the capital, one comes to the Deserters – a people whose name is *Asmach*, a word which would mean in Greek 'those who stand on the left hand of the king'. They were a body of men two hundred and forty thousand strong, of the Egyptian warrior class, who went over to the Ethiopians during the reign of Psammetichus. The Egyptians had guard-posts in various parts of the country: one at Elephantine against the Ethiopians, another in Daphnae at Pelusium against the Arabians and Assyrians, and a third at Marea to keep a watch on Libya. The Persians have similar garrisons to-day both at Elephantine and Daphnae. Now it happened in Psammetichus' time that the Egyptians were kept on garrison duty for three years without being relieved, and this was the cause of their desertion. They discussed their grievances, came to a unanimous resolution, and went off in a body to Ethiopia. The king, on hearing the news, gave chase and overtook them; and the story goes that when he besought them to return and used every argument to dissuade them from abandoning their wives and children and the gods of their country, one of their number pointed, in reply, to his private parts and said that wherever *those* were, there would be no lack of wives and children. So they continued their journey to Ethiopia and put themselves at the disposal of the Ethiopian king, by whom they were well rewarded, for he gave them permission to expel certain Ethiopians with whom he was on bad terms, and to settle on their land. The result of their living there was that the Ethiopians learned Egyptian manners and became more civilized.

The course of the Nile is, then, known not only where it traverses Egypt but as much further southward as one can travel by land or water in four months; for calculation will show that that is the time it takes to go from Elephantine to the Deserters. At that point the river runs from west to east; beyond, nobody knows its course with any certainty, for the country is uninhabited because of the heat. I did, however, hear a story from some people of Cyrene, who told me that during a visit to the oracle of Ammon they happened, in the course of conversation with Etearchus the Ammonian king, to get on to the subject of the Nile and the riddle of its source. Etearchus told them that he had once had a visit from certain Nasamonians, a people who live in Syrtis and the country a little to the eastward. Being asked if there was anything more they could tell him about the uninhabited parts of Libya, these men declared that a group of wild young fellows, sons of chieftains in their country, had on coming to manhood planned amongst themselves all sorts of extravagant adventures, one of which was to draw lots for five of their number to explore the Libyan desert and try to penetrate further than had ever been done before. The whole Mediterranean coast of Libya from Egypt to Cape Soloïs,[1] where it ends, is inhabited by many different tribes of Libyans, except the portion which is possessed by Greeks and Phoenicians; but in the inland parts lying to the southward of the inhabited coastal district only wild beasts are to be found, and further still to the southward there is a waterless and sandy desert without life of any kind. The story then was that the young men, sent off by their companions on their travels with a good supply of food and water, passed through the inhabited parts of the country to the region of wild beasts and then came to the desert, which they proceeded to cross in a westerly direction. After travelling for many days over the sand they saw some trees growing on a level spot; they approached and began to pick the fruit which the trees bore, and while they were doing so were attacked by some little men – of less than middle height – who seized them and carried them off. The speech of these dwarfs was unintelligible, nor could they understand the Nasamonians. They took their captives through a vast tract of marshy country, and beyond it came to a town, all the inhabitants of which were of the same small stature, and all black. A great river with crocodiles in it flowed past the town from west to east.

I have said enough about Etearchus the Ammonian and his story, and will merely add his statement – which I repeat on the authority of the men from Cyrene – that the explorers got safely home again,

1. Cape Spartel.

and that the people whose country they visited were a nation of wizards. The river which flows past their town was supposed by Etearchus, reasonably enough, to be the Nile; for the Nile does in fact flow from Libya, dividing it in two and (to argue by analogy from the known to the unknown) I am willing to believe that it rises at the same distance from its mouth as the Danube, which has its source amongst the Celts near Pyrene and flows right through the middle of Europe, to reach the Black Sea at the Milesian colony of Istria. (The Celts live beyond the Pillars of Hercules, next to the Cynesians who are the most westerly people of Europe.) Its course is quite familiar because it flows through inhabited country; but nobody, on the other hand, knows anything about the source of the Nile, because that river runs through a part of Libya which is uninhabited and desert. All I could possibly learn by inquiry about its course, I have here set down. It enters Egypt from the country beyond. Egypt is more or less opposite to, or south of, the mountainous part of Cilicia, from which the direct route to Sinope on the Black Sea takes five days for a man travelling light;[1] and Sinope lies opposite the mouth of the Danube. It is my belief, then, that the Nile, as it traverses the whole of Libya, is equal in length to the Danube – and on that subject I shall say no more.

About Egypt I shall have a great deal more to relate because of the number of remarkable things which the country contains, and because of the fact that more monuments which beggar description are to be found there than anywhere else in the world. That is reason enough for my dwelling on it at greater length. Not only is the Egyptian climate peculiar to that country, and the Nile different in its behaviour from other rivers elsewhere, but the Egyptians themselves in their manners and customs seem to have reversed the ordinary practices of mankind. For instance, women attend market and are employed in trade, while men stay at home and do the weaving. In weaving the normal way is to work the threads of the weft upwards, but the Egyptians work them downwards. Men in Egypt carry loads on their heads, women on their shoulders; women pass water standing up, men sitting down. To ease themselves they go indoors, but eat outside in the streets, on the theory that what is un-

1. Greatly underestimated.

seemly but necessary should be done in private, and what is not unseemly should be done openly. No woman holds priestly office, either
in the service of goddess or god; only men are priests in both cases.
Sons are under no compulsion to support their parents if they do
not wish to do so, but daughters must, whether they wish it or not.
Elsewhere priests grow their hair long; in Egypt they shave their
heads. In other nations the relatives of the deceased in time of mourning cut their hair, but the Egyptians, who shave at all other times,
mark a death by letting the hair grow both on head and chin. They
live with their animals – unlike the rest of the world, who live apart
from them. Other men live on wheat and barley, but any Egyptian
who does so is blamed for it, their bread being made from spelt, or
Zea as some call it. Dough they knead with their feet, but clay with
their hands – and even handle dung. They practise circumcision,
while men of other nations – except those who have learnt from
Egypt – leave their private parts as nature made them. Men in Egypt
have two garments each, women only one. The ordinary practice at
sea is to make sheets fast to ring-bolts fitted outboard; the Egyptians
fit them inboard. In writing or calculating, instead of going, like the
Greeks, from left to right, the Egyptians go from right to left – and
obstinately maintain that theirs is the dexterous method, ours being
left-handed and awkward. They have two sorts of writing, the sacred
and the common. They are religious to excess, beyond any other
nation in the world, and here are some of the customs which illus-
trate the fact; they drink from brazen cups which they scour every
day – everyone, without exception. They wear linen clothes which
they make a special point of continually washing. They circumcise
themselves for cleanliness' sake, preferring to be clean rather than
comely. The priests shave their bodies all over every other day to
guard against the presence of lice, or anything else equally unpleasant,
while they are about their religious duties; the priests, too, wear linen
only, and shoes made from the papyrus plant – these materials, for
dress and shoes, being the only ones allowed them. They bath in cold
water twice a day and twice every night – and observe innumerable
other ceremonies besides. Their life, however, is not by any means all
hardship, for they enjoy advantages too: for instance, they are free
from all personal expense, having bread made for them out of the

sacred grain, and a plentiful daily supply of goose-meat and beef, with wine in addition. Fish they are forbidden to touch; and as for beans, they cannot even bear to look at them, because they imagine they are unclean (in point of fact the Egyptians never sow beans, and even if any happen to grow wild, they will not eat them, either raw or boiled). They do not have a single priest for each god, but a number, of which one is chief-priest, and when a chief-priest dies his son is appointed to succeed him. Bulls are considered the property of the god Epaphus – or Apis – and are therefore tested in the following way: a priest appointed for the purpose examines the animal, and if he finds even a single black hair upon him, pronounces him unclean; he goes over him with the greatest care, first making him stand up, then lie on his back, after which he pulls out his tongue to see if that, too, is 'clean' according to the recognized marks – what those are I will explain later.[1] He also inspects the tail to make sure the hair on it grows properly; then, if the animal passes all these tests successfully, the priest marks him by twisting round his horns a band of papyrus, which he seals with wax and stamps with his signet ring. The bull is finally taken away, and the penalty is death for anybody who sacrifices an animal which has not been marked in this manner. The method of sacrifice is as follows: they take the beast (one of those marked with the seal) to the appropriate altar and light a fire; then, after pouring a libation of wine and invoking the god by name, they slaughter it, cut off its head, and flay the carcase. The head is loaded with curses and taken away – if there happen to be Greek traders in the market, it is sold to them; if not, it is thrown into the river. The curses they pronounce take the form of a prayer that any disaster which threatens either themselves or their country may be diverted and fall upon the severed head of the beast. Both the libation and the practice of cutting off the heads of sacrificial beasts are common to all Egyptians in all their sacrifices, and the latter explains why it is that no Egyptian will use the head of any sort of animal for food. The methods of disembowelling and burning are various, and I will describe the one which is followed in the worship of the goddess whom they consider the greatest and honour with the most important festival. In this case, when they have flayed the bull, they first pray

1. In Book III, chapter 29 (p. 215).

and then take its paunch out whole, leaving the intestines and fat in-side the body; next they cut off the legs, shoulders, neck, and rump, and stuff the carcase with loaves of bread, honey, raisins, figs, frank-incense, myrrh, and other aromatic substances; finally they pour a quantity of oil over the carcase and burn it. They always fast before a sacrifice, and while the fire is consuming it they beat their breasts. That part of the ceremony done, they serve a meal out of the portions left over.

All Egyptians use bulls and bull-calves for sacrifice, if they have passed the test for 'cleanness'; but they are forbidden to sacrifice cows, on the ground that they are sacred to Isis. The statues of Isis show a female figure with cow's horns, like the Greek representations of Io, and of all animals cows are universally held by the Egyptians in the greatest reverence. This is the reason why no Egyptian, man or woman, will kiss a Greek, or use a Greek knife, spit, or cauldron, or even eat the flesh of a bull known to be clean, if it has been cut with a Greek knife.

They have a curious method of disposing of dead bulls and cows: cows are thrown into the river, but bulls are buried on the outskirts of towns, with one horn, or sometimes both, sticking out from the ground to mark the place. In due time, when the carcase has rotted, a barge comes from the island called Prosopitis to collect the bones. This island is part of the Delta and is nine *schoeni* in circumference; it contains a number of towns, the one from which the barges come being Atarbechis, where there is a temple of much sanctity dedicated to Aphrodite.[1] From Atarbechis many people go round to the various towns to dig up the bones, which they take away and bury again all together in one spot. Other cattle which die a natural death are disposed of in the same way as bulls – for that is the law. None of them are slaughtered. The Egyptians who possess a temple dedicated to the Theban Zeus, or live in the province of Thebes, never sacrifice sheep but only goats; for not all Egyptians worship the same gods – the only two to be universally worshipped are Isis and Osiris, who, they say, is Dionysus. On the other hand, those who have a temple dedicated to Mendes, or live in the Mendesian province, never sacri-fice goats but only sheep. The Thebans and those who follow them

1. Hathor.

explain the origin of their custom of abstaining from the sacrifice of sheep by a story of Heracles,[1] who, they say, wished above all things to see Zeus. Zeus, however, was unwilling that his wish should be gratified. Heracles persisted, and Zeus had to devise a means of getting out of the difficulty. His plan was to skin a ram and cut off its head; then, holding the head before him and covering himself in the fleece, he showed himself to Heracles. This story explains why the Egyptians represent Zeus with a ram's head – a practice which has extended to the Ammonians, who are a joint colony of Egyptians and Ethiopians and speak a language which has points of resemblance to both. So far as I can see, the Ammonians took their name too from this circumstance; for *Amun* is the Egyptian name for Zeus. So much, then, for the reason why the Thebans do not sacrifice rams but consider them to be sacred animals. Nevertheless on the festival of Zeus, which occurs once a year, they break this custom and do, in fact, slaughter a ram – but only one. They cut the animal in pieces, skin it, and put the fleece upon the statue of Zeus, just as Zeus once put it upon himself, and then confront the statue of Zeus with a statue of Heracles. Then all who are engaged in the ceremony beat their breasts as if in mourning for the ram's death, and afterwards bury the carcase in a sacred sepulchre.

I was told that this Heracles was one of the twelve gods. Of the other Heracles, with whom the Greeks are familiar, I could get no information anywhere in Egypt. Nevertheless it was not the Egyptians who took the name Heracles from the Greeks. The opposite is true: it was the Greeks who took it from the Egyptians – those Greeks, I mean, who gave the name to the son of Amphitryon. There is plenty of evidence to prove the truth of this, in particular the fact that both the parents of Heracles – Amphitryon and Alcmene – were of Egyptian origin. Again, the Egyptians say they do not know the names of Poseidon or the Dioscuri, or receive them as gods amongst the rest. But surely, if they had taken the name of any gods from the Greeks, it is precisely these they would have been most likely to notice – unless I am greatly mistaken in my belief that the Egyptians were already at that time a sea-faring nation, and that some of the Greeks, too, used the sea. Being sailors, the Egyptians would have

1. Perhaps Chunsu, a war-god, son of Amun at Thebes.

learnt the name of Poseidon and the Dioscuri even before that of Heracles.

Nevertheless the Egyptians have had a god named Heracles from time immemorial. They say that seventeen thousand years before the reign of Amasis the twelve gods were produced from the eight; and of the twelve they hold Heracles to be one. To satisfy my wish to get the best information I possibly could on this subject, I made a voyage to Tyre in Phoenicia, because I had heard that there was a temple there, of great sanctity, dedicated to Heracles. I visited the temple, and found that the offerings which adorned it were numerous and valuable, not the least remarkable being two pillars, one of pure gold, the other of emerald which gleamed in the dark with a strange radiance. In the course of conversation with the priests I asked how long ago the temple had been built, and found by their answer that they, too, did not share the Greek view; for they said that the temple was as ancient as Tyre itself, and that Tyre had already stood for two thousand three hundred years. I also saw another temple there, dedicated to the Thasian Heracles; and I have also been to Thasos, where I found a temple of Heracles built by the Phoenicians who settled there after they had sailed in search of Europa. Even this was five generations before Heracles the son of Amphitryon made his appearance in Greece. The result of these researches is a plain proof that the worship of Heracles is very ancient; and I think that the wisest course is taken by those Greeks who maintain a double cult of this deity, with two temples, in one of which they worship him as Olympian and divine, and in the other pay him such honour as is due to a demi-god, or hero. The Greeks have many stories with no basis of fact. One of the silliest is the story of how Heracles came to Egypt and was taken away by the Egyptians to be sacrificed to Zeus,[1] with all due pomp and the sacrificial wreath upon his head; and how he quietly submitted until the moment came for the beginning of the actual ceremony at the altar, when he exerted his strength and killed them all. For me at least such a tale is proof enough that the Greeks know nothing whatever about Egyptian character and custom. The Egyptians are forbidden by their religion even to kill animals for sacrifice, except sheep and such bulls and bull-calves as have passed

1. See Introduction, p. 27; the story told of an imaginary 'King Busiris'.

the test for 'cleanness' – and geese: is it likely, then, that they would sacrifice human beings? Besides, if Heracles was a mere man (as they say he was) and single-handed, how is it conceivable that he should have killed tens of thousands of people? And now I hope that both gods and heroes will forgive me for saying what I have said on these matters!

I mentioned the fact that certain Egyptians (the Mendesians) will not sacrifice goats, either male or female. The reason is this: they believe Pan to be one of the eight gods who existed before the subsequent twelve, and painters and sculptors represent him just as the Greeks do, with the face and legs of a goat. Not that they think he is, in fact, like that – on the contrary they do not believe he differs in form from the rest of the gods. But that is how they paint him – why, I should prefer not to mention. The Mendesians hold all goats in veneration, especially male ones, whose keepers enjoy special honours. One of them is held in particular reverence, and when he dies the whole province goes into mourning. Mendes[1] is the Egyptian name both for Pan and for a goat. In this province not long ago a goat tupped a woman, in full view of everybody – a most surprising incident.

Pigs are considered unclean. If anyone touches a pig accidentally in passing, he will at once plunge into the river, clothes and all, to wash himself; and swineherds, though of pure Egyptian blood, are the only people in the country who never enter a temple, nor is there any intermarriage between them and the rest of the community, swineherds marrying their daughters and taking their wives only from amongst themselves.

The only deities to whom the Egyptians consider it proper to sacrifice pigs are Dionysus and the Moon. To both of these they offer pigs at the same time, at the same full moon, and afterwards eat the flesh. To explain the reason why they abhor the notion of sacrificing swine at any festival except this one, there is a legend current amongst them, which I know but think it seemly not to mention it. The method of sacrificing a pig to the Moon is to slaughter the animal, put together the tip of the tail, the spleen, and the caul, cover them with all the fat found in the belly, and burn them; the rest of

1. Min of Chemmis.

the meat is eaten on the same day as the sacrifice is offered – the day of the full moon; on no other day would they consent to taste it. People of slender means make models of pigs out of dough, which they bake and offer in sacrifice instead of real ones.

Everyone, on the eve of the festival of Dionysus, sacrifices a hog before the door of his house. When the animal is slaughtered, it is given back to the swineherd from whom it was procured. The swineherd then removes the carcase. In other ways the Egyptian method of celebrating the festival of Dionysus is much the same as the Greek, except that the Egyptians have no choric dance. Instead of the phallus they have puppets, about eighteen inches high; the genitals of these figures are made almost as big as the rest of their bodies, and they are pulled up and down by strings as the women carry them round the villages. Flutes lead the procession, and the women as they follow sing a hymn to Dionysus. There is a religious legend to account for the size of the genitals and the fact that they are the only part of the puppet's body which is made to move.

Now I have an idea that Melampus the son of Amythaon knew all about this ceremony; for it was he who introduced the name of Dionysus into Greece, together with the sacrifice in his honour and the phallic procession. He did not, however, fully comprehend the doctrine, or communicate it in its entirety; its more perfect development was the work of later teachers. Nevertheless it was Melampus who introduced the phallic procession, and from Melampus the Greeks learned the rites which they now perform. Melampus, in my view, was an able man who acquired the art of divination and brought into Greece, with little change, a number of things which he had learned in Egypt, and amongst them the worship of Dionysus. I will never admit that the similar ceremonies performed in Greece and Egypt are the result of mere coincidence – had that been so, our rites would have been more Greek in character and less recent in origin. Nor will I allow that the Egyptians ever took over from Greece either this custom or any other. Probably Melampus got his knowledge of the worship of Dionysus through Cadmus of Tyre and the people who came with him from Phoenicia to the country now called Boeotia. The names of nearly all the gods came to Greece from Egypt. I know from the inquiries I have made that they came from abroad, and it seems most likely that it was from Egypt, for the names of all the gods have been known in Egypt from the beginning of time, with the exception (as I have already said) of Poseidon and the Dioscuri – and also of Hera, Hestia, Themis, the Graces, and the Nereids. I have the authority of the Egyptians themselves for this. I think that the gods of whom they profess no knowledge were named by the Pelasgians – with the exception of Poseidon, of whom they learned from the Libyans; for the Libyans are the only people who have always known Poseidon's name, and always worshipped him. Heroes[1] have no place in the religion of Egypt.

These practices, then, and others which I will speak of later, were borrowed by the Greeks from Egypt. This is not the case, however, with the Greek custom of making images of Hermes with the phallus erect; it was the Athenians who took this from the Pelasgians, and from the Athenians the custom spread to the rest of Greece. For just at the time when the Athenians were assuming Hellenic nationality, the Pelasgians joined them, and thus first came to be regarded as Greeks. Anyone will know what I mean if he is familiar with the mysteries of the Cabiri – rites which the men of Samothrace learned from the Pelasgians, who lived in that island before they moved to Attica, and communicated the mysteries to the Athenians. This will show that the Athenians were the first Greeks to make statues of Hermes with the erect phallus, and that they learned the practice from the Pelasgians – who explained it by a certain religious doctrine, the nature of which is made clear in the Samothracian mysteries.

In ancient times, as I know from what I was told at Dodona, the Pelasgians offered sacrifices of all kinds, and prayed to the gods, but without any distinction of name or title – for they had not yet heard of any such thing. They called the gods by the Greek word *theoi* – 'disposers' – because they had 'disposed' and arranged everything in due order, and assigned each thing to its proper division. Long afterwards the names of the gods were brought into Greece from Egypt and the Pelasgians learnt them – with the exception of Diony-sus, about whom they knew nothing till much later; then, as time went on, they sent to the oracle at Dodona (the most ancient and, at

1. i.e. men who have been subsequently worshipped.

that period, the only oracle in Greece) to ask advice about the propriety of adopting names which had come into the country from abroad. The oracle replied that they would be right to use them. From that time onward, therefore, the Pelasgians used the names of the gods in their sacrifices, and from the Pelasgians the names passed to Greece.

But it was only – if I may so put it – the day before yesterday that the Greeks came to know the origin and form of the various gods, and whether or not all of them had always existed; for Homer and Hesiod are the poets who composed our theogonies and described the gods for us, giving them all their appropriate titles, offices, and powers, and they lived, as I believe, not more than four hundred years ago. The poets who are said to have preceded them were, I think, in point of fact later.[1] This is my personal opinion, but for the former part of my statement on these matters I have the authority of the priestesses of Dodona.

About the oracles – that of Dodona in Greece and of Ammon in Libya – the Egyptians have the following legend: according to the priests of the Theban Zeus, two women connected with the service of the temple were carried off by the Phoenicians and sold, one in Libya and the other in Greece, and it was these women who founded the oracles in the two countries. I asked the priests at Thebes what grounds they had for being so sure about this, and they told me that careful search had been made for the women at the time, and that though it was unsuccessful, they had afterwards learned that the facts were just as they had reported them. At Dodona, however, the priestesses who deliver the oracles have a different version of the story: two black doves, they say flew away from Thebes in Egypt, and one of them alighted at Dodona, the other in Libya. The former, perched on an oak, and speaking with a human voice, told them that there, on that very spot, there should be an oracle of Zeus. Those who heard her understood the words to be a command from heaven, and at once obeyed. Similarly the dove which flew to Libya told the Libyans to found the oracle of Ammon – which is also an oracle of Zeus. The people who gave me this information were the three priestesses at

---

1. Herodotus is not deceived by the religious poetry ascribed to 'Orpheus' and 'Musaeus' and alleged to be much older than Homer.

Dodona – Promeneia the eldest, Timarete the next, and Nicandra the youngest – and their account is confirmed by the other Dodonaeans connected with the temple. Personally, however, I would suggest that if the Phoenicians really carried off the women from the temple and sold them respectively in Libya and Greece, the one who was brought to Greece (or Pelasgia as it was then called) must have been sold to the Thesprotians; and later, while she was working as a slave in that part of the country, she built, under an oak that happened to be growing there, a shrine to Zeus; for she would naturally remember in her exile the god whom she had served in her native Thebes. Subsequently, when she had learned to speak Greek, she established an oracle there, and mentioned, in addition, that the same Phoenicians who had sold her, also sold her sister in Libya. The story which the people of Dodona tell about the doves came, I should say, from the fact that the women were foreigners, whose language sounded to them like the twittering of birds; later on the dove spoke with a human voice, because by that time the woman had stopped twittering and learned to talk intelligibly. That, at least, is how I should explain the obvious impossibility of a dove using the language of men. As to the bird being black, they merely signify by this that the woman was an Egyptian. It is certainly true that the oracles at Thebes and Dodona are similar in character. Another form of divination – by the inspection of sacrificial victims – also came from Egypt.

It was the Egyptians too who originated, and taught the Greeks to use, ceremonial meetings, processions, and liturgies: a fact which can be inferred from the obvious antiquity of such ceremonies in Egypt, compared with Greece, where they have been only recently introduced. The Egyptians meet in solemn assembly not once a year only, but on a number of occasions, the most important and best attended being the festival of Artemis at Bubastis: second in importance is the assembly at Busiris – a city in the middle of the Delta, containing a vast temple dedicated to Isis, the Egyptian equivalent of Demeter, in whose honour the meeting is held. Then there are the assemblies in honour of Athene at Sais, of the Sun at Heliopolis, of Leto at Buto, and of Ares[1] at Papremis. The procedure at Bubastis is

1. Artemis = Bast (Bu = city); Athene, Neith; the Sun, Ra; Leto, Uat; Ares, Set.

this: they come in barges, men and women together, a great number in each boat; on the way, some of the women keep up a continual clatter with castanets and some of the men play flutes, while the rest, both men and women, sing and clap their hands. Whenever they pass a town on the river-bank, they bring the barge close in-shore, some of the women continuing to act as I have said, while others shout abuse at the women of the place, or start dancing, or stand up and hitch up their skirts. When they reach Bubastis they celebrate the festival with elaborate sacrifices, and more wine is consumed than during all the rest of the year. The numbers that meet there, are, according to native report, as many as seven hundred thousand men and women – excluding children. I have already mentioned the fes-tival of Isis at Busiris: it is here that everybody – tens of thousands of men and women – when the sacrifice is over, beat their breasts: in whose honour, however, I do not feel it is proper for me to say.[1] Any Carians who happen to live in Egypt go even further and cut their foreheads with knives, thus proving that they are foreigners and not Egyptians. At Sais, on the night of the sacrifices, everybody burns a great number of lights in the open air round the houses; the lamps they use are flat dishes filled with oil and salt, with a floating wick which keeps burning throughout the night. The festival is called the Festival of Lamps, and even the Egyptians who cannot attend it mark the night of the sacrifice by lighting lamps, so that on that night lamps are burning not in Sais only but throughout the country. There is a sacred tradition which accounts both for the date and for the manner of these observances.

At Heliopolis and Buto the assemblies are for the purpose of sacri-fice only; but at Papremis there is a special ceremony in addition to the ordinary rites and sacrifices as practised elsewhere. As the sun draws towards setting, only a few of the priests continue to employ themselves about the image of the god, while the majority, armed with wooden clubs, take their stand at the entrance of the temple; opposite these is another crowd of men, more than a thousand strong, also armed with clubs and consisting of men who have vows

1. Osiris. His 'passion play' was probably so much like some Greek 'mys-teries' that Herodotus feels it improper to talk about it, though he mentions Osiris in his 'public' capacity (p. 145 etc.). Cf. p. 148.

to perform. The image of the god, in a little wooden gold-plated shrine, is conveyed to another sacred building on the day before the ceremony. The few priests who are left to attend to it, put it, together with the shrine which contains it, in a four-wheeled cart which they drag along towards the temple. The others, waiting at the temple gate, try to prevent it from coming in, while the votaries take the god's side and set upon them with their clubs. The assault is resisted, and a vigorous tussle ensues in which heads are broken and not a few actually die of the wounds they receive. That, at least, is what I believe, though the Egyptians told me that nobody is ever killed. The origin of this festival is explained locally by the story that the mother of Ares once lived in the temple; Ares himself was brought up elsewhere, but when he grew to manhood he wished to get to know his mother and for that purpose came to the temple where she was. Her attendants, however, not knowing him by sight, refused him admission, and succeeded in keeping him out until he fetched help from another town and forced his way in by violence. This, they say, is why the battle with clubs is part of the ceremony at the festival of Ares.

It was the Egyptians who first made it an offence against piety to have intercourse with women in temples, or to enter temples after intercourse without having previously washed. Hardly any nation except the Egyptians and Greeks has any such scruple, but nearly all consider men and women to be, in this respect, no different from animals, which, whether they are beasts or birds, they constantly see coupling in temples and sacred places – and if the god concerned had any objection to this, he would not allow it to occur. Such is the theory, but, in spite of it, I must continue to disapprove the practice. The Egyptians are meticulous in their observance of this point, as indeed they are in everything else which concerns their religion.

There are not a great many wild animals in Egypt, in spite of the fact that it borders on Libya. Such as there are – both wild and tame – are without exception held to be sacred. To explain the reason for this, I should have to enter into a discussion of religious principles which is a subject I particularly wish to avoid – any slight mention I have already made of such matters having been forced upon me by the needs of my story. But, reasons apart, how they actually behave towards animals I will proceed to describe. The various sorts have guardians appointed for them, sometimes men, sometimes women, who are responsible for feeding them; and the office of guardian is handed down from father to son. Their manner, in the various cities, of performing vows is as follows: praying to the god to whom the particular creature, whichever it may be, is sacred, they shave the heads of their children – sometimes completely, sometimes only a half or a third part – and after weighing the hair in a pair of scales, give an equal weight of silver to the animals' keeper, who then cuts up fish (the animals' usual food) to an equivalent value and gives it to them to eat. Anyone who deliberately kills one of these animals, is punished with death; should one be killed accidentally, the penalty is whatever the priests choose to impose; but for killing an ibis or a hawk, whether deliberately or not, the penalty is inevitably death.

The number, already large, of domestic animals would have been greatly increased, were it not for an odd thing that happens to the cats. The females, when they have kittens, avoid the toms; but the toms, thus deprived of their satisfaction, get over the difficulty very ingeniously, for they either openly seize, or secretly steal, the kittens and kill them – but without eating them – and the result is that the females, deprived of their kittens and wanting more (for their maternal instinct is very strong), go off to look for mates again. What happens when a house catches fire is most extraordinary: nobody takes the least trouble to put it out, for it is only the cats that matter: everyone stands in a row, a little distance from his neighbour, trying to protect the cats, who nevertheless slip through the line, or jump over it, and hurl themselves into the flames. This causes the Egyptians deep distress. All the inmates of a house where a cat has died a natural death shave their eyebrows, and when a dog dies they shave the whole body including the head. Cats which have died are taken to Bubastis, where they are embalmed and buried in sacred receptacles; dogs are buried, also in sacred burial-places, in the towns where they belong. Weasels are buried in the same way as dogs; field-mice and hawks are taken to Buto, ibises to Hermopolis. Bears, which are scarce, and wolves (which in Egypt are not much bigger than jackals) are buried wherever they happen to be found lying dead.

The following is an account of the crocodile. During the four winter months it takes no food. It is a four-footed, amphibious creature, lays and hatches its eggs on land, where it spends the greater part of the day, and stays all night in the river, where the water is warmer than the night-air and the dew. The difference in size between the young and the full-grown crocodile is greater than in any other known creature; for a crocodile's egg is hardly bigger than a goose's, and the young when hatched is small in proportion, yet it grows to a size of some twenty-three feet long or even more. It has eyes like a pig's but great fang-like teeth in proportion to its body, and is the only animal to have no tongue and a stationary lower jaw; for when it eats it brings the upper jaw down upon the under. It has powerful claws and a scaly hide, which on its back is impenetrable. It cannot see under water, though on land its sight is remarkably quick. One result of its spending so much time in the water is that the inside of its mouth gets covered with leeches. Other animals avoid the crocodile, as do all birds too with one exception – the sandpiper, or Egyptian plover; this bird is of service to the crocodile and lives, in consequence, in the greatest amity with him; for when the crocodile comes ashore and lies with his mouth wide open (which he generally does facing towards the west), the bird hops in and swallows the leeches. The crocodile enjoys this, and never, in consequence, hurts the bird. Some Egyptians reverence the crocodile as a sacred beast; others do not, but treat it as an enemy. The strongest belief in its sanctity is to be found in Thebes and round about Lake Moeris; in these places they keep one particular crocodile, which they tame, putting rings made of glass or gold into its ears and bracelets round its front feet, and giving it special food and ceremonial offerings. In fact, while these creatures are alive they treat them with every kindness, and, when they die, embalm them and bury them in sacred tombs. On the other hand, in the neighbourhood of Elephantine crocodiles are not considered sacred animals at all, but are eaten. In the Egyptian language these creatures are called *champsae*. The name crocodile – or 'lizard' – was given them by the Ionians, who saw they resembled the lizards commonly found on stone walls in their own country.

Of the numerous different ways of catching crocodiles I will describe the one which seems to me the most interesting. They bait a hook with a chine of pork and let it float out into midstream, and at the same time, standing on the bank, take a live pig and beat it. The crocodile, hearing its squeals, makes a rush towards it, encounters the bait, gulps it down, and is hauled out of the water. The first thing the huntsman does when he has got the beast on land is to plaster its eyes with mud; this done, it is dispatched easily enough – but without this precaution it will give a lot of trouble.

The hippopotamus is held sacred in the district of Papremis, but not elsewhere. This animal has four legs, cloven hoofs like an ox, a snub nose, a horse's mane and tail, conspicuous tusks, a voice like a horse's neigh, and is about the size of a very large ox. Its hide is so thick and tough that when dried it can be made into spear-shafts. Otters, too, are found in the Nile; they, and the fish called lepidotus, and eels are all considered sacred to the Nile, as is also the bird known as the fox-goose. Another sacred bird is the phoenix; I have not seen a phoenix myself, except in paintings, for it is very rare and visits the country (so at least they say at Heliopolis) only at intervals of 500 years, on the occasion of the death of the parent-bird. To judge by the paintings, its plumage is partly golden, partly red, and in shape and size it is exactly like an eagle. There is a story about the phoenix; it brings its parent in a lump of myrrh all the way from Arabia and buries the body in the temple of the Sun. To perform this feat, the bird first shapes some myrrh into a sort of egg as big as it finds, by testing, that it can carry; then it hollows the lump out, puts its father inside and smears some more myrrh over the hole. The egg-shaped lump is then just of the same weight as it was originally. Finally it is carried by the bird to the temple of the Sun in Egypt. Such, at least, is the story.

Near Thebes a species of snake is found said to be sacred to Zeus; these snakes are small and quite harmless, and have two horns growing from the top of their heads. Such as are found dead are buried in the temple of Zeus.

There is a place in Arabia[1] more or less opposite the city of Buto, where I went to try to get information about the flying snakes. On my arrival I saw their skeletons in incalculable numbers; they were piled in heaps, some of which were big, others smaller, others – the

---

1. i.e. in the desert east of the Delta. Just what Herodotus saw and was told about it is a mystery. Had he seen fish-bones in a dried-up lake and been told about swarms of locusts?

most numerous – smaller still. The place where these bones lie is a narrow mountain pass leading to a broad plain which joins on to the plain of Egypt, and it is said that when the winged snakes fly to Egypt from Arabia in spring, the ibises meet them at the entrance to the pass and do not let them get through, but kill them. According to the Arabians, this service is the reason for the great reverence with which the ibis is regarded in Egypt, and the Egyptians themselves admit the truth of what they say. The ibis is jet-black all over; it has legs like a crane's, a markedly hooked beak, and is about the size of a landrail. That, at any rate, is what the black ibis is like – the kind namely that attacks the winged snakes; there is, however, another sort, more commonly found in inhabited districts; this has a bald head and neck and is white except for the head, throat, wing-tips, and rump, which are jet-black; its legs and beak are similar to those of the black ibis. The winged snakes resemble watersnakes; their wings are not feathered, but are like a bat's. I will now leave the subject of sacred animals and say something of the people.

The Egyptians who live in the cultivated parts of the country, by their practice of keeping records of the past, have made themselves much the most learned of any nation of which I have had experience. I will describe some of their habits: every month for three successive days they purge themselves, for their health's sake, with emetics and clysters, in the belief that all diseases come from the food a man eats; and it is a fact – even apart from this precaution – that next to the Libyans they are the healthiest people in the world. I should put this down myself to the absence of changes in the climate; for change, and especially change of weather, is the prime cause of disease. They eat loaves made from spelt – *cyllestes* is their word for them – and drink a wine made from barley, as they have no vines in the country. Some kinds of fish they eat raw, either dried in the sun, or salted; quails, too, they eat raw, and ducks and various small birds, after pickling them in brine; other sorts of birds and fish, apart from those which they consider sacred, they either roast or boil. When the rich give a party and the meal is finished, a man carries round amongst the guests a wooden image of a corpse in a coffin, carved and painted to look as much like the real thing as possible, and anything from eighteen inches to three foot long; he shows it to each guest in turn, and says: 'Look upon this body as you drink and enjoy yourself; for you will be just like it when you are dead.'

The Egyptians keep to their native customs and never adopt any from abroad. Many of these customs are interesting, especially, perhaps, the 'Linus'[1] song. This person, under different names, is celebrated in song not only in Egypt but in Phoenicia, Cyprus, and other places, and appears to be the person whom the Greeks celebrate as Linus; if this is so, it is yet one more of the many surprises that Egypt has to offer: for where did the Egyptians get this song from? It is clearly very ancient; the Egyptian name for Linus is Maneros, and their story is that their first king had an only son, who died young, and that this dirge – their first and, at the time, their only melody – was invented to be sung in his honour.

There is another point in which the Egyptians resemble one section of the Greek people – the Lacedaemonians: I mean the custom of young men stepping aside to make room for their seniors when they meet them in the street, and of getting up from their seats when older men come in. But they are unlike any of the Greeks in that they do not greet one another by name in the streets, but make a low bow and drop one hand to the knee. The clothes they wear consist of a linen tunic with a fringe hanging round the legs (called in their language *calasiris*), and a white woollen garment on top of it. It is, however, contrary to religious usage to be buried in a woollen garment, or to wear wool in a temple. This custom agrees with the rites known as Orphic and Bacchic (actually Egyptian and Pythagorean); for anyone initiated into these rites is similarly debarred from burial in a garment of wool. They have a myth which explains the reason for this.

The Egyptians were also the first to assign each month and each day to a particular deity, and to foretell by the date of a man's birth his character, his fortunes, and the day of his death – a discovery which Greek poets have turned to account. The Egyptians, too, have made more use of omens and prognostics than any other nation; they keep written records of the observed results of any unusual

1. The names 'Linus' and 'Maneros' are not Egyptian. Herodotus may here be repeating popular but garbled Greek beliefs about various Levantine 'dying god' rituals.

phenomenon, so that they come to expect a similar consequence to follow a similar occurrence in the future. The art of divination is not attributed by them to any man, but only to certain gods: for instance, Heracles, Apollo, Athena, Artemis, Ares, and Zeus[1] all have an oracle in the country, while the oracle of Leto in Buto is held in greater repute than any of them. The method of delivering the responses varies in the different shrines.

The practice of medicine they split up into separate parts, each doctor being responsible for the treatment of only one disease. There are, in consequence, innumerable doctors, some specializing in diseases of the eyes, others of the head, others of the teeth, others of the stomach, and so on; while others, again, deal with the sort of troubles which cannot be exactly localized. As regards mourning and funerals, when a distinguished man dies all the women of the household plaster their heads and faces with mud, then, leaving the body indoors, perambulate the town with the dead man's female relatives, their dresses fastened with a girdle, and beat their bared breasts. The men too, for their part, follow the same procedure, wearing a girdle and beating themselves like the women. The ceremony over, they take the body to be mummified.

Mummification is a distinct profession. The embalmers, when a body is brought to them, produce specimen models in wood, painted to resemble nature, and graded in quality; the best and most expensive kind is said to represent a being whose name I shrink from mentioning in this connexion;[2] the next best is somewhat inferior and cheaper, while the third sort is cheapest of all. After pointing out these differences in quality, they ask which of the three is required, and the kinsmen of the dead man, having agreed upon a price, go away and leave the embalmers to their work. The most perfect process is as follows: as much as possible of the brain is extracted through the nostrils with an iron hook, and what the hook cannot reach is rinsed out with drugs; next the flank is laid open with a flint knife and the whole contents of the abdomen removed; the cavity is then thoroughly cleansed and washed out, first with palm wine and again with an infusion of pounded spices. After that it is filled with pure

1. For the gods' names see pp. 146 and 152 and notes.
2. Osiris; cf. p. 153.

bruised myrrh, cassia, and every other aromatic substance with the exception of frankincense, and sewn up again, after which the body is placed in natrum, covered entirely over, for seventy days – never longer. When this period, which must not be exceeded, is over, the body is washed and then wrapped from head to foot in linen cut into strips and smeared on the under side with gum, which is commonly used by the Egyptians instead of glue. In this condition the body is given back to the family, who have a wooden case made, shaped like the human figure, into which it is put. The case is then sealed up and stored in a sepulchral chamber, upright against the wall. When, for reasons of expense, the second quality is called for, the treatment is different: no incision is made and the intestines are not removed, but oil of cedar is injected with a syringe into the body through the anus which is afterwards stopped up to prevent the liquid from escaping. The body is then pickled in natrum for the prescribed number of days, on the last of which the oil is drained off. The effect of it is so powerful that as it leaves the body it brings with it the stomach and intestines in a liquid state, and as the flesh, too, is dissolved by the natrum, nothing of the body is left but the bones and skin. After this treatment it is returned to the family without further fuss.

The third method, used for embalming the bodies of the poor, is simply to clear out the intestines with a purge and keep the body seventy days in natrum. It is then given back to the family to be taken away.

When the wife of a distinguished man dies, or any woman who happens to be beautiful or well known, her body is not given to the embalmers immediately, but only after the lapse of three or four days. This is a precautionary measure to prevent the embalmers from violating the corpse, a thing which is said actually to have happened in the case of a woman who had just died. The culprit was given away by one of his fellow workmen. If anyone, either an Egyptian or a foreigner, is found drowned in the river or killed by a crocodile, there is the strongest obligation upon the people of the nearest town to have the body embalmed in the most elaborate manner and buried in a consecrated burial-place; no one is allowed to touch it except the priests of the Nile – not even relatives or friends; the priests alone prepare it for burial with their own hands and place it in the tomb, as if it were something more sacred than the body of a man.

The Egyptians are unwilling to adopt Greek customs, or, to speak generally, those of any other country. There is, however, one exception to this almost universal rule in the case of Chemmis, a large town near Neapolis in the district of Thebes. In this place there is a square of enclosed ground sacred to Perseus the son of Danae; palm trees grow round it, and there is a stone gateway of great size surmounted by two very large stone figures. Within the enclosure is a shrine containing a statue of Perseus. According to the local legend, Perseus is frequently to be seen in the neighbourhood, and also within the temple; sometimes a sandal which he has worn, three feet long, is found – a sign, they say, of the approach of a period of great prosperity for the whole of Egypt. In the worship of Perseus Greek ceremonies are used, athletic contests with all the usual events, and prizes of cattle, cloaks, and skins. When I asked why it was that Perseus revealed himself only to the people of Chemmis, and why they alone of the Egyptians celebrated games in his honour, the answer was that Perseus belonged by birth to their city; Danaus and Lynceus, they said, were Chemmites before they sailed to Greece, and from them they traced Perseus' descent. Further, when he came to Egypt from Libya with the Gorgon's head (which is the reason the Greeks also assign for his going there) he paid a visit to Chemmis, having previously learned the name of the place from his mother, and there acknowledged all his kinsmen. On his arrival he instructed them to to celebrate games in his honour, and they accordingly did so.

Up to this point I have described the life of the Egyptians who live south of the marsh-country; those who inhabit the marshes are in most things much the same as the rest; and they also practise monogamy, as the Greeks do; nevertheless they are peculiar in certain ways which they have discovered of living more cheaply: for instance, they gather the water-lilies (called lotus by the Egyptians), which grow in great abundance when the river is full and floods the neighbouring flats, and dry them in the sun; then from the centre of each blossom they pick out something which resembles a poppy-head, grind it, and make it into loaves which they bake. The root of this plant is also edible; it is round, about as big as an apple, and tastes fairly sweet.

There is another kind of lily to be found in the river; this resembles a rose, and its fruit is formed on a separate stalk from that which bears the blossom, and has very much the look of a wasps' comb. The fruit contains a number of seeds, about the size of an olive-stone, which are good to eat either green or dried. They pull up the annual crop of papyrus-reed which grows in the marshes, cut the stalks in two, and eat the lower part, about eighteen inches in length, first baking it in a closed pan, heated red-hot, if they want to enjoy it to perfection. The upper section of the stalk is used for some other purpose. Some of these people, however, live upon nothing but fish, which they gut as soon as they catch them, and eat after drying them in the sun.

Gregarious fish are not found in large numbers in the rivers; they frequent the lakes, which they leave at the breeding season to swim in shoals to the sea. In front go the males, dropping their milt, which the females, following behind, gulp down. It is this that causes the females to conceive, and after a period in the sea, when they are about to spawn, the whole shoal returns to its former haunt in the inland lakes. This time, however, it is the females who lead the way, and as they swim along in their hundreds they do just what the males did on the way out, dropping their grains of spawn, a little here, a little there, while the males who follow behind swallow them up. Each of these grains of spawn is a fish in embryo; some of them escape and are not swallowed by the males, and it is these which afterwards grow to maturity. Fish which are caught on their way to the sea are found to have their heads bruised on the left side, while those taken as they return upstream have similar bruises on the right side. The reason is that as they swim down river to the sea they keep close to the bank on their left, and still stick to the same side of the river on their return, keeping as near the bank as they possibly can and continually brushing against it, for fear of being carried out of their course by the strength of the stream.

When the Nile begins to rise, the hollows and marshy ground close beside it are the first to fill, the water from the river seeping through the banks, and no sooner are these low-lying bits of ground formed into lakes than they are found to contain a multitude of small fish. I think I understand the probable reason for this: the fish, I should say, when the river is falling the previous year, lay their eggs in the mud

just before they get away with the last of the water, so that when
the flood comes round again in due course, the eggs at once
hatch and produce the fish. These are the facts about the fish in the
Nile.

The Egyptians who live in the marsh-country use an oil extracted
from the castor-oil plant. This plant, which grows wild in Greece,
they call *Kiki*, and the Egyptian variety is very prolific and has a disagreeable smell. Their practice is to sow it along the banks of rivers
and lakes, and when the fruit is gathered it is either bruised and
pressed, or else boiled down, and the liquid thus obtained is of an
oily nature and quite as good as olive-oil for burning in lamps,
though the smell is unpleasant.

The country is infested by swarms of gnats, and the people have invented various methods of dealing with them; south of the marshes
they sleep at night on raised structures, which is a great benefit to
them because the gnats are prevented by the wind from flying high;
in the marsh-country itself they do not have these towers, but everyone, instead, provides himself with a net, which during the day he
uses for fishing, and at night fixes up round his bed, and creeps in
under it before he goes to sleep. For anyone to sleep wrapped in a
cloak or in linen would be useless, for the gnats would bite through
them; but they do not even attempt to get through the net.

The Nile boats used for carrying freight are built of acacia [?] wood
– the acacia resembles in form the lotus of Cyrene, and exudes gum.
They cut short planks, about three feet long, from this tree, and the
method of construction is to lay them together like bricks and
through-fasten them with long spikes set close together, and then,
when the hull is complete, to lay the deck-beams across on top. The
boats have no ribs and are caulked from inside with papyrus. They
are given a single steering-oar, which is driven down through the
keel; the masts are of acacia wood, the sails of papyrus. These vessels
cannot sail up the river without a good leading wind, but have to be
towed from the banks; and for dropping downstream with the current
they are handled as follows: each vessel is equipped with a raft made of
tamarisk wood, with a rush mat fastened on top of it, and a stone with
a hole through it weighing some four hundredweight; the raft and
the stone are made fast to the vessel with ropes, fore and aft respec-

tively, so that the raft is carried rapidly forward by the current and pulls the 'baris' (as these boats are called) after it, while the stone, dragging along the bottom astern, acts as a check and gives her steerage-way. There are a great many of these vessels on the Nile, some of them of enormous carrying capacity.

When the Nile overflows, the whole country is converted into a sea, and the towns, which alone remain above water, look like the islands in the Aegean. At these times water transport is used all over the country, instead of merely along the course of the river, and any-one going from Naucratis to Memphis would pass right by the pyramids instead of following the usual course by Cercasorus and the tip of the Delta. If you go by boat from Canopus on the coast across the flats to Naucratis, you will pass Anthylla and Archandropolis, of which the former, a city of some repute, has been made over ever since the Persian conquest of Egypt to the wife of the reigning mon-arch to keep her in shoes. The latter town, I fancy, took the name of Archandropolis from Archander the son of Phthius, grandson of Achaeus and son-in-law of Danaus. There may, of course, have been another Archander; but the name in any case is not Egyptian.

Up to this point I have confined what I have written to the results of my own direct observation and research, and the views I have formed from them; but from now on the basis of my story will be the accounts given to me by the Egyptians themselves – though here, too, I shall put in one or two things which I have seen with my own eyes.

The priests told me that it was Min, the first king of Egypt, who raised the dam which protects Memphis from the floods. The river used to flow along the base of the sandy hills on the Libyan border, and this monarch, by damming it up at the bend about a hundred furlongs south of Memphis, drained the original channel and di-verted it to a new one half-way between the two lines of hills. To this day the elbow which the Nile forms here, where it is forced into its new channel, is most carefully watched by the Persians, who strengthen the dam every year; for should the river burst it, Mem-phis might be completely overwhelmed. On the land which had been drained by the diversion of the river, King Min built the city which is now called Memphis – it lies in the narrow part of Egypt – and afterwards on the north and west sides of the town excavated a lake, communicating with the river, which itself protects it on the east. In addition to this the priests told me that he built there the large and very remarkable temple of Hephaestus.[1]

Next, the priests read to me from a written record the names of three hundred and thirty monarchs, in the same number of generations, all of them Egyptians except eighteen, who were Ethiops, and one other, who was an Egyptian woman. This last had the same name – Nitocris – as the queen of Babylon. The story was that she ensnared to their deaths hundreds of Egyptians in revenge for the king her brother, whom his subjects had murdered and forced her to succeed; this she did by constructing an immense underground chamber, in which, under the pretence of opening it by an inaugural ceremony, she invited to a banquet all the Egyptians whom she knew to be chiefly responsible for her brother's death; then, when the banquet was in full swing, she let the river in on them through a large concealed conduit-pipe. The only other thing I was told about her was that after this fearful revenge she flung herself into a room full of ashes, to escape her punishment. The other kings, the priests told me, were in no way distinguished and left nothing to commemorate their reigns, with the exception of the last of them, Moeris, who is remembered by the northern gateway he built for the temple of Hephaestus and the lake with the pyramids in it, which were constructed by his orders. The extent of the lake and the size of the pyramids I will mention later on. As none of the other kings on the priests' roll left any memorial at all, I will pass on to say something of Sesostris, who succeeded them. Sesostris, the priests said, sailed first with a fleet of warships from the Arabian gulf along the coast of the Indian Ocean, subduing the coastal tribes as he went, until he found that shoal water made further progress impossible; then on his return to Egypt (still according to the priests' account) he raised a powerful army and

1. Sir Flinders Petrie believed (followed by J. L. Myres and others) that §§124–136 (pp. 178–180 of this edition), on the Pyramid Builders, should stand here, but have been misplaced. The change would have the effect of making Herodotus' informants get their popular history of the Old Kingdom, including the Pyramid Builders, Middle Kingdom (Sesostris, a 'blown up' version of Senosret, Dynasty XII) and New Kingdom (with the Ramessids represented by Rhampsinitus) in the right order.

marched across the continent, reducing to subjection every nation in his path. Whenever he encountered a courageous enemy who fought valiantly for freedom, he erected pillars on the spot inscribed with his own name and country, and a sentence to indicate that by the might of his armed forces he had won the victory; if, however, a town fell easily into his hands without a struggle, he made an addition to the inscription on the pillar – for not only did he record upon it the same facts as before, but added a picture of a woman's genitals, meaning to show that the people of that town were no braver than women. Thus his victorious progress through Asia continued, until he entered Europe and defeated the Scythians and Thracians; this, I think, was the furthest point the Egyptian army reached for the memorial columns are to be seen in this part of the country but not beyond. On his way back Sesostris came to the river Phasis, and it is quite possible that he here detached a body of troops from his army and left them behind to settle – or, on the other hand, it may be that some of his men were sick of their travels and deserted. I cannot say with certainty which supposition is the right one, but it is undoubtedly a fact that the Colchians are of Egyptian descent. I noticed this myself before I heard anyone else mention it, and when it occurred to me I asked some questions both in Colchis and in Egypt, and found that the Colchians remembered the Egyptians more distinctly than the Egyptians remembered them. The Egyptians did, however, say that they thought the original Colchians were men from Sesostris' army. My own idea on the subject was based first on the fact that they have black skins and woolly hair (not that that amounts to much, as other nations have the same), and secondly, and more especially, on the fact that the Colchians, the Egyptians, and the Ethiopians are the only races which from ancient times have practised circumcision. The Phoenicians and the Syrians of Palestine themselves admit that they adopted the practice from Egypt, and the Syrians who live near the rivers Thermodon and Parthenius, as well as their neighbours the Macronians, say that they learnt it only a short time ago from the Colchians. No other nations use circumcision, and all these are without doubt following the Egyptian lead. As between the Egyptians and the Ethiopians, I should not like to say which learned from the other, for the custom is evidently a very ancient one; but I have no doubt that the other nations adopted it as a result of their intercourse with Egypt, and in this belief I am strongly supported by the fact that Phoenicians who have contact with Greece drop the Egyptian usage, and allow their children to go uncircumcised.

And now I think of it, there is a further point of resemblance between the Colchians and Egyptians: they share a method of weaving linen different from that of any other people; and there is also a similarity between them in language and way of living. The linen made in Colchis is known in Greece as Sardonian linen; that which comes from Egypt is called Egyptian.

Most of the memorial pillars which King Sesostris erected in the conquered countries have disappeared, but I have seen some myself in Palestine,[1] with the inscription I mentioned, and the drawing of a woman's genitals. In Ionia also there are two images of Sesostris cut on rock, one on the road from Ephesus to Phocaea, the other between Sardis and Smyrna; in each case the carved figure is nearly seven feet high and represents a man with a spear in his right hand and a bow in his left, and the rest of his equipment to match – partly Egyptian, partly Ethiopian. Across the breast from shoulder to shoulder runs an inscription, cut in the Egyptian sacred script: *By the strength of my shoulders I won this land.* The name and country of the conqueror are not here recorded, and some who have seen the image suppose it to represent Memnon; however, they are wide of the mark, for Sesostris has made the truth plain enough elsewhere.

The priests went on to tell me that Sesostris, on his return home with a host of prisoners from the conquered countries, was met at Daphnae, near Pelusium, by his brother, whom he had left to govern Egypt during his absence, and invited with his sons to a banquet. While they were at dinner, his brother piled faggots round the building and set them on fire. Seeing what had happened, Sesostris at once asked his wife (for she too was a member of the party) what he should do about it, and was advised by her to take two of their sons – of whom there were six – and lay them out over the burning wood to make a bridge by which they might walk through the fire to safety. The king took her advice, with the result that two of his sons were

1. Herodotus could have seen hieroglyphic monuments here, but the 'genitals' are imaginary.

burnt to death, while the others, together with their father, were saved.

Once home again in Egypt, Sesostris punished his brother and proceeded to employ his prisoners of war in various tasks. It was they who were forced to drag the enormous masses of stone which were brought during Sesostris' reign for the temple of Hephaestus, and to dig the dykes which one finds there to-day, thereby depriving Egypt – though it was far from their intention to do so – of the horses and carriages which were formerly in such common use throughout the country. All Egypt is flat; yet from that time onwards it has been unfit for horses or wheeled traffic because of the innumerable dykes, running in all directions, which cut the country up. The king's object was to supply water to the towns which lay inland at some distance from the river; for previously the people in these towns, when the level of the river fell, had to go short and to drink brackish water from wells. It was this king, moreover, who divided the land into lots and gave everyone a square piece of equal size, from the produce of which he exacted an annual tax. Any man whose holding was damaged by the encroachment of the river would go and declare his loss before the king, who would send inspectors to measure the extent of the loss, in order that he might pay in future a fair proportion of the tax at which his property had been assessed. Perhaps this was the way in which geometry was invented, and passed afterwards into Greece – for knowledge of the sundial and the gnomon and the twelve divisions of the day came into Greece from Babylon.

Sesostris was the only Egyptian king to rule Ethiopia. As memorials of his reign he left stone statues of himself and his wife, each forty-five feet high, and statues thirty feet high of each of his four sons. They were erected in front of the temple of Hephaestus. Long afterwards the priest of Hephaestus would not allow Darius the king of Persia to erect a statue of himself in front of these, because (as he put it) his deeds had not been as great as the deeds of Sesostris the Egyptian; the conquests of Sesostris, no less extensive than those of Darius, included the Scythians, whom Darius had been unable to subdue; it was not right, therefore, that he should put his statue in front of those dedicated by a monarch, whose achievements he had failed to surpass. Darius, they say, admitted the truth of this.

When Sesostris died, he was succeeded by his son Pheros,[1] a prince who undertook no military adventures. He went blind, and the reason for it is explained in the following tale: one year the Nile rose to an excessive height, as much as twenty-seven feet, and when all the fields were under water it began to blow hard, so that the river got very rough. The king in insensate rage seized a spear and hurled it into the swirling waters, and immediately thereafter he was attacked by a disease of the eyes, and became blind. He was blind for ten years, after which he received an oracle from the city of Buto to the effect that the time of his punishment being now ended, he would recover his sight, if he washed his eyes with the urine of a woman who had never lain with any man except her husband. He tried his wife first, but without success – he remained as blind as ever; then he tried other women, a great many, one after another, until at last his sight was restored. Then he collected within the walls of a town, now called Red Clod, all the women except the one whose urine had proved efficacious, set the place on fire, and burnt them to death, town and all; afterwards he married the woman who had been the means of curing him. In gratitude for his recovery he dedicated a number of offerings in all the temples of repute; but the most remarkable of them were two stone obelisks which he set up in the precinct of the temple of Hephaestus. These are well worth seeing; they are twelve feet broad and a hundred and fifty feet high, each hewn from a single block of stone.[2]

Pheros was succeeded by a native of Memphis, whose name in the Greek language was Proteus. To this day there is a sacred precinct of his at Memphis, very fine and richly adorned, and situated south of the temple of Hephaestus. The whole district hereabouts is known as the Camp of the Tyrians, because the houses in the neighbourhood are occupied by Phoenicians from Tyre. Within the enclosure there is a temple dedicated to Aphrodite the Stranger. I should guess, myself, that it was built in honour of Helen the daughter of Tyndareus, not only because I have heard it said that she passed some time at the court of Proteus, but also, and more particularly, because of the

1. Simply the title 'Pharaoh'.
2. Probably an exaggerated estimate; but that now before the Lateran in Rome is over 100 feet high.

description of Aphrodite as 'the stranger', a title never given to this goddess in any of her other temples. I questioned the priests about the story of Helen, and they told me in reply that Paris was on his way home from Sparta with his stolen bride, when, somewhere in the Aegean sea, he met foul weather, which drove his ship towards Egypt, until at last, the gale continuing as bad as ever, he found himself on the coast, and managed to get ashore at the Salt-pans, in the mouth of the Nile now called the Canopic. Here on the beach there was a temple, which still exists, dedicated to Heracles, and in connexion with it there is a very ancient custom, which has remained unaltered to the present day. If a runaway slave takes refuge in this shrine and allows the sacred marks, which are the sign of his submission to the service of the god, to be set upon his body, his master, no matter who he is, cannot lay hands on him. Now some of Paris' servants found out about this and, wishing to get him into trouble, deserted, and fled as suppliants to the temple and told against him the whole story of his abduction of Helen and his wicked treatment of Menelaus. They brought these charges against their master not only before the temple priests, but also before the warden of that mouth of the Nile, a man named Thonis. Thonis at once sent a dispatch to Proteus at Memphis. 'A Trojan stranger (the message ran) has arrived here from Greece, where he has been guilty of an abominable crime: first he seduced the wife of his host, then carried her off together with a great deal of valuable property; and now stress of weather has forced him to land on this coast. Are we to let him sail away again in possession of his stolen goods, or should we confiscate them?' Proteus answered: 'No matter who it is that has committed this crime against his friend, arrest him and send him to me, that I may hear what he can say for himself.' Thonis accordingly arrested Paris, held his ships, and took both him and Helen to Memphis, together with the stolen property and the servants who had taken sanctuary in the temple. On their arrival Proteus asked Paris who he was and where he had come from, and Paris gave him his name and all the details of his family and a true account of his voyage; but when he was further asked how he had got possession of Helen, then, instead of telling the truth, he began to shilly-shally, until the runaway servants convicted him of lying and told the whole story of his crime. Finally Proteus gave his judgement: 'If,' he said, 'I did not consider it a matter of great importance that I have never yet put to death any stranger who has been forced upon my coasts by stress of weather, I should have punished you for the sake of your Greek host. To be welcomed as a guest, and to repay that kindness by so foul a deed! You are a villain. You seduced your friend's wife, and, as if that were not enough, persuaded her to escape with you on the wings of passion you roused. Even that did not content you – but you must bring with you besides the treasure you have stolen from your host's house. But though I cannot punish a stranger with death, I will not allow you to take away your ill-gotten gains: I will keep this woman and the treasure, until the Greek to whom they belong chooses to come and fetch them. As for you and the companions of your voyage, I give you three days in which to leave my country – and to find an anchorage elsewhere. If you are not gone by then, I shall treat you as enemies.'

This was the account I had from the priests about the arrival of Helen at Proteus' court. I think Homer[1] was familiar with the story; for though he rejected it as less suitable for epic poetry than the one he actually used, he left indications that it was not unknown to him. For instance, when he describes the wanderings of Paris in the *Iliad* (and he has not elsewhere contradicted his account), he says that in the course of them he brought Helen to Sidon in Phoenicia. The passage occurs in the section of the poem called the *Deeds of Diomed*, and runs like this:

> There were the bright robes woven by the women of Sidon,
> Whom the hero Paris, splendid as a god to look on,
> Brought from that city when he sailed the wide sea
> Voyaging with high-born Helen, when he took her home.

There is also a passage in the *Odyssey* alluding to the same fact:

> These drugs of subtle virtue the daughter of Zeus was given
> By an Egyptian woman, Polydamna, wife of Thon;
> For the rich earth of Egypt bears many herbs
> Which steeped in liquor have power to cure, or to kill.

1. Cf. *Iliad* VI, 289 ff. and *Odyssey* IV.

and, again, Menelaus is made to say to Telemachus:

> *In Egypt the gods still stayed me, though I longed to return,*
> *For I had not paid them their due of sacrifice.*

Homer makes it quite clear in these passages that he knew about Paris going out of his way to Egypt – the point of the first I have quoted being that Syria borders on Egypt, and the Phoenicians, to whom Sidon belongs, live in Syria. Another thing which is proved by these passages, and especially by the one about Sidon, is that Homer was not the author of the *Cypria*; for in that poem it is stated that Paris reached Troy with Helen three days after he left Sparta, having had a good voyage with a fair wind and calm sea, whereas we learn from the *Iliad* that he was forced to take her far out of his way – but I must not waste any more time on Homer and the *Cypria*.

I asked the priests if the Greek story of what happened at Troy had any truth in it, and they gave me in reply some information which they claimed to have had direct from Menelaus himself. This was, that after the abduction of Helen, the Greeks sent a strong force to the Troad in support of Menelaus' cause, and as soon as the men had landed and established themselves on Trojan soil, ambassadors, of whom Menelaus was one, were dispatched to Troy. They were received within the walls of the town, and demanded the restoration of Helen together with the treasure which Paris had stolen, and also satisfaction for the injuries they had received. The Trojans, however, gave them the answer which they always stuck to afterwards – sometimes even swearing to the truth of it: namely, that neither Helen nor the treasure was in their possession, but both were in Egypt, and there was no justice in trying to force them to give satisfaction for property which was being detained by the Egyptian king Proteus. The Greeks, supposing this to be a merely frivolous answer, laid siege to the town, and persisted until it fell; but no Helen was found, and they were still told the same story, until at last they believed it and sent Menelaus to visit Proteus in Egypt. He sailed up the river to Memphis, and when he had given a true account of all that had happened, he was most hospitably entertained and Helen, none the worse for her adventures, was restored to him with all the rest of his property. Nevertheless, in spite of this generous treatment, Menelaus proved himself no friend to Egypt; for when he wished to leave, but was delayed for a long time by contrary winds, he took two Egyptian children and offered them in sacrifice. The discovery of this foul act turned the friendship of the Egyptians to hatred; he was pursued, but managed to escape with his ships to Libya. Where he went afterwards the Egyptians could not say. They told me that they had learned of some of these events by inquiry, but spoke with certain knowledge of those which had taken place in their own country.

This, then, is the version the Egyptian priests gave me of the story of Helen, and I am inclined to accept it for the following reason: had Helen really been in Troy, she would have been handed over to the Greeks with or without Paris' consent; for I cannot believe that either Priam or any other kinsman of his was mad enough to be willing to risk his own and his children's lives and the safety of the city, simply to let Paris continue to live with Helen. If, moreover, that had been their feeling when the troubles began, surely later on, when the Trojans had suffered heavy losses in every battle they fought, and there was never an engagement (if we may believe the epic poems) in which Priam himself did not lose two of his sons, or three, or even more: surely, I repeat, in such circumstances as these, there can be little doubt that, even if Helen had been the wife of Priam the king, he would have given her back to the Greeks, if to do so offered a chance of relief from the suffering which the war had caused. Again, Paris was not heir to the throne, and so could not have been acting as regent for his aged father; for it was Hector, his elder brother and a better man than he, who was to have succeeded on Priam's death, and it was not likely that Hector would put up with his brother's lawless behaviour, especially as it was the cause of much distress both to himself and to every other Trojan besides. The fact is, they did not give Helen up because they had not got her; what they told the Greeks was the truth, and I do not hesitate to declare that the refusal of the Greeks to believe it came of divine volition in order that their utter destruction might plainly prove to mankind that great sins meet with great punishments at the hands of God. That, at least, is my own belief.

The next king after Proteus was Rhampsinitus, who is remembered by the entrance gates which he erected at the western end of the temple of Hephaestus, and by two statues which face them, each about thirty-eight feet high; the more northerly of the two is called by the Egyptians Summer; the more southerly, Winter. The former they treat with reverence and every ceremony of respect, but their behaviour towards the latter is quite the reverse.

Rhampsinitus possessed a vast fortune in silver, so great that no subsequent king came anywhere near it – let alone surpassed it. In order to keep the treasure safe, he proposed to have a stone building put up, with one of its walls forming a part of the outer wall of his palace. The builder he employed had designs upon the treasure and ingeniously contrived to construct the wall in such a way that one of the stone blocks of which it was composed could easily be removed by a couple of men – or even by one. When the new treasury was ready, the king's money was stored away in it; and after the lapse of some years the builder, then on his death-bed, called his two sons and told them how clever he had been, saying that he had planned the device of the movable stone entirely for their benefit, that they might live in affluence. Then he gave the precise measurements, and instructions for its removal, and told them that if only they kept the secret well, they would control the Royal Exchequer as long as they lived. So the father died and his sons lost no time in setting to work; they came by night to the palace, found the stone in the treasury wall, took it out easily enough and got away with a good haul of silver. The king, on his next visit to the treasury, was surprised to see that some of the vessels in which the money was stored were no longer full, but as the seals were unbroken and all the locks in perfect order, he was at a loss to find the culprit. When the same thing happened again, and yet again, and he found that each time he visited the chamber the level of the money in the jars had still further fallen (for the thieves persisted in their depredations), he ordered traps to be made and set near the money-jars. The thieves came as usual, and one of them made his way into the chamber; but, as soon as he approached the money-jar he was after, the trap got him. Realizing his plight, he at once called out to his brother to tell him what had happened, and begged him to come in as quickly as he could and cut off his head, lest the recognition of his dead body should involve both of them in ruin. The brother, seeing the sense of this request, acted upon it without delay; then, having fitted the stone back in its place, went home tak-ing the severed head with him. Next morning the king visited his treasury, and what was his astonishment when he saw in the trap the headless body of the thief, and no sign of damage to the building, or any apparent means of entrance or exit! Much perplexed, he finally decided to have the thief's body hung up outside the wall, and a guard set with orders to arrest and bring before him anyone they might see thereabouts in tears, or showing signs of mourning. Now the young man's mother was deeply distressed by this treatment of her dead son's body, and begged the one who was still alive to do all he possibly could to think of some way of getting it back, and even threatened, if he refused to listen to her, to go to the king and de-nounce him as the thief. The young man made many excuses, but to no purpose; his mother continued to pester him, until at last he thought of a way out of the difficulty. He filled some skins with wine and loaded them on to donkeys, which he drove to the place where the soldiers were guarding his brother's corpse. Arrived there, he gave a pull on the necks of two or three of the skins, which undid the fastenings. The wine poured out, and he roared and banged his head, as if not knowing which donkey to deal with first, while the soldiers, seeing the wine streaming all over the road, seized their pots and ran to catch it, congratulating themselves on such a piece of luck. The young man swore at them in pretended rage, which the soldiers did their best to soothe, until finally he changed his tune, and, appearing to have recovered his temper, drove the donkeys out of the roadway and began to rearrange the wine-skins on their backs. Meanwhile, as he chatted with the soldiers, one of them cracked a joke at his expense and made him laugh, whereupon he made them a present of a wine-skin, and without more ado they all sat down to enjoy themselves, and urged their benefactor to join the party and share the drink. The young man let himself be persuaded, and soon, as cup succeeded cup and the soldiers treated him with increasing familiarity, he gave them another skin. Such a quantity of wine was too much for the guards; very drunk and drowsy, they stretched themselves out at full length and fell asleep on the spot. It was now well after dark, and the thief took down his brother's body and as an insult shaved the right cheek of each of the guards. Then he put the corpse on the donkeys' backs and returned home, having done successfully what his mother demanded.

The king was very angry when he learnt that the thief's body had been stolen, and determined at any cost to catch the man who had been clever enough to bring off such a coup. I find it hard to believe the priests' account of the means he employed to catch him – but here it is: he sent his own daughter to a brothel with orders to admit all comers, and to compel each applicant, before granting him her favours, to tell her what was the cleverest and wickedest thing that he had ever done; and if anyone told her the story of the thief, she was to get hold of him and not allow him to escape. The girl obeyed her father's orders, and the thief, when he came to know the reason for what she was doing, could not resist the temptation to go one better than the king in ingenuity. He cut the hand and arm from the body of a man who had just died, and, putting them under his cloak, went to visit the king's daughter in her brothel. When she asked him the question which she had asked all the others, he replied that his wickedest deed was to cut off his brother's head when he was caught in a trap in the king's treasury, and his cleverest was to make the soldiers drunk, so that he could take down his brother's body from the wall where it was hanging. The girl immediately clutched at him; but under cover of the darkness the thief pushed towards her the hand of the corpse, which she seized and held tight in the belief that it was his own. Then, leaving it in her grasp, he made his escape through the door.

The cleverness and audacity of this last exploit filled the king with astonishment and admiration; soon after the news of it reached him, he went to every town in Egypt with a promise to the thief, should he give himself up, not only of a free pardon but of a rich reward. The thief trusted him and presented himself, and Rhampsinitus signalized his admiration for the most intelligent of all mankind by giving him his daughter in marriage. The Egyptians, he said, were the cleverest nation in the world, but this fellow beat the lot.

Another story I heard about Rhampsinitus was, that at a later period he descended alive into what the Greeks call Hades, and there played dice with Demeter, sometimes winning and sometimes losing, and returned to earth with a golden napkin which she had given him as a present. I was told that to mark his descent into the underworld and subsequent return, the Egyptians instituted a festival, which they certainly continued to celebrate in my own day – though I cannot state with confidence that the reason for it is what it was said to be. The priests weave a robe, taking one day only over the process; then they bandage the eyes of one of their number, put the robe into his hands, and lead him to the road which runs to the temple of Demeter. Here they leave him, and it is supposed that he is escorted to the temple, twenty furlongs from the city, by two wolves which afterwards bring him back to where they found him. Anyone may believe these Egyptian tales, if he is sufficiently credulous; as for myself, I keep to the general plan of this book, which is to record the traditions of the various nations just as I heard them related to me.

The Egyptians say that Demeter and Dionysus are the chief powers in the underworld; and they were also the first people to put forward the doctrine of the immortality of the soul, and to maintain that after death it enters another creature at the moment of that creature's birth. It then makes the round of all living things – animals, birds, and fish – until it finally passes once again, at birth, into the body of a man. The whole period of transmigration occupies three thousand years. This theory has been adopted by certain Greek writers, some earlier, some later, who have put it forward as their own. Their names are known to me, but I refrain from mentioning them.

Up to the time of Rhampsinitus, Egypt was excellently governed and very prosperous; but his successor Cheops (to continue the account which the priests gave me) brought the country into all sorts of misery. He closed all the temples, then, not content with excluding his subjects from the practice of their religion, compelled them without exception to labour as slaves for his own advantage. Some were forced to drag blocks of stone from the quarries in the Arabian hills to the Nile, where they were ferried across and taken over by others, who hauled them to the Libyan hills. The work went on in three-monthly shifts, a hundred thousand men in a shift. It took ten years of this oppressive slave-labour to build the track along which the blocks were hauled – a work, in my opinion, of hardly less magnitude than the pyramid itself, for it is five furlongs in length, sixty feet wide, forty-eight feet high at its highest point, and constructed of polished stone blocks decorated with carvings of animals. To build it took, as I said, ten years – including the underground sepulchral chambers on the hill where the pyramids stand; a cut was made from the Nile, so that the water from it turned the site of these into an island. To build the pyramid itself took twenty years; it is square at the base, its height (800 feet) equal to the length of each side; it is of polished stone blocks beautifully fitted, none of the blocks being less than thirty feet long. The method employed was to build it in steps, or, as some call them, tiers or terraces. When the base was complete, the blocks for the first tier above it were lifted from ground level by contrivances made of short timbers; on this first tier there was another, which raised the blocks a stage higher, then yet another which raised them higher still. Each tier, or storey, had its set of levers, or it may be that they used the same one, which, being easy to carry, they shifted up from stage to stage as soon as its load was dropped into place. Both methods are mentioned, so I give them both here. The finishing-off of the pyramid was begun at the top and continued downwards, ending with the lowest parts nearest the ground. An inscription is cut upon it in Egyptian characters recording the amount spent on radishes, onions, and leeks for the labourers, and I remember distinctly that the interpreter who read me the inscription said the sum was 1600 talents of silver. If this is true, how much must have been spent in addition on bread and clothing for the labourers during all those years the building was going on – not to mention the time it took (not a little, I should think) to quarry and haul the stone, and to construct the underground chamber?

But no crime was too great for Cheops: when he was short of money, he sent his daughter to a bawdy-house with instructions to charge a certain sum – they did not tell me how much. This she actually did, adding to it a further transaction of her own; for with the intention of leaving something to be remembered by after her death, she asked each of her customers to give her a block of stone, and of these stones (the story goes) was built the middle pyramid of the three which stand in front of the great pyramid. It is a hundred and fifty feet square.

Cheops reigned for fifty years, according to the Egyptians' account, and was succeeded after his death by his brother Chephren. Chephren was no better than his predecessor; his rule was equally oppressive, and, like Cheops, he built a pyramid, but of a smaller size (I measured both of them myself). It has no underground chambers, and no channel was dug, as in the case of Cheops' pyramid, to bring to it the water from the Nile. The cutting of the canal, as I have already said, makes the site of the pyramid of Cheops into an island, and there his body is supposed to be. The pyramid of Chephren lies close to the great pyramid of Cheops; it is forty feet lower than the latter, but otherwise of the same dimensions; its lower course is of the coloured stone of Ethiopia. Both these pyramids stand on the same hill, which is about a hundred feet in height. Chephren reigned for fifty-six years – so the Egyptians reckon a period of a hundred and six years, all told, during which the temples were never opened for worship and the country was reduced in every way to the greatest misery. The Egyptians can hardly bring themselves to mention the names of Cheops and Chephren, so great is their hatred of them; they even call the pyramids after Philitis, a shepherd who at that time fed his flocks in the neighbourhood.

The next king of Egypt after Chephren was Mycerinus, the son of Cheops. Mycerinus, reversing his father's policy of which he did not approve, reopened the temples and allowed his subjects, who had been brought into such abject slavery, to resume the practice of their religion and their normal work. Of all kings who ruled in Egypt he had the greatest reputation for justice in the decision of legal causes, and for this the Egyptians give him higher praise than any other monarch; for apart from the general equity of his judgements, he used to compensate out of his own property any man who was dissatisfied with the result of his suit, and so leave him nothing to complain of.

Such were the generosity and mild rule of Mycerinus, when the first of his troubles fell upon him: his daughter, who was his only child, died. Wishing, in the excess of his grief at this calamity, to give his daughter a tomb which should be different from any other, he had a wooden cow made, hollow inside and plated on the outside with gold, to receive her body. The cow was not buried, but was still to be seen in my day at Sais, standing in a richly decorated chamber of the royal palace; incense of all kinds is burnt before it every day, and at night a lamp is kept always lighted in the room. Close by in another chamber, the priests told me, are some statues, which represent the concubines of Mycerinus: there are, indeed, twenty or so naked wooden figures of great size in this chamber, but as to whom they represent I can only pass on such information as was given me.

There is another, and quite different, story about the cow and the statues; according to this, Mycerinus conceived a passion for his daughter and violated her, and distress at the outrage drove her to hang herself; she was entombed in the cow, and her mother cut off the hands of the servants who had allowed the king access to her. The statues represent the servants, and, like their living originals, they have no hands. Personally I think this story is nonsense, especially in its explanation of the statues' missing hands; I could see for myself that they had simply dropped off through age. They are still there, plainly visible – lying on the ground near the statues' feet.

The cow is covered with a purple cloth, all but the head and neck, which are bare and very thickly coated with gold. Between its horns there is a gold disk representing the sun. The figure is not erect but in a kneeling posture, and is of the size of a large live cow. Once a year, at the festival on which the Egyptians beat themselves in honour of that deity whom I must not name in this connexion, the cow is taken from the chamber into the sunlight; for it is said that the girl on her deathbed begged her father Mycerinus to be allowed once a year to see the sun.

After the death of his daughter a second calamity fell upon Mycerinus: he received an oracle from Buto to the effect that he was destined to live only for six more years and to die within the seventh. He sent back an angry message to the shrine, and reproached the god with the injustice of allowing a man so pious as himself to die so soon, when his father and uncle, who had closed the temples, forgotten the gods, and afflicted their fellow men, had lived to a good old age. In answer to this there was another message from the oracle, which declared that his life was being shortened precisely because he had not done what he ought to have done: for it was fated that Egypt should suffer for a hundred and fifty years – a thing which his two predecessors, unlike himself, had understood very well. Mycerinus, convinced by this that his doom was sealed, had innumerable lamps made, by the light of which he set himself every evening to drink and be merry, and never ceased day or night from the pursuit of pleasure, travelling about from place to place amongst the pools and wood-lands, wherever he heard of a particularly delightful spot. His object in this was by turning night into day to extend the six remaining years of his life to twelve, and so to convict the oracle of falsehood. He, too, left a pyramid, built square, with its lower half of Ethiopian stone; it is much smaller than his father's, each side at the base being only about 280 feet long.

There are people in Greece who say that this pyramid was erected by the courtesan Rhodopis. They are quite wrong, and I do not think they even know who Rhodopis was; for if they did, they could never have attributed to her the erection of such a monument, which must have cost a sum of money vast beyond reckoning. Besides this, they show their ignorance of the fact that Rhodopis lived during the reign of Amasis, not in Mycerinus' time – much later than the period of the kings who built these pyramids. She was by birth a Thracian, the slave of Iadmon, son of Hephaestopolis of Samos, and fellow-slave of Aesop the fable-writer. The clearest proof that Aesop was the slave of Iadmon is the fact that when the Delphians, in obedience to the oracle's command, repeatedly advertised for someone to claim compensation for Aesop's murder, the only person to come forward was the grandson of Iadmon (a man of the same name).

She was brought to Egypt by Xanthus the Samian, to follow her trade, and Charaxus of Mytilene, son of Scamandronymus and brother of Sappho the poetess, paid a large sum to redeem her from slavery. Having in this way obtained her freedom, she remained in Egypt and succeeded by her great beauty in amassing a fortune which – for her – was a considerable one, but certainly not sufficient for building a pyramid. There is no sense in pretending she was ex-cessively rich, for the tenth part of her property can be seen to-day by anyone who cares to go and look at it: for wishing to be remembered in Greece by some sort of temple-offering such as nobody had ever thought of before, she spent a tenth of her money on as many iron roasting-spits as it would buy, and sent them to Delphi. They still lie in a heap behind the altar which the Chians dedicated, opposite the actual shrine. The prostitutes of Naucratis seem to be particularly attractive; for not only did Rhodopis live there, and become so famous that every Greek was familiar with her name, but, at a later period, there was Archidice who, though less a subject of common gossip than Rhodopis, figured in poetry from one end of Greece to the other. When Charaxus returned to Mytilene after purchasing Rhodopis' freedom, he was ridiculed by Sappho in one of her poems. So much, then, for Rhodopis.

The successor of Mycerinus, the priests told me, was Asychis, and he it was who added to the temple of Hephaestus its eastern entrance-gate, much the finest and biggest of the four. Like the other gates, but to a much greater extent, it is decorated with carvings and an enormous quantity of other architectural adornment. During the reign of Asychis money was so short and trade so bad, that a law was passed allowing a man to borrow on the security of his father's dead body, with the further provision, added later, that the lender should have power over the family vault of the borrower in its entirety, so that anyone who borrowed on this security and died before he could re-pay the loan, was excluded from burial either in his own family tomb, or anywhere else – nor was he allowed to bury in his own vault any of his relatives.

Wishing to go one better than his predecessors on the throne, Asychis built a pyramid of brick to commemorate his reign, and on it cut an inscription in stone to the following effect: 'Do not com-pare me to my disadvantage with the stone pyramids. I surpass them as far as Zeus the other gods. They pushed a pole to the bottom of a lake, and the mud which stuck on it they collected and made into bricks. That was how they built me.'

Having no further achievements of this monarch to recount, I will pass to the next. This was Anysis, a blind man who came from a city of the same name. During his reign Egypt was invaded in great force by the Ethiopians under Sabacos,[1] their king. The blind Anysis fled and took refuge in the marsh-country, leaving Egypt in the hands of the Ethiopian, who remained master of it for fifty years. When an Egyptian committed a crime, it was not the custom of Sabacos to punish him with death; but instead of the death-penalty he compelled

1. The historical Shabaka, one of the Nubian kings of Dynasty XXV (725–667 B.C.).

the offender, according to the seriousness of the offence, to raise the level of the soil in the neighbourhood of his native town. In this way the cities came to stand even higher than they did before; for the level of the ground had already been raised once, in Sesostris' reign, when the canals were dug. This was the second time, and the result was that the cities came to stand very high indeed. None of the Egyptian cities, I think, was raised so much as Bubastis, where there is a temple of Bubastis (the Greek Artemis) which is well worth describing. Other temples may be larger, or have cost more to build, but none is a greater pleasure to look at. The site of the building is almost an island, for two canals have been led from the Nile and sweep round it, one on each side, as far as the entrance, where they stop short without meeting; each canal is a hundred feet wide and shaded with trees. The gateway is sixty feet high and is decorated with remarkable carved figures some nine feet in height. The temple stands in the centre of the city, and, since the level of the buildings everywhere else has been raised, but the temple itself allowed to remain in its original position, the result is that one can look down and get a fine view of it from all round. It is surrounded by a low wall with carved figures, and within the enclosure stands a grove of very tall trees about the actual shrine, which is large and contains the statue of the goddess. The whole en-closure is a furlong square. The entrance to it is approached by a stone-paved road about four hundred feet wide, running eastward through the market-place and joining the temple of Bubastis to the temple of Hermes. The road is lined on both sides with immense trees – so tall that they seem to touch the sky.

It was a dream which finally caused the departure, or, rather, the flight, of the Ethiopian Sabacos from Egypt. He dreamt that a man stood by his bed and advised him to assemble all the priests in Egypt and cut them in half, and he is supposed to have said that he believed the dream to have been sent by the gods, to provoke him to sacrilege and involve him in some disaster at the hands of either gods or men. He refused, therefore, to do what was advised; on the contrary, he pre-ferred to leave Egypt, as the destined period of his rule there had now come to an end – for before he left Ethiopia, he had received a pro-phecy from the Ethiopian oracle that he was fated to govern Egypt for fifty years. The fifty years were now up; and that fact, added to the disquieting effect of his dream, caused him to leave Egypt of his own accord.

After the departure of the Ethiopian, the blind Anysis returned from the marsh-country, where for fifty years he had lived on an island which he had built up of earth and ashes, and resumed the government of Egypt. During those years of exile, he had instructed all the Egyptians whose duty it was to smuggle food to him without Sabacos knowing of it, to bring with them, as an additional present, a certain quantity of ashes. Amyrtaeus was the first, in after days, to discover this island, the site of which was unknown for more than seven hundred years, in spite of attempts by previous kings to find it. It is called Elbo, and is about ten furlongs across in each direction.

Next on the throne after Anysis was Sethos,[1] the high priest of Hephaestus. He is said to have neglected the warrior class of the Egyptians and to have treated them with contempt, as if he had been unlikely to need their services. He offended them in various ways, not least by depriving them of the twelve acres of land which each of them had held by special privilege under previous kings. As a result, when Egypt was invaded by Sennacherib, the king of Arabia and Assyria, with a great army, not one of them was willing to fight. The situation was grave; not knowing what else to do, the priest-king entered the shrine and, before the image of the god, complained bitterly of the peril which threatened him. In the midst of his lamentations he fell asleep, and dreamt that the god stood by him and urged him not to lose heart; for if he marched boldly out to meet the Arabian army, he would come to no harm, as the god himself would send him helpers.

By this dream the king's confidence was restored; and with such men as were willing to follow him – not a single one of the warrior class, but a mixed company of shopkeepers, artisans, and market-people – he marched to Pelusium, which guards the approaches to Egypt, and there took up his position. As he lay here facing the Assyrians, thousands of field-mice[2] swarmed over them during the night, and ate their quivers, their bowstrings, and the leather handles

---

1. No Egyptian king called Sethos (Sethi) is known at this time.

2. The 'field-mice', it has often been suggested, might have been plague-carrying rodents; cf. 2 Kings XIX.

of their shields, so that on the following day, having no arms to fight with, they abandoned their position and suffered severe losses during their retreat. There is still a stone statue of Sethos in the temple of Hephaestus; the figure is represented with a mouse in its hand, and the inscription: 'Look upon me and learn reverence.'

Up to this point I have relied on the accounts given me by the Egyptians and their priests. They declare that three hundred and forty-one generations separate the first king of Egypt from the last I have mentioned – the priest of Hephaestus – and that there was a king and a high priest corresponding to each generation. Now to reckon three generations as a hundred years, three hundred generations make ten thousand years, and the remaining forty-one generations make 1340 years more; thus one gets a total of 11,340 years, during the whole of which time, they say, no god ever assumed mortal form; nothing of the sort occurred either under the former or under the later kings. They did say, however, that four times within this period the sun changed his usual position, twice rising where he normally sets, and twice setting where he normally rises. They assured me that Egypt was quite unaffected by this: the harvests, and the produce of the river, were the same as usual, and there was no change in the incidence of disease or death.

When the historian Hecataeus was in Thebes, the priests of Zeus, after listening to the attempt he made to trace his family back to a god in the sixteenth generation, did to him precisely what they did to me – though, unlike Hecataeus, I kept clear of personal genealogies. They took me into the great hall of the temple, and showed me the wooden statues there, which they counted; and the number was just what I have said, for each high priest has a statue of himself erected there before he dies. As they showed them to me, and counted them up, beginning with the statue of the high priest who had last died, and going on from him right through the whole number, they assured me that each had been the son of the one who preceded him. When Hecataeus traced his genealogy and connected himself with a god sixteen generations back, the priests refused to believe him, and denied that any man had ever had a divine ancestor. They countered his claim by tracing the descent of their own high priests, pointing out that each of the statues represented a 'piromis' (a word which means something like 'gentleman') who was the son of another 'piromis', and made no attempt to connect them with either a god or a demigod. Such, then, were the beings represented by the statues; they were far from being gods – they were men.

Nevertheless, before their time Egypt was, indeed, ruled by gods, who lived on earth amongst men, sometimes one of them, sometimes another being supreme above the rest. The last of them was Horus the son of Osiris – Horus is the Apollo, Osiris the Dionysus, of the Greeks. It was Horus who vanquished Typhon and was the last god to sit upon the throne of Egypt.

In Greece, the youngest of the gods are thought to be Heracles, Dionysus, and Pan; but in Egypt Pan is very ancient, and one of the 'eight gods' who existed before the rest; Heracles is one of the 'twelve' who appeared later, and Dionysus one of the third order who were descended from the twelve. I have already mentioned the length of time which by the Egyptian reckoning elapsed between the coming of Heracles and the reign of Amasis; Pan is said to be still more ancient, and even Dionysus, the youngest of the three, appeared, they say, 15,000 years before Amasis. They claim to be quite certain of these dates, for they have always kept a careful written record of the passage of time. But from the birth of Dionysus, the son of Semele, daughter of Cadmus, to the present day is a period of about 1600 years only; from Heracles the son of Alcmena, about 900 years; from Pan the son of Penelope – he is supposed by the Greeks to be the son of Penelope and Hermes – not more than about 800 years, a shorter time than has elapsed since the Trojan war.

It is open to anyone to believe whichever of these two traditions he prefers; I have already stated my own opinion. If indeed these gods had been publicly known and had grown old in Greece, like Heracles, the son of Amphitryon, and Dionysus, the son of Semele, and Pan, the son of Penelope, it might have been said that the two last-mentioned were men who bore the names of previously existing gods; but the Greek tradition is that Dionysus, as soon as he was born, was sewn up in Zeus' thigh and taken to Nysa, which is in Ethiopia above Egypt; and as to what happened after the birth of Pan, tradition is silent. It is clear to me, therefore, that the names of these gods became known in Greece later than the rest, and that the

Greeks trace their genealogy from the time when they first acquired the knowledge of them.

So far the Egyptians themselves have been my authority; but in what follows I shall relate what other people, too, are willing to accept in the history of this country, with a few points added from my own observation.[1] After the reign of Sethos, the priest of Hephaestus, the Egyptians for a time were freed from monarchical government. Unable, however, to do without a king, for long they divided Egypt into twelve regions and appointed a king for each of them. United by intermarriage, the twelve kings governed in mutual friendliness on the understanding that none of them should attempt to oust any of the others, or to increase his power at the expense of the rest. They came to the understanding, and ensured that the terms of it should be rigorously kept, because, at the time when the twelve kingdoms were first established, an oracle had declared that the one who should pour a libation from a bronze cup in the temple of Hephaestus would become master of all Egypt. They held their meetings in all the temples.

To strengthen the bond between them, they decided to leave a common memorial of their reigns, and for this purpose constructed a labyrinth a little above Lake Moeris, near the place called the City of Crocodiles. I have seen this building, and it is beyond my power to describe; it must have cost more in labour and money than all the walls and public works of the Greeks put together – though no one would deny that the temples at Ephesus and Samos are remarkable buildings. The pyramids, too, are astonishing structures, each one of them equal to many of the most ambitious works of Greece; but the labyrinth surpasses them. It has twelve covered courts – six in a row facing north, six south – the gates of the one range exactly fronting the gates of the other, with a continuous wall round the outside of the whole. Inside, the building is of two storeys and contains three thousand rooms, of which half are underground, and the other half directly above them. I was taken through the rooms in the upper

1. With Psammetichus (pp. [129, 190] etc.) begins Dynasty XXVI (c. 660–529), after the withdrawal of the Assyrians (whose occupation Herodotus' Egyptian informants did not mention), and under which Egypt became well known to the Greeks (p. 191).

storey, so what I shall say of them is from my own observation, but the underground ones I can speak of only from report, because the Egyptians in charge refused to let me see them, as they contain the tombs of the kings who built the labyrinth, and also the tombs of the sacred crocodiles. The upper rooms, on the contrary, I did actually see, and it is hard to believe that they are the work of men; the baffling and intricate passages from room to room and from court to court were an endless wonder to me, as we passed from a court-yard into rooms, from rooms into galleries, from galleries into more rooms, and thence into yet more courtyards. The roof of every chamber, courtyard, and gallery is, like the walls, of stone. The walls are covered with carved figures, and each court is exquisitely built of white marble and surrounded by a colonnade. Near the corner where the labyrinth ends there is a pyramid, two hundred and forty feet in height, with great carved figures of animals on it and an underground passage by which it can be entered. Marvellous as the labyrinth is, the so-called Lake of Moeris beside which it stands is perhaps even more astonishing; the circumference of it is 3600 *stades*, or sixty *schoeni*: a distance, that is to say, of about 420 miles, equal to the length of the whole Egyptian coastline; in shape it is elongated, running north and south, and its greatest depth is fifty fathoms. Now this immense basin is obviously artificial, for nearly in the middle of it are two pyramids, standing three hundred feet out of the water (with their bases an equal depth below the surface), and each surmounted by the stone image of a man sitting on a throne. The water in the lake is not supplied by natural springs (the country hereabouts being excessively dry), but has been brought from the Nile through an artificial duct, and flows in during six months of the year, and out again into the river during the other six. For the half-year that the water runs out, the lake pays the treasury a talent of silver for the fish that are caught; for the other half, only twenty *minae* – one-third of the amount.

The people who live here told me that there is a subterranean pass-age, running westward into the interior along the hills above Mem-phis, by which the water of the lake reaches the Libyan Syrtis. I was anxious to know what had been done with the soil which had been removed when the lake was excavated, for I could see no sign of it; and when I asked the people who live nearest the lake to enlighten

me about this, I had no difficulty in believing their answer – for I remembered the story of a similar thing that happened at Nineveh, the
capital of Assyria. King Sardanapalus had a vast treasure, which he
kept in a strong-room underground, and some thieves plotted to
steal it. They tunnelled a passage to the strong-room from the house
where they lived, making as good a guess as possible at the distance
and direction, and every night dumped the soil they took out into the
Tigris, which flows past the city, until their purpose was achieved.
Just the same method, I was told, was adopted in the excavation of
the lake – except, indeed, that there was no need to wait for darkness
before dumping the soil: they dug it out, and flung it into the Nile,
and knew well enough that the Nile would carry it away and get rid
of it.

Now as time went on, the twelve kings, who had kept their compact not to molest one another, met to offer sacrifice in the temple of
Hephaestus. It was the last day of the festival, and when the moment
for pouring the libation had come, the high priest, in going to fetch
the golden cups which were always used for the purpose, made a
mistake in the number and brought one too few, so that Psammetichus, who was standing last in the row, did not get one. As their
custom was, all the kings were wearing their bronze helmets, and
Psammetichus, finding himself without a cup, quite innocently and
without any ulterior motive took his helmet off, held it out to receive the wine, and so made his libation. The other kings at once
connected this action with the oracle, which had declared that
whichever of them poured his libation from a bronze cup, should
become sole monarch of Egypt. They proceeded to question him,
and when they were satisfied that he had acted with no thought of
malice, they decided not to put him to death, but to strip him of the
greater part of his power and banish him to the marsh-country, forbidding him to leave it or to have any communication with the rest
of Egypt.

This was the second time that Psammetichus had been exiled; the
first was when he fled the country to escape Sabacos, the Ethiopian,
who had killed Necos his father; on that occasion he took refuge in
Syria, and after the departure of Sabacos in consequence of his dream,
he was brought back by the Egyptians of the province of Sais. And

now it was his ill-luck to be driven again from his throne by the eleven kings, and exiled to the marshes – all because of what he did with his helmet. In bitter resentment at the treatment he had received, Psammetichus planned revenge. He sent for advice to the oracle at Buto (the most veracious in Egypt) and was told in reply that vengeance would come from the sea, whence bronze men would appear. Psammetichus did not believe a word of this, and thought it most improbable that he would get any help from bronze men; but not long afterwards it so happened that a company of sea-raiders from Ionia and Caria were forced by bad weather to land on the Egyptian coast. They wore bronze armour, and an Egyptian, who had never seen such a thing before, hurried off to the marshes and told Psammetichus that bronze men had come from the sea and were plundering the country. Seeing in this the fulfilment of the oracle, Psammetichus made friends with the raiders, and by the promise of rich rewards persuaded them to enter his service, and by their help and the help of his supporters in Egypt defeated and deposed his eleven enemies.

Having become sole master of Egypt, Psammetichus built the southern gateway of the temple of Hephaestus at Memphis, and opposite to it a court for Apis – or Epaphus, which is the Greek name. Apis is kept in this court whenever he appears; it has a colonnade round it, with statues eighteen feet high instead of pillars, and is richly carved with figures.

To the Ionians and Carians who helped him to gain the throne Psammetichus granted two pieces of land, opposite one another on each side of the Nile, which came to be known as the Camps, and in addition to the grant of land kept all the other promises he had made them. He even went so far as to put some Egyptian boys into their charge, to be taught Greek; and their learning of the language was the origin of the class of Egyptian interpreters. The tracts of land where the Ionians and Carians settled, and where they lived for many years, lie a little distance seaward from Bubastis, on the Pelusian mouth of the Nile. Amasis subsequently turned them out and brought them to Memphis, to protect him from his own people. They were the first foreigners to live in Egypt, and after their original settlement there, the Greeks began regular intercourse with the Egyptians, so that we have accurate knowledge of Egyptian history from the time of Psammetichus onward. The docks and ruined houses of their first home, where they lived before Amasis moved them to Memphis, were still to be seen in my day. This, then, is the story of how Psammetichus won the throne of Egypt.

I have already referred more than once to the Egyptian oracle, but it is sufficiently interesting to warrant further notice. The temple, which is dedicated to Leto, stands in a great city called (as I have already mentioned) Buto, at the Sebennytic mouth of the Nile, on the right-hand side as one enters the river from seaward. The city also contains two other temples, one of Apollo, the other of Artemis. The shrine of Leto, where the oracle is, is a building of great size with a gateway sixty feet high, but the most remarkable sight it has to offer is not the temple itself, but a small shrine within the enclosure made out of a single block of stone; it is cubical in shape, each side sixty feet long and sixty high. The roof is formed of another single block, which projects beyond the walls to a distance of six feet. This was certainly the most marvellous thing I actually saw here; after it, what impressed me most was the island called Chemmis. This lies in a deep, broad lake by the temple, and the Egyptians say that it floats. I never saw it move, and it did not actually look as if it were floating, and I wondered very much, when I heard about it, if there could be such a thing as a floating island. There is a large temple of Apollo on it with three separate altars, and numerous date-palms and other trees, some of them fruit trees, some not. The Egyptians have a legend to explain how the island came to float: in former times Leto, one of the eight original deities, lived in Buto, where her oracle now is, and having received Apollo, son of Osiris, as a sacred trust from Isis, she saved him from Typhon when he came there in his world-wide search, by hiding him in the island. The Egyptians say that Apollo and Artemis are the children of Isis and Dionysus, and that Leto saved them and brought them up. In Egyptian, Apollo is Horus, Demeter is Isis, Artemis is Bubastis. It was from this tradition that Aeschylus, son of Euphorion, borrowed the idea (not found in earlier poets) of making Artemis the daughter of Demeter. This is why it was made to float, and is to-day called the floating island.

The reign of Psammetichus lasted for fifty-four years, during twenty-nine of which he was engaged in the siege of Azotus, a large town in Syria, until he finally took it. The siege of Azotus was the longest of any in history known to us.

Psammetichus left a son, Necos, who succeeded him. It was Necos who began the construction of the canal to the Arabian gulf, a work afterwards completed by Darius the Persian. The length of the canal is four days' journey by boat, and its breadth sufficient to allow two triremes to be rowed abreast. The water is supplied from the Nile, and the canal leaves the river at a point a little south of Bubastis and runs past the Arabian town of Patumus, and then on to the Arabian gulf. The first part of its course is along the Arabian side of the Egyptian plain, a little to the northward of the chain of hills by Memphis, where the stone-quarries are; it skirts the base of these hills from west to east, and then enters a narrow gorge, after which it trends in a southerly direction until it enters the Arabian gulf. The shortest distance from the Mediterranean, or Northern Sea, to the Southern Sea – or Indian Ocean – namely, from Mt Casius between Egypt and Syria to the Arabian gulf, is just a thousand *stades*.[1] This is the most direct route – by the canal, which does not keep at all a straight course, the journey is much longer. The construction of the canal in the time of King Necos cost the lives of 120,000 Egyptians. Necos did not complete the work, but broke it off in deference to an oracle, which warned him that his labour was all for the advantage of the 'barbarian' – as the Egyptians call anyone who does not speak their language. He then turned his attention to war; he had triremes built, some on the Mediterranean coast, others on the Arabian gulf, where the docks are still to be seen, and made use of his new fleets as occasion arose; and in addition he attacked the Syrians by land and defeated them at Magdolus, afterwards taking Gaza, a large town in Syria. The clothes he happened to wear on this occasion he sent as an offering to Apollo at Branchidae in Milesia. Then, after a reign of sixteen years, he died, and was succeeded by his son Psammis.

After his accession to the throne, Psammis was visited by a deputation from Elis. These men had come to boast of the excellence of the organization of the Olympic Games, which, they thought, could not possibly be run better or more fairly, even by the Egyptians

1. About 125 miles.

themselves, who were the ablest people in the world. When the Eleans had explained the reason for their visit, the king summoned a meeting of the most learned of his subjects, who proceeded to ask questions of the Eleans, and received in reply a full account of their method of organizing the Games. Having described in detail everything they did, the Eleans then said that they had come to find out if the Egyptians could think of anything fairer to suggest. The Egyptians, after considering the matter, asked if the Eleans allowed any people from their own city to compete in the Games, and when they were informed that competition was free and open to members of all the Greek states, including Elis, they expressed the opinion that to organize the games on such a principle was not fair at all; for it was quite impossible, when men from one's own city took part in some event, not to favour them at the expense of the strangers. If they really wanted fair play at the Games, and if that was indeed the purpose of their visit to Egypt, then (they said) they should open the various events to visitors only, and not allow anyone from Elis to compete.

During the six short years of his reign, Psammis attacked Ethiopia; but soon after the expedition he died and was succeeded by his son Apries. Except his great-grandfather Psammetichus, Apries was more prosperous than any of the former kings; his reign lasted for twenty-five years, and in the course of it he sent an army against Sidon and fought a naval battle with the Tyrians. He was not, however, to escape misfortune in the end; the occasion of it, when it came, I will describe more fully in my account of Libya, only touching upon it here. The facts, to put them as briefly as I can, were these: an expedition which he sent against Cyrene failed disastrously, and he was held personally responsible for the defeat; the Egyptians believed that he had deliberately sent them to certain destruction, and desired their deaths in order to strengthen his grip on those of his subjects who were left alive. In their indignation at this, the survivors who got home and the friends of the men who had been killed at once broke into rebellion. Apries sent Amasis to try to argue the rebels into submission, and while Amasis was doing his best to persuade them to return to their duty, a man who was standing behind him as he spoke put a helmet on his head and said that he was crowning him king. Amasis was not altogether displeased by this, as he soon showed; for when the rebels had actually offered him the throne, he prepared to lead them against Apries, who, hearing of the danger which threatened him, sent Patarbemis, a distinguished member of his court, with orders to bring Amasis alive into his presence. Amasis, however, in answer to Patarbemis' summons, rose in his saddle (he was on horseback at the time), broke wind, and told him to take *that* back to his master. Patarbemis persisted in his request that the rebel should obey the king's command and go along with him, whereupon Amasis replied that that was precisely what he had long been intending to do: the king would have no cause of complaint upon that score – he would come, sure enough, and bring others with him. This answer, and the preparations he saw already going on, were enough to convince Patarbemis of Amasis' intentions; he hurried back to the court, to inform the king with the least possible delay of the turn events had taken. On his arrival there without Amasis, Apries fell into a violent rage and, on the spur of the moment, ordered his nose and ears to be cut off. The Egyptians, who up to then had been loyal to the king, seeing a fellow countryman of such distinction treated in this shameful way, immediately went over to the rebels and put themselves at the disposal of Amasis. At the news of their defection, Apries armed his mercenaries (a body of 30,000 Carians and Ionians, who were with him at Sais, where his palace was – a large and noteworthy building), and advanced to the attack, the Egyptians under Amasis marching to meet them. The two forces encountered one another at Momemphis, and prepared for the coming battle

The Egyptians are divided into seven classes named after their occupations: priests, warriors, cowherds, swineherds, tradesmen, interpreters, and pilots. The warrior-class, known as Calasirians and Hermotybians, come from the following districts (all Egypt is divided into districts): the Hermotybians from the districts of Busiris, Sais, Chemmis, Papremis, the island of Prosopitis, and half of Natho. At their most numerous, they numbered 160,000 men. None of them touch trade of any kind, but all have a purely military education. The Calasirians are from the districts of Thebes, Bubastis, Aphthis, Tanis, Mendes, Sebennytus, Athribis, Pharbaethus, Thmuis, Onuphis, Anysis, and Myecphoris (this last is an island, opposite Bubastis). At their most numerous, the Calasirians numbered 250,000. They, like the Hermotybians, are forbidden to follow any trade or craft, and have an exclusively military training, son following father. I could not say for certain whether the Greeks got their ideas about trade, like so much else, from Egypt or not; the feeling is common enough, and I have observed that Thracians, Scythians, Persians, Lydians – indeed, almost all foreigners – reckon craftsmen and their descendants as lower in the social scale than people who have no connexion with manual work: only the latter, and especially those who are trained for war, do they count amongst the 'nobility'. All the Greeks have adopted this attitude, especially the Spartans; the feeling against handicraft is least strong in Corinth.

The Egyptian warrior-class had certain privileges, shared by no other class except the priests: each man had a grant of twelve *arurae* of land, free of tax (an *arura* is 100 Egyptian – or Samian – cubits square).[1] Other privileges were enjoyed, not by the whole class together, but in rotation, no one man enjoying them twice: for instance, a thousand Calasirians and a thousand Hermotybians served each year in the king's bodyguard, and received during their service, in addition to the grant of land, a daily allowance of 5 lb. of bread, 2 lb. of beef, and 4 cupfuls of wine.

In the fight which ensued the foreign mercenaries gave a good account of themselves but were greatly outnumbered and defeated. Apries is said to have believed that his power was so firmly established, that not even a god could have brought him down; nevertheless, he had the worst of the engagement, was taken prisoner, and conveyed to his former royal palace at Sais – his no longer, but now the property of the victorious Amasis. Here he was kept for a time, and well treated by his conqueror, but in the end the Egyptians objected to the injustice of maintaining a man who was his – and their – worst enemy, and persuaded Amasis to surrender the prisoner. They strangled him, and buried his body in the family tomb in the temple of Athene, nearest the shrine, on the left-hand side as one goes in. The people of Sais buried all the kings who came from the province inside this precinct – the tomb of Amasis, too, though further from the shrine than that of Apries and his ancestors, is in the temple court, a great cloistered building of stone, decorated with pillars carved in

1. About ¾ acre.

imitation of palm-trees, and other costly ornaments. Within the cloister is a chamber with double doors, and behind the doors stands the sepulchre. Here too, in Athene's precinct at Sais, is the tomb of one whose name I prefer not to mention in such a connexion; it stands behind the shrine and occupies the whole length of the wall. Great stone obelisks stand in the enclosure, and there is a stone-bordered lake near by, circular in shape and about the size, I should say, of the lake called the Wheel on the island of Delos. It is on this lake that the Egyptians act by night in what they call their Mysteries the Passion of that being whose name I will not speak.[1] All the details of these performances are known to me, but – I will say no more. Similarly I propose to hold my tongue about the mysterious rites of Demeter, which the Greeks call Thesmophoria, though in this case there are one or two points which may be mentioned without impiety. I may say, for instance, that it was the daughters of Danaus who brought this ceremony from Egypt and instructed the Pelasgian women in it, and that after the Dorian conquest of the Peloponnese it was lost; only the Arcadians, who were not driven from their homes by the invaders, continued the celebration of it.

When Apries had been deposed in the way I have described, Amasis came to the throne. He belonged to the district of Sais and was a native of the town called Siuph. At first the Egyptians were inclined to be contemptuous, and did not think much of him because of his humble and undistinguished origin; but later on he cleverly brought them to heel, without having recourse to harsh measures. Amongst his innumerable treasures, he had a gold footbath, which he and his guests used on occasion to wash their feet in. This he broke up, and with the material had a statue made to one of the gods, which he then set up in what he thought the most suitable spot in the city. The Egyptians constantly coming upon the statue, treated it with profound reverence, and as soon as Amasis heard of the effect it had upon them, he called a meeting and revealed the fact that the deeply revered statue was once a foot-bath, which they washed their feet and pissed and vomited in. He went on to say that his own case was much the same, in that once he had been only an ordinary person and was now their king; so that just as they had come to revere the transformed

1. Cf. pp. 148, 153.

foot-bath, so they had better pay honour and respect to him too. In this way the Egyptians were persuaded to accept him as their master.

He used to organize his working day on a regular principle: from dawn till the time when the markets filled up, at mid-morning, he gave all his attention to such business as was brought to him, after which he spent the rest of the day in frivolous amusements, drinking and joking with friends. His well-wishers were pained by this behaviour, and advised him to mend his ways; 'My lord,' they said, 'this excessive levity is not the thing to maintain your royal dignity. You ought rather to sit all day in state upon a stately throne, attending to your kingly affairs; for then the Egyptians would feel that a great man ruled them, and you would have a better name amongst them. Your present conduct, on the contrary, is not at all suitable for a king.'

'Archers,' Amasis replied, 'string their bows when they wish to shoot, and unstring them after use. A bow kept always strung would break, and so be useless when it was needed. It is the same with a man; anyone who was always serious, and never allowed himself a fair share of relaxation and amusement, would suddenly go off his head, or get a stroke. It is because I know this that I divide my time between duty and pleasure.'

It is said that Amasis in his private life, before he came to the throne, was just as fond of his joke and his glass, and was never inclined to serious pursuits; indeed, if ever he found himself short of means to continue his round of drinking and enjoyment, he would go out on the prowl and steal, and people who claimed that property of theirs was in his possession would, if he denied it, take him off to the nearest oracle. Sometimes the oracle would convict him, sometimes not. In consequence of this, when he came to the throne, he had a low opinion of the gods who had acquitted him of theft; he neglected their temples, contributed nothing to their adornment, and never frequented them for sacrifice, on the ground that their oracles were false and they were worth nothing; those on the other hand who had convicted him, he held in the highest honour – for their oracles were true, and they were gods indeed.

His first work was the marvellous gateway for the temple of Athene in Sais. He left everyone else far behind him by the size and height of this building, and by the size and quality of the blocks of stone of which it was constructed. He then presented to the temple some large statues and immense men-sphinxes, and brought for its repair other enormous blocks of stone, some from the quarries near Memphis, and the biggest of all from Elephantine, which is twenty days' voyage by river from Sais. But what caused me more astonishment than anything else was a room hollowed from a single block of stone; this block also came from Elephantine, and took three years to bring to Sais, two thousand men, all of the pilot-class, having the task of conveying it. The outside measurements of this chamber are: length, 21 cubits; breadth, 14 cubits; height, 8 cubits. Inside, its length is $18\frac{5}{8}$ cubits, its breadth 12, and its height 5. It lies by the entrance to the temple, for the story goes that it was not dragged inside the enclosure, because, during the process of moving it, the man chiefly responsible for its construction groaned with vexation at the amount of time and labour which was being wasted, and Amasis took this for a bad omen and refused to have it brought any further. Another story is that it was left outside, because one of the workmen who were levering it along with crowbars got crushed to death underneath it.

To all the temples of note Amasis presented a number of works remarkable for their size; I might mention particularly the recumbent image, seventy-five feet long, in front of the temple of Hephaestus at Memphis. On the same base stand two images in Ethiopian stone, one on each side, both twenty feet high. At Sais there is another recumbent image of the same size as the one at Memphis. It was also Amasis who built the spacious and very remarkable temple of Isis at Memphis.

It is said that the reign of Amasis was a time of unexampled material prosperity for Egypt; the river gave its riches to the earth and the earth to the people. The total number of inhabited towns, they say, was twenty thousand. Amasis established an admirable custom, which Solon borrowed and introduced at Athens where it is still preserved; this was that every man once a year should declare before the Nomarch, or provincial governor, the source of his livelihood; failure to do this, or inability to prove that the source was an honest one, was punishable by death.

Amasis favoured the Greeks and granted them a number of privileges, of which the chief was the gift of Naucratis as a commercial
headquarters for any who wished to settle in the country. He also
made grants of land upon which Greek traders, who did not want to
live permanently in Egypt, might erect altars and temples. Of these
latter the best known and most used – and also the largest – is the
Hellenium; it was built by the joint efforts of the Ionians of Chios,
Teos, Phocaea, and Clazomenae, of the Dorians of Rhodes, Cnidos,
Halicarnassus, and Phaselis, and of the Aeolians of Mytilene. It is to
these states that the temple belongs, and it is they who have the right
of appointing the officers in charge of the port. Other cities which
claim a share in the Hellenium do so without any justification; the
Aeginetans, however, did build a temple of Zeus separately, the
Samians one in honour of Hera, and the Milesians another in honour
of Apollo.

In old days Naucratis was the only port in Egypt, and anyone who
brought a ship into any of the other mouths of the Nile was bound
to state on oath that he did so of necessity and then proceed to the
Canopic mouth; should contrary winds prevent him from doing so,
he had to carry his freight to Naucratis in barges all round the Delta,
which shows the exclusive privilege the port enjoyed. And when the
Amphictyons, after the accidental destruction by fire of the temple
at Delphi, contracted to have it rebuilt at a cost of three hundred
talents (a quarter of that sum to be furnished by the Delphians), and
the Delphians went round from city to city asking for contributions,
Egypt was by no means least in giving assistance. Amasis gave them
a thousand talents of alum, and the Greeks who had settled in Egypt,
twenty *minae*.

After the conclusion of a pact of friendship and alliance with Cyrene, Amasis, as a token of his goodwill – or perhaps merely because
he wanted a Greek wife – decided to marry a woman from that city.
The woman he chose was Ladice, daughter either of Battus, or (for
accounts differ) of Arcesilaus, or of Critobulus, one of the leading
citizens. For a time the marriage was not consummated; for whenever the king went to bed with her, he was unable to have intercourse,
while with his other wives he did. This happened frequently, until at
last Amasis told her that she must have bewitched him, and there was

no escape for her, in consequence, from a most miserable death. Ladice denied the charge, but in vain; the king's anger was not softened, so she made a silent vow to Aphrodite that if that very night – the last which could save her from death – the marriage could be consummated, she would present a statue to the temple of the goddess of Cyrene. Her prayer was at once answered; Amasis lay with her successfully, and continued to do so on every occasion afterwards, and came to love her deeply. Ladice fulfilled her vow to Aphrodite; she had the statue made and sent it to Cyrene, where it still remained up to my own time, looking outward from the city. Ladice herself suffered no harm when Cambyses conquered Egypt; for when he learnt who she was, Cambyses sent her back safely to her native Cyrene.

Amasis further showed his goodwill to Greece by sending presents to be dedicated in Greek temples; to Cyrene he sent a gold-plated statue of Athene and a painting of himself; to the temple of Athene at Lindos, two statues in stone and a remarkable linen corslet; and to the goddess Hera in Samos two likenesses of himself, in wood, which until my own time stood behind the doors in the great temple. These last were a mark of his friendship with the ruler of Samos, Polycrates, son of Aeaces; but the gifts to Lindos in Rhodes were not the expression of any personal feeling, but were given because of the tradition that the temple of Athene there was founded by the daughter of Danaus, who touched at the island during their flight from the sons of Aegyptus.

Amasis was also the first man to take Cyprus and compel it to pay tribute.

BOOK THREE

IT was against Amasis, then, that Cyrus' son Cambyses marched at the head of an army drawn from various subject nations and including both Ionian and Aeolian Greeks. His pretext was as follows. Cyrus had sent to Amasis to ask for the services of the best oculist in Egypt, and the one who was selected, in resentment at being torn from his wife and family and handed over to the Persians, suggested to Cambyses by way of revenge that he should ask for Amasis' daughter in marriage, knowing that consent would cause the Egyptian king personal distress, and that refusal would embroil him with Cambyses. Cambyses did as the man suggested, and sent a representative to Egypt to make the request. Amasis, who dreaded the power of Persia, and was well aware that Cambyses wanted his daughter not as a wife but as a concubine, found himself in an awkward position, and unable to say either yes or no. Now there was a daughter of the late King Apries, a tall and beautiful girl named Nitetis, the last survivor of her family, and Amasis, after thinking the matter over, decided to dress her up like a princess in fine clothes adorned with gold, and send her to Persia as his own daughter. This he did; and some time later, when Cambyses happened to address her by her father's name, she replied: 'My lord, you do not know how Amasis has cheated you; he dressed me in gorgeous clothes and sent me to you as his own daughter – but indeed I am not; I am the daughter of Apries, his master, whom he killed when he led the Egyptians to rebel against him.' It was these words, and the cause of quarrel they disclosed, which, according to the Persian account, brought down upon Egypt the wrath of Cambyses, son of Cyrus. The Egyptians, on the other hand, claim that Cambyses was the son of Nitetis, Apries' daughter, and was thus a native of their own country – for it was Cyrus, they say, not Cambyses, who sent to Amasis to demand his daughter. The claim, however, is not justified by facts; for knowing as they do – none better – the laws of Persia, they could not fail to be aware, first, that Persian usage bars a bastard from the succession so long as there is a legitimate heir, and, secondly, that Cambyses was the son of Cassandane, daughter of Pharnaspes, one of the Achaemenidae, and not of this Egyptian woman. The fact is, they wish to claim kinship with Cyrus, and pervert the truh to justify their claim. There is also another story current, but not, I think, a convincing one: namely, that a Persian woman paid a visit to Cyrus' wives, and greatly admired the fine tall sons which she saw standing by Cassandane's side. Hearing her praises, Cassandane, who was jealous of Nitetis, said: 'In spite of my beautiful children Cyrus treats me with contempt and gives all his attention to that woman he got from Egypt.' 'Well then, mother,' exclaimed Cambyses, the elder of her two sons, 'when I'm a man, I'll turn Egypt upside-down for you.' He was only about ten when he astonished the women by making this promise, but he never forgot it; for when he grew up and had ascended the throne, he did, indeed, invade Egypt.

There was another thing, quite different from all this, which helped to bring about the Egyptian expedition. One of the Greek mercenaries of Amasis, a Halicarnassian called Phanes, a brave and intelligent soldier, being dissatisfied for some reason or other with his conditions of service, deserted, and escaped from Egypt by sea, with the object of getting an interview with Cambyses. As he was a person of consequence in the army and had very precise knowledge of the internal condition of Egypt, Amasis was anxious to catch him and sent the most trustworthy of his eunuchs to pursue him in a warship. He was caught in Lycia but not brought back; for getting his guards to drink themselves stupid, he outwitted his captor and made good his escape to Persia. Cambyses was anxious to launch his attack on Egypt and was wondering how best he could cross the desert, when Phanes arrived, and not only revealed to him all the secrets of Amasis, but also advised him that the best way of getting his army through the desert would be to send to the Arabian king and ask for a safe-conduct.

The only entrance into Egypt is through this desert. From Phoenicia to the boundaries of Gaza the country belongs to the Syrians known as 'Palestinian': from Gaza, a town, I should say, not much smaller than Sardis, the seaports as far as Ienysus belong to the king of Arabia; from there as far as Lake Serbonis, near which Mt Casius runs down to the sea, it is once more Syrian territory; and after Lake Serbonis (where Typhon is supposed to be buried) Egypt begins. The whole area between Ienysus on the one side, and Mt Casius and the Lake on the other – and it is of considerable extent, not less than three days' journey – is desert and completely without water.

I will now mention something of which few voyagers to Egypt are aware. Throughout the year, not only from all parts of Greece but from Phoenicia as well, wine is imported into Egypt in earthenware jars; yet one might say that not a single empty wine-jar is to be seen anywhere in the country. The obvious question is: what becomes of them? I will explain. The mayor of each place has orders to collect all the jars from his town and send them to Memphis, and the people of Memphis have to fill them with water and send them to this tract of desert in Syria. In this way every fresh jar of wine imported into Egypt, and there emptied of its content, finds its way into Syria to join the previous ones. It was the Persians, immediately after their conquest of Egypt, who devised this means of storing water in the desert, and so making the passage into the country practicable; but at the time of which I am speaking there was no water at all, so Cambyses took the advice of his Halicarnassian friend Phanes, and sent to the Arabian king with a request for safe-conduct. The request was granted, and pledges were exchanged between the two parties.

No nation regards the sanctity of a pledge more seriously than the Arabs. When two men wish to make a solemn compact, they get the service of a third, who stands between them and with a sharp stone cuts the palms of their hands near the base of the thumb; then he takes a little tuft of wool from their clothes, dips it in the blood and smears the blood on seven stones which lie between them, invoking as he does so, the names of Dionysus and Urania; then the person who is giving the pledge, commends the stranger – or fellow citizen, as the case may be – to his friends, who in their turn consider themselves equally bound to honour it. The only gods the Arabs recognize are

Dionysus and Urania; the way they cut their hair – all round in a circle, with the temples shaved – is, they say, in imitation of Dionysus. Dionysus in their language is Orotalt, and Urania Alilat.

When the Arabian king had made his vow of friendship with the messengers of Cambyses, the method he devised of helping the Egyptian army was to fill camel-skins with water, load them on to all his live camels, and so convey them to the desert, where he awaited the arrival of the troops. That, at any rate, is the more credible account of his procedure; there is also another, which I ought to mention, though it is not so easy to believe. According to this, the Arabian king had cowhides and other skins stitched together to form a pipe long enough to reach from the Corys – a large river in Arabia which runs into the Red Sea – all the way to the desert; here he had large reservoirs constructed, filled them by means of the pipe, and so stored the water. The water was brought to three separate places, over a total distance – between river and desert – of a twelve days' journey.

Psammenitus, Amasis' son, took up a position on the Pelusian mouth of the Nile, to await the attack of Cambyses. Amasis had died before the invasion actually began, after a reign of forty-four years, during which he had suffered no serious disaster. His body was embalmed and buried in the sepulchre he had himself built in the temple of Athene in Sais. In the reign of his successor Psammenitus, an unparalleled event occurred – rain fell at Thebes, a thing which the men of that city say had never happened before, or has ever happened since till the present day. Normally, in upper Egypt no rain falls at all; but on this occasion it did – a light shower.

The Persians crossed the desert, took up a position near the Egyptian army, and prepared for an engagement. Before the battle the Greek and Carian mercenaries who were serving with the Egyptians planned a dreadful revenge upon Phanes in their anger at his bringing a foreign army against Egypt: they seized his sons, whom he had left behind, and brought them to the camp, where they made sure their father could see them; then, placing a bowl in the open ground between the two armies, they led the boys up to it one by one, and cut their throats over it. Not one was spared, and when the last was dead, they poured wine and water on to the blood in the bowl, and every man in the mercenary force drank. That done, the fight began; and after a hard struggle and heavy casualties on both sides, the Egyptians were routed.

At the place where this battle was fought I saw a very odd thing, which the natives had told me about. The bones still lay there, those of the Persian dead separate from those of the Egyptian, just as they were originally divided, and I noticed that the skulls of the Persians are so thin that the merest touch with a pebble will pierce them, but those of the Egyptians, on the other hand, are so tough that it is hardly possible to break them with a blow from a stone. I was told, very credibly, that the reason was that the Egyptians shave their heads from childhood, so that the bone of the skull is indurated by the action of the sun – this is also why they hardly ever go bald, bald-ness being rarer in Egypt than anywhere else. This, then, explains the thickness of their skulls; and the thinness of the Persians' skulls rests upon a similar principle: namely that they have always worn felt skull-caps, to guard their heads from the sun. I also observed the same thing at Papremis, where the Persians serving under Achaemenes, the son of Darius, were destroyed by Inarus the Libyan.

After their defeat, the Egyptians fled in disorder and shut them-selves up in Memphis. Cambyses called upon them to come to terms, sending a Persian herald up the river to the town in a Mytilenean vessel; but directly they saw the ship coming into the town, they rushed out in a body, smashed up the ship, tore everyone on board limb from limb, and carried the bits back inside the walls. They then stood a siege, but after a time surrendered. The neighbouring Libyans were alarmed by the fate of Egypt and gave themselves up without a blow, agreeing to pay tribute and sending presents. A similar fear caused the people of Cyrene and Barca to follow their example. Cambyses graciously accepted what the Libyans sent him; the offer-ing from Cyrene, on the contrary, he treated with contempt. I sup-pose he objected to the smallness of the amount – it was only 500 *minae* of silver; anyway, he snatched the money into his own hands and flung it to his men.[1]

1. 50,000 silver drachmas would have taken a good deal of 'snatching'. Herodotus is perhaps again emphasizing the difference of scale between Greek and Asiatic ideas of wealth.

Ten days passed, and Cambyses, wishing to see what stuff the Egyptian king Psammenitus was made of – he had been but six months on the throne – forced him, with other Egyptians, to witness from a seat in the city suburbs a spectacle deliberately devised to humiliate him. First, he had his daughter dressed like a slave and sent out with a pitcher to fetch water, accompanied by other young girls similarly dressed and chosen from noble families. The girls cried bitterly as they passed the place where their fathers sat watching them, and the fathers, in their turn – all but Psammenitus himself – wept and lamented no less bitterly at the sight of such an insult to their children. Psammenitus, however, after a single glance of recognition, bent to the ground in silence. The girls with their pitchers passed on, and then came the king's son with two thousand others of the same age, their mouths bridled and a rope round their necks, on their way to execution for the murder of the Mytileneans at Memphis and the destruction of the ship – for the sentence of the royal judges had been that for each man ten Egyptian noblemen should die. Psammenitus watched them pass, and knew that his son was going to his death; but, though the other Egyptians who were sitting near him continued to weep and to show every sign of distress, he did just what he had done before at the sight of his daughter. So the young men, too, passed on; and then there chanced to walk by the place where Psammenitus, son of Amasis, sat with the others in the city suburbs, an old man who had once been the king's friend and had dined at his table, but had been stripped of his fortune and was now nothing more than a beggar trying to get what he could from the soldiers. At the sight of him Psammenitus burst into tears, and called him by name, and beat his head in distress. Guards were standing near, whose duty it was to report to Cambyses exactly how Psammenitus behaved as each of the processions went by, and Cambyses was so much surprised at what he heard, that he sent a messenger to Psammenitus to ask how he could behave as he did. 'Your master Cambyses,' the messenger said, 'asks why it is, that you made no sound and shed no tear when you saw your daughter insulted and your son going to his death, yet honoured with those signs of grief a beggar who, he understands, is not even related to you.' 'Son of Cyrus,' was the answer, 'my own suffering was too great for tears, but I could not but weep

LIBRARY   MONEY
LANTERN ?   MAPS
CAR   CAMERA
COLEMAN FUEL HATCHET
RAIN —   BLANKET

$$\frac{65}{}\overline{)5}$$

65
15
5
325
6
97.5

for the trouble of a friend, who has lost great wealth and been reduced to beggary on the threshold of old age.'

When this answer was reported, it was recognized as just, and the Egyptians relate that Croesus – who, as it happened, had accompanied Cambyses in the expedition against Egypt – wept when he heard it, as did the Persians who were present, and that even Cambyses felt a touch of pity – for he at once gave orders that Psammenitus' son should be reprieved from the sentence of death, and that Psammenitus himself should be brought before him from the place where he sat in the city suburbs.

The messengers were too late to save the young man, for he had been the first to be killed; but they brought Psammenitus to Cambyses, at whose court he lived from that time onward. Here he was well treated; and indeed, if he had only had the sense to keep out of mischief, he might have recovered Egypt and ruled it as governor; for the Persians are in the habit of treating the sons of kings with honour, and even of restoring to their sons the thrones of those who have rebelled against them. There are many instances from which one may infer that this sort of generosity is usual in Persia: one obvious one is the case of Thannyras, the son of Inarus the Libyan, who was allowed to succeed his father. Pausiris, the son of Amyrtaeus,[1] is another example: to him, too, his father's kingdom was restored – and all this in spite of the fact that nobody ever caused the Persians more trouble and loss than Inarus and Amyrtaeus. Psammenitus, however, did not refrain from stirring up trouble, and was properly paid for it. He was caught trying to raise a revolt amongst the Egyptians, and as soon as his guilt was known by Cambyses, he drank bull's blood and died on the spot. And that was the end of Psammenitus.

Cambyses now left Memphis and went on to Sais, fully resolved on what he would do when he got there. This intention he at once carried out, for no sooner had he entered the palace of Amasis than he gave orders for his body to be taken from the tomb where it lay. This done, he proceeded to have it treated with every possible indignity, such as lashing with whips, pricking with goads, and the plucking of its hairs. All this was done till the executioners were weary, and at last, as the

1. This is after 449 B.C., when Amyrtaeus was still holding out; cf. Thucydides I, 112.

corpse had been embalmed and would not fall to pieces under the blows, Cambyses ordered it to be burnt. This was a wicked thing to do, because the Persians believe that fire is a god, and never burn their dead. Indeed, such a practice is unheard of either amongst them or the Egyptians: in the former case for the reason I mentioned, and because the Persians think it is wrong to give a man's dead body to a god; in the latter, because the Egyptians believe fire to be a living creature which devours whatever it gets, and, when it has eaten enough, dies with the food it feeds on. It is wholly contrary to Egyptian custom to allow dead bodies to be eaten by animals: that is why they embalm them – to prevent them from being eaten in the grave by worms. Cambyses, therefore, in giving this order, was running counter to the religious belief of both nations. The Egyptians have a story that it was not Amasis at all whose body received this treatment; it was another man's, of about the same stature, but the Persians thought it was the king's when they committed the outrage upon it. For Amasis, according to this story, had learnt from an oracle of the fate which threatened him after his death, and, in order to avert it, buried close to the doors, just within his tomb, the body of this man who was lashed with the Persian whips, but his own body he instructed his son to place in the furthest possible recess of the burial-chamber. I do not myself believe that Amasis ever gave these orders at all – it is just a tale the Egyptians tell to save their face.

Cambyses next made plans for three separate military ventures: one against the Carthaginians, another against the Ammonians, and the third against the long-lived Ethiopians, on the coast of the Indian Ocean, south of Libya. He proposed to send his fleet against the Carthaginians and a part of his land forces against the Ammonians; to Ethiopia he decided first to send spies, ostensibly with presents to the king, but actually to collect what information they could; in particular he wanted them to find out if the so-called Table of the Sun really existed. (The story about the Table of the Sun is that there is a meadow, situated in the outskirts of the city, where a plentiful supply of boiled meat of all kinds is kept; it is the duty of the magistrates to put the meat there at night, and during the day anybody who wishes may come and eat it. Local legend has it that the meat appears spontaneously and is the gift of the earth.)

Having decided that the spies should go, Cambyses sent to Elephantine for some men of the Fish-Eaters who were acquainted with
the Ethiopian language, and, while they were being fetched, gave
orders for the fleet to sail against Carthage. The Phoenicians, however, refused to go, because of the close bond which connected
Phoenicia and Carthage, and the wickedness of making war against
their own children. In this way, with the Phoenicians out of it and
the remainder of the naval force too weak to undertake the campaign
alone, the Carthaginians escaped Persian domination. Cambyses did
not think fit to bring pressure to bear, because the Phoenicians had
taken service under him of their own free will, and his whole naval
power was dependent on them. The Cyprians, too, had given their
services to Persia and took part in the Egyptian campaign.

The Fish-Eaters who had been summoned from Elephantine were
sent off to Ethiopia with instructions on what they were to say on
their arrival: they took with them as presents for the king a scarlet
robe, a gold chain-necklace and bracelets, an alabaster casket of
myrrh, and a jar of palm-wine. The Ethiopians, who were the objects
of all this attention, are said to be the tallest and best-looking people
in the world. Their laws and customs are peculiar to themselves, and
the strangest is the method they have of choosing for their king the
man whom they judge to be the tallest, and strong in proportion to
his height. The Fish-Eaters duly arrived in the country and presented
their gifts to the king with the following words: 'Cambyses, King of
Persia, wishing to be your friend and guest, has sent us here with
orders to have speech with you, and these gifts he offers you are just
the things which he himself takes most pleasure in using.'

But the Ethiopian king knew the men were spies, and answered:
'The king of Persia has not sent you with these presents because he
puts a high value upon being my friend. You have come to get information about my kingdom; therefore, you are liars, and that king
of yours is a bad man. Had he any respect for what is right, he would
not have coveted any other kingdom than his own, nor made slaves
of a people who have done him no wrong. So take him this bow, and
tell him that the king of Ethiopia has some advice to give him: when
the Persians can draw a bow of this size thus easily, then let him raise
an army of superior strength and invade the country of the long-lived

Ethiopians. Till then, let him thank the gods for not turning the thoughts of the children of Ethiopia to foreign conquest.' He then un-strung the bow, put it into the hands of the Fish-Eaters, and picked up the scarlet robe, asking what it was and how it was made. The men explained about the dye and how the material was dipped in it, whereupon the king replied that both the dyers and the garments they dyed were pretending to be what they were not, and were therefore cheats. Then he asked about the gold chain and the bracelets, and when the Fish-Eaters explained their use as ornaments he laughed and, supposing them to be fetters, remarked that they had stronger ones in their own country. Next he asked about the myrrh, and after hearing how it was prepared and how people rubbed it on their bodies for a perfume, he repeated the comment he had made about the scarlet robe. Finally he came to the wine and, having learnt the process of its manufacture, drank some and found it delicious; then, for a last question, he asked what the Persian king ate and what was the greatest age that Persians could attain. Getting in reply an account of the nature and cultivation of wheat, and hearing that the Persian king ate bread, and that people in Persia did not commonly live be-yond eighty, he said he was not surprised that anyone who ate dung should die so soon, adding that Persians would doubtless die younger still, if they did not keep themselves going with that drink – and here he pointed to the wine, the one thing in which he admitted the superiority of the Persians.

The Fish-Eaters, in their turn, asked the king how long the Ethio-pians lived and what they ate, and were told that most of them lived to be a hundred and twenty, and some even more, and that they ate boiled meat and drank milk. When they expressed surprise that any-one should live to such an advanced age, they were taken to a spring, the water from which smelt like violets and caused a man's skin, when he washed in it, to glisten as if he had washed in oil. They said the water of this spring lacked density to such a degree that nothing would float in it, neither wood nor any lighter substance – every-thing sank to the bottom. If this account is true, then their constant use of it must be the cause of the Ethiopians' longevity. After the visit to the spring the king conducted them to a prison in which all the prisoners were bound with gold chains – for in Ethiopia the rarest

and most precious metal is bronze. Inspection of the prison was followed by inspection of the Table of the Sun, and last of all they were
taken to see the coffins. These coffins are said to be made of crystal,
and the method the Ethiopians follow is first to dry the corpse, either
by the Egyptian process or some other, then cover it all over with
gypsum and paint it to resemble as closely as possible the living man;
then they enclose it in a shaft of crystal which has been hollowed out,
like a cylinder, to receive it. The stuff is easily worked and is mined
in large quantities. The corpse is plainly visible inside the cylinder;
there is no disagreeable smell, or any other cause of annoyance, and
every detail can be as distinctly seen as if there were nothing between
one's eyes and the body. The next-of-kin keep the cylinder in their
houses for a year, offering it the first fruits and sacrificing to it; then
they carry it out and set it up near the town.

Having now seen all they could, the spies returned to Egypt to
make their report, which so angered Cambyses that he at once began
his march against Ethiopia, without any orders for the provision of
supplies, and without for a moment considering the fact that he was
to take his men to the ends of the earth. He lost his wits completely
and, like the madman he was, the moment he heard what the Fish-
Eaters had to say, off he went with his whole force of infantry, leaving behind the Greeks who were serving under him. Arrived at
Thebes, he detached a body of 50,000 men with orders to attack the
Ammonians, reduce them to slavery, and burn the oracle of Zeus;
then with his remaining forces he continued his march towards
Ethiopia. They had not, however, covered a fifth of the distance,
when everything in the nature of provisions gave out, and the men
were forced to eat the pack-animals until they, too, were all gone.
If Cambyses, when he saw what the situation was, had changed his
mind and returned to his base, he would, in spite of his original error,
have shown some sense; but as it was, he paid not the least attention
to what was happening and continued his advance. The troops kept
themselves alive by eating green-stuff so long as there was any to be
had in the country, but once they had reached the desert, some of
them were reduced to the dreadful expedient of cannibalism. One
man in ten was chosen by lot to be the victim. This was too much
even for Cambyses; when it was reported to him, he abandoned the

expedition, marched back, and arrived at Thebes with greatly reduced numbers. From Thebes he went down to Memphis and allowed the Greeks to sail home. So ended the expedition against
Ethiopia.

The force which was sent against the Ammonians started from
Thebes with guides, and can be traced as far as the town of Oasis,
which belongs to Samians supposed to be of the Aeschrionian tribe,
and is seven days' journey across the sand from Thebes. The place is
known in Greek as the Island of the Blessed. General report has it
that the army got as far as this, but of its subsequent fate there is no
news whatever. It never reached the Ammonians and it never returned to Egypt. There is, however, a story told by the Ammonians
themselves and by others who heard it from them, that when the men
had left Oasis, and in their march across the desert had reached a point
about mid-way between the town and the Ammonian border, a
southerly wind of extreme violence drove the sand over them in
heaps as they were taking their mid-day meal, so that they disappeared for ever.

After the arrival of Cambyses at Memphis, Apis – the Greek
Epaphus – appeared to the Egyptians. Immediately the whole people
put on their best clothes and went on holiday, and Cambyses, seeing
the festivities and convinced that the Egyptians were rejoicing over
recent disaster, summoned the officers in charge of Memphis and
asked them why it was that the Egyptians had done nothing of the
kind during his previous visit to the city, but had waited to celebrate
their holiday until the present occasion, when he had returned after the
loss of a large part of his army. They replied that a god had appeared
amongst them; he was wont to reveal himself only at long intervals
of time, and whenever he did so, all Egypt rejoiced and celebrated a
festival. Cambyses' answer to this was, that the men were liars, and
as such he had them executed. Then he called the priests into his
presence, and when they made precisely the same assertion, he replied
that if some tame god or other had really revealed himself to the
Egyptians he would find out about it soon enough; and without
another word he ordered the priests to fetch Apis – which they
did.

This Apis – or Epaphus – is the calf of a cow which is never afterwards able to have another. The Egyptian belief is that a flash of light descends upon the cow from heaven, and this causes her to receive Apis. The Apis-calf has distinctive marks: it is black, with a white diamond on its forehead, the image of an eagle on its back, the hairs on its tail double, and a scarab under its tongue. The priests brought the animal and Cambyses, half mad as he was, drew his dagger, aimed a blow at its belly, but missed and struck its thigh. Then he laughed, and said to the priests: 'Do you call that a god, you poor creatures? Are your gods flesh and blood? Do they feel the prick of steel? No doubt a god like that is good enough for the Egyptians; but you won't get away with trying to make a fool of me.' He then ordered the priests to be whipped by the men whose business it was to carry out such punishments, and any Egyptian who was found still keeping holiday to be put to death. In this way the festival was broken up, the priests punished, and Apis, who lay in the temple for a time wasting away from the wound in his thigh, finally died and was buried by the priests without the knowledge of Cambyses.

Even before this Cambyses had been far from sound in his mind; but the Egyptians are convinced that the complete loss of his reason was the direct result of this crime. Of the outrages he subsequently committed the first was the murder of his brother Smerdis (his father's son by the same mother as himself). He had already sent Smerdis back to Persia, because he was jealous of him for being the only Persian to succeed in drawing – though only a very little way, about two fingers' breadth – the bow which the Fish-Eaters brought from Ethiopia. After his arrival there, Cambyses dreamt that a messenger came to him from Persia with the news that Smerdis was sitting on the royal throne and that his head touched the sky. In alarm lest the dream should mean that his brother would kill him and reign in his stead, Cambyses sent Prexaspes, the most trusted of his Persian friends, to make away with him. Prexaspes went up-country to Susa and did the deed – according to one account he took his victim out hunting, according to another he lured him down to the Persian Gulf and drowned him. This, they say, was the beginning; and the next crime Cambyses committed was the murder of his sister who had come with him to Egypt. This woman was his sister by both parents, and also his wife, though it had never before been a Persian custom for brothers and sisters to marry. Cambyses got over the difficulty in the following way: having fallen in love with one of his sisters and wishing afterwards to take the illegal step of making her his wife, he summoned the royal judges and asked them if there was any law in the country which allowed a man to marry his sister if he wished to do so. These royal judges are specially chosen men, who hold office either for life or until they are found guilty of some misconduct; their duties are to determine suits and to interpret the ancient laws of the land, and all points of dispute are referred to them. When, therefore, Cambyses put his question, they managed to find an answer which would neither violate the truth nor endanger their own necks: namely, that though they could discover no law which allowed brother to marry sister, there was undoubtedly a law which permitted the king of Persia to do what he pleased. In this way they avoided breaking any established law, in spite of their fear of Cambyses; and at the same time, by bringing in a particular law to help the king to realize his wish, they escaped the danger to themselves which a too rigid attention to ancestral usage would have involved. Cambyses accordingly married the sister he was in love with, and not long afterwards married another one as well – and this, the younger of the two, was the one who went with him to Egypt.

As in the case of Smerdis, there are two accounts of her death; the Greeks say that Cambyses set a puppy and a lion-cub to fight, and that his wife was amongst the spectators; the puppy was getting the worst of it, when another from the same litter broke its chain and came to its brother's help, and the two together proved too much for the cub. Cambyses enjoyed watching the fight, but his sister, who was sitting beside him, began to cry. Noticing her tears, Cambyses asked the reason for them, and she replied that it was the sight of the puppy coming to help its brother that had made her weep; for she could not but remember Smerdis, and think how there was nobody now to come to help her husband. It was this remark which, according to the Greek version, made Cambyses put her to death. The Egyptians, on the other hand, say that the two were sitting at table, when the woman took a lettuce and, after pulling off the leaves, asked her husband whether he thought it looked better with its leaves on or off. Cambyses said that he preferred it before it was stripped, whereupon his sister replied that he had treated the house of Cyrus just as she had treated the lettuce – he had stripped it bare. Cambyses, in a fury, kicked her; and, as she was pregnant at the time, she had a miscarriage and died.

These two crimes were committed against his own kin; both were the acts of a madman – whether or not his madness was due to his treatment of Apis. It may, indeed, have been the result of any one of the many maladies which afflict mankind, and there is, in fact, a story that he had suffered from birth from the serious compliant which some call 'the sacred sickness'.[1] There would then be nothing strange in the fact that a serious physical malady should have affected his brain. But in addition to the two crimes already mentioned, there were other Persians, too, whom he treated with the savagery of a lunatic; for instance, there was the case of Prexaspes, a man who was highly valued by the king and used to bring him his dispatches, and whose son was the king's cupbearer – also a position of no small honour. On one occasion Cambyses said to this distinguished official: 'What sort of man do the Persians think I am, and what do they say about me?' 'Master,' Prexaspes replied, 'you are highly praised by them, and they have but one criticism to make: they say you are too fond of wine.' This enraged Cambyses; 'So now,' he said, 'the Persians say that excessive drinking has driven me mad. They said something quite different before; but I see it was a lie.' For on a former occasion, when a number of Persians were sitting with him, and Croesus was also present, he had asked what they thought of him compared with his father, and they had answered that he was better than his father, because he had kept all Cyrus' possessions and acquired Egypt and the command of the sea into the bargain. Croesus, however, was not satisfied with this opinion, and said: 'Son of Cyrus, I at least do not think you are equal to your father; for you have not yet a son like the son he left behind him in yourself.' Cambyses was delighted with this, and praised Croesus' judgement, and it was the memory of this incident which made him, on the present occasion, say in a rage to Prexaspes: 'I'll soon show you if the Persians speak the truth, or if what they say is not a sign of their own madness rather than of mine. You see your son standing there by the door? If

1. Epilepsy?

I shoot him through the middle of the heart, I shall have proved the Persians' words empty and meaningless; if I miss, then say, if you will, that the Persians are right, and my wits are gone.'

Without another word he drew his bow and shot the boy, and then ordered his body to be cut open and the wound examined; and when the arrow was found to have pierced the heart, he was delighted, and said with a laugh to the boy's father: 'There's proof for you, Prexaspes, that I am sane and the Persians mad. Now tell me if you ever saw anyone else shoot so straight.'

Prexaspes knew well enough that the king's mind was unbalanced, so in fear for his own safety he answered: 'Master, I do not believe that God himself is a better marksman.' On another occasion he arrested twelve Persians of the highest rank on some trifling charge, and buried them alive, head downwards. For this action Croesus the Lydian thought fit to give him some advice. 'My lord,' he said, 'do not always act on the passionate impulse of youth. Check and control yourself. There is wisdom in forethought, and a sensible man looks to the future. If you continue too long in your present course of killing your countrymen for no sufficient cause – and of killing children too – then beware lest the Persians rise in revolt. Again and again your father Cyrus urged me to give you whatever advice I might think would help you.'

In spite of the fact that Croesus spoke in all friendship, Cambyses answered: 'So even you dare tell me how I ought to behave! You – who governed your own country so finely, and gave such excellent advice to my father to cross the Araxes and attack the Massagetae, when all they wanted was to come over themselves and attack us! You – who ruined yourself by your own bad government, and ruined Cyrus simply because he took your advice! But now you are going to pay for it – I have long wanted an excuse to get even with you.' He was just reaching for his bow to shoot him down, when Croesus leapt from his seat and ran from the room. Robbed of his shot, Cambyses sent his servants to catch him and kill him; but they knew their master's moods and hid him instead, so that if Cambyses changed his mind and asked for Croesus, they would be able to produce him and get a reward for saving his life; for they knew they could kill him later, if the king kept to his purpose and showed no signs of regret.

And it did in fact happen that quite soon afterwards Cambyses missed Croesus, and his servants, as soon as they noticed it, let him know that he was still alive. Cambyses said that he rejoiced to hear it, but the men who saved him would not get off so lightly: he would punish them with death – which he did.

All this may pass for a sample of the maniacal savagery with which Cambyses treated the Persians and his allies during his stay in Memphis; amongst other things, he broke open ancient tombs and examined the bodies, and even entered the temple of Hephaestus and jeered at the god's statue. This statue closely resembles the Pataici which the Phoenicians carry about on the prows of their warships – but I should make it clearer to anyone who has never seen these, if I said it was like a pygmy. He also entered the temple of the Cabiri, which no one but the priest is allowed to do, made fun of the images there (they resemble those of Hephaestus, and are supposed to be his sons), and actually burnt them.

In view of all this, I have no doubt whatever that Cambyses was completely out of his mind; it is the only possible explanation of his assault upon, and mockery of, everything which ancient law and custom have made sacred in Egypt. For if anyone, no matter who, were given the opportunity of choosing from amongst all the nations in the world the set of beliefs which he thought best, he would inevitably, after careful consideration of their relative merits, choose that of his own country. Everyone without exception believes his own native customs, and the religion he was brought up in, to be the best; and that being so, it is unlikely that anyone but a madman would mock at such things. There is abundant evidence that this is the universal feeling about the ancient customs of one's country. One might recall, in particular, an anecdote of Darius. When he was king of Persia, he summoned the Greeks who happened to be present at his court, and asked them what they would take to eat the dead bodies of their fathers. They replied that they would not do it for any money in the world. Later, in the presence of the Greeks, and through an interpreter, so they they could understand what was said, he asked some Indians, of the tribe called Callatiae, who do in fact eat their parents' dead bodies, what they would take to burn them. They uttered a cry of horror and forbade him to mention such a dreadful thing. One can see by this what custom can do, and Pindar, in my opinion, was right when he called it 'king of all'.

While Cambyses was occupied with the Egyptian expedition, the Lacedaemonians made an expedition to Samos against Polycrates, the son of Aeaces. Polycrates had seized power in the island, and at the outset had divided his realm into three and gone shares with his brothers, Pantagnotus and Syloson; later, however, he killed the former, banished the latter (the younger of the two) and held the whole island himself. Once master of it, he concluded a pact of friendship with Amasis, king of Egypt, sealing it by a mutual exchange of presents. It was not long before the rapid increase of his power became the talk of Ionia and the rest of Greece. All his campaigns were victorious, his every venture a success. He had a fleet of a hundred fifty-oared galleys and a force of a thousand bowmen. His plundering raids were widespread and indiscriminate – he used to say that a friend would be more grateful if he gave him back what he had taken, than if he had never taken it. He captured many of the islands and a number of towns on the mainland as well. Amongst other successes, he defeated at sea the Lesbians, who had sent their whole fleet to the help of Miletus; the prisoners he took were forced to dig, in chains, the whole moat which surrounds the walls of Samos.

Amasis was fully aware of the remarkable luck which Polycrates enjoyed, and it caused him some uneasiness; accordingly when he heard of his ever-mounting tale of successes, he wrote him the following letter, and sent it to Samos: 'Amasis to Polycrates: – It is a pleasure to hear of a friend and ally doing well, but, as I know that the gods are jealous of success, I cannot rejoice at your excessive prosperity. My own wish, both for myself and for those I care for, would be to do well in some things and badly in others, passing through life with alternate success and failure; for I have never yet heard of a man who after an unbroken run of luck was not finally brought to complete ruin. Now I suggest that you deal with the danger of your continual successes in the following way: think of whatever it is you value most – whatever you would most regret the loss of – and throw it away: throw it right away, so that nobody can ever see it again. If, after that, you do not find that success alternates with failure, then go on using the remedy I have advised.'

Polycrates read the letter and approved of the advice which it contained; so he began to look around amongst his treasures for what he felt he would be most grieved to lose, and finally hit upon a ring. This was a signet-ring he used to wear, an emerald set in gold, the work of a Samian named Theodorus, the son of Telecles. Having decided that this was the thing to get rid of, he manned a galley, went aboard, and gave orders to put to sea. When the vessel was a long way off-shore, he took the ring from his finger, in full view of everyone on board, and threw it into the water. Then he rowed back to the island, returned to his house, and lamented his lost treasure.

Five or six days later it happened that a fisherman caught a fine big fish and thought it would make a worthy present for Polycrates. He took it to the door and asked for an audience; this being granted, he offered the fish, and said: 'My King, I did not think it right to take this fish I caught to market, poor working man though I am; it is such a fine one that I thought it good enough for you and your greatness. So I have brought it here to give you.'

Polycrates, much pleased with what the fisherman said, replied: 'You have done very well, and I thank you twice over – once for your words, and again for your present. I invite you to take supper with me.'

The fisherman then went home, very proud of the honour done him. Meanwhile Polycrates' servants cut up the fish, and found the signet-ring in its belly. The moment they saw it, they picked it up, and taking it to Polycrates in triumph, told him how it had been found. Seeing in this the hand of providence, Polycrates wrote a letter to Amasis in Egypt, and related to him everything he had done and what the result had been. Amasis read the letter, and at once replied how impossible it is for one man to save another from his destiny, and how certain it was that Polycrates, whose luck held even to the point of finding again what he deliberately threw away, would one day die a miserable death. He forthwith sent a messenger to Samos to say that the pact between Polycrates and himself was at an end. This he did in order that when the destined calamity fell upon

Polycrates, he might avoid the distress he would have felt, had Polycrates still been his friend.

This, then, was the man, still in the enjoyment of unbroken success, with whom the Lacedaemonians were at war, having been called in by the Samians, who afterwards founded Cydonia in Crete. For Polycrates, at the time when Cambyses the son of Cyrus was raising the force for his Egyptian expedition, had secretly sent him a request to apply to Samos for a contingent of troops to join him, and Cambyses had gladly complied, sending to the island to ask Polycrates to contribute a naval force for the coming campaign against Egypt. Polycrates thereupon manned forty triremes with carefully selected crews, every man of which he had particular reason to suspect of disloyalty to himself, and sent them off, with instructions to Cambyses never to allow them to return to Samos. According to one account, these people never arrived in Egypt, but having got as far as Carpathus, talked things over and decided not to continue their voyage; according to another, they did reach Egypt, where they were put under guard, and later escaped and sailed back to Samos. Off the island Polycrates met them with his own fleet, and a battle was fought in which they were victorious; after their success they landed on the island, but the fight which then ensued went against them, and they finally took to their ships again and sailed to Lacedaemon. There are some who maintain that these men who came back from Egypt actually defeated Polycrates; I think, however, that this is unlikely to be true, because if they were strong enough to have dealt with Polycrates unaided, there would have been no need for them to call on the Lacedaemonians for assistance; moreover, it is unreasonable to suppose that a man with so large a paid army and force of native bowmen could be defeated by the exiled Samians, who were but few in number. To prevent the Samians who were still subject to him from playing traitor and joining the returned exiles, Polycrates had their wives and children shut up in the boat-sheds, and was prepared to burn them, sheds and all, in case of need.

When those who had been forced to leave the island reached Sparta, they procured an audience with the magistrates and made a long speech to emphasize the urgency of their request. The Spartans, however, at this first sitting, answered the speech by saying that they had forgotten the beginning of it, and could not understand the end; so the Samians had to try again. At the second sitting they brought a bag, and merely remarked that the bag needed flour – to which the Spartans replied that the word 'bag' was superfluous. All the same, they decided to grant the request for assistance, and began their pre-parations for the expedition.

The Samians claim that the Spartans undertook the campaign in return for the service they had themselves rendered them in sending ships on a previous occasion to assist them against the Messenians; the Spartans, however, deny that their motive was gratitude: it was not so much the wish to grant the request for help, as the determina-tion to punish the Samians for the theft of the bowl which they had sent to Croesus, and of the corslet, which the Egyptian king Amasis had sent them as a present. The Samians had carried off this corslet in a raid a year before they took the bowl; it was of linen, embroidered with gold thread and cotton, and had a number of figures of animals woven into the fabric. The most remarkable thing about it was that each fine thread of which the material was woven was made up of three hundred and sixty separate strands, all distinctly visible. Similar to it was the corslet which Amasis presented to the temple of Athene at Lindos.

The Corinthians, too, were very willing to lend help in the ex-pedition against Samos, in revenge for an insult which they had suf-fered at the hands of the Samians a generation before, about the time of the seizure of the bowl. Periander, the son of Cypselus, had sent off to Alyattes at Sardis three hundred boys belonging to the leading families in Corcyra, to be made into eunuchs. The Corinthians in charge touched at Samos on the way, and the people of the island, when they heard why the boys were being taken to Sardis, told them to take refuge in a temple of Artemis and refused to allow the Corinthians to drag them away from it. The Corinthians tried to starve them out, but the Samians were too clever for them: they im-provised a festival (it is still celebrated in the original way) in which every night during the whole period that the boys remained as sup-pliants, they organized dances close to the temple, and the dancers – boys and young girls – carried cakes made of millet-seed and honey, which they let the Corcyraean boys snatch as they passed, and so get enough to eat to keep them alive. This went on until the Corinthian guards got tired of it and left the island, leaving behind the boys, who were afterwards taken by the Samians back home to Corcyra.

If, after the death of Periander, relations between Corinth and Corcyra had been friendly, the Corinthians would never, on account of this incident, have taken part in the expedition against Samos; but the fact is that ever since the original settlement of the island the two peoples have been on bad terms; so the incident was remembered and the Corinthians bore the Samians a grudge for it. Periander had chosen the boys from amongst the leading families in Corcyra, and sent them to Sardis for eunuchs in revenge for a brutal crime by which the Corcyraeans had started the quarrel. Periander had murdered his wife Melissa; and another misfortune was to follow. He had two sons by Melissa, one seventeen years old, the other eighteen, and these young men, after their mother's death, were sent for by Procles, who was their maternal grandfather and lord of Epidaurus. Procles treated them with all the kindness due to his daughter's children, and when the time came for them to say goodbye, he accompanied them a part of the way, and asked them if they knew who had killed their mother. The elder of the two took no notice of this question, but the younger, whose name was Lycophron, was profoundly disturbed – so much so, indeed, that when he was back in Corinth, convinced that his father was his mother's murderer, he refused to greet him, or answer his questions, or to have any talk with him whatever. This went on until Periander, in a rage, turned him out of the house. Then he asked his other son, the elder, what it was that their grandfather had said to them. The young man described the kindly welcome they had received; but as to what Procles had said at the moment of bidding them goodbye, he had quite forgotten it – it had gone in at one ear and out of the other. Periander, however, was not satisfied; he continued to press his questions, saying it was quite impossible that this was all, and that Procles must have given them some hint or other, until at last the young man remembered what it was, and told him. Periander thought this over, and, having no intention of relenting his harshness, sent a message to the people with whom his younger son was staying and forbade them to keep him in their house. So once more Lycophron was turned out, and had to find another refuge, when the same thing happened again, Periander commanding his hosts, upon pain of his displeasure, to shut their doors against him. In this way the boy was driven from one friend's house to another's, and each family in turn, in spite of their fear of the consequences, took him in on the strength of his being Periander's son, until at last Periander made a proclamation to the effect that anyone who gave the boy shelter, or even spoke to him, should be fined a certain sum, the money to be dedicated to the service of Apollo. This was enough to make everyone refuse to talk to him or let him into the house, and even Lycophron himself did not think that he ought to attempt to break the prohibition, but made the best of a bad job and found what shelter he could by lying on the ground under the porticoes. Four days later Periander saw him; he was dirty and hungry, and the father's heart melted at the sight. Going up to him, he said: 'Which is better, my son – the wretched condition you are now in, or the prospect of inheriting the wealth and power which I enjoy, merely on the condition of obeying me, your father? You are my son and I am king of the rich city of Corinth; but in spite of that you have chosen a beggar's life, because you set yourself up in resistance and resentment against the one person you least ought to treat in such a way. If anything unfortunate has occurred to make you suspect me, remember that I am a sufferer from it as well as you – indeed more than you, because it was I who caused it. It is much more agreeable to be the object of envy than of pity, and you now know the consequence of being angry with one's parents and one's betters – so go back home.' Lycophron's only answer to this attempt to win him over was to tell his father that he owed the fine to Apollo, for having spoken to him. Then, realizing that the boy's trouble was desperate and incurable, Periander put him aboard ship and sent him away out of his sight to Corcyra, which was also a part of his dominions. Having got rid of Lycophron, Periander made war against his father-in-law Procles, as the chief cause of his present difficulties. He captured Epidaurus, and took Procles himself prisoner.

Time passed, and when Periander was an old man and no longer felt himself equal to the task of managing his affairs, he sent to Corcyra to invite Lycophron to return to Corinth and take over the sovereign power, passing over his elder son, who seemed to him a dull-witted fellow without any sort of ability. Lycophron, however, did not deign even to answer the messenger: so Periander, who was now very anxious to be reconciled to him, sent his daughter, the boy's sister, to plead with him, in the belief that he would be more likely to listen to her than to anyone else. 'Brother,' she said, 'would you rather see our father's power pass into strange hands, and the family fortune's broken up than come back to Corinth and enjoy them yourself? Stop punishing yourself, and come home with me. Obstinacy never got a man anywhere. Do not to try to cure one evil by another. Many think that mercy is a better thing than justice, and many a man, too, by pushing his mother's claims has thrown away his father's fortune. Power is a slippery thing, and has never lacked lovers to woo it. Our father is an old man now and far past his prime. Take then what belongs to you, and keep it – do not abandon it to strangers.' Periander had told the girl to use these arguments, as most likely to influence her brother; but his only reply was that he would never return to Corinth while he knew that his father was still alive. Periander, when he heard of it, made a third and last effort: he sent a messenger to say that he was willing to come to Corcyra himself, if his son would return to Corinth and there take over the government of the state. To this Lycophron agreed, and each began his preparations for leaving – Periander for Corcyra, Lycophron for Corinth; but the Corcyraeans, when they got wind of what was happening, murdered the young man in order to keep Periander away. It was for this deed that Periander took his vengeance on them.

The Lacedaemonians arrived with a powerful force and laid siege to Samos. In an assault on the defences they fought their way forward to the tower near the sea, on the side of the town where the suburbs are, but Polycrates brought a strong party to meet the threat and drove them off. At the upper tower on the ridge which joins on to the high ground, the mercenaries and many of the Samians sallied out, and for a short time held the attack; but they were soon forced to retreat, and the Lacedaemonians followed up their advantage and killed many of them. If all the Lacedaemonians that day had shown the spirit of Archias and Lycopes, Samos would have fallen; for these two men, unsupported by any of their companions, pressed forward upon the retreating Samians and entered the town with them, where they were cut off and killed. I myself once met at Pitana – his native village – the grandson of this Archias; he bore the same name, and was the son of Samius and grandson of the original Archias, and professed a greater admiration for the Samians than for any other foreigners. He told me his father had been called Samius in memory of his grandfather's heroic death in Samos, and his respect for the Samians was due to the fact that they had honoured his grandfather with a public funeral.

After an unsuccessful siege of forty days the Lacedaemonians returned to the Peloponnese. A foolish story got about that Polycrates coined a large amount of the local money in lead, which he then gilded, and offered to buy them off with it; they took it – and that was the reason for their departure. This was the first military expedition to Asia undertaken by the Dorians of Lacedaemon.

The Samians who had fought against Polycrates, seeing that the Lacedaemonians were about to leave them in the lurch, also abandoned the campaign and sailed to Siphnos. They were in need of money, and the Siphnians at that time were at the height of their prosperity; they were richer than any other of the island peoples, having gold and silver mines so productive that a tenth part of their output was enough to furnish a treasury at Delphi not inferior in value to the most splendid to be found there.[1] The remainder of the yield was shared out each year amongst the islanders themselves. When they began depositing money in their treasury at Delphi, they asked the oracle if it was possible that their present prosperity could last for any length of time, and the Priestess gave them the following answer:

> When the council-chamber in Siphnos shines white,
> And white too is the forehead of the market-place,
> Then is there need of a man of foresight to beware.
> Danger threatens from a wooden host and a scarlet messenger.

Now it was a fact that at that time the council-chamber and market-place in Siphnos had recently been adorned with Parian marble. The islanders could make nothing of the oracle, either when it was given, or later when the Samians came; for as soon as they arrived off the

1. Its opulent productions may still be seen in the museum.

island, they sent one of their ships to the city with a delegation on board. Here, then, was the explanation of the oracle: all ships in the old days had their topsides painted scarlet – so that was what the Priestess meant when she warned the Siphnians to beware of a 'wooden host and a scarlet messenger'.

On their arrival the Samian envoys asked the Siphnians to lend them ten talents, and, the request being refused, set about harrying the country. The Siphnians at once came out in force to save their crops, but got the worst of it, and many of them were cut off from the town. The Samians then exacted a hundred talents. With this money the Samians bought from the Hermionians the island of Hydrea, off the Peloponnese, and handed it over in trust to the people of Troezen, while they themselves went on to Crete where they founded the city of Cydonia. Their object, when they sailed, was not to settle in Crete, but to drive out the Zacynthians from their islands; settle, however, they did, and enjoyed five years of great prosperity in the island. It was they who built the temples, including the shrine of Dictyna, which are still to be seen in Cydonia. But in the sixth year they were attacked by the Aeginetans, who with the help of the Cretans beat them in an engagement at sea and reduced them to slavery. They sawed off the boars' heads which the Samian ships carried on their prows, and laid them up in the temple of Athene in Aegina. The attack was made to pay off an old score; for some time previously, when Amphicrates was king of Samos, the Samians had attacked Aegina and inflicted great damage on the island – though not without suffering heavy loss themselves.

I have dwelt longer upon the history of the Samians than I should otherwise have done, because they are responsible for three of the greatest building and engineering feats in the Greek world: the first is a tunnel nearly a mile long, eight feet wide and eight feet high, driven clean through the base of a hill nine hundred feet in height. The whole length of it carries a second cutting thirty feet deep and three broad, along which water from an abundant source is led through pipes into the town. This was the work of a Megarian named Eupalinus, son of Naustrophus. Secondly, there is the artificial harbour enclosed by a breakwater, which runs out into twenty fathoms of water and has a total length of over a quarter of a mile;

and, last, the island has the biggest of all known Greek temples. The first architect of it was Rhoecus, son of Phileus, a Samian. These three works seemed to me sufficiently important to justify a rather full account of the history of the island.

Cambyses, son of Cyrus, after going out of his mind, still lingered on in Egypt; and while he was there, two brothers, who belonged to the caste of the Magi, rose in rebellion against him at home. One of them – Patizeithes – had been left by Cambyses as controller of his household during his absence, and this was the one who planned the revolt. Aware that Smerdis was dead, but that his death was concealed from all but a few of the Persians, most of whom believed that he was still alive, he took advantage of this state of affairs to make a bid for the throne. The brother, whom I have already mentioned as his confederate, bore a close resemblance to Cyrus' son Smerdis, Cambyses' murdered brother. Besides the physical likeness, it also happened that he bore the same name. Patizeithes having persuaded this brother of his that he would successfully carry the business through, made him take his seat upon the royal throne, and then sent out a proclamation to the troops, not only throughout Persia but also in Egypt, that they should take their orders in future not from Cambyses but from Smerdis. The proclamation was duly published; and the herald who was instructed to take it to Egypt happened to find Cambyses and his army at Ecbatana in Syria. Here he took his stand before the assembled troops and proclaimed the new order. When Cambyses got to know of it, he at once supposed that what the herald said was true and that Prexaspes, whom he had sent to Persia to get rid of Smerdis, had failed to do so, and betrayed him. He looked at Prexaspes and said: 'So that is the way you carried out my orders!'

'Master,' Prexaspes replied, 'this is a lie. Your brother Smerdis has not rebelled against you, and you will never again have cause of quarrel with him, big or little. I did what you told me to do, and buried him with my own hands. If dead men rise from their graves, you may believe, if you will, that Astyages the Mede may return to fight against you; but if the course of nature continues unchanged, I can promise you that from Smerdis at least you will never have anything more to fear. My advice to you is, that we catch this herald and examine him, to find out who it was that sent him with this order to obey King Smerdis.'

Cambyses agreed, and a party was at once sent in pursuit of the herald. When he was brought in, Prexaspes said to him: 'You claim to have come with a message from Smerdis the son of Cyrus; now, my good fellow, if you want to get away safe, you had better tell us the truth – did Smerdis in person give you these orders, or was it one of his subordinates?'

'Since King Cambyses went with the army to Egypt,' the man replied, 'I have never set eyes upon Smerdis the son of Cyrus. It was the Magus, whom Cambyses made steward of his household, who gave me my instructions; but he said it was on the authority of Smerdis that I was to give the message which I have.' This statement was perfectly true. Cambyses then said: 'Prexaspes, you have carried out my orders like an honest man, and no blame attaches to you; but tell me – who can it be who has assumed Smerdis' name and risen in revolt against me?'

'I think, my lord,' he replied, 'that I understand what has happened: the rebels are the two Magi – Patizeithes, whom you left in control of your household, and his brother Smerdis.'

The moment Cambyses heard the name, he was struck with the truth of what Prexaspes had said, and realized that his dream of how somebody told him that Smerdis was sitting on the throne with his head touching the sky, had been fulfilled. It was clear to him now that the murder of his brother had been all to no purpose; he lamented his loss, and at last, in bitterness and anger at the whole miserable set of circumstances, he leapt upon his horse, meaning to march with all speed to Susa and attack the Magus. But as he was springing into the saddle, the cap fell off the sheath of his sword, exposing the blade, which pierced his thigh – just in the spot where he had previously struck Apis the sacred Egyptian bull. Believing the wound to be mortal, Cambyses asked what the name of the town was, and was told it was Ecbatana. There had been a prophecy from the oracle at Buto that he would die at Ecbatana; and he had supposed that to mean the Median Ecbatana, his capital city, where he would die in old age. But, as it turned out, the oracle meant Ecbatana in Syria. After the mention of the name, the double shock of his wound and of Patizeithes' rebellion brought him back to his senses. The meaning of the oracle became clear, and he said: 'Here it is fated that Cambyses, son of Cyrus, should die.' At the moment he said nothing more; but some twenty days later he sent for the leading Persians who were present with the army and addressed them in the following words: 'Men of Persia, circumstances compel me to reveal to you something which I have done my utmost to conceal. When I was in Egypt I had a dream – and would that I had never dreamt it! The dream was, that a messenger from Persia came to tell me that Smerdis was sitting on my throne and that his head touched the sky. Fearing my brother would rob me of the crown, I acted with more haste than judgement – for I now realize that it is not in human power to avert what is destined to be. In my folly I sent Prexaspes to Susa to kill Smerdis. The dreadful deed was done, and I lived without fear, never imagining that when Smerdis was dead another man would rise against me. Failing to grasp the true nature of what was in store for me, I murdered my brother for nothing, and have lost my kingdom just the same. It was Smerdis the Magus, not my brother, of whose rebellion God warned me in my dream. Well – I did the deed, and you may be sure you will never see Smerdis the son of Cyrus again. You have the two Magi to rule you now: Patizeithes, whom I left in control of my household, and his brother Smerdis. The one man who of all others should have helped me against the shameful plot of the two Magi, has come to a horrid end at the hands of those nearest and dearest to him. But since he is dead, I must do that next best thing and tell you with my last breath what I would wish you to do. In the name of the gods who watch over our royal house, the command I lay upon all of you, and especially upon those of the Achaemenidae who are here present, is this: do not allow the dominion to pass again into the hands of the Medes. If they have won it by treachery, with the same weapon take it from them; if by force, then play the man and by force recover it. If you do as I bid you, I pray that the earth may be fruitful for you, your wives bear you children, your flocks multiply and freedom be yours for ever: but if you fail to recover, or make no attempt to recover, the sovereign power, then my curse be upon you – may your fate be just the opposite, and, in addition to that, may every Persian perish as miserably as I.' Having said this, Cambyses bitterly lamented the cruelty of his lot, and when the Persians saw the king in tears, they tore their clothes, and showed their sympathy by a great deal of crying and groaning. Shortly afterwards gangrene and mortification of the thigh set in, and Cambyses died, after a reign in all of seven years and five months. He had no children, either sons or daughters.

The Persians who were with Cambyses at his death found it difficult to believe that the Magi had seized power; it seemed to them much more likely that Cambyses' story about the death of Smerdis was a malicious invention designed to set the whole of Persia against him. They were convinced that it was Smerdis the son of Cyrus who was on the throne – and all the more so because Prexaspes vehemently denied the murder, knowing, as he did, that it would be dangerous, now that Cambyses was gone, to admit that a son of Cyrus had died by his hand. The result was that the Magus, after assuming the name of Smerdis, son of Cyrus, found himself securely on the throne, and continued there for the seven months which were needed to make up the eighth year of Cambyses. During this time his subjects received great benefits from him, and he was regretted after his death by all the Asiatics under his rule, except by the Persians themselves, for to every nation within his dominion he proclaimed, directly he came to the throne, a three years' remission of taxes and military service. But after seven months of power, the following circumstances led to his exposure.

The first person to suspect that he was not the son of Cyrus, but an impostor, was a certain Otanes, the son of Pharnaspes, one of the wealthiest members of the Persian nobility, and his suspicions were aroused by the fact that Smerdis never ventured outside the central fortifications of the capital, and never summoned any eminent Persians to a private audience.

Now when the Magus usurped the throne, he took over all Cambyses' wives, amongst whom there was a daughter of Otanes called Phaidime. Otanes, to test the truth of his suspicions, sent a message to this daughter, and asked her who it was she slept with – Smerdis the son of Cyrus, or some other man. She replied that she did not know; she had never seen Smerdis the son of Cyrus, and had no idea who her husband was. Otanes sent a second message: 'If,' it ran, 'you do not yourself know Smerdis the son of Cyrus, ask Atossa who it is with whom you both live. She can hardly fail to know her own brother.' Phaidime replied: 'I have no means of speaking to Atossa, nor of seeing any other of the king's wives; for as soon as this man, whoever he may be, came to the throne, he separated us and gave us all different quarters.' This was a further indication of the truth of what Otanes suspected, so he sent a third message to his daughter. 'Phaidime,' he wrote, 'you have noble blood in your veins, and must not shrink from any danger your father asks you to face. If your husband is the man I think he is, and not the son of Cyrus, he must not get away with sharing your bed and sitting on the throne of Persia. He must be punished. This, then, is what you must do: next time he spends the night with you, wait till you are sure he is asleep and then feel for his ears. If you find that he has got ears, consider yourself the wife of Smerdis, son of Cyrus; but if he has none, then you will know you are married to Smerdis the Magus.' Phaidime answered that it would be an extremely risky thing to do; for if her husband proved to have no ears, and she were caught feeling for them, he would be certain to kill her. Nevertheless she was willing to take the risk. Now when Cyrus was on the throne he had punished Smerdis the Magus for some serious crime by having his ears cut off.

Phaidime, then, kept the promise she had made to her father Otanes; when her turn came to sleep with the Magus (in Persia a man's wives share his bed in rotation), she entered the bedroom, lay down, and then, as soon as the Magus was soundly asleep, felt for his ears. She quickly satisfied herself that he had not got any; so next morning she lost no time in letting her father know the result of the experiment. Otanes took into his confidence Aspathines and Gobryas, two eminent Persians whom he had special reason to trust, and told them of his discovery. Both these men already had their suspicions of the truth, and were ready enough, in consequence, to accept what Otanes said, and it was then agreed that each of the three should choose his most trustworthy friend and bring him in as an accomplice. Otanes chose Intaphrenes, Gobryas Megabyzus, and Aspathines Hydarnes. The number of conspirators was thus raised to six, and on the arrival at Susa from Persia of Darius, whose father Hystaspes was governor there, it was decided to add him to the number.

The seven conspirators now met to pledge loyalty to one another and discuss the measures they were to take. When it was Darius' turn to express his views, he said that he had supposed himself to be the only person who knew that Smerdis the son of Cyrus was dead, and that the present king was the Magus. 'And for that very reason,' he went on, 'I hurried to Susa in order to arrange to get rid of him. Now, as it turns out that I am not the only one in the secret, my opinion is that we should act promptly. There would be nothing but danger in delay.'

Otanes answered: 'You are the son of a brave father, Darius, and seem likely to prove as good a man as he; nevertheless I advise you not to be rash or in too much of a hurry. What we need is prudence – and we must add to our number before we strike the blow.'

'Listen, all of you,' Darius replied; 'if you take Otanes' advice, the result will be ruin for everyone. Somebody is sure to seek advantage for himself by betraying us to the Magus. You ought really to have done this thing entirely on your own; but as you have seen fit to let others in on it, and have communicated your intentions to me, I have only one thing to say – let us act immediately. If we let a single day slip by, I promise you one thing: nobody will have time to be-tray *me* – for I will myself denounce you all to the Magus.'

Otanes was alarmed by the passionate urgency of Darius. 'I see,' he said, 'that you are determined to rush this business through, and will not allow us a moment's delay for deliberation. But can you tell us how to get into the palace to make our attack? Doubtless you know as well as we do that there are guards everywhere; even if you haven't seen them, you have surely heard of them. How are we to get past?'

'Otanes,' Darius answered, 'there are many occasions when words are useless, and only deeds will make a man's meaning plain; often enough, too, it is easy to talk – and only to talk, for no brave act fol-lows. You know there will be no difficulty in passing the guards. Who will dare to refuse admission to men of our rank and distinction, if not from respect, then from fear of the consequences? Besides, I have a perfect excuse for getting us in: I will say I have just come from Persia and have a message from my father for the king. If a lie is necessary, why not speak it? We are all after the same thing, whether we lie or speak the truth: our own advantage. Men lie when they think to profit by deception, and tell the truth for the same reason – to get something they want, and to be the better trusted for their honesty. It is only two different roads to the same goal. Were there no question of advantage, the honest man would be as likely to lie as the liar is, and the liar would tell the truth as readily as the honest man. Any sentry who lets us through without question, will be rewarded later; anyone who tries to stop us must be treated instantly as an enemy. We must force our way past him and set to work at once.'

'Friends,' said Gobryas, 'will there ever be a better moment than now to save the throne – or, if we fail, to die in the attempt? Are Persians to be ruled by a Mede – a Magus – a fellow who has had his ears chopped off? Those of you who stood by the deathbed of Cambyses are not likely to forget his dying curse upon the Persians who should make no effort to save the throne. We took it lightly then – thinking Cambyses was speaking slander. But now the situation has changed, and I propose that we follow Darius' advice, and break up the meeting for no other purpose than to march straight to the palace and attack the Magus.' All the conspirators agreed to this proposal.

While this discussion was in progress, events had been taking place elsewhere. The two Magi had been thinking things over and had decided to take Prexaspes into their confidence. There were several reasons for this decision: first, Prexaspes had been cruelly treated by Cambyses, who shot his son dead; then, as he had been directly responsible for the murder of Smerdis the son of Cyrus, he was the only person in the secret of his death; and, lastly, he was highly respected in Persian society. They summoned him therefore to their presence and began to bargain for his support; they tried to get from him a promise upon oath never to say a word to anybody about the hoax they had practised upon the Persians, and offered to pay him enormous sums as the price of his silence. Prexaspes agreed, whereupon the Magi made the further proposal that they should themselves call upon all the Persians to meet at the base of the palace wall, and that Prexaspes should proclaim, from the top of a tower, that the king was none other than Smerdis the son of Cyrus. In giving Prexaspes these instructions, the Magi relied on the fact that the Persians would be more likely to believe him than anyone else, seeing that he had frequently denied the murder and expressed the opinion that Smerdis was still alive. Again Prexaspes agreed; so the Magi summoned the people to assemble, and told Prexaspes to climb to the top of the tower and make his declaration. But then Prexaspes, deliberately ignoring everything which the Magi had asked him to say, made a speech in which he traced the genealogy of Cyrus right back from Achaemenes, went on to describe the great services which Cyrus had rendered to his country, and finally revealed the true state of affairs, adding that he had concealed it hitherto out of regard to his own safety, but that the time had now come when it was no longer possible to hold his tongue. He kept back nothing; he himself, he said, had been forced by Cambyses to kill Smerdis the son of Cyrus, and the country was now in the power of the two Magi. Finally, with a prayer that the Persians might suffer untold misery if they did not recover the throne and punish the usurpers, he threw himself headlong from the tower to the ground. Such was the end of Prexaspes, who throughout his life had been a man of high distinction.

Meanwhile the seven conspirators, having reached their decision to attack the Magi without a moment's delay, had prayed for luck and were on their way to the palace. They knew nothing about the affair of Prexaspes, and were half-way there before they learnt the truth. The news pulled them up, for they thought it advisable to discuss this new element in the situation. The supporters of Otanes urged delay and the risk of making their attempt until things calmed down again; but Darius and his party were still for immediate action and opposed to any change of plan. The argument was growing hot, when they suddenly saw seven pairs of hawks chasing two pairs of vultures, which they tore at, as they flew, with both beak and claw. It was an omen; forthwith the plan of Darius was unanimously accepted, and with renewed confidence the seven men hurried on towards the palace. When they reached the gates, everything turned out just as Darius had foreseen: the sentries, out of respect for their exalted rank and having no suspicion of the real purpose of their visit, allowed them to pass without question – almost as if they were under the special protection of heaven. In the great court, however, they were met by some of the eunuchs – the king's messengers – who stopped them and asked their business, at the same time threatening the guards for having let them through. The check was momentary; eager to press on, the seven, with a word of mutual encouragement, drew their daggers, stabbed the eunuchs who were trying to hold them up, and ran forward into the hall.

Both the Magi were at this time indoors, discussing the situation which had been brought about by Prexaspes' treachery. They heard the eunuchs crying out in evident alarm, and sprang up to see what the matter was; then, realizing their danger, they at once prepared to fight it out. One just had time to get his bow down, the other seized his spear. The one with the bow had no chance to use it – the fight was at much too close quarters; the other, however, used his spear to advantage, keeping off his attackers and wounding Aspathines in the leg, and Intaphrenes in the eye – Intaphrenes, as a result of the wound, lost his eye but survived. His companion, unable to use his bow and finding himself defenceless, ran into a bedroom, which opened out of the hall, and tried to shut the doors on his pursuers; but two of them, Darius and Gobryas, managed to force their way in with him, and Gobryas got his arms round the Magus. It was dark in the room, and Darius, standing over the two men locked together on the floor, hesitated to intervene; for he was afraid that, if he struck, he might kill the wrong man. But Gobryas, aware of his hesitation, cried out: 'What's your hand for – if you don't use it?'

'I dare not strike,' said Darius, 'for fear of killing you.'

'Fear nothing,' answered Gobryas; 'spit both of us at once – if need be.'

Darius then drove his dagger home – by good luck into the body of the Magus.

When both the Magi had been killed, the confederates decapitated them, and ran out into the street, shouting and making a great noise, with the severed heads in their hands. The two wounded men had been left behind in the palace, being too weak to move – they were needed, moreover, to keep a watch upon the citadel. Once outside, the five who were unhurt appealed to their fellow citizens, told them what had happened, and showed them the heads – and then set about murdering every Magus they came across. The other Persians, once they had learnt of the exploit of the seven confederates, and understood the hoax which the two brothers had practised on them, were soon ready to follow their example: they, too, drew their daggers and killed every Magus they could find – so that if darkness had not put an end to the slaughter, the whole tribe would have been exterminated. The anniversary of this day has become a red-letter day in the Persian calendar, marked by an important festival known as the Magophonia, or Killing of the Magi, during which no Magus is allowed to show himself – every member of the tribe stays indoors till the day is over.

Five days later, when the excitement had died down, the conspirators met to discuss the situation in detail. At the meeting certain speeches were made – some of our own countrymen refuse to believe they were actually made at all; nevertheless they were.[1] The first speaker was Otanes, and his theme was to recommend the establishment in Persia of democratic government. 'I think,' he said, 'that the time has passed for any one man amongst us to have absolute power. Monarchy is neither pleasant nor good. You know to what lengths the pride of power carried Cambyses, and you have personal experience of the effect of the same thing in the conduct of the Magus. How can one fit monarchy into any sound system of ethics, when it allows a man to do whatever he likes without any responsibility or control? Even the best of men raised to such a position would be bound to change for the worse – he could not possibly see things as he used to do. The typical vices of a monarch are envy and pride; envy, because it is a natural human weakness, and pride, because excessive wealth and power lead to the delusion that he is something more than a man. These two vices are the root cause of all wickedness: both lead to acts of savage and unnatural violence. Absolute power ought, by rights, to preclude envy on the principle that the man who possesses it has also at command everything he could wish for; but in fact it is not

1. The speeches that follow, totally Greek in tone – and interesting, as the earliest extant of the many *Greek* arguments on forms of government – are obviously fantastic. Herodotus' contemporary critics were right, and if we wish to pillory him as a liar, this is the strongest ground. If we wish to believe in his honesty, we must suppose that he had the substance of the speeches from someone whom he trusted. But it is not totally impossible that the Persians, who were not far in time from tribal life, may have considered abolishing the despotic monarchy as they had seen it under Cambyses.

so, as the behaviour of kings to their subjects proves: they are jealous of the best of them merely for continuing to live, and take pleasure in the worst; and no one is readier than a king to listen to tale-bearers. A king, again, is the most inconsistent of men; show him reasonable respect, and he is angry because you do not abase yourself before his majesty; abase yourself, and he hates you for being a toady. But the worst of all remains to be said – he breaks up the structure of ancient tradition and law, forces women to serve his pleasure, and puts men to death without trial. Contrast with this the rule of the people: first, it has the finest of all names to describe it – equality under law; and, secondly, the people in power do none of the things that monarchs do. Under a government of the people a magistrate is appointed by lot and is held responsible for his conduct in office, and all questions are put up for open debate. For these reasons I propose that we do away with the monarchy, and raise the people to power; for the state and the people are synonymous terms.'

Otanes was followed by Megabyzus, who recommended the principle of oligarchy in the following words: 'In so far as Otanes spoke in favour of abolishing monarchy, I agree with him; but he is wrong in asking us to transfer political power to the people. The masses are a feckless lot – nowhere will you find more ignorance or irresponsibility or violence. It would be an intolerable thing to escape the murderous caprice of a king, only to be caught by the equally wanton brutality of the rabble. A king does at least act consciously and deliberately; but the mob does not. Indeed how should it, when it has never been taught what is right and proper, and has no knowledge of its own about such things? The masses have not a thought in their heads; all they can do is to rush blindly into politics like a river in flood. As for the people, then, let them govern Persia's enemies; but let us ourselves choose a certain number of the best men in the country, and give *them* political power. We personally shall be amongst them, and it is only natural to suppose that the best men will produce the best policy.'

Darius was the third to speak. 'I support,' he said, 'all Megabyzus' remarks about the masses but I do not agree with what he said of oligarchy. Take the three forms of government we are considering – democracy, oligarchy, and monarchy – and suppose each of them to

be the best of its kind; I maintain that the third is greatly preferable
to the other two. One ruler: it is impossible to improve upon that –
provided he is the best. His judgement will be in keeping with his
character; his control of the people will be beyond reproach; his
measures against enemies and traitors will be kept secret more easily
than under other forms of government. In an oligarchy, the fact that
a number of men are competing for distinction in the public service
cannot but lead to violent personal feuds; each of them wants to get
to the top, and to see his own proposals carried; so they quarrel. Personal quarrels lead to open dissension, and then to bloodshed; and
from that state of affairs the only way out is a return to monarchy – a
clear proof that monarchy is best. Again, in a democracy, malprac-
tices are bound to occur; in this case, however, corrupt dealings in
government services lead not to private feuds, but to close personal
associations, the men responsible for them putting their heads together and mutually supporting one another. And so it goes on, until
somebody or other comes forward as the people's champion and
breaks up the cliques which are out for their own interests. This wins
him the admiration of the mob, and as a result he soon finds himself
entrusted with absolute power – all of which is another proof that
the best form of government is monarchy. To sum up: where did we
get our freedom from, and who gave it us? Is it the result of democracy, or of oligarchy, or of monarchy? We were set free by one man,
and therefore I propose that we should preserve that form of government, and, further, that we should refrain from changing ancient
laws, which have served us well in the past. To do so would lead only
to disaster.'

These were the three views set out in the three speeches, and the
four men who had not spoken voted for the last. Otanes (who had
urged equality before the law), finding the decision against him, then
made another speech. 'My friends,' he said, 'it is clear that the king
will have to be one of ourselves, whether we draw lots for it, or ask
the people of Persia to make their choice between us, or use some
other method. I will not compete with you for the crown, for I have
no wish to rule – or to *be* ruled either. I withdraw, therefore, upon
one condition: that neither I myself, nor any of my descendants,
shall be forced to submit to the rule of that one of you, whoever he

is, who becomes king.' The other six agreed to this condition, and Otanes stood down. To this day the family of Otanes continues to be the only free family in Persia, and submits to the king only so far as the members of it may choose, while not disobeying the laws of the Persians.

The other six then discussed the fairest way of deciding who should have the throne. They agreed that, if it fell to any of themselves, Otanes and his descendants should receive, every year, a suit of Median clothes and such other gifts as are held to be of most value by the Persians, as a mark of honour for the part he had played in the plot against the Magi, of which he was the prime mover and principal organizer. These privileges were for Otanes only; they also agreed upon another to be shared by all: permission, namely, for any of the seven to enter the royal presence unannounced, except when the king was in bed with a woman. They further agreed that the king should not marry outside the families of the seven confederates. To choose which should be king, they proposed to mount their horses on the outskirts of the city, and he whose horse neighed first after the sun was up should have the throne.

Darius had a clever groom called Oebares. After the meeting had broken up, he went to see this fellow, and told him of the arrangement they had come to, whereby they should sit on their horses' backs and the throne should be given to the one whose horse neighed first as the sun rose. 'So if,' he added, 'you can think of some dodge or other, do what you can to see that this prize falls to me, and to no one else.'

'Well, master,' Oebares answered, 'if your chance of winning the throne depends upon nothing but that, you may set your mind at rest; you may be perfectly confident – you, and nobody else, will be king. I know a charm which will just suit our purpose.'

'If,' said Darius, 'you really have got something which will do the trick, you had better hurry and get it all worked out, for to-morrow is the day.'

Oebares, accordingly, as soon as it was dark, took from the stables the mare which Darius' horse was particularly fond of, and tied her up on the outskirts of the city. Then he brought along the stallion and led him round and round the mare, getting closer and closer in narrowing circles, and finally allowed him to mount her. Next morning just before dawn the six men, according to their agreement, came riding on their horses through the city suburb, and when they reached the spot where the mare had been tethered on the previous night, Darius' horse started forward and neighed. At the same instant, though the sky was clear, there was a flash of lightning and a clap of thunder: it was a sign from heaven; the election of Darius was assured, and the other five leapt from their saddles and bowed to the ground at his feet.

That is one account of how Oebares made the horse neigh. The Persians also have another, namely that he rubbed the mare's genitals and then kept his hand covered inside his breeches. When the sun was rising and the horses were about to be released, he drew his hand out and put it to the nostrils of Darius' horse, which at the smell of the mare at once snorted and neighed.

In this way Darius became king of Persia. Following the conquests of Cyrus and Cambyses, his dominion extended over the whole of Asia, with the exception of Arabia. The Arabs had never been reduced to subjection by the Persians, but friendly relations had continued between the two countries ever since the Arabs let Cambyses pass through their territory on his Egyptian campaign; for without this service the invasion of Egypt would have been impracticable.

The first women Darius married were Cyrus' two daughters Atossa and Artystone; the former had previously been the wife of her brother Cambyses and also of the Magus; the latter was a virgin. Subsequently he married Parmys, a daughter of Cyrus' son Smerdis, and, in addition to these, the daughter of Otanes, the man who had exposed the Magus.

Now that his power was felt in every corner of his dominions, his first act was to erect a stone monument with a carving of a man on horseback, and the following inscription: *Darius, son of Hystaspes, by the virtue of his horse and of his groom Oebares, won the throne of Persia.* The horse's name was included. This was in Persia; he then proceeded to set up twenty provincial governorships, called satrapies. The several governors were appointed and each nation assessed for taxes; for administrative purposes neighbouring nations were joined in a single unit; outlying peoples were considered to belong to this nation or that, according to convenience.

Before I record the amount of the annual tribute paid by the various provinces, I should mention that those who paid in silver were instructed to use the Babylonian talent as the measure of weight, while the Euboean talent was the standard for gold – the Babylonian being worth 1⅙ of the Euboean. During the reigns of Cyrus and Cambyses there was no fixed tribute at all, the revenue coming from gifts only; and because of his imposition of regular taxes, and other similar measures, the Persians have a saying that Darius was a tradesman, Cambyses a tyrant, and Cyrus a father – the first being out for profit wherever he could get it, the second harsh and careless of his subjects' interests, and the third, Cyrus, in the kindness of his heart always occupied with plans for their well-being.

Now for the account of the tribute paid by the twenty provinces:

First: The Ionians, the Magnesians in Asia, the Aeolians, Carians, Lycians, Milyans, and Pamphylians contributed together a total sum of 400 talents of silver.

Second: the Mysians, Lydians, Lasonians, Cabalians, and Hytennians, 500 talents.

Third: the people on the southern shore of the Hellespont, the Phrygians, the Thracians of Asia, the Paphlagonians, Mariandynians, and Syrians, 360 talents.

Fourth: the Cilicians paid 500 talents of silver, together with 360 white horses (one for each day in the year); of the money, 140 talents were used to maintain the cavalry force which guarded Cilicia, and the remaining 360 went to Darius.

Fifth: from the town of Posidium, which was founded by Amphilochus, son of Amphiaraus, on the border between Cilicia and Syria, as far as Egypt – omitting Arabian territory, which was free of tax – came 350 talents. This province contains the whole of Phoenicia and that part of Syria which is called Palestine, and Cyprus.

Sixth: Egypt, together with the Libyans on the border and the towns of Cyrene and Barca (both included in the province of Egypt) paid 700 talents, in addition to the money from the fish in Lake Moeris, and the 120,000 bushels of corn allowed to the Persian troops and their auxiliaries who were stationed in the White Castle at Memphis.

Seventh: the Sattagydians, Gandarians, Dadicae, and Aparytae paid a joint tax of 170 talents.

Eighth: Susa, with the rest of Cissia – 300 talents.

Ninth: Babylon and Assyria – 1000 talents of silver and 500 eunuch boys.

Tenth: Ecbatana and the rest of Media, with the Paricanians and Orthocorybantes – 450 talents.

Eleventh: Caspians, Pausicae, Pantimathi, and Daritae – a joint sum of 200 talents.

Twelfth: the Bactrians and their neighbours as far as the Aegli – 360 talents.

Thirteenth: Pactyica, together with the Armenians and their neighbours as far as the Black Sea – 400 talents.

Fourteenth: the Sagartians, Sarangians, Thamanaeans, Utians, Myci, together with the inhabitants of the islands in the Persian gulf where the king sends prisoners and others displaced from their homes in war – 600 talents.

Fifteenth: the Sacae and Caspians – 250 talents.

Sixteenth: the Parthians, Chorasmians, Sogdians, and Arians – 390 talents.

Seventeenth: the Paricanians and Asiatic Ethiopians – 400 talents.

Eighteenth: the Matienians, Saspires, and Alarodians – 200 talents.

Nineteenth: the Moschi, Tibareni, Macrones, Mosynoeci, and Mares – 300 talents.

Twentieth: the Indians, the most populous nation in the known world, paid the largest sum: 360 talents of gold-dust.

If the Babylonian talents here referred to are reduced to the Euboean scale, they will make a total of 9880; and if gold is reckoned at thirteen times the value of silver, the Indian gold-dust will be found to amount to 4680 talents. Thus the grand total of Darius' annual revenue comes to 14,560 Euboean talents – omitting the odd ones.

This was the revenue derived from Asia and a few parts of Libya; but as time went on, more came in from the islands and from the peoples in Europe as far as Thessaly. The method adopted by the Persian kings of storing their treasure is to melt the metal and pour it into earthenware jars; the jar is then chipped off, leaving the solid metal. When the money is wanted, the necessary amount is coined for the occasion.

That completes the list of provinces, with the amounts they had to contribute in taxation. The one country I have not mentioned as paying taxes is Persia herself – for she does not pay any. A few peoples upon whom no regular tax was imposed made a contribution in the form of gifts; the Ethiopians, for instance, on the Egyptian border; these people were subdued by Cambyses during his campaign against Ethiopia proper – the 'long-lived' Ethiopians – and occupy the country round about the sacred mountain of Nysa, and hold festivals in honour of Dionysus. The grain which they and their next neighbours use is the same as that used by the Calantian Indians – and they live underground. Every second year these two nations brought – and still bring to-day – about two quarts of unrefined gold, two hundred logs of ebony, and twenty elephant tusks. Again, a voluntary contribution was undertaken by the Colchians and the neighbouring tribes between them and the Caucasus the limit of the empire in this direction, everything to the northward being outside the range of Persian influence. In their case the contribution consisted (and still does) in the gift, every fourth year, of a hundred boys and a hundred girls. Lastly, the Arabians brought a thousand talents of frankincense every year. This, then, was the revenue which the king received over and above what was produced by regular taxation.

I will say something of the method by which the Indians get their large supplies of gold, which enable them to bring to Persia the gold-dust I have already mentioned. Eastward of India lies a desert of sand; indeed of all the inhabitants of Asia of whom we have any reliable information, the Indians are the most easterly – beyond them the country is uninhabitable desert. There are many tribes of Indians, speaking different languages, some pastoral and nomadic, others not. Some live in the marsh-country by the river and eat raw fish, which they catch from boats made of reeds – each boat made from a single joint. The people of this tribe make their clothes from a sort of rush which grows in the river, gathering it and beating it out, and then weaving it into a kind of matting which they wear to cover their chests, like a breastplate. Another tribe further to the east is nomadic, known as the Padaei; they live on raw meat. Among their customs, it is said that when a man falls sick, his closest companions kill him, because, as they put it, their meat would be spoilt if he were allowed to waste away with disease. The invalid, in these circumstances, protests that there is nothing the matter with him – but to no purpose. His friends refuse to accept his protestations, kill him and hold a banquet. Should the sufferer be a woman, her woman friends deal with her in the same way. If anyone is lucky enough to live to an advanced age, he is offered in sacrifice before the banquet – this, however, rarely happens, because most of them will have had some disease or other before they get old, and will consequently have been killed by their friends.

There is another tribe which behaves very differently: they will not take life in any form; they sow no seed, and have no houses and live on a vegetable diet. There is a plant which grows wild in their country, and has seeds in a pod about the size of millet seeds; they gather this, and boil and eat it, pod and all. In this tribe, a sick man will leave his friends and go away to some deserted spot to die – and nobody gives a thought either to his illness or death.

All the Indian tribes I have mentioned copulate in the open like cattle; their skins are all of the same colour, much like the Ethiopians'. Their semen is not white like other peoples', but black like their own skins – the same peculiarity is to be found in the Ethiopians. Their country is a long way from Persia towards the south, and they were never subject to Darius.

There are other Indians further north, round the city of Caspatyrus and in the country of Pactyica, who in their mode of life resemble the Bactrians. These are the most warlike of the Indian tribes, and it is they who go out to fetch the gold – for in this region there is a sandy desert. There is found in this desert a kind of ant of great size – bigger than a fox, though not so big as a dog. Some specimens, which were caught there, are kept at the palace of the Persian king. These creatures as they burrow underground throw up the sand in heaps, just as our own ants throw up the earth, and they are very like ours in shape. The sand has a rich content of gold, and this it is that the Indians are after when they make their expeditions into the desert. Each man harnesses three camels abreast, a female, on which he rides, in the middle, and a male on each side in a leading-rein, and takes care that the female is one who has as recently as possible dropped her young. Their camels are as fast as horses, and much more powerful carriers. There is no need for me to describe the camel, for the Greeks are familiar with what it looks like; one thing, however, I will mention, which will be news to them: the camel in its hind legs has four thighs and four knees, and its genitals point backwards towards its tail. That, then, is how these Indians equip themselves for the expedition, and they plan their time-table so as actually to get their hands on the gold during the hottest part of the day, when the heat will have driven the ants underground. In this part of the world the sun is not, as it is elsewhere, hottest at noon, but in the morning: from dawn, that is, until closing-time in the market. During this part of the day the heat is much fiercer than it is at noon in Greece, and the natives are said to soak themselves in water to make it endurable. At midday the heat diminishes and is much the same here as elsewhere, and, as the afternoon goes on, it becomes about equal to what one finds in other countries in the early morning. Towards evening it grows cooler and cooler, until at sunset it is really cold.

When the Indians reach the place where the gold is, they fill the bags they have brought with them with sand, and start for home again as fast as they can go; for the ants (if we may believe the Persians' story) smell them and at once give chase; nothing in the world can touch these ants for speed, so not one of the Indians would get home alive, if they did not make sure of a good start while the ants were mustering their forces. The male camels, who are slower movers than the females, soon begin to drag and are left behind, one after the other, while the females are kept going hard by the memory of their young, who were left at home.

According to the Persians, most of the gold is got in the way I have described; they also mine a certain quantity – but not so much – within their own territory.

It would seem to be a fact that the remotest parts of the world have the finest products, whereas Greece has far the best and most temperate climate. The most easterly country in the inhabited world is, as I said just now, India; and here both animals and birds are much bigger than elsewhere – if we except the Indian horse, which is inferior in size to the Median breed known as the Nisaean. Gold, too,

is found here in immense quantity, either mined, or washed down
by rivers, or stolen from the ants in the manner I have described; and
there are trees growing wild which produce a kind of wool better
than sheep's wool in beauty and quality, which the Indians use for
making their clothes. Again, the most southerly country is Arabia;
and Arabia is the only place that produces frankincense, myrrh, cassia,
cinnamon, and the gum called ledanon. All these, except the myrrh,
cause the Arabians a lot of trouble to collect. When they gather
frankincense, they burn storax (the gum which is brought into Greece
by the Phoenicians) in order to raise a smoke to drive off the flying
snakes; these snakes, the same which attempt to invade Egypt, are
small in size and of various colours, and great numbers of them keep
guard over all the trees which bear the frankincense, and the only
way to get rid of them is by smoking them out with storax. The
Arabians say that the whole world would swarm with these creatures
were it not for a certain peculiar fact – the same thing, incidentally,
as keeps down the spread of adders. And indeed it is hard to avoid the
belief that divine providence, in the wisdom that one would expect
of it, has made prolific every kind of creature which is timid and
preyed upon by others, in order to ensure its continuance, while
savage and noxious species are comparatively unproductive. Hares,
for instance, which are the prey of all sorts of animals, not to mention
birds and men, are excessively prolific; they are the only animals in
which superfetation occurs, and you will find in a hare's womb young
in all stages of development, some with fur on, others with none,
others just beginning to form, and others, again, barely conceived. A
lioness, on the contrary, the most bold and powerful of beasts, produces but a single cub, once in her life – for she expels from her body
not only the cub, but her womb as well – or what is left of it. The
reason for this is that when the unborn cub begins to stir, he scratches
at the walls of the womb with his claws, which are sharper than any
other animal's, and as he grows bigger scrabbles his way further and
further through them until, by the time he is about to be born, the
womb is almost wholly destroyed. In the same way, if adders and
the Arabian flying snakes were able to replace themselves naturally,
it would be impossible for men to live. Fortunately, however, they
are not; for when they couple, the female seizes the male by the neck

at the very moment of the release of the sperm, and hangs on until she has bitten it through. That finishes the male; and the female, too, has to pay for her behaviour, for the young in her belly avenge their father by gnawing at her insides, until they end by eating their way out. Other species of snakes, which are harmless to men, lay eggs and hatch out their young in large numbers. The reason why flying snakes seem so numerous in Arabia is that they are all concentrated in that country – you will not find them anywhere else, whereas adders are common all over the world.

When the Arabians go out to collect cassia, they cover their bodies and faces, all but their eyes, with ox-hides and other skins. The plant grows in a shallow lake which, together with the ground round about it, is infested by winged creatures like bats, which screech alarmingly and are very pugnacious. They have to be kept from attacking the men's eyes while they are cutting the cassia. The process of collecting cinnamon is still more remarkable. Where it comes from and what country produces it, they do not know; the best some of them can do is to make a fair guess that it grows somewhere in the region where Dionysus was brought up. What they say is that the dry sticks, which we have learnt from the Phoenicians to call cinnamon, are brought by large birds, which carry them to their nests, made of mud, on mountain precipices, which no man can climb, and that the method the Arabians have invented for getting hold of them is to cut up the bodies of dead oxen, or donkeys, or other animals into very large joints, which they carry to the spot in question and leave on the ground near the nests. They then retire to a safe distance and the birds fly down and carry off the joints of meat to their nests, which, not being strong enough to bear the weight, break and fall to the ground. Then the men come along and pick up the cinnamon, which is subsequently exported to other countries. Still more surprising is the way of getting ledanon – or ladanon, as the Arabians call it. Sweet-smelling substance though it is, it is found in a most malodorous place; sticking, namely, like glue in the beards of he-goats who have been browsing amongst the bushes. It is used as an ingredient in many kinds of perfume, and is what the Arabians chiefly burn as incense.

So much for the perfumes: let me only add that the whole country exhales a more than earthly fragrance. One other thing is remarkable enough to deserve a mention – the sheep. There are two kinds, such as are found nowhere else: one kind has such long tails – not less than 4½ feet – that if they were allowed to trail on the ground, they would develop sores from the constant friction; so to obviate this, the shepherds have devised the art of making little carts of wood, and fix one of them under the tail of each sheep. The other kind have flat tails, eighteen inches broad.

The furthest inhabited country towards the south-west is Ethiopia; here gold is found in great abundance, and huge elephants, and ebony, and all sorts of trees growing wild; the men, too, are the tallest in the world, the best-looking, and longest-lived.

So much for the countries at the furthest limits of Asia and Libya. About the far west of Europe I have no definite information, for I cannot accept the story of a river called by non-Greek peoples the Eridanus, which flows into the northern sea, where amber is supposed to come from; nor do I know anything of the existence of islands caled the Tin Islands, whence we get our tin. In the first place, the name Eridanus is obviously not foreign but Greek, and was invented by some poet or other; and, secondly, in spite of my efforts to do so, I have never found anyone who could give me first-hand information of the existence of a sea beyond Europe to the north and west. Yet it cannot be disputed that tin and amber do come to us from what one might call the ends of the earth. It is clear that it is the northern parts of Europe which are richest in gold, but how it is procured is another mystery. The story goes that the one-eyed Arimaspians steal it from the griffins who guard it; personally, however, I refuse to believe in one-eyed men who in other respects are like the rest of us. In any case it does seem to be true that the countries which lie on the circumference of the inhabited world produce the things which we believe to be most rare and beautiful.

There is a plain in Asia surrounded by a ring of hills, which are broken by clefts in five separate places. This tract of land used to belong to the Chorasmians and lies on the boundaries of five different tribes: the Chorasmians themselves, the Hyrcanians, the Parthians, the Sarangians, and the Thamanaeans; but ever since the Persian rise to power it has been the property of the Persian king. In the ring of hills a considerable river rises – the Aces – which used to supply

water to the five tribes I have mentioned, being split into five channels and flowing out to each of them through a different gorge;
now, however, that the Persians are masters of the country, all these
people find themselves in a serious difficulty, for the king has blocked
up the gorges and constructed sluice-gates to contain the flow of
water, so that what used to be a plain has now become a large lake,
the river flowing in as before but no longer having any means of
egress. The result of this for the people who depended upon the use
of the water, but are now deprived of it, has been disastrous. In winter,
to be sure, they get rain like anyone else, but they need the river
water when they are sowing their millet and sesame in the summer.
When therefore they find themselves waterless, they go in a body
with their wives to the Persians, and stand howling in front of the
gates of the king's palace, until the king gives orders to open the
sluices and allow the water to flow to whichever tribe it may be that
needs it most. Then, when the land has drunk all the water it wants,
the sluices are shut, and the king orders others to be opened in turn,
according to the needs of the remaining tribes. I am told he opens the
sluices only upon receipt of a heavy payment over and above the
regular tax.

Soon after the rising of the seven Persians against the Magus, one of
their number, Intaphrenes, was executed for a failure to show proper
respect to the king's authority. Having business to transact with
Darius, he wished to enter the palace. Now it had already been agreed
that any of the conspirators might visit the king unannounced, provided that he was not, at the moment, in bed with a woman; and in
view of this Intaphrenes refused to have his name sent in by a messenger, and claimed it as his right, as one of the seven, to walk straight in.
He was, however, stopped by the king's chamberlain and the sentry
on duty at the palace gate, who told him that Darius had, in fact, a
woman with him at the time. Thinking this was only a trumped-up
excuse to keep him out, Intaphrenes drew his scimitar and cut off
their ears and noses, strung them on his horse's bridle, tied the bridle
round their necks, and sent them packing. The poor fellows showed
themselves to Darius and explained the reason for their plight, which
at once suggested to the king the alarming possibility of a fresh con-

spiracy. Thinking his six former confederates might all be in this business together, he sent for each of them in turn, and sounded them to see if they approved of what Intaphrenes had done. None of them did; so as soon as he was satisfied that Intaphrenes had acted entirely on his own initiative, he had him arrrested with his children and all his near relations, in the strong suspicion that he and his family were about to raise a revolt. All the prisoners were then chained, as condemned criminals. After his arrest, Intaphrenes' wife came to the palace and began to weep and lament outside the door, and continued so long to do so that Darius, moved to pity by her incessant tears, sent someone out to speak to her. 'Lady,' the message ran, 'the king is willing to spare the life of one member of your family – choose which of the prisoners you wish to save.' Having thought this offer over, the woman answered that, if the king granted her the life of one only of her family, she would choose her brother. The answer surprised Darius, and he sent again and asked why it was that she rejected her husband and children, and preferred to save her brother, who was neither so near to her as her children, nor so dear as her husband. 'My lord,' she replied, 'God willing, I may get another husband, and other children when these are gone. But as my father and mother are both dead, I can never possibly have another brother. That was the reason for what I said.' Darius appreciated the lady's good sense, and, to mark his pleasure, granted her not only the life she asked, but also that of her eldest son. The rest of the family were all put to death. This, then, was the early end of one of the seven confederates.

About the time of Cambyses' last sickness the following events occurred. A Persian called Oroetes who had been appointed by Cyrus governor of Sardis, conceived a purpose of peculiar barbarity – the murder of Polycrates of Samos. He was determined to capture and kill him, in spite of the fact that he had never received any injury at his hands, either by word or deed, and had never even met him in person. This outrage is generally supposed to have been the result of a quarrel between Oroetes and another Persian named Mitrobates, governor of the province of Dascyleium. The two men, the story goes, were sitting near the palace entrance, engaged in talk; their talk grew heated, and they were soon quarrelling over the question of

which of them was the better man, when Mitrobates said with a
sneer: 'What? You call yourself a man, when you have neglected to
add Samos to the king's dominions, though it lies so near your province
and is so easy to subdue? Why, one of the islanders with fifteen soldiers at his back raised a revolt and took it, and is now master there.'
Oroetes was stung by this reproach; but instead of having his revenge
upon the man who uttered it, he conceived the desire of removing the
cause of it by destroying Polycrates.

According to another account, less generally accepted, Oroetes sent
a messenger to Samos to make some request or other (what it was is
not stated), and on his arrival Polycrates was at table in the hall with
Anacreon, the poet of Teos. It so happened that Polycrates sat facing
the wall of the room with his back to the man as he came forward to
say what he had to say; and – either to show his contempt for Oroetes'
power, or perhaps merely by chance – he not only omitted to give an
answer, but did not even bother to turn round while the messenger
was speaking. Both stories are told to account for Polycrates' death
and the reader may take his choice between them.

However, when Oroetes was living at Magnesia on the Maeander,
he had already got to know of the design which Polycrates had in
mind – for Polycrates was the first Greek we know of to plan the
dominion of the sea, unless we count Minos of Cnossus and any
other who may possibly have ruled the sea at a still earlier date. In
ordinary human history at any rate, Polycrates was the first; and he
had high hopes of making himself master of Ionia and the islands.
Knowing, then, of Polycrates' ambition, Oroetes sent a Lydian
named Myrsus, the son of Gyges, to Samos with a message to the
following effect: 'I understand, Polycrates, that you have an important enterprise in mind, but your resources are not equal to your designs. I have a proposal to make which, if you adopt it, will ensure
your success – and my own safety, for it is clear from reports I have
received that Cambyses is plotting my death. Come, then, and get me
out of the country; I promise you a share in everything I possess, and
that will give you money enough to get control of the whole of
Greece. If you have any doubts about my wealth, send whoever it is
you most trust, and I will show him what I have.' Polycrates, who
was very fond of money, was delighted by this proposal and did not

hesitate to accept it. He sent his secretary, a Samian called Maeandrius, son of a father of the same name, to see if Oroetes' claim was true – it was Maeandrius who not long afterwards sent as an offering to the temple of Hera the magnificent furniture from Polycrates' hall. Oroetes, however, as soon as he knew that someone was actually on the way and must shortly be expected to come and view his treasure, filled eight chests with stones very nearly to the brim, topped them up with a thin layer of gold, fastened them securely and kept them ready for inspection. Maeandrius arrived, saw the gold, and returned with his report to Polycrates.

In spite of many attempts by his friends and by professional soothsayers to dissuade him, Polycrates now prepared to visit Oroetes in person. His daughter, too, did her best to stop him; for she had dreamt she saw her father hanging in the air, washed by Zeus and anointed by the sun-god Helios, and the dream had frightened her so much that she would have done anything in the world to prevent her father from going to Oroetes; and she did, in fact, follow him to the ship with words prophetic of disaster. Polycrates, however, in irritation, merely threatened that, if he got home safely, he would delay her marriage for many years – to which she answered that she prayed the threat might be fulfilled, for she would rather be a maiden all her life than lose her father. But all warnings were lost upon Polycrates; taking with him a number of friends, amongst whom was Democedes of Crotona, the son of Calliphon, and the most distinguished physician of his day, he sailed for Magnesia, where he met an end in dreadful contrast with his personal distinction and high ambition. For apart from the lords of Syracuse, no other petty king in the Greek world can be compared with Polycrates for magnificence. Somehow or other – the precise manner need not be told – Oroetes had him murdered, and the dead body hung on a cross. Of the men who accompanied him, Oroetes let the Samians go, and told them they could be grateful to him for their freedom; the rest, who were either foreigners or slaves, he reckoned as prisoners of war and detained.

The dream of Polycrates' daughter was thus fulfilled by his crucifixion; when rain fell he was 'washed by Zeus', and he was 'anointed by Helios' when under the sun's heat the moisture was sweated out from his body. This, then, was the end of the long-continued prosperity of Polycrates: it was just as Amasis, king of Egypt, had previously foretold.

It was not long before Oroetes had to pay for this murder. After the death of Cambyses, and throughout the period when Persia was controlled by the Magi, he had lived in Sardis and offered no help to his countrymen in resisting the Median usurpation. He had, moreover, during these unsettled times, procured the death of Mitrobates, the governor of Dascyleium, who had taunted him about Polycrates, and of Mitrobates' son Cranaspes, both distinguished Persians. Nor were these two murders by any means his only acts of violence; he also, for instance, made away with one of Darius' couriers; the man had come with a message which was not to Oroetes' taste, so he sent a party to waylay him on his return journey. He was killed, and neither his body, nor that of his horse, was ever discovered. Darius, once his power was established, was anxious to punish Oroetes for his many crimes, and not least for the murder of Mitrobates and his son. He thought it would be unwise, things being as they were, to send an armed force openly against him; for the country was still in an unsettled state; he himself had only recently come to the throne, and he knew that Oroetes was a powerful man, being governor of Phrygia, Lydia, and Ionia, with a thousand Persians in his bodyguard. Darius had recourse, in consequence, to subtler methods, and called a meeting of the leading men in the country, whom he addressed in the following words: 'It is my wish, gentlemen, that one of you should undertake on my behalf a matter which calls for tact rather than the combined force of numbers. Force is always beside the point when subtlety will serve. Which of you will kill Oroetes for me, or bring him to me alive? He is a man who has never yet lifted a finger to help his country: on the contrary, he has done us grave disservice. He has made away with two of our friends, Mitrobates and his son; and now he kills my own messengers whom I send to summon him. This is a defiance of authority which is not to be tolerated. Before he can do us further harm, he must be stopped, by death.'

Thirty of the company who were present competed so hotly for the privilege of undertaking this service, that Darius was forced to make them draw lots, to stop the argument. This they did, and the lucky man proved to be Bagaeus, the son of Artontes, who at once set about having a number of documents prepared on various subjects, which he sealed with the king's seal, and took with him to Sardis. Here he called upon Oroetes, and in his presence opened the papers one by one, handing them to the king's secretary (an officer who forms part of every governor's establishment), with instructions to read them aloud. His object in this was to test the loyalty of Oroetes' bodyguard in case they might be willing to act against their master. When, therefore, he noticed that they regarded the documents with respect – and, still more, the words they heard read from them – he passed one to the secretary which contained an order, purporting to come from Darius, to the effect that the guards were to refuse service to Oroetes. The order was read out, and the guards promptly laid their spears at Bagaeus' feet. Then Bagaeus, seeing the written order obeyed, ventured to hand to the secretary the paper he had reserved till last. This contained the words: 'King Darius commands the Persians in Sardis to kill Oroetes.' The guards immediately drew their scimitars, and despatched him – and that was how Oroetes the Persian was punished for his betrayal of Polycrates.

Soon after Oroetes' money had been confiscated and conveyed to Susa, Darius was out hunting and happened to twist his foot as he dismounted from his horse. The injury was serious, the ankle being actually dislocated. It had been his custom for some time to keep in attendance certain Egyptian doctors, who had a reputation for the highest eminence in their profession, and these men he now consulted. But in their efforts to reduce the joint, they wrenched the foot so clumsily that they only made matters worse. For seven days and nights Darius was unable to sleep for pain, and was very ill; on the eighth day, however, being informed about the skill of Democedes of Crotona by someone who had previously heard of him in Sardis, he ordered him to be fetched immediately. The man was found in a neglected condition amongst Oroetes' slaves, and brought to the palace just as he was, dressed in rags and dragging his chains. When he came into the royal presence and Darius asked him if he understood the art of medicine, he replied that he did not, for he was afraid that if he declared himself he would never be allowed to return home to Greece. Darius, however, was not deceived; realizing that

Democedes was concealing his knowledge, he told the men who had brought him to fetch the whips and the iron spikes. This was enough to force an admission – up to a point; for Democedes still maintained that he had no thorough medical knowledge, but had merely acquired a smattering of it by living with a doctor. All the same, Darius put himself in his hands, and Democedes, by using Greek methods and substituting milder remedies for the rough-and-ready treatment of the Egyptian doctors, enabled the king to get some sleep, and very soon cured him completely. Darius, who had never expected to be able to use his foot again, presented him with two sets of gold chains, a gift which caused Democedes to ask if the king was determined to double his sufferings as a reward for the cure he had effected. This amused Darius, who thereupon sent him off to visit his wives, and when the eunuchs who conducted him to their apartments told them that this was the man who had saved the king's life, they each scooped a cupful of gold coins from a chest and gave them to Democedes. There was such a lot of the money that a servant called Sciton, by picking up the coins which spilt over the cups, managed to collect quite a fortune.

Democedes had left Crotona and gone to live with Polycrates in order to escape from his father, who was a man of savage temper. Unable to bear the treatment he received, he cleared out and went first to Aegina, where within a year he proved himself the best doctor in the island, in spite of the fact that he had no equipment or surgical instruments. In the second year of his residence the Aeginetans gave him a state appointment at a salary of a talent; a year later the Athenians employed him at a salary of 100 *minae*; and a year after that Polycrates offered him two talents; and that was how he came to Samos. It was chiefly because of Democedes' success that Crotoniate doctors came to have such a high reputation. Darius' accident happened during the period when the physicians of Crotona were considered the best in Greece, and those of Cyrene the next best. During the same period the Argives were considered the best musicians.

After his successful treatment of Darius, Democedes lived in a large house in Susa, took his meals at the king's table, and enjoyed every privilege but one – the liberty of returning to Greece. The Egyptian doctors who had tried to cure Darius in the first place were about to be impaled as a punishment for being outdone by a Greek; but so great was Democedes' influence with the king, that they were let off as a result of his intercession in their favour; and – another instance of his power – he procured the release of a professional soothsayer from Elis, who had gone with Polycrates and was lying neglected amongst his slaves. He stood very high with the king.

But the story of Democedes is not yet by any means finished. Shortly after this Atossa, the daughter of Cyrus and wife of Darius, developed on her breast an abscess, which later burst and began to spread. Shame had induced her to conceal it, and to say nothing about it to anyone, while it was still small; but when it got worse and she found herself dangerously ill, she sent for Democedes and let him see it. He said he could cure her, but before he did so he made her swear to do him in return any service he might choose to ask, adding that he would not ask for anything she could blush to give. On these terms he treated the abscess, effected a cure, and told the queen what he wished her to do. Then when in bed with Darius she began the following conversation: 'My lord, with the immense resources at your command, the fact that you are making no further conquests to increase the power of Persia, must mean that you lack ambition. Surely a young man like you, who is master of great wealth, should be seen engaged in some active enterprise, to show the Persians that they have a man to rule them. Indeed, there are two reasons for ending this inactivity: for not only will the Persians know their leader to be a man, but, if you make war, you will waste their strength and leave them no leisure to plot against you. Now is the time for action, while you are young; for as the body grows in strength, so does the mind; but as the years pass and the body weakens, the mind ages too and loses its edge.'

This, of course, was what Democedes had instructed Atossa to say; and Darius replied: 'What you have said is precisely what I intend to do. I have already decided to bridge the straits between Asia and Europe, and attack the Scythians. You will not have long to wait before it is done.'

'Never mind about the Scythians for the moment,' Atossa went on; 'they are yours for the asking at any moment you please. Look – what I want you to do is to invade Greece. I have heard people talk of the women there, and I should like to have Spartan girls, and girls from Argos and Attica and Corinth, to wait upon me. You have a man better fitted than anyone in the world to give you full information about Greece and to act as guide – I mean the doctor who cured your foot.'

'Lady,' Darius answered, 'as you think Greece should be my first objective, I had better begin by sending a party of Persians over to Greece to reconnoitre, together with the man you mentioned. They can then bring me back a full report of everything they see and hear. After that, when I have the information I need, I will begin the war.'

It was no sooner said than done. At dawn the next morning he sent for fifteen Persians, all men of distinction, and gave them instructions to cruise along the Greek coast, taking Democedes with them to show them the way. He added a strict order that Democedes should not be allowed to escape, but should be brought back at all costs. He then summoned Democedes himself, and begged him to give the reconnoitring party such guidance and information as they needed, and afterwards to return to Persia. He told him to take all his household furniture with him and make a present of it to his father and brothers, promising to replace it at double its value when he came back, and adding a further offer of a merchant vessel which should sail in company with them, loaded with valuable goods.

I do not myself believe that Darius' motive, when he made these promises, was anything but genuine and straightforward; Democedes, however, was afraid he might be laying a trap to make him reveal his true intentions, so instead of accepting with open arms everything Darius offered, he said he would leave his property where it was, to await his return to claim it; the ship, however, and its cargo, which Darius wished to give as a present to his brothers, he was willing to take.

Democedes and the Persians, having received their orders from Darius, were now sent down to the coast. At Sidon in Phoenicia they lost no time in fitting out two warships, and a merchant vessel which they loaded with a rich assortment of goods; then, when all was ready for sea, they got under way for Greece, made a written record of the results of a careful survey of most of the notable features of the coast, and finally arrived at Tarentum in Italy. Here Aristophilides, who was in control of the town, showed himself a good friend to Democedes by getting the steering-gear removed from the Persian ships, and the Persians themselves arrested as spies, so that while they were under restraint Democedes was able to get away to Crotona. Once he was safe home, Aristophilides released his prisoners and restored the gear he had taken from the ships, whereupon they put to sea in pursuit of Democedes, found him in the market-place at Crotona, and laid hands on him. Some of the people in the town were prepared to give him up through fear of Persia; but others took his part, and setting about his captors with their sticks, did their best to drag him away. The Persians tried to scare them by pointing out that the man they wanted to save was a runaway slave of Darius. 'Do you realize what you are doing?' they cried. 'Do you suppose the king will be content to submit to this high-handed treatment? What good will it do you, if you take this fellow from us? Won't your city be the first objective in the war which is bound to ensue – and the first we shall reduce to slavery?' Their threats, however, were of no avail; forced to abandon not only Democedes himself but also the merchant vessel which had accompanied them, they returned to Asia, making no further attempt, now that they had lost their guide, to pursue their survey of the Greek coasts. Just before they left, Democedes told them to let Darius know that he was engaged to be married to the daughter of Milo, the wrestler, whose name was in high esteem at the Persian court. I think myself that Democedes was determined to make this marriage, however much money it cost him, in order to show Darius that he was a man of mark in his own country as well as abroad.

After sailing from Crotona, the Persians were wrecked on the Iapygian coast and taken as slaves, but were afterwards ransomed and brought home to the court of Darius by a man named Gillus, a Tarentine exile. In gratitude for their recovery Darius was willing to grant any request that Gillus might make, and Gillus, after relating the story of his political misfortunes, declared that what he most wished for was to be enabled to return to Tarentum, and added that, to prevent setting Greece by the ears if a powerful armament sailed to Italy on his behalf, he would be quite content to be escorted home by the people of Cnidos only; their help, he thought, would be most likely to ensure the success of his enterprise, as Cnidos and Tarentum were on very friendly terms. Darius complied with his wishes and sent an order to Cnidos for the necessary steps to be taken. The order was obeyed, but the Cnidians failed to induce the people of Tarentum to agree to the exile's return, and were not strong enough to use force.

These Persians of whom I have just written were the first who ever came from Asia to Greece; their object was to collect information, for the reasons I have given.

These events were followed by the capture of Samos, which was the first place, either inside or outside the Greek world, to fall to Darius, and this was why: during the campaign of Cambyses in Egypt, a great many Greeks visited that country for one reason or another: some, as was to be expected, for trade, some to serve in the army, others, no doubt, out of mere curiosity, to see what they could see. Amongst the sightseers was Aeaces' son Syloson, the exiled brother of Polycrates of Samos. While he was in Egypt, Syloson had an extraordinary stroke of luck: he was hanging about the streets of Memphis dressed in a flame-coloured cloak, when Darius, who at that time was a member of Cambyses' guard and not yet of any particular importance, happened to catch sight of him and, seized with a sudden longing to possess the cloak, came up to Syloson and made him an offer for it. His extreme anxiety to get it was obvious enough to Syloson, who was inspired to say: 'I am not selling this for any money, but if you must have it, I will give it to you free.' Darius thereupon thanked him warmly and took it. Syloson at the moment merely thought he had lost it by his foolish good-nature; then came the death of Cambyses and the revolt of the seven against the Magus, and Darius ascended the throne. Syloson now had the news that the man, whose request for the flame-coloured cloak he had formerly gratified in Egypt, had become king of Persia. He hurried to Susa, sat down at the entrance of the royal palace, and claimed to be included in the official list of the King's Benefactors. The sentry on guard reported his claim to Darius, who asked in surprise who the man might be. 'For surely,' he said, 'as I have so recently come to the throne, there cannot be any Greek to whom I am indebted for a service. Hardly any of them have been here yet, and I certainly cannot remember owing anything to a Greek. But bring him in all the same, that I may know what he means by this claim.'

The guard escorted Syloson into the royal presence, and when the interpreters asked him who he was and what he had done to justify the statement that he was the king's benefactor, he reminded Darius of the story of the cloak, and said that he was the man who had given it him. 'Sir,' exclaimed Darius, 'you are the most generous of men; for while I was still a person of no power or consequence you gave me a present – small indeed, but deserving then as much gratitude from me as would the most splendid of gifts to-day. I will give you in return more silver and gold than you can count, that you may never regret that you once did a favour to Darius the son of Hystaspes.' 'My lord,' replied Syloson, 'do not give me gold or silver, but recover Samos for me, my native island, which now since Oroetes killed my brother Polycrates is in the hands of one of our servants. Let Samos be your gift to me – but let no man in the island be killed or enslaved.'

Darius consented to Syloson's request, and dispatched a force under the command of Otanes, one of the seven, with orders to do everything that Syloson had asked; and Otanes, accordingly, went down to the coast to make his preparations.

In Samos power was in the hands of Maeandrius, the man whom Polycrates on leaving the island had appointed to attend to his affairs. When he learned of Polycrates' death, he would have liked, had he been allowed, to behave with exemplary regard for justice; but he was not given the chance. His first act was to erect an altar to Zeus the Liberator, and to enclose it in a piece of ground just outside the city, where it is still to be seen; then he called a meeting of all the citizens of Samos and addressed them in the following terms: 'You know as well as I do that the sceptre of Polycrates, and the power it represents, have passed into my hands, so that I may, if I wish, become your absolute master. So far as I am able, however, I shall refrain from doing myself what I should object to in another. I did not approve the conduct of Polycrates, nor should I that of any other man who sought irresponsible power over people as good as himself; therefore, now that Polycrates has met his end, I intend to surrender the power to which I am entitled, and to proclaim you equal before the law. All I claim as a special privilege for myself, is the sum of six talents from Polycrates' fortune, together with the right of keeping for myself and my posterity the priesthood of Zeus the Liberator to whom I built the shrine; I who now offer you your liberty.'

One of his audience, a man of repute named Telesarchus, at once sprang to his feet. 'What?' he cried; 'that's a fine speech to hear from a guttersnipe like you! Far from being fit to govern us, you ought rather to account for the money you have had your hands on.' This was enough to show Maeandrius that, if he surrendered the sovereign power, somebody else would be sure to seize it; so he changed his mind and determined to hold on to what he had got. Withdrawing to the citadel, he sent for each one of the leading men in turn, making out that he intended to show them his accounts, arrested them all, and put them in irons.

Shortly after the arrests Maeandrius fell ill, and his brother Lycaretus thought he was going to die; so in order to facilitate his own seizure of power, he had all the prisoners put to death. So, it seems, the people of Samos did not want liberty.

The result was that when the Persians arrived in Samos to restore the exiled Syloson, nobody lifted a finger against them. Maeandrius and his party professed themselves willing to leave the island upon certain terms, which were agreed to by Otanes; a truce was made, and the Persians of the highest rank then had chairs of state placed for them opposite the citadel, and took their seats upon them.

Now Maeandrius had a crazy brother called Charilaus, who for some fault or other had been shut up in a dungeon; this fellow, hearing what was going on, put his head out through the bars of his prison, and when he saw the Persian grandees peacefully sitting on their chairs of state, he shouted out that he had something which he wanted to say to Maeandrius. Maeandrius, on being told of this, sent word to have his brother taken out of gaol and brought to him. The moment he arrived he began with much violent and abusive language to urge Maeandrius to set upon the Persians. 'What a coward you are!' he exclaimed. 'Here am I, your own brother, who has never done you the least harm, whom you think fit to keep chained up in a dungeon, while you have not spirit enough to punish those foreigners who would throw you out of house and home! Why – you could crush them easily! If you're afraid of them, give me command of the soldiers and I will soon see they get what they deserve for daring to come here. As for you, I am quite willing to see you safely out of the island.'

Maeandrius agreed to his brother's proposal, not, I imagine, because he was foolish enough to think himself able to get the better of the Persian force, but rather out of spite – for he did not relish the idea of Syloson recovering control of the city without any loss or damage, and without even striking a blow. What he wanted was to incense the Persians against Samos, so that he could hand over to Syloson when things were in a state of the greatest possible weakness and confusion, knowing that the Persians would be savage for revenge if they were roughly handled. As for himself, he was sure of getting away safely at any time he wished, by means of a secret tunnel which he had made, leading from the citadel to the sea.

Maeandrius then escaped from Samos on shipboard, and his brother Charilaus armed the soldiers, opened the city gates, and fell upon the unsuspecting Persians, who thought that everything had been peacefully settled. So the leading Persians were killed where they sat. But the rest of the Persian force now came to the rescue, and Charilaus' men, hard pressed, were driven back into the citadel. When Otanes saw the serious loss which the Persians had suffered, he deliberately put out of his mind all memory of the instructions he had received from Darius before the expedition started – that is, not to kill or capture any Samian, but to hand the island over to Syloson intact – and commanded his troops to kill everyone they could catch, boy or man. The order was obeyed; and while some of the Persian force laid siege to the citadel, others began the massacre, killing all they fell in with, inside or outside sacred ground, without discrimination.

After his escape Maeandrius sailed to Lacedaemon, taking with him the various articles of value which he had brought out of the island. Arrived here, he angled for the help of Cleomenes, the son of Anaxandrides, the king of Sparta, in the following way: he would set out gold and silver drinking cups on his table and, while his servants were polishing them, would get into conversation with

Cleomenes and induce him to come to the house. Every time Cleomenes, at the sight of the cups, was struck with admiration and
astonishment, and every time Maeandrius would ask him to take
away as many of them as he pleased. Cleomenes, however, after being subjected two or three times to this temptation, showed a quite
extraordinary sense of propriety and refused to accept the offered
gift. Knowing, moreover, that Maeandrius would be sure to get assistance if he made a similar offer to other Spartans, he went to the
magistrates and said that it would be better for Sparta if the visitor
from Samos left the country, before he succeeded in persuading either
him or some other Spartan to disgrace himself. The suggestion was
accepted, and it was publicly proclaimed that Maeandrius must go.
As for Samos, the Persians took the entire population like fish in a
drag-net, and presented Syloson with an empty island. Some years
later, however, Otanes contracted some sort of disease of the genital
organs and that, in conjunction with a dream he had, induced him to
repopulate the place.

After the Persian fleet had sailed for Samos, Babylon revolted.
The revolt had been long and carefully planned; indeed, preparations
for withstanding a siege had been going quietly on all through the
reign of the Magus and the disturbances which followed the rising of
the seven against him, and somehow or other the secret never leaked
out. When the moment finally came to declare their purpose, the
Babylonians, in order to reduce the consumption of food, herded
together and strangled all the women in the city – each man exempt-
ing only his mother, and one other woman whom he chose out of his
household to bake his bread for him. When the news reached Darius,
he marched against them with all the forces at his disposal, and laid
siege to the city. The Babylonians, however, were unimpressed; they
climbed gaily on to their battlements and hurled insulting jibes at
Darius and his army, calling out: 'What are you sitting there for,
men of Persia? Why don't you go away? Oh yes, you will capture
our city – when mules have foals.'

Now whoever it was who made this last remark, naturally supposed that no mule would ever have a foal.

A year and seven months went by, and Darius and his army began
to chafe at their inability to make any progress towards taking the

city. Every trick of strategy, every possible device, had been tried; but to no purpose. The town could not be taken, not even when Darius, after all else had failed, attempted to repeat the method which Cyrus had previously used with success. The Babylonians were always on the watch with extraordinary vigilance, and gave the enemy no chance.

At last, in the twentieth month of the siege, a marvellous thing happened to Zopyrus, son of the Megabyzus who was one of the seven conspirators who killed the Magus: one of his sumpter-mules foaled. When Zopyrus was told of this, he refused to believe it till he had seen the foal with his own eyes; then, forbidding the others who had seen it to say a word to anyone of what had occurred, he began to think hard, and came to the conclusion that the time had come when Babylon could be taken – for had not that Babylonian, at the beginning of the siege, said that the city would fall when mules foaled? That the man should have used the phrase, and that the miracle should actually have happened – surely that meant that the hand of God was in it.

Convinced, therefore, that Babylon was now doomed to destruction, he went to Darius and asked him if the capture of the city was really of supreme importance to him, and, on being told that it was, set himself to devise a way of bringing it about by his own sole act and initiative; for in Persia any special service to the king is very highly valued. Accordingly he passed in review every scheme he could think of, and finally decided that there was one way only in which he could bring the place under, namely by maiming himself and then going over to the enemy as a deserter. Taking this dreadful expedient as a mere matter of course, he at once put it into practice, and there were no half-measures in the way he set about it: he cut off his nose and ears, shaved his hair like a criminal's, raised weals on his body with a whip, and in this condition presented himself to Darius. Darius was shocked at the sight of a man of Zopyrus' eminence so fearfully mutilated, and springing from his chair with an exclamation of horror, asked who it was that inflicted this punishment upon him, and what Zopyrus had done to deserve it. 'My lord,' Zopyrus answered, 'there is no one but yourself who has power enough to reduce me to this condition. The hands that disfigured me were none other than my own, for I could not bear to hear the Assyrians of Babylon laugh the Persians to scorn.'

'You speak like a madman,' said Darius; 'to say you did this horrible thing because of our enemies in the beleaguered city, is merely to cloak a shameful act in fine words. Are you fool enough to think that the mutilation of your body can hasten our victory? When you did that to yourself, you must have taken leave of your senses.'

'Had I told you of my intention,' Zopyrus answered, 'you would not have allowed me to proceed. So I acted upon my own initiative. And now – if you too will play your part – we will capture Babylon. I will go as I am to the city walls, pretending to be a deserter, and I will tell them that it was you who caused my misery. They will believe me readily enough – and they will put their troops under my command. Now for your part: wait till the tenth day after I enter the town, and then station by the gates of Semiramis a detachment of a thousand men, whose loss will not worry you. Then, seven days later, send 2000 men to the Nineveh gates and, twenty days after that, another 4000 to the Chaldaean gates. None of these three detachments must be armed with anything but their daggers – let them carry daggers only. And then, after a further interval of twenty days, order a general assault upon the city walls from every direction, taking care that our own Persian troops have the sectors opposite the Belian and Cissian gates. It is my belief that the Babylonians, when they see that I have done them good service, will increase my responsibility – even to trusting me with the keys of the gates. And after that – I and the Persians will attend to what must be done.'

Having given these directions to the king, Zopyrus fled towards the gates of Babylon, glancing over his shoulder as he ran, like a deserter in fear of pursuit. When the soldiers on watch saw him, they hurried down from the battlements, and opening one of the gates just a crack, asked him his name and business. Saying he was Zopyrus and had deserted from the Persian army, he was let in, and conducted by the sentries to the magistrates. Here he poured out his tale of woe, pretending that the injuries he had done to himself had been inflicted upon him by Darius, and all because he had advised him to abandon the siege, as there appeared to be no means of ever bringing it to a successful conclusion. 'And now,' he added, 'here I am, men of Babylon; and my coming will be gain to you, but loss – and that the severest – to Darius and his army. He little knows me if he thinks he can get away with the foul things he has done me – moreover, I know all the ins and outs of his plans.'

The Babylonians, seeing a Persian of high rank and distinction in such a state – his nose and ears cut off and his body a mess of blood from the lash of whips – were quick to believe that he spoke the truth and had really come to offer them his services, and in this belief were prepared to give him whatever he asked. At once he asked for the command of some troops, and, when the request was granted, proceeded to put into practice the plan he had arranged with Darius. The tenth day after his arrival he marched his force out of the city, and surrounded and killed the first detachment of a thousand men which he had instructed Darius to send. This was enough to show the Babylonians that his deeds were as good as his words; they were in high glee, and ready to put themselves under his orders in anything he might propose. After waiting, therefore, the agreed number of days, he picked another party from the troops in the city, marched out, and killed the two thousand Persians which Darius had posted by the Nineveh gates. As a result of this second service, the reputation of Zopyrus went up with a jump and his name was on everybody's lips. Then once more, after the agreed interval, he marched his men out through the Chaldaean gates, and surrounded the four thousand. After this achievement Zopyrus was the one and only soldier in Babylon, the city's hero, and was created General in Chief and Guardian of the Wall.

And now Darius, as had been agreed, ordered a general assault upon the walls from every direction – which was the signal for Zopyrus to reveal the full extent of his cunning. Waiting till the Babylonian forces had mounted the battlements to repel Darius' onslaught, he opened the Cissian and Belian gates and let the Persians in. Those of the Babylonians who were near enough to see what had happened, fled to the temple of Bel; the rest remained at their posts until they, too, realized that they had been betrayed.

Thus Babylon was captured for the second time, and Darius after his victory – unlike Cyrus, its previous conqueror – destroyed its defences, pulled down all the city gates, and impaled the leading citizens to the number of about three thousand. The rest he allowed to remain in their homes. I mentioned at the beginning of my account how the Babylonians strangled their women to save food, and it was in consequence of this that Darius, in order to prevent the race from dying out, compelled the neighbouring peoples each to send a certain stated number of women to Babylon. In all, as many as fifty thousand were collected there. It is from these that the present inhabitants are descended.

In the judgement of Darius no Persian surpassed Zopyrus, either before his time or after, as a benefactor of his country, except only Cyrus – with whom nobody in Persia has ever dreamt of comparing himself. We are told that Darius often said that he would rather have Zopyrus without his frightful wounds than twenty more Babylons. He rewarded him with the highest honours, giving him every year the sort of gifts which are most prized amongst the Persians, and, amongst much else, the governorship of Babylon, free from tax, for as long as he lived.

Megabyzus, who held the command in Egypt against the Athenians and their allies, was Zopyrus' son; and the other Zopyrus, who deserted from the Persian army and came to Athens, was the son of Megabyzus.

BOOK FOUR

After the capture of Babylon Darius invaded Scythia. The Scythians, having on a previous occasion invaded and conquered Media, had been, in some sense, the aggressors, and Darius, having an immense revenue in money and an unlimited number of men to draw upon in his Asiatic dominions, found himself anxious to have his revenge. There had been a period of twenty-eight years, as the reader will remember, during which the Scythians were in control of upper Asia after destroying the power of the Medes, its previous masters. They entered the country in pursuit of the Cimmerians, and, on their return home after the long gap of twenty-eight years, found trouble waiting for them hardly less serious than their struggle with the Medes. This was in the shape of a large hostile army, which opposed their entrance; for the Scythian women, wearied with their menfolk's protracted absence, had intermarried with the slaves.

The Scythians blind their slaves, a practice in some way connected with the milk which they prepare for drinking in the following way: they insert a tube made of bone and shaped like a flute into the mare's anus, and blow; and while one blows, another milks. According to them, the object of this is to inflate the mare's veins with air and so cause the udder to be forced down. They make the blind men stand round in a circle, and then pour the milk into wooden casks and stir it; the part which rises to the top is skimmed off, and considered the best; what remains is not supposed to be so good. The reason why they blind their prisoners of war is connected with the fact that the Scythians are not an agricultural people, but nomadic.

From the union of these slaves with the women of Scythia a new generation had grown to manhood, and when they learned the circumstances of their birth they resolved to oppose the return of the army from Media. As a preliminary measure of defence they dug a broad trench from the Tauric mountains to the widest part of Lake Maeotis; then, taking up defensive positions along it, resisted all attempts to force an entrance. Many engagements were fought, but the invading army could make no headway until one of their number thought of a new plan of attack. 'My friends,' he said, 'what we are doing is absurd. In this war with our own slaves we stand to lose both ways, by the casualties we inflict no less than by the casualties we suffer; for the more we kill of them, the fewer we shall have, when we are once again their masters. I propose, therefore, that we should stop using spears and bows, and go for them each one of us with a horse-whip. When they saw us armed, they naturally felt that they were as good as we are, and were meeting us on equal terms; but when they see us coming with whips instead, they will remember they are slaves. Once they admit that, they will never try to stand up to us.'

The Scythians put the plan into action with immediate success; the opposing army was dumbfounded; every man forgot he was a soldier and fled. This, then, is the story of how the Scythians dominated Asia, were expelled by the Medes, and returned to Scythia; and it was to punish them for their original invasion that Darius was now raising an army against them.

The Scythians say that they are the youngest of all nations, and the following is the account they give of their origin. The first man to live in their country, which before his birth was uninhabited, was a certain Targitaus, the son of Zeus and of a daughter of the river Borysthenes – I merely repeat the tradition, and do not myself believe it. Targitaus had three sons, Lipoxais, Arpoxais, and Colaxais, the youngest; and during their reign in Scythia there fell from the sky a golden plough, a golden yoke, a golden battle-axe, and a golden cup. The eldest of the three was the first to see these treasures, and as he went to pick them up the gold caught fire. At this he retired, and the second of the brothers approached; but the gold caught fire and blazed, just as before. Lastly, when the two elder brothers had been kept off by the flames, the youngest came along, and this time the fire went out, so that he was able to pick up the golden imple-ments and carry them home. The elder brothers accepted this as a sign from heaven and made over the whole kingdom to Colaxais.

The descendants of Lipoxais were those Scythians now known as Auchatae; those of the second brother, Arpoxais, are the Catiari and Traspies; those of the youngest brother are the Royal Scythians, now called Paralatae. They are known indiscriminately under the general name of Scoloti, after one of their kings, and the Greeks call them Scythians. Such is the Scythians' account of their origin, and they add that the period from Targitaus, their first king, to Darius' crossing of the Hellespont to attack them, is just a thousand years. The gold which fell from heaven is guarded by the kings with the utmost care, and every year they visit it and offer it magnificent sacrifices. There is a legend in the country that any guardian of the gold who falls asleep in the open air during the festival will die within the year, and because of this the person concerned is given as much land as he can ride round in a day. In view of the great size of Scythia, Colaxais split it up into three separate kingdoms for his sons, making the one where the gold was kept larger than the other two. It is said to be impossible to travel through the region which lies further north, or even to see it, because of falling feathers – both earth and air are thick with them and they shut out the view.

The Greeks of Pontus give a different account of Scythia and the country beyond it. According to them, Heracles came into this part of the world, which was then uninhabited, with the oxen of Geryon. Geryon's home was far away, on an island which the Greeks call Erythea, near Gades, which lies on the Ocean beyond the Pillars of Heracles. Legend says that Ocean is a great river running from the east all round the world; but there is nothing to prove this. When Heracles reached the country which is now Scythia, the weather was bad and it was bitterly cold, so he drew his lion's skin over him and went to sleep. While he slept, the horses which he had unharnessed from his chariot and turned loose to graze mysteriously disappeared. As soon as he awoke Heracles began to look for them, and roamed all over the country until he came at last to a place called Hylaea, or the Woodland, where in a cave he found a viper-maiden – a creature which from the buttocks upwards was a woman, but below them a snake. For a moment he looked at her in astonishment; then asked if she had seen his mares straying around. She replied that they were in her own keeping, and promised to return them to him on condition that he lay with her. Heracles complied. The viper-woman, however, did not at once give him back the mares, but put off the fulfilment of her bargain in order to keep Heracles as long as possible for her lover, though all he wanted himself was to get the horses and go. At last she let him have them, and said: 'I kept these horses safe for you, when I found them here; and you have given me my reward, for I have three sons by you. Now tell me what I am to do with them: when they grow up, shall I settle them here in this country, of which I am mistress, or send them to you?' 'When the boys are grown to be men,' Heracles answered, 'you will not be far wrong if you do what I will now tell you. Whichever of them you find can draw this bow as I do, and put on this girdle in the way I will show you, should be settled here in this country; but any of them who fail to do these two things must be sent away. Do this, and you will not only show proper obedience to me but find happiness for yourself as well.'

Heracles then strung one of his bows – up to that time he always carried two – and showed her how to put on the girdle, after which he put into her hands both bow and girdle, and went away. The girdle had a little gold cup for the tongue of its buckle. When the boys grew up, their mother named the eldest Agathyrsus, the next Gelonus, and the youngest Scythes, and carried out the instructions which she remembered Heracles had given her. Two of the young men, Agathyrsus and Gelonus, failed to accomplish the task assigned them and were therefore banished from the country by their mother; but the youngest brother, Scythes, succeeded and was allowed to remain. In this way Scythes, the son of Heracles, became father of the line of Scythian kings; and to this day the Scythians wear belts with little cups attached, in memory of the belt of their ancestor Heracles. This was the only thing the mother of Scythes did for him.

Besides the story which the Greeks of Pontus tell, there is another which I myself consider the most likely of the three. This relates how the nomadic tribes of Scythians who lived in Asia, being hard pressed by the Massagetae, were forced across the Araxes into Cimmeria (what is now Scythia is said to have been once inhabited by Cimmerians). The Cimmerians could not agree upon what line to take when they saw the hordes of Scythians flooding into their country, but split into two sharply opposed parties, the Princes – or Royal

Tribe – on the one side, and the rest of the people on the other. Each party urged its view with equal insistence, the people maintaining that the proper course was to clear out without risking an engagement against so powerful an invader, the princes – more courageously – calling upon everyone to make a stand and fight for their country. Neither party, however, could win the other's acceptance of its view, so the one decided to take to its heels and surrender the country to the invader without a blow, while the other, the princes, remembering the blessings they had enjoyed in the past, and imagining the misery they must expect to suffer if they left their homes, refused to accompany the fugitives and preferred to die where they were and be buried in the earth which belonged to them. Accordingly they divided themselves into two equal bodies, and fought until every man of them was dead. The people buried them by the river Hyras, where their tomb may still be seen, and then left the country, so that when the Scythians entered soon afterwards to take possession they found it uninhabited. There are still traces of the Cimmerians in Scythia: one finds, for instance, remains of fortifications, a Cimmerian strait, a Cimmerian Bosphorus, and a tract of land called Cimmeria.

It is clear that the Cimmerians entered Asia to escape the Scythians, and built settlements on the peninsula where the Greek town of Sinope now stands; and there is no doubt that the reason why the Scythians in the course of their pursuit entered Median territory was that they took the wrong route by mistake; for whereas the Cimmerians kept along the coast, the Scythians took the inland road, keeping the Causcasus on their right, until they found themselves in Media. These facts are admitted by Greeks and Asians alike.

More information about this part of the world is to be found in a poem by Aristeas, son of Caÿstrobius, a native of Marmora island. He tells us that 'inspired by Phoebus' he journeyed to the country of the Issedones, and that beyond the Issedones live the one-eyed Arimaspians, and beyond them the griffins which guard the gold, and beyond the griffins the Hyperboreans, whose land comes down to the sea. All these, except the Hyperboreans, were continually encroaching upon one another's territory, beginning with the Arimaspians, so that the Issedones were expelled by the Arimaspians, the Scythians by the Issedones, and the Cimmerians by the Scythians, who forced them from their homes along the shores of the Black Sea. Here, then, is further evidence against the Scythians' account of this region.

I have mentioned the birthplace of Aristeas, the author of this poem; now here is a story I heard about him in Marmora and Cyzicus. He belonged to one of the first families in his home town, and one day, upon entering a fuller's shop, he fell down dead. The fuller closed his shop and hurried out to inform his relatives of what had occurred, but no sooner had the news of Aristeas' death got about, than a person from Cyzicus, who had just arrived from the town of Artaca, contradicted the rumour and declared that he had met him going towards Cyzicus and had talked to him. He was absolutely certain of this and would take no denial. Meanwhile, Aristeas' relatives were on their way to the shop with what was necessary for the funeral, intending to take the body away; they opened the door, and the room was empty – Aristeas was not there, either dead or alive. Seven years later he reappeared in Marmora, wrote the peom we now call *The Tale of the Arimaspians*, and again vanished. I will add something which I know happened to the people of Metapontum in Italy two hundred and forty years (as I found by computation) after the second disappearance of Aristeas. There the story goes that Aristeas appeared and told them to erect an altar to Apollo, with a statue beside it bearing the name of Aristeas of Marmora; then, after explaining that they were the only people in Italy whom Apollo had visited, and that he himself on the occasion of his visit had accompanied the god in the form of a raven, he vanished. The Metapontines sent to Delphi to ask the oracle what the apparition signified, and were advised that they had better do what it recommended. This advice they took, with the result that in the market-square of the town a statue inscribed with the name of Aristeas stands to-day by the side of the image of Apollo, surrounded by myrtle bushes.

No one has any accurate information about what lies beyond the region I am now discussing, and I have never met anyone who claims first-hand acquaintance with it. Even Aristeas, whom I have just mentioned, does not pretend in his poem to have gone further than the country of the Issedones, and admits that his account of what lies beyond is mere hearsay, founded on tales which the Issedones told him. I will, nevertheless, put down everything which careful inquiry about these remote parts has brought to my notice. West of the seaport at the mouth of the Borysthenes[1] – which lies in the middle of the Scythian coastline – the first people are the Graeco-Scythian tribe called Callipidae, and their neighbours to the eastward are the Alizones. Both these peoples resemble the Scythians in their way of life, and also grow grain for food, as well as onions, leeks, lentils, and millet. North of the Alizones are agricultural Scythian tribes, growing grain not for food but for export; beyond these are the Neuri, and north of the Neuri the country, so far as we know, is uninhabited. So much for the peoples along the Hypanis,[2] west of the Borysthenes; east of the Borysthenes, starting from the sea one comes first to Hvlaea – the Woodland – to the northward of which are Scythians who get their living from the land and are known to the Greeks on the river Hypanis as Borysthenites. They call themselves Olbiopolites. These Scythians extend eastward as far as a river named the Panticapes – the distance of a three days' journey – and northward as far up the Borysthenes as a boat can sail in eleven days. Further north is a great tract of uninhabited desert, beyond which live the Androphagi – the Maneaters – who have no connexion with the Scythians but are a quite distinct race. Northward again, so far as we can tell, there is utter desert without trace of human life. Eastward of the Scythians who lived off the land, and on the other side of the Panticapes, are the nomadic Scythians, who know nothing of agriculture. All this region with the exception of Hylaea is treeless. The nomadic tribes are to be found over a stretch of country extending eastward fourteen days' journey as far as the river Gerrhus, on the further side of which lies what is called the country of the Kings, and the Royal Scythians, who are the most warlike and numerous section of their race, and look upon the others as their slaves. Their territory runs south as far as Taurica[3] and east to the trench which was dug by the sons of the blind slaves, and to Cremni, the trading post on the shore of the Sea of Azov. Part of it reaches as far as the river Tanais.[4] North of the

1. The Dnieper.
2. The Bug.
3. The southern part of the Crimea.
4. The Don.

Royal Scythians is a non-Scythian race called Melanchlaeni, or Black-Cloaks, and north of them, so far as one knows, is a region of lakes and uninhabited country.

Once across the Tanais, one has left Scythia behind, and comes first to the Sauromatae, who occupy a stretch of country which runs northward fifteen days' journey from the northern tip of the Sea of Azov, and is entirely bare of trees, wild or cultivated. The next region beyond the Sauromatae belongs to the Budini, and is plenti-fully supplied with timber of all sorts. Northward again the country is uninhabited over the distance of a seven days' journey, until by turning a little easterly one comes to the Thyssagetae, a distinct and numerous race which gets its living by hunting. These folk live along-side another tribe called Iyrcae, who, like them, are hunters, and climb trees, of which there are many in the country, to wait for their game. Each man is provided with a dog and a horse, which has been trained to crouch flat on its belly to keep out of view, and when, from his hiding-place in the branches, the huntsman catches sight of the game, he lets fly, jumps down on to his horse, and gives chase, the dog following.

Further to the north and east lives another Scythian tribe, which moved into these parts after some trouble with the Royal Scythians to which it originally belonged. As far as this, the country I have been describing is a level plain with good deep soil, but further on it becomes rugged and stony; beyond this region, which is of great extent, one comes to the foothills of a lofty mountain chain, and a nation of bald men. They are said to be bald from birth, women and men alike, and to have snub noses and long chins; they speak a pecu-liar language, dress in the Scythian fashion, and live on the fruit of a tree called ponticum – a kind of cherry – which is about the size of a fig-tree and produces a stoned fruit as large as a bean. They strain the ripe fruit through cloths and get from it a thick dark-coloured juice which they call *aschy*. They lap the juice up with their tongues, or mix it with milk for a drink, and make cakes out of the thick sediment which it leaves. They have but few sheep, as the grazing is poor. Every man lives under his ponticum-tree, which he protects in winter with bands of thick white felt, taking them off in the summer. These people are supposed to be protected by a mysterious sort of sanctity;

they carry no arms and nobody offers them violence; they settle disputes amongst their neighbours, and anybody who seeks asylum amongst them is left in peace. They are called Argippaei.

As for the bald men, a great deal is known of the country and of the people to the south and west from the reports, which are easy enough to come by, of Scythians who visit them, and of Greeks who frequent the port on the Dnieper and other ports along the Black Sea coast. The Scythians who penetrate as far as this do their business through interpreters in seven languages. Beyond the Argippaei, however, lies a region of which no one can give an accurate account, for further progress is barred by a lofty and impassable range of mountains. The bald men themselves tell the improbable tale that the mountains are inhabited by a goat-footed race, beyond which, still further north, are men who sleep for six months in the year – which to my mind is utterly incredible. East of the Argippaei, however, the country is definitely known to be inhabited by the Issedones; but the region north of those two nations is unknown, apart from the stories they themselves tell of it.

Some knowledge of the practices of the Issedones has come through to us: for instance, when a man's father dies, his kinsmen bring sheep to his house as a sacrificial offering; the sheep and the body of the dead man are cut into joints and sliced up, and the two sorts of meat, mixed together, are served and eaten. The dead man's head, however, they gild, after stripping off the hair and cleaning out the inside, and then preserve it as a sort of sacred image, to which they offer sacrifice. Son does this to father, just as the Greeks observe ancestral commemoration.

In other respects the Issedones appear to have a sound enough sense of the difference between right and wrong, and a remarkable thing about them is that men and women have equal authority. It is amongst the Issedones themselves that the strange tales of the distant north originate – tales of the one-eyed men and the griffins which guard the gold – and the Scythians have passed them on to the rest of us, which explains why we call the one-eyed men by the Scythian name of Arimaspians – *arima* being the Scythian word for 'one', and *spu* for 'eye'.

The whole region I have been describing has excessively hard winters; for eight months in the year the cold is intolerable; the ground is frozen iron-hard, so that to turn earth into mud requires not water but fire. The sea freezes over, and the whole of the Cimmerian Bosphorus; and the Scythians, who live outside the trench which I mentioned previously, make war upon the ice, and drive waggons across it to the country of the Sindi. Even apart from the eight months' winter, the remaining four months are cold; and a further point of difference between the winters here and in all other parts of the world is that here, in Scythia, no rain worth mentioning falls during the season when one would naturally expect it, whereas throughout the summer it never stops. There are no thunderstorms during what is the usual season for them elsewhere, but only in the summer, when they are very violent; a winter thunderstorm is looked upon as a prodigy, as are earthquakes whether in summer or winter. Horses stand the winter well, but mules and donkeys cannot stand it at all; this is unusual, for elsewhere mules and donkeys bear cold easily, but horses kept standing during hard weather, are subject to frostbite. I think the cold may explain the fact that the cattle in this part of the world have no horns: a verse in Homer's *Odyssey* supports this view, where the poets speak of

Libya, where horns grow quickly on the foreheads of lambs;

a sensible remark, indicating that a hot climate favours the rapid growth of horns; whereas in severe cold cattle do not grow them at all, or hardly at all.

A remarkable fact occurs to me (I need not apologize for the digression – it has been my plan throughout this work) that mules cannot be bred in Elis, though Elis is not a cold place, and there is apparently nothing else to account for it. The people there say it is the result of some curse or other. Their practice is to wait for the breeding season and drive their mares over the border, and put the donkeys to them in their neighbours' land; then, when they are pregnant, they drive them home again. About the feathers which the Scythians say fill the air, and make it impossible to traverse, or even to see, the more northerly parts of the continent – I think myself that it must be always snowing in these northerly regions, though less, of course, in summer than in winter. Anyone who has seen heavy snow at close quarters

will know what I mean – it is very like feathers; and it is because of
the severity of these northern winters that the country is uninhabited.
No doubt the Scythians and their neighbours when they talk of the
feathers really mean snow – because of the likeness between the two.
I have now related the utmost which can be gathered from report.

Of the Hyperboreans we get no information from the Scythians
or anyone else in that part of the world, except, perhaps, from the
Issedones. Not that the Issedones really tell us anything; for if they
did, we should have it from the Scythians too, like the story of the
one-eyed men. There is, however, a mention of the Hyperboreans
in Hesiod, and in Homer's *Epigoni* – if, indeed, Homer was the author
of that poem. But the people who tell us by far the most about them
are the Delians; for, according to them, certain sacred offerings
wrapped up in wheat-straw come from the Hyperboreans into
Scythia, whence they are taken over by the neighbouring peoples in
succession until they get as far west as the Adriatic; from there they
are sent south, and the first Greeks to receive them are the Dodonaeans. Then, continuing southward, they reach the Malian gulf,
cross to Euboea, and are passed on from town to town as far as
Carystus. Then they skip Andros, the Carystians take them to Tenos,
and the Tenians to Delos. That is how these things are said to reach
Delos at the present time; but on the first occasion they were sent in
charge of two girls, whose names the Delians say were Hyperoche
and Laodice. To protect the girls on the journey, the Hyperboreans
sent five men to accompany them – the people now known as 'Per-
pherees', and greatly honoured in Delos. Later, however, when the
Hyperboreans found that their messengers did not return, they
changed their plan, and, disliking the idea that they might always lose
whoever it was that they sent away on this long journey, began the
practice of wrapping the offerings in straw and taking them to the
border, with instructions to their neighbours to see them conveyed to
their destination by a process of relay, from one nation to another.
And that is how they arrive in Delos to-day. I know of something
similar to this in Thrace and Paeonia: the women there, in their
sacrifices to Artemis the Queen, always bring wheat-straw with their
offerings.

The two Hyperborean girls died in Delos, and the boys and girls of the island still cut their hair as a sign of mourning for them – the girls, before they marry, cutting off a lock, which they twist round a spindle and lay upon the tomb (it stands on the left, as one enters the temple of Artemis, and has an olive growing on it); the boys twisting a strand of hair round a new shoot from some plant which, like the girls, they too lay on the tomb. There is also a story that before the time of Hyperoche and Laodice, two other Hyperborean girls, Arge and Opis, came to Delos by the same route. Hyperoche and Laodice came to bring to Ilithyia, who presides over childbirth, the thank-offering which they had promised for easy labour, but Arge and Opis came to the island at the same time as Apollo and Artemis, and are therefore honoured in a different way; for the women of Delos make collections for them, and name them in the hymn which Olen of Lycia wrote in their honour – a ceremony which the other islanders, and the Ionians too, have learned from the women of Delos; Olen of Lycia was also the author of the other ancient hymns which are sung in Delos. The ashes from the thigh-bones burnt upon the altar are all scattered upon the tomb of Opis and Arge, where it stands behind the temple of Artemis, facing east, close to the banqueting-hall of the Ceians.

So much, then, for the Hyperboreans; for I will not tell the tale of Abaris, who was supposed to have been a Hyperborean, and carried his arrow all round the world without eating a bite. Let me just add, however, that, if Hyperboreans exist 'beyond the north-wind' there must also be Hypernotians 'beyond the south'.

I cannot help laughing at the absurdity of all the map-makers – there are plenty of them – who show Ocean running like a river round a perfectly circular earth, with Asia and Europe of the same size. Let me spend a few words in giving a proper notion of the size and shape of these two continents. Persian territory extends south-ward to the Red Sea, as it is called; north of them are the Medes, then the Saspires, then the Colchians, who go as far as the northern sea,[1] where the mouth of the Phasis is. These four nations fill the area between the Black Sea and the Persian Gulf. Thence run westward two great continental promontories, one of which stretches from the Phasis on the north along the Black Sea and the Hellespont to the

1. The Black Sea.

Mediterranean at Sigeum in the Troad, and again, in the south, along the Mediterranean coast from the Myriandic gulf, near Phoenicia, to Cape Triopium. This branch of the continent contains thirty different nations. The other starts from Persia, and embraces successively Persia, Assyria, and Arabia, and ends – or is assumed to end – at the Arabian gulf,[1] which Darius connected by canal with the Nile. Between Persia and Phoenicia lies a very large area of country; and from Phoenicia the branch I am speaking of runs along the Mediterranean coast through Palestine-Syria to Egypt, where it ends. It contains three nations only. Such is Asia from Persia westward; eastward, beyond Media and the territories of the Saspires and Colchians, lies the Red Sea[2] and, at the northern limit, the Caspian Sea and the river Araxes, which flows eastwards. Asia is inhabited as far as India; further east the country is uninhabited, and nobody knows what it is like. Such, then, are the shape and size of Asia. Libya is a part of the second branch I mentioned, for it adjoins Egypt; Egypt itself forms a narrow neck, only about 120 miles across from the Mediterranean to the Red Sea; but it soon broadens out, and what is known as Libya covers a very large area.

In view of what I have said, I cannot but be surprised at the method of mapping Libya, Asia, and Europe which I mentioned a page or two back. The three continents do, in fact, differ very greatly in size. Europe is as long as the other two put together, and for breadth is not, in my opinion, even to be compared with them. As for Libya, we know that it is washed on all sides by the sea except where it joins Asia, as was first demonstrated, so far as our knowledge goes, by the Egyptian king Neco, who, after calling off the construction of the canal between the Nile and the Arabian gulf, sent out a fleet manned by a Phoenician crew with orders to sail round and return to Egypt and the Mediterranean by way of the Pillars of Heracles.[3] The Phoenicians sailed from the Red Sea into the southern ocean, and every autumn put in where they were on the Libyan coast, sowed a patch of ground, and waited for next year's harvest. Then, having got in their grain, they put to sea again, and after two full

1. The Red Sea.
2. The Indian Ocean.
3. The Straits of Gibraltar.

years rounded the Pillars of Heracles in the course of the third, and returned to Egypt. These men made a statement which I do not myself believe, though others may, to the effect that as they sailed on a westerly course round the southern end of Libya, they had the sun on their right – to northward of them. This is how Libya was first discovered to be surrounded by sea, and the next people to make a similar report were the Carthaginians; for Sataspes, son of Teaspes, the Achaemenian, though sent out for the purpose, took fright at the length and loneliness of the voyage and turned back. It was Sataspes' mother who sent him upon this venture; he had raped a daughter of Megabyzus' son Zopyrus, and was about to be impaled as a punishment by Xerxes, when his mother, who was a sister of Darius, begged him off by promising to inflict upon him a punishment even more severe; this was to force him to circumnavigate Libya, returning by way of the Arabian gulf. Xerxes agreed; and Sataspes, on his arrival in Egypt, procured a vessel and crew and sailed to the Straits of Gibraltar. Passing through the Straits, he doubled Cape Soloeis[1] and continued on a southerly course for many months; but when he found that, far though he had sailed, there was always need to sail further yet, he put about and returned to Egypt. From Egypt he went to Xerxes' court, where he reported that at the most southerly point they had reached they found the coast occupied by small men, who wore clothes made from palm leaves. When they landed, the pygmies used to abandon their settlements and escape to the hills. Sataspes' men had done them no harm, beyond entering their villages and taking some of their cattle. As to his failure to complete the circumnavigation, Sataspes declared that the reason was that his ship was brought to a standstill and was unable to make headway. Xerxes, however, refused to pardon him, and, on the ground that he had failed to accomplish his set task, exacted the original penalty and had him impaled. A eunuch in Sataspes' service, when he learned of his master's death, escaped to Samos with a great deal of money. It was all seized, however, by a certain Samian, whose name I willingly forget – though I know it well.

The greater part of Asia was discovered by Darius. He wanted to find out where the Indus joins the sea – the Indus is the only river

1. Spartel.

other than the Nile where crocodiles are found – and for this purpose
sent off on an expedition down the river a number of men whose
word he could trust. Led by a Caryandian named Scylax, the expedition sailed from Caspatyrus in the district of Pactyica, following
the course of the river eastward until it reached the sea; then, turning
westward, the ships followed the coast, and after a voyage of some
thirty months reached the place from which the king of Egypt had
sent out the Phoenicians, whom I have already mentioned, to circumnavigate Libya. After this voyage was completed, Darius subdued the
Indians and made regular use of the southern ocean. In this way all
Asia, with the exception of the easterly part, has been proved to be
surrounded by sea, and so to have a general geographical resemblance
to Libya.

　　With Europe, however, the case is different; for no one has ever
determined whether or not there is sea either to the east or to the
north of it; all we know is that in length it is equal to Asia and Libya
combined. Another thing that puzzles me is why three distinct
women's names should have been given to what is really a single land-
mass; and why, too, the Nile and the Phasis – or, according to some,
the Maeotic Tanais and the Cimmerian Strait[1] – should have been
fixed upon for the boundaries. Nor have I been able to learn who it
was that first marked the boundaries, or where they got the names
from. Most Greeks assume that Libya was so called after a native
woman and that Asia was named after the wife of Prometheus; the
Lydians, however, claim the latter name for themselves, and say that
Asia was named not after the wife of Prometheus, but after Asies, the
son of Cotys and grandson of Manes, who passed it on besides to the
tribe called Asias in Sardis. As for Europe, nobody knows if it is surrounded by sea, or where it got its name from, or who gave it, unless
we are to say that it came from Europa, the Tyrian woman, and before
that was nameless like the rest. This, however, is unlikely; for Europa
was an Asiatic and never visited the country which we now call
Europe, but only sailed from Phoenicia to Crete and from Crete to
Lycia. But that is quite enough on this subject – and in any case I
shall continue to use the names which custom has made familiar.

　　Round the Black Sea – the scene of Darius' campaign – are to be

1. The Kertch.

found, if we except Scythia, the most uncivilized nations in the world. No one could claim that the rest have any of the arts of civilized life, or have produced any man of distinction – again with a simple exception: namely, Anacharsis. The Scythians, however, though in most respects I do not admire them, have managed one thing, and that the most important in human affairs, better than anyone else on the face of the earth: I mean their own preservation. For such is their manner of life that no one who invades their country can escape destruction, and if they wish to avoid engaging with an enemy, that enemy cannot by any possibility come to grips with them. A people without fortified towns, living, as the Scythians do, in waggons which they take with them wherever they go, accustomed, one and all, to fight on horseback with bows and arrows, and dependent for their food not upon agriculture but upon their cattle: how can such a people fail to defeat the attempt of an invader not only to subdue them, but even to make contact with them? They have been helped in this by the nature of their country and by the rivers which it contains, the land consisting of a rich and well-watered plain, with excellent pasture, and the rivers being almost as numerous as canals are in Egypt. The best known of the rivers, those, namely, which are navigable by sea-going ships, I will mention: they are the Ister[1] which has five mouths, the Tyras, the Hypanis,[2] the Borysthenes,[3] the Panticapes, Hypacyris, Gerrhus, and Tanais.[4] The Danube, which is the mightiest river in the known world, and never varies, summer or winter, in the volume of its waters, is the most westerly of the Scythian rivers, and owes its great size to the tributary streams which join it. Of these tributaries, five are genuine Scythian rivers and have their source in the country: namely, the Pyretus (or Porata, as the Scythians call it), the Tiarantus, the Araros, the Naparis, and the Ordessus. The first of these – a big river – is the most easterly of the five; the second, the Tiarantus, is smaller and further to the west, while the Araros, the Naparis, and the Ordessus join the Danube somewhere between the two. In addi-

1. The Danube.
2. The Bug.
3. The Dnieper.
4. The Don.

tion to the tributaries which can properly be called Scythian, there are also many others: the Maris, flowing from the country of the Agathyrsi; three large rivers, the Atlas, the Auras, and the Tibisis, which flow with a northerly course from the heights of Haemus; the Athrys, the Noes, and the Artanes from Thrace and the country of the tribe of Thracians called Crobyzi; the Scios, flowing from Paeonia and Mt Rhodope through the Haemus mountains; the Angrus, running northward from Illyria through the Triballian plain, to join the Brongus, thus making two more, both of considerable size; the Carpis and the Alpis, flowing northward, too, from the country beyond the Umbrians.[1] All these rivers discharge into the Danube, that mighty stream which, rising amongst the Celts, the most westerly, after the Cynetes, of all European nations, traverses the whole length of the continent before it enters Scythia. No wonder that with all the tributaries I have mentioned, and many others besides, the Danube is the greatest of rivers – though if we discount the tributaries and compare the single stream of the Danube with the single stream of the Nile, the latter is the greater of the two; for no river, or even rivulet, flows into the Nile to increase its volume. The fact that the height of the Danube remains constant summer and winter, I think I can explain in the following way: in winter the volume of water is normal, or slightly above normal, for though there is much snow, the rainfall is negligible; but in summer the great mass of the previous winter's snow melts, and the water from it, pouring into the river, combined with frequent heavy rains – which at this season are common – increases its volume. So though there is more evaporation in summer than in winter, the effect of it is offset by the increased volume of the tributary streams; thus a balance is produced, and the level of water is kept constant, throughout the year.

The next river, the Tyras, runs southward from its source in a

1. The 'river Alpis' perhaps preserves the name of the Alps, and 'Carpis', still more speculatively, that of the Carpathians; but Greek knowledge of central Europe lagged far behind that of the Mediterranean and Black Sea lands; the Alps as mountains remain unknown not only to Herodotus but even to Apollonius of Rhodes in his account of the wanderings of the Argonauts 200 years later.

large lake, which forms the boundary between Scythia and the
country of the Neuri. Greeks called Tyritae have established a settlement at its mouth. The third river, the Hypanis, has its source in
Scythia, in another great lake, round the borders of which wild
white horses graze. The lake is called – very properly – the Mother
of Hypanis. Five days' sail from the lake the water continues fresh
and shallow; but thence on towards the sea, a distance of four days'
journey, it is excessively salt; the sudden change is caused by a spring
which here joins the river and is so salt that, though it is quite small,
it taints the entire volume of water – and the Hypanis is a pretty big
stream. The spring, or rivulet, rises where the territory of the Scythian
agricultural tribes borders on that of the Alizones; its name, and the
name of the place in the immediate neighbourhood of its source, is in
the Scythian language Exampaeus, which might be rendered in
Greek as 'Sacred Ways'. The Tyras and the Hypanis draw close
together in the country of the Alizones, but afterwards diverge,
leaving a wider and wider space between them.

The Borysthenes, the second largest of the Scythian rivers, is, in
my opinion, the most valuable and productive not only of the
rivers in this part of the world, but anywhere else, with the sole exception of the Nile – with which none can be compared. It provides
the finest and most abundant pasture, by far the richest supply of the
best sorts of fish, and the most excellent water for drinking – clear
and bright, whereas that of other rivers in the vicinity is turbid; no
better crops grow anywhere than along its banks, and where grain
is not sown the grass is the most luxuriant in the world. An unlimited supply of salt is formed by natural processes at the mouth of
the river, which also produces a very large spineless fish, good for
pickling and known locally as *antacaeus*, and a number of other most
remarkable things. The course of the river is southerly, and it is
known as far as the place called Gerrhus, forty days' voyage up;
beyond that, nobody can say through what countries it flows. We do
know, however, that it enters the territory of the agricultural
Scythians after crossing an uninhabited region; for these Scythians
live along its banks as far as would take a boat ten days to cover. This
river and the Nile are the only ones of which I do not know the
source; nor, I think, does any other Greek. Not far from the sea the

Borysthenes and Hypanis unite and flow through low-lying marsh-country, and the pointed spit of land between them is called Cape Hippolaus; there is a temple of Demeter upon it, and opposite the temple, on the Hypanis, is the settlement of the Borysthenites.

The fifth river, the Panticapes, also rises in a lake and flows in a southerly direction through Hylaea – the Woodland – to join the Borysthenes. The country between it and the Borysthenes is occupied by the Scythian agricultural tribes. The Hypacyris, the sixth river, flows from a lake right through the territory of the Scythian nomads, and reaches the sea near Carcinitis, leaving Hylaea and the place called Achilles' Racecourse to the right. The Gerrhus splits off from the Borysthenes, far to the north at a spot which goes by the same name and lies somewhere about the region where the Borysthenes begins to be known. It forms the boundary between the Nomad and the Royal Scythians, and runs into the Hypacyris. The eighth river, the Tanais, has its source far up country in a large lake, and empties itself into a larger one still, Lake Maeotis.[1] It divides the Royal Scythians from the Sauromatae, and is joined by yet another river, the Hyrgis. These, then, are the most notable of the rivers with which Scythia is provided. The grass which grows hereabouts is more apt to cause bile in cattle than any other we know of, as can be seen plainly enough when the carcasses are cut open.

Having described the natural resources of the country, I will go on to give some account of the people's customs and beliefs. The only gods the Scythians worship are Hestia (their chief deity), Zeus, and Earth (whom they believe to be the wife of Zeus), and, as deities of secondary importance, Apollo, Celestial Aphrodite, Heracles, and Ares. These are recognized by the entire nation; the Royal Scythians also offer sacrifice to Poseidon. In the Scythian language Hestia is *Tabiti*, Zeus (very properly, in my opinion) *Papaeus*,[2] Earth *Api*, Apollo *Oetosyrus*, Aphrodite *Argimpasa*, Poseidon *Thagimasadas*.

It is not their custom to make statues, or to build altars and temples, in honour of any god except Ares. The method of sacrifice is every-

1. The Sea of Azov.
2. i.e. 'Father'; Nausicaa in the Odyssey addresses her father as 'Pappa', and there was a native god whom the Greeks called 'Zeus Papas' also in north-west Asia Minor.

where and in every case the same: the victim has its front feet tied together, and the person who is performing the ceremony gives a pull on the rope from behind and throws the animal down, calling, as he does so, upon the name of the appropriate god; then he slips a noose round the victim's neck, pushes a short stick under the cord and twists it until the creature is choked. No fire is lighted; there is no offering of first-fruits, and no libation. As soon as the animal is strangled, he is skinned, and then comes the boiling of the flesh. This has called for a little inventiveness, because there is no wood in Scythia to make a fire with; the method the natives adopt after skinning the animal is to strip the flesh from the bones and put it into a cauldron – if, that is, they happen to possess one: these cauldrons are made in the country, and resemble Lesbian mixing-bowls in shape, though they are much larger – and then make a fire of the bones underneath it. In the absence of a cauldron, they put all the flesh into the animal's paunch, mix water with it, and boil it like that over the bone-fire. The bones burn very well, and the paunch easily contains all the meat once it has been stripped off. In this way an ox, or any other sacrificial beast, is ingeniously made to boil itself. When the meat is cooked, the sacrificer offers a portion of both flesh and entrails by throwing it on the ground in front of him. All sorts of cattle are offered in sacrifice, but most commonly horses.

Ceremonies in honour of Ares are conducted differently. In every district, at the seat of government. Ares has his temple; it is of a peculiar kind, and consists of an immense heap of brushwood, three furlongs each way and somewhat less in height. On top the heap is levelled off square, like a platform, accessible on one side but rising sheer on the other three. Every year a hundred and fifty waggon-loads of sticks are added to the pile, to make up for the constant settling caused by rains, and on the top of it is planted an ancient iron sword, which serves for the image of Ares. Annual sacrifices of horses and other cattle are made to this sword, which, indeed, claims a greater number of victims than any other of their gods. Prisoners of war are also sacrificed to Ares, but in their case the ceremony is different from that which is used in the sacrifice of animals: one man is chosen out of every hundred; wine is poured on his head, and his throat cut over a bowl; the bowl is then carried to the platform on top of the woodpile, and the blood in it poured out over the sword. While this goes on above, another ceremony is being enacted below, close against the pile: this consists in cutting off the right hands and arms of the prisoners who have been slaughtered, and tossing them into the air. This done, and the rest of the ceremony over, the worshippers go away. The victims' arms and hands are left to lie where they fall, separate from the trunks. They never use pigs for sacrifice and will not even breed them anywhere in the country.

As regards war, the Scythian custom is for every man to drink the blood of the first man he kills. The heads of all enemies killed in battle are taken to the king; if he brings a head, a soldier is admitted to his share of the loot; no head, no loot. He strips the skin off the head by making a circular cut round the ears and shaking out the skull; he then scrapes the flesh off the skin with the rib of an ox, and when it is clean works it in his fingers until it is supple, and fit to be used as a sort of handkerchief. He hangs these handkerchiefs on the bridle of his horse, and is very proud of them. The finest fellow is the man who has the greatest number. Many Scythians sew a number of scalps together and make cloaks out of them, like the ones peasants wear, and often, too, they take the skin, nails and all, off the right hands and arms of dead enemies and use it to cover their quivers with – having discovered the fact that human skin is not only tough, but white, as white as almost any skin. Sometimes they flay a whole body, and stretch the skin on a wooden frame which they carry around with them when they ride. They have a special way of dealing with the actual skulls – not with all of them, but only those of their worst enemies: they saw off the part below the eyebrows, and after cleaning out what remains stretch a piece of rawhide round it on the outside. If a man is poor, he is content with that, but a rich man goes further and gilds the inside of the skull as well. In either case the skull is then used to drink from. They treat the skulls of their kinsmen in the same way, in cases where quarrels have occurred and a man has been beaten in fight in the presence of the king. When important visitors arrive, these skulls are passed round and the host tells the story of them: how they were once his relatives and made war against him, and how he defeated them – all of which passes for a proof of courage. Once a year the governor of each district mixes a bowl of wine, from which every Scythian who has killed his man in battle has the right to drink. Those who have no dead enemy to their credit are not allowed to touch the wine, but have to sit by themselves in disgrace – the worst, indeed, which they can suffer. Any man, on the contrary, who has killed a great many enemies, has two cups and drinks from both of them at once.

There are many soothsayers in Scythia, and their method is to work with willow rods. They bring great bundles of them, which they put down on the ground; then they untie them, lay out each rod separately, and pronounce their prophecy. While they are speaking it, they collect the rods into a bundle again as before. This is the native mode of divination in Scythia; but the class of effeminate persons called 'Enarees' use a different method, which they say was taught them by Aphrodite: these people take a piece of the inner bark of the lime-tree and cut it into three pieces, which they keep twisting and untwisting round their fingers as they prophesy.

When the king of Scythia falls sick, he sends for three of the most reputable soothsayers, who proceed to practise their arts in the way I have described; more often than not they declare that such and such a person (whose name they mention) has sworn falsely by the king's hearth – it being customary in Scythia to use this form of oath for the most solemn purposes. The supposed culprit is at once arrested and brought into the king's presence, where he is charged by the soothsayers, who tell him that their powers of divination have revealed that he has sworn by the king's hearth and perjured himself, and that his perjury is the cause of the king's sickness. The man, of course, denies the charge, and makes a great fuss, whereupon the king sends for more soothsayers – six this time instead of three – who also bring their skill to bear. Should they convict the accused of perjury, he is beheaded without more ado, and his property is divided by lot amongst the first three soothsayers; if, however, the new six acquit him, more are brought in, and, if need be, still more again, and if, in the final result, the majority declare for the man's innocence, the law is that the three original ones should be executed. The method of execution is this: a cart is filled with sticks and harnessed to oxen; the guilty men, gagged and bound hand and foot, are thrust down amongst the sticks, which are then set alight, and the oxen scared off at a run. Often the oxen are burnt to death together with the sooth-sayers; often, too, the pole of the cart is burnt through soon enough to allow them to escape with a scorching. Peccant soothsayers – 'lying prophets' as they are called – are burnt to death in this way for other crimes besides the one I have described. When the king orders an execution, he does not allow the criminal's sons to survive him: all males are put to death, but not the females, who are in no way harmed.

When Scythians swear an oath or make a solemn compact, they fill a large earthenware bowl with wine and drop into it a little of the blood of the two parties to the oath, having drawn it either by a prick with a awl or a slight cut with a knife; then they dip into the bowl a sword, some arrows, a battle-axe, and a javelin, and speak a number of prayers; lastly, the two contracting parties and their chief followers drink the mixture of wine and blood.

The burial-place of the Scythian kings is in the country of the Gerrhi, near the spot where the Borysthenes first becomes navigable. When a king dies, they dig a great square pit, and, when it is ready, they take up the corpse, which has been previously prepared in the following way: the belly is slit open, cleaned out, and filled with various aromatic substances, crushed galingale, parsley-seed, and anise; it is then sewn up again and the whole body coated over with wax. In this condition it is carried in a waggon to a neighbouring tribe within the Scythian dominions, and then on to another, taking the various tribes in turn; and in the course of its progress, the people who successively receive it, follow the custom of the Royal Scythians and cut a piece from their ears, shave their hair, make circular incisions on their arms, gash their foreheads and noses, and thrust arrows through their left hands. On each stage of the journey those who have already been visited join the procession, until at last the funeral cortège, after passing through every part of the Scythian dominions, finds itself at the place of burial amongst the Gerrhi, the most northerly and remote of Scythian tribes. Here the corpse is laid in the tomb on a mattress, with spears fixed in the ground on either side to support a roof of withies laid on wooden poles, while in other parts of the great square pit various members of the king's household are buried beside him: one of his concubines, his butler, his cook, his groom, his steward, and his chamberlain – all of them strangled. Horses are buried too, and gold cups (the Scythians do not use silver or bronze), and a selection of his other treasures.[1] This ceremony over, everybody with great enthusiasm sets about raising a mound of earth, each competing with his neighbour to make it as big as possible. At the end of a year another ceremony takes place: they take fifty of the best of the king's remaining servants, strangle and gut them, stuff the bodies with chaff, and sew them up again – these servants are native Scythians, for the king has no bought slaves, but chooses people to serve him from amongst his subjects. Fifty of the finest horses are then subjected to the same treatment. The next step is to cut a number of wheels in half and to fix them in pairs, rim-downwards, to stakes driven into the ground, two stakes to each half-wheel; then stout poles are driven lengthwise through the horses from tail to neck, and by means of these the horses are mounted on the wheels, in such a way that the front pairs support the shoulders and the rear pairs the belly between the thighs. All four legs are left dangling clear of the ground. Each horse is bitted and bridled, the bridle being led forward and pegged down. The bodies of the men are dealt with in a similar way: straight poles are driven up through the neck, parallel with the spine, and the lower protruding ends fitted into sockets in the stakes which run through the horses; thus each horse is provided with one of the young servants to ride him. When horses and riders are all in place around the tomb, they are left there, and the mourners go away. When an ordinary person dies, the nearest relatives lay the corpse in a cart and take it round to visit their friends. The various families in turn entertain their guests to a meal, and serve the corpse with food just like the rest. The round of visits lasts forty days, and then the body is buried. After a burial the Scythians go through a process of cleaning themselves; they wash their heads with soap, and their bodies in a vapour-bath, the nature of which I will describe. First, however, I must mention that hemp grows in Scythia, a plant resembling flax, but much coarser and taller. It grows wild

---

1. The account of Scythian royal burials and chamber-tombs is accurate. For the findings of archaeology, see modern illustrated books, such as Rostovtsev, *Iranians and Greeks in South Russia* (1922), T. Talbot Rice, *The Scythians* (text must be used with care) or E. D. Phillips, *The Royal Hordes*.

as well as under cultivation, and the Thracians make clothes from it very like linen ones – indeed, one must have much experience in these matters to be able to distinguish between the two, and anybody who has never seen a piece of cloth made from hemp, will suppose it to be of linen. And now for the vapour-bath: on a framework of three sticks, meeting at the top, they stretch pieces of woollen cloth, taking care to get the joins as perfect as they can, and inside this little tent they put a dish with red-hot stones in it. Then they take some hemp seed, creep into the tent, and throw the seed on to the hot stones. At once it begins to smoke, giving off a vapour unsurpassed by any vapour-bath one could find in Greece. The Scythians enjoy it so much that they howl with pleasure. This is their substitute for an ordinary bath in water, which they never use. The women grind up cypress, cedar, and frankincense on a rough stone, mix the powder into a thick paste with a little water, and plaster it all over their bodies and faces. They leave it on for a day, and then, when they remove it, their skin is clean, glossy, and fragrant.

Like the Egyptians, the Scythians are dead-set against foreign ways, especially against Greek ways. An illustration of this is what happened to Anacharsis – and, later, to Scylas. The former was a great traveller, and a man of great and varied knowledge; he had given proof of this in many parts of the world, and was on his way home to Scythia when, as he was passing through the Hellespont, he broke his journey at Cyzicus. Finding the people of this town engaged in celebrating a magnificent festival in honour of the Mother of the Gods, Anacharsis made a vow that, if he got home safe and sound, he would himself celebrate a night-festival and offer sacrifice to this goddess in exactly the same way as he had seen it done at Cyzicus. On his arrival in Scythia, he entered the Woodland – that forest of all sorts of trees, which lies near Achilles' Racecourse – and, according to his promise, went through the ceremony with all the proper rites and observances, drum in hand and the images fastened to his dress. He happened to be noticed by some Scythian or other, who at once went and told Saulius, the king; Saulius then came in person, and, seeing Anacharsis occupied with these outlandish rites, shot him dead. To-day, if anyone asks about Anacharsis, the Scythians say they never heard of him – all because he travelled abroad into Greece and adopted foreign practices. But as I was told by Tymnes, the agent of Ariapithes, Anacharsis was the uncle of the Scythian king Idanthyrsus, and son of Gnurus, grandson of Lycus, and great-grandson of Spargapithes. If he was really a member of this family, he must have been killed by his own brother; for Idanthyrus was a son of Saulius, and it was Saulius who shot him. There is also a different story about Anacharsis which I have heard in the Peloponnese; according to this, he was sent abroad by the king of Scythia to find out what he could about Greece, and told the king on his return that all the Greeks were too busy to study any branch of learning, with the sole exception of the Lacedaemonians, who were the only ones to be able to keep up a sensible conversation. This story, however, is only a frivolous Greek invention; the plain truth is that Anacharsis was killed in the way I have described, for associating with Greeks and adopting foreign ways.

Many years later Scylas came to grief in a similar manner. He was one of the sons of the Scythian king Ariapithes, and his mother, who was not a native woman but came from Istria, taught him to speak and read Greek. As time went on, Ariapithes was treacherously murdered by Spargapithes, the king of the Agathyrsi, and Scylas succeeded to the throne and married Opoea, one of his father's wives. This woman was a native of Scythia, and Ariapithes had a son by her, named Oricus. During his reign, Scylas, as a result of the education his mother had given him, found himself discontented with the traditional way of life in Scythia, and powerfully attracted by Greek ideas. Whenever, therefore, he went with his army to the Greek settlement of the Borysthenites – these people claim to have come originally from Miletus – his custom was to leave his men outside the wall and enter the town himself. Then, when the gates were barred behind him, and the townspeople on the watch to prevent any of the Scythians seeing what he was up to, he would change into Greek clothes, stroll about the streets without any sort of bodyguard or personal attendant, take part in religious ceremonies and behave in every way just as if he were a Greek himself. Often a month or more would go by, before he would change back into his Scythian clothes and leave for home. He was constantly doing this, and even built himself a house there, and married a woman from the neighbourhood to look after it for him. Fate, however, had its revenge in store, as the sequel will show. It happened one day that Scylas conceived the desire to be initiated into the mysteries of Dionysus, and just as he was on the point of beginning the ritual, a terrible thing occurred: the house I mentioned, which he had built in the city – it was a very large and expensive building, set about with marble sphinxes and griffins – was struck from heaven by a thunderbolt and burnt to the ground. In spite of this, however, Scylas carried through the ceremony of initiation.

Now the Greek custom of indulging in Dionysiac orgies is, in Scythian eyes, a shameful thing; and no Scythian can see sense in imagining a god who drives people out of their wits. On this occasion, therefore, at the initiation of Scylas, one of the Borysthenites slipped away and told the Scythians, who were waiting outside the town, of what was going on. 'You laugh at us,' he said, 'for being possessed by the spirit of Dionysus when we celebrate his rites. Well, this same spirit has now taken hold of your own king; he is under its influence – Dionysus has driven him mad. If you don't believe it, come along and I will let you see for yourselves.' The chief Scythians present accepted the offer, and the man took them secretly to the top of a high building, from which they could get a good view of what was happening in the streets. Presently a party of revellers came by, with Scylas amongst them; and when the Scythians saw their king in the grip of the Bacchic frenzy, they were profoundly disturbed and, returning to the army, let every man know of the disgraceful spectacle they had witnessed. Later, when Scylas was at home again, the Scythians put themselves under the protection of his brother Octamasades, the son of Teres' daughter, and rose in rebellion, and Scylas himself, when he learnt what was afoot and understood the reason for it, fled the country and took refuge in Thrace. Octamasades started in pursuit at the head of an army, and made contact with the Thracian forces on the Ister; but before the battle could begin, Sitalces[1] sent a message in the following terms: 'There is really no

1. Sitalces, mentioned here without introduction as well known, is the king of the Odrysians still active in 429 (Thucydides II, 29, 95 ff., and below, p. 486), and killed in battle in 424. This incident, then, must be after c. 460, and may be a later addition to his story by Herodotus.

need for us to begin hostilities. You are my sister's son, and my
brother is with you' (this, I should mention, was the truth: Sitalces'
brother had fled from Thrace and was living with Octamasades).
'Give me back my brother, and I will do the same with Scylas; then
neither of us need risk his army in an engagement.' Octamasades
agreed to the proposal and the exchange was effected, whereupon
Sitalces went off with his brother, and Octamasades, there and then,
had Scylas beheaded. These two stories will show the importance
which the Scythians attach to their national traditions, and the severity
of the punishments they inflict upon anyone who introduces alien
customs.

I was never able to learn exactly what the population of Scythia
is. The reports I have heard are not consistent, some putting it very
high, others comparatively low – considering, that is, the power and
importance of Scythia. They did, however, actually show me
something, which gave me a notion of their numbers: between the
rivers Borysthenes and Hypanis there is a place called Exampaeus,
which I mentioned a little further back in connexion with the salt
spring which rises there and makes the water of the Hypanis undrink-
able. In this place there stands a brazen bowl, six times as big as the one
which was set up as a dedicatory offering at the entrance to the Black
Sea by Pausanias, son of Cleombrotus. Anyone who has not seen
Pausanias' bowl will understand me better if I say that the Scythian
bowl can easily hold 5000 gallons and is of metal about four inches
thick. The people of the district told me that this huge vessel was
made out of arrowheads; for one of their kings, named Ariantes,
wishing to know how many men there were in Scythia, gave orders
that each of them should bring him a single arrowhead, failure to do
so being punishable by death. An enormous number were brought,
and Ariantes decided to turn them into something which might
serve as a permanent record. The result was the brazen bowl, which
he set up at Exampaeus.

Scythia has few really remarkable features, except its rivers,
which are more numerous, and bigger, than anywhere else in the
world. There is, however, one other interesting thing besides the
rivers and the vast extent of the plains – a footprint left by Heracles.
The natives show this to visitors on a rock by the river Tyras. It is

like a man's footprint, but is three feet long. I must now leave this subject and get back to the story which I set out to tell.

While Darius was preparing his invasion of Scythia, and sending messengers to every part of his dominions with orders to raise troops here, ships there, and labourers somewhere else to work on the bridge over the Bosphorus, his brother Artabanus did his utmost to make him abandon the enterprise, on the ground that the Scythians were such difficult people to get at. Good though the advice was, it had no effect upon Darius; Artabanus stopped trying to persuade him, and Darius completed his preparations and marched from Susa at the head of his army. A Persian named Oeobazus, who had three sons, all of them in the army, asked Darius to let one of them stay behind, and Darius, as if in answer to a modest request from a personal friend, said he would willingly leave all three. Oeobazus, supposing his sons to be excused service, was delighted, but the king ordered his officers to put the three young men to death. So they were indeed left behind – with their throats cut.

Darius continued his march from Susa to Chalcedon on the Bosphorus, where the bridge was, and then took ship and sailed to the Cyanean rocks – those rocks which according to the Greek story used to be constantly changing their position. Here, seated in the temple which stands by the straits, he looked out over the Black Sea – a sight indeed worth seeing. No sea can equal the Black Sea; it is 1380 miles long, and 410 wide in its widest part. Its mouth is half a mile wide, and the length of the Bosphorus, the narrow strait which leads into it (and where the bridge was), is nearly fifteen miles. The Bosphorus joins the Propontis, which is about sixty miles wide and a hundred and seventy long, and runs into the Hellespont, a narrow strait nearly fifty miles long but less than one mile wide. The Hellespont leads into the broad sea we call the Aegean. The foregoing measurements were arrived at in the following way: in a summer day a ship can cover a distance of approximately 70,000 fathoms, and in a night 60,000. To sail from the entrance of the Black Sea to Phasis – which represents a voyage along its greatest length – takes nine days and eight nights; this would make a distance of 1,110,000 fathoms, or 11,100 furlongs.[1] Across the broadest part, from Sindica

1. 1,380 miles.

to Themiscyra on the Thermodon, it is a voyage of three days and two nights; this comes to 330,000 fathoms, or 3300 furlongs.[1]

I have now given the measurements – and the method of arriving at them – of the Black Sea, Bosphorus, and Hellespont; it remains to add that the Black Sea is connected with a lake nearly as big as itself, called Maeotis, or Mother of the Pontus.

When he had looked on the waters of the Black Sea, Darius returned by ship to the bridge, which had been designed by a Samian named Mandrocles. Then, after seeing what he could of the Bosphorus, he had two marble columns erected, on one of which was an inscription in Assyrian characters showing the various nations which were serving on the campaign; the other had a similar inscription in Greek. These nations were, in fact, all over which he had dominion, and made a total force, including cavalry but excluding the naval contingent, of 700,000 men. There were 600 ships. Years afterwards the people of Byzantium removed these columns and used them in their own city to build the altar of Artemis the Protectress; a single plinth, however, covered with Assyrian characters, was left lying near the temple of Dionysus in Byzantium. I imagine, though I do not know for certain, that Darius' bridge was half-way between Byzantium and the temple which stands on the strait between the Bosphorus and the Black Sea.

Darius was so pleased with the bridge that he loaded its designer with presents, and Mandrocles spent a certain portion of what he received in having a picture painted, showing the whole process of the bridging of the strait, and Darius himself sitting on his throne, with the army crossing over. This picture he presented as a dedicatory offering to the temple of Hera, with the following verses inscribed upon it, to serve as a permanent record of his achievement:

> Goddess, accept this gift from Mandrocles,
> Who bridged the Bosphorus' fish-haunted seas.
> His labour, praised by King Darius, won
> Honour for Samos, for himself a crown.

Darius, having rewarded Mandrocles, then crossed over into Europe. Before he went, he gave orders to the Ionians – who, with

1. About 410 miles.

other Greeks from Aeolia and the Hellespont, were in charge of the fleet – to sail into the Black Sea as far as the Danube, where they were to bridge the river and await his arrival. The orders were obeyed: the naval contingent, passing through the Cyanean Islands, carried right on to the Danube, sailed up the river for two days as far as the point where the main stream divides, and here built the bridge. Darius, after passing over the Bosphorus bridge, marched through Thrace and stopped for three days at the source of the Tearus, a river which has the local reputation of being the best in the world for its curative properties, especially in cases of scab in both men and horses. It originates in thirty-eight separate springs, some hot, some cold, and all issuing from the same rock, which lies at a spot two days' journey both from Heraeum, near Perinthus, and from Apollonia on the Black Sea. The river is a tributary of the Contadesdus which, in its turn, joins the Agrianes, the two streams subsequently uniting with the Hebrus, which falls into the sea near Aenus.

Darius was so greatly charmed with the Tearus, that he erected another pillar close to its source with this inscription: 'The springs of the Tearus, whose water is the finest in action and noblest in appearance of all rivers, was visited in the course of his march against Scythia by Darius son of Hystaspes, finest in action and noblest in appearance of all men, King of Persia and the whole continent.'

Continuing his march, Darius came to another river, the Artiscus, which flows through the country of the Odrysians. Here he indicated a certain spot where every man in the army was ordered to deposit a stone as he passed by. This was done, with the result that when Darius moved on he left great hills of stones behind him.

Before he reached the Danube, the first people he subdued were the Getae, who believe that they never die. The Thracians of Salmydessus and those who live beyond Apollonia and Mesembria, known as the Scyrmiadae and Nipsaeans, surrendered without fighting; but the Getae, who are the most manly and law-abiding of the Thracian tribes, offered fierce resistance and were at once reduced to slavery. The belief of these people in their immortality takes the following form: they never really die, but every man, when he takes leave of this present life, goes to join Salmoxis, a divine being who is also called by some of them Gebeleizis. Every five years they choose one of their number by lot and send him to Salmoxis as a messenger, with instructions to ask him for whatever they may happen to want. To effect the dispatch, some of them with javelins in their hands arrange themselves in a suitable position, while others take hold of the messenger by his hands and feet, and swing him up into the air in such a way as to make him fall on the upturned points of the javelins. If the man is killed, they take it as a sign that Salmoxis is in a favourable mood; if he escapes, they put it down to his own bad character, tell him what they think of him, and send another messenger instead. The instructions, of course, are given to the messenger while he is still alive. This same tribe of Thracians will, during a thunderstorm, shoot arrows up into the sky, and utter threats against the lord of the lightning and the thunder, because they recognize no god but their own.

I myself have heard a very different account of Salmoxis from the Greeks who live on the Hellespont and the Black Sea. According to this, he was a man, and lived in Samos, where he was a slave in the household of Pythagoras, the son of Mnesarchus. He subsequently gained his freedom, amassed a fortune, and returned to his native country of Thrace, where he found the people in great poverty and ignorance. As he had gained, from living with Greeks and from his association with one of their more influential teachers, an insight into Ionian ideas and a more civilized way of living than was to be found in Thrace, he built himself a hall in which he used to entertain the leading men of the country with much liberality, and endeavour to teach them that neither he nor they, who were his guests, nor any of their descendants, would ever die, but would go to a place where they would live in perpetual enjoyment of every blessing. All the time that he was trying to promulgate this new doctrine, he was occupied in the construction of an underground chamber, and when it was ready he entered it and disappeared from sight. For three years he lived in this room underground, and his fellow countrymen missed him sadly, and mourned for him as if he were dead; then in the fourth year he reappeared, and in this way persuaded the Thracians that the doctrine he had taught was true. For my part I neither put entire faith in this story of Salmoxis and his underground chamber, nor wholly disbelieve it; I think, however, that Salmoxis lived long before Pythagoras' time. In any case, whether there was once a man of that name, or whether he is a local god belonging to the Getae, that is enough of him.

The Getae, whose practices I have described, were defeated by the Persians and forced to accompany the army of Darius, who then continued his march with all his land forces to the Danube. When they had crossed the river, he ordered the Ionians to break up the bridge and join him in his march across country together with all the men from the ships. They were about to carry out this order and destroy the bridge, when Coes the son of Erxander, who was in command of the contingent from Mytilene, obtained an interview with Darius, after first satisfying himself that the king was willing to listen to other people's suggestions. 'My lord,' he said, 'you are going to attack a country without a single town in it, and no part of which is under cultivation. Surely it would be wiser to leave this bridge intact, and under the guard of the men who built it; for whether we make contact with the Scythians and succeed in what we hope to do, or not, we should then, in either case, have a safe means of getting back by the same route. I have never been afraid of direct defeat by the Scythians in battle; the danger, to my mind, is rather that we should fail to find them, and that endless and indeterminate marching in the attempt to do so would get us into difficulty. Some may think that I make this suggestion for my own advantage, in the hope of being left behind to guard the bridge; but that is not true: I am merely putting forward, my lord, what I believe to be the best plan for you to follow, and as for myself, I have no intention of staying here, but will accompany your army in its march.'

Darius was highly pleased with Coes' advice. 'When I am safely home again, my Lesbian friend,' he answered, 'be sure to come and see me, so that I may make some practical return for your excellent counsel.' Soon after, he called a meeting of the Ionian commanders and showed them a long leather strap in which he had tied sixty knots. 'Men of Ionia,' he said, 'my orders to you about the bridge are now cancelled; I want you to take this strap, and every day undo one of the knots, beginning with the day on which you see me start my march against the Scythians. Should I fail to return before all the knots have given out, you are at liberty to sail home; meanwhile, in accordance with my change of plans, guard the bridge with every possible care for its safety. This will be the greatest service you can do me.'

After giving his new orders, Darius pressed on without further delay.

Scythia is divided from us by Thrace, which comes down to the sea. Then the coast sweeps round in a great bend where Scythia begins and the Danube flows eastward into the sea. I will now give some indication of the extent of the Scythian coastline, starting from the Danube: across the Danube eastward, ancient Scythia begins, and continues, with the Black Sea as its southern boundary, as far as the town called Carcinitis. Then, still on the Black Sea, the land runs out in a great mountainous promontory and is inhabited by the Tauri, as far as what is known as the Rugged Chersonese which comes down into the eastern sea, Lake Maeotis.[1] For Scythia is bounded on two sides by two different seas, one to the south, the other to the east, much as Attica is; and the position of the Tauri in Scythia is – if I may compare small things with great – as if the promontory of Sunium from Thoricus to Anaphlystus in Attica projected rather further into the sea and were inhabited by some race other than Athenians. Or, to give a different illustration for the benefit of those who have not sailed along this bit of the Attic coast, it is as if some race other than the present inhabitants were to draw a line between the port of Brundisium and Tarentum in Iapygia, and occupy the promontory to seaward of it. These two examples may suggest many others, where the shape of the land resembles the Tauric peninsula. North of the Tauri, and along the sea-coast to the eastward, is again Scythian territory, as is also the country west of the Cimmerian Bosphorus and Lake Maeotis as far as the river Tanais, which flows into the far corner of the lake. On the landward side Scythia is bounded, starting from the Danube, by the following tribes: first the Agathyrsi, next the Neuri, then the Androphagi, and lastly the Melanchlaeni. In shape it is a square, of which the two sides touch the sea; all four sides are equal, those on the sea and those inland. It is a ten days' journey from the Danube to the Borysthenes, and another ten on to Lake Maeotis, making twenty; and it is also

1. The Sea of Azov.

a twenty days' journey inland from the Black Sea to the Melanchlaeni whose territory forms the northern boundary. I reckon a day's journey at 200 furlongs, so the two sides of the square which run inland, and the two transverse ones running east and west, are each 4000 furlongs in length.

The Scythians, after discussing the situation and concluding that by themselves they were unequal to the task of coping with Darius in a straight fight, sent off messengers to their neighbours, whose chieftains had already met and were forming plans to deal with what was evidently a threat to their safety on a very large scale. The conference was attended by the chieftains of the following tribes: the Tauri, Agathyrsi, Neuri, Androphagi, Melanchlaeni, Geloni, Budini, and Sauromatae. It is the custom of the Tauri to sacrifice to the Maiden Goddess all shipwrecked sailors and such Greeks as they happen to capture upon their coasts; their method of sacrifice is, after the preliminary ceremonies, to hit the victim on the head with a club. Some say that they push the victim's body over the edge of the cliff on which their temple stands, and fix the head on a stake; others, while agreeing about the head, say the body is not pushed over the cliff, but buried. The Tauri themselves claim that the goddess to whom these offerings are made is Agamemnon's daughter, Iphigenia. Any one of them who takes a prisoner in war, cuts off his head and carries it home, where he sets it up high over the house on a long pole, generally above the chimney. The heads are supposed to act as guardians of the whole house over which they hang. War and plunder are the sources of this people's livelihood.

The Agathyrsi live in luxury and wear gold on their persons. They have their women in common, so that they may all be brothers and, as members of a single family, be able to live together without jealousy or hatred. In other respects their way of life resembles that of the Thracians.

The Neuri share the customs of Scythia. A generation before the campaign of Darius they were forced to quit their country by snakes, which appeared all over the place in great numbers, while still more invaded them from the uninhabited region to the north, until life became so unendurable that there was nothing for it but to move out, and take up their quarters with the Budini. It appears that these people practise magic; for there is a story current amongst the Scythians and the Greeks in Scythia that once a year every Neurian turns into a wolf for a few days, and then turns back into a man again. I do not believe this tale; but all the same, they tell it, and even swear to the truth of it. The Androphagi are the most savage of men, and have no notion of either law or justice. They are herdsmen without fixed dwellings; their dress is Scythian, their language peculiar to themselves, and they are the only people in this part of the world to eat human flesh. The Melanchlaeni all wear black cloaks – hence their name. In all else they resemble the Scythians. The Budini, a numerous and powerful nation, all have markedly blue-grey eyes and red hair; there is a town in their territory called Gelonus, all built of wood, both dwelling-houses and temples, with a high wooden wall round it, thirty furlongs each way. There are temples here in honour of Greek gods, adorned after the Greek manner with statues, altars, and shrines – though all constructed of wood; a triennial festival, with the appropriate revelry, is held in honour of Dionysus. This is to be accounted for by the fact that the Geloni were originally Greeks, who, driven out of the seaports along the coast, settled amongst the Budini. Their language is still half Scythian, half Greek. The language of the Budini is quite different, as, indeed, is their culture generally: they are a pastoral people who have always lived in this part of the country (a peculiarity of theirs is eating lice), whereas the Geloni cultivate the soil, eat grain, and keep gardens, and resemble them neither in appearance nor complexion. In spite of these facts the Greeks lump the Budini and Geloni together under the name of the latter; but they are wrong to do so.

The country here is forest with trees of all sorts. In the most densely wooded part there is a big lake surrounded by reedy marshland; otters and beavers are caught in the lake, and another sort of creature with a square face, whose skin they use for making edgings for their jackets; its testicles are good for affections of the womb.

About the Sauromatae there is the following story. In the war between the Greeks and the Amazons, the Greeks, after their victory at the river Thermodon, sailed off in three ships with as many Amazons on board as they had succeeded in taking alive. (The Scythians call the Amazons *Oeorpata*, the equivalent of *mankillers*, *oeor* being the Scythian word for 'man', and *pata* for 'kill'.) Once at sea, the women murdered their captors, but, as they had no knowledge of boats and were unable to handle either rudder or sail or oar, they soon found themselves, when the men were done for, at the mercy of wind and wave, and were blown to Cremni – the Cliffs – on Lake Maeotis, a place within the territory of the free Scythians. Here they got ashore and made their way inland to an inhabited part of the country. The first thing they fell in with was a herd of horses grazing; these they seized, and, mounting on their backs, rode off in search of loot. The Scythians could not understand what was happening and were at a loss to know where the marauders had come from, as their dress, speech, and nationality were strange to them. Thinking, however, that they were young men, they fought in defence of their property, and discovered from the bodies which came into their possession after the battle that they were women. The discovery gave a new direction to their plans; they decided to make no further attempt to kill the invaders, but to send out a detachment of their youngest men, about equal in number to the Amazons, with orders to camp near them and take their cue from whatever it was that the Amazons then did: if they pursued them, they were not to fight, but to give ground; then, when the pursuit was abandoned, they were once again to encamp within easy range. The motive behind this policy was the Scythians' desire to get children by the Amazons. The detachment of young men obeyed their orders, and the Amazons, realizing that they meant no harm, did not attempt to molest them, with the result that every day the two camps drew a little closer together. Neither party had anything but their weapons and their horses, and both lived the same sort of life, hunting and plundering.

Towards midday the Amazons used to scatter and go off to some little distance in ones and twos to ease themselves, and the Scythians, when they noticed this, followed suit; until one of them, coming upon an Amazon girl all by herself, began to make advances to her. She, nothing loth, gave him what he wanted, and then told him by signs (being unable to express her meaning in words, as neither understood the other's language) to return on the following day with a friend, making it clear that there must be two men, and that she herself would bring another girl. The young man then left her and told the others what had happened, and on the next day took a friend to the same spot, where he found his Amazon waiting for him and another one with her. Having learnt of their success, the rest of the young Scythians soon succeeded in getting the Amazons to submit to their wishes. The two camps were then united, and Amazons and Scythians lived together, every man keeping as his wife the woman whose favours he had first enjoyed. The men could not learn the women's language, but the women succeeded in picking up the men's; so when they could understand one another, the Scythians made the following proposal: 'We', they said, 'have parents and property. Let us give up our present way of life and return to live with our people. We will keep you as our wives and not take any others.' The Amazons replied: 'We and the women of your nation could never live together; our ways are too much at variance. We are riders; our business is with the bow and the spear, and we know nothing of women's work; but in your country no woman has anything to do with such things – your women stay at home in their waggons occupied with feminine tasks, and never go out to hunt or for any other purpose. We could not possibly agree. If, however, you wish to keep us for your wives and to behave as honourable men, go and get from your parents the share of property which is due to you, and then let us go off and live by ourselves.' The young men agreed to this, and when they came back, each with his portion of the family possessions, the Amazons said: 'We dread the prospect of settling down here, for we have done much damage to the country by our raids, and we have robbed you of your parents. Look now – if you think fit to keep us for your wives, let us get out of the country altogether and settle somewhere on the other side of the Tanais.' Once again the Scythians agreed, so they crossed the Tanais and travelled east for three days, and then north, for another three, from Lake Maeotis, until they reached the country where they are to-day, and settled down there. Ever since then the women of the Sauromatae have kept to their old ways, riding to the hunt on horseback sometimes with, sometimes without, their menfolk, taking part in war and wearing the same sort of clothes as men. The language of these people is the Scythian, but it has always been a corrupt form of it because the Amazons were never able to learn to speak it properly.

They have a marriage law which forbids a girl to marry until she has killed an enemy in battle; some of their women, unable to fulfil this condition, grow old and die in spinsterhood.

These, then, were the nations whose chieftains had met together to discuss the common danger; and to them the envoys from Scythia brought the news that the Persian king, having overrun the whole of the other continent, had bridged the Bosphorus and crossed into Europe, where he had already brought Thrace into subjection and was now engaged in throwing a bridge across the Danube, with the intention of making himself master of all Europe too. 'We beg you,' they said, 'not to remain neutral in this struggle; do not let us be destroyed without raising a hand to help us. Let us rather form a common plan of action, and meet the invader together. If you refuse, we shall be forced to yield to pressure and either abandon our country or make terms with the enemy. Without your help, what else could we do? What will become of us? Moreover, if you stand aside, you will not on that account get out of things any more lightly; for this invasion is aimed at you just as much as at us, and, once we have gone under, the Persians will never be content to leave you unmolested. There is plain proof of the truth of this: for had the Persian attack been directed against us alone in revenge for the old wrong we did them when we enslaved their country, they would have been bound to come straight for Scythia without touching any other nation on the way. By doing that they would have made it plain to everyone that the object of their attack was Scythia, and Scythia alone; but, as things are, they no sooner crossed into Europe than they have begun to bring under their heel in turn every nation through whose territory they pass. Not to mention the other Thracians, even our neighbours the Getae have been enslaved.'

The assembled chieftains deliberated upon what the Scythian envoys had reported, but failed to reach a unanimous conclusion. Those of the Geloni, Budini, and Sauromatae agreed to stand by the Scythians, but the rest – the chieftains, namely, of the Agathyrsi, Neuri, Androphagi, Melanchlaeni, and Tauri – returned the following answer. 'Had you not yourselves been the aggressors in your trouble with Persia, we should have considered your request justified; we should have granted what you ask and been willing enough to fight at your side. But the fact is, you invaded Persia without consulting us, and remained in possession of it as long as heaven allowed you, and now the same power is urging the Persians to pay you back in your own coin. We did the Persians no injury on that former occasion, and we will not be the first to start trouble now. Of course, should they prove to be the aggressors and actually invade us, we shall do our best to keep them out; but until we see that happen, we shall stay where we are and do nothing. In our opinion, the invasion is directed not against us, but against you, who were the aggressors in the first place.'

When this reply was reported to the Scythians, seeing that these nations refused to support them, they decided to avoid a straight fight, and to retire, blocking up all the wells and springs which they passed and trampling the pasture. They organized their forces in two divisions. One, under the command of Scopasis, was to be joined by the Sauromatae, and had orders if the Persians turned against them to withdraw along the coast of Lake Maeotis toward the river Don, and, should the Persians themselves retreat, to attack them in their turn. This was one division, and this was the route it was to take. Of the other, the two sections – the greater under Idanthyrsus and the second under Taxacis – were to unite forces and, after joining up with the Geloni and Budini, were, like the first division, to withdraw before the Persian advance at the distance of a day's march, and carry out as they went the same strategy. This division was to begin by retiring in the direction of those nations who had refused to join the alliance, with the idea of involving them in the war against their will, if they would not fight on their own initiative. Subsequently, this second force was to go back to their own country and launch an attack, if the situation seemed to justify it.

Having determined on this plan of action, the Scythians marched out to meet Darius, sending their best horsemen in advance. The waggons which served as houses for the women and children, and all the cattle, except what they needed for food, were ordered to move northward at once, in advance of their future line of retreat. The advance-guard made contact with the Persians about three days' march from the Danube, and at once encamped at a distance of a single day's march in front of them, devastating the land. The Persians, on the appearance of the Scythian cavalry, gave chase and continued to follow in their tracks as they withdrew before them. The Persian advance was now directed against the single division of the Scythian army under Scopasis, and was consequently eastward towards the Don. The Scythians crossed the river, and the Persians followed in pursuit, until they had passed through the territory of the Sauro-matae and reached that of the Budini, where they came across the wooden fortified town of Gelonus, abandoned and empty of defend-ers, and burnt it. Previously, so long as their route lay through the country of the Scythians and Sauromatae, they had done no damage, because the country was barren and there was nothing to destroy. After burning the town, they continued to press forward on the enemy's heels until they reached the great uninhabited region which lies beyond the territory of the Budini. This tract of land is seven days' journey across, and on the further side of it lies the country of the Thyssagetae, from which four great rivers, Lycus, Oarus, Tanais, and Syrgis, flow through the land of the Macotae to empty them-selves into Lake Maeotis.

When he reached this uninhabited area, Darius called a halt on the banks of the Oarus, and began eight large forts, spaced at regular intervals of approximately eight miles. The remains of them were still to be seen in my day. While these forts were under construction, the Scythians whom he had been following changed the direction of their march, and by a broad sweep through the country to the northward returned to Scythia and completely disappeared. Unable to see any sign of them, Darius left his forts half finished and himself turned back towards the west, supposing that the Scythians he had been chasing were the whole nation, and that they were now trying to escape in that direction. He made the best speed he was capable of, and on reaching Scythia fell in with the other two combined divisions of the Scythian army; at once he gave chase, and they, as before, withdrew a day's march in front of him. As Darius continued to press forward in hot pursuit, the Scythians now carried out their plan of leading him into the territory of the people who had refused, in the first instance, to support them in their resistance to Persia. The first were the Melanchlaeni, and the double invasion of their country, first by the Scythians and then by the Persians, caused great disturbance; the turn of the Androphagi came next, and then the Neuri, with the same result. Finally, still withdrawing before the Persian advance, the Scythians approached the frontiers of the Agathyrsi. These people, unlike their neighbours, of whose terrified attempt to escape they had been witness, did not wait for the Scythians to invade them, but sent a representative to forbid them to cross the frontier, adding a warning that, if they attempted to do so, they would be resisted by force of arms. This challenge they followed up by manning their frontiers in arms. The other tribes – the Melanchlaeni, Androphagi, and Neuri – offered no resistance to the successive invasions of Scythians and Persians, but forgot their former threats and in great confusion fled northwards into the waste. The Scythians, finding the Agathyrsi prepared to keep them out, then changed direction, and, from the land of the Neuri, drew the Persians back into Scythia.

Finding no end of this, Darius at last dispatched a rider with a message for Idanthyrsus, the Scythian king. 'Why on earth, my good sir,' the message ran, 'do you keep on running away? You have, surely, a choice of two alternatives: if you think yourself strong enough to oppose me, stand up and fight, instead of wandering all over the world in your efforts to escape me; or, if you admit that you are too weak, what is the good, even so, of running away? You should rather send earth and water to your master, as the sign of your submission, and come to a conference.'

'Persian,' Idanthyrsus replied, 'I have never yet run from any man in fear; and I am not doing so now from you. There is, for me, nothing unusual in what I have been doing: it is precisely the sort of life I always lead, even in times of peace. If you want to know why I will not fight, I will tell you: in our country there are no towns and no cultivated land; fear of losing which, or seeing it ravaged, might indeed provoke us to hasty battle. If, however, you are determined upon bloodshed with the least possible delay, one thing there is for which we will fight – the tombs of our forefathers. Find those tombs, and try to wreck them, and you will soon know whether or not we are willing to stand up to you. Till then – unless for good reason – we shall continue to avoid a battle. This is my reply to your challenge; and as for your being my master, I acknowledge no masters but

Zeus from whom I sprang, and Hestia the Scythian queen. I will send you no gifts of earth and water, but others more suitable; and your claim to be my master is easily answered – be damned to you!' This was the message which was carried back to Darius.

The mere suggestion of slavery filled the Scythian chieftains with rage, and they dispatched the division under Scopasis, which included the Sauromatae, with orders to seek a conference with the Ionians, who were guarding the bridge over the Danube. Those who remained decided to stop leading the Persians the usual dance, and to attack them whenever they found them foraging. This policy they carried out, waiting for the proper opportunities to present themselves. On every occasion the Scythian cavalry proved superior to the Persian, which would give ground and fall back on the infantry for support; this checked the attack, for the Scythians knew the Persian infantry would be too much for them, and regularly turned tail after driving in the cavalry. Similar raids were made at night.

I must mention one very surprising thing which helped the Persians and hampered the Scythians in these skirmishes: I mean the unfamiliar appearance of the mules and the braying of the donkeys. As I have already pointed out, neither donkeys nor mules are bred in Scythia – indeed, there is not a single specimen of either in the whole country, because of the cold. This being so, the donkeys' braying caused great confusion amongst the Scythian cavalry; often, in the course of an attack, the sound of it so much upset the horses, which had never heard such a noise before or seen such a creature as that from which it proceeded, that they would turn short round, ears pricked, in consternation. This gave the Persians some small advantage in the campaign.

Seeing the Persians disorganized by these continual raids, the Scythians hit upon a stratagem to keep them longer in the country and reduce them in the end to distress from lack of supplies. This was to slip away from time to time to some other position leaving behind a few cattle in the charge of shepherds; the Persians would come and take the animals, and be much encouraged by the momentary success. This happened again and again, until at last Darius did not know where to turn, and the Scythians, seeing his acute embarrassment, sent him the promised presents – a bird, a mouse, a frog, and five arrows. The Persians asked the man who brought these things what they signified, but got no reply. The man's orders – so he said – were merely to deliver them, and to return home as quickly as he could: the Persians themselves, if they were clever, could find out what the presents meant. Thereupon the Persians put their heads together, and Darius expressed the view that the Scythians were giving him earth and water and intended to surrender: mice, he reasoned, live on the ground and eat the same food as men; frogs live in water; birds are much like horses – and the arrows symbolized the Scythian power, which they were giving into his hands. Gobryas, however (one of the seven conspirators who put down the Magus), by no means agreed with him, but interpreted the gifts as saying: 'Unless you Persians turn into birds and fly up in the air, or into mice and burrow under ground, or into frogs and jump into the lakes, you will never get home again, but stay here in this country, only to be shot by the Scythian arrows.'

While the Persians were thus interpreting the gifts, the division of the Scythian force which had previously had orders to keep watch along the shore of Lake Maeotis, and had now been sent to confer with the Ionians on the Danube, made its way to the bridge. 'Men of Ionia,' began the Scythian spokesman, 'we bring you freedom, if only you will do what we suggest. We understand that your orders from Darius were to guard the bridge for sixty days – no more; and after that if he failed to put in an appearance, to go home. Now, therefore, the obvious thing for you to do is to wait till the sixty days have passed and then clear out – neither Darius nor ourselves will have anything to reproach you for in that.' The Ionians agreed and the Scythians rode back without loss of time.

After the presents had been sent to Darius, the Scythians who had not gone to the Danube drew up their cavalry and infantry with the apparent intention of offering the Persians battle. But as soon as their dispositions were made, a hare started up between the two armies and began running. The Scythians were after it in a moment – company after company of them, directly they caught sight of it – while the army was reduced to a shouting rabble. Darius inquired what all the noise and fuss were about, and upon learning that the enemy was engaged in hunting a hare, he turned to those of his officers he was in

the habit of talking with, and said: 'These fellows have a hearty contempt for us, and I am now ready to believe that Gobryas' interpretation of those things they sent me was the right one. Well then – as I
have come round to his opinion, it is time to think of the best way
of getting out of this country in safety.'

'My lord,' Gobryas answered. 'I already knew pretty well from
hearsay how difficult the Scythians were to deal with, and now that
I am on the spot and can see how they fool us with their tricks, I
know it all the better. As to our next move, my proposal is this: as
soon as it is dark, I suggest that we should light the camp-fires as
usual, and then, tethering the donkeys and leaving behind on some
pretext or other those of our men who are least fit to face the hardship
and privation, clear out before the Scythians advance to the Danube
and destroy the bridge, and before the Ionians on guard can take any
measures which may lead to our destruction.'

Darius adopted this proposal, and as soon as night fell began the
homeward march, leaving behind the sick and such other of his troops
as he could most easily spare, as well as the donkeys all tethered in
their usual places. His object in leaving the donkeys was to let their
braying disguise the fact of his withdrawal; as for the men, they were
incapacitated by sickness and he did want not them – though he gave
it out that they were to guard the camp, while he, with his best
troops, launched an attack on the Scythians. Having thus explained
his departure to the men whom he was, in point of fact, deserting,
Darius had the camp-fires lighted and moved off at his best speed
towards the Danube. The donkeys made more noise than ever when
they were aware that the main body of the army had gone; and when
the Scythians heard it they never suspected any change in the situation, but were confident that the whole Persian army was still there.
Dawn came; and the Persian remnant, realizing that Darius had
betrayed them, held out their arms in sign of surrender, and told the
Scythians of what had occurred. On hearing the news, the whole
Scythian force – all the three divisions of it, joined by the Sauromatae, the Budini, and Geloni – without a moment's delay set off for
the Danube in pursuit of the Persians. The greater part of the Persian
army was travelling on foot, and, in the absence of regular roads, was
uncertain of the way; and the consequence was that the Scythians,

who were all mounted, and perfectly familiar with the most direct route, reached the bridge long before them. The two armies had missed each other on the way, and the Scythians, realizing that the Persians had not yet arrived, seized the opportunity of another word with the Ionians on the ships. 'Men of Ionia,' they said, 'your sixty days are now up, and you have no business to wait any longer. Hitherto you stayed at your post because you feared the consequences of desertion; but now things have changed – break up the bridge and be off. Good luck go with you, and thank the gods and the Scythians for your freedom. As for your former master, we will settle with him in such a way that his present campaign will prove his last.'

In the discussion which followed, Miltiades the Athenian, who was lord of the Chersonese on the Hellespont and in command of its contingent, expressed the opinion that they should take the Scythians' advice, and so liberate Ionia; he was opposed, however, by Histiaeus of Miletus, who pointed out that each one of them owed his position as head of a state to Darius, and, in the event of Darius' fall, he himself would be unable to maintain his power at Miletus, nor would any of the rest of them. Each state would be sure to turn against absolute government, and choose democracy. The meeting had begun by supporting Miltiades; but no sooner had Histiaeus put forward this view than everyone present changed his mind and it was unanimously adopted. The voters on this occasion were these: Daphnis of Abydos, Hippoclus of Lampsacus, Herophantus of Parium, Metrodorus of Proconnesus, Aristagoras of Cyzicus, and Ariston of Byzantium – all men highly esteemed by Darius, and all despots of their states on the Hellespont; in addition to these there were, from Ionia, Strattis of Chios, Aeaces of Samos, Laodamas of Phocaea, and Histiaeus of Miletus – the same who opposed Miltiades. The only distinguished Aeolian present was Aristagoras of Cyme.

Once they had accepted the view put forward by Histiaeus, they decided upon the next step to be taken, and how they would disguise its true purpose. The plan was to remove a portion of the bridge – about the length of a bowshot – on the Scythian side of the river, which would serve the double purpose of appearing to be doing something which they were not, and of preventing the Scythians from forcing a passage over, and to assure the Scythians, while the work of demolition was going on, that they would do all they were asked. This was how they intended to work out in practice the proposal of Histiaeus; and when the decision was made, Histiaeus himself was chosen to address the Scythians. 'Men of Scythia,' he said, 'you bring good news, and it is lucky you have got here so soon. Everything is going ahead well, and to our mutual benefit – your service to us, and ours to you. As you see, we are demolishing the bridge, and we shall spare no effort to recover our freedom. The best thing you can do, while we are busy with the demolition, is to go and look for the Persian army; then, when you have found it, you can punish the invaders as they deserve, both for your own sakes and for ours.' Once again the Scythians believed in the good faith of the Ionians; they went back in search of the Persian army, but completely failed to make contact with it anywhere. The failure was their own fault, for they could easily have found the Persians if they had not blocked up the wells and destroyed everything which the horses could eat – precisely the move on which they most congratulated themselves. But as it turned out, it was the one thing that wrecked their chances; for in their search for the Persian army they followed a route through a part of the country where there was both pasture and water, thinking that the Persians, in their attempt to escape, would naturally do the same. The Persians, however, kept strictly to the route they had originally followed. They had great difficulty in reaching the crossing. It was dark when they arrived, and the discovery that the bridge was broken caused a panic, for they at once supposed that the Ionians had left them in the lurch. Darius, however, told an Egyptian he happened to have with him, a man with a tremendous voice, to stand on the river bank and shout for Histiaeus. The fellow obeyed, and Histiaeus, who heard him at the very first hail, set all the ships to the task of ferrying the army over, and made good the broken section of the bridge. In this way the Persians got safely out of the country, having twice avoided the Scythians' attempt to make contact with them. The Scythians have a low opinion of the men of Ionia in consequence of all this: to consider them as a free people, they are, they say, the most despicable and craven in the world; and, considered as slaves, the most subservient to their masters and the least likely to run away.

Darius now marched through Thrace to Sestos in the Chersonese, where he took ship for Asia, leaving a distinguished Persian named Megabazus to command in Europe. Darius had once paid this man a high compliment: wishing to eat some pomegranates, he had just opened the first of them, when his brother Artabanus asked him which of his possessions he would like to be multiplied to a number as great as the seeds in a pomegranate. Darius' answer was 'Megabazus': he would rather, he said, have such a number of men like Megabazus than be master of Greece. It was in Persia that Darius paid him this compliment, and on the present occasion he left him in Europe with a corps of the army 80,000 strong. This same Megabazus once made a remark for which the people along the Hellespont have never forgotten him: he was in Byzantium, and on hearing that Chalcedon was settled seventeen years earlier than that city, he said the men of Chalcedon must have been blind at the time; for if they had had any eyes, they would never have chosen an inferior site, when a much finer one lay ready to hand. Megabazus, then, as I have said, being left behind in command on the Hellespont, began the reduction of such communities as did not submit to Persia.

While Megabazus was thus occupied, another powerful force was on its way against Libya. Before I explain the reason for this, I have some preliminary matters to relate. The grandsons of the crew of the ship *Argo* were expelled from Lemnos by the Pelasgians who had kidnapped the Athenian women from Brauron. Leaving Lemnos, they sailed to Lacedaemon, where they encamped on Mount Taygetus. The Lacedaemonians, seeing the fires that these men had kindled on the ridge, sent someone to find out who they were and where they had come from. On being questioned, they said they were Minyae, descendants of the heroes who had sailed in the *Argo* and had put in at Lemnos, where they started the families to which they belonged. When the Lacedaemonians heard this account of their parentage, they sent a second messenger to ask what their object was in coming to Lacedaemon and lighting their fire. To this they replied that, having been thrown out of Lemnos by the Pelasgians, they had come to the land of their fathers – which was the most reasonable thing they could do; and that now they wanted to settle down there, and have a share in the land and in the privileges of government. The

Lacedaemonians, moved in particular by the fact that the sons of Tyndareus had sailed in the *Argo*, consented to receive the Minyae on the terms they proposed, and gave them grants of land and divided them amongst the various tribes. At once the Minyae married Spartan wives, and gave the women they had brought from Lemnos to Spartan husbands. It was not long, however, before the Minyae, in the pride of their newly won privileges, began to go too far, even claiming a share in the royal power, and doing other things no less improper. The Lacedaemonians, therefore, decided to kill them, and, with this purpose in view, arrested them and threw them into prison. Now judicial killings at Sparta are always carried out at night, never by day; so just before sentence could be executed on the Minyae, their wives asked leave to be admitted into the prison, in order to have a word with their husbands. These women were all natives of Sparta and daughters of leading Spartan citizens, so no one suspected treachery, and they succeeded in getting their request granted. Once inside the prison, however, they changed clothes with the men, who were enabled by this disguise to pass themselves off as women and get out. Then, having made their escape, they once more established themselves on Taygetus.

While all this was going on, Theras the son of Autesion (Autesion's father Tisamenus was the son of Thersander and grandson of Polyneices) was preparing to leave Lacedaemon to found a settlement elsewhere. Theras was a Cadmeian by descent, and maternal uncle of Eurysthenes and Procles, the two sons of Aristodemus, and acted as regent in Sparta during his nephews' infancy; but when the boys grew up and took over the reins of government, he so deeply resented finding himself, after a taste of power, in a subordinate position, that he refused to stay in Lacedaemon and declared that he would sail away to join his kinsfolk in the island of Thera. This island used to be known as Callista, and certain descendants of Membliarus, son of the Phoenician Poiciles, were living in it. Cadmus, the son of Agenor, touched at it during his search for Europa and, whether because he liked the place or for some other reason, left there a number of Phoenicians with his own kinsman Membliarus amongst them. These men and their descendants lived in Callista for eight generations before Theras came from Lacedaemon, and it was to join with them that Theras was now preparing to sail with a party of colonists chosen from the various tribes in Sparta. He had no intention of turning them out – he insisted strongly that he meant to settle down with them as a kinsman.

It was just at this time that the Minyae escaped from prison and sat themselves down on Taygetus; and the Lacedaemonians were planning their destruction, when Theras, wishing to prevent bloodshed, begged them off and undertook to carry them away out of the country. The Lacedaemonians agreed, so he set sail to join the descendants of Membliarus in three thirty-oared galleys, taking with him the Minyae – or, rather, some few of them; for the great number went off to the country of the Paroreatae and Caucones, whom they drove from their home, and afterwards built six towns of their own, to correspond to the six groups into which they had divided themselves. The towns were Lepreum, Macistus, Phrixae, Pyrgus, Epium, and Nudium: most of them were destroyed within my own time by the people of Elis. Callista was renamed Thera after Theras, who settled there.

Theras' son refused to accompany the expedition, and Theras said he would be leaving him behind like a sheep amongst wolves: the remark caught on, and led to the young man being known as Oeolycus – a name which stuck to him. He was later the father of Aegeus, who gave his name to the Aegidae, a powerful Spartan clan – the men of this clan were advised by an oracle to build a shrine to the Furies of Oedipus and Laius, because their children never survived. The remedy was successful and the mortality ceased. The same thing happened to their descendants in Thera.

Up to this point the Lacedaemonians and the Theraeans tell the same story; what follows is on the authority of the latter only. Grinnus, the son of Aesanius, a descendant of Theras and king of the island, went to Delphi to offer a sacrifice of a hundred victims on behalf of the community. Amongst the people of the island who accompanied him was Battus, son of Polymnestus, a member of the Minyan family of the Euphemidae. During his stay at Delphi, Grinnus consulted the oracle on quite different matters, and received from the Priestess the apparently irrelevant answer that he must found a city in Libya. 'Lord Apollo,' he replied, 'I am too old and inactive to start on such a journey; can you not tell one of these

younger men to undertake it instead of me?' And as he spoke he
pointed at Battus. For the moment, nothing further occurred; they
left Delphi, put the oracle out of their minds, and did nothing about
it – for they did not even know where Libya was, and shrank from
sending out a party of settlers merely, as it were, into the blue.
During the seven years that followed not a drop of rain fell in Thera,
and every tree on the island, except one, withered and died. In this
difficult situation the Theraeans sent to Delphi for advice, and were
reminded about the colony which they had omitted to send to Libya.
There was now nothing else to be done, so they sent some men to
Crete to inquire if any native of that island, or any stranger living
there, had ever been to Libya. In the course of their travels about
Crete, the party from Thera came to Itanus, where they met a certain
Corobius, a purple-fisher, who told them that he had once been
blown out of his course and had fetched up at the island of Platea,
just off the Libyan coast. This man they paid to return with them to
Thera, and shortly afterwards a small reconnoitring party, with Corobius as pilot, set sail. They reached Platea and put Corobius ashore
with enough supplies for a stated number of months, and then made
sail again with all speed for home, to bring the news about the island.
They had agreed with Corobius to be away a definite length of time;
this period, however, was exceeded, and Corobius was in distress
from lack of supplies, until a Samian vessel bound for Egypt, under
the command of a man called Colaeus, was forced by the weather to
run for Platea. The Samians listened to Corobius' story, left him
enough food to last a year, and resumed their voyage to Egypt, which
they were anxious to reach. Easterly winds, however, prevented
them from getting there, and continued so long that they were driven
away to the westward right through the Pillars of Heracles until, by
a piece of more than human luck, they succeeded in making Tartessus.
This place had not at that period been exploited, and the consequence
was that the Samian merchants, on their return home, made a greater
profit on their cargo than any Greeks of whom we have precise
knowledge, with the exception of Sostratus of Aegina, the son of
Laodamas – with him, nobody can compare. A tenth part of their pro-
fits, amounting to six talents, they spent on the manufacture of a
bronze vessel, shaped like an Argive wine-bowl, with a continuous

row of griffins' heads round the rim; this bowl, supported upon three kneeling figures in bronze, eleven and a half feet high, they placed as an offering in the temple of Hera. The help given by the Samian merchants to Corobius was the origin of the strong bond of friendship between Samos on the one hand, and Cyrene and Thera on the other.

The Theraeans who had left Corobius in Platea told their compatriots, when they reached home, that they had established a settlement on an island off the Libyan coast, and it was thereupon decided to send a party to join the new colony; the party was to represent all the seven villages in Thera, and brothers were to draw lots to determine which should join it. It was to be under the sole authority of Battus. Two fifty-oared galleys then got under way for Platea.

I have related the foregoing on the authority of the Theraeans only; for the sequel, the people of Cyrene are in agreement with them. Nevertheless, in what concerns Battus, they tell a different story. Etearchus, they say, the ruler of a city in Crete called Oaxus, had a daughter named Phronima, and, when the girl's mother died, married a second wife. This woman had no sooner entered the family than she thought fit to make herself a proper stepmother to Phronima, in deed as well as name, and thought of everything she possibly could to torment her. To crown all, she accused her of fornication and persuaded her husband that it was true. Etearchus planned, in consequence, to get rid of poor Phronima in a most abominable manner. He made friends with a man called Themison, a Theraean merchant living in Oaxus, and obtained from him a promise upon oath to perform whatever service should be asked of him. Then, as soon as he had got him to take the oath, he fetched his daughter, put her into Themison's charge, and told him to take her away and throw her into the sea. Themison was very angry at the way he had been caught, and broke off his friendship with Etearchus; then, in order to clear himself of the obligation under which his oath had laid him, he put to sea with the girl and, when they were clear of the land, lowered her into the water on the end of a rope, hauled her up again, and sailed home with her to Thera, where a distinguished Theraean named Polymnestus afterwards made her his mistress. In course of time she gave birth to a son, who lisped and stammered, and this child – according, at any rate, to what is said at

Thera and Cyrene – was called Battus. My own view, however, is that he was never known as Battus until after he went to Libya, where he assumed the name in consequence of the words spoken by the Delphic oracle, and of the high position he held there – for 'battus' in the Libyan language means 'king', and that, I fancy, is why the Priestess at Delphi, when she spoke the prophecy, addressed him by the Libyan word, knowing, as she did, that he was to become a king in Libya. For after he had grown to manhood he went to Delphi to consult the oracle about his defective speech, and was answered by the lines:

> O Battus, for a voice you come; but the lord Apollo
> Sends you to Libya, nurse of flocks, to build a city –

which would have been the equivalent of saying in Greek, 'O King, for a voice you come'. Battus replied: 'Lord, I consulted your oracle about my speech, and you tell me, quite irrelevantly, to found a settlement in Libya! It is impossible. What resources have I? What men?' But his complaint was useless; he could get no other answer from the oracle, and when the same command was repeated, he left the temple before the Priestess had finished speaking and returned to Thera. Subsequently, however, he had no better luck than before; indeed, everything began to go wrong both with Battus himself and the others on the island. What was the cause of their distress they could not understand, and, when they sent to Delphi for enlightenment, the old answer was yet again repeated: if, the Priestess said, they would join Battus in founding a settlement at Cyrene in Libya, their fortunes would mend. So then they sent Battus off, and he and a party of men sailed for Libya in two fifty-oared galleys; they reached the coast, but, unable to decide what their next move should be, sailed home again to Thera. The islanders, however, refused to allow them to come ashore; they threw things at them as they were making up for the harbour, and shouted that they must put about and go back again; so, as there was nothing else for it, they once more got under way for Libya. This time, they established themselves on Platea, the island off the coast which I mentioned before. It is said to be of the same size as the city of Cyrene is to-day.

The settlers stayed in Platea for two years; but they failed to prosper in their new home, and all made sail again for Delphi, leaving one man behind on the island. They went to the oracle, and declared that, in spite of the fact that they were living in Libya, they were no better off than before. To this the Priestess replied:

> If you know sheep-breeding Libya better than I do,
> Not having been there – I have – I marvel much at your cunning!

On this, Battus and his men sailed away once more for Platea, for it was plain that Apollo would not let them off until they established a settlement actually on the Libyan mainland. After calling, therefore, at the island and taking off the man they had left there, they crossed to the mainland and built a town on the coast, just south of Platea, at a spot called Aziris – a charming place with a river on one side and lovely valleys on both. Here they lived for six years, but were then persuaded to leave by the Libyans, who undertook to show them a better place. After getting them to consent to the move, the Libyans took them further west, and so timed the journey as to pass through the finest bit of country – called Irasa – in the dark, in order to prevent them from seeing it. Finally they reached the spring called Apollo's Fountain and the Libyan guides said to the Greeks: 'This is the place for you to settle in, for here there is a hole in the sky.'

During the lifetime of Battus, the founder of Cyrene, who ruled there for forty years, and of his son Arcesilaus, who ruled for sixteen, the number of people in the town remained equal to that of the original settlers; but under the rule of its third king – known as Battus the Fortunate – an oracle delivered at Delphi was the cause of a great rush amongst the Greeks generally to join the colony. For the people of Cyrene themselves were offering land to new settlers, and the oracle declared that whoever came to delightful Libya after the land was parcelled out, should one day rue it.

In this way the population of the place greatly increased, and it began to encroach upon the territory of its neighbours. Its expansion continued, until the Libyans under their king, Adicran, in resentment at their loss of territory and the domineering attitude of Cyrene, dispatched an embassy to Egypt and put themselves at the disposal of the Egyptian king Apries, who collected a strong force and sent it against Cyrene. The Cyrenaeans took the field and, marching to the Well of Thestis in Irasa, engaged and defeated the Egyptian army. This severe defeat – so severe that few of them returned home alive – was doubtless due to the fact that the Egyptians had had no previous experience of Greek fighting and were not prepared to treat it seriously. Apries' subjects blamed him personally for this disastrous campaign, and it was the reason for their rebellion against him.

Battus the Fortunate had a son named Arcesilaus, who on coming to power quarrelled with his brothers, until they left him and went off to another part of the country, where they founded on their own initiative a second settlement – the town called, then as now, Barca. While the town was still building, they persuaded the Libyans to withdraw their allegiance from Cyrene, and Arcesilaus made war upon those of them who had consented to do so. Alarmed by the approach of the troops from Cyrene, the Libyans hastily withdrew to the eastward, and Arcesilaus gave chase as far as the place in Libya called Leucon, where the Libyans decided to attack him. In the fight which ensued the Cyrenaeans were soundly beaten, losing as many as 7000 heavy-armed men. Following this severe blow, Arcesilaus fell ill and, after taking some drug, was strangled by his brother Learchus, who, in his turn, was murdered by Eryxo, Arcesilaus' wife. The lordship of Cyrene then passed to Arcesilaus' son Battus – a lame man with a limp. These misfortunes prompted the Cyrenaeans to send to the oracle at Delphi for advice – how, they asked, should they order their affairs so as to secure the most satisfactory sort of government? In reply, the Priestess told them to call in a man from Mantinea in Arcadia to put things right for them; so they applied for a suitable person and were given the services of a certain Demonax, who enjoyed the highest reputation amongst the citizens of Mantinea. Demonax, accordingly, went to Cyrene and, after making himself familiar with all the facts of the situation there, took the following measures: he divided the population into three sections, or tribes, the first consisting of the emigrants from Thera and their neighbours, the second of men from the Peloponnese and Crete, and the third of men from the islands. Next, he appropriated to Battus, the ruler of the city, certain special lands and priestly offices, and threw open to the people in general all the other privileges which had previously been enjoyed by the kings. These arrangements remained unaltered during Battus' lifetime, but under his son and successor Arcesilaus there was a great rumpus about the various state offices and privileges, and Arcesilaus (the son, that is, of Battus the lame and Pheretima) refused to put up with the new order introduced by Demonax, and demanded the restoration of his ancestral rights. In the civil struggles which followed, he was defeated and fled to Samos, and his mother sought refuge at Salamis in Cyprus – a town which was controlled at that period by Euelthon, who dedicated the remarkable censer in the Corinthian treasure-house at Delphi. Pheretima went to Euelthon's court and asked for an army to put the party she represented back in power at Cyrene; but an army was the one thing Euelthon was unwilling to give her. Other things he gave her generously enough, and each time she accepted a present she said it was a fine one, but not so fine as to give her what she really wanted – an army. As she continued on every occasion to make the same remark, Euelthon ended by sending her a golden spindle and distaff, with wool on it. Pheretima repeated the same words as before, which drew from Euelthon the reply that he had sent her a present which, unlike an army, he thought suitable to her sex.

Arcesilaus, meanwhile, was in Samos, collecting all manner of men, with promises of a general share-out of the land. When he had got a large force together he set off for Delphi to ask the oracle about the chances of his return to Cyrene. 'Apollo Loxias,' the Priestess replied, 'grants you power in Cyrene over a period of eight generations under four rulers named Battus and four named Arcesilaus; but he advises you to make no attempt to keep your power beyond that period. As for yourself, when you return to your country, be gentle. If you find the oven full of jars, do not bake them but send them away downwind. But if you do heat the oven, enter not the land surrounded by water, for otherwise you will die, and the best of the bulls with you.' Having heard this oracular utterance, Arcesilaus went back to Cyrene with his Samian supporters and recovered possession of supreme power. But once there, he forgot the warning of the oracle and took proceedings against his political opponents, who had driven him into exile. Some of them left the country for good; others fell into his hands and were sent to their death in Cyprus. These last, however, were forced by the weather to put in at Cnidus, and were rescued by the islanders and sent to Thera. Others shut themselves up in a high tower, the private stronghold of one Aglomachus, and Arcesilaus stacked wood round the place and burnt them alive. After this deed, realizing, too late, that this was what the oracle had meant when the Priestess warned him, if he should find the jars in the oven, not to bake them, he deliberately kept away from Cyrene, because he thought it might be the 'land surrounded by water' which the oracle had spoken of, and he was afraid the prophecy of his death might be fulfilled. Nevertheless, he was not to escape: he had a wife related to him by blood, the daughter of Alazir, the ruler of Barca; to this man he went, and the people of Barca, with some of the exiles from Cyrene, saw him in the market and killed him. They also killed his father-in-law Alazir. So Arcesilaus, whether he would or not, missed the meaning of the oracle and fulfilled his destiny.

While Arcesilaus was in Barca after doing the deed which was to bring him to ruin, his mother Pheretima represented him at Cyrene, enjoying his privileges, attending to the business of government, and taking her seat in the council; but on hearing of her son's death, she fled to Egypt on the strength of certain services which Arcesilaus had rendered to Cambyses, the son of Cyrus; for it was he who had put Cyrene under Cambyses' control and fixed a rate of tribute. On her arrival there she flung herself on the mercy of Aryandes, justifying her request for help by the argument that it was Arcesilaus' friendship with Persia that had caused his death. Aryandes had been made governor of Egypt by Cambyses: he subsequently lost his life as the result of an attempt to rival Darius. Aware by what he had seen and heard that Darius wished to perpetuate his memory by something no other king had previously done, Aryandes started to follow his example – but he soon got what he deserved for his impudence. The facts were these: Darius had issued a gold coinage, of which the metal was of the greatest possible purity, and Aryandes as governor of Egypt had followed suit by a similar issue of silver – and indeed to this day the purest silver coinage is the Aryandic. Darius, when he came to know of this, disguised the real cause of his anger by bringing a charge of rebellion against Aryandes, and had him executed.

Now, however, Aryandes took pity on Pheretima and put at her service all the forces in Egypt, both army and fleet, with Amasis, a man of the Maraphian tribe, to command the former, and Badres, of the Pasargadae, to command the latter; then, before giving the order to move, he sent a herald to Barca to inquire the name of the man who had murdered Arcesilaus. To this the people of the town replied that they were all equally responsible – for they had received many injuries at his hands. At that Aryandes ordered the troops to march with Pheretima. This, at any rate, was the cause which served as a pretext for the expedition; its real object, I fancy, was the sub-jugation of Libya. The races of men in Libya are many and various, and only a few of them were subject to the Persian king; the greater number never gave Darius a moment's thought.

The following is a description of the Libyan tribes in their order: starting from Egypt, the first are the Adyrmachidae, whose way of living is more or less Egyptian in character. They dress like the rest of the Libyans. Their women wear a bronze ring on each leg, and grow their hair long; when they catch a bug on their persons, they give it bite for bite before throwing it away. They are the only Libyan tribe to follow this practice, as also that of taking girls who are about to be married to see the king. Any girl who catches his fancy, leaves him a maid no longer. This tribe extends from the Egyptian border as far as the port called Plynus.

Next come the Giligamae, whose territory runs westward as far as the island of Aphrodisias. In between lies Platea, the island off the coast where the Cyrenaeans first settled, and on the mainland is the Harbour of Menelaus, and Aziris where the Cyrenaeans also lived for a time. It is in this part of the country that silphium begins to be found, and extends all the way from Platea to the mouth of the Syrtis. The Giligamae live in much the same sort of way as the other tribes. Next to the westward are the Asbystae; their territory lies further inland than Cyrene, and does not extend to the coast, which is occu-pied by the Cyrenaeans. This tribe is conspicuous amongst the Libyans for its use of four-horse chariots, and in its general way of life does its best to imitate that of Cyrene. Westward, again, are the Auschisae, who live south of Barca and touch the sea near Euesperides. Within their territory is the small tribe of the Bacales, who reach the coast near Tauchira, a town belonging to Barca; they live in the same sort of way as the people south of Cyrene. Still proceeding in a westerly direction, one comes next to the Nasamones, a numerous tribe, who in the summer leave their cattle on the coast and go up country to a place called Augila for the date harvest. The date-palms here grow in large numbers and to a great size, and are all of the fruit-bearing kind. These people also catch locusts, which they dry in the sun and grind up fine; then they sprinkle the powder on milk and drink it. Each of them has a number of wives, which they use in common, like the Massagetae – when a man wants to lie with a woman, he puts up a pole to indicate his intention. It is the custom, at a man's first marriage, to give a party, at which the bride is enjoyed by each of the guests in turn; they take her one after another, and then give her a present – something or other they have brought with them from home. In the matter of oaths, their practice is to swear by those of their countrymen who had the best reputation for integrity and valour, laying their hands upon their tombs; and for purposes of divination they go to sleep, after praying, on the graves of their forebears, and take as significant any dream they may have. When two men make a solemn compact, each drinks from the other's hand, and if there is no liquor available, they take some dust from the ground and lick it up.

The neighbours of the Nasamones are the Psylli – but they no longer exist. There is a story which I repeat as the Libyans tell it: that the south wind dried up the water in their storage tanks, so that they were left with none whatever, as their territory lies wholly within the Syrtis. Upon this they held a council, and having unanimously decided to declare war on the south wind, they marched out to the desert, where the wind blew and buried them in sand. The whole tribe was wiped out, and the Nasamones occupied their former domain.

Further inland to the southward, in the part of Libya where wild beasts are found, live the Garamantes, who avoid all intercourse with men, possess no weapons of war, and do not know how to defend themselves.[1] Along the coast to the westward the neighbours of

1. Garamantes: this is inconsistent with the account of their chariots on p. 332; the name of the tribe here is probably corrupt.

the Nasamones are the Macae. These people wear their hair in the form of a crest, shaving it close on either side of the head and letting it grow long in the middle; in war they carry ostrich skins for shields. The river Cinyps, which rises on a hill called the Hill of the Graces, runs through their territory to the sea. The Hill of the Graces is about twenty-five miles inland, and is densely wooded, unlike the rest of Libya so far described, which is bare of trees.

Next come the Gindanes. The women of this tribe wear leather bands round their ankles, which are supposed to indicate the number of their lovers: each woman puts on one band for every man she has gone to bed with, so that whoever has the greatest number enjoys the greatest reputation for success in love. Within the territory of the Gindanes a headland runs into the sea, and it is here that the Lotophagi live, a tribe which lives exclusively on the fruit of the lotus. The lotus fruit is about as big as a mastic-berry, and as sweet as a date. The Lotophagi also make wine from it.

Next along the coast are the Machlyes, who also make use of the lotus, but to a lesser extent than the Lotophagi. Their territory reaches to a large river called Triton, which flows into the great lagoon of Tritonis. In the lagoon there is an island named Phla, and there is said to have been an oracle to the effect that the Lacedaemonians should send settlers there. The story is also told of how Jason, when he had finished building the *Argo* under Mount Pelion, put on board, in addition to the usual offerings, a bronze tripod, and set sail to round the Peloponnese on his way to Delphi. Off Cape Malea he was caught by a northerly blow and carried to Libya, where, before he could get his bearings, he found himself in the shoal water off the lagoon of Tritonis. How to get clear was a problem; but at that moment Triton appeared and told Jason to give him the tripod, in return for which he would show him the channel and let them all get away in safety. Jason did as he was asked, whereupon Triton showed him the course to steer in order to clear the shallows. He then placed the tripod in his own temple, after uttering over it in full detail, for the benefit of Jason's crew, the prophecy that when a descendant of the *Argo*'s company should carry off the tripod, it was unavoidably decreed by fate that a hundred Grecian cities should then be built on the shores of Lake Tritonis. The Libyans in the neighbourhood got to know of this prophecy, and hid the tripod.

The people next to the Machlyes are the Auses; both these tribes live on the shores of the lagoon, and the river Triton forms the boundary between them. The Machlyes let the hair grow on the back of their heads, the Auses on the front. They hold an annual festival in honour of Athene, at which the girls divide themselves into two groups and fight each other with stones and sticks; they say this rite had come down to them from time immemorial, and by its performance they pay honour to their native deity – which is the same as our Greek Athene. If any girl, during the course of the battle, is fatally injured and dies, they say it is a proof that she is no maiden. Before setting them to fight, they pick out the best-looking girl and dress her up publicly in a full suit of Greek armour and a Corinthian helmet; then they put her in a chariot and drive her round the lagoon. How they dressed these girls before there were Greeks settled in the neighbourhood, I cannot say; presumably the armour they used was Egyptian – for I am prepared to maintain that both shields and helmets were introduced into Greece from Egypt. There is a belief amongst these people that Athene is the daughter of Poseidon and the lake, but that having some quarrel with her father she put herself at the disposal of Zeus, who made her his own daughter. The women of the tribe are common property; there are no married couples living together, and intercourse is casual – like that of animals. When a child is fully grown, the men hold a meeting, and it is considered to belong to the one it most closely resembles.

I have now mentioned all the pastoral tribes along the Libyan coast. Up country further to the south lies the region where wild beasts are found, and beyond that there is a great belt of sand, stretching from Thebes in Egypt to the Pillars of Heracles. Along this belt, separated from one another by about ten days' journey, are little hills formed of lumps of salt, and from the top of each gushes a spring of cold, sweet water. Men live in the neighbourhood of these springs – beyond the wild beasts' region, they are the furthest south, towards the desert, of any human beings. The first of them, ten days' journey from Thebes, are the Ammonians, with their temple derived from that of the Theban Zeus – I have already pointed out how the image of Zeus in both temples has a ram's face. They have another spring there, of which the water is tepid in the early morning and cools down towards market time; by noon it is very cold, and that is the moment when they water their gardens; then, as the days draw towards evening, the chill gradually goes off it, until by sunset it is tepid again; after that it gets hotter and hotter as the night advances, and at midnight it boils furiously. Then, after midnight, the process is reversed, and it steadily cools off until dawn. The spring is known as the Fountain of the Sun.

Ten days' journey west of the Ammonians, along the belt of sand, there is another similar salt-hill and spring. This place, called Augila, is also inhabited, and it is here that the Nasamonians come for their date harvest. Again at the same distance to the west is a salt-hill and spring, just as before, with date-palms of the fruit-bearing kind, as in the other oases; and here live the Garamantes, a very numerous tribe of people, who spread soil over the salt to sow their seed in. From these people is the shortest route – thirty days' journey – to the Lotophagi; and it is amongst them that the cattle are found which walk backwards as they graze. The reason for this curious habit is provided by the formation of their horns, which bend forwards and downwards; this prevents them from moving forwards in the ordinary way, for, if they tried to do so, their horns would stick in the ground. In other respects they are just like ordinary cattle – except for the thickness and toughness of their hide. The Garamantes hunt the Ethiopian hole-men, or troglodytes, in four-horse chariots, for these troglodytes are exceedingly swift of foot – more so than any people of whom we have any information. They eat snakes and lizards and other reptiles and speak a language like no other, but squeak like bats.

Ten days' journey from the Garamantes is yet another hill and spring – this time the home of the Atarantes, the only people in the world, so far as our knowledge goes, to do without names. Atarantes is the collective name – but individually they have none. They curse the sun as it rises and call it by all sorts of opprobrious names, because it wastes and burns both themselves and their land. Once more at a distance of ten days' journey there is a salt-hill, a spring, and a tract of inhabited country, and adjoining it rises Mount Atlas. In shape the mountain is a slender cone, and it is so high that according to report the top cannot be seen, because summer and winter it is never free of cloud. The natives (who are known as the Atlantes, after the mountains) call it the Pillar of the Sky. They are said to eat no living creature, and never to dream.

Thus far I am able to give the names of the tribes who inhabit the sand-belt, but beyond this point my knowledge fails. I can affirm, however, that the belt continues to the Pillars of Heracles and beyond, and that at regular intervals of ten days' journey are salt-hills and springs, with people living in the neighbourhood. The houses are all built of salt-blocks – an indication that there is no rain in this part of Libya; for if there were, salt walls would collapse. The salt which is mined there is of two colours, white and purple. South of the sand-belt, in the interior, lies a waterless desert, without rain or trees or animal life, or a drop of moisture of any kind.

The coast of Libya, then, between Egypt and Lake Tritonis is occupied by nomads living on meat and milk – though they do not breed pigs, and abstain from cows' meat for the same reason as the Egyptians. Even at Cyrene women think it is wrong to eat cows' meat, out of respect for the Egyptian Isis, in whose honour they celebrate both fasts and festivals. At Barca the women avoid eating pigs' flesh, as well as cows'. West of Tritonis, nomad tribes are no longer found; the people are quite different, not only in their general way of life, but in the treatment of their children. Many of the nomads – perhaps all, but I cannot be certain about this – when their children are four years old, burn the veins on their heads, and sometimes on their temples, with a bit of greasy wool, as a permanent cure for catarrh. For this reason they are said to be the healthiest people in the world – indeed, it is true enough that they are healthier than any other race we know of, though I should not care to be too certain that this is the reason. Anyway, about the fact of their health there is no doubt. Should the cauterizing of the veins bring on convulsions, they have discovered that the effective remedy is to sprinkle goat's urine on the child – I repeat in all this what is said by the Libyans. When the nomad tribes sacrifice, the process is to begin by cutting off the victim's ear, which they throw over the house as a preliminary offering, and then to wring the animal's neck. They sacrifice to the sun and moon, the worship of which is common to all the Libyans, though those who live round Lake Tritonis sacrifice chiefly to Athene, and, after her, to Triton and Poseidon. It is evident, I think, that the Greeks took the 'aegis' with which they adorn statues of Athene from the dress of the Libyan women; for except that the latter is of leather and has fringes of leather thongs instead of snakes, there is no other point of difference. Moreover, the word 'aegis' itself shows that the dress represented in statues of Athene is derived from Libya; for Libyan women wear goatskins with the hair stripped off, dyed red and fringed at the edges, and it was from these skins that we took our word 'aegis'. I think too that the crying of women at religious ceremonies also originated in Libya – for the Libyan women are much addicted to this practice, and they do it very beautifully. Another thing the Greeks learnt from Libya was to harness four horses to a chariot. The nomad Libyans – except the Nasamonians – bury their dead just as we do in Greece; the Nasamonians, however, bury them in a sitting position, and take care when anyone is dying to make him sit up, and not to let him die flat on his back. Their houses, which are portable, are made of the dry haulms of some plant, knit together with rush ropes.

West of the Triton, and beyond the Auses, Libya is inhabited by tribes who live in ordinary houses and practise agriculture. First come the Maxyes, a people who grow their hair on the right side of their heads and shave it off on the left. They stain their bodies red and claim to be descended from the men of Troy. The country round here, and the rest of Libya to the westward, has more forest and a greater number of wild animals than the region which the nomads occupy. The latter – that is, eastern Libya – is low-lying and sandy as far as the river Triton, whereas the agricultural region to the west is very hilly, and abounds with forest and animal life. It is here that the huge snakes are found – and lions, elephants, bears, asps, and horned asses, not to mention dog-headed men, headless men with eyes in their breasts (I don't vouch for this, but merely repeat what the Libyans say), wild men and wild women, and a great many other creatures by no means of a fabulous kind. In the nomads' country none of these occur; instead, one finds white-rump antelopes, gazelles, deer, asses – not the horned sort but a different species which can do without water; it is a fact that they do not drink – another kind of antelope, about as big as an ox, the horns of which are used for making the curved sides of lyres, foxes, hyaenas, hedgehogs, wild rams, jackals, panthers, and others, including land-crocodiles like huge lizards, four and a half feet long, ostriches, and small snakes with a single horn. All these are found, together with other animals common elsewhere, with the exception of the stag and the wild boar, of which there are none at all in Libya. There are, however, three kinds of mice, called respectively *dipodes*, *zegeries*, and *echines* – also weasels which are found amongst the silphium, and resemble those at Tartessus. So much, then, for the animal life in that part of Libya where the nomads are: I have made it as full and accurate as my extensive inquiries permit.

Continuing westward from the Maxyes, one comes next to the Zaueces: amongst this people the drivers of the war-chariots are the women. Their neighbours are the Gyzantes, whose country is very well supplied with honey – much of it made by bees, but even more by some process which the people have discovered. Everybody here paints himself red and eats monkeys, of which there is an abundant supply in the hills. Off the coast, according to the Carthaginian account, is an island called Cyrauis, about twenty-five miles long, but narrow, which can be reached on foot from the mainland and is full of olive-trees and vines. In the island is a lake, and the native girls dip feathers smeared with pitch into the mud at the bottom of it, and bring up gold dust – again, I merely record the current story, without guaranteeing the truth of it. It may, however, be true enough; for I have myself seen something similar in Zacynthus, where pitch is fetched up from the water in a lake. There are a number of lakes – or ponds – in Zacynthus, of which the largest measures seventy feet each way and has a depth of two fathoms. The process is to tie a branch of myrtle on to the end of a pole, which is then thrust down to the bottom of this pond; the pitch sticks to the myrtle, and is thus brought to the surface. It smells like bitumen, but in all other respects it is better than the pitch of Pieria. It is then poured into a trench near the pond, and when a good quantity has been collected, it is removed from the trench and transferred to jars. Anything that falls into this pond, passes underground and comes up again in the sea, a good half mile distant. In view of all this, the account of what happens in the island off Libya may quite possibly be true.

The Carthaginians also tell us that they trade with a race of men who live in a part of Libya beyond the Pillars of Heracles. On reaching this country, they unload their goods, arrange them tidily along the beach, and then, returning to their boats, raise a smoke. Seeing the smoke, the natives come down to the beach, place on the ground a certain quantity of gold in exchange for the goods, and go off again to a distance. The Carthaginians then come ashore and take a look at the gold; and if they think it represents a fair price for their wares, they collect it and go away; if, on the other hand, it seems too little, they go back aboard and wait, and the natives come and add to the gold until they are satisfied. There is perfect honesty on both sides; the Carthaginians never touch the gold until it equals in value what they have offered for sale, and the natives never touch the goods until the gold has been taken away.

I have now mentioned all the Libyans whose names I am acquainted with; most of them cared nothing for the king of Persia, either then or now. One other thing I can add about this country: so far as one knows, it is inhabited by four races, and four only, of which two are indigenous and two not. The indigenous peoples are the Libyans and Ethiopians, the former occupying the northerly, the latter the more southerly, parts; the immigrants are the Phoenicians and Greeks. I do not think the country can be compared for the fertility of its soil with either Asia or Europe, with the single exception of the region called Cinyps – so named after the river which waters it. This region, however, is quite different from the rest of Libya, and is as good for cereal crops as any land in the world. The soil here, unlike the soil elsewhere, is black and irrigated by springs; it has no fear of drought on the one hand, or of damage, on the other, from excessive rain (it does, by the way, rain in that part of Libya). The yield of the harvests is equal to the yield in Babylonia. There is also good soil at Euesperides – in the best years it will yield a hundred-fold – but the yield in Cinyps is three times as great. The land of Cyrene, the highest of that part of Libya which is inhabited by nomads, has the remarkable peculiarity of three separate harvest-seasons: first, the crops near the coast ripen and are ready for cutting or picking; then, when these are in, the crops in what they call the hill-country – the middle region above the coastal belt – are ready for harvesting; and lastly, when this second harvest is over, the crops in the highest tract of country are ripe and ready, so that by the time the first harvest is all eaten or drunk, the last comes in – making, for the fortunate people of Cyrene, a continuous harvest of eight months on end. So much for this subject.

On their arrival at Barca, the troops sent from Egypt by Aryandes to assist Pheretima laid siege to the town and called upon the inhabitants to surrender the men who were responsible for the murder of Arcesilaus. The Barcaeans, however, refused, on the ground that every one of them was equally responsible. The siege therefore continued for nine months, the Persians endeavouring to effect an entrance by mining operations as well as by direct assault. A metalworker very ingeniously discovered the saps in the following way: he went all round the inner circuit of the town wall with a bronze shield, with which he kept tapping the ground, and getting a dull, dead sound in every place except over the saps, where the bronze of the shield echoed and rang. In these places the Barcaeans dug countermines and killed the Persian sappers; and they also succeeded in beating off the direct attacks. When the siege had dragged on for a long time with much misery and loss on both sides, especially in the Persian army, Amasis, who was in command of the infantry, decided on a change of tactics: realizing that Barca could not be taken by force, but might nevertheless fall to fraud, he waited for darkness and dug up a broad trench, over which he laid thin planks, finally making up the surface with earth to the level of the ground on either side. At dawn next morning he invited the Barcaeans to a conference, to which they gladly came; and the conference ended in an agreement on the following terms: standing upon the concealed trench, they entered into solemn covenant to the effect that the Barcaeans should pay a fair sum to the Persian king, and that the Persians, in their turn, should do no further harm to Barca – and that this covenant should stand so long as the earth beneath their feet remained firm. As soon as the oaths were sworn, the Barcaeans, without any thought of treachery, came out of the town and, throwing open all the gates, invited any Persian to enter it at will. The Persians accepted the invitation and hurried in – but not before they had broken up the hidden trench; for they wished to keep the oath which they had sworn to the people of Barca, that the covenant should stand as long as the ground under their feet. Well – the ground had given way, so the oath no longer held.

The men of Barca who were most deeply involved in the murder of Arcesilaus were delivered up by the Persians to Pheretima, who impaled them on stakes all round the city wall. She also cut off their wives' breasts, and stuck those up, too, in the same position. The rest of the people she gave over to the Persian soldiery to pillage, with the exception of those who belonged to the house of Battus and were not implicated in the murder. To these last she gave control of the town. Everyone else the Persians reduced to slavery, and then started on their march for home.

The people of Cyrene, on the appearance of the Persian army before the town, decided, in fulfilment of some oracle or other, to let it through. As they marched along the streets Badres, the commander of the fleet, recommended the seizure of the place, but Amasis, the commander of the infantry, refused on the ground that the objective of the expedition had been the single Greek city of Barca. Nevertheless, when they had passed through the town and come to a halt on the hill of Lycaean Zeus, they regretted their missed opportunity, and attempted to get into Cyrene again. This time, however, the Cyrenaeans refused to admit them, whereupon, though there was no fighting of any kind, the Persians were seized with panic and hastily retreated a distance of some seven miles before they dared come to a halt. Here the army encamped, and a message from Aryandes arrived, ordering them home; they applied to Cyrene for supplies, succeeded in obtaining them, and set off on their return to Egypt. But the Libyans harried their march, cutting off stragglers for the sake of their clothes and equipment, all the way to the border.

The furthest point in Libya reached by this Persian army was Euesperides. The Barcaeans who were taken as slaves were sent from Egypt to the Persian King Darius, who gave them a village in Bactria to live in. They named the village Barca, and it was still inhabited in my time.

Pheretima's web of life was also not woven happily to the end. No sooner had she returned to Egypt after her revenge upon the people of Barca, than she died a horrible death, her body seething with worms while she was still alive. Thus this daughter of Battus, by the nature and severity of her punishment of the Barcaeans, showed how true it is that all excess in such things draws down upon men the anger of the gods.

BOOK FIVE

THE Persians whom Darius had left in Europe under Megabazus' command began hostilities against the Greeks on the Hellespont by subduing the Perinthians, who refused to accept Persian domination. Before this time they had already been roughly handled by the Paeonians. An oracle had told the Paeonians from the river Strymon to march on Perinthus, and if the Perinthians, once the armies faced each other, called them on by name, then they were to go for them; otherwise, they should hold back. The Perinthians took up their position on the outskirts of their town, a challenge was issued, and three champions from each side – a man, a horse, and a dog – engaged respectively in single combat. Seeing that two of their three champions were getting the better of the tussle, the Perinthians in great delight shouted out *Io Paean*, the cry of victory, whereupon the Paeonians at once supposed that this was what the oracle had meant. 'Now,' they said to each other, 'the oracle is fulfilled – and it's up to us.' They attacked immediately, won a resounding victory, and left few of their enemies alive. This incident took place a long time before; on the present occasion, in spite of a brave attempt to secure their freedom, the force of numbers was too much for them and they were defeated by Megabazus and the Persians. After the subjection of Perinthus, Megabazus marched through Thrace, bringing every city and every people in that country under the control of the Persian king. All this was according to orders; for he had received instructions from Darius to conquer Thrace.

The population of Thrace is greater than that of any country in the world except India. If the Thracians could be united under a single ruler, or combine, they would be the most powerful nation on earth, and no one could cope with them – that, at any rate, is my own opinion; but in point of fact such a thing is impossible – there is no way of its ever being realized, and the result is that they are weak. They go by various names in different parts of the country, but they all live in much the same way with the exception of the Getae, the Trausi, and the people north of Creston. The customs of the Getae, who believe themselves immortal, I have already described; the Trausi follow the normal practices of Thracians in general, except in one particular – their behaviour, namely, on the occasion of a birth or a death. When a baby is born the family sits round and mourns at the thought of the sufferings the infant must endure now that it has entered the world, and goes through the whole catalogue of human sorrows; but when somebody dies, they bury him with merriment and rejoicing, and point out how happy he now is and how many miseries he has at last escaped.

With the Thracians who live beyond Creston, it is customary for a man to have a number of wives; and when a husband dies, his wives enter into keen competition, in which his friends play a vigorous part on one side or the other, to decide which of them was most loved. The one on whom the honour of the verdict falls is first praised by both men and women, and then slaughtered over the grave by her next of kin and buried by her husband's side. For the other wives, not to be chosen is the worst possible disgrace, and they grieve accordingly. The rest of the Thracians carry on an export trade in their own children; they exercise no control over young girls, allowing them to have connexions with any man they please; their wives, on the other hand, whom they purchase at high prices from their parents, they watch very strictly. They consider tattooing a mark of high birth, the lack of it a mark of low birth; the best man, in their opinion, is the idle man, and the sort least worthy of consideration is the agricultural labourer. The most reputable sources of income are war and plunder. So much for their most striking ideas. The only deities they worship are Ares, Dionysus, and Artemis – though their kings, in contrast to the people generally, pay particular reverence to Hermes;[1] they swear by no other deity but Hermes, and claim their own descent from him. When a rich Thracian is buried, the custom is to lay out the body for three days, during

1. A wanderer-god? Cf. German Wotan.

which, after a preliminary period of mourning, a feast is held of all sorts of animals slaughtered for the purpose; then the body is buried, with or without cremation, a mound is raised over it, and elaborate games set on foot. The most valuable prizes in the games are awarded for single combat.

Of the country north of Thrace, and of who lives in it, there is no precise information; but it would seem that beyond the Danube lies a boundless tract of uninhabited land. One people only have I been able to hear of on the other side of the Danube: these are the Sigynnae, who dress, it is said, in the Median fashion,[1] and have little, snub-nosed, shaggy horses, with hair about four inches long all over their bodies. These horses cannot carry a man, but are very fast in harness, with the result that driving is here the rule. The borders of this country reach almost to the Veneti on the Adriatic. The Sigynnae claim to be colonists from Media, but how that can be so I cannot myself imagine – though there is room for anything in the course of time. The word 'Sigynna' is used by the Ligurians above Marseilles for 'tradesman': in Cyprus it means 'spear'. According to the Thracian account the country beyond the Danube is infested by bees, which make further progress impossible; to my mind, however, this is an improbable story, as bees are not creatures which can stand the cold. I prefer to believe that it is cold which prevents men from living under the Great Bear. Such are the facts I have heard reported about this part of the world, the coastal region of which Megabazus was now bringing under Persian control.

As soon as Darius had crossed the Hellespont and arrived at Sardis, the recollection of the service rendered him by Histiaeus of Miletus, and of the good advice of the Mytilenean Coes, prompted him to send for the two men, and to ask them what they would like him to do for them in return. Histiaeus already possessed sole authority over Miletus, and did not ask for power over any other state in addition; instead, he put in a request for Myrcinus in the country of the Edoni, because he wished to found a city there; Coes, on the other hand, who was a private person without any authority, asked for supreme power over Mytilene. Both petitions were granted, and the two men went off to the places of their choice.

1. i.e. in trousers and jacket.

Meanwhile Darius happened to see something which prompted him to order Megabazus to effect the transfer of the whole Paeonian nation from Europe to Asia. Two Paeonians called Pigres and Mastyes wanted to seize power in their country; so when Darius had crossed into Asia, they went to Sardis with a sister of theirs, a tall and beautiful girl. Awaiting the moment when Darius should take his seat in state before the Lydian capital, they dressed the girl as finely as they could and sent her off with a jar on her head to fetch water, leading a horse by a halter round her arm and spinning flax as she went. The sight of her as she passed was sufficiently remarkable to catch Darius' eye; for what she was doing was not what one would expect of a Persian or a Lydian, or any other Asiatic woman. Darius, indeed, did more than notice her: he sent some of his bodyguard to see what she would do with the horse. The men followed her, and the girl, on reaching the river, watered the horse, filled her pitcher, and started back by the same way as she had come, with the pitcher of water on her head, leading the horse and turning her spindle. Darius, much surprised both by what his men had witnessed and by what he saw with his own eyes, gave orders for the girl to be brought into his presence. Soon she came, and with her her two brothers, who had kept at hand to watch: Darius asked what nation the girl belonged to, and the young men replied that they were Paeonians and that she was their sister. The king then wanted to know who the Paeonians were, and where their country was, and why the two brothers had come to Sardis, and was told in reply that the Paeonians were Teucrian settlers from Troy, that their country was on the Strymon, not far from the Hellespont, and that the reason for their coming to Sardis was to put themselves under his power. Darius then asked if all the women in Paeonia were as hard-working as this one, and the young men eagerly asserted – which was, of course, the whole point of their proceedings – that they were.

The result of this was that Darius wrote to Megabazus, whom he had left in command in Thrace, instructing him to turn the Paeonians, men, women, and children, out of their homes and bring them to him. A messenger rode off with all speed to the Hellespont, crossed the water, and delivered the letter to Megabazus, who the moment he had read it provided himself with Thracian guides and marched against Paeonia. On hearing the news of his approach the Paeonians took the field in a body on the coast road, under the impression that the Persians would try to force their way in from that direction. They were fully prepared to resist Megabazus had he done what they expected; but the Persians no sooner learned of their concentration to guard the seaward approaches to their country than they procured guides and, taking the inland route, gave the Paeonians the slip and launched an attack on their towns, which, being undefended, fell an easy prey. At the news that their towns were in enemy hands, the Paeonian army disintegrated; the men went off on their own and surrendered individually to the Persians. The result of the campaign was that a number of Paeonian tribes – the Siriopaeones, Paeoplae, and the others as far as Lake Prasias – were transferred bodily to Asia. The tribes in the neighbourhood of Mt Pangaeum and on the lake itself were not subjugated by Megabazus – though he did attempt the conquest of the latter. The houses of these lake-dwellers are actually in the water, and stand on platforms supported on long piles and approached from the land by a single narrow bridge. Originally the labour of driving the piles was presumably undertaken by the tribe as a whole, but later they adopted a different method; now the piles are brought from Mt Orbelus and every man drives in three for each wife he marries – and each has a great many wives. Each member of the tribe has his own hut on one of the platforms, with a trap-door opening on to the water underneath. To prevent their babies from tumbling in, they tie a string to their legs. Their horses and other pack-animals they feed on fish, which are so abundant in the lake that, when they open the trap-door and let down an empty basket on a rope, they have only a minute to wait before they pull it up again, full. The fish are of two kinds – they call them *papraces* and *tilones*.

The captured Paeonians were taken to Asia, and Megabazus, after his successful campaign, sent to Amyntas of Macedonia a demand for earth and water, as a sign of his submission to Darius. The seven most distinguished Persians in the army, after himself, were entrusted with the task of conveying the message. It is a very short way from Lake Prasias to Macedonia; next to the lake is the mine which later produced a talent of silver every day for Alexander, and then one has only to cross a mountain named Dysorum to get there. On their arrival the seven Persian envoys obtained an audience with Amyntas and made their demands for earth and water. It was not refused; Amyntas, moreover, invited them to a magnificent dinner which he had prepared, and entertained them most hospitably. After dinner, while the wine was still going round, one of the Persians said: 'At important dinners like this, my Macedonian friend, it is our custom in Persia to get our wives and mistresses to come and sit with us in the dining-room. You have welcomed us kindly, provided us with an excellent dinner, and offered earth and water to our King Darius; come then – won't you do as we do?'

'Gentlemen,' Amyntas replied, 'what you mention is by no means the custom in Macedonia; with us, men and women are kept separate. However, you are our masters, and, as you ask for this favour, you shall not be refused.'

Amyntas sent for the women, and they came in and sat down in a row opposite the Persians, who, finding them very charming, remarked to Amyntas that such an arrangement was by no means a good one: it would surely have been better for the women not to have come at all if, instead of sitting beside them, they merely intended to sit opposite. It was a painful thing only to be allowed to look at them. Amyntas, of necessity, told the women to move over and sit with the guests, and as soon as they did so, the Persians, who were very drunk, began to touch their breasts, and even, in some cases, to try to kiss them. Amyntas saw what was going on, but his great fear of the Persians helped him, in spite of his anger, to hold his tongue; his son Alexander, however, who was also present and a witness of the Persians' behaviour, was quite unable to restrain himself – he was a young man, ignorant of the harsh ways of the world, and in his resentment he said to Amyntas: 'You are an old man, father, and should look after yourself. Don't try to sit out the drinking, but go and rest. I will stay at table, and give our guests all they need.' Amyntas, convinced that his son was about to do something rash, said he could tell by the way the boy spoke that he was all on fire, and wanted to get his father out of the way only to commit some violence. 'But,' he added, 'I beg you not to do these men any mischief; for if you do, you will ruin us all. Have the courage to endure the sight of their behaviour. As for myself, I will leave the room as you suggest.'

With this warning, Amyntas went out, and Alexander turned to the Persians. 'My friends,' he said, 'these women are entirely at your service; you may go to bed with any of them you like – indeed, with all of them. You have but to say the word. Now, however, as it is nearly bedtime and you are, as I observe, agreeably primed with drink, perhaps you will allow me to send them away to take a bath – after which you may have them back again.' The Persians agreed, and Alexander, after telling the women to return to their quarters, dressed in their clothes an equal number of smooth-chinned young men, gave them a dagger each, took them back into the dining-room, and said to the Persians: 'Gentlemen, you have had, I think, a really perfect dinner. Everything we had, and everything we could get, has been yours; and now, to put the finishing touch to your entertainment, we make you a free and generous offer of our mothers and sisters, that you may know without any doubt that we honour you as you deserve, and that you may tell your king, who sent you, that a Greek, the lord of Macedonia, entertained you royally both with bed and board.' Alexander then put a Macedonian by the side of each Persian; and when the Persians, thinking they were women, tried to touch them, they were stabbed.

That was the end of the Persian envoys to Macedon – and of their servants too; servants, and carriages, and a great deal of luggage of every kind – all disappeared together. Not long afterwards the Persians went to much trouble in an attempt to trace the lost envoys; but Alexander cleverly succeeded in keeping the affair dark by giving Bubares, the Persian commander of the search-party, a large sum of money and his own sister Gygaea. In this way the murder was hushed up and never discovered.

I happen to know, and will prove in a subsequent chapter of this history,[1] that these descendants of Perdiccas are, as they themselves claim, of Greek nationality. This was, moreover, recognized by the managers of the Olympic games, on the occasion when Alexander wished to compete and his Greek competitors tried to exclude him on the ground that foreigners were not allowed to take part. Alex-

1. In Book VIII, ch. 137 ff.

ander, however, proved his Argive descent, and so was accepted as a Greek and allowed to enter for the foot-race. He came in equal first.

Megabazus took the Paeonians to the Hellespont, crossed over, and continued his march to Sardis. Histiaeus of Miletus was already engaged in the fortification of Myrcinus, the place which he had asked Darius to give him for his services in guarding the bridge over the Danube. Myrcinus is on the Strymon. His proceedings did not escape Megabazus' attention; so as soon as he reached Sardis with the Paeonians, he said to Darius: 'I am astonished, my lord, at your rashness in allowing an able Greek like Histiaeus to found a settle-ment in Thrace. The site, with its silver mines, and abundance of timber for building ships and making oars, is a very valuable one. The neighbourhood is thickly populated both with Greeks and barbarians, all of whom will accept him as their master and do what he tells them, night and day. I beg you to put a stop to what he is doing, or you will find yourself involved in a war with your own subjects. Send for him, so that he can't go on with it – and let your message be a tactful one; but once you have him, see that he never has a chance to get back to Greece.' Megabazus, who showed admir-able foresight in this, had no difficulty in persuading Darius to do as he asked, and a courier was dispatched to Myrcinus with the following message: 'Darius the King to Histiaeus: On thinking the matter over, I find that I have no friend more loyal than yourself, or more devoted to my prosperity; and the proof of it has been deeds, not words. Therefore, as I have an important enterprise in hand, I beg you to come to me without fail, in order that I may communicate it to you.'

Histiaeus took the message as genuine and was much flattered at being a King's Counsellor. He obeyed the summons, and on his arrival at Sardis, Darius said to him: 'I will tell you, Histiaeus, why I sent for you. Ever since I lost sight of you after my return from Scythia I have never desired anything so much as to see and talk to you again; for I am convinced that a man's most precious possession is a wise and loyal friend, and that you are both these things my own experience has shown me. Now, therefore, as you have been kind enough to come to Sardis, I have a proposal to make: forget about Miletus and this new settlement of yours in Thrace, and come with me to Susa. All I have will there be yours. You will eat at my table and be my counsellor.'

Darius then left for Susa and made Histiaeus accompany him. Before he went, he appointed Artaphernes, his brother by the same father, as governor of Sardis, and gave Otanes the command of the coast. Otanes' father Sisamnes had been put to death by Cambyses: he was one of the royal judges, and as a punishment for taking a bribe and perverting justice Cambyses had him flayed; all his skin was torn off and cut into strips, and the strips stretched across the seat of the chair which he used to sit on in Court. Cambyses then appointed his son to be judge in his place, and told him not to forget what his chair was made of, when he gave his judgements. This Otanes – the one who had the remarkable chair – after taking over Megabazus' command, captured Byzantium and Chalcedon, and also Antandrus in the Troad, and Lamponium; then with Lesbian ships he captured Lemnos and Imbros, both of which islands were at that time still occupied by Pelasgians. The men of Lemnos put up a stiff resistance, but were finally crushed, and the Persians appointed Lycaretus, the brother of Maendrius the ruler of Samos, to take charge of those of them who were left alive. Lycaretus died as governor in Lemnos. The reason Otanes gave for subjugating and enslaving all these people was that some had shirked service in the Scythian expedition, while others had molested Darius' army on its way home.

Such were the exploits of Otanes after he took over the command. Then trouble ceased for a while, until it broke out again in Ionia. This time it came from Naxos and Miletus. Naxos, just then, was the richest island in the Aegean, and Miletus during the same period had reached the peak of her prosperity and was the glory of Ionia. Previously Miletus had been terribly weakened by civil disorders, which lasted some sixty years, until a commission from Paros was asked in to put her on her feet again. The Parians, whom the people of Miletus had chosen out of all the Greeks to settle their disputes, managed the business in the following way: their best men visited the place, and when they saw the widespread ruin there they asked to be allowed to make a thorough inspection of all the land. This they did, and whenever in the desolated countryside they saw a bit of well-cultivated ground, they made a note of its owner's name. Of such farms, however, though they examined the whole Milesian territory, they found very few. After their inspection the commissioners returned to the city and lost no time in calling a general assembly, at which they announced their decision to entrust the government to the men whose land they had found in good order – for there was no doubt, in their opinion, that such men would manage public business as efficiently as they had managed their own. The other Milesians were told to take their orders from the new government.

But to return from this business of the Parians to the Ionian troubles I mentioned just now – to those, I mean, which originated in Naxos and Miletus. Certain substantial citizens of Naxos, forced by the popular party to leave the island, took refuge in Miletus, which had been put under Aristagoras, son of Molpagoras, as deputy governor. He was nephew and son-in-law of Histiaeus, the son of Lysagoras, who was being detained by Darius at Susa. Power in Miletus actually belonged to Histiaeus – but, as I said, he was in Susa when the Naxian exiles, formerly his friends, arrived. The first thing they did when they got there was to ask Aristagoras to lend them some troops, in the hope of recovering their position at home. This suggested to Aristagoras that if he helped the exiles to return he himself would be lord of Naxos; so using their friendship with Histiaeus to cloak his purpose, he made them an offer. 'Personally,' he said, 'I cannot engage to furnish enough troops to force your return to Naxos against the wishes of the party now in power. They have, I understand, eight thousand armoured men, and they have a powerful fleet. I will, however, do my very best to find a means of helping you. My idea is this: Artaphernes is a friend of mine – and Artaphernes, you must know, is the son of Hystaspes and the brother of Darius, and is in command of the whole coastal district of Asia, with a large army and navy. This, I think, is the man who will do our business for us.'

On this, the Naxians authorized Aristagoras to make the best arrangements he could, and told him to promise certain sums of money which they would themselves furnish, and pay for the troops; for they had great hopes that, when they appeared in Naxos, the people would submit to their orders, and then the other islands of the Cyclades, for none of these had yet been subdued by Darius.

Aristagoras then went to Sardis and told Artaphernes that Naxos, in spite of its small size, was a fine and fertile island, close to the Ionian coast, and rich both in treasure and slaves. 'Therefore,' he went on, 'I suggest that you attack it, and restore the exiles. If you do this, two advantages will accrue: first, I have a large sum of money for you, over and above the expenses of the expedition (which would naturally be met by us who undertake it), and, secondly, you will add to the King's dominions not only Naxos itself but the other islands of the Cyclades, such as Paros and Andros, which are dependent on it. Then with the Cyclades as your base you will have no difficulty in attacking Euboea, a large island – as large as Cyprus – and very prosperous and easy to take. For the whole enterprise you will need not more than a hundred ships.'

'The plan you propose,' Artaphernes replied, 'is likely to be of great benefit to our royal house, and I think your advice is excellent, except in one particular – the size of the fleet. Instead of a hundred, I shall have two hundred ready for you next spring. The only other thing we need is to get the king's approval.'

Aristagoras returned to Miletus much pleased with this answer, and Artaphernes at once communicated with Susa. He laid the proposal of Aristagoras before the king, obtained his consent, and set about his preparations, equipping two hundred ships of war and a strong force of Persian and allied troops, the whole of which he put under the command of Megabates, one of the Achaemenidae, and a cousin both of Darius and himself. Megabates' daughter – if there is any truth in the story – was subsequently betrothed to Pausanias, son of Cleombrotus, when he had his set heart on making himself master of Greece.

After the appointment of Megabates to the command, Artaphernes gave him instructions to proceed to Miletus, where he took Aristagoras on board together with the Ionian contingent and the Naxian exiles. He then made sail ostensibly for the Hellespont; but, on reaching Chios, he brought up at Caucasa, meaning to make a passage from there to Naxos as soon as he got a northerly wind. However, the Naxians were not destined to come to grief as a result of this expedition. What happened was this: Megabates, on making his rounds to inspect the watch, found a Myndian vessel on which no watch had been set. Angry at this neglect of duty, he ordered his guard to find the captain – a man named Scylax – and to put him in irons with his head sticking out through an oar-port in the ship's side. Somebody told Aristagoras about this ignominious punishment of his Myndian friend, and Aristagoras went to Megabates and tried to get him released. Megabates refused, so Aristagoras released the man with his own hands. The Persian commander was furious – and said so with great vigour; to which Aristagoras answered: 'All this is none of our business. Didn't Artaphernes put you under my orders when he sent you out here? Didn't he tell you to sail wherever I thought fit? Why are you meddling?'

Megabates was angry at this; and as soon as it was dark he sent off a party of men in a boat to Naxos, to warn the people of their danger; for they had no idea that it was against them that the expedition was directed. On receipt of the warning, however, they lost no time in preparing for a siege; all the stuff from the open country was brought inside the city walls, a stock of food and drink was laid in, and the defences strengthened. As a result of these preparations for imminent war, the enemy, after making the passage from Chios, found the islanders in a strong position and quite ready to receive them. The siege began and continued for four months; by that time all the stores which the Persians had brought with them were exhausted; Aristagoras had spent a great deal of money from his private funds – and still more was needed, if the siege was to continue. The Persians, therefore, decided to give up. They built some forts for the exiles and withdrew to the mainland. The expedition had been a failure.

Aristagoras was now unable to keep his promise to Artaphernes. The call upon him to meet the expenses of the men's pay had landed him in difficulties and he was afraid that, owing to the failure of the attempt on Naxos and his quarrel with Megabates, he might lose his position in Miletus. These various causes of alarm were already making Aristagoras contemplate rebellion, when something else occurred to confirm his purpose: this was the arrival from Susa of a slave, sent by Histiaeus, the man with the tattooed scalp,[1] urging him to do precisely what he was thinking of, namely, to revolt. Histiaeus had been wanting to make Aristagoras take this step, but

1. 'The man, etc.'; the story must have been well known.

was in difficulty about how to get a message safely through to him, as the roads from Susa were watched; so he shaved the head of his most trustworthy slave, pricked the message on his scalp, and waited for hair to grow again. Then, as soon as it had grown, he sent the man to Miletus with instructions to do nothing when he arrived except to tell Aristagoras to shave his hair off and look at his head. The message found there was, as I have said, an order to revolt. What prompted Histiaeus to do this was his distress at being detained in Susa, and he hoped that, if a rebellion were started, he might be sent down to the coast to deal with it, whereas if nothing of the sort occurred he had little expectation of ever seeing Miletus again. With this purpose in mind he sent off the messenger; and so Aristagoras found himself faced with a combination of circumstances, all of which urged him in the same direction. Accordingly, he called a council of his supporters, declared his views, and told them of Histiaeus' message. His friends were unanimous in their approval, and all recommended revolt – with a single exception: the historian Hecataeus. Hecataeus was strongly opposed to war with Persia, emphasizing the resources at Darius' command, and supporting his point with a long list of the nations under Persian dominion. This argument, however, failed to convince the meeting, so, as second best, he advised them to work for control of the sea. He then went on to say that, in view of the weakness of Miletus, of which he was well aware, there was, in his opinion, only one way in which this could be done: namely, by taking from the temple at Branchidae the treasure which had been deposited there by the Lydian King Croesus. If that were done, he had good hope that they might succeed in gaining command of the sea – in any case they would themselves have the use of the money, and prevent it from falling into enemy hands. This treasure was of great value, as I have shown in the early part of my History.[1]

Hecataeus' proposal was not adopted; but they did decide, none the less, to throw off the Persian yoke, and, as a first step, to send one of their number to Myus, where the army was which had returned from Naxos, and there to try to seize the fleet's commanders. The man they sent was Iatragoras, and a number fell into the trap he laid – Oliatus, the son of Ibanolis of Mylasa, Histiaeus, son of

1. In Book I, ch. 92.

Tymnes of Termera, Coes, son of Erxander (to whom Darius had given Mytilene), Aristagoras, son of Heracleides, of Cyme: all these and many more he managed to get into his hands. After that all disguise was thrown off, and Aristagoras, in open rebellion, set himself to damage Darius in every way he could think of. To induce the Milesians to support him, he began by abdicating his own position in favour of a democratic government, and then went on to do the same thing in the other Ionian states, where he got rid of the political bosses. Some of them he drove out; those he had arrested on the ships which had joined his expedition to Naxos he handed over to the cities to which they respectively belonged, hoping thereby to get the goodwill of their former subjects. At Mytilene, Coes was taken out and stoned to death the moment the people got their hands on him; at Cyme, however, Aristagoras was allowed to go free, and most of the other cities showed a similar leniency.

Having thus put down the despots in the various states of Ionia, Aristagoras of Miletus first had generals appointed, and then, as he needed to find some powerful ally, embarked in a warship and set sail on a mission to Lacedaemon.

Anaxandrides, son of Leon, was no longer king of Sparta, for he had died and his son Cleomenes had succeeded him – not, indeed, by right of merit but merely by right of birth. Anaxandrides had married his sister's daughter, to whom he was devoted; but the marriage was childless, and in view of this fact he was summoned to appear before the Ephors, who declared that even if he chose to neglect his own interests, they, at least, could not allow the family of Eurysthenes to die out. 'As your wife bears no children,' they said, 'you had better get rid of her and marry someone else, if you wish to please the Spartans.' Anaxandrides answered that he had no intention of doing either; his wife had been guilty of no fault, and the magistrates' advice that he should send her away and marry another woman instead was most improper – he would do nothing of the kind. At this, the Ephors and Elders began to think again, and finally made another proposal. 'It is clear,' they said, 'that you are much attached to your wife. You would be wise, therefore, to make no objection to what we are now about to suggest – to refuse again might make it necessary for the Spartans to take unpleasant measures against you. As for your present wife, we do not ask you to divorce her; you may continue to give her all the privileges she now enjoys; but you must marry another woman as well, to bear you children.' Anaxandrides consented, and from that time had two wives and two separate households – an unheard-of thing in Sparta.

Not long after, his second wife gave birth to Cleomenes, and no sooner had she presented the Spartans with an heir to the throne than, strangely enough, his first wife, who had formerly been child-less, also happened to become pregnant. The relatives of the second wife made a great fuss when they heard the news, and maintained – what was quite untrue – that she was pretending to be pregnant for the sake of her reputation, and meant to pass off a supposititious baby as her own. So great was the outcry they made that when her time came the Ephors, who were not convinced one way or the other, sat round her bed while the child was actually being born. The child was named Dorieus; and almost immediately after his birth she was again pregnant, this time with Leonidas, and yet again, after a very short interval, with Cleombrotus – though some have said that the two latter were twins. Anaxandrides' second wife, however, the mother of Cleomenes – she was a daughter of Prinetades, son of Demarmenus – never had another child.

But to return to Cleomenes: he was, the story goes, not quite right in his head – even, indeed, on the verge of madness, whereas Dorieus was the finest young man of his generation and confident that his merits would assure his succession. As a result of this he was naturally indignant when, on the death of Anaxandrides, the Spartans followed their usual custom and put the eldest son, Cleomenes, on the throne. Unable to bear the prospect of being ruled by Cleomenes, he asked the Spartans for a body of men and took them off to found a settlement elsewhere, without previously consulting the Delphic oracle on a suitable site, or observing any of the usual formalities: he just went off, in a fit of temper, to Libya, with some men from Thera to act as guides. Arrived there, he settled by the river Cinyps, on a piece of excellent land belonging to the Libyans. Within three years, however, he was driven out by the Macae (a Libyan tribe) and the Carthaginians, and returned to the Peloponnese.

Here he was advised by a certain Antichares of Eleon, on the strength of the oracles given to Laius, to found the city of Heracles in Sicily; for, according to this person, all the country of Eryx in Western Sicily belonged to the Heraclids, as Heracles himself was its original conqueror. Dorieus, accordingly, went to Delphi to consult the oracle on his chance of acquiring the land which he was after, and was told by the Priestess that it would certainly be his, whereupon he fetched the band of settlers whom he had taken to Libya and sailed with them along the Italian coast.

The people of Sybaris say that just about this time they and their ruler Telys were contemplating war against Croton; the Crotoniates in great alarm asked, and obtained, the assistance of Dorieus, who joined them in their campaign and helped them to capture Sybaris. This, as I said, is the account the Sybarites give; but the Crotoniates say that they had no foreign ally in their war with Sybaris, except the Elean sooth-sayer Callias, one of the Iamidae, who joined after deserting Telys, because he found, on offering sacrifice, that the omens were unfavourable for an attack on Croton. Both parties produce evidence to support their stories: the Sybarites, first, show a piece of consecrated ground, with a temple in it, near the dry bed of the Crathis, and declare that it was Dorieus who, after the capture of the town, dedicated it to Athene Crathias; and, secondly, adduce as the strongest proof of all the death of Dorieus, who, they maintain, lost his life because he transgressed the instructions of the oracle. Had he done only what he was sent to do, and not allowed himself to be led into incidental adventures, he would have taken and held the country of Eryx, and neither he nor his army would have perished. The Crotoniates, on the other hand, point to the extensive lands in their territory which were granted to Callias (they were still, within my own memory, in the possession of his family), whereas Dorieus and his descendants were granted none at all. Yet if – they argue – Dorieus really did help in the war, a great deal more would have been given to him than to Callias. In this conflict of evidence, you may agree with whichever party you think is telling the truth.

Other Spartans sailed with Dorieus to assist in founding the new settlement. These were Thessalus, Paraebates, Celeas, and Euryleon. They reached Sicily, but were defeated and killed, with all the men

under their command, in a battle with the Phoenicians and the
people of Egesta. The only one of them to escape was Euryleon, who
collected the few survivors of the army and captured Minoa, a colony
of Selinus, and helped the people of Selinus to free themselves
from their ruler Peithagoras. Later, after the expulsion of Peithagoras,
he attempted to seize power in Selinus himself, and did actually enjoy
it for a while, until the people of the town organized a revolt and
killed him, though he took sanctuary at the altar of Zeus of the
Market Place.

Another man who accompanied Dorieus, and shared his fate, was
Philippus, the son of Butacides and a native of Croton; he had been
engaged to marry a daughter of Telys of Sybaris; but the marriage
came to nothing, as he was banished from Croton. In his disappointment he sailed for Cyrene, and it was from there that he equipped a
warship, which he manned at his own expense, to join in Dorieus'
expedition. This Philippus was an Olympic victor and the best-
looking man of his day; and because of his good looks he received
from the people of Egesta the unparalleled honour of a hero's shrine
erected on his tomb, at which religious ceremonies are still held to win
his favour.

This, then, was the end of Dorieus, who might have been king of
Sparta had he only stayed there and put up for a time with being a
subject of Cleomenes; for Cleomenes' reign was a brief one,[1] and he
died without a son to succeed him, leaving only a daughter, whose
name was Gorgo.

Cleomenes, however, was on the throne when Aristagoras of
Miletus came to Sparta. According to the Spartan account, Aristagoras brought to the interview a map of the world engraved on
bronze, showing all the seas and rivers, and opened the conversation
in the following way: 'I hope, Cleomenes, that you will not be too
much surprised at my anxiety to visit you. The circumstances are
these. That Ionians should have lost their liberty is a bitter shame and
grief not only to us, but to the rest of Greece, and especially to you,
who are the leaders of the Greek world. We beg you, therefore, in

---

1. Actually he reigned *c.* 520 to 490 B.C. Herodotus has been misled
by Spartan informants hostile to Cleomenes, as later by Athenians hostile to
Themistocles; cf. p. 489 and n.

the name of the gods we all worship, to save from slavery your Ionian kinsmen. It will be an easy task, for these foreigners have little taste for war, and you are the finest soldiers in the world. The Persian weapons are bows and short spears; they fight in trousers and turbans – that will show you how easy they are to beat! Moreover, the inhabitants of that continent are richer than all the rest of the world put together – they have everything, gold, silver, bronze, elaborately embroidered clothes and beasts of burden and slaves. All this you may have if you wish. I will show you the relative positions of the various nations.'

Here Aristagoras produced the map he had brought with him. 'Look,' he continued, pointing to it, 'next to the Ionians here are the Lydians – theirs is a fine country, rich in money. Then come the Phrygians, farther east, richest in cattle and crops of all the nations we know. And here, adjoining them are the Cappadocians – Syrians, we Greeks call them; and next to them the Cilicians, with their territory extending to the coast – see, here's the island of Cyprus – who pay annual tribute to the Persian king of five hundred talents. Now, the Armenians – they, too, have cattle in abundance; and next to them, here, the Matieni. Again, farther east, lies Cissia: you can see the Choaspes marked, with Susa on its banks, where the Great King lives, and keeps his treasure. Why, if you take Susa, you need not hesitate to compete with God himself for riches. You should suspend your wars over a scrap of land – and poor land at that – with your rivals the Messenians and Arcadians and Argives, who have nothing whatever in the nature of gold or silver which is worth fighting and dying for, when you are offered the chance of an easy conquest of the whole land of Asia. Is there really any choice between the two?'

'Sir,' Cleomenes replied, 'I will wait two days before I give you an answer.'

That was as far as they got at the moment; but when the day came on which Cleomenes had agreed to give his decision and they met at the appointed place, he asked Aristagoras how far off Susa was, and how many days it took to reach it from the Ionian coast. Up to this, Aristagoras had been clever, and had led Cleomenes on with great success; but in answering this question he made a bad mistake. If he wanted to induce the Spartans to invade Asia, he never ought to have told the truth; but he did, and said it took three months. Cleomenes stopped Aristagoras from saying any more of the road to Susa. 'Milesian,' he cried, 'you must leave Sparta before sunset. Your proposal to take Lacedaemonians a three months' journey from the sea is a highly improper one.'

Cleomenes then went home, and Aristagoras followed him with a branch of olive in his hand, like a suppliant, made his way in, and besought Cleomenes to listen, and send away the child – for his only daughter Gorgo, a little girl of eight or nine, happened to be standing by her father's side. Cleomenes told him to say what he wished and not to mind the child, and Aristagoras, in answer, began with an offer of ten talents, to be paid to Cleomenes if he consented to do what he asked. Cleomenes shook his head, and Aristagoras gradually increased his offer. When he went as high as fifty talents the little girl suddenly exclaimed: 'Father, you had better go away, or the stranger will corrupt you'. Cleomenes appreciated his daughter's warning, and went into another room, and Aristagoras left Sparta for good, without succeeding in saying any more about the road to Susa.

That information I will now supply myself. At intervals all along the road are recognized stations, with excellent inns, and the road itself is safe to travel by, as it never leaves inhabited country. In Lydia and Phrygia, over a distance of 94½ parasangs – about 330 miles – there are 20 stations. On the far side of Phrygia one comes to the river Halys; there are gates here, which have to be passed before one crosses the river, and a strong guard-post. Once over the river and into Cappadocia, a distance of 104 parasangs, with 28 stations, brings one to the Cilician border, where the road passes through two sets of gates, both guarded. These left behind, the distance through Cilicia is 15½ parasangs, with three stations. Separating Cilicia from Armenia is a river, the Euphrates, which has to be crossed in a boat, and the distance across Armenia itself is 56½ parasangs, with 15 stations or stopping-places. Here, too, there is a guard. Through this part of the country four rivers run, all of which have to be crossed by a ferry: the first is the Tigris; the second and third both have the same names – Zabatus – though they are different rivers and flow from distinct sources, one rising in Armenia, the other in Matiene; and the fourth is the Gyndes – the river which Cyrus once split up into three hundred and sixty channels. Leaving Armenia and entering Matiene, one has 137 parasangs to go, with 34 stations, and, passing from thence into Cissia, another 42½ with 11 stations, which bring one to the river Choaspes – another navigable stream – on which the city of Susa stands. Thus the total number of stations, or posthouses, on the road from Sardis to Susa is 111. If the measurement of the Royal Road in parasangs is correct, and if a parasang is equal (as indeed it is) to 30 furlongs, then the distance from Sardis to the Palace of Memnon (450 parasangs) will be 13,500 furlongs. Travelling, then, at the rate of 150 furlongs a day, a man will take just ninety days to make the journey. So one can see that Aristagoras of Miletus was quite right when he told the Spartan Cleomenes that it took three months to reach Susa from the sea. But, if anyone wants still greater accuracy, I would point out that the distance from Ephesus to Sardis should be added to the total, so that one gets, as a final measurement of the distance from the Aegean to Susa – the 'city of Memnon' – 14,040 furlongs, Ephesus to Sardis being 540 furlongs, which increase the three months' journey by three days.

Repulsed from Sparta, Aristagoras went on to Athens, which had been liberated from autocratic government in the way which I will now describe. Hipparchus, the son of Pisistratus and brother of the despot Hippias, in spite of a vivid dream which warned him of his danger, was murdered by Harmodius and Aristogiton, two men belonging to the family of the Gephyraei; the murder, however, did the Athenians no good, for the oppression they suffered during the four succeeding years was worse than before. Hipparchus had dreamt, on the night before the Panathenaic festival, that the tall and beautiful figure of a man stood over his bed and spoke to him these obscure and riddling words:

> O lion, endure the unendurable with enduring heart;
> No man does wrong and shall not pay the penalty.

At dawn next morning he was seen communicating his dream to the interpreters; but later he put it out of his mind and took part in the procession, during which he was killed.

The Gephyraei, to whom the two men who killed Hipparchus

belonged, came, by their own account, originally from Eretria; but I have myself looked into the matter and find that they were really Phoenicians, descendants of those who came with Cadmus to what is now Boeotia, where they were allotted the district of Tanagra to make their homes in. After the expulsion of the Cadmeans by the Argives, the Gephyraei were expelled by the Boeotians and took refuge in Athens, where they were received into the community on certain stated terms, which excluded them from a few privileges not worth mentioning here. The Phoenicians who came with Cadmus – amongst whom were the Gephyraei – introduced into Greece, after their settlement in the country, a number of accomplishments, of which the most important was writing, an art till then, I think, unknown to the Greeks. At first they used the same characters as all the other Phoenicians, but as time went on, and they changed their language, they also changed the shape of their letters. At that period most of the Greeks in the neighbourhood were Ionians; they were taught these letters by the Phoenicians and adopted them, with a few alterations, for their own use, continuing to refer to them as the Phoenician characters – as was only right, as the Phoenicians had introduced them. The Ionians also call paper 'skins' – a survival from antiquity when paper was hard to get, and they did actually use goat and sheep skins to write on. Indeed, even to-day many foreign peoples use this material. In the temple of Ismenian Apollo at Thebes in Boeotia I have myself seen cauldrons with inscriptions cut on them in Cadmean characters – most of them not very different from the Ionian. There were three of these cauldrons; one was inscribed: 'Amphityron dedicated me from the spoils of the Teleboae', and would date from about the time of Laius, son of Labdacus, grandson of Polydorus and great-grandson of Cadmus. Another had an inscription of two hexameter verses:

> *Scaeus the boxer, victorious in the contest,*
> *Gave me to Apollo, the archer God, a lovely offering.*

This might be Scaeus the son of Hippocoön; and the bowl, if it was dedicated by him and not by someone else of the same name, would be contemporary with Laius' son Oedipus. The third was also inscribed in hexameters:

Laodamas, while he reigned, dedicated this cauldron
To the good archer Apollo – a lovely offering.

It was during the reign of this Laodamas, the son of Eteocles, that the Cadmeans were expelled by the Argives and took refuge with the Encheles. The Gephyraei remained in the country, but were later forced by the Boeotians to withdraw to Athens, where they have certain temples set apart for their own special use, which the other Athenians are forbidden to enter; one of them is the temple of Demeter Achaeia, in which secret rites are performed.

Having told the story of Hipparchus' dream, and traced the descent of the Gephyraei, the family to which the men who murdered him belonged, I must now get back to my original theme: the liberation of Athens from despotic rule, and how that liberation was brought about. Hippias was still in power and embittered against the Athenians because of the murder of his brother. The Alcmaeonidae, an Athenian family which had been driven into exile by the house of Pisistratus, attempted with the help of the other exiles to procure their return by force and liberate Athens. They seized and fortified Leipsydrium above Paeonia, but the enterprise met with disaster. Resolved to attempt any device which might help them against the Pisistratidae, they got a contract from the Amphictyons to build the temple which stands to-day at Delphi, but at that time did not exist. They were wealthy men, and came of a long and distinguished line; and the temple they built was better in various respects than the plan required; in particular, they gave it a façade of Parian marble, whereas the agreement had been to use freestone for the whole. The Athenians say that these men, during their stay at Delphi, bribed the Priestess to tell any Spartans that might happen to consult the oracle, either on state or private business, that it was their duty to liberate Athens; and the Spartans, as a result of the constant repetition of the same injunction, sent Anchimolius, the son of Aster, a distinguished citizen, at the head of an army to drive out the Pisistratidae. The Pisistratidae were good friends of theirs: but no matter – the commands of God were more important to them than human ties. Anchimolius and his force were sent by sea, and landed at Phalerum; but the Pisistratidae, who already knew of their intentions, had sent for help to Thessaly, with which country they had an alliance. The Thessalians responded to the appeal, and dispatched a troop of cavalry, a thousand strong, under their king, Cineas of Conia. The plan the Pisistratidae adopted, on the strength of this reinforcement, was to clear the ground round Phalerum of trees so as to give horses freedom of movement, and then to launch a cavalry attack. The attack succeeded; many Lacedaemonians were killed, Anchimolius amongst them, and the survivors driven back to their ships. That was the end of the first Spartan attempt; Anchimolius was buried at Alopecae in Attica, and his tomb can be seen near the temple of Heracles in Cynosargos. Later, however, they tried again; and this time the expedition was on a larger scale; it was commanded by their king, Cleomenes the son of Anaxandrides, and went by land instead of by sea. The army crossed the border into Attica, and was met by the Thessalian cavalry, which withdrew after a short engagement, leaving more than forty dead; the remainder made their way straight back to Thessaly. Cleomenes then marched to Athens, and, together with the Athenians who wished for freedom, besieged Hippias and his party on the Acropolis. The Lacedaemonians had not intended to undertake a siege, and the Pisistratidae had ample supplies of food and drink; it is likely, therefore, that, but for an unexpected accident, Cleomenes would have kept up the siege for days and then retired to Sparta; but, luckily for the Spartans and unluckily for their enemies, the children of the Pisistratidae were caught as they were being smuggled out of the country for safety. This disaster upset all their plans; in order to recover the children, they were forced to accept the Athenians' terms, and agreed to leave Attica within five days. They afterwards withdrew to Sigeum on the Scamander. The family had enjoyed despotic power in Athens for thirty-six years. The family was descended from Neleus of Pylos, as were Melanthus and Codrus, who in ancient times became kings of Athens, after settling in the country. It was in memory of this that Hippocrates named his son Pisistratus after the Pisistratus who was a son of Nestor.

This, then, is the story of how Athens was freed from despotism. I will now proceed to relate whatever is memorable in Athenian history from the time of the liberation to the revolt of Ionia, and the arrival in Athens of Aristagoras of Miletus, with his request for aid against Persia.

Athens had been great before; now, her liberty won, she grew greater still. The most powerful men in the city were two: Clisthenes, a member of the Alcmaeonid family – it was he, the story goes, who bribed the priestess at Delphi – and Isagoras, son of Tisander, a man of reputable family, though I do not know the origin of it; however members of his family offer sacrifice to Carian Zeus. These two were rivals for power, and Clisthenes, who was getting the worst of it, took the people into his party. He then changed the number of Athenian tribes from four to ten, and abolished the old names – previously the four tribes had been called after Geleon, Aegicores, Argades, and Hoples, the four sons of Ion; but now he named the new tribes after other heroes, all native Athenian except Ajax, whom, though a foreigner, he admitted into the list as a neighbour and ally. I think that in taking this step he was following the example of his maternal grandfather, Clisthenes the despot of Sicyon; for he, after his war with Argos, stopped the rhapsodists' competitions in reciting from Homer's poems in Sicyon, because they were full of praise for Argos and the Argives. Again, he would have liked on similar grounds – because, that is, he was an Argive – to abolish the influence of Adrastus the son of Talaus, who had, and still has, a shrine dedicated to him in the market-place at Sicyon. He did, in fact, visit Delphi to ask the oracle if he might 'expel' him, but the prophetess answered: 'Adrastus was King of Sicyon, but you are merely a stone-thrower'. As the god would not allow this, Clisthenes went home and began to think out some means whereby Adrastus might leave Sicyon of his own accord. Presently he hit on something which he thought would do. He sent to Thebes in Boeotia and informed the Thebans that he wished to invite the hero Melanippus, the son of Astacus, to Sicyon. The Thebans allowed him to do this, so Clisthenes then invited Melanippus, and consecrated for him a sanctuary actually inside the government house, where he was established in the greatest possible security. I must not omit to explain that Clisthenes picked on Melanippus as the person to introduce into Sicyon, because he was a bitter enemy of Adrastus, having killed both Mecistes, his brother, and Tydeus his son-in-law.[1] After settling him in his new

---

1. In the disaster of the Seven against Thebes, described in the *Thebaid*, an ancient epic popularly ascribed to Homer.

shrine, he transferred to him the religious honours of sacrifice and festival which had previously been paid to Adrastus.

The people of Sicyon had always regarded Adrastus with great reverence, because the country had once belonged to Polybus, his maternal grandfather, who died without an heir and bequeathed the kingdom to him. One of the most important of the tributes paid him was the tragic chorus, or ceremonial dance and song, which the Sicyonians celebrated in his honour; normally, the tragic chorus belongs to the worship of Dionysus; but in Sicyon it was not so – it was performed in honour of Adrastus, treating his life-story and sufferings. Clisthenes, however, changed this: he transferred the choruses to Dionysus, and the rest of the ceremonial to Melanippus. In addition to all this, he changed the names of the Dorian tribes, in order to make a distinction between the Argive and the Sicyonian; moreover, the distinction was a highly invidious one, and designed to make fools of the Sicyonians, for the names he chose were derived from the words 'donkey' and 'pig', with only the endings changed. This applied to all the tribes except his own, which he named the Archelai – 'rulers of the people' – after his own royal office; the others he named Hyatae – 'pig-men', Oneatae – 'donkey-men', and Choereatae – 'swine-men'. These names continued to be used in Sicyon, not only during Clisthenes' reign but for sixty years after his death; then the matter was discussed, and the tribes were renamed Hylles, Pamphyli, and Dymanatae, with the addition of a fourth, the Aegiales, named after Adrastus' son Aegialeus.

Now Clisthenes of Athens, following the lead of his grandfather and namesake Clisthenes of Sicyon, decided, out of contempt, I imagine, of the Ionians, that his tribes should not be the same as theirs, so as soon as he had won the support of the common people of Athens, previously held in contempt, he renamed the tribes and increased their number, appointing ten presidents – 'phylarchs' – instead of the original four, and incorporating ten local subdivisions – 'demes' – in each tribe. Having once got the masses to support him, he found himself much more powerful than his rivals. Isagoras, beaten in his turn, then appealed to Cleomenes the Spartan, who had stayed in his house during the siege of the Pisistratidae (he was indeed rumoured to have had illicit relations with Isagoras' wife). Cleomenes then first sent an order to Athens for the expulsion of Clisthenes, together with a large number of other Athenians, calling them the 'Accursed'. This was a suggestion of Isagoras; for the Alcmaeonidae and their allies were held to be involved in the blood-guilt it referred to, but Isagoras and his friends were not.

The Accursed had got their name as follows: There was an Athenian called Cylon, who had been a victor at the Olympic games. This man began to plume himself on his chances of becoming master of Athens, and, with that end in view, collected a band of friends and tried to seize the Acropolis. The attempt failed, and he took sanctuary as a suppliant at the feet of the statue there. The officers in charge of the administrative districts of Attica, who at that period were in control of affairs, persuaded Cylon and the other fugitives to leave the statue and submit themselves to justice, promising, however, to spare their lives. Nevertheless, they were killed, and the Alcmaeonidae are said to have done the deed. This happened before the time of Pisistratus.

On the arrival of Cleomenes' order for the expulsion of Clisthenes and the 'Accursed', Clisthenes himself left Athens, but his departure did not prevent Cleomenes from coming to the city with a small force of men and banishing, as accursed, seven hundred Athenian families, whose names had been given him by Isagoras. Then he attempted to abolish the Council, and transfer power to a body of three hundred supporters of Isagoras. The Council resisted, and refused to obey his orders, whereupon he, together with Isagoras and his party, occupied the Acropolis. This united the rest of Athens against them; they were blockaded in the Acropolis for two days, but, on the day after, a truce was made, and all of them who were Lacedaemonians were allowed to leave the country. Omens come true, and the end of this affair had already been foretold; for when Cleomenes climbed the hill to seize the Acropolis, he was just going into Athene's temple to say a prayer when the Priestess, before he could get through the door, rose from her chair and cried: 'Spartan stranger, go back. Do not enter the holy place. No Dorian is permitted to come in.' Answering that he was not a Dorian but an Achaean, Cleomenes paid no attention to the warning, and made his attempt upon the Acropolis, and, as I have said, he and his Spartans were flung out. The rest were put in prison by the Athenians and executed, amongst them Timesitheus of Delphi, a man of whose prowess and courage I could, if I would, tell great things.

After the execution of the prisoners, the Athenians recalled Clisthenes and the seven hundred families which had been expelled by Cleomenes; they were well aware that they were now in a state of war with Cleomenes and Sparta, so to strengthen their position they sent representatives to Sardis, in the hope of concluding an alliance with Persia. When they got there and delivered their message, Artaphernes the governor asked in reply who these Athenians were that sought an alliance with Persia, and in what part of the world they lived. Then, having been told, he put the Persian case in a nutshell by remarking that, if the Athenians would signify their submission by the usual gift of earth and water, then Darius would make a pact with them; otherwise they had better go home. Eager that the pact should be concluded, the envoys acted on their own initiative and accepted Artaphernes' terms – for which they were severely censured on their return to Athens.

Meanwhile Cleomenes, who felt that he had been insulted by the Athenians both in word and deed, was busy collecting an army from every part of the Peloponnese. His purpose, though he kept it to himself and did not publish it, was to have his revenge upon Athens and to set up Isagoras, who had escaped with him from the Acropolis, in power there. His preparations completed, he marched as far as Eleusis with a strong force, and at the same moment, by a previously concerted plan, the Boeotians seized the two outlying Attic villages of Oenoe and Hysiae, while the Chalcidians broke in from another direction and devastated part of Attica. Threatened though they were from two sides at once, the Athenians decided to oppose the Spartans at Eleusis, and to deal with the Boeotians and Chalcidians later. Just before the battle could begin, the Corinthian contingent, reflecting that they were acting wrongfully, changed their minds and withdrew. Then Demaratus, the son of Ariston, one of the two Spartan kings and joint commander of the expedition, though he had had no previous difference with Cleomenes, followed suit. This divergence in a matter of policy gave rise to a new law in Sparta; previously both kings had gone out with the army, but this was now made illegal, and it was further provided that, as one had to remain in the capital, one of the Tyndaridae as well should stay behind – both of whom had hitherto accompanied the army as auxiliaries. Then the other allied troops, when they saw the split between the Spartan kings and the desertion of the Corinthians, also abandoned their positions and left the field. This was the fourth time a Spartan army had been seen on Attic soil: two of the occasions had been acts of war; the other two, attempts to do service to the people of Athens. The first invasion was when they founded Megara, and is rightly assigned to the period when Codrus was King of Athens; the second and third were the expeditions from Sparta to drive out the Pisistratidae; the fourth and last was this present one, when Cleomenes with a Peloponnesian army marched as far as Eleusis.

Having witnessed this inglorious dispersal of the invading army, the Athenians wanted revenge, and decided to march first against the Chalcidians; but as the Boeotians were coming to their aid, towards the Euripus strait, the Athenians decided to tackle them first. In the fight which followed the Athenians won an overwhelming victory, killing a great many and taking seven hundred prisoners. The same day they crossed into Euboea, engaged the Chalcidians, and beat them too. After the victory they settled 4000 men, each with a piece of land assigned him, on the estates of the 'hippobotae', or 'horse-owners', as the wealthy Chalcidians were called. The prisoners taken in this second engagement, together with the seven hundred Boeotians, were kept under guard in chains, but afterwards ransomed at 200 drachmas apiece. The fetters they were bound with, the Athenians hung up in the Acropolis; they were still there in my day, hanging on the walls which the Persian fire had scorched, opposite the shrine which faces westward. With a tenth of the ransom money they had a chariot-and-four made in bronze, and consecrated it as an offering to Athene. It is the first thing you see on the left as you pass through the Propylaea on the Acropolis. The inscription on it is as follows:

> *Athens with Chalcis and Boeotia fought,*
> *Bound them in chains and brought their pride to naught.*
> *Prison was grief, and ransom cost them dear –*
> *One tenth to Pallas raised this chariot here.*

Thus Athens went from strength to strength, and proved, if proof were needed, how noble a thing freedom is, not in one respect only, but in all; for while they were oppressed under a despotic government, they had no better success in war than any of their neighbours, yet, once the yoke was flung off, they proved the finest fighters in the world. This clearly shows that, so long as they were held down by authority, they deliberately shirked their duty in the field, as slaves shirk working for their masters; but when freedom was won, then every man amongst them was interested in his own cause.

Meanwhile the Thebans were anxious to pay off their score with Athens. They sent to Delphi for advice, and were told by the priestess of the oracle that they would be unable to get their revenge if they tried to act alone: they must, she said, bring the matter forward to be discussed by 'the many voices', and ask their 'nearest' to help them. When, therefore, the messengers returned, the Theban magistrates called a general assembly and announced what the oracle had advised. The people, hearing that this advice was to appeal for help to their 'nearest', and knowing that their nearest neighbours were the men of Tanagra, Coronea, and Thespia, wondered what could be meant by it. 'Surely,' they said to each other, 'these neighbours of ours need no asking; they have always been our allies and have fought at our side all through the war with the best will in the world. Perhaps the oracle has some other meaning.' As they were debating the matter, one of them suddenly realized the truth. 'I believe,' he exclaimed, 'that I know what it means. Asopus, it is said, had two daughters, Thebe and Aegina. Thebe and Aegina – two sisters: *that* is what "nearest" signifies. The god has advised us to ask the Aeginetans for aid.' No better solution being offered, the Thebans at once sent a request for assistance to Aegina, as being their 'nearest' according to the intention of the oracle, and the Aeginetans met the request by agreeing to lend them the support of their national heroes, the sons of Aeacus. Relying upon this powerful aid, the Thebans made their attempt, but were soundly beaten by the Athenians. Thereupon they sent a second message to Aegina, giving back the sons of Aeacus and asking for some men instead. The Aeginetans at that period enjoyed very great prosperity; this fact, together with the memory of their old quarrel with Athens, encouraged them to comply with the

Thebans' request and to begin hostilities without a formal declaration of war. While the Athenians were attending to the Boeotians, they sent a squadron of warships to Attica, wrecked the port of Phalerum and a number of villages along the neighbouring coast, and did considerable damage.

The desire of the Aeginetans to pay off their old score against Athens arose from the following circumstances. Once, long before, the crops had failed in Epidaurus, and the Epidaurians consulted the Delphic oracle upon what they should do to meet their troubles. The Priestess replied that things would go better for them if they set up statues of Damia and Auxesia. They then asked if the statues should be made in bronze or in stone, and were advised that neither of these materials should be used: the statues should be made from the wood of the cultivated olive. In consequence of this they asked the Athenians for permission to fell some olive trees, in the belief that the olives of Attica were of peculiar sanctity – or it may be that in those days Athens was the only place where olives grew. The Athenians gave them permission to fell the trees, on condition that they offered an annual sacrifice to Erechtheus and Athene Polias. The Epidaurians agreed, got what they wanted, and made the statues from the olive-wood. The statues were erected, their harvests improved, and the promise made to the Athenians was duly kept.

Now at this period, as in the past, Aegina was subject to Epidaurus: so much so, indeed, that the Aeginetans used to cross to Epidaurus for the hearing of their own private law-suits. A little later, however, the islanders built a fleet and, growing headstrong, rebelled against Epidaurus. Their superiority at sea enabled them, once the struggle had begun, to do much damage to the Epidaurians; amongst other things they carried off the statues of Damia and Auxesia and put them up at a place called Oea, in the interior of their island, about twenty furlongs from the town. Here they instituted in their honour certain ceremonies, consisting partly of sacrifices, partly of companies of female dancers and singers in the satirical and abusive mode, whose attacks were directed not against men, but against the women of the place. Ten 'choregi' were appointed to pay and train the dancers for each of the two deities. Similar modes of worship were in use also at Epidaurus, as well as other – secret – sorts.

After the theft of the statues the Epidaurians ceased to fulfil their undertaking to send an annual tribute to the gods of Athens. The Athenians remonstrated, but to no purpose, for the people of Epidaurus proved that they were in no way in the wrong. They had fulfilled their obligations so long as the statues were in their possession; but now they were gone, the obligation was at an end. Now, the Aeginetans had the statues; so the proper thing was to make the Aeginetans pay. At this, the Athenians sent a demand to Aegina for the return of the statues, but were told in reply that Aegina was not interested in Athens. The Athenians claim that, after they had asked for the statues, they sent a party to Aegina in a single warship, who attempted to bring the statues away, on the ground that, being made of Athenian wood, they were Athenian property. First they tried to wrench them off their pedestals; then, having failed to do so, they made ropes fast to them, and hauled. As they were heaving, there was a clap of thunder and an earthquake, and the ship's company suddenly went mad and began to kill each other, until only one was left, who returned by himself to Phalerum. The Athenian story is, however, contradicted by the Aeginetans, who deny that it was a single warship – they could easily have kept off a single ship, or several, for that matter, even if they had no navy themselves; on the contrary, the Athenians came with a large fleet, and they themselves made no attempt to oppose them. They are not clear as to whether they avoided battle because they acknowledged their inferiority at sea or because they were planning what they then did. In any case, the Athenians landed unopposed and made for the statues; then, having failed to wrench them from their bases, they attached their ropes and began heaving – and continued to heave until an extraordinary thing happened. Personally I do not believe it, though perhaps somebody may – but the story is that each statue fell upon its knees, and in that attitude both have remained ever since. The Aeginetans go on to affirm that as soon as they got wind of the intended attack from Athens, they sought aid from Argos, so that when the Athenians landed, Argive reinforcements were already on the spot to oppose them; they had slipped across from Epidaurus, fell upon the Athenians before they knew they were there, and cut off their retreat to their ships. It was at that moment that the earthquake occurred, and the thunderclap. The Argives and Aeginetans agree in this account, and the Athenians, too, admit that only one of their men returned to Attica alive: the only point of dispute is the occasion of his escape, the Argives saying that he got away after they had destroyed the rest of the Athenian force, the Athenians claiming that the whole thing was an act of God. Even the sole survivor soon came to a bad end; for when he reached Athens with a report of the disaster, the wives of the other men who had gone with him to Aegina, in grief and anger that he alone should have escaped, crowded round him and thrust the brooches, which they used for fastening their dresses, into his flesh, each one, as she struck, asking him where her husband was. So he perished, and the Athenians were more horrified at his fate than at the defeat of their troops in Aegina. The only way they could punish their women for the dreadful thing they had done was to make them adopt Ionian dress; previously Athenian women had worn Dorian dress, very similar to the fashion at Corinth; now they were made to change to linen tunics, to prevent them from wearing brooches. Actually this kind of dress is not originally Ionian, but Carian; for in ancient times all women in Greece wore the costume now known as Dorian. But the Argives and Aeginetans passed a law that in both their countries brooch-pins should be made half as long again as they used to be, and that brooches should be the principal things offered by women in the shrines of these two deities; also, nothing from Attica was to be taken to the temple, not even pottery, and thenceforward only drinking vessels made in the country should be used. From that time to the present day the women of Argos and Aegina have worn brooches with longer pins than in the past – and all because of their quarrel with Athens.

The origin, then, of the mutual hatred of Athens and Aegina was such I have described. And now the Aeginetans, who had not forgotten the affair of the statues, eagerly responded to the Theban call for assistance, and began making raids on the Attic coast. The Athenians were about to start counter-measures when they were advised by an oracle from Delphi to hold their hand: they should wait, the oracle ran, for thirty years, and then, in the thirty-first year after the Aeginetans had started the trouble, they should consecrate a piece of ground to Aeacus, and declare war. If they followed this advice everything would go as they wished; if, on the other hand, they attacked Aegina forthwith they would, indeed, ultimately be victorious, but not without suffering in the meantime as much loss as they inflicted. On hearing this warning the Athenians did so far take it as to consecrate to Aeacus that precinct which is still to be seen by the market-place in Athens; but, in view of the intolerable injury they had received at the hands of the Aeginetans, they could not bear to be told to wait thirty years for their revenge. They began their preparations accordingly, but were checked by new trouble from Sparta. This arose from the discovery by the Spartans that the Alcmaeonidae had corrupted the priestess at Delphi, and what she had done against Sparta and the Pisistratidae. The Spartans were doubly distressed; for they had driven their own friends into exile, and they now realized that by doing so they had not gained the goodwill of Athens. Moreover they were spurred to action by the discovery of certain prophecies of coming disasters at the hands of the Athenians – prophecies of which they had known nothing until Cleomenes brought them to Sparta. These prophecies had formerly been in the possession of the Pisistratidae, who left them in the temple on the Acropolis when they were expelled from Athens. It was here that Cleomenes found them and picked them up. When, therefore, the Spartans got hold of them, and saw at the same time the growth of Athenian power with the unlikelihood it brought of Athens submitting to their authority, they realized that a free Attica would be a match for them, and that the only way of weakening their rivals and reducing them to obedience was to establish a despotic government in Athens. On this realization they acted, and sent to Sigeum on the Hellespont to recall Pisistratus' son Hippias. Hippias responded to the summons; the Spartans then sent for representatives from their other allied states, and the assembly was addressed in the following words: 'We acknowledge to you, our comrades in arms, that we have made a mistake. On the strength of certain oracles, which have proved to be a swindle, we expelled from their country men who were our friends, men who undertook to keep Athens dependent upon us; these gone, we put power into the hands of an ungrateful rabble, which had no sooner raised its head by our generous act of liberation than it turned against us and flung us out, ourselves and our king, with every mark of insult. Since then these people have been growing in reputation and strength, as their neighbours the Boeotians and Chalcidians have learnt to their cost, and as others perhaps will also discover, unless they mind their step. This was the mistake we made; and now, with your help, we will try to make up for it. Our object when we invited you and Hippias, whom you see before you, to attend this meeting, was to agree to unite our forces for his restoration. Together we will take him to Athens and give him back the power of which we formerly robbed him.'

Most of the allied representatives disapproved of the substance of this speech, but the only one to raise his voice in protest was Sosicles of Corinth. 'Upon my word, gentlemen,' he exclaimed, 'this is like turning the universe upside-down. Earth and sky will soon be changing places – men will be living in the sea and fish on land, now that you Spartans are proposing to abolish democratic government and restore despotism in the cities. Believe me, there is nothing wickeder or bloodier in the world than despotism. If you think it is a good thing for other people, why not give a lead by adopting it yourselves before trying to establish it elsewhere? Without any experience of it – indeed, you have taken the utmost care that it should never happen in Sparta – you are wronging your friends; if only you knew, as we know, what irresponsible government can be, your advice about it now would be better than it is.

'The government of Corinth was once an oligarchy: one clan – the Bacchiadae, who intermarried only amongst themselves – were in power there. Amphion, a member of this clan, had a lame daughter, Labda, whom none of the Bacchiadae was willing to marry, so she was taken by Eëtion, the son of Echecrates, a man from the village of Petra, but belonging by descent to the Lapithae and the family of Caeneus. Having no children either by Labda or any other wife, Eëtion went to Delphi to ask the oracle about his chance of an heir, and the moment he entered the shrine the priestess addressed him in these words:

> *Eëtion, worthy of honour, no man honours you.*
> *Labda is with child, and her child will be a millstone*
> *which will fall upon the rulers and will bring justice to Corinth.*

The prophecy, though addressed to Eëtion, happened to reach the ears of the Bacchiadae, who till then had failed to grasp the meaning of an earlier prophecy about the future of Corinth. Now, however, it became apparent that both referred to the same event. The earlier one went like this:

> *An eagle in the rocks has conceived, and shall bring forth a lion,*
> *Mighty, ravening; and he will loose the knees of many.*
> *Give heed to these things, Corinthians, you who dwell*
> *About lovely Pirene and the rock-set town of Corinth.*

This earlier prophecy, as I have said, had been unintelligible to the Bacchiadae; but as soon as they heard the second one, which was given to Eëtion, they saw the point of it and realized the similarity of the two. The meaning of both prophecies being now clear, they kept quiet, but resolved to make away with Eëtion's child as soon as it should be born. The moment, therefore, that Labda was brought to bed they sent ten of their number to the village where Eëtion lived, to kill the baby. Arrived at Petra, they entered the house, and asked to see the child; and Labda, who had no idea why they had come and supposed that they wished to see her baby out of affection for its father, gave it to one of them to hold. Now the plan they had made on the way to Petra was, that whoever first got hold of the baby should dash it to the ground; but chance – or providence – saved it, for as soon as Labda put it into the man's arms, it smiled at him, and he, seeing it smile, was touched, and could not bring himself to kill it, but passed it to his neighbour who, in his turn, passed it on again until all ten had had it in their arms, and not one could bring himself to kill it. So they gave the baby back to its mother and went out of the room. Close by the door they stopped and began to reproach one another, especially the man who had been the first to hold the baby, for not doing what they had decided to do, until at last, after a considerable time, they made up their minds to go back and all take a share in the killing. Fate, however, had decreed that Eëtion's child should live and be a cause of misery to Corinth; for Labda, who had been standing close behind the door, heard everything that the men were saying, and, in fear lest the second time they got hold of her baby they might feel differently and actually destroy it, she hid it in a chest, which was the most unlikely place she could think of, knowing, as she did, that if the men came back they would be sure to make a thorough search. And this is just what happened: they entered the room, and after hunting everywhere without success, decided to go away and to tell the people who had sent them that their orders had been carried out. This they did; and Eëtion's son grew up, and was named Cypselus after the chest, by means of which he had escaped the danger which threatened him.

'One day, after he had grown to maturity, Cypselus happened to consult the oracle, and on the strength of the answer he received – an answer which cut, as it were, both ways – set to work and made himself master of Corinth. The prophecy went like this:

> Fortunate is he who steps down into my house,
> Cypselus, son of Eëtion, lord of famous Corinth:
> Fortunate he and his sons, but not the sons of his sons.

Such was the prophecy which induced Cypselus to seize power, and I will now tell you what use he made of it when he got it: many of the Corinthians he drove into exile, many he deprived of their property, and still more, by a long way, of their lives. He ruled in Corinth for thirty years, died in the height of prosperity, and was succeeded by his son Periander. To begin with, Periander was less violent than his father, but soon surpassed him in bloody-mindedness and savagery. This was the result of a correspondence which he entered into with Thrasybulus, the master of Miletus. He sent a representative to the court of this despot, to ask his opinion on how best and most safely to govern his city. Thrasybulus invited the man to walk with him from the city to a field where corn was growing. As he passed through this cornfield, continually asking questions about why the messenger had come to him from Corinth, he kept cutting off all the tallest ears of wheat which he could see, and throwing them away, until the finest and best-grown part of the crop was ruined. In this way he went right through the field, and then sent the messenger away without a word. On his return to Corinth, Periander was eager to hear what advice Thrasybulus had given, and the man replied that he had not given any at all, adding that he was surprised at being sent to visit such a person, who was evidently mad and a wanton destroyer of his own property – and then he described what he had seen Thrasybulus do. Periander seized the point at once; it was perfectly plain to him that Thrasybulus recommended the murder of all the people in the city who were outstanding in influence or ability. Moreover, he took the advice, and from that time forward there was no crime against the Corinthians that he did not commit; indeed, anything that Cypselus had left undone in the way of killing or banishing, Periander completed for him. Once, on a single day, he stripped every woman in the town naked, on account of his wife Melissa – but let me explain: Periander had mislaid something which a friend had left in his charge, so he sent to the oracle of the dead, amongst the Thesproti on the river Acheron, to ask where he had put it. The ghost of Melissa appeared and said that she would not tell, either by word or sign; for she was cold and naked, the clothes, which had been buried with her, having been of no use at all, since they had not been burnt. Then, as evidence for her husband that she spoke the truth, she added that Periander had put his loaves into a cold oven. The messengers reported what they had seen and heard, and Periander, convinced by the token of the cold oven and the loaves (because he had lain with her after she was dead), immediately issued a proclamation to the effect that every woman in Corinth should come to the temple of Hera. The women obeyed, crowding to the temple in their best clothes as if to a festival, and Periander, who had hidden some of his guards for the purpose, had them all stripped – every one of them, mistresses and maids alike – and their clothes collected into a pit and burnt, while he prayed to the spirit of his wife Melissa. After this he sent to the oracle again, and Melissa's ghost told him where he had put whatever it was that his friend had left with him.

'Well, gentlemen, now you can see what despotic government is, and the sort of things it can do. As for us in Corinth, we were astonished enough when we saw you were sending for Hippias; but our amazement is even greater now, at hearing you speak as you do. We implore you, in the name of the gods of Greece, not to saddle our cities with despotic institutions. If you refuse to desist from your purpose – if you still attempt to restore Hippias to power, contrary to all law and justice – you may at least be certain that you have no support from Corinth.'

When the Corinthian representative had finished his speech, Hippias, who was more familiar than anyone else with the prophecies, swore by the same gods that the day would come when Corinth would find herself plagued by the Athenians, and that then the Corinthians would long for the Pisistratidae more than for anyone else in the world, and long in vain. The representatives of the other allied states had made no comment until they heard Sosicles; then, however, every one of them held his tongue no longer, but spoke in Sosicles' support, and urged the Spartans not to meddle with the affairs of any city in Greece. This settled the matter; the Spartans abandoned their purpose, and Hippias left the country. Before he went, Amyntas of Macedon offered him Anthemus, and the Thessalians Iolcus; but he returned to Sigeum without accepting either offer. This place Pisistratus had taken by force of arms from the Mytilenaeans, and had afterwards put it under the control of Hegesistratus, a natural son of his by an Argive woman. Hegesistratus did not manage to enjoy his father's gift without a good deal of trouble; for there was constant war over a long period between the Athenians at Sigeum and the Mytilenaeans at Achilleum, the latter claiming the restoration of their lost territory, the former disputing the claim and endeavouring to prove that Aeolians had no more right to the country in the neighbourhood of Troy than they themselves had, or any other Greeks who helped Menelaus to avenge the rape of Helen. Amongst the various incidents of this war, one in particular is worth a mention: in the course of a battle in which the Athenians were victorious, the poet Alcaeus ran away, but left his arms in the hands of the victors, who hung them up in the temple of Athene at Sigeum. Alcaeus wrote some verses, describing his little accident to his friend Melanippus, and sent it to him at Mytilene. The war between Mytilene and Athens was brought to an end by Periander, who was invited by both parties to act as arbitrator; the condition he proposed was that each side should retain what it at the moment possessed. In this way Sigeum passed into the power of Athens.

Hippias, on his return to Asia, moved heaven and earth to set Artaphernes against the Athenians, and to procure the subjection of

Athens to himself and Darius; and the Athenians, when they learnt of the efforts he was making against them, sent to Sardis to urge the Persians not to listen to the exiles. Artaphernes replied that, if they valued their safety, they must take Hippias back. The Athenians refused, and made up their minds to accept the consequence — open hostility to Persia.

It was at this moment, when the Athenians had made their decision and were already on bad terms with Persia, that Aristagoras of Miletus, who had been turned out of Sparta by Cleomenes, arrived in Athens. He knew that Athens at this time was the next most powerful state in Greece; accordingly he appeared before the people and made a speech, in which he repeated the arguments he had previously used at Sparta, about the good things to be found in Asia, and the Persian methods of warfare – how they used neither shields nor spears and were easy to beat. In addition to this he pointed out that Miletus had been founded by Athenian settlers, so it was only natural that the Athenians, powerful as they were, should help her in her need. Indeed, so anxious was he to get Athenian aid, that he promised everything that came into his head, until at last he succeeded. Apparently it is easier to impose upon a crowd than upon an individual, for Aristagoras, who had failed to impose upon Cleomenes, succeeded with thirty thousand Athenians. Once persuaded to accede to Aristagoras' appeal, the Athenians passed a decree for the dispatch of twenty warships to Ionia, under the command of Melanthius, a distinguished Athenian.

The sailing of this fleet was the beginning of trouble not only for Greece, but for other peoples.

Aristagoras sailed in advance of the contingent, and, on reaching Miletus, adopted a plan of action from which no advantage could possibly accrue to the Ionians – indeed, he did not intend that it should, his only object being to annoy Darius. He sent a man to Phrygia, with a message to the Paeonians from the Strymon, who had been taken prisoner by Megabazus and were then living there with a tract of land and a village of their own. The man duly delivered the message, which ran as follows: 'Men of Paeonia, Aristagoras, lord of Miletus, has sent me to propose a way by which you may save yourselves, if you will adopt it. All Ionia is in revolt against the Persian king, and you have the chance of getting back home. You must make your own way to the sea; after that, we will look after you.' The Paeonians were delighted, and taking their women and children with them, made off for the coast – all but a few whose hearts failed them, and who stayed behind. From the coast they crossed to Chios, and while they were there, a large troop of Persian cavalry, which had started in pursuit of them, arrived in their track; having failed to overtake them, the Persians sent a message across to the island and urged them to return. The Paeonians refused, and were taken on to Lesbos by the Chians, and from there the Lesbians took them to Doriscus. Thence they made their own way on foot to Paeonia.

The Athenian squadron of twenty sail now reached Miletus. It was accompanied by five other warships belonging to the Eretrians, who had joined the expedition not for the Athenians' sake, but to pay a debt of honour to the people of Miletus, who some time previously had fought at their side all through their war with the Chalcidians – who, in their turn, had the support of Samos. On the arrival, therefore, of these two contingents, Aristagoras, as soon as the rest of his allies had assembled, proceeded to attack Sardis. He did not himself accompany the expedition, but stayed in Miletus, having appointed to the command his brother Charopinus and another Milesian named Hermophantus.

The fleet sailed for Ephesus, where the ships were left at Coressus in Ephesian territory; the troops, a strong force, then began their march up-country with Ephesian guides. They followed the course of the Cayster, crossed the ridge of Tmolus, and came down upon Sardis, which they took without opposition, except for the central stronghold of the town, which was defended by Artaphernes in person, with a considerable force. But they were prevented from sacking the place after its capture by the fact that most of the houses in Sardis were constructed of reeds, reed-thatch being used even on the few houses which were built of brick. One house was set alight by a soldier, and the flames rapidly spread until the whole town was ablaze. The outlying parts were all burning, so the native Lydians and such Persians as were there, caught in a ring of fire and unable to get clear of the town, poured into the market-square on either bank of the Pactolus, where they were forced to stand on their defence. The Pactolus is the river which brings the gold dust down from Tmolus. It flows through the market at Sardis, and then joins the Hermus, which, in its turn, flows into the sea. The Ionians, seeing some of the enemy defending themselves, and others approaching in large numbers, then became alarmed, and withdrew to Tmolus; and thence, just before nightfall, they marched off to rejoin their ships. In the conflagration at Sardis a temple of Cybebe, a goddess worshipped in that part of the world, was destroyed, and the Persians later made this a pretext for their burning of Greek temples.

All the Persians this side of the Halys, already alerted, were mustering to rescue the Lydians; finding the Ionians already gone from Sardis, they followed on their tracks and came up with them at Ephesus. The Ionians formed up to meet the attack, but were severely beaten. Amongst the large numbers of well-known men who were killed was Eualcides, the Eretrian commander, a man who more than once had been crowned as winner in the games, and had been highly praised in the poetry of Simonides of Ceos. The survivors scattered to their cities.

After this battle the Athenians would have nothing more to do with the Ionian rebellion, and in spite of frequent appeals from Aristagoras refused to help him. But the Ionians, in view of the injury they had already done Darius, pressed on the war with no less vigour, even without Athenian aid. They sailed to the Hellespont and got control of Byzantium and all the other towns thereabouts, then, by an expedition outside those seas, they won over the greater part of Caria; even Caunus, which had previously held off, now, after the burning of Sardis, joined the rebel cause. With the exception of Amathus, all Cyprus, too, volunteered assistance and rebelled against Persia. The origin of the Cyprian revolt was this: a man named Onesilus, a younger brother of Gorgus the ruler of Salamis, and son of Chersis (whose father was Siromus, and grandfather Euelthon) had repeatedly urged Gorgus to throw off the Persian yoke, and then, on hearing the news of the revolt of the Ionians, had redoubled his appeals with the utmost importunity; but Gorgus refused to listen. Onesilus, therefore, with the help of his supporters, waited until he went out of town and then shut the gates on him. Having thus lost his city, Gorgus fled to the Persians, and Onesilus, becoming master of Salamis, tried to induce all the Cyprians to join in the revolt. His only failure was with Amathus; the men of this town refused to listen to him, so he laid siege to it.

While Onesilus was busy with the siege of Amathus, news was brought to Darius that Sardis had been taken and burnt by the Athenians and Ionians, and that the prime mover in the joint enterprise was Aristagoras of Miletus. The story goes that when Darius learnt of the disaster, he did not give a thought to the Ionians, knowing perfectly well that the punishment for their revolt would come; but he asked who the Athenians were, and then, on being told, called for his bow. He took it, set an arrow on the string, shot it up into the air and cried: 'Grant, O God, that I may punish the Athenians'. Then he commanded one of his servants to repeat to him the words, 'Master, remember the Athenians', three times, whenever he sat down to dinner. After that he sent for Histiaeus the Milesian, whom he had already detained for a long time at his court, and said: 'I understand, Histiaeus, that your deputy, whom you put in charge of Miletus, has thrown off his allegiance to me. He has brought against me men from the continent across the sea, and has persuaded the Ionians – who shall assuredly pay for it – to join them in his service, and he has taken Sardis from me. Come now – was this well done? And could it have happened without your knowledge and advice? The time may come when you will blame yourself for this.'

'My lord,' Histiaeus replied, 'how can you say such a thing? Is it likely that I should plan to do anything which might injure you in any way whatever, small or great? I have all I want, so what motive could there be for such treachery? Is not what is yours, mine? And have I not the honour of sharing all your counsels? If my deputy at Miletus is indeed guilty of this thing, you may be very sure that he has acted entirely on his own initiative. Personally I find it impossible to believe that he and the Milesians are acting against your interests; if, however, they really are doing so – if you have really been told the truth – then, my lord, you can see how unwisely you acted when you forced me to leave the coast; for it appears that the Ionians have waited till I was out of sight to do what they have long passionately desired to do. If only I had still been there, not a single city would have stirred. Give me leave, therefore, at once to return to Ionia; I will put everything right for you, and deliver into your hands this deputy-governor of Miletus, who has caused all the trouble. Moreover, I will not only do this to your entire satisfaction, but I also swear by the gods of your royal house not to take off the clothes I am wearing on my arrival in Ionia, until I have forced Sardinia, the biggest island in the world, to pay tribute to you.'

The purpose of this was to deceive Darius – and it was successful. The King believed Histiaeus and let him go, telling him to return to Susa when he had done what he promised.

Meantime – while, that is, the report on Sardis was on its way to the king, and the king, after shooting the arrow, was conferring with Histiaeus, and Histiaeus by Darius' permission was on his way to the coast – the following events took place. During the siege of Amathus, Onesilus of Salamis got news that a Persian named Artybius was expected to arrive in Cyprus with a strong Persian force. Onesilus, therefore, dispatched messengers to all parts of Ionia with an appeal for help. The Ionians quickly made up their minds and came over to the island in strength. No sooner had they arrived than the Persians crossed from Cilicia and marched on Salamis, while the Phoenicians sailed round the promontory called the Keys of Cyprus. Thereupon the city-chief of Cyprus called a meeting of the Ionian commanders and addressed them in these words: 'Men of Ionia, we of Cyprus offer you the choice of engaging either the Persians or the Phoenicians. Should you prefer to try your strength on land against the Persians, now is the time to disembark and make your dispositions, while we, in our turn, go aboard your ships and fight the Phoenicians at sea. If, on the contrary, you would rather tackle the Phoenicians – by all means do so; but whichever you choose, take care to fight well. Let it not be your fault if Ionia and Cyprus fail to preserve their liberty.'

The Ionians replied: 'The common council of Ionia sent us here to guard the sea, not to hand over our ships to you and to fight the Persians on land. We will therefore keep the station assigned to us, and in that try to do our duty. And as for you – remember what you suffered from your masters the Persians, and be men.'

The Persian army arrived on the plain of Salamis, and the Cyprian kings made their dispositions to meet them. Picked troops from Salamis and Soli they drew up to face the Persians, leaving the remainder from other Cyprian towns to deal with the other enemy groups. Onesilus volunteered in person to oppose the Persian commander Artybius. Artybius rode a horse which had been trained, when attacking an infantryman, to rear and go for the man with his fore-hooves. Onesilus got to know of this, and had a word about it with his armour-bearer, a Carian by nationality and a very fine and courageous soldier. 'I am told,' he said, 'that Artybius' horse rears, and savages with his teeth and hooves anyone he comes on. Now think a moment, and tell me which of the two – Artybius or his horse – you would rather watch for a chance of striking.'

'My lord,' the attendant answered, 'I am quite ready to attack both or either – indeed, I will do anything you bid me; but I will tell you none the less what I think will be best for you. What I say is, a prince and a general should fight with another prince, or another general. If you kill a general, it will be a great thing for you; and if he kills you – which God forbid – even death from a worthy hand is only half as bad as it might otherwise have been. You, then, must fight Artybius; we underlings will go for our equals – and for the horse. Don't be afraid of his tricks: I promise you, he will never rear up against anybody again.'

Shortly afterwards began the battle on land and at sea. In the latter, the Ionians that day were in magnificent fettle – especially the Samian contingent – and beat the Phoenicians; on land, while the struggle was going on, Artybius on his horse came charging down upon Onesilus, who, according to the arrangement with his armour-bearer, aimed a blow at the rider's body; as Onesilus struck, the horse reared and brought its fore-feet down upon his shield – and at that instant the Carian swung his curved sword and sheared its feet clean off. The horse fell, and Artybius, the Persian commander, with him. Elsewhere on the field, Stesenor the ruler of Curium (Curium is said to have been a colony from Argos), with a considerable body of troops under his command, played traitor; and his lead was immediately followed by the war-chariots from Salamis. The result was a victory for Persia, and in the rout of the Cyprian army many were killed, including Onesilus, the son of Chersis and originator of the Cyprian revolt, and Aristocyprus, the prince of Soli. (Aristocyprus was the son of Philocyprus, whom Solon the Athenian, when he visited Cyprus, praised in a poem more highly than any other prince.)

The people of Amathus, in revenge for his having laid siege to their town, severed the head from the dead body of Onesilus and hung it up above their gates. In time it became hollow, and was occupied by a swarm of bees, who filled it with honeycomb. In consequence of this the townspeople consulted an oracle, and were advised to take the head down and bury it, and, if they wished to prosper, to regard Onesilus thenceforward as a hero, and to honour him with an annual sacrifice. This was done, and the ceremony was still observed in my own day. The Ionians who had won the action at sea, faced with the total failure of Onesilus' cause and the fact that all the towns in Cyprus were now under siege – with the one exception of Salamis, which the people of the town restored to their former ruler Gorgus – lost no time in returning home to Ionia. Of the Cyprian towns the one to hold out longest was Soli; the Persians took it after more than four months, by undermining the wall.

Thus after a year of freedom Cyprus was once more brought into subjection. Meanwhile Daurises, who had married a daughter of Darius, and two other Persian commanders, Hymaees and Otanes, who had also married daughters of the king, pursued the Ionian force which had attacked Sardis, cut it up, and drove the survivors into their ships; the three commanders then divided their attentions between the various towns and proceeded to sack them. Daurises made for the settlements on the Hellespont, and took in as many days the five towns of Dardanus, Abydus, Percote, Lampsacus, and Paesus. Then, on his way from Paesus to Parium, hearing that the Carians had made common cause with the Ionians and thrown off the Persian yoke, he turned about, and marched against Caria. Somehow or other the Carians got wind of the movement before he arrived, and massed at a place called White Pillars on the Marsyas – a tributary of the Maeander, rising in Idrian territory. When the assembled Carians were debating how to deal with the danger which threatened them, what I think was the best suggestion came from Pixodarus, son of Mausolus, a man of Cindya, who had married a daughter of the Cilician King Syennesis. The proposal was that the army should cross the Maeander and fight with the river in their rear; this would

prevent them from running away, and every man, forced to remain
at his post, would be even braver than nature made him. But this
plan was not adopted: it was decided, instead, that the Persians, not
the Carians, should have the Maeander at their backs – for if the
Persians were defeated and compelled to retire, they would then fail
to get away and be driven into the river. Soon the Persians arrived,
crossed the Maeander, and were engaged by the Carians on the
Marsyas. The struggle was long and violent, but the Carians were
finally overwhelmed by weight of numbers. Some 2000 Persians
were killed, and about 10,000 Carians. The Carian survivors shut
themselves up at Labraunda, in the great grove of sacred plane-trees
known as the precinct of Zeus Stratius. The Carians are the only
people we know of who sacrifice to Zeus Stratius.[1] While they were
there, they discussed plans for saving themselves – not knowing if
it would be better for them to surrender to the Persians or to leave
Asia for good. However, during the course of their deliberations the
Milesians and their allies came to offer assistance, and the Carians
changed thir minds entirely and prepared for fresh resistance. The
Persians attacked, and there was a second battle; but the result of it
was even more disastrous than before. The whole Carian and allied
force suffered severe losses, but the Milesian contingent the worst of
all. The Carians, however, recovered from this blow and later fought
another action. Learning of the Persian intention to attack their
towns, they laid a trap on the Pedasus road. The Persians fell into it
during a night march and were cut to pieces. Three of their commanders, Daurises, Amorges, and Sisimaces, were killed – also Gyges'
son Myrsus. The man who planned this ambush was Heracleides of
Mylasa, a son of Ibanollis.

Meanwhile Hymaeës – another of the Persian officers who went
in pursuit of the Ionians after their attack on Sardis – marched to the
Propontis and captured Cius in Mysia. Hearing, after its capture,
that Daurises had left the Hellespont and was on his way to Caria,
he went to the Hellespont himself with the troops under his command, and crushed all the Aeolians in the neighbourhood of Troy,
and also the Gergithes, a remnant of the ancient Teucrians. During
these campaigns he died of disease in the Troad. Meanwhile Arta-

1. Zeus of the Host.

phernes, the governor of Sardis, and Otanes, the third commander, attacked Ionia and the part of Aeolis which adjoins it, capturing Clazomenae in Ionia and Cyme in Aeolis.

It now plainly appeared that Aristagoras of Miletus was, after all, but a poor-spirited creature: himself responsible for setting Ionia by the ears and all the subsequent trouble, nevertheless, when he saw these towns falling one after another, and realized that he had no chance against Darius, he began to look about for means of escape. He called a meeting of his supporters, and, saying they ought to have some place of refuge in the event of their being pushed out of Miletus, asked their advice on the most suitable place for a new settlement. The two alternatives he himself had in mind were Sardinia and Myrcinus, the Edonian town which Histiaeus had fortified when it was given him by Darius. Hecataeus the historian, the son of Hegesander, objected to both, and proposed that Aristagoras should construct a fortress on the island of Leros and lie low there as long as necessary, if he should be driven from Miletus: then, with it as a base, he might return. Aristagoras, however, decided that the best chance was to go for Myrcinus; accordingly, he turned over affairs at Miletus to Pythagoras, a man of distinction, and himself sailed to Thrace with all who were willing to accompany him. There he gained control of the territory he was after, but on a subsequent venture, while he was besieging a neighbouring town, he was killed with all his men by the Thracians who had been willing to leave it under a truce.

BOOK SIX

THUS died Aristagoras, the author of the Ionian rebellion. Meanwhile Histiaeus, the ruler of Miletus, went to Sardis. He had obtained leave from Darius to quit Susa, and on his arrival at Sardis, Artaphernes, the governor, asked him what, in his opinion, had caused the Ionian revolt. Histiaeus pretended complete ignorance of the whole situation, and said he was astonished that such a thing should have occurred. Artaphernes, however, who knew that he was lying, and had, indeed, full knowledge of the history of the revolt, had his answer ready. 'I will tell you how it is, Histiaeus,' he said, 'you made the shoe – Aristagoras put it on.' This remark, proving as it did that Artaphernes knew the truth, was alarming, and Histiaeus that very night made his escape to the coast. The promise he had made to Darius to bring Sardinia, the biggest island in the world, under Persian rule was thus broken; his real purpose was to take over command of the Ionians in their war against the king.

Crossing to Chios, Histiaeus was arrested by the islanders on suspicion of a plot against them in the Persian interest, but was subsequently released when the Chians had heard the whole story and were convinced of his hostility to Darius. Then they asked him why he had been so anxious to urge Aristagoras to start the revolt which had caused Ionia so much distress, and Histiaeus, taking care to conceal the real reason, declared in reply that he had done so because Darius had been planning a transfer of population, intending to settle the Phoenicians in Ionia and Ionians in Phoenicia. This was quite untrue, but it was enough to alarm the Ionians.

Histiaeus now sent letters to some Persians in Sardis, as if they had previously discussed the rebellion with him. His messenger was a certain Hermippus, a man from Atarneus. Hermippus, however, instead of delivering the letters at the proper addresses, gave them to Artaphernes, who, realizing what was afoot, instructed Hermippus to take them on to the people for whom they were intended and then bring back to him the answers which each of them wrote to Histiaeus. When he had seen them he executed many of the Persians, and Sardis was in chaos.

After this disappointment, the Chians, at Histiaeus' request, were prepared to take him back to Miletus; but the people there had had a taste of liberty and were too well pleased to have got rid of Aristagoras to be willing to welcome another ruler of the same stamp. When Histiaeus attempted to force his way into the town under cover of darkness, one of the Milesians wounded him in the thigh. His next move, when he found himself excluded from his own town, was to return to Chios, from which, having failed to persuade the Chians to give him ships, he crossed to Mytilene in Lesbos. Here he was successful; the Lesbians put eight triremes into commission and sailed with him to Byzantium, which they made their base for the seizure of all ships bound out from the Black Sea, except those whose crews promised to obey his orders.

While they were thus engaged, Miletus itself was in expectation of a heavy combined attack by land and sea. The Persian commanders had united their forces and were marching against it, counting the lesser cities of secondary importance. Amongst those who sailed with the fleet, it was the Phoenicians whose heart was most in the business, though there were also contingents from Cyprus (which had recently been subjugated), Cilicia, and Egypt.

The Ionians, learning of the Persians' intentions, sent their representatives to the Panionium. In their deliberations it was decided to raise no troops to oppose the Persians on land; the actual defence of Miletus was to be left to its people, while they themselves should man every available ship, and concentrate them at the little island of Lade, just off the coast opposite Miletus. Here they would fight a naval action in defence of the town.

Presently the Ionian fleet began to arrive, and the ships took station in the following order: at the eastern end of the line were 80 vessels from Miletus; next to them came 12 from Priene and 3 from Myus, then 17 from Teos, and 100 from Chios. The contingents from Erythrae and Phocaea followed, consisting of 8 and 3 vessels respectively; and next to these lay the Lesbian contingent, 70 strong. Finally, on the western end of the line were 60 vessels from Samos – making a grand total of 353 triremes, against the 600 which the Persians had at their disposal.

On the arrival of the combined Persian force, both ships and troops, the officers in command had something of a shock; the size of the Ionian fleet was greater than they had expected, and they were afraid they might be unable to defeat it. If they did not get command of the sea, they might fail to take Miletus and be punished by Darius for their failure. So they collected the autocrats of the various Ionian cities, who, after they were turned out by Aristagoras, had fled to the Persians; these men were now with the army before Miletus, and it was to them that the Persian commanders turned in their difficulty. Having called them to a conference, they said: 'Men of Ionia, now is the time for you to show yourselves true servants of the king. Each of you must do his best to detach his own countrymen from the Ionian alliance. Make your proposals to them, and promise that, if they abandon their allies, there will be no disagreeable consequences for them; we will not set fire to their houses or their temples, or treat them with any greater harshness than before this trouble occurred. If, however, they refuse, and insist upon fighting, then you must resort to threats, and say exactly what we will do to them: tell them, that is, that when they are beaten they will be sold as slaves, their boys will be made eunuchs, their girls carried off to Bactria, and their land given to others.'

The exiled autocrats agreed to the Persian proposal, and each of them sent a message by night to the people of his town. The scheme, however, did not prosper; for in each town the recipients of the letters thought that they were the only ones to be addressed, with the result that all of them firmly refused the invitation to treachery. This incident occurred immediately after the arrival of the Persian force at Miletus.

Soon afterwards meetings were held by the Ionians who had assembled at Lade, and amongst the various speeches which were made, one of the most notable was that of the Phocaean commander, Dionysius. 'Fellow countrymen,' he said, 'our fate balances on a razor's edge between being free men or slaves – and runaway slaves at that. Come then: if you are willing to submit for a while to strict discipline and to spend a few laborious days, you will thereby be enabled to defeat the Persians and keep your liberty. If, on the other hand, you continue to live soft and to go as you please, then I see no hope whatever of your escaping punishment at the king's hands for your revolt. Now take my advice; put yourselves under my orders, and, if heaven gives us a fair deal, I promise you either that the enemy will refuse battle altogether, or, if he fights, that he will be soundly beaten.' The appeal succeeded; the Ionians agreed to take orders from Dionysius, who at once got to work. Every day he had ships and crews out for training, making the fleet sail in line ahead, keeping the troops on board under arms, practising the oarsmen on the man-oeuvre of 'breaking the line', and insisting that all ships, for the remainder of the day, should lie to their anchors instead of being hauled ashore. Thus the men got no rest from morning to night. For seven days they continued to obey orders; but after that, being unaccustomed to such hard work and worn out with toiling away under the hot sun, they began to grumble. 'What god have we offended,' they said, 'to be punished like this? We must have taken leave of our senses, to have put ourselves into the hands of this swollen-headed Phocaean who provides no more than three ships for the fleet! Yet here he is, taking complete charge; the way he treats us is outrageous: we shall never recover from it – many of us are ill already, and many more expect to be. Anything would be preferable to the misery we now endure – if it's a choice between two sorts of slavery, then the one we are threatened with, however bad it turns out to be, could hardly be worse than what we are putting up with now. Now then – let us refuse to obey his orders.'

It was no sooner said than done. Every seaman in the fleet refused duty. They pitched tents, like soldiers, in the island, lounged about in the shade, and refused to go aboard their vessels or to continue their training in any way whatever.

The commanders of the Samian contingent, when they realized how the Ionians were behaving and were aware of the complete lack of discipline amongst them, changed their minds about the pro-posal which had previously been made to them by Aeaces, the son of Syloson, at the request of the Persians. This proposal – to with-draw, namely, from the Ionian confederacy – they now decided to accept, convinced, as they were, that it would be impossible to get the better of the Persian fleet, and, even if they did, that Darius would soon send another fleet against them five times as great. The moment, therefore, that they saw the Ionians shirking their duty, they thought that the most profitable thing to do was to save their houses and temples, while they had the chance. Aeaces, who proposed the desertion, was the son of Syloson and grandson of Aeaces. He had been ruler of Samos, and along with the other autocrats in the Ionian states was banished from power by Aristagoras of Miletus.

Then the Phoenician fleet came forward, and the Ionians sailed in line ahead to meet them. They were soon at close quarters, and, once the fight had begun, I cannot say for certain which of the Ionian contingents fought well and which fought ill; for the reports are confused, everybody blaming everybody else. As for the Samians, it is said that in accordance with their agreements with Aeaces they abandoned their place in the line, got sail on their vessels, and made for home – with the exception of eleven triremes, whose officers stayed and fought contrary to orders from their superiors. (To com-memorate the courage of these men, the government at Samos had a column erected, with their names and parentage inscribed upon it. The column still stands in the public square.)

The sight of the Samians under sail for home was too much for the Lesbians, who were next in the line; they soon followed suit, as, indeed, did the majority of the Ionian fleet. Of those who remained at their posts and fought it out, the most roughly handled were the Chians who fought a brilliant and most valiant action. As mentioned before, they contributed a hundred ships to the combined fleet. Aboard each were forty picked men, of citizen class, serving as marines. Though they saw the greater number of the confederate fleet playing traitor, they scorned to imitate such cowardly behaviour, but with the few friends still fighting beside them again and again broke the enemy line and continued the struggle, until, having captured a number of enemy ships, they had lost nearly all their own; after which, with the few that remained afloat, they made their escape to Chios. Those of their ships which were crippled made for Mycale, with the enemy in pursuit, and here they were run ashore and abandoned, the crews continuing their journey overland on foot. On the way, they entered the territory of Ephesus. It was after dark, and the women of the place were celebrating the Thesmophoria, and the Ephesians, having had no news of the Chians' predicament, and seeing that a company of armed men had crossed their borders, at once supposed them to be brigands who were after their women. They therefore hurried to the rescue with every available man, and the Chians were killed.

Such was their fate. Meanwhile the Phocaean commander Dionysius, who had captured three enemy vessels in the course of the engagement, also made good his escape once he realized that all was lost. He did not, however, make for Phocaea, because he knew his people would share the fate of all the other Ionians and be reduced to slavery; instead he set his course, without further preparation, straight for Phoenicia, where he sank a number of cargo-vessels and took from them property of considerable value; he then sailed for Sicily, which he made his base for piratical raids against Carthaginian and Tyrrhenian shipping – Greek ships he never molested.

After their victory over the Ionian fleet, the Persians invested Miletus by land and sea. They dug saps under the walls, brought up rams of all kinds, and, five years after the revolt of Aristagoras, overwhelmed it. So Miletus was reduced to slavery, and the oracle's prediction was fulfilled. The prediction was as follows: the people of Argos had consulted the oracle at Delphi on a matter which concerned the safety of their own city, and had received an answer in which others were involved besides themselves; for while a part of it concerned Argos, there was an additional passage which referred to Miletus. The former I will mention when I reach the proper moment in my story;[1] the latter was in these words:

> Thou then, Miletus, contriver of wicked deeds,
> Shalt be a feast for many, and a splendid prize;
> Thy wives shall wash the feet of many a long-haired man,
> And others shall care for our shrine at Didyma.

1. Book VI, ch. 77; see p. 415. The 'double oracle' sounds as if Argos too had been approached by Aristagoras, and consulted the oracle on that account.

This is just what happened to the Milesians; most of the men were killed by the Persians – and the Persians wear their hair long; the women and children were made slaves, and the temple at Didyma, both shrine and oracle, was plundered and burnt. The wealth of this temple I have frequently spoken of elsewhere in my story. The men in the city whose lives were spared were sent as prisoners to Susa; Darius did them no harm, and settled them in Ampe on the Persian Gulf, near the mouth of the Tigris. The Persians themselves occupied the land in the immediate neighbourhood of the town, and the rest of the cultivated region which belonged to it, and made over the mountainous interior to the Carians of Pedasus.

The people of Sybaris who, after the loss of their city, lived in Laus and Scidrus, failed to show proper sympathy with the Milesians in their misfortune; for at the capture of Sybaris by the Crotoniates, the whole male population of Miletus, from the boys upwards, had shaved their heads and gone into deep mourning, as a mark of the friendly connexion between the two towns – and indeed I know of no two towns more closely bound together by mutual ties. The Athenians, on the contrary, showed their profound distress at the capture of Miletus in a number of ways, and in particular, when Phrynichus produced his play, *The Capture of Miletus*, the audience in the theatre burst into tears. The author was fined a thousand drachmae for reminding them of a disaster which touched them so closely, and they forbade anybody ever to put the play on the stage again.

In this way Miletus was emptied of its inhabitants.

In Samos the wealthier citizens were by no means pleased by the way their officers had come to an understanding with the Persians. Immediately after the fight off Lade they met in conference, and decided not to wait for the arrival of Aeaces, but to abandon the island and settle elsewhere rather than to stay and be slaves to Aeaces and his Persian masters. It happened that about this time the people of Zancle in Sicily had sent to Ionia to invite settlers to Kale-Acte, or Fair Shore, a place on the north coast of the island facing Tyrrhenia, and inhabited by Sicilian natives. Their purpose was to found an Ionian settlement on this spot. The people of Samos were the only Ionians to accept the invitation, and they set sail in company with such of the Milesians as had escaped. The expedition had, however, an unexpected sequel. In the course of their voyage, they reached Western Locri, in southern Italy, just at the moment when Scythes, the ruler of Zancle, was attempting, with all his men, to capture by siege a Sicel town. Anaxilaus, ruler of Rhegium, who was at that period on bad terms with Zancle, and knew what was going on, got into touch with the Samians and persuaded them to forget about the Fair Shore, their original objective, and seize Zancle itself instead, while it was undefended. The Samians agreed; the town was taken, and the Zanclaeans, as soon as the news reached them, hurried back to recover it and called upon Hippocrates, despot of Gela, as an ally of theirs, to support them. Hippocrates responded to the appeal, but when he arrived at Zancle with his army, he repaid Scythes for the loss of the town he ruled by flinging him into chains and sending him off with his brother Pythogenes to Inyx; he then entered into negotiation with the Samians and, after an exchange of guarantees, completed the betrayal of the people of Zancle. His reward for this treachery was to be half of all the movable property and slaves in the town, and all in the open country. The greater number of the townspeople he thus kept as slaves; the three hundred leading citizens he handed over to the Samians to have their throats cut. The Samians, however, did not do this.

Scythes escaped from Inyx to Himera, and from there made his way to Asia and up-country to the court of Darius, who came to consider him the most honourable man who had ever come to him from Greece; for having got leave from Darius to revisit Sicily, he returned to Persia of his own accord, where he died in old age and great prosperity.

This, then, is the story of how the Samians escaped from Persian domination, and acquired without effort the lovely town of Zancle.

After the sea-fight off Miletus, the Phoenicians, on instructions from Persia, restored Aeaces, the son of Syloson, to his previous authority in Samos, as a reward for the great and valuable services which he had rendered. Samos itself was not burnt by the Persians, neither the town nor the temples; of all the Ionian rebels the Samians alone escaped, because of the desertion of their ships during the battle of Lade. After capturing Miletus the Persians quickly occupied Caria, some of the towns being taken by force, others without resistance.

Meanwhile news of events at Miletus reached Histiaeus, who was still around Byzantium seizing Ionian merchantmen outward bound from the Black Sea. Leaving his business in the Hellespont in the hands of Bisaltes of Abydos, the son of Apollophanes, he at once sailed for Chios with a number of Lesbians, and attacked a Chian garrison, which refused to admit him, at a place called the Hollows. A great many of the garrison were killed, and Histiaeus, basing himself on Polichne, soon, with the help of his Lesbians, got the better of the rest of the Chians, weakened, as they were, by the sea battle.

It seems that there is nearly always a warning sign of some kind, when disaster is about to overtake a city or a nation. Chios was no exception – for before this happened the warnings it received were far from negligible. The Chians had sent a choir of a hundred young men to Delphi; ninety-eight of them caught the plague and died, and only two returned. Again, in the capital city of the island, at about the same time, a little before the sea battle, the roof of a school fell in on some children who were learning their letters, and of a hundred and twenty children only one escaped. Both these events were acts of God to forewarn the people of Chios; they were followed by the battle of Lade, which brought the community to its knees, and then by the arrival of Histiaeus with his Lesbians, who, in their weakened state, had easily conquered them.

Histiaeus' next act was a campaign against Thasos with a considerable force of Ionians and Aeolians. While he was engaged in the blockade, news came that the Phoenician fleet had left Miletus and was sailing to attack the other Ionian states. He promptly raised the blockade of Thasos and hurried to Lesbos with all his troops. From Lesbos, finding his men short of supplies, he crossed to the mainland with the intention of cutting the crops round about Atarneus, and in the Mysian territory along the valley of the Caicus. It happened, however, that the Persian general Harpagus, who was in the neighbourhood at the head of a large army, fell in with Histiaeus' party as they came ashore, took Histiaeus prisoner, and killed most of his men. The circumstances of his capture were these: the Greek and Persian forces were engaged at Malene, in Atarnean territory: for a long time it was an even struggle, until at last the Persian cavalry, arriving late on the scene, fell upon the enemy; this victory was their work. The Greeks fled; and Histiaeus, who did not expect Darius to punish his fault with death, made a last bid to save himself. He was overtaken by a Persian as he ran, and, just as he was about to be speared, he cried out in Persian, 'I am Histiaeus, the Milesian'. Now if after his capture he had been taken to Darius, he would not, in my opinion, have found himself in serious trouble, but Darius would have pardoned him; but as it was, for this very reason – to prevent him, that is, from rising once more to a position of influence in Darius' court – Artaphernes, the governor of Sardis, and Harpagus, his actual captor, resolved upon his death. As soon as he reached Sardis he was impaled; his head was cut off, pickled, and sent to Darius in Susa. Darius, when he learned what Artaphernes and Harpagus had done, was angry with them for not bringing Histiaeus to him alive; he gave orders for the head to be washed and tended, and buried with all the honour due to a man who had done good service to Persia and the king. So ends the story of Histiaeus.

The Persian fleet lay during the winter at Miletus. The following year it put to sea again, and took without difficulty the islands of Chios, Lesbos, and Tenedos off the Asiatic coast. Each island, as soon as it was occupied, was gone through with the drag-net – a process in which men join hands and make a chain right across the island from north to south, and then move from one end to the other, hunting everybody out. The Persians also took the Ionian towns on the mainland – but without the netting process, as it was not practicable. The threats which the Persian commanders had uttered against the Ionians when they found them resolved upon opposition were now carried into effect; once the towns were in their hands, the best-looking boys were chosen for castration and made into eunuchs; the handsomest girls were dragged from their homes and sent to Darius' court, and the towns themselves, temples and all, were burnt to the ground. In this way the Ionians were reduced for the third time to slavery – first by the Lydians, and then, twice, by the Persians.

Leaving Ionia, the fleet proceeded to take all the places on the left-hand coast of the Hellespont, as one enters the strait. The towns on the opposite side had already fallen to the Persians by assault from inland. The places on the European side of the Hellespont are the Chersonese, which contains a great many towns, Perinthus, the strongholds on the Thracian coast, Selymbria, and Byzantium. The people of Byzantium, and their opposite neighbours in Chalcedon, instead of awaiting the attack of the Phoenicians by sea, abandoned their homes and fled to the Black Sea coast, where they established themselves at Mesembria. The Phoenicians, after destroying by fire the places I have mentioned, turned their attention to Proconnesus and Artace; then, having burnt these too, they returned to the Chersonese to take such places as had escaped destruction on their previous visit. The one exception was Cyzicus; for before the Phoenicians entered the strait, the people of this town had made their submission to Darius by coming to terms with Oebares, the son of Megabazus, who was governor of Dascyleium. Thus all the towns of the Chersonese, except Cardia, were taken by the Phoenicians.

Up to this period, the man who had exercised absolute power over this part of the world was Miltiades, the son of Cimon and grandson of Stesagoras. He had inherited his position from Miltiades the son of Cypselus, who had come into possession of it in the following way. The Dolonci, a Thracian people to whom the Chersonese then belonged, finding themselves in difficulties in a war with the Apsinthians, sent their chiefs to Delphi, to ask advice from the oracle. The Priestess replied by recommending them to take home with them, in order to resettle their affairs, the first man who, after they left the temple, should invite them to enter his house. The chiefs of the Dolonci, travelling by the Sacred Road, passed through Phocis and Boeotia, and then, as nobody asked them in, turned off and made for Athens.

Supreme power in Athens was at this time in the hands of Pisistratus, but a position of considerable importance was also enjoyed by Cypselus' son, Miltiades. Miltiades belonged to a family whose fortune was great enough to allow them to enter a four-horse chariot for the Games, and traced his descent back to Aeacus of Aegina; but further down the line his ancestry was Athenian, and Philaeus, the son of Ajax, was the first of the family to be naturalized in Athens. Now it happened that as the Dolonci passed his house, Miltiades, who was sitting in his porch, caught sight of them, and noticing that they were dressed like foreigners and carried spears, called out to them. The men came up to where he was sitting, whereupon he invited them in and offered them shelter and hospitality. The invitation was accepted, and, while they were staying in the house, they told Miltiades all about the oracle, and then begged him to act upon the advice which God had given. Miltiades had no sooner heard their story than he agreed to do as they wished – for he disliked Pisistratus' government and was very willing to be out of the way. He lost no time, therefore, in going to Delphi, where he asked the oracle if he was right in acceding to the request which the Dolonci had made him. The Priestess replied in the affirmative, and the matter was settled: and so Miltiades, son of Cypselus – who before this time had won the four-horse chariot race at Olympia – collected everybody in Athens who was willing to take part in the venture, and sailed with the Dolonci. He took possession of the country, and the chieftains who had brought him over made him their prince.

Miltiades' first act was to build a wall across the neck of the peninsula from Cardia to Pactya, to stop the Apsinthians from breaking into the Chersonese on plundering raids. Here at the neck the peninsula is some 4½ miles wide, its total length being about 52½ miles. Having completed the wall and shut out the Apsinthians, Miltiades next attacked Lampsacus; but he was ambushed and taken prisoner.

The Lydian King Croesus had had Miltiades much in his thoughts, so when he learned of his capture, he sent a command to the people of Lampsacus to set him at liberty; if they refused, he was determined, he added, to 'cut them down like a pine-tree'. The people of the town were baffled by Croesus' threat, and at a loss to understand what being cut down like a pine-tree might mean, until at last the true significance of the phrase dawned upon a certain elderly man: the pine, he explained, was the only kind of tree which sent up no new shoots after being felled – cut down a pine and it will die off completely. The explanation made the Lampsacenes so frightened of Croesus that they let Miltiades go.

Miltiades thus escaped, thanks to Croesus; nevertheless he died childless, leaving his authority and possessions to Stesagoras, the son of his half-brother on his mother's side, Cimon. Ever since his death the people of the Chersonese have offered in his honour the sacrifices commonly due to the Founder of a state, with chariot-races and athletic contests, in which nobody from Lampsacus is allowed to compete.

During the war with Lampsacus it was the fate of Stesagoras, too, to die without an heir – he was hit on the head with a chopper in the Council chamber by a man who pretended to be a deserter, but was actually an enemy of his, and a pretty hot one. Stesagoras having thus met his end, Miltiades the son of Cimon and brother of the murdered Stesagoras was dispatched by the Pisistratidae in a warship to the Chersonese, to assume the direction of affairs. The Pisistratidae had treated Miltiades well while he was in Athens, just as if they had not been guilty of his father's death – *that* incident, however, I will treat of later on.[1]

On his arrival in the Chersonese Miltiades kept within doors, on the pretence of showing respect for his dead brother, and the leading men from every town all over the country met together, when they heard of this, and came in a body to show their sympathy with him. Miltiades then had every one of them arrested. He then made himself master of the Chersonese, kept a body of 500 mercenaries, and married Hegesipyle, daughter of the Thracian King Olorus.

This Miltiades – that is, Cimon's son – had not been long in the Chersonese before he was involved in more serious difficulties, for two years after his arrival he was obliged to take to his heels to escape from the Scythian nomads who, incensed by the attack of Darius, joined forces and marched as far as the Chersonese. Miltiades did not await their attack, but fled, and remained away until they withdrew, when the Dolonci sent and fetched him back. This had occurred two years previously;[2] and now, when he learned that the Phoenicians were at Tenedos, he shipped his property on board five triremes and made sail for Athens, starting from Cardia. He sailed down the Black Gulf, and, just as he got clear of the peninsula, fell in with the Phoenician fleet. Miltiades himself got away to Imbros with four of his five triremes, but the fifth, commanded by his eldest son Metio-

1. Book VI, ch. 103, p. 424.
2. If the text is correct, Miltiades was in exile for 15 years, *c.* 511–496; but it may be corrupt. The story is anyhow flagrantly inconsistent with that in Book IV (p. 316), where Miltiades is said to have done his best to let the Scythians destroy Darius.

chus (his mother was not the daughter of Olorus the Thracian, but another woman), was overhauled and captured. The Phoenicians thought that they had a prize indeed, when they found that, together with the ship, they had caught Miltiades' son; for it was Miltiades who, when the Scythians urged the Ionians to break the bridge over the Danube and sail home, had advised them to consent. Remembering this, the Phoenicians brought Metiochus to Darius, in confident expectation of the royal favour. The king, however, far from doing any harm to Metiochus, treated him with the greatest liberality: he presented him with a house and property, and a Persian wife by whom he had children, who lived as Persians.

Miltiades himself sailed from Imbros and arrived safely at Athens.

During the course of this year no further hostile measures were undertaken by the Persians against Ionia; on the contrary, something was done greatly to its advantage. Artaphernes, governor of Sardis, sent for representatives from all the Ionian states and forced them to bind themselves by oath to settle their differences by arbitration, instead of raiding. In addition to this, he had their territories surveyed and measured in parasangs (the Persian equivalent of 30 furlongs), and settled the tax which each state was to pay at a figure which has remained unaltered down to my time. The amount was, moreover, much the same as it had previously been.

These measures were conducive to peace. Then, in the following spring, Darius superseded all his other generals and sent Mardonius, the son of Gobryas, down to the coast in command of a very large force, both military and naval. Mardonius was still a young man, and had recently married Darius' daughter Artozostra. Reaching Cilicia with his army, he took ship and continued along the coast in company with the fleet, leaving other officers to conduct the troops to the Hellespont. When in the course of his voyage along the Asiatic coast he reached Ionia, he did something which will come as a great surprise to those Greeks who cannot believe that Otanes declared to the seven conspirators that Persia should have a democratic government: he suppressed the despots in all the Ionian states and set up democratic institutions in their place. He then hurried on towards the Hellespont. Having got together a formidable fleet and army, he ferried the troops across the strait and began his march through Europe, with Eretria and Athens as his main objectives. At any rate, these two places were the professed object of the expedition, though in fact the Persians intended to subjugate as many Greek towns as they could. Their fleet subdued Thasos without resistance, and the troops on land added the Macedonians to the list of Darius' subjects. All the peoples on the hither side of Macedonia were subjects already.

From Thasos the fleet stood across to the mainland and proceeded along the coast to Acanthus, and from there attempted to double Athos; but before they were round this promontory, they were caught by a violent northerly gale, which proved too much for the ships to cope with. A great many of them were driven ashore and wrecked on Athos – indeed, report says that something like three hundred were lost with over twenty thousand men. The sea in the neighbourhood of Athos is full of monsters, so that those of the ships' companies who were not dashed to pieces on the rocks, were seized and devoured. Others, unable to swim, were drowned; others, again, died of cold.

While this disaster was overtaking the fleet, on land Mardonius and his army in Macedonia were attacked in camp one night by the Brygi, a Thracian tribe. The Persian losses were heavy, and Mardonius himself was wounded. But even so the Brygi did not escape subjection; for Mardonius did not leave their country until he had subdued them.

However, the casualties his army had suffered by the attack of the Brygi, and the fearful losses of the fleet at Athos, now induced Mardonius to begin his retreat. The whole force, therefore, returned to Asia in disgrace.

Next year Darius, on the strength of a tale put about by their neighbours that the people of Thasos were planning a revolt, sent them an order to dismantle their defences and bring their fleet across to Abdera. The islanders of Thasos after they had been blockaded by Histiaeus of Miletus had determined to apply their ample resources to building warships and stronger fortifications. The island's revenue was derived partly from property on the mainland and partly from mines: the gold mines at Scapte Hyle yielded in all eighty talents a year, those in the island itself rather less, but a good sum all the same, so that the islanders, without raising any tax on their own produce, enjoyed, from the mines and the mainland. a revenue of two hundred talents – and, in a particularly good year, of as much as three hundred. I have seen these mines myself; much the most remarkable are those discovered by the Phoenicians who came with Thasus the son of Phoenix to colonize the island, which has since borne his name. These Phoenician mines lie between Coenyra and a place called Aenyra, on the south-eastern side of Thasos, facing Samothrace. A whole mountain has been turned upside down in the search for gold. In spite of all this, however, the islanders obeyed Darius' order, pulled down their fortifications and sent their whole fleet over to Abdera.

Darius now began to put out feelers to test the attitude of the Greeks, and to find out whether they were likely to resist or surrender. He sent heralds to the various Greek states to demand earth and water for the king, and at the same time he sent orders to the Asiatic coast towns, which were already tributary, for the provision of warships and transport vessels to carry cavalry. While these were being prepared, the heralds in Greece obtained what they asked from many of the towns on the mainland and from all the islanders whom they visited with their request. Amongst the islanders, moreover, who gave the sign of submission, were the Aeginetans.

This act on the part of Aegina produced an immediate reaction from the Athenians, who supposed that the Aeginetans had submitted out of enmity to themselves and intended to join the Persian attack upon them; at once, therefore (and they were not sorry to have the excuse), they entered into correspondence with Sparta and accused the Aeginetans of being traitors to Greece. Having heard the accusation, Cleomenes, the son of Anaxandrides and one of the Spartan kings, crossed to Aegina with the intention of arresting the men chiefly responsible; but when he attempted the arrest, he found a number of other people in the island hotly opposed to him. Conspicuous amongst these was a son of Polycritos – a man called Crius (Ram) – who declared that Cleomenes would never get away with the arrest of a single man on the island – for what he was doing had not the authority of the Spartan government behind it. He had been bribed, the man added, by Athens – otherwise both kings would have come together to make the arrest. He did this on the instigation of Demaratus. As Cleomenes was leaving the island, he asked the man his name. 'Ram,' came the answer. 'Very well, Master Ram,' said Cleomenes, 'you had better get your horns sheathed in metal. There's trouble coming for you.'

Meanwhile Demaratus, who had stayed behind in Sparta, was talking against Cleomenes. Demaratus was the other of the two Spartan kings, but he belonged to the less honoured of the two houses: his family was not, indeed, actually of lower origin than the other, for both have a common ancestor; but the house of Eurysthenes, being the elder branch, is held in higher respect. The Spartans maintain (unlike all the poets) that when they originally settled in their present territory, Aristodemus – son of Aristomachus, grandson of Cleodaeus, and great-grandson of Hyllus – was himself their king, and not Aristodemus' sons. Shortly afterwards, his wife Argeia (who is said to have been the daughter of Autesion, the son of Tisamenos, grandson of Thersander and great-grandson of Polynices) gave birth to twins. Aristodemus lived to see the children, but immediately afterwards fell ill and died. The Spartans of that time determined, as the custom is, to make the elder of the two children king, but as they were both the same size and each exactly like the other, it was impossible to tell which to choose. Thus baffled, or perhaps even before trying, they asked the mother; but she said that she was no more able to tell them apart herself. Actually, of course, she knew perfectly well which was which, and only pretended not to, in the hope that both of them might somehow be made kings. At a loss what to do next, the Spartans sent to the Delphic oracle for advice, and the Priestess replied that they must let both the children be kings, but give the elder one the greater honour. The answer of the oracle by no means solved the puzzle, for the Spartans were no better able than before to determine which baby had been born first. At last, however, a suggestion was made by a man from Messenia called Panites: this was, that they should watch the mother and see which she fed and washed first. If she always kept to the same order, that fact alone would tell them all they wanted to know; if, on the contrary, she varied it, and attended sometimes to one child first and sometimes to the other, then it would be clear that she knew no more than they did and they would have to try some other plan.

The Spartans did as the man from Messenia advised. Keeping a watch on the mother, who was quite unaware of their reason for doing so, they found that she invariably fed and washed the two children in the same order; so they took the one which was singled out for preference – which was of course the elder – and had it brought up at the public expense. The child was named Eurysthenes, and its brother Procles. When the children grew up, the story goes that they quarrelled as long as they lived, in spite of the fact that they were brothers; and their descendants continued the family feud.

This version of the story is found only in Sparta. The common Greek tradition is, that the Dorian kings as far back as Perseus, the son of Danae (thus not including the god), are as they stand in the accepted Greek lists, and are rightly considered as of Greek nationality, because even at this early date they ranked as such. I am justified in saying 'as far back as Perseus', and no father, because Perseus has no human father by whose name he can be called, as Heracles, for instance, has Amphitryon. If, on the other hand, we trace the ancestry of Danae, the daughter of Acrisius, we find that the Dorian chieftains are genuine Egyptians. This is the accepted Greek version of the genealogy of the Spartan royal house; the Persians, however, maintain that Perseus was an Assyrian who adopted Greek nationality; his ancestry, therefore, was not Greek; and the forebears of Acrisius were not related to Perseus at all, but were Egyptian – which accords with the Greek version of the story. But there is no need to pursue this subject further. How it happened that Egyptians came to the Peloponnese, and what they did to make themselves kings in that part of Greece, has been chronicled by other writers; I will add nothing, therefore, but proceed to mention some points which no one else has yet touched upon.

The prerogatives of the Spartan kings are these: two priesthoods, of Zeus Lacedaemon and of Zeus Uranius, and the power of declaring war on whom they please. In this, no Spartan may attempt to oppose their decision, under pain of outlawry. On service, the kings go first and return last; they have a bodyguard of a hundred picked men, and are allowed for their own use as many cattle as they wish. To them personally are allotted the skins and chines of all animals offered for sacrifice. In peace-time their privileges are as follows: at all public religious celebrations they are the first to sit down at the dinner which follows the sacrifice; they are served first, each getting twice as much of every dish as anybody else. Theirs is the right to make the first ceremonial libation, and to them belong the hides of all animals offered in sacrifice. On the first and seventh days of every month each king is given a full-grown animal to offer in sacrifice in the temple of Apollo, also a bushel of barley-meal and a Laconian quart of wine. At all public games seats of honour are reserved for them. It is their duty to select and appoint the officials who see to the entertainment of foreign visitors, and each of them nominates two 'Pythians' – officials, that is, whose duty it is to visit Delphi when occasion arises, and who take their meals with the kings at the public expense.

If the kings happen not to attend the usual state dinner, two quarts of meal and half a pint of wine are sent to each of them at his house; when they do attend, they are served with double quantities of everything, a privilege they also enjoy when they are invited to dinner at a private house.

They are responsible for the safe-keeping of all oracles (the 'Pythians' also have knowledge of them), and certain definite legal matters are left to their sole decision. These are as follows: first, if a girl inherits her father's estate and has not been betrothed by him to anybody, the kings decide who has the right to marry her;[1] secondly, all matters connected with the public roads are in their hands; and, thirdly, anyone who wishes to adopt a child must do it in the king's presence.

They sit with the twenty-eight Elders in the Council chamber, and, in the event of their absence from a meeting, those of the Elders

---

1. She would no doubt be married to her nearest relation on the father's side, an uncle or cousin, so that the property might remain in the clan. The same rule held at Athens, where the kinsman, if already married, was actually compelled to divorce his wife. Adoption by a childless man is controlled, for the same reason. The kings, like the Athenian chief Archon, appear as guardians of property-rights.

who are nearest of kin to them take over their privilege and cast two votes, in addition to their own.

Besides these public marks of distinction during his lifetime, special ceremonies are also observed upon a king's death. News of the death is carried by riders all over the country, and women go the rounds of the capital beating cauldrons. This is the signal for two people, one man and one woman, from every citizen's household to put on mourning – which they are compelled to do under penalty of a heavy fine. One custom is observed on the occasion of a king's death, which is the same in Sparta as in Asia: this is, that when a death occurs, not only Spartans but a certain number of the country people from all over Laconia are forced to attend the funeral. A huge crowd assembles, consisting of many thousands of people – Spartan citizens, country folk, and serfs – and men and women together strike their foreheads with every sign of grief, wailing as if they could never stop and continually declaring that the king who has just died was the best they ever had.

If a king is killed in war, they make a statue of him, and carry it to burial on a richly-draped bier. After a king's funeral there are no public meetings or elections for ten days, all of which are spent in mourning. When a new king comes to the throne on the death of his predecessor, he follows a custom which obtains in Persia on similar occasions: he remits, that is, all debts owed by Spartan citizens either to the king or to the treasury. This corresponds with the Persian custom whereby a king, on his accession, remits arrears of tribute from all his subject states.

The Spartans resemble the Egyptians in that they make certain callings hereditary: town-criers, flute-players, and cooks are all, respectively, sons of fathers who followed the same profession. A man cannot, for instance, merely because he has a loud voice, adopt the profession of town-crier, or herald, to the exclusion of a competitor; he can be a herald only if his progenitors have been heralds.

At this time, then, when Cleomenes was in Aegina working for the common good of Greece, Demaratus continued to spread malicious stories about him – not because he felt any kindness towards Aegina, but simply out of envy and spite. Accordingly, on his return to Sparta Cleomenes began to consider ways of depriving Demaratus of his office, and he soon found something upon which he could base his attack. When Ariston was king of Sparta, although he married twice, he had no children. Unwilling to admit that this might be his own fault, he married a third time – and in the following circumstances: he had a friend, a Spartan citizen, with whom he was particularly intimate, and this friend's wife was much the most beautiful woman in Sparta. Oddly enough, she had been as a child extremely plain, and owed the transformation to her nurse, who, seeing that she was ugly, and that her parents, who were people of substance, were distressed about it, conceived the idea of carrying her every day to the shrine of Helen. (This is at Therapne, above the temple of Apollo.) She would then take the baby in, lay it down in front of Helen's statue, and pray the goddess to take away its ugliness. One day as the nurse left the shrine, a woman appeared and asked her what it was that she had in her arms. The nurse replied that it was a baby. The woman asked to see it, but the nurse refused, for the child's parents had forbidden her to show it to anybody. The woman, however, persisted, and at last the nurse, seeing how extremely anxious she was to have a look at the baby, showed it to her; and she stroked the baby's head and declared that it would grow to be the most beautiful woman in Sparta.

From that very day there was a change in its appearance. The child grew up, and, as soon as she was old enough, was married to Agetus, the son of Alcides – Ariston's friend, whom I mentioned before.

Now Ariston fell in love with Agetus' wife, and, as his desire for her gave him no peace, he hit upon the following plan: going to his friend, the woman's husband, he offered to let him choose anything he possessed, and promised to make him a present of it, provided that his friend would do the like for him. Agetus agreed – for, as Ariston had a wife already, it never occurred to him that his own might be in danger. The compact was confirmed by oath, and Ariston handed over whatever it was that Agetus chose. Then, when his turn came to say what he wanted in exchange, he tried to take his friend's wife. Agetus protested that he had consented to anything else, but not that. However, he had sworn an oath; and that, together with Ariston's trick, forced him to let his wife go.

Thus Ariston married his third wife, after divorcing his second;

and quite shortly this woman, before her ten months were up, gave birth to a son – Demaratus. Ariston was with the Ephors, sitting on his state chair, when a servant brought him the news. Counting on his fingers the number of months since his marriage – the date of which he had not forgotten – he exclaimed with an oath: 'The child can't be mine'. The Ephors heard what he said, but, at the moment, paid little attention to it. Later on, when Demaratus grew older, Ariston regretted the remark he had made, for he had come to believe that the boy really was his son. Some time before all this happened, the whole Spartan people had joined in prayer that Ariston, whom they considered to be the most distinguished of the kings who had ever reigned in Sparta, might have a son: this was why, when the son was born, he was named Demaratus.[1]

In course of time Ariston died and Demaratus succeeded to the throne. Apparently, however, it was fated that the whole story should come to light and lead to the deposition of Demaratus, through the quarrel between him and Cleomenes – first on the occasion when Demaratus brought the army back from Eleusis, and again when Cleomenes crossed to Aegina to deal with the islanders who had taken sides with Persia.

Eager to have his revenge, Cleomenes entered into an agreement with Demaratus' kinsman Leotychides, the son of Menares and grandson of Agis, whereby he undertook to make Leotychides king in place of Demaratus, on condition of getting his support in the attack upon Aegina.

Now Leotychides was a bitter enemy of Demaratus; and this was why. Leotychides had been engaged to marry Percalus, a daughter of Chilon, the son of Demarmenus, but Demaratus by a bold stroke had got in first, carried off the girl by force, and married her himself. This was the origin of the quarrel between the two men, and now Leotychides, at Cleomenes' urgent request, declared upon oath that Demaratus was not Ariston's son, and had no right to the throne. He followed this up by reminding people of what Ariston had said when the servant told him of the child's birth – how he had counted the months, and sworn that he could not be its father. This was the ground on which Leotychides tried to prove that Demaratus, not

1. 'The People's prayer'.

being Ariston's son, had therefore no right to the throne, and he produced as witnesses the Ephors who had been present on the occasion and had heard what Ariston said. The case caused violent disputes, until finally the Spartans determined to settle the question of Demaratus' parentage by consulting the Delphic oracle. Upon the decision to refer the matter to Delphi, Cleomenes, who was mainly responsible for getting the Spartans to take this step, secured the support of Cobon, who was a very influential person in Delphi; and he persuaded Perialla the prophetess to give the answer which Cleomenes wanted. She replied, accordingly, to the messengers' question that Demaratus was not the son of Ariston. Afterwards, the true facts of this transaction became known. Cobon was exiled, and Perialla deprived of her office.

These were the events which led to the deposition of Demaratus; but his leaving the country for Persia was the result of a later humiliation. After his deposition, Demaratus had been elected to some other office in the state, and once when he was sitting amongst the spectators at the festival of the Naked Boys, Leotychides, who was now king in his place, sent his servant to ask him what it felt like to be a magistrate after being a king. Stung by this question, the only point of which was to jeer at and humiliate him, Demaratus replied that, though he himself had had experience of both offices, Leotychides had not. 'Nevertheless,' he added, 'this question will be the beginning of great things for Sparta – either for good or evil.' Then, wrapping his head in his cloak, he left the theatre and went home, where he prepared an ox for sacrifice and offered it to Zeus. That done, he sent for his mother and, putting into her hand a portion of the beast's entrails, said to her with great earnestness: 'Mother, I beseech you by all the gods, and especially by Zeus the guardian of this home of ours, to tell me the truth; who was really my father? Leotychides, in the dispute we had, said that when you married Ariston you were already pregnant by your previous husband – and there is an even worse story told by some, that you became the lover of a servant – a stableman, who looked after the asses – and that I am his son. For God's sake, do not lie to me. Even if you have done what you are said to have done, you are not the only one – many women have done the same. Besides, there are many here in Sparta who say that

Ariston was impotent; had the seed been in him, he would have had children by his other wives.'

'My son,' his mother answered, 'since you beg me so earnestly to tell you the truth, nothing shall be hidden from you. On the third night after Ariston brought me to his house, I was visited by a phantom exactly resembling him. The phantom came to my bed, and afterwards took the wreath it was wearing and put it on me. Then it vanished, and when Ariston came in later, he asked who had given me the wreath. I said he had given it me himself, but he denied it; then I solemnly swore that it was so, and reproached him for his denial, since so short a time before he had had me in his arms and given me the wreath. Hearing me take my oath, Ariston was convinced, and realized that the hand of God was in this; moreover, the wreath proved to have come from the shrine of the hero Astrabacus, by the courtyard gate, and when we questioned the diviners, their answer was that the phantom who had visited me was Astrabacus himself. There, my son; now you know everything which you wish to know. Either the hero Astrabacus is your father, or Ariston; for that was the night when you were conceived. As for the particular ground of your enemies' attack – I mean the fact that Ariston himself, when he was told of your birth, denied in the presence of witnesses that you could be his son, because the ten months were not up – it was merely ignorance of such things which made him say what he did say. A woman does not always carry her child till the tenth month; sometimes only seven – you yourself, my son, were a seven-months child. Ariston, too, realized soon afterwards that he had spoken in ignorance. There now: what I have told you is the truth – so listen to no other story about your parentage. As for stable-boys, may their children be born to Leotychides' wife, and the wives of all who say such things.'

Now that he had learned from his mother all that he wanted to know, Demaratus made provision for a journey and went to Elis, giving out that he was going to Delphi to consult the oracle. The Spartans, who suspected that he meant to flee the country, started in pursuit of him. But Demaratus was too quick for them, and got across from Elis to Zacynthus. The Spartans followed, laid hands on him, and took away his servants; but, as the people of Zacynthus refused to give him up, he afterwards crossed to Asia and presented himself at the court of Darius, who welcomed him with a magnificent gift of land and cities. Such, then, were the chances which brought Demaratus to Asia; he had been a man of the highest distinction in Sparta, both in action and in counsel – he had, moreover, given his country a victory at Olympia in the four-horse chariot race, and was the only king of Sparta ever to achieve this honour.

Leotychides succeeded Demaratus after his deposition. He had a son, Zeuxidamus, who was known to some of the Spartans by the nickname 'Puppy'; he did not succeed to the throne, as he died before his father, leaving a son, Archidamus. After Zeuxidamus' death Leotychides married again; his second wife, who was Eurydame, sister of Menius and daughter of Diactorides, brought him no male issue, but only a daughter, Lampito, whom he gave in marriage to Archidamus, Zeuxidamus' son.

Leotychides himself did not end his days in Sparta; Demaratus was to be avenged as follows. While in command of the army in an expedition against Thessaly,[1] just as complete success was within his grasp, he allowed himself to be heavily bribed. He was caught red-handed, sitting in his tent on a glove stuffed full of coins, whereupon he was brought to trial and banished, and his house was demolished. He took refuge in Tegea, where he afterwards died. All this, however, took place some time later, and I must now return to Cleomenes.

After the success of his scheme against Demaratus, Cleomenes, with Leotychides' support, went promptly to Aegina, embittered by the affront which had been put upon him. Now that both kings had come the Aeginetans thought it best to offer no further resistance. Cleomenes and his colleague chose ten of their wealthiest and most distinguished citizens, brought them over into Attica, and put them in charge of their bitterest enemies, the Athenians. Amongst the ten were the two most powerful men in the island: Crius (Ram) the son of Polycritus, and Casambus the son of Aristocrates.

Later on, when his machinations against Demaratus became known in Sparta, Cleomenes took fright and slipped away into Thessaly. From there he passed into Arcadia, where he began to stir

1. Perhaps in the allied expedition to northern Greece in 478. Cf. Introduction, p. 20.

up trouble and tried to win the support of the Arcadians for an attack on Sparta. He made them swear oaths to follow him wherever he might choose to take them, and even did his utmost to get the leading men to Nonacris, in order to make them swear by the water of Styx – for it is here at Nonacris that the Arcadians believe the waters of the Infernal River to be visible. It is, indeed, a fact that one can see a little water trickling out of a rock into a basin surrounded by a circular wall. Nonacris, where this spring is to be found, is an Arcadian town near Pheneus.

The Spartans, alarmed by the news of Cleomenes' proceedings in Arcadia, brought him home and restored him to the same power as he had before possessed. He had always been a little queer in the head, but no sooner had he returned to Sparta than he went quite mad, and began poking his staff into the face of every full Spartiate he met. As a result of this lunatic behaviour his relatives put him in the stocks. As he was lying there, fast bound, he asked his jailer, when no one else was there, to give him a knife. At first the man, who was a serf, refused, but Cleomenes, by threats of what he would do to him when he recovered his liberty, so frightened him that he at last consented. As soon as the knife was in his hands, Cleomenes began to mutilate himself, beginning on his shins. He sliced his flesh into strips, working upwards to his thighs, and from them to his hips and sides, until he reached his belly, and while he was cutting that into strips he died. Most people in Greece think that that was a punishment for having corrupted the Priestess at Delphi and inducing her to say what she did say about Demaratus; the Athenians, however, put it down to his devastating the sacred land of Demeter and Persephone, when he marched to Eleusis; while the Argives maintain that it was a punishment for his sacrilege when, after a battle, he fetched the Argive fugitives from the holy ground of Argos, and cut them to pieces, and then showed such contempt for the grove itself that he burned it down.

The story of this incident is as follows. Cleomenes had been told by the Delphic oracle that he would take Argos. Thereupon at the head of a Spartan army he marched to the river Erasinus – a stream which is supposed to flow from Lake Stymphalis, whose waters drain into an unseen chasm and reappear in Argos, where they are known locally as the Erasinus. Arrived at the bank of this stream, Cleomenes offered sacrifice to it before venturing to cross. The appearance of the omens was not favourable. 'Very well,' said Cleomenes; 'I admire the god of the river for refusing to betray his countrymen. All the same, the Argives will not get away with it so lightly.'

He then withdrew his troops and marched to Thyrea, and after sacrificing a bull to the sea went on in boats to the territory of Tiryns and Nauplia. The Argives, learning of his movements, marched to the coast to defend their country, and on reaching the place called Sepia, near Tiryns, took up a position within easy range of the Spartan army. They were not now afraid of a pitched battle, though a certain oracle they had received made them apprehensive of treachery. The oracle was the one which was pronounced by the Priestess for the joint benefit of the Argives and Milesians, and ran as follows:

> But when the female subdues the male and drives him out,
> And wins thereby great glory amongst the Argives,
> Then shall she cause many Argive women to tear their cheeks;
> And thus shall they speak in the generations yet to come:
> ' The fearful thrice-coiled snake was tamed by the spear and slain.'

Alarmed by this conjunction of circumstances, the Argives decided to adopt an unusual plan. This was to conform to the orders called out to the Spartan army by its herald. Every time, therefore, that the Spartan herald repeated an order, the Argives did the same. Cleomenes, however, soon observed what was going on, and issued a command to his men, the next time his herald should pass the word for breakfast, not to obey it, but to take up arms and attack the enemy instead. The plan succeeded perfectly; the Argives, having heard the Spartan army's call to breakfast, were sitting quietly at their own when they were suddenly assaulted; many were killed, and many more escaped to the little wood which was held sacred to the hero Argos. Here they were surrounded and closely watched.

Next Cleomenes, having learnt from Argive deserters some names of men who had found sanctuary in the wood, sent a herald to tell individuals, by name, that he had received their ransom money, and

to invite them, on the strength of that, to come out. (The regular
Peloponnesian ransom is 2 minae for each prisoner.) In this way
Cleomenes got about fifty of them to come out, one at a time, and
had them all butchered. The men who were still inside had no idea
of what was taking place, because the wood was so thick that they
could not see the fate of their comrades outside it. At last, however,
one of them climbed a tree – and saw. After that, the invitation to
come out was no longer accepted. Cleomenes then ordered all his
serfs to pile faggots round the wood, set fire to them, and burn it to
the ground. The order was obeyed, and while the fire was raging,
Cleomenes asked one of the Argive deserters to what god the wood
was held sacred. 'To Argos,' was the reply. Cleomenes groaned when
he heard the name. 'Apollo,' he cried, 'O God of prophecy, you did
indeed deceive me when you said I should take Argos, for now I
believe that your prophecy to me is fulfilled.'

After this Cleomenes sent the greater part of his army home, and
with a thousand of his best troops went to the temple of Hera, to
offer sacrifice. But the priest of the temple refused to allow him to
do so, on the ground that to sacrifice in that temple was forbidden
to strangers. Cleomenes thereupon made his serfs drag the priest away
from the altar and thrash him, and then performed the sacrifice
himself and marched off.

On his return to Sparta he was brought by his enemies before the
magistrates; the charge against him was that he had accepted a bribe
not to take Argos, when he might easily have done so. His answer –
whether true or false I cannot be sure – was that when he had destroyed the shrine of the hero Argos, he supposed that the prophecy
was already fulfilled, and on that account he did not think it proper
to make an attempt on the *town* of Argos, until he had further consulted the god's wishes, and found out, by means of a sacrifice,
whether he would grant him this further success or not. When,
however, he attempted to get a favourable sign by offering a sacrifice
in the temple of Hera, a flame shot out from the breast of the goddess'
statue, and he knew from this with absolute certainty that he was not
to capture Argos. Had the flame flashed from the statue's head, it
would have meant that he was to capture the city completely; but
the flash that came from the breast signified that he had already done

all that God intended him to do. The Spartans accepted this as a credible and reasonable defence, and Cleomenes was fully acquitted.

Argos, in consequence of these events, was left so short of men that the management of the town's affairs fell into the hands of the slaves, who filled all the government posts until the sons of those who had been killed grew up and ejected them. These now resumed control, and the slaves, when driven out by force, occupied Tiryns. For a time Tiryns and Argos lived on friendly terms; but a certain Cleander, a soothsayer from Phigalea in Arcadia, joined the slaves in Tiryns and persuaded them to attack their former masters. The result was a protracted struggle, and it was with much difficulty that the Argives finally got the upper hand.

Cleomenes' behaviour in this episode was, according to the Argives, the cause of his subsequent madness and miserable death. His own countrymen, however, deny that his madness was a punishment from heaven; they are convinced, on the contrary, that he lost his wits because, in his association with the Scythians, he had acquired the habit of drinking his wine neat. These nomads, anxious for revenge upon Darius for his invasion of their country, had sent proposals to Sparta for a combined effort against him; the suggestion was that they themselves should try to invade Persia by way of the river Phasis, and that the Spartans should march inland from Ephesus and effect a junction with them. The story is, that when the Scythian representatives came to discuss this scheme, Cleomenes spent much time with them and from too close association with them acquired the habit of taking wine without water – and went off his head in consequence. The Spartans tell us that ever since then they have used the phrase 'Scythian fashion' when they want a stronger drink than usual.

There, then, is the Spartan story; my own opinion is that Cleomenes came to grief as a punishment for what he did to Demaratus.

When the Aeginetans heard that Cleomenes was dead, they sent envoys to Sparta to decry Leotychides about their friends who were being held as hostages in Athens. The Spartans submitted the matter to a court of law, and the verdict was that the people of Aegina had been monstrously abused by Leotychides. They condemned him, therefore, to be given up and taken away to Aegina in exchange for the Aeginetans who were held in Athens. The envoys were on the point of marching him off when a well-known Spartan, Theasides, son of Leoprepes, intervened. 'Men of Aegina,' he cried, 'what is this you are proposing to do? Will you dare to carry off the king of Sparta? True – he has been put into your hands by his own country-men, because at the moment they are angry with him and have condemned him to this indignity; but I warn you – the time may come when, if you do this, they will destroy you utterly in revenge.' The warning words made the Aeginetans change their minds; instead of taking Leotychides along with them as a prisoner, they entered into an agreement with him, to the effect that he should accompany them to Athens and bring about the surrender of the hostages. But when, on his arrival there, he asked for the men whom he had left in trust to be given back to him, the Athenians were unwilling to comply; they temporized and made excuses, and said that as two kings had put the men in their keeping, they could not feel it was right to give them up to only one. In fact, they refused; and their refusal drew from Leotychides the following story. 'Gentle-men,' he said, 'you must act as you see fit. Surrender your charge like honourable men; or refuse to surrender it – *not* like honourable men. In either case, I should like to tell you what happened in Sparta once in connexion with some property left in trust. According to our belief, there lived in Sparta three generations ago a man named Glaucus, the son of Epicydes; he was in every respect an admirable person, and had, in particular, a reputation for honest dealing beyond any other Spartan of his day. Time, however, had something in store for him – you shall hear the story as we tell it. One day a man from Miletus came to Sparta and expressed a wish to talk to Glaucus. "I am a Milesian," he said, "and I have come to you because I should like to profit by your honesty. People all over Greece – yes, and in Ionia too – are always talking of your honesty, and that set me thinking. Ionia, I told myself, is never safe from sudden change – and property never stays long in the same hands; but the Peloponnese, on the contrary, is stable. This led me to make a decision, namely, to realize one-half of my property and to put the money in your hands, in full confidence that it will be safe there. I ask you, therefore, to take the money and with it these tallies, which you must please keep care-fully. Then you can return the money to whoever brings you the corresponding halves." Glaucus listened to what the stranger from Miletus said, and accepted the trust on the terms he proposed. Years went by, and one day there came to Sparta the sons of the Milesian who had made Glaucus his trustee. They sought an interview with him, produced their halves of the tallies, and asked for the money. "But," said Glaucus, trying to put them off, "I don't remember this transaction, and nothing you say has any effect in awakening my memory. Of course, when I *do* recollect it, I will act as an honest man should: I will pay the money back properly, if I received it, and, if I did not, I will prosecute you according to the law of my country. I promise to settle the matter, one way or the other, in three months' time."

'When the Milesians, supposing their money lost to them, had gone home in great disappointment, Glaucus visited Delphi to ask the oracle's advice; and his question, whether or not he should perjure himself and so rob the Milesians of their property, was met by the Priestess with a rebuke, in the following words:

> *To-day, indeed, Glaucus, it is more profitable*
> *To prevail by false-swearing and rob them of their money.*
> *Swear if you will; for death awaits even the true-swearer.*
> *Yet an oath has a son, nameless, without hands or feet,*
> *But swift to pursue until he has seized and destroyed*
> *Utterly the race and house of the perjured one.*
> *The children of him who keeps his oath are happier hereafter.*

'Glaucus on hearing this answer begged the god to forgive him for this question; but the Priestess told him that to seek God's approval of a sin came to the same thing as committing it. So Glaucus sent for the Milesians and gave them back their money.

'And now, gentlemen, I come to the real point of my story. To-day Glaucus has not a single living descendant; not a family in Sparta bears his name; it has been totally rooted out. That will show you how wise a thing it is, where covenants are concerned, not to hesitate, even in thought, to make proper restitution.'

However, the Athenians would not listen even to this; so Leotychides went home.

The Aeginetans had never yet been punished for the unprovoked attack which they had previously made upon the Athenians at the request of Thebes. Now, however, on the ground that it was Athens which was in the wrong, and they themselves the injured party, they made their preparations for revenge. The Athenians held a festival every four years at Sunium; on this occasion, therefore, the Aeginetans set a trap for their state vessel, and captured her with a number of leading Athenians on board, whom they seized and imprisoned. The outrage stirred the Athenians to immediate action, and they prepared to use every resource they possessed against Aegina.

There was in Aegina a well-known man called Nicodromus, the son of Cnoethus, who had previously been banished from the island and still nursed resentment against his compatriots. When this person got to know that the Athenians were preparing to attack Aegina, he agreed to betray the island, and fixed the day upon which he would strike his blow and expect the arrival of Athenian troops to support him. In due course he carried out his part of the bargain by occupying what is called the Old Town; but the Athenians failed to keep their appointment. Finding their fleet was not a match for the Aeginetans, they had asked the Corinthians to lend them ships; but this took time, and meanwhile the whole undertaking was ruined. The Corinthians were on the best of terms with Athens at this period, and when the Athenians asked them for ships they had put twenty at their disposal, charging five drachmae apiece (for it was illegal to make a free gift of them); and with these and what they already possessed the Athenians manned seventy vessels, and sailed for Aegina. They were one day too late.

Nicodromus, as soon as he found that the Athenians had not appeared at the time agreed upon, escaped from the island in a boat together with a number of other Aeginetans. Later on, these people were allowed by the Athenians to settle at Sunium, which they made their base for raids upon their compatriots in Aegina.

In this way, then, the property-owning class in Aegina defeated the revolt of the commons under Nicodromus, arrested a number of the revolutionaries and led them out to execution; but in the process of doing so they committed an act of sacrilege, which stuck to them in spite of all efforts to remove it by propitiatory sacrifices. Before they could regain the favour of the outraged goddess, they were driven from their island. What happened was this: seven hundred prisoners were about to be executed when one of them broke loose. He ran for sanctuary into the doorway of the shrine of Demeter the Lawgiver and held on to the door-handle with both hands. His pursuers tried to drag him away, and, when they failed to detach his grip, cut his hands off. Then they led him away; and those hands stayed there, still clutching the handle.

That was how the Aeginetans dealt with each other. When the Athenians arrived, seventy Aeginetan ships engaged them, but were defeated, whereupon a call for help was sent to Aegina's old ally, Argos. But this time the Argives refused to send assistance, on the ground that some Aeginetan ships which had been seized by Cleomenes had put in at ports in the Argolid, and helped the Spartan invasion. In this descent upon Argos the Spartans had also been joined by men from Sicyonian ships, and the Argives had imposed a joint fine of a thousand talents – five hundred upon each guilty party. The people of Sicyon acknowledged that they were in the wrong and agreed to pay a hundred talents to clear themselves, but not so the Aeginetans: they refused to humiliate themselves by any sort of admission. This was why, on the present occasion, the Argives refused the call for help; officially, not a single man was sent, though about a thousand volunteered, and went to Aegina under the command of Eurybates, a man who had trained for the *pentathlon*. Most of these volunteers were killed by the Athenians in Aegina and never returned; and their commander Eurybates, in a series of single combats, killed his man in the first three, but in the fourth was himself killed by a man from Decelea, named Sophanes.

Later, the Aeginetans caught the Athenian fleet off its guard and beat it, capturing four ships with their crews.

While Athens and Aegina were at each other's throats, the king of Persia continued to mature his plans. His servant never failed to repeat to him the word 'Remember Athens'; the Pisistratidae, with their slanderous attacks upon the Athenians, were still with him, and besides, he himself was anxious to have an excuse to conquer all the Greek communities which refused to give earth and water. In consequence of the ill success of his previous expedition, he relieved Mardonius of his command, and appointed other generals, whom he proposed to send against Eretria and Athens, Datis, a Mede, and his own nephew, Artaphernes, son of the other Artaphernes, and their orders were to reduce Athens and Eretria to slavery and to bring the slaves before the king.

The new commanders left the court and with a powerful and well-equipped force made for the Aleian plain in Cilicia. Here they halted and were joined by the naval contingent – all the ships and men which the various subject communities had been ordered to supply – including the horse-transports which Darius had requisitioned from his tributary states the year before. The horses were embarked in the transports, the troops in the ships of war, and, six hundred vessels strong, they sailed to Ionia. From there they did not follow the coast to the Hellespont and Thrace, but started from Samos and sailed across the Icarian sea and through the islands, presumably because the commanders dreaded the passage round Athos, which in the previous year had been the cause of so terrible a disaster. Another reason which constrained them to take this course was their previous failure to capture Naxos, which was now their first objective in the war. On their arrival at the island from the sea of Icaria, the Naxians offered no resistance, but fled to the hills. The Persians caught some of them, carried them off to slavery, and burnt the city, temples and all. They then put to sea again, to attack the other islands.

While the Persians were thus employed, the inhabitants of Delos left their island and fled to Tenos; and as the Persian fleet was coming in from seaward, Datis sailed on in advance and issued an order to the ships to come to anchor not at Delos, but at Rhenaea, opposite. He then ascertained where the Delians were, and sent them a message in the following words: 'Reverend sirs, what strange opinion have you conceived of me, thus to disappear? I surely have sense enough – even without the king's orders – to spare the island in which Apollo and Artemis were born, and to do no harm either to its soil or to its people. I beg you, therefore, to return to your homes, in the island which belongs to you.' Datis followed the message by piling three hundred talents-weight of frankincense upon the altar, and burning it as an offering. He then left Delos and sailed with his army for Eretria, taking with him both Ionians and Aeolians.

The Delians declared that after his departure the island was shaken by an earthquake – the first and (so far) the last shock ever experienced there. It may well be that the shock was an act of God to warn men of the troubles that were on the way; for indeed, during the three generations comprising the reigns of Darius the son of Hystaspes, and of his son Xerxes and his grandson Artaxerxes, Greece suffered more misery than in the twenty generations before Darius was born – partly from the Persian wars, partly from her own internal struggles for supremacy. In view of this, it is not surprising that there should have been an earthquake in Delos, where there had never been an earthquake before. Besides, there was an oracle, which contained the words,

> *Delos too I will shake, though it has never been shaken.*

Sailing from Delos the Persians proceeded to make the rounds of the other islands, touching at each, pressing troops for service, and taking the islanders' children as hostages. They also visited Carystus and, when the people of the place refused to give hostages or supply men to fight against neighbours – by which they meant Athens and Eretria – they laid siege to the town and destroyed the crops in the surrounding country, until the Carystians were forced to do what the Persians demanded.

In Eretria at the news of the Persian approach the people at once called to Athens for help and the call was not refused, for the Athenians sent to their assistance the four thousand men whom they had previously settled on the estates of the wealthier Chalcideans. Nevertheless, in spite of the appeals to Athens, things at Eretria were not in a healthy state; there was no firm resolve, and counsels were divided; one party proposed abandoning the town and taking refuge in the Euboean hills, another – having an eye to the main chance – was preparing to betray the city. When Aeschines the son of Nothon, one of the leading men of Eretria, came to know of what was afoot, he at once proceeded to act: he disclosed the whole situation to those of the Athenians who had already arrived, and urged them to go home again before they were involved in the catastrophe which was bound to come. They took Aeschines' advice, and got safe away by crossing to Oropus.

Meanwhile the Persian fleet brought up at Tamynae, Choereae, and Aegilia – all three places in Eretrian territory. The horses were immediately put ashore, and preparations for an assault began. The Eretrians had no intention of leaving their defences to meet the coming attack in the open; their one concern (the proposal not to abandon the town having been carried) was to defend their walls – if they could.

The assault soon came, and there was weight behind it. For six days fighting continued with many killed on both sides; then, on the seventh, two well-known Eretrians, Euphorbus the son of Alcimachus and Philagrus the son of Cyneas, betrayed the town to the enemy. The Persians entered, and, in accordance with Darius' orders, stripped the temples bare and burnt them in revenge for the burnt temples of Sardis, and carried off all the inhabitants as prisoners.

Having mastered Eretria the Persians waited a few days and then sailed for Attica, flushed with victory and confident that they would treat Athens in the same way.

The part of Attic territory nearest Eretria – and also the best ground for cavalry to manoeuvre in – was at Marathon. To Marathon, therefore, Hippias directed the invading army, and the Athenians, as soon as the news arrived, hurried to meet it.

The Athenian troops were commanded by ten generals, of whom the tenth was Miltiades. Miltiades' father, Cimon the son of Stesagoras, had been banished from Athens by Pisistratus, the son of Hippocrates. While in exile he had the good fortune to win the chariot race at Olympia, thereby gaining the same distinction as his half-brother Miltiades. At the next games he won the prize again with the same team of mares, but this time waived his victory in favour of Pisistratus, and for allowing the latter to be proclaimed the winner was given leave to return to Athens. At a later Olympic festival he won a third time, still with the same four mares. Soon after, Pisistratus having died, he was murdered by Pisistratus' sons, who sent some men to waylay him one night near the Council House. He was buried outside Athens, beyond what is called the Sunk Road, and opposite his grave were buried the mares which had thrice won the chariot race. This triple victory had once before been achieved by a single team, that of Euagoras the Laconian; but there are no other instances of it. At the time of Cimon's death, Stesagoras, the elder of his two sons, was living in the Chersonese with Miltiades his uncle, and the younger son, who was called Miltiades after the founder of the settlement in the Chersonese, was with his father in Athens.

It was this Miltiades who was now an Athenian general. He had recently escaped from the Chersonese and twice nearly lost his life – once when the Phoenicians chased him as far as Imbros in their anxiety to catch him and take him to Darius, and again when, after escaping that danger and getting home to what looked like safety, he found his enemies waiting for him and was prosecuted in the courts for his unconstitutional and despotic government in the Chersonese. But he escaped this too, and after the trial was elected a general by the people.

Before they left the city, the Athenian generals sent off a message to Sparta. The messenger was an Athenian named Pheidippides, a professional long-distance runner. According to the account he gave the Athenians on his return, Pheidippides met the god Pan on Mount Parthenium, above Tegea. Pan, he said, called him by name and told him to ask the Athenians why they paid him no attention, in spite of his friendliness towards them and the fact that he had often been useful to them in the past, and would be so again in the future. The Athenians believed Pheidippides' story, and when their affairs were once more in a prosperous state, they built a shrine to Pan under the Acropolis, and from the time his message was received they have held an annual ceremony, with a torch-race and sacrifices, to court his protection.

On the occasion of which I speak – when Pheidippides, that is, was sent on his mission by the Athenian commanders and said that he saw Pan – he reached Sparta the day after he left Athens and delivered his message to the Spartan government. 'Men of Sparta' (the message ran), 'the Athenians ask you to help them, and not to stand by while the most ancient city of Greece is crushed and sub-dued by a foreign invader; for even now Eretria has been enslaved, and Greece is the weaker by the loss of one fine city.' The Spartans, though moved by the appeal, and willing to send help to Athens, were unable to send it promptly because they did not wish to break their law. It was the ninth day of the month, and they said they could not take the field until the moon was full. So they waited for the full moon, and meanwhile Hippias, the son of Pisistratus, guided the Persians to Marathon.

The previous night Hippias had dreamed that he was sleeping with his mother, and he supposed that the dream meant that he would return to Athens, recover his power, and die peacefully at home in old age. So much for his first interpretation. On the following day when he was acting as guide to the invaders, he put the prisoners from Eretria ashore on Aegilia, an island belonging to the town of Styra, led the fleet to its anchorage at Marathon, and got the troops into position when they had disembarked. While he was busy with all this, he happened to be seized by an unusually violent fit of sneezing and coughing, and, as he was an oldish man, and most of his teeth were loose, he coughed one of them right out of his mouth. It fell somewhere in the sand, and though he searched and searched in his efforts to find it, it was nowhere to be seen. Hippias then turned to his companions, and said with a deep sigh: 'This land is not ours; we shall never be able to conquer it. The only part I ever had in it my tooth possesses.' So the meaning of the dream was now clear to him.

The Athenian troops were drawn up on a piece of ground sacred to Heracles, when they were joined by the Plataeans, who came to support them with every available man. Some time before this the Plataeans had surrendered their independence to the Athenians, who had, in their turn, already rendered service to Plataea on many occasions and in difficult circumstances. The way it happened was this: Plataea was being hard pressed by Thebes, and as Cleomenes the son of Anaxandrides happened to be in the neighbourhood with a Spartan army, the Plataeans first thought of putting themselves into Spartan hands. The Spartans, however, refused the offer: 'We live too far apart'; – their argument ran – 'an alliance with us would be but cold comfort to you; you might be carried off into slavery several times over before any of us even heard of it. Our advice is that you make your surrender to Athens – Athens is your neighbour, and Athenian help is by no means to be despised.' The advice did not proceed from goodwill towards Plataea, but merely from the Spartans' desire to embroil Athens in quarrels with the Boeotians. Nevertheless the advice was taken: representatives from Plataea, while the Athenians were engaged in offering sacrifice to the Twelve Gods, came and sat by the altar, to make their solemn request, and the act of surrender was completed.

When the Thebans heard what the Plataeans had done, they at once sent an army against them. The Athenians hurried to their defence, and a fight was on the point of beginning when the Corinthians intervened. They came up, and as both sides submitted the dispute to their arbitration, they fixed the boundary between the two countries, with the condition that there should be no interference from Thebes with any Boeotians who might not wish to belong to the Boeotian state. The Corinthians after making this decision left for home, and the Athenians had also started on their return march, when they were set upon by the Boeotians. In the fight which ensued the Athenians were victorious, and they followed up their victory by crossing the borderline which the Corinthians had fixed for Plataea, and making the river Asopus the frontier between the territory of Thebes on the one side, and of Plataea and Hysiae on the other. These were the circumstances under which the people of Plataea put themselves into Athenian hands, and which led to their coming to the support of Athens at Marathon.

Amongst the Athenian commanders opinion was divided: some were against risking a battle, on the ground that the Athenian force was too small to stand a chance of success; others – and amongst them Miltiades – urged it. It seemed for a time as if the more faint-hearted policy would be adopted – and so it would have been but for the action of Miltiades. In addition to the ten generals, there was another person entitled to a vote, namely the polemarch, or War Archon, appointed by lot.[1] This office (which formerly carried an equal vote in military decisions with the generals) was held at this time by Callimachus of

1. According to the Aristotelian *Constitution of Athens*, §22, the appointment of the Archons, including the War Archon, by lot was not introduced till three years later. Herodotus, not interested in constitutional details, has fallen into an anachronism. Callimachus was commander-in-chief, and accordingly had pride of place in the near-contemporary mural painting in the Painted Stoa at Athens, as described by the traveller Pausanias (I, 15). (This is the only *description*; some other *mentions* of it are in contexts concerned not with the picture, but with Miltiades, and naturally mention only him.) Herodotus does, however, know that the War Archon's position was different from that in his own time, when the office had lost all military importance. Thus (p. 428), he has the commander-in-chief's regular position on the right wing; but the idea of the generals 'presiding' (which *might* include giving the executive orders) on successive days is that of Herodotus' own time.

Aphidnae. To Callimachus, therefore, Miltiades turned. 'It is now in your hands, Callimachus,' he said, 'either to enslave Athens, or to make her free and to leave behind you for all future generations a memory more glorious than even Harmodius and Aristogeiton left. Never in our history have we Athenians been in such peril as now. If we submit to the Persians, Hippias will be restored to power – and there is little doubt what misery must then ensue: but if we fight and win, then this city of ours may well grow to pre-eminence amongst all the cities of Greece. If you ask me how this can be, and how the decision rests with you, I will tell you: we commanders are ten in number, and we are not agreed upon what action to take; half of us are for a battle, half against it. If we refuse to fight, I have little doubt that the result will be bitter dissension; our purpose will be shaken, and we shall submit to Persia. But if we fight before the rot can show itself in any of us, then, if God gives us fair play, we can not only fight but win. Yours is the decision; all hangs upon you; vote on my side, and our country will be free – yes, and the mistress of Greece. But if you support those who have voted against fighting, that happiness will be denied you – you will get the opposite.'

Miltiades' words prevailed, and by the vote of Callimachus the War Archon the decision to fight was made.

The generals held the presiding position in succession, each for a day; and those of them who had voted with Miltiades, offered, when their turn for duty came, to surrender it to him. Miltiades accepted the offer, but would not fight until the day came when he would in any case have presided. When it did come, the Athenian army moved into position for the coming struggle. The right wing was commanded by Callimachus – for it was the regular practice at that time in Athens that the War Archon should lead the right wing; then followed the tribes, in their regular order; and, finally, on the left wing, were the Plataeans. Ever since the battle of Marathon, when the Athenians offer sacrifice at their quadrennial festival, the herald links the names of Athens and Plataea in the prayer for God's blessing.

One result of the disposition of Athenian troops before the battle was the weakening of their centre by the effort to extend the line sufficiently to cover the whole Persian front; the two wings were strong, but the line in the centre was only a few ranks deep. The dispositions made, and the preliminary sacrifice promising success, the word was given to move, and the Athenians advanced at a run towards the enemy, not less than a mile away. The Persians, seeing the attack developing at the double, prepared to meet it, thinking it suicidal madness for the Athenians to risk an assault with so small a force – rushing in with no support from either cavalry or archers. Well, that was what they imagined; nevertheless, the Athenians came on, closed with the enemy all along the line, and fought in a way not to be forgotten. They were the first Greeks, so far as I know, to charge at a run, and the first who dared to look without flinching at Persian dress and the men who wore it; for until that day came, no Greek could hear even the word Persian without terror.

The struggle at Marathon was long drawn out. In the centre, held by the Persians themselves and the Sacae, the advantage was with the foreigners, who were so far successful as to break the Greek line and pursue the fugitives inland from the sea; but the Athenians on one wing and the Plataeans on the other were both victorious. Having got the upper hand, they left the defeated enemy to make their escape, and then, drawing the two wings together into a single unit, they turned their attention to the Persians who had broken through in the centre. Here again they were triumphant, chasing the routed enemy, and cutting them down until they came to the sea, and men were calling for fire and taking hold of the ships. It was in this phase of the struggle that the War Archon Callimachus was killed, fighting bravely, and also Stesilaus, the son of Thrasylaus, one of the generals; Cynegirus, too, the son of Euphorion,[1] had his hand cut off with an axe as he was getting hold of a ship's stern, and so lost his life, together with many other well-known Athenians. The Athenians secured in this way seven ships; but the rest got off, and the Persians aboard them, after picking up the Eretrian prisoners whom they had left on Aegilia, laid a course round Sunium for Athens, which they hoped to reach in advance of the Athenian army. In Athens the Alcmaeonidae were accused of suggesting this move; they had, it was said,

1. And thus brother of Aeschylus, who himself, in an epitaph for his own tomb, gave Marathon as his one claim to distinction.

an understanding with the Persians, and raised a shield as a signal to them when they were already on board.

While the Persian fleet was on its way round Sunium, the Athenians hurried back with all possible speed to save their city, and succeeded in reaching it before the arrival of the Persians. Just as at Marathon the Athenian camp had been a plot of ground sacred to Heracles, so now they fixed their camp on another, also sacred to the same god, at Cynosarges. When the Persian fleet appeared, it lay at anchor for a while off Phalerum (at that time the chief harbour of Athens) and then sailed for Asia.

In the battle of Marathon some 6400 Persians were killed; the losses of the Athenians were 192. During the action a very strange thing happened: Epizelus, the son of Cuphagoras, an Athenian soldier, was fighting bravely when he suddenly lost the sight of both eyes, though nothing had touched him anywhere – neither sword, spear, nor missile. From that moment he continued blind as long as he lived. I am told that in speaking about what happened to him he used to say that he fancied he was opposed by a man of great stature in heavy armour, whose beard overshadowed his shield; but the phantom passed him by, and killed the man at his side.

When Datis was on his way back to Asia with his army, he stopped at Myconos, where he had a dream. What the dream was is not recorded; but at the first light of dawn next morning he ordered the ships to be searched, and discovered, in a Phoenician vessel, a statue of Apollo, overlaid with gold. He made inquiries about where it had been stolen from, and as soon as he learned to which temple it belonged, he sailed in his own ship to Delos. The Delians by that time had returned to the island, so he had the statue placed in their temple for safe keeping, and instructed the islanders to take it back to Delium, a place in Theban territory, on the sea opposite Chalcis. Datis then left the island; but the Delians did not restore the statue. It was brought back to Delium by the Thebans themselves twenty years later, on the advice of an oracle.

Datis and Artaphernes, on their arrival in Asia, conveyed the prisoners taken in Eretria up-country to Susa. Before their capture Darius had nursed bitter resentment against the Eretrians, because they had injured him without provocation; now, however, when he saw them brought before him in defeat and knew that they were in his power, his anger vanished. He did them no further harm, but settled them on some land of his, called Ardericca, in Cissia, about twenty-six miles from Susa. Some five miles from Ardericca is the well which produces three different substances – bitumen, salt, and oil. They draw the liquid with a swipe;[1] instead of a bucket, half a wineskin is attached to the rope at one end, and they dip with this, draw up the stuff, and pour it into a tank; from the tank it is drained off into another receptacle, and the three substances become separated: the bitumen and salt solidify at once. The Persian word for the oil is *rhadinace*; it is very dark in colour, and has a strong smell. Here, then, in Ardericca, the Eretrians were given their new home; they have continued to live there to my own day, and still speak their original language.

After the full moon, two thousand Spartans set off for Athens. They were so anxious not to be late that they were in Attica on the third day after leaving Sparta. They had, of course, missed the battle; but such was their passion to see the Persians, that they went to Marathon to have a look at the bodies. That done, they complimented the Athenians on their good work, and returned home.

The tale of the Alcmaeonidae treacherously signalling to the Persians with a shield is, to me, quite extraordinary, and I cannot accept it. Is it likely that these men, who were obviously greater tyrant-haters even than Callias the son of Phaenippus and father of Hipponicus, should have wished to see Athens ruled by Hippias under foreign control? Callias was the only man in Athens who at the expulsion of Pisistratus dared to buy any of his property when it was put up for public sale, besides showing the most violent hostility to him in other ways. Not even Callias, I repeat, could surpass the Alcmaeonidae in hatred of absolute government, so the charge that they could have been guilty of the treacherous signal is mere slander, and I confess it surprises me. They were men who remained in exile throughout the period of absolute government in Athens[2] – and it was they who thought of the plan which deprived the Pisistratidae

1. A long pole balanced horizontally on a pivot.

2. This is in all probability quite untrue (see Introduction, p. 32); evidence on Herodotus' dependence on his oral sources.

of their power. Indeed, in my judgement it was the Alcmaeonidae much more than Harmodius and Aristogeiton who liberated Athens; for the two latter by their murder of Hipparchus merely exasperated the remaining members of the clan, without in any way checking their despotism, while the Alcmaeonidae did, in plain fact, actually bring about the liberation – always provided that what I said further back is true, namely that it was the Alcmaeonidae who bribed the Delphic priestess to keep on telling the Spartans that they must set Athens free. Perhaps it might be argued that they betrayed their country because of some grudge they bore the Athenian commons; but that is nonsense – they were better thought of and more respected than anybody else in Athens. It is unreasonable, therefore, to suppose that they gave the signal for any reason of that sort. A shield *was* held up: that is a fact and cannot be denied; but as to who did it, I can add nothing to what I have already said.

Even in very early days the Alcmaeonidae were a distinguished family in Athens, and from the time of Alcmaeon, and afterwards of Megacles, they became very distinguished indeed. Alcmaeon, the son of Megacles, gave all the assistance in his power to the Lydians who came from Croesus at Sardis to consult the oracle at Delphi; and Croesus, when the Lydians told him of the good service he had rendered, invited him to Sardis and offered him, as a reward, as much gold as he could carry on his person at one time. Alcmaeon thought of a fine way of taking advantage of this unusual offer: he put on a large tunic, very loose and baggy in front, and a pair of the widest top-boots that he could find, and, thus clad, entered the treasury to which the king's servants conducted him. Here he attacked a heap of gold dust; he crammed into his boots, all up his legs, as much as they would hold, filled the baggy front of his tunic full, sprinkled the dust all over his hair, stuffed some more into his mouth, and then staggered out, scarcely able to drag one foot after another and looking, with his bulging cheeks and swollen figure, like anything rather than a man. When Croesus saw him he burst out laughing, and gave him all the gold he was carrying, and as much again in addition. In this way Alcmaeon's family suddenly found itself rich, and Alcmaeon was able to keep race-horses, with which he won the chariot race at Olympia.

In the next generation the family became much more famous than before through the distinction conferred upon it by Cleisthenes the master of Sicyon. Cleisthenes, the son of Aristonymus, grandson of Myron, and great-grandson of Andreas, had a daughter, Agarista, whom he wished to marry to the best man in all Greece. So during the Olympic games, in which he had himself won the chariot race, he had a public announcement made, to the effect that any Greek who thought himself good enough to become Cleisthenes' son-in-law should present himself in Sicyon within sixty days – or sooner if he wished – because he intended, within the year following the sixtieth day, to betroth his daughter to her future husband. Cleisthenes had had a race-track and a wrestling-ring specially made for his purpose, and presently the suitors began to arrive – every man of Greek nationality who had something to be proud of either in his country or in himself. From Sybaris in Italy, then at the height of its prosperity, came Smindyrides the son of Hippocrates, a man noted above all others for delicate and luxurious living, and from Siris, also in Italy, came Damasus the son of Amyris who was nick-named the Philosopher. Then there was Amphimnestus, the son of Epistrophus, from Epidamnus on the Ionian Gulf, and Males from Aetolia – Males, the brother of Titormus who was the strongest man in Greece and went to live in the remotest part of Aetolia to avoid intercourse with his kind. From the Peloponnese came Leocedes the son of Pheidon, who was ruler of Argos and the man who brought in the system of weights and measures for the Peloponnese – and also turned out the Eleians whose duty it was to manage the Olympic games and proceeded to manage them himself – the wickedest and most arrogant thing ever done by a Greek. Next there was Amiantus, the son of Lycurgus, from Trapezus in Arcadia, and Laphanes, an Azanian from Paeus, whose father Euphorion, the story goes, received Castor and Pollux under his own roof and afterwards kept open house for all comers; and then Onomastus of Elis, the son of Agaeus. From Athens there were two: Megacles, whose father Alcmaeon visited the court of Croesus, and Tisander's son Hippocleides, the wealthiest and best-looking man in Athens. Euboea provided but a single suitor, Lysanias from Eretria, which at that time was at the height of its prosperity; then there was a Thessalian,

Diactorides, one of the Scopadae, from Crannon, and, lastly, Alcon from Molossia. This was the list of suitors.

Cleisthenes began by asking each in turn to name his country and parentage; then he kept them in his house for a year, to get to know them well, entering into conversation with them sometimes singly, sometimes all together, and testing each of them for his manly qualities and temper, education and manners. Those who were young he would take to the gymnasia – but the most important test of all was their behaviour at the dinner-table. All this went on throughout their stay in Sicyon, and all the time he entertained them handsomely.

For one reason or another it was the two Athenians who impressed Cleisthenes most favourably, and of the two Tisander's son Hippocleides came to be preferred, not only for his manly virtues but also because he was related some generations back to the family of Cypselus of Corinth.

At last the day came which had been fixed for the betrothal, and Cleisthenes had to declare his choice. He marked the day by the sacrifice of a hundred oxen, and then gave a great banquet, to which not only the suitors but everyone of note in Sicyon was invited. When dinner was over, the suitors began to compete with each other in music and in talking in company. In both these accomplishments it was Hippocleides who proved by far the doughtiest champion, until at last, as more and more wine was drunk, he asked the fluteplayer to play him a tune and began to dance to it. Now it may well be that he danced to his own satisfaction; Cleisthenes, however, who was watching the performance, began to have serious doubts about the whole business. Presently, after a brief pause, Hippocleides sent for a table; the table was brought, and Hippocleides, climbing on to it, danced first some Laconian dances, next some Attic ones, and ended by standing on his head and beating time with his legs in the air. The Laconian and Attic dances were bad enough; but Cleisthenes, though he already loathed the thought of having a son-in-law like that, nevertheless restrained himself and managed to avoid an outburst; but when he saw Hippocleides beating time with his legs, he could bear it no longer. 'Son of Tisander,' he cried, 'you have danced away your marriage.' 'I could hardly care less,' was the cheerful reply. Hence the common saying, 'It's all one to Hippocleides.'

Cleisthenes now called for silence and addressed the company. 'Gentlemen,' he said, 'you are here as suitors for my daughter's hand. I have the highest opinion of you all; to distinguish one and reject the rest is not an agreeable task, and I would gladly, were it possible, show my favour to every one of you. Unfortunately, it is not possible; I have only one girl to dispose of, so how can I please you all? To each man, therefore, who has failed to win the bride I propose to give a talent of silver, to mark my appreciation of the honour he has done me by wishing to marry into my family, and to compensate him for his long absence from home; and my daughter Agarista I betroth, according to the Athenian law, to Megacles the son of Alcmaeon.' Megacles declared that he accepted her, and the formalities of the betrothal were completed.

Such is the story of the Trial of the Suitors, and this was the way in which the Alcmaeonidae came to be talked of throughout Greece. The issue of the marriage was that Cleisthenes (named after his grandfather, Cleisthenes of Sicyon) who reorganized the Athenian tribes and instituted the democracy in Athens. A second son of Megacles was Hippocrates, who became the father of another Megacles and another Agarista – the namesake of Cleisthenes' daughter – who married Xanthippus the son of Ariphron. This second Agarista dreamt during her pregnancy that she gave birth to a lion, and a few days later became the mother of Pericles.

After the slaughter at Marathon, the already high reputation of Miltiades in Athens was greatly increased. Consequently, when he asked for a fleet of seventy ships together with troops and money, without even telling the Athenians the object of the expedition he had in mind, but merely saying he would enrich them if they followed him, because it was a place where they could easily get as much money as they wanted, they were so carried away by excitement that they made no objections whatever. They let him have the ships and the men, whereupon he set sail for Paros. Ostensibly the reason for the attack was the fact that the Parians had been the aggressors in that they had sent a trireme to Marathon with the Persian fleet; this, however, was only a cloak for his real purpose; for the truth of the matter was that he was angry with the Parians because Lysagoras the son of Teisias, a Parian by birth, had told tales against him to Hydarnes the Persian.

Arrived at the island, Miltiades drove the Parians within their defences and began the siege, at the same time sending in a demand for a hundred talents with the threat that, if they refused to pay, he would persist in the blockade until the town fell. The Parians, however, had not the least intention of giving Miltiades any money; instead, they began to exercise their ingenuity for the defence of the town. In this they were full of resource – they raised the wall by night to twice its original height in any section where it was assailable.

So far I have told the story of this episode as it is commonly accepted by everyone; for the sequel, the Parians themselves are my only authority. Miltiades was making no progress in the siege of the town, and while he was puzzling himself about his next move, a prisoner – a Parian woman named Timo, who had been a Priestess of subordinate rank to the Earth Goddesses – sought an interview with him. This she obtained and suggested to Miltiades that, if he really wanted to capture Paros, he had better do as she advised. She proceeded to make her proposal, and Miltiades, in accordance with it, made his way to the hill in front of the town, where the shrine of Demeter the Lawgiver stood. Unable to open the door in the fence which surrounded the precinct, he jumped over and made straight for the shrine. Precisely what he intended to do there, I really don't know – perhaps to meddle with some of the things which it is sacrilege to touch – but, whatever it was, when he reached the doors of the shrine, he was seized with a sudden fit of trembling, ran back the way he had come, and, in jumping down from the top of the fence, fell and twisted his thigh – or, as some think, smashed his knee. So when he returned to Athens he was in a poor way, and all he had achieved after twenty-six days' siege was to destroy the crops in the countryside; he had failed to annex the island, and he did not bring home a single penny.

When the Parians found out that the Priestess Timo had made her treacherous suggestion to Miltiades, they wanted to punish her; so as soon as the siege was raised they sent to Delphi to inquire if they would be right in putting her to death for giving to the enemy information which might have led to the ruin of her country, and for revealing to Miltiades the mysteries which no one of the male sex was allowed to know. The Priestess at Delphi told them in reply that Timo was not guilty of these crimes; on the contrary, Miltiades was destined to come to a bad end, and she had merely put in an appearance to lead him into trouble.

Miltiades on his return to Athens became the talk of the town; many were loud in their censure of him, and especially Xanthippus, who brought him before the people to be tried for his life on the charge of defrauding the public. Miltiades, though present in court, was unable to speak in his own defence because his leg was gangrened; he lay on a couch and his friends spoke for him, basing their defence upon his past services to his country. They had much to say about the battle of Marathon and the capture of Lemnos, recalling how he had punished the Pelasgians and brought the island under Athenian control. The popular verdict was to spare his life, but to fine him fifty talents for his offence. Shortly afterwards the gangrene in his thigh grew worse; mortification set in and he died. The fifty talents were paid by his son Cimon.

The events which led to Miltiades' capture of Lemnos were as follows. The Athenians had forced certain Pelasgians to leave Attica. Whether or not they were justified in doing this is not clear; all I can offer are two contradictory accounts, that of the Athenians themselves, on the one side, and of Hecataeus the son of Hegesander on the other. Hecataeus in his History maintains that the Athenians were in the wrong. According to him, they had given the Pelasgians in payment for building the wall round the Acropolis a tract of land, of poor quality and in bad condition, at the foot of Mount Hymettus; the Pelasgians had improved the land, and when the Athenians saw it changed out of recognition and in first-rate order, they grudged the gift and longed to take it back, until without any further justification they forcibly ejected the occupants. The Athenians, on the contrary, claim that right was on their side; their account is that the Pelasgians used to leave their settlement under Hymettus and come after the Athenian girls when they went to fetch water from the Nine Springs. Neither the Athenians nor anyone else had house-slaves in those days, so their own daughters used to go for the water; and whenever they did so, the Pelasgians, regardless of decency or respect, used to rape them. Nor was even this the end of it, for they were finally caught in the act of plotting an attempt upon Athens. In this situation the Athenians go on to point out the superiority of their own behaviour; they might easily have killed the Pelasgians when they discovered their plot, but all they did was to tell them to go. The Pelasgians accordingly left Attica and settled, amongst other places, in Lemnos. There, then, are the two accounts: that of the Athenians on the one side, and of Hecataeus on the other.

When the Pelasgians had been settled for some time in Lemnos, they began to wish to have their revenge on the Athenians. Familiar as they were with the Athenian festivals, they fitted out some galleys and sailed to Brauron, where the Athenian women were celebrating the festival of Artemis; they surprised and seized a number of them, and sailed off with them to Lemnos, where they kept them as concubines. In time these women had numerous children, whom they brought up to behave like Athenians and to speak Attic Greek. The boys as they grew older would not mix with the children of the Pelasgian women, and all supported one another when it came to blows and a Pelasgian boy hit a Greek one. Indeed the children of the Greek mothers fancied themselves lords and masters of the rest and completely dominated them. The situation gave the Pelasgians something to think about; if these bastard children were already determined to support one another and to lord it over their legitimate children, what would they do when they were grown up? They decided in consequence to kill the Attic women's children; then, having done so, they murdered their mothers as well. This crime – together with the former one when the women of Lemnos murdered their husbands (and Thoas too) – is the origin of the Greek custom of referring to any specially horrible crime as a 'Lemnian deed'.

As a result of these murders the crops in Lemnos failed, the birth-rate declined, and the cattle no longer increased as rapidly as before, so that the islanders began to suffer severely from lack of food and dwindling population. In these circumstances they sent to Delphi to ask for advice on the best way of escaping from their troubles, and were told by the Priestess to submit to whatever punishment the Athenians might choose to impose upon them. So they went to

Athens and declared their readiness to give full satisfaction for their offence. The Athenians spread the richest coverings they possessed on a couch in the Council House and, placing a table beside it loaded with good things, told the Pelasgians to surrender their land to them in a similar condition. 'We will do so,' the Pelasgians answered, 'when a ship sails from Attica to Lemnos with a northerly wind in a single day.' This, of course, they knew was impossible, because Attica is a long way south of Lemnos. Nothing further happened at the time; but many years later, when the Chersonese was under Athenian control, Miltiades the son of Cimon during the period of the northerly winds sailed in a day from Elaeus in the Chersonese to Lemnos. On his arrival he ordered the Pelasgians out of the island, reminding them of the prophetic words which they had been so confident could never come true. The people of Hephaestia obeyed; in Myrina no one would admit that the Chersonese was part of Attica, so the town was besieged until it, too, was forced to yield. Thus it was that the Athenians, with the help of Miltiades, got possession of Lemnos.

BOOK SEVEN

WHEN the news of the battle of Marathon reached Darius, son of Hystaspes and king of Persia, his anger against Athens, already great enough on account of the assault on Sardis, was even greater, and he was more than ever determined to make war on Greece. Without loss of time he dispatched couriers to the various states under his dominion with orders to raise an army much larger than before; and also warships, transports, horses, and grain. So the royal command went round; and all Asia was in an uproar for three years, with the best men being enrolled in the army for the invasion of Greece, and with the preparations. In the year after that, a rebellion in Egypt, which had been conquered by Cambyses, served only to harden Darius' resolve to go to war, not only against Greece but against Egypt too.

Both expeditions were ready to start when a violent quarrel broke out between Darius' sons on the question of priority and succession; for according to Persian law the king may not march with his army until he has named his successor. Darius before his accession had three sons by his former wife, Gobryas' daughter, and four more after his accession by Atossa the daughter of Cyrus. The eldest of the first three was Artabazanes, and of the last four Xerxes. It was between these two, therefore, being sons of different mothers, that the dispute arose, Artabazanes basing his claim to the succession on the argument that he was the eldest of all Darius' sons and therefore, by universal custom, entitled to inherit his father's position, Xerxes urging in reply that he was the son of Atossa the daughter of Cyrus, who won the Persians their freedom.

Darius had not yet declared his mind, when Demaratus the son of Ariston arrived in Susa, after being deposed as king of Sparta and having gone into voluntary exile; and the story goes that when he heard about the dispute between Darius' sons, he went to see Xerxes and advised him to point out, in addition to the arguments he was already using, that Darius was already on the throne of Persia when he was born, whereas Artabazanes was born before his father held any public office at all. It was therefore neither reasonable nor fair that the crown should pass to anyone but Xerxes. Even in Sparta, he went on to suggest, the custom was that if sons were born before the father came to the throne, and another was born afterwards when he was king, the latter should succeed him. Xerxes adopted the suggestion and Darius, recognizing the justice of the argument, proclaimed him heir to the throne. Personally, I believe that even without this advice from Demaratus, Xerxes would have become king, because of the immense influence of Atossa.

Xerxes, then, was publicly proclaimed as next in succession to the crown, and Darius was free to turn his attention to the war. Death, however, cut him off before his preparations were complete; he died in the year following this incident and the Egyptian rebellion, after a reign of thirty-six years, and so was robbed of his chance to punish either Egypt or the Athenians. After his death the crown passed to his son Xerxes.

Xerxes at first was not at all interested in invading Greece but began his reign by building up an army for a campaign in Egypt. But Mardonius – the son of Gobryas and Darius' sister and thus cousin to the king – who was present in court and had more influence with Xerxes than anyone else in the country, used constantly to talk to him on the subject. 'Master,' he would say, 'the Athenians have done us great injury, and it is only right that they should be punished for their crimes. By all means finish the task you already have in hand; but when you have tamed the arrogance of Egypt, then lead an army against Athens. Do that, and your name will be held in honour all over the world, and people will think twice in future before they invade your country.' And to the argument for revenge he would add that Europe was a very beautiful place; it produced every kind of garden tree; the land there was everything that land should be – it was, in short, too good for anyone in the world except the Persian king. Mardonius' motive for urging the campaign was love of mischief and adventure and the hope of becoming governor of Greece himself; and after much persistence he persuaded Xerxes to make the attempt. Certain other occurrences came to his aid. In the first place, messengers arrived from the Aleuadae in Thessaly (the Aleuadae were the Thessalian reigning family) with an invitation to Xerxes, promising zealous assistance; at the same time the Pisistratidae in Susa spoke to the same purpose and worked upon him even more strongly through the agency of an Athenian named Onomacritus, a collector of oracles, who had arranged and edited the oracles of Musaeus. The Pisistratidae had made up their quarrel with him before coming to Susa. He had been expelled from Athens by Hipparchus for inserting in the verses of Musaeus a prophecy that the islands off Lemnos would disappear under water – Lasus of Hermione had caught him in the very act of the forgery. Before his banishment he had been a close friend of Hipparchus. Anyway, he went to Susa; and now, whenever he found himself in the king's presence, the Pisistratidae would talk big about his wonderful powers and he would recite selections from his oracles. Any prophecy which implied a setback to the Persian cause he would carefully omit, choosing for quotation only those which promised the brightest triumphs, describing to Xerxes how it was fore-ordained that the Hellespont should be bridged by a Persian, and how the army would march from Asia into Greece. Subjected, therefore, to this double pressure, from Onomacritus' oracles on the one side, and the advice of the Pisistratidae and Aleuadae on the other, Xerxes gave in and allowed himself to be persuaded to undertake the invasion of Greece.

First, however, in the year after Darius' death, he sent an army against the Egyptian rebels and decisively crushed them; then, having reduced the country to a condition of worse servitude than it had ever been in in the previous reign, he turned it over to his brother Achaemenes, who long afterwards, while he was still Governor, was killed by a son of Psammetichus, a Libyan.

After the conquest of Egypt, when he was on the point of taking in hand the expedition against Athens, Xerxes called a conference of the leading men in the country, to find out their attitude towards the war and explain to them his own wishes. When they met, he addressed them as follows: 'Do not suppose, gentlemen, that I am departing from precedent in the course of action I intend to undertake. We Persians have a way of living, which I have inherited from my predecessors and propose to follow. I have learned from my elders that ever since Cyrus deposed Astyages and we took over from the Medes the sovereign power we now possess, we have never yet remained inactive. This is God's guidance, and it is by following it that we have gained our great prosperity. Of our past history you need no reminder; for you know well enough the famous deeds of Cyrus, Cambyses, and my father Darius, and their additions to our empire. Now I myself, ever since my accession, have been thinking how not to fall short of the kings who have sat upon this throne before me, and how to add as much power as they did to the Persian empire. And now at last I have found a way to win for Persia not glory only but a country as large and as rich as our own – indeed richer than our own – and at the same time to get satisfaction and revenge. That, then, is the object of this meeting – that I may disclose to you what it is that I intend to do. I will bridge the Hellespont and march an army through Europe into Greece, and punish the Athenians for the outrage they committed upon my father and upon us. As you saw, Darius himself was making his preparations for war against these men; but death prevented him from carrying out his purpose. I therefore on his behalf, and for the benefit of all my subjects, will not rest until I have taken Athens and burnt it to the ground, in revenge for the injury which the Athenians without provocation once did to me and my father. These men, you remember, came to Sardis with Aristagoras the Milesian, a subject of ours, and burnt the temples and sacred groves; and you know all too well how they served our troops under Datis and Artaphernes, when they landed upon Greek soil. For these reasons I have now prepared to make war upon them, and, when I consider the matter, I find several advantages in the venture; if we crush the Athenians and their neighbours in the Peloponnese, we shall so extend the empire of Persia that its boundaries will be God's own sky, so that the sun will not look down upon any land beyond the boundaries of what is ours. With your help I shall pass through Europe from end to end and make it all one country. For if what I am told is true, there is not a city or nation in the world which will be able to withstand us, once these are out of the way. Thus the guilty and the innocent alike shall bear the yoke of servitude.

'If, then, you wish to gain my favour, each one of you must present himself willingly and in good heart on the day which I shall name; whoever brings with him the best equipped body of troops I will reward with those marks of distinction held in greatest value by our countrymen. That is what you must do; but so that I shall not appear to consult only my own whim, I will throw the whole matter into open debate, and ask any of you who may wish to do so, to express his views.'

The first to speak after the king was Mardonius. 'Of all Persians who have ever lived,' he began, 'and of all who are yet to be born, you, my lord, are the greatest. Every word you have spoken is true and excellent, and you will not allow the wretched Ionians in Europe to make fools of us. It would indeed be an odd thing if we who have defeated and enslaved the Sacae, Indians, Ethiopians, Assyrians, and many other great nations for no fault of their own, but merely to extend the boundaries of our empire, should fail now to punish the Greeks who have been guilty of injuring us without provocation. Have we anything to fear from them? The size of their army? Their wealth? The question is absurd; we know how they fight; we know how slender their resources are. People of their race we have already reduced to subjection – I mean the Greeks of Asia, Ionians, Aeolians, and Dorians. I myself before now have had some experience of these men, when under orders from your father I invaded their country; and I got as far as Macedonia – indeed almost to Athens itself – without a single soldier daring to oppose me. Yet, from what I hear, the Greeks are pugnacious enough, and start fights on the spur of the moment without sense or judgement to justify them. When they declare war on each other, they go off together to the smoothest and levellest bit of ground they can find, and have their battle on it – with the result that even the victors never get off without heavy losses, and as for the losers – well, they're wiped out. Now surely, as they all talk the same language, they ought to be able to find a better way of settling their differences: by negotiation, for instance, or an interchange of views – indeed by anything rather than fighting. Or if it is really impossible to avoid coming to blows, they might at least employ the elements of strategy and look for a strong position to fight from. In any case, the Greeks, with their absurd notions of warfare, never even thought of opposing me when I led my army to Macedonia.

'Well then, my lord, who is likely to resist you when you march against them with the millions of Asia at your back, and the whole Persian fleet? Believe me, it is not in the Greek character to take so desperate a risk. But should I be wrong and they be so foolish as to do battle with us, then they will learn that we are the best soldiers in the world. Nevertheless, let us take this business seriously and spare no pains; success is never automatic in this world – nothing is achieved without trying.'

Xerxes' proposals were made to sound plausible enough by these words of Mardonius, and when he stopped speaking there was a silence. For a while nobody dared to put forward the opposite view, until Artabanus, taking courage from the fact of his relationship to the king – he was a son of Hystaspes and therefore Xerxes' uncle – rose to speak. 'My lord,' he said, 'without a debate in which both sides of a question are expressed, it is not possible to choose the better course. All one can do is to accept whatever it is that has been proposed. But grant a debate, and there is a fair choice to be made. We cannot assess the purity of gold merely by looking at it: we test it by rubbing it on other gold – then we can tell which is the purer. I warned your father – Darius my own brother – not to attack the Scythians, those wanderers who live in a cityless land. But he would not listen to me. Confident in his power to subdue them he invaded their country, and before he came home again many fine soldiers who marched with him were dead. But you, my lord, mean to attack a nation greatly superior to the Scythians: a nation with the highest reputation for valour both on land and at sea. It is my duty to tell you what you have to fear from them: you have said you mean to bridge the Hellespont and march through Europe to Greece. Now suppose – and it is not impossible – that you were to suffer a reverse by sea or land, or even both. These Greeks are said to be great fighters – and indeed one might well guess as much from the fact that the Athenians alone destroyed the great army we sent to attack them under Datis and Artaphernes. Or, if you will, suppose they were to succeed upon one element only – suppose they fell upon our fleet and defeated it, and then sailed to the Hellespont and destroyed the bridge: then, my lord, you would indeed be in peril. It is no special wisdom of my own that makes me argue as I do; but just such a disaster as I have suggested did, in fact, very nearly overtake us when your father bridged the Thracian Bosphorus and the Danube to take his army into Scythia. You will remember how on that occasion the Scythians went to all lengths in their efforts to induce the Ionian guard to break the Danube bridge, and how Histiaeus, the lord of Miletus, merely by following the advice of the other Ionian despots instead of rejecting it, as he did, had it in his power to ruin Persia. Surely it is a dreadful thing even to hear said, that the fortunes of the king once wholly depended upon a single man.

'I urge you, therefore, to abandon this plan; take my advice and do not run any such terrible risk when there is no necessity to do so. Break up this conference; turn the matter over quietly by yourself, and then, when you think fit, announce your decision. Nothing is more valuable to a man than to lay his plans carefully and well; even if things go against him, and forces he cannot control bring his enterprise to nothing, he still has the satisfaction of knowing that it was not his fault – the plans were all laid; if, on the other hand, he leaps headlong into danger and succeeds by luck – well, that's a bit of luck indeed, but he still has the shame of knowing that he was ill prepared.

'You know, my lord, that amongst living creatures it is the great ones that God smites with his thunder, out of envy of their pride. The little ones do not vex him. It is always the great buildings and the tall trees which are struck by lightning. It is God's way to bring the lofty low. Often a great army is destroyed by a little one, when God in his envy puts fear into the men's hearts, or sends a thunderstorm, and they are cut to pieces in a way they do not deserve. For God tolerates pride in none but Himself. Haste is the mother of failure – and for failure we always pay a heavy price; it is in delay our profit lies – perhaps it may not immediately be apparent, but we shall find it, sure enough, as time goes on.

'This, my lord, is the advice I offer you. And as for you, Mardonius, I warn you that the Greeks in no way deserve disparagement;

so say no more silly things about them. By slandering the Greeks you increase the king's eagerness to make war on them, and, as far as I can see, this is the very thing you yourself most passionately desire. Heaven forbid it should happen! Slander is a wicked thing: in a case of slander two parties do wrong and one suffers by it. The slanderer is guilty in that he speaks ill of a man behind his back; and the man who listens to him is guilty in that he takes his word without troubling to find out the truth. The slandered person suffers doubly – from the disparaging words of the one and from the belief of the other that he deserves the disparagement.

'Nevertheless, if there is no avoiding this campaign in Greece, I have one final proposal to make. Let the king stay here in Persia; and you and I will then stake our children on the issue, and you can start the venture with the men you want and as big an army as you please. And if the king prospers, as you say he will, then I consent that my sons should be killed, and myself with them; if my own prediction is fulfilled, let *your* sons forfeit their lives – and you too – if you ever get home.

'Maybe you will refuse this wager, and still persist in leading an army into Greece. In that case I venture a prophecy: the day will come when many a man left at home will hear the news that Mardonius has brought disaster upon Persia, and that his body lies a prey to dogs and birds somewhere in the country of the Athenians or the Spartans – if not upon the road thither. For that is the way you will find out the quality of the people against whom you are urging the king to make war.'

Xerxes was exceedingly angry. 'Artabanus,' he replied, 'you are my father's brother, and that alone saves you from paying the price your empty and ridiculous speech deserves. But your cowardice and lack of spirit shall not escape disgrace: I forbid you to accompany me on my march to Greece – you shall stay at home with the women, and everything I spoke of I shall accomplish without help from you. If I fail to punish the Athenians, let me be no child of Darius, the son of Hystaspes, the son of Arsames, the son of Ariaramnes, the son of Teispes, the son of Cyrus, the son of Cambyses, the son of Teispes, the son of Achaemenes! I know too well that if we make no move, the Athenians will – they will be sure to invade our country. One has but to make the inference from what they did before; for it was they who marched into Asia and burnt Sardis. Retreat is no longer possible for either of us: if we do not inflict the wound, we shall assuredly receive it. All we possess will pass to the Greeks, or all they possess will pass to us. That is the choice before us; for in the enmity between us there is no middle course. It is right, therefore, that we should now revenge ourselves for the injury we once received; and no doubt in doing so I shall learn the nature of this terrible thing which is to happen to me, if I march against men whom Pelops the Phrygian, a mere slave of the Persian kings, once beat so soundly that to this very day both people and country bear the conqueror's name.'

So ended the speeches at the conference. Later on that evening Xerxes began to be worried by what Artabanus had said, and during the night, as he turned it over in his mind, he came to the conclusion that the invasion of Greece would not, after all, be a good thing. Having reached this decision he fell asleep; and the Persians say that before the night was over he dreamed that the figure of a man, tall and of noble aspect, stood by his bed. 'Lord of Persia,' the phantom said, 'have you changed your mind and decided not to lead an army against Greece, in spite of your proclamation to your subjects that troops should be raised? You are wrong to change; and there is one here who will not forgive you for doing so. Continue to tread the path which you chose yesterday.' The visionary figure then flew away, and next morning Xerxes put the dream out of his mind and summoned a meeting of the same people as before. 'Gentlemen,' he said to them, 'I ask your forbearance for changing my mind so quickly. My understanding has hardly yet grown to its full strength, and those who would force me into this war do not leave me alone for a moment. When I heard what Artabanus said, my hot young blood boiled up for the moment, and I flung some words at him such as a young man ought not to address to his senior. But now I acknowledge the justice of what he said, and I will take his advice. I have changed my mind; there will be no war against Greece. Peace is to continue.'

The Persians were delighted at this, and bowed low before their master; but the following night Xerxes dreamed that the same figure as before stood by his bed and spoke to him. 'Son of Darius,' it said, 'so you have openly, in the presence of your subjects, renounced the campaign and made light of what I said to you, as if it had never been said at all. Now let me tell you what the result will be, if you do not at once undertake this war: just as in a moment you rose to greatness and power, so in a moment will you be brought low again.'

Terrified by the dream Xerxes leapt out of bed and sent for Artabanus. 'Artabanus,' he said, 'when you first gave me your good advice, I lost control of myself and answered wildly and foolishly. But I soon thought better of it and realized that I ought to do as you suggested. Now, however, I cannot do so, much as I should like it; for since I changed my mind I have been haunted by a dream which will not allow me to act as you advised. The last time I saw the vision, it left me with threats of disaster. Now if God sent the dream, and it is God's pleasure that we should invade Greece, the same vision will appear to you and will give you the same commands as it gave to me. And this, I think, is most likely to happen if you put on my clothes, take your seat on my throne, and then go to sleep in my bed.'

Artabanus, who thought it was improper for him to sit on the royal throne, did not at once do as Xerxes bade; but at last he was forced to yield – though not until he had addressed Xerxes in the following words: 'In my belief, my lord, readiness to listen to good advice comes to much the same thing as being wise oneself. You of course have both virtues; but you are led astray by the companionship of bad men. Their advice to you is like the gales of wind which do not allow the sea to be what it is meant to be – the thing, namely, in all the world most useful to us. As for myself, I was not so much hurt by your abuse of me as by the fact that when we were offered a choice between two courses, of which one tended to flatter our arrogance and the other to check it by pointing out how wrong it is to teach the heart always to seek for more than it possesses, you chose the one which is the more likely to lead both yourself and your country to disaster. Now you lean toward the better course; but you tell me that since you gave up your intention of attacking Greece, you have been haunted by a dream which will not let you lay your purpose aside. You imagine, my son, that your dream was ent by some god or other; but dreams do not come from God. I, who am older than you by many years, will tell you what these visions are that float before our eyes in sleep: nearly always these drifting phantoms are the shadows of what we have been thinking about during the day; and during the days before your dream we were, you know, very much occupied with this campaign. Nevertheless it is possible that your dream cannot be explained as I have explained it: perhaps there is, indeed, something divine in it – in which case what you have said sums the matter up completely: let it appear to me as well as to you, with its commands.

'All the same, if it means to come at all, it should not be more likely to come if I wear your clothes than if I wear my own, or if I sleep in your bed than if I sleep in mine. For surely this phantom of your dreams, whatever it may be, is not so foolish as to think that I am you simply because I wear your clothes. But, apart altogether from the question of clothes, should the phantom ignore me and not think fit to appear, but should nevertheless come again to you – well, that indeed is something we must take note of! For if it visits you often, even I shall admit that it is sent by God.

'As for the rest, if your mind is made up and I cannot turn you from your purpose: if I really must sleep in your bed – so be it. I will do what you command – and then let us see if the phantom comes. But until it does, I shall keep my own opinion on the matter.'

Then Artabanus, hoping to prove that Xerxes was mistaken, did as he had been bidden. He dressed himself in the king's clothes and took his seat upon the royal throne; and afterwards when he had gone to bed and fallen asleep, he dreamt that the very same figure which had twice visited the king stood over him. 'Are you the man,' said the phantom, 'who in would-be concern for the king is trying to dissuade him from making war on Greece? You will not escape unpunished, either now or hereafter, for seeking to turn aside the course of destiny; and as for Xerxes, he has been told already what will happen to him if he disobeys me.' The phantom after uttering these threats was on the point of burning out Artabanus' eyes with hot irons, when he leapt up with a shriek, and ran to find Xerxes. Then, sitting beside him, he recounted the dream in detail and went on to speak in the following words: 'Sire, like other men I have seen in my time powerful kingdoms struck down by weaker ones, and it was for that reason I tried to prevent you from giving way to the hot blood of youth. There is danger in insatiable desire, and I could not but remember the fate of Cyrus' campaign against the Massagetae and Cambyses' invasion of Ethiopia. Yes, and did I not march with Darius, too, against the Scythians? My memory of those disasters forced me to believe that the world would call you happy only if you lived in peace. But now I know that God is at work in this matter; and since apparently heaven itself is about to send ruin upon Greece, I admit that I was mistaken. Tell the Persians about the vision which God has sent us; make them prepare for war according to the orders which you previously gave them, and, as God is offering you this great opportunity, play your own part to the full in realizing it.'

Both Artabanus and Xerxes now placed the fullest confidence in the dream. The king, at the first light of dawn, laid the whole matter before the Persians, and Artabanus who had been the only one openly to oppose the project of war, now no less openly supported it.

After Xerxes had made his decision to fight, he had a third dream. The Magi were consulted about its significance and expressed the opinion that it portended the conquest of the world and its total subjection to Persia. In the dream, Xerxes had imagined himself crowned with olive, of which the branches spread all over the earth; then the crown had suddenly vanished from his head. After the Magi's favourable interpretation, all the Persian nobles who had attended the conference hurried home to their respective provinces; and as every one of them hoped to win the reward which Xerxes had offered, no pains were spared in the subsequent preparations, and Xerxes, in the process of assembling his armies, had every corner of the continent ransacked. For the four years following the conquest of Egypt the mustering of troops and the provision of stores and equipment continued, and towards the close of the fifth Xerxes, at the head of his enormous force, began his march.

The army was indeed far greater than any other in recorded history. It dwarfed the army Darius commanded on his Scythian campaign, and the great host of Scythians who burst into Media on the heels of the Cimmerians and brought nearly all upper Asia under their control. (It was this inroad which Darius' invasion was designed to avenge.) It was incomparably larger than the armies which the stories tell us Agamemnon and Menelaus led to Troy, or than those of the Mysians and Teucrians which before the Trojan War crossed the Bosphorus into Europe, overwhelmed Thrace, and, coming down to the Adriatic coast, drove as far south as the river Peneus. All these armies together, with others like them, would not have equalled the army of Xerxes. There was not a nation in Asia that he did not take with him against Greece; save for the great rivers there was not a stream his army drank from that was not drunk dry. Some nations provided ships, others formed infantry units; from some cavalry was requisitioned, from others horse-transports and crews; from others, again, warships for floating bridges, or provisions and naval craft of various kinds.

In view of the previous disaster to the fleet off Mt Athos, preparations had been going on in that area for the past three years. A fleet of triremes lay at Elaeus in the Chersonese, and from this base men of the various nations of which the army was composed were sent over in shifts to Athos, where they were put to the work of cutting a canal under the lash. The natives of Athos also took part. Bubares the son of Megabazus and Artachaees the son of Artaeus were the Persian officers in charge.

Mt Athos is a high and famous mountain running out into the sea. People live on it, and where the high land ends on the landward side it forms a sort of isthmus with a neck about a mile and a half wide, all of which is level ground or low hillocks, across from the sea by Acanthus to the sea facing Torone. On this isthmus where Athos peters out stands the Greek town of Sane, and south of it, on Athos itself, are Dium, Olophyxus, Acrothoon, Thyssus, and Cleonae – the inhabitants of which Xerxes now proposed to turn into islanders.

I will now describe how the canal was cut. The ground was divided into sections for the men of the various nations, on a line taped across the isthmus from Sane. When the trench reached a certain depth, the labourers at the bottom carried on with the digging and passed the soil up to others above them, who stood on terraces and passed it on to another lot, still higher up, until it reached the men at the top, who carried it away and dumped it. All the nations except the Phoenicians had their work doubled by the sides falling in, as they naturally would, since they made the cutting the same width at the top as it was intended to be at the bottom. But the Phoenicians, in this as in Xerxes' other works, gave a signal example of their skill. They, in the section allotted to them, took out a trench double the width prescribed for the actual finished canal, and by digging at a slope contracted it as they got further down, until at the bottom their section was the same width as the rest.

In a meadow near by the workmen had their meeting-place and market, and grain ready ground was brought over in great quantity from Asia.

Thinking it over I cannot but conclude that it was mere ostentation that made Xerxes have the canal dug – he wanted to show his power and to leave something to be remembered by. There would have been no difficulty at all in getting the ships hauled across the isthmus on land; yet he ordered the construction of a channel for the sea broad enough for two warships to be rowed abreast. The same people who had to cut the canal also had orders to bridge the river Strymon. At the same time other work too was in progress: cables, some of papyrus, some of white flax, were being prepared for the bridges – a task which Xerxes entrusted to the Phoenicians and Egyptians; and provision dumps were being formed for the troops, lest either men or animals should go hungry on the march to Greece. For these dumps the most convenient sites were chosen after a careful survey, the provisions being brought from many different parts of Asia in merchantmen or transport vessels. The greatest quantity was collected at a place called the White Cape in Thrace; other dumps were at Tyrodiza in Perinthian territory, Doriscus, Eion on the Strymon, and in Macedonia.

So the work went on, and meanwhile the great army – all the troops from the continent which were to take part in the expedition – had assembled according to orders at Critalla in Cappadocia, and from there began to move forward with Xerxes to Sardis. Which of the Persian provincial governors received the king's prize for the best-equipped contingent, I am not able to say; nor do I even know if the matter was ever decided.

After crossing the Halys the army passed through Phrygia to Celaenae. In this place the springs of the river Maeander rise – and another river, too, of equal size, called (as its proper name) the Cataract. This latter stream rises in the actual market-square of Celaenae and joins the Maeander. Here, too, the skin of Marsyas the Silenus is exhibited; according to the Phrygian legend Apollo flayed Marsyas and hung the skin up here in the market-place. Here at Celaenae a Lydian named Pythius, the son of Atys, was awaiting Xerxes, and on his arrival entertained him and the whole army with most lavish hospitality, and promised besides to furnish money for the expenses of the war. The mention of money caused Xerxes to ask the Persians present who Pythius was and if he was really rich enough to make such an offer. 'My lord,' was the answer, 'it was this man who gave your father Darius the golden plane-tree and the golden vine; and still, so far as we know, he is the wealthiest man in the world, after yourself.'

Xerxes was surprised by this latter statement, and repeated his question, this time asking Pythius himself how much money he possessed. 'Sire,' said Pythius, 'I will be open with you and not pretend that I do not know the amount of my fortune. I do know it, and I will tell you exactly what it is. When I learned that you were on your way to the Aegean coast, my immediate wish was to make a contribution towards the expenses of the war; so I went into the matter of my finances and found upon calculation that I possessed 2000 talents of silver, and 3,993,000 gold Darics. This it is my intention to give you; I can live quite comfortably myself on my slaves and the produce of my estates.'

Xerxes was much pleased. 'My Lydian friend,' he replied, 'you are the only man I have met since I left Persian territory who has been willing to entertain my army, and nobody but you has come into my presence with an offer to contribute money for the war of his own free will. But you have done both, and on a magnificent scale. Therefore, as a reward for your generosity, I make you my personal friend and, in addition, I will give you from my own coffers 7000 gold Darics which are needed to make your fortune up to the round sum of 4,000,000. Continue, then, to possess what you have acquired; and have the wisdom to remain always the man you have proved yourself to-day. You will never regret it, now or hereafter.'

Having carried out this promise, Xerxes moved on. Passing the Phrygian town of Anaua, and a lake from which salt is extracted, Xerxes now arrived at the large city of Colossae, where the river Lycus disappears underground to reappear about half a mile further on, where it, too, joins the Maeander. Leaving Colossae the army made for the Lydian border and arrived next at Cydrara, where a column with an inscription upon it set up by Croesus defines the boundary between Phrygia and Lydia. The road as it enters Lydia divides, one track leading left towards Caria, the other to the right towards Sardis. A traveller by the latter road has to cross the Maeander and pass Callatebus, a town where the manufacture of honey out of tamarisk-syrup and wheat flour is carried on. This was the road which Xerxes took, and it was hereabouts that he came across a plane-tree of such beauty that he was moved to decorate it with golden ornaments and to appoint a guardian for it in perpetuity. The following day he reached the Lydian capital.

In Sardis Xerxes' first act was to send representatives to every place in Greece except Athens and Sparta with a demand for earth and water and a further order to prepare entertainment for him against his coming. This renewed demand for submission was due to his confident belief that the Greeks who had previously refused to comply with the demand of Darius would now be frightened into complying with his own. It was to prove whether or not he was right that he took this step.

He then prepared to move forward to Abydos, where a bridge had already been constructed across the Hellespont from Asia to Europe. Between Sestos and Madytus in the Chersonese there is a rocky headland running out into the water opposite Abydos. It was here not long afterwards that the Greeks under Xanthippus the son of Ariphron took Artaÿctes the Persian governor of Sestos, and nailed him alive to a plank – he was the man who collected women in the temple of Protesilaus at Elaeus and committed various acts of sacrilege. This headland was the point to which Xerxes' engineers carried their two bridges from Abydos – a distance of seven furlongs. One was constructed by the Phoenicians using flax cables, the other by the

Egyptians with papyrus cables. The work was successfully completed, but a subsequent storm of great violence smashed it up and carried everything away. Xerxes was very angry when he learned of the disaster, and gave orders that the Hellespont should receive three hundred lashes and have a pair of fetters thrown into it. I have heard before now that he also sent people to brand it with hot irons. He certainly instructed the men with the whips to utter, as they wielded them, the barbarous and presumptuous words: 'You salt and bitter stream, your master lays this punishment upon you for injuring him, who never injured you. But Xerxes the King will cross you, with or without your permission. No man sacrifices to you, and you deserve the neglect by your acid and muddy waters.' In addition to punishing the Hellespont Xerxes gave orders that the men responsible for building the bridges should have their heads cut off. The men who received these invidious orders duly carried them out, and other engineers completed the work. The method employed was as follows: galleys and triremes were lashed together to support the bridges – 360 vessels for the one on the Black Sea side, and 314 for the other. They were moored slantwise to the Black Sea and at right angles to the Hellespont, in order to lessen the strain on the cables. Specially heavy anchors were laid out both upstream and downstream – those to the eastward to hold the vessels against winds blowing down the straits from the direction of the Black Sea, those on the other side, to the westward and towards the Aegean, to take the strain when it blew from the west and south. Gaps were left in three places to allow any boats that might wish to do so to pass in or out of the Black Sea.

Once the vessels were in position, the cables were hauled taut by wooden winches ashore. This time the two sorts of cable were not used separately for each bridge, but both bridges had two flax cables and four papyrus ones. The flax and papyrus cables were of the same thickness and quality, but the flax was the heavier – half a fathom of it weighed 114 lb. The next operation was to cut planks equal in length to the width of the floats, lay them edge to edge over the taut cables, and then bind them together on their upper surface. That done, brushwood was put on top and spread evenly, with a layer of soil, trodden hard, over all. Finally a paling was constructed along each side, high enough to prevent horses and mules from seeing over and taking fright at the water.

The bridges were now ready; and when news came from Athos that work on the canal was finished, including the breakwaters at its two ends, which had been built to prevent the surf from silting up the entrances, the army, after wintering at Sardis and completing its preparations, started the following spring on its march to Abydos.

No sooner had the troops begun to move than the sun vanished from his place in the sky and it grew dark as night, though the weather was perfectly clear and cloudless. Xerxes, deeply troubled, asked the Magi to interpret the significance of this strange phenomenon, and was given to understand that God meant to foretell to the Greeks the eclipse of their cities – for it was the sun which gave warning of the future to Greece, just as the moon did to Persia. Having heard this Xerxes continued the march in high spirits.

The army, however, had not gone far when Pythius the Lydian, in alarm at the sign from heaven, was emboldened by the presents he had received to come to Xerxes with a request. 'Master,' he said, 'there is a favour I should like you to grant me – a small thing, indeed, for you to perform, but to me of great importance, should you consent to do so.' Xerxes, who thought the request would be almost anything but what it actually turned out to be, agreed to grant it and told Pythius to say what it was he wanted. This generous answer raised Pythius' hopes, and he said, 'My lord, I have five sons, and it happens that every one of them is serving in your army in the campaign against Greece. I am an old man, Sire, and I beg you in pity to release from service one of my sons – the eldest – to take care of me and my property. Take the other four – and may you return with your purpose accomplished.'

Xerxes was furiously angry. 'You miserable fellow,' he cried, 'have you the face to mention your son, when I, in person, am marching to the war against Greece with my sons and brothers and kinsmen and friends – *you*, my slave, whose duty it was to come with me with every member of your house, including your wife? Mark my words: it is through the ears you can touch a man to pleasure or rage – let the spirit which dwells there hear good things, and it will fill the body with delight; let it hear bad, and it will swell with fury. When you did me good service, and offered more, you cannot boast that you were more generous than I; and now your punishment will be less than your impudence deserves. Yourself and four of your sons are saved by the entertainment you gave me; but you shall pay with the life of the fifth, whom you cling to most.'

Having answered Pythius in these words Xerxes at once gave orders that the men to whom such duties fell should find Pythius' eldest son and cut him in half and put the two halves one on each side of the road, for the army to march out between them. The order was performed.

And now between the halves of the young man's body the advance of the army began: first came the men with the gear and equipment, driving the pack-animals, and behind these a host of troops of all nationalities indiscriminately mixed. When more than half the army had passed, a gap was left in the marching column to keep these troops from contact with the king, who was immediately preceded by a thousand horsemen, picked out of all Persia, followed by a thousand similarly picked spearmen with spears reversed. Then came ten of the sacred horses, known as Nisaean, in magnificent harness. (The horses are so called because they come from the great Nisaean plain in Media, where horses of unusual size are bred.) They were followed by the holy chariot of Zeus drawn by eight white horses, with a charioteer on foot behind them holding the reins – for no mortal man may mount into that chariot's seat. Then came the king himself, riding in a chariot drawn by Nisaean horses, his charioteer, Patiramphes, son of Otanes the Persian, standing by his side.

That was how Xerxes rode from Sardis – and, when the fancy took him, he would leave his chariot and take his seat in a covered carriage instead. Behind him marched a thousand spearmen, their weapons pointing upwards in the usual way – all men of the best and noblest Persian blood; then a thousand picked Persian cavalry, then – again chosen for quality out of all that remained – a body of Persian infantry ten thousand strong. Of these a thousand had golden pomegranates instead of spikes on the butt-end of their spears, and were arrayed surrounding the other nine thousand, whose spears had silver pomegranates. The troops mentioned who marched with spears reversed also had golden pomegranates on the butt-end of their weapons, while those immediately behind Xerxes had golden apples. The ten thousand infantry were followed by a squadron of ten thousand Persian horse, after which there was a gap of two furlongs, and then came the remainder of the army, in a miscellaneous mass.

From Lydia the army made for the river Caicus and Mysia and thence proceeded through Atarneus to Carene, keeping Mt Cane on its left; then crossing the level country near Thebe it passed Atramyttium and the Pelasgian town of Antandrus, and with Mt Ida on its left entered Trojan territory. During a night in camp at the foot of Mt Ida a heavy storm of thunder and lightning caused the death of a considerable number of men. When the army reached the Scamander, the first river since the march from Sardis began which failed to provide enough water for men and beasts, Xerxes had a strong desire to see Troy, the ancient city of Priam. Accordingly he went up into the citadel, and when he had seen what he wanted to see and heard the story of the place from the people there, he sacrificed a thousand oxen to the Trojan Athene, and the Magi made libations of wine to the spirits of the great men of old. During the night which followed there was panic in the camp. At dawn the march continued; and the army after leaving on the left Rhoeteum, Ophryneum, and Dardanus which is next to Abydos, and the Teucrians of Gergithos on the right, arrived at Abydos.

Xerxes now decided to hold a review of his army. On a rise of ground near by, a throne of white marble had already been specially prepared for his use by the people of Abydos; so the king took his seat upon it and, looking down over the shore, was able to see the whole of his army and navy at a single view. As he watched them he was seized with the desire to witness a rowing-match. The match took place and was won by the Phoenicians of Sidon, to the great delight of Xerxes who was as pleased with the race as with his army. And when he saw the whole Hellespont hidden by ships, and all the beaches and plains of Abydos filled with men, he congratulated himself – and the moment after burst into tears. Artabanus his uncle, the man who in the first instance had spoken his mind so freely in trying to dissuade Xerxes from undertaking the campaign, was by his side; and when he saw how Xerxes wept, he said to him: 'My lord, surely there is a strange contradiction in what you do now and

what you did a moment ago. They you called yourself a lucky man –
and now you weep.'

'I was thinking,' Xerxes replied; 'and it came into my mind how
pitifully short human life is – for of all these thousands of men not
one will be alive in a hundred years' time.'

'Yet,' said Artabanus, 'there are sadder things in life even than
that. Short as it is, there is not a man in the world, either here or elsewhere, who is happy enough not to wish – not once only but again
and again – to be dead rather than alive. Troubles come, diseases
afflict us; and this makes life, despite its brevity, seem all too long.
So heavy is the burden of it that death is a refuge which we all desire,
and it is common proof amongst us that God who gave us a taste
of this world's sweetness has been a niggard in his giving.'

'Artabanus,' Xerxes replied, 'the lot of men here upon earth is
indeed as you have described it; but let us put aside these gloomy
reflections, for we have pleasant things in hand. Now tell me – if
that figure had not appeared to you so vividly in your dream, would
you have clung to your original opinion and tried to prevent me
from making war on Greece, or would you have changed your
mind? Answer me truly.'

'Sire,' said Artabanus, 'I pray that the dream we had may not
disappoint either my hopes or your own. But ever since that night
I have been beside myself with dread; many things contribute to
the cause of it, but nothing so much as my knowledge that the two
mightiest powers in the world are against you.'

'What a strange man you are,' said Xerxes; 'tell me, what powers
do you mean? Have you any fault to find with my army? Isn't it big
enough? Do you think the Greek army will be several times as large,
or our navy smaller than theirs? Which are you afraid of? Both
perhaps! But if you feel that our force is inadequate, another army
could easily be mustered with little delay.'

'No man of sense, my lord,' Artabanus answered, 'could find any
fault with the size of your army or the number of your ships. If you
increase your forces, the two powers I have in mind will be even
worse enemies to you than they are now. I will tell you what they
are – the land and the sea. So far as I know there is not a harbour anywhere big enough to receive this fleet of ours and give it protection

HERODOTUS · BOOK SEVEN [49

in the event of storms: and indeed there would have to be not merely one such harbour, but many – all along the coast by which you will sail. But there is not a single one; so I would have you realize, my lord, that men are at the mercy of circumstance, and not their master.

'Now let me tell you of your other great enemy, the land. If you meet with no opposition, the land itself will become more and more hostile to you the further you advance, drawn on and on; for men are never satisfied by success. What I mean is this – if nobody stops your advance, the land itself – the mere distance growing greater and greater as the days go by – will ultimately starve you. No: the best man, in my belief, is he who lays his plans warily, with an eye for every disaster which might occur, and then, when the time comes, acts boldly.'

'There is good sense,' Xerxes answered, 'in everything you have said; nevertheless you ought not to be so timid always, or to think of every accident which might possibly overtake us. If upon the proposal of a plan you were always to weigh equally all possible chances, you would never do anything. I would much rather take a risk and run into trouble half the time than keep out of any trouble through being afraid of everything.

'If you dispute whatever is said to you, but can never prove your objections, you are as likely to be wrong as the other man – indeed there is nothing to choose between you. And as for proof – how can a man ever be certain? Certainty, surely is beyond human grasp. But however that may be, the usual thing is that profit comes to those who are willing to act, not to the overcautious and hesitant. Just think how the power of Persia has grown: if my predecessors had felt as you do – or even if they had not, but had taken the advice of men who did – you would never have seen our country in its present glory. No indeed: it was by taking risks that my ancestors brought us to where we stand to-day. Only by great risks can great results be achieved. We, therefore, are following in the footsteps of our fathers; we are marching to war at the best season of the year; we shall conquer all Europe, and – without being starved to death anywhere or having any other unpleasant experience – we shall return home in triumph. For one thing, we are carrying ample stores with us; for another, we will have the grain belonging to any country we may enter, no matter who lives there. Our enemies, remember, are not nomad tribes – they are agricultural peoples.'

'Sire,' said Artabanus, 'though you will not listen to my fears, take, at least, one piece of advice from me – for when there is much to talk of, many words are needed. Cyrus, the son of Cambyses, conquered and made tributary to Persia all Ionia except Athens; I urge you therefore on no account to take these Ionians to attack men of their own blood. We are well able to defeat our enemy without their help. If the Ionians come with us, they will have two courses open to them: either to prove themselves scoundrels by helping to enslave their mother country, or to prove themselves honest men by helping to keep her free. By choosing the former course they will do us little good; by choosing the latter they will be able to cause serious injury to your army. Remember, I beg you, the truth of the old saying, that the end is not always to be seen in the beginning.'

Xerxes answered: 'Artabanus, of all the views you have put forward you are most mistaken in your fear that the Ionians will desert our cause. We have the best possible proof of their reliability, and you yourself like everybody else who took part in Darius' Scythian campaign can bear witness to it. On that occasion, when the Ionians had it in their power to save or destroy the whole Persian army, they did us no harm but acted with loyalty and honour. Besides, there is another reason for trusting them: for is it conceivable that they will try to wreck our cause, when they have left their wives, children, and property in our country? You may, therefore, dismiss this fear from your mind. Doubt nothing, and keep safe for me my house and dominions; for to you, and you alone, I give my sovereignty in trust.'

After this conversation Xerxes sent Artabanus back to Susa and then summoned a meeting of the leading Persians. 'Gentlemen,' he said to them, 'I have brought you here because I wished to ask you to show courage in what lies before us; you must not disgrace our countrymen, who in former days did so much that was great and admirable. Let each and all of us exert ourselves to the utmost; for the noble aim we are striving to achieve concerns every one of us alike. Fight this war with all your might – and for this reason: our enemies, if what I hear is true, are brave men, and if we defeat them, there is no other army in the world which will ever stand up to us again. And now let us pray to the gods who have our country in their keeping – and cross the bridge.'

All that day the preparations for the crossing continued; and on the following day, while they waited for the sun which they wished to see as it rose, they burned all sorts of spices on the bridges and laid boughs of myrtle along the way. Then sunrise came, and Xerxes poured wine into the sea out of a golden goblet and, with his face turned to the sun, prayed that no chance might prevent him from conquering Europe or turn him back before he reached its utmost limits. His prayer ended, he flung the cup into the Hellespont and with it a golden bowl and a Persian *acinaces*, or short sword. I cannot say for certain if he intended the things which he threw into the water to be an offering to the Sun-god; perhaps they were – or it may be that they were a gift to the Hellespont itself, to show he was sorry for having caused it to be lashed with whips.

This ceremony over, the crossing began. The infantry and cavalry went over by the upper bridge – the one nearer the Black Sea; the pack-animals and underlings by the lower one towards the Aegean. The first to cross were the Ten Thousand, all with wreaths on their heads, and these were followed by the mass of troops of all the nations. Their crossing occupied the whole of the first day. On the next day the first over were the thousand horsemen, and the contingent which marched with spears reversed – these, too, all wearing wreaths. Then came the sacred horses and the sacred chariot, and after them Xerxes himself with his spearmen and his thousand horsemen. The remainder of the army brought up the rear, and at the same time the ships moved over to the opposite shore. According to another account I have heard, the king crossed last.

From the European shore Xerxes watched his troops coming over under the whips. The crossing occupied seven days and nights without a break. There is a story that some time after Xerxes had passed the bridge, a native of the country thereabouts exclaimed: 'Why, O God, have you assumed the shape of a man of Persia, and changed your name to Xerxes, in order to lead everyone in the world to the conquest and devastation of Greece? You could have destroyed Greece without going to that trouble.'

After the whole army had reached the European shore and the forward march had begun, an extraordinary thing occurred – a mare gave birth to a hare. Xerxes paid no attention to this omen, though the significance of it was easy enough to understand. Clearly it meant that he was to lead an army against Greece with the greatest pomp and circumstance, and then to come running for his life back to the place he started from. There had previously been another strange and ominous occurrence in Sardis, when a mule dropped a foal with a double set of sexual organs, male and female – the former uppermost. Xerxes, however, ignored both omens and continued his march at the head of the army. The fleet followed the coast in a westerly direction down the Hellespont and then on to Cape Sarpedon, where it had orders to wait, and thus started in the opposite direction to the army, which marched eastwards through the Chersonese, keeping on its right the tomb of Helle, the daughter of Athamas, and on its left the town of Cardia. After passing through a place called The Market, it skirted the Black Gulf and crossed the river which gives the gulf its name – and which failed on that occasion to supply enough water for the army's needs. From that point it turned west, past the Aeolian settlement of Aenus and Lake Stentoris, to Doriscus.

Doriscus is the name given to a strip of coast in Thrace backed by a large plain through which flows the large river Hebrus. A fortress – also called Doriscus – had been built here, and a Persian garrison left in it by Darius ever since his invasion of Scythia. It occurred to Xerxes, therefore, that it would be a convenient place for organizing and numbering his troops, and this he proceeded to do.

The naval captains had orders from Xerxes to move all the ships from Doriscus to the adjoining beach where Zone stands, and the Samothracian town of Sale – the beach, that is, which runs out to the well-known headland of Serreum. In ancient times this whole district belonged to the Cicones. Here the ships were all hauled ashore and allowed to dry out.

Meanwhile Xerxes at Doriscus was occupied in numbering his troops. As nobody has left a record, I cannot state the precise number of men provided by each separate nation, but the grand total, excluding the naval contingent, turned out to be 1,700,000. The counting was done by first packing ten thousand men as close together as they could stand and drawing a circle round them on the ground; they were then dismissed, and a fence, about navel-high, was constructed round the circle; finally other troops were marched into the area thus enclosed and dismissed in their turn, until the whole army had been counted. After the counting, the army was reorganized in divisions according to nationality.

The nations of which the army was composed were as follows. First the Persians themselves: the dress of these troops consisted of the tiara, or soft felt cap, embroidered tunic with sleeves, a coat of mail looking like the scales of a fish, and trousers; for arms they carried light wicker shields, quivers slung below them, short spears, powerful bows with cane arrows, and daggers swinging from belts beside the right thigh. They were commanded by Otanes, the father of Xerxes' wife Amestris. In ancient times the Greek name for the Persians was Cephenes, though they were known to themselves and their neighbours as Artaei. It was not till Perseus, the son of Zeus and Danae, on a visit to Cepheus, the son of Belus, married his daughter Andromeda and had by her a son whom he named Perses (and left behind in that country because Cepheus had no male heir) that the Persians took, from this Perses, their present name.

The Median contingent, commanded by Tigranes the Achaemenid, was equipped in the same way as the Persian – in point of fact this mode of dress was originally Median and not Persian at all. The Medes were once universally known as Arians, but they, too, changed their name. In their case the change, according to their own account, followed the visit of Medea the Colchian, who went to their country from Athens.

The dress of the Cissian contingent was like the Persian, except that instead of caps they wore turbans. They were commanded by Anaphes, the son of Otanes. The Hyrcanians were armed in the same way as the Persians, and their commander was Megapanus, who afterwards became governor of Babylon. The Assyrians were equipped with bronze helmets made in a complicated outlandish way which is hard to describe, shields, spears, daggers (like the Egyptian ones), wooden clubs studded with iron, and linen corslets. These people used to be called Syrians by the Greeks, Assyrians being the name for them elsewhere. With them were the Chaldeans. Their commander was Otaspes, the son of Artachaees.

The Bactrians had caps almost exactly like those worn by the Medes, and were armed with their native cane bows and short spears. The Sacae (a Scythian people) wore trousers and tall pointed hats set upright on their heads, and were armed with the bows of their country, daggers, and the *sagaris*, or battle-axe. 'Sacae' is the name the Persians give to all Scythian tribes: these were the Amyrgian Scythians. They, together with the Bactrians, were under the command of Hystaspes, the son of Darius and of Cyrus' daughter Atossa.

The Indians were dressed in cotton; they carried cane bows and cane arrows tipped with iron, and marched under the command of Pharnazathres, the son of Artabates. The Arians, under Hydarnes' son Sisamnes, were armed with Median bows, the rest of their equipment being the same as the Bactrians'; also in Bactrian equipment were the Parthians and Chorasmians under Artabazus son of Pharnaces, the Sogdians under Azanes son of Artaeus, the Gandarians and Dadicae under Artyphius son of Artabanus. Then there were the Caspians and the Sarangians, the former commanded by Ariomardus, the brother of Artyphius, dressed in leather jackets and armed with the *acinaces* and the cane bow of their country; the latter, under Megabazus' son Pherendates, armed with bows and Median spears, and conspicuous for their brightly coloured clothes and high boots reaching to the knee. The Utians and Myci under the command of Arsamenes son of Darius, and the Paricanians under Oeobazus' son Siromitres were equipped, like the Pactyans, with leather jackets, bows, and daggers. The Pactyan commander was Artaÿntes, the son of Ithamitres.

The Arabians wore the *zeira*,[1] caught in with a belt; their weapon was the bow, carried at the right side – a long bow, which assumed a reverse curve when unstrung. The Ethiopians, in their leopard skins and lion skins, carried long bows made of palm-wood – as much as six feet long – which were used to shoot small cane arrows tipped not with iron but with stone worked to a fine point, like the stone they use for engraving seals. They also had spears with spearheads of antelope horn, and knotted clubs. When going to battle they

1. A sort of long flowing garment.

smeared half their bodies with chalk and half with vermilion. The Arabians and the Ethiopians from the country south of Egypt were commanded by Arsames, the son of Darius – his mother was Cyrus' daughter Artystone, the favourite wife of Darius, who had a statue made of her in beaten gold.

The eastern Ethiopians – for there were two sorts of Ethiopians in the army – served with the Indians. These were just like the southern Ethiopians, except for their language and their hair: their hair is straight, while that of the Ethiopians in Libya is the crispest and curliest in the world. The equipment of the Ethiopians from Asia was in most respects like the Indian, except that they wore headdresses consisting of horses' scalps, stripped off with the ears and mane attached – the ears were made to stand erect and the mane served as a crest. For shields they used the skins of cranes.

The Libyans were clothed in leather and carried javelins hardened with fire. Their commander was Massages, the son of Oarizus. The Paphlagonians wore wicker helmets, small shields, fairly short spears, javelins, and daggers. They wore the native high boot reaching half-way to the knee. Similarly equipped were the Ligyans, Matieni, Mariandynians, and Syrians (or Cappadocians, as the Persians call them). In command of the Paphlagonians and Matieni was Dotus, the son of Megasidrus, and in command of the Mariandynians, Ligyans, and Syrians was Gobryas, the son of Darius and Artystone.

The dress of the Phrygians was, with a few small differences, like the Paphlagonian. This people, according to the Macedonian account, were known as Briges during the period when they lived in Macedonia, and changed their name at the same time as, by migrating to Asia, they changed their country. The Armenians, who are Phrygian colonists, were armed in the Phrygian fashion and both contingents were commanded by Artochmes, the husband of one of Darius' daughters.

The Lydian equipment closely resembled the Greek. These people were known anciently as Maeonians, and took their present name from Lydus, the son of Atys. The Mysians wore the native helmet and were armed with small shields and javelins made of wood hardened in fire. They are Lydian colonists, and are known as Olympieni after Mt Olympus.[1] The two latter contingents were led by Arta-phernes, son of the same Artaphernes who landed with Datis at Marathon.

The Thracian troops wore fox skins as a headdress, tunics with the *zeira*, or long cloak, in this case brightly coloured, thrown over them, and high fawnskin boots; their weapons were the javelin, light shield, and small dagger. The Thracians after their migration to Asia became known as Bithynians; previously, according to their own account, they were called Strymonians, after the river Strymon upon which they lived, and from which they were driven by the Teucrians and Mysians. The commander of these Asiatic Thracians was Bassaces, the son of Artabanus.

The Pisidians[2] carried little ox-hide shields and a pair of hunting-spears of Lycian workmanship, and wore bronze helmets, crested, and decorated with the ears and horns of an ox, also in bronze. Their legs were bound with strips of crimson cloth. In the country where these people live there is an oracle of Ares.

The Cabalians (who are really Maeonians but are known as Lasonians) had the same kind of equipment as the Cilicians – I will describe it when I come to the Cilicians in the course of this catalogue. The Milyans carried short spears and had their clothes fastened with brooches; some of them were also armed with Lycian bows and wore leather casques. All these troops were led by Badres, the son of Hystanes.

The Moschians had wooden helmets and were armed with shields and short spears with long heads. Similarly equipped were the Tibareni, Macrones, and Mossynoeci; the officers who organized and commanded these troops were, for the two former, Ariomardus, the son of Darius and Parmys (who was daughter of Smerdis and granddaughter of Cyrus), and, for the two latter, Artayctes, the son of Cherasmis, governor of Sestos on the Hellespont.

1. The Mysian Olympus is one of at least eight scattered round the Aegean, all, perhaps, named after the great 'abode of the gods' in Thessaly – as was, when there was no mountain handy, Olympia in the Peloponnese.

2. Not actually in the text as preserved, but a neat attempt to fill a gap where a name is wanted; it has some resemblance to the adjacent word 'shields', and this may have helped a copyist to omit it.

The Marians wore the peculiar plaited helmets of their country and were armed with little leather shields and javelins; the Colchians had wooden helmets, small shields made of rawhide, short spears, and swords. These two contingents were under the command of Pharandates, the son of Teaspis. Similarly armed were the Alarodians and Saspires, under Masistius, the son of Siromitras. The troops from the islands in the Persian Gulf (the islands, that is, where the Persian king settles people he has expelled from their homes) were dressed and armed very much in the Median fashion, and were commanded by Bagaeus' son Mardontes, who in the following year held a command at Mycale and was killed in the battle.

Such, then, were the troops of the various nations which made up the infantry. The names of their chief commanders I have already recorded; it was they who organized and numbered the troops, and appointed the commanders of thousands and myriads of men. The latter were responsible for appointing men to take charge of small units – squads of ten or a hundred. There were also other officers commanding contingents and nations, but those whom I mentioned above were the commanders.

Over them, and in general command of the infantry, were Mardonius, the son of Gobryas, Tritantaechmes, the son of Artabanus (the man who voted against the campaign), Smerdomenes, the son of Otanes (both nephews of Darius and Xerxes' cousins), Masistes, the son of Darius and Atossa, Gergis, the son of Ariazus, and Megabyzus, the son of Zopyrus. These six commanded all the infantry except the Ten Thousand – a body of picked Persian troops under the leadership of Hydarnes, the son of Hydarnes. This corps was known as the Immortals, because it was invariably kept up to strength; if a man was killed or fell sick, the vacancy he left was at once filled, so that its strength was never more nor less than 10,000.

Of all the troops in the army the native Persians were not only the best but also the most magnificently equipped; their dress and armour I have mentioned already, but should add that every man glittered with the gold which he carried about his person in unlimited quantity. They were accompanied, moreover, by covered carriages containing their women and servants, all elaborately fitted out. Special food, separate from that of the rest of the army, was brought along for them on camels and mules.

The nations above mentioned use cavalry, but for this expedition only the following provided it: first the Persians – armed in the same way as their infantry, except that some of them wore devices of hammered bronze or iron on their heads. Secondly, a nomad tribe called Sagartians, a people who speak Persian and dress in a manner half Persian, half Pactyan: these furnished a contingent 8000 strong. Their custom is to carry no weapons of bronze or iron except daggers; the special weapon upon which they chiefly rely is the lasso made of plaited strips of hide. In action, the moment they are in contact with the enemy, they throw their lassos, which have a noose at the end, and haul towards them whatever they catch, horse or man. The victim, tied up and helpless, is then dispatched. The Sagartian contingent was attached to the Persian. The Medes and Cissians were equipped like their infantry. The Indians, also armed like the Indian foot, rode, some on horseback, some in chariots drawn by either horses or wild asses. The Bactrians and Caspians were equipped like their infantry. The Libyans were like their infantry in equipment, but all riding in chariots. The Caspeirians and Paricanians again had the same arms as their infantry. The Arabians, equipped like their infantry, rode camels, which in speed are not inferior to horses.

These were the only nations which provided cavalry, and the total strength, not counting camels and chariots, was 80,000. The cavalry was drawn up in squadrons, and the Arabian contingent brought up the rear to avoid spreading panic amongst the horses, who cannot endure the presence of camels.

In command of the cavalry were Datis' two sons, Harmamithras and Tithaeus. The third general of cavalry, Pharnuches, had been injured and left behind in Sardis. When the army was leaving Sardis, he met with an unhappy accident: a dog ran under his horse's feet, and the horse, taken by surprise, reared and threw its rider. As a result of the fall Pharnuches began to spit blood; and his sickness finally turned to consumption. His servants at once dealt with the horse according to his orders – bringing him to the spot where he had thrown his master, and cutting his legs off at the knees. So Pharnuches lost his command.

The fleet, apart from transport vessels, consisted of 1207 triremes. They were furnished as follows: (i) the Phoenicians, with the Syrians of Palestine, contributed 300. The crews wore helmets very like the Greek ones, and linen corslets; they were armed with rimless shields and javelins. These people have a tradition that in ancient times they lived on the Persian Gulf, but migrated to the Syrian coast, where they are found to-day. This part of Syria, together with the country which extends southward to Egypt, is all known as Palestine.

(ii) The Egyptians contributed 200. They wore reticulated helmets and were armed with concave, broad-rimmed shields, boarding-spears, and heavy axes. Most of the crews wore corslets and carried long knives.

(iii) The Cyprians contributed 150. Their princes wore turbans, the common sailors peaked hats. The rest of their equipment resembled the Greek. According to the Cyprians' own account, some of them came originally from Salamis and Athens, some from Arcadia, some from Cythnus, some from Phoenicia and Ethiopia.

(iv) The Cilicians contributed 100. The crews wore the native helmet and woollen corslets and carried light rawhide shields. Each man was armed with two javelins and a sword which closely resembled the Egyptian long knife.

The ancient name of the Cilicians was Hypachaei; their present name they took from Cilix, the son of Agenor, a Phoenician.

(v) The Pamphylians contributed 30. Their armour was Greek. These people are descended from the Greeks who followed Amphilochus and Calchas when the army was dispersed after the capture of Troy.

(vi) The Lycians contributed 50. They wore greaves and corslets; they carried bows of cornel wood, cane arrows without feathers, and javelins. They had goatskins slung round their shoulders, and hats stuck round with feathers. They also carried daggers and riphooks. The Lycians are of Cretan origin; their old name was Termilae, and they took their present one from Lycus son of Pandion, an Athenian.

(vii) The Asiatic Dorians contributed 30. Coming originally from the Peloponnese, they were armed in the Greek fashion.

(viii) The Carians contributed 70. Their equipment was similar to the Greek, except that they carried riphooks and daggers. Their old name I have already mentioned in an early chapter of this history.

(ix) The Ionians contributed 100. Their equipment was Greek. These people, according to the Greek account, as long as they lived in what is now known as Achaea in the Peloponnese, before the coming of Danaus and Xuthus, were called Pelasgians of the Coast. They took their present name from Xuthus' son Ion.

(x) The islanders – also wearing Greek armour – contributed 17. They, too, are a Pelasgian people; they were later known as Ionians for the same reason as those who inhabited the twelve cities founded from Athens.

(xi) The Aeolians (also, as the Greeks suppose, originally a Pelasgian people) contributed 60. Their equipment was similar to the Greek.

(xii) The towns on the Hellespont and Bosphorus (the people in these places are Ionian and Dorian colonists) contributed 100 – all furnished with Greek equipment and armour. Abydos, however, was not included: the men of this town had orders from Xerxes to stay at home and guard the bridges.

All the ships also carried Persians, Medes, or Sacae as marines. The fastest ships were the Phoenician and of these the Sidonian were the best. The men who served with the fleet like those who served with the army had their own native officers; but, as my story does not require it, I do not propose to mention their names. Some of them were far from distinguished, and every nation had as many officers as it had towns. In any case, these native officers were not really commanders; like the rest of the troops, they merely served under compulsion. The names of the Persian generals who had the real command and were at the head of the contingents sent by the various nations, I have already recorded.

The naval commanders were as follows: Ariabignes son of Darius; Prexaspes son of Aspathines; Megabazus son of Megabates; Achaemenes son of Darius. Ariabignes, who was Darius' son by a daughter of Gobryas, commanded the Ionian and Carian contingent, Achaemenes, who was Xerxes' brother by both parents, the Egyptian. The rest of the fleet was under the other two. Galleys of thirty and fifty oars, horse-transports, and boats made the total number of the fleet up to 3000.

Next to the commanders the following were the best known of those who sailed with the fleet: Tetramnestus son of Anysus, from Sidon; Matten son of Siromus, from Tyre; Marbalus son of Agbalus, from Aradus; Syennesis son of Oromedón, from Cilicia; Cyberniscus son of Sicas, from Lycia; Gorgus son of Chersis and Timonax son of Timagoras, from Cyprus; and Histiaeus son of Tymnes, Pigres son of Hysseldomus, and Damasithymus son of Candaules, from Caria.

There is no need for me to mention all the other subordinate officers, but there is one name which I cannot omit – that of Artemisia. It seems to me a most strange and interesting thing that she – a woman – should have taken part in the campaign against Greece. On the death of her husband the sovereign power had passed into her hands, and she sailed with the fleet in spite of the fact that she had a grown-up son and that there was consequently no necessity for her to do so. Her own spirit of adventure and manly courage were her only incentives. She was the daughter of Lygdamis, a Halicarnassian; on her mother's side she was Cretan. She sailed in command of the men of Halicarnassus, Cos, Nisyra, and Calydna, and furnished five ships of war. They were the most famous in the fleet, after the contingent from Sidon, and not one of the confederate commanders gave Xerxes sounder advice than she did. The places I mentioned as being under her rule are all Dorian – the Halicarnassians being colonists from Troezen, and the rest from Epidaurus.

I have now finished what I had to say about the fleet.

When the counting and marshalling of the troops had been completed, Xerxes thought he would like to hold a general review. Accordingly he drove in his chariot past the contingents of all the various nations, asking questions, the answers to which were taken down by his secretaries, until he had gone from one end of the army to the other, both horse and foot. Next the ships were launched, and Xerxes dismounting from his chariot went aboard a Sidonian vessel, where he took his seat under a canopy of gold and sailed along the line of the anchored fleet, asking questions about each ship and having the answers recorded, just as he had done with the army. The ships' masters had taken their vessels some four hundred feet from the beach, and brought up there in a single line with the bows turned shoreward and the fighting men drawn up on deck fully armed as for war. To hold his review, Xerxes passed along between the line and the shore.

Having sailed from one end to the other of the line of anchored ships, Xerxes went ashore again and sent for Demaratus, the son of Ariston, who was accompanying him in the march to Greece. 'Demaratus,' he said, 'it would give me pleasure at this point to put to you a few questions. You are a Greek, and a native, moreover, of by no means the meanest or weakest city in that country – as I learn not only from yourself but from the other Greeks I have spoken with. Tell me, then – will the Greeks dare to lift a hand against me? My own belief is that all the Greeks and all the other western peoples gathered together would be insufficient to withstand the attack of my army – and still more so if they are not united. But it is your opinion upon this subject that I should like to hear.'

'My lord,' Demaratus replied, 'is it a true answer you would like, or merely an agreeable one?'

'Tell me the truth,' said the king: 'and I promise that you will not suffer by it.' Encouraged by this Demaratus continued: 'My lord, you bid me speak nothing but the truth, to say nothing which might later be proved a lie. Very well then; this is my answer: poverty is my country's inheritance from of old, but valour she won for herself by wisdom and the strength of law. By her valour Greece now keeps both poverty and bondage at bay.

'I think highly of all Greeks of the Dorian lands, but what I am about to say will apply not to all Dorians, but to the Spartans only. First then, they will not under any circumstances accept terms from you which would mean slavery for Greece; secondly, they will fight you even if the rest of Greece submits. Moreover, there is no use in asking if their numbers are adequate to enable them to do this; suppose a thousand of them take the field – then that thousand will fight you; and so will any number, greater than this or less.'

Xerxes laughed. 'My dear Demaratus,' he exclaimed, 'what an extraordinary thing to say! Do you really suppose a thousand men would fight an army like mine? Now tell me, would *you*, who were once, as you say, king of these people, be willing at this moment to fight ten men single-handed? I hardly think so; yet, if things in

Sparta are really as you have described them, then, according to
your laws, you as king ought to take on a double share – so that if
every Spartan is a match for ten men of mine, I should expect you
to be a match for twenty. Only in that way can you prove the truth
of your claim. But if you Greeks, who think so much of yourselves,
are all of the size and quality of those I have spoken with when they
have visited my court – and of yourself, Demaratus – there is some
danger of your words being nothing but an empty boast. But let
me put my point as reasonably as I can – how is it possible that a
thousand men, or ten thousand, or fifty thousand, should stand up
to an army as big as mine, especially if they were not under a single
master, but all perfectly free to do as they pleased? Suppose them to
have five thousand men: in that case we should be more than a
thousand to one! If, like ours, their troops were subject to the control
of a single man, then possibly for fear of him, in spite of the disparity
in numbers, they might show some sort of factitious courage, or let
themselves be whipped into battle; but, as every man is free to follow
his fancy, it is not conceivable that they should do either. Indeed, my
own opinion is that even on equal terms the Greeks could hardly face
the Persians alone. We, too, have this thing that you were speaking
of – I do not say it is common, but it does exist; for instance, amongst
the Persians in my bodyguard there are men who would willingly
fight with three Greeks together. But you know nothing of such
things, or you could not talk such nonsense.'

'My lord,' Demaratus answered, 'I knew before I began that if
I spoke the truth you would not like it. But, as you demanded the
plain truth and nothing less, I told you how things are with the
Spartans. Yet you are well aware that I now feel but little affection
for my countrymen, who robbed me of my hereditary power and
privileges and made me a fugitive without a home – whereas your
father welcomed me at his court and gave me the means of livelihood
and somewhere to live. Surely it is unreasonable to reject kindness;
any sensible man will cherish it. Personally I do not claim to be able
to fight ten men – or two; indeed I should prefer not even to fight
with one. But should it be necessary – should there be some great
cause to urge me on – then nothing would give me more pleasure
than to stand up to one of those men of yours who claim to be a match

for three Greeks. So it is with the Spartans; fighting singly, they are as good as any, but fighting together they are the best soldiers in the world. They are free – yes – but not entirely free; for they have a master, and that master is Law, which they fear much more than your subjects fear you. Whatever this master commands, they do; and his command never varies: it is never to retreat in battle, however great the odds, but always to stand firm, and to conquer or die. If, my lord, you think that what I have said is nonsense – very well; I am willing henceforward to hold my tongue. This time I spoke because you forced me to speak. In any case, I pray that all may turn out as you desire.'

Xerxes burst out laughing at Demaratus' answer, and good-humouredly let him go.

After the conversation I have recorded above, Xerxes appointed Mascames, son of Megadostes, to the governorship of Doriscus in place of the man who had been given that post by Darius, and then continued his march through Thrace towards Greece. Mascames was later to prove himself a very remarkable person; so much so, in fact, that Xerxes used to send a special present every year in recognition of his superiority to all the governors appointed either by himself or by Darius; moreover his son Artaxerxes showed the same favour to Mascames' descendants. Persian governors had held posts in Thrace and on the Hellespont before Xerxes' expedition, but in the years which succeeded it all of them except the governor of Doriscus were driven out by the Greeks – Mascames no one has yet been able to expel, though many have tried to do so. This is the reason for the annual present from the Persian king. Of the governors who were expelled by the Greeks the only one whom Xerxes considered as a man of any worth was Boges, governor of Eion. Boges he was never tired of praising, and those of his sons who were left in Persia and survived him he treated with marked respect. This man did, indeed, deserve the highest praise; for when he was besieged by the Athenians under Cimon, son of Miltiades, and the chance was offered him of leaving the town on terms and returning to Asia, he refused to do so, because he was afraid the king might think that he had shirked his duty to save his skin; so, rather than surrender, he held out to the last extremity. When all supplies were consumed, he made a huge pile of timber, set it on fire, and then, cutting the throats of his children, wife, concubines, and servants, flung their bodies into the flames; then he collected all the gold and silver in the town, scattered it broadcast from the walls into the Strymon, and ended by leaping into the fire himself. For this behaviour his name is still mentioned in Persia with respect; and it is right that it should be.

From Doriscus Xerxes marched on towards Greece, pressing into his service the men of every nation which lay in his path; for, as I have already recorded, the whole country as far as Thessaly had been forced into subjection and made tributary to Persia by the conquests, first, of Megabazus and, later, of Mardonius. After leaving Doriscus the army passed first by the Samothracian forts, the most westerly of which is Mesembria; the next place is Stryme, a town belonging to the Thasians. Between the two runs the Lisus, a stream which on that occasion failed to provide sufficient water for Xerxes' army. It was drunk dry. This part of the country was once called Gallacia instead of its present name of Briantica; strictly, however, it too belongs to the Cicones. Having crossed the dried-up channel of the Lisus, Xerxes moved on past the Greek towns of Maronia, Dicaea, and Abdera, passing also some well-known lakes in that neighbourhood, namely Ismaris, between Maronia and Stryme, and Bistonis near Dicaea, a lake into which flow the rivers Trauos and Compsatus. At Abdera there was not, to be sure, any well-known lake for him to pass, but he crossed the river Nestus, which there enters the sea. Next he reached the settlements owned by the Thasians upon the continent, in one of which there is a lake about four miles in circumference, full of fish and very salt. It was drunk dry by the pack-animals alone. The town by this lake is called Pistyrus. All these Greek coastal settlements Xerxes kept on his left as he marched westward. The Thracian tribes lying along his route were the Paeti, Cicones, Bistones, Sapaei, Dersaei, Edoni, and Satrae; some of these lived on the coast and furnished ships for the king's fleet, but others lived inland, and of these all the tribes I have mentioned except the Satrae were forced to serve in the army. The Satrae, so far as one knows, have never yet been reduced to subjection, and are the only Thracian people to have kept their independence right down to the present day. The reason for this is the nature of their country, which consists of high mountains, thickly wooded with timber of all sorts and covered with snow. They are also first-rate fighters. It is in the territory of this people that there is an oracle of Dionysus, situated on the loftiest mountain range. The service of the temple belongs to the Bessi, a branch of the Satrae; and there is a Priestess, as at Delphi, to deliver the oracles – which, by the way, are not more involved than the Delphic.

Once through the region mentioned above, Xerxes next passed the Pierian forts, one of which is called Phagres and another Pergamus. His route led him close by the walls, as he kept on his right the great range of Pangaeum, where there are gold and silver mines worked partly by the Pierians and Odomanti but mostly by the Satrae. Then he passed through the country of the Doberes and Paeoplae (Paeonian tribes living north of Pangaeum), and continued in a westerly direction as far as the Strymon and the town of Eion, where Boges, whom I mentioned just now, was governor during his lifetime. The country in the neighbourhood of Mt Pangaeum is known as Phyllis; it extends westward to the Angites, a stream which flows into the Strymon, and southward as far as the Strymon itself. This latter river the Magi tried to propitiate by a sacrifice of white horses, and after performing many other magical tricks in the hope of winning the river's favour, they crossed it by the bridges which they found at Nine Ways, a place in the territory of the Edoni; and when they learnt that Nine Ways was the name of the place, they took nine native boys and nine girls and buried them alive there. Burying people alive is a Persian custom; I understand that Xerxes' wife Amestris in her old age did it to fourteen Persian boys of distinguished family, by way of a present which she hoped the supposed god of the underworld would accept instead of herself.

From the Strymon the army came to a strip of coast running westward, on which stands the Greek town of Argilus. The country here, and for some distance inland, is called Bisaltia. Thence, keeping the Gulf of Posidium on his left, Xerxes marched through the plain of Syleus, past the Greek town of Stagirus, until he arrived at Acanthus. Like the others whom I mentioned before, the inhabitants of these places and of the country round Mt Pangaeum were pressed into his service, those on the coast being forced to sail with the fleet, those inland to march with the army. The road which the Great King took remains untouched to this day; the Thracians hold it in profound reverence and never plough it up or sow crops on it.

At Acanthus Xerxes issued a proclamation of friendship to the people and made them a present of a suit of Median clothes, with many expressions of approval for their enthusiastic support of the war and for the work they had done on the canal. It was while Xerxes was here that Artachaees fell sick and died. He was a man of the Achaemenid family, much respected by Xerxes, and had been in charge of the construction of the canal. He was the biggest man in Persia – about 8 ft 2 ins. high – and had the loudest voice in the world, so that Xerxes was greatly distressed at his death and had him carried out and buried with all pomp and ceremony. The whole army helped to raise a mound over his grave. The people of Acanthus, in obedience to an oracle, offer sacrifice to Artachaees, as to a demi-god, and call upon his name in prayer.

The death of Artachaees was, as I said, very distressing for Xerxes; but things were even worse for the Greeks who had to entertain the Persian army and provide a dinner for the king. They were utterly ruined, and were obliged to leave house and home. For instance, when the Thasians, on behalf of their towns on the mainland, billeted and fed the army, Antipater, the son of Orgeus, a citizen of the highest repute, to whom the arrangements had been entrusted, proved that the meal cost 400 talents of silver. And similar accounts were returned by the officers in the other towns. A great deal of fuss had been made about the meal, and orders for its preparation had been issued a long time in advance; accordingly, the moment that word came from the officers who carried the king's commands, people in every town distributed their stores of grain and employed themselves for months on end in making barley and wheat flour, in buying up and fattening the best cattle they could find, and feeding poultry in coops and waterfowl in ponds, to be ready for the army when it came. In addition to this they ordered the manufacture of drinking cups and mixing-bowls of gold and silver, and of everything else that is needed to adorn the table. All this, of course, was for the king himself and those who dined with him; for the troops in general the preparations were confined to food. On the arrival of the army, there was always a tent ready for Xerxes to take his rest in, while the men bivouacked in the open; but it was when dinner-time came that the real trouble for the unfortunate hosts began. The guests ate their fill and, after spending the night in the place, pulled up the tent next morning, seized the cups and table-gear and everything else it contained, and marched off without leaving a single thing behind. A man of Abdera called Megacreon spoke to the point on this subject, when he advised all the people of the town to take their wives to the temples and pray heaven to continue to spare them one half of their troubles, with proper gratitude for the blessing already received, that King Xerxes was not in the habit of taking *two* dinners a day. It was clear enough that if the orders had been to prepare a morning meal as well as an evening one, the people of Abdera would have had to clear out altogether before Xerxes arrived, or else be hopelessly crushed by the burden of the expense. Nevertheless the various places along the route did manage to carry out their orders, though not without severe suffering.

At Acanthus Xerxes sent the fleet on separately, and ordered the commanders to wait for him at Therma – the town on the gulf to which it has given its name. It was through Therma that he had ascertained his shortest route to lie. From Doriscus to Acanthus the army had been marching in three divisions, of which one under Mardonius and Masistes took the coast road and kept in close touch with the fleet, another under Tritantaechmes and Gergis a parallel route some distance inland, and the third under Smerdomenes and Megabyzus a route between the two. This third division Xerxes himself accompanied.

Having received from Xerxes its orders to proceed, the fleet passed through the Athos canal, which led to the deep bight on which stand the towns of Assa, Pilorus, Singus, and Sarte; from all these places reinforcements were taken on board, and a course was set for the Gulf of Therma. Rounding Ampelus in Torone, they sailed past the towns of Torone, Galepsus, Sermyle, Mecyberna, and Olynthus (the country round here is known as Sithonia), levying more ships and men; but the main body of the fleet sailed direct from Cape Ampelus to Canastraeum (the southernmost point of Pallene), and then took over more reinforcements in both ships and men from Potidaea, Aphytis, Nea, Aege, Therambo, Scione, Mende, and Sane – all towns in what is now called Pallene, but used to be called Phlegra. From here they continued to follow the coast towards the rendezvous at Therma, taking over on the way more men from the towns near Pallene and the Thermaic Gulf – namely Lipaxus, Combreia, Lisae, Gigonus, Campsa, Smila, and Aeneia. All this region is still known as Crossaea. After passing the last of these towns – Aeneia – the fleet found itself off Mygdonia and actually within the gulf, and proceeded to the rendezvous at Therma. The ships also called at Sindus and Chalestra on the river Axius, which forms the boundary between Mygdonia and Bottiaeis. This latter district has a small strip of coastline occupied by the towns of Ichnae and Pella.

While the fleet waited near Therma and the Axius and the intervening towns, Xerxes with the army was on his way from Acanthus by the inland road to the rendezvous. He passed through Paeonia and Crestonia to the river Echeidorus, which rises in the latter country and flows through Mygdonia, to reach the sea by way of the marshland at the mouth of the Axius. It was during this march that his pack-camels were attacked by lions, which came down from their haunts at night and never molested either the men or any of the other animals, but only the camels. I am puzzled at what it could have been that made the lions ignore every other living creature and set only upon the camels – beasts which they had never seen, or had any experience of, before. This part of the country – namely the region between the river Nestus which runs through Abdera and the Achelous which runs through Acarnania – abounds with lions, and also with wild oxen, which have those enormous horns that are imported into Greece. There are no lions anywhere in Europe east of the Nestus, or in the continent west of the Achelous; they exist only in the country between those rivers.

At Therma Xerxes halted his army, and the troops went into camp. They occupied the whole seaboard from Therma in Mygdonia to the Lydias and Haliacmon – two rivers which unite and form the boundary between Bottiaeis and Macedonia. While they were encamped here, all the rivers I have mentioned supplied enough water for their needs except the Echeidorus, which failed.

Xerxes could see from Therma the Thessalian mountains – the

towering peaks of Olympus and Ossa – and on being informed that between the two mountains there was a narrow gorge through which the river Peneus ran, and also a road leading into Thessaly, he suddenly felt that he would like to go by sea and inspect the mouth of the river. His intention was to take the army by the upper road through the inland parts of Macedonia into Perrhaebia, past the town of Gonnus; for that, he heard, was the safest route. No sooner, therefore, had the fancy taken him than he acted upon it; and going aboard the Sidonian vessel which he always used for any such occasion, he gave the signal to the rest of the fleet to put to sea, leaving the army behind in its encampments. The appearance of the river-mouth, on his arrival there, was a great surprise to him, so that he called the guides and asked them if it was possible to turn the course of the river so as to bring it to the sea at some other point. Now it is said that in the remote past Thessaly was a lake – a not unreasonable supposition, as the whole country is enclosed by lofty hills. To the eastward is the great barrier of Pelion and Ossa, two mountains whose bases form a continuous chain; then there is the range of Olympus on the north, Pindus on the west, and Othrys on the south. In the centre of this ring of mountains lies the low plain of Thessaly. A number of rivers pour their waters into it, the best known being the Peneus, Apidanus, Onochonus, Enipeus, and Pamisus; all these flow down from the surrounding mountains, unite into a single stream, and find their way to the sea through one narrow gorge. After the junction the other names are all dropped and the river is known simply as the Peneus. The story then is, that, ages ago, before the gorge existed and while there was as yet no outlet for the water, these rivers, though, like Lake Boebeis, they had yet no names, poured down from the hills as much water as they do to-day, and so made Thessaly an inland sea. The natives of Thessaly have a tradition that the gorge which forms the outlet for the river was made by Poseidon, and the story is a reasonable one; for if one believes that it is Poseidon who shakes the earth and that chasms caused by earthquake are attributable to him, then the mere sight of this place would be enough to make one say that it is Poseidon's handiwork. It certainly appeared to me that the cleft in the mountains had been caused by an earthquake.

So when Xerxes asked if there was any other outlet by which the Peneus could reach the sea, the guides, who were perfectly familiar with the facts, replied, 'No, my lord; there is no other outlet but this, because the whole of Thessaly is surrounded with a ring of hills, like a crown.' At this Xerxes is said to have remarked: 'The Thessalians are sensible men; it was with this very danger in view that they made their submission to me in good time – they realized, amongst other things, that their country is easy to take and very vulnerable. Nothing more would have been needed than to flood the country by damming the gorge, and so forcing the river from its present channel; that would have put all Thessaly except the mountains under water.' In saying this he had, of course, the Aleuadae in mind – the Thessalian family who were the first Greeks to submit to the Persian king. Doubtless he thought that they had made the offer of friendship in the name of the people generally.

Then, having seen the place, and having made this comment, Xerxes returned by sea to Therma.

His stay in Pieria lasted a number of days, during which one third of his army was felling the forest through the mountains of Macedonia, making a route for his troops to follow into Perrhaebia. Meanwhile the representatives who had been sent to Greece to demand submission rejoined the army – some empty-handed, others bringing the earth and water. Those who gave the tokens of submission were the following: the Thessalians, Dolopes, Aenianes, Perrhaebi, Locrians, Magnetes, Malians, Achaeans of Phthiotis, Thebans, and all the other Boeotians except the people of Plataea and Thespiae. Against these the Greeks who determined to resist the invader swore an oath to the effect that, once the war was fought to a successful conclusion, they would punish all men of Greek blood, who without compulsion yielded to the Persians, and dedicate a tenth part of their property to the God at Delphi.

To Athens and Sparta Xerxes sent no demand for submission because of what happened to the messengers whom Darius had sent on a previous occasion: at Athens they were thrown into the pit like criminals, at Sparta they were pushed into a well – and told that if they wanted earth and water for the king, to get them from there. This time, therefore, Xerxes refrained from sending a request. Just what disagreeable consequences were suffered by the Athenians for this treatment of the king's messengers, I am unable to say; perhaps it was the destruction of their city and the countryside around it – though I do not myself believe that this happened as a direct result of their crime. The case is clear, however, with respect to the Spartans: upon them fell the anger of Agamemnon's herald Talthybius. There is in Sparta a temple dedicated to Talthybius, and a family – the Talthybiadae – descended from him, which enjoys the sole privilege of holding the office of herald. Now there was a long period after the incident I have mentioned above, during which the Spartans were unable to obtain favourable signs from their sacrifices; this caused them deep concern, and they held frequent assemblies at which the question 'Is there any Spartan who is willing to die for his country?' was put by the public crier. Thereupon two Spartans, Sperchias, the son of Aneristus, and Bulis, the son of Nicolas, both men of good family and great wealth, volunteered to offer their lives to Xerxes in atonement for Darius' messengers who had been killed in Sparta. They were dispatched accordingly to Persia to meet their doom. The courage of these two men is indeed admirable, and what followed is no less so. On their way to Susa they visited Hydarnes, a Persian by birth who was in command of the whole Asiatic seaboard; and by him they were given a hospitable welcome and invited to dinner. During the meal Hydarnes said: 'Why is it, gentlemen, that you refuse to be friends with the king? You have only to look at me and the position I enjoy to see that he knows how to reward merit. Now Xerxes believes that you, too, are men of merit; and both of you, if only you would submit, might find yourselves in authority over lands in Greece which he would give you.'

'Hydarnes,' came the answer, 'the advice you give us does not spring from a full knowledge of the situation. You know one half of what is involved, but not the other half. You understand well enough what slavery is, but freedom you have never experienced, so you do not know if it tastes sweet or bitter. If you ever did come to experience it, you would advise us to fight for it not with spears only, but with axes too.'

After this they continued their journey to Susa, and the first thing that happened when they entered the presence of the king was that the men of the royal bodyguard ordered – and, indeed, attempted to compel – them to fall flat on the ground in the act of worship. The two Spartans, however, declared that they would never do such a thing, even though the guards should push their heads down on to the floor. It was not, they said, the custom in Sparta to worship a mere man like themselves, and it was not for that purpose that they had come to Persia. So they persisted in their refusal, adding words to the following effect: 'My lord King of the Medes, the Spartans sent us here to suffer punishment in reparation for the murder of the Persian messengers in Sparta'; to which Xerxes with truly noble generosity replied that he would not behave like the Spartans, who by murdering the ambassadors of a foreign power had broken the law which all the world holds sacred. He had no intention of doing the very thing for which he blamed them, or, by taking reprisals, of freeing the Spartans from the burden of their crime.

This conduct on the part of the Spartans succeeded for a time in allaying the anger of Talthybius, in spite of the fact that Sperchias and Bulis returned home alive; long afterwards, however, during the war between Athens and the Peloponnese, the Spartans believe that it was aroused again – and in this, I think, the hand of God was clearly to be seen. That Talthybius' anger should have fallen upon *ambassadors*, and should not have ceased until it was fully satisfied, was only right; but that it should have struck the sons of the very men who visited the Persian king because of it – that the objects of it should have been Bulis' son Nicolaus and Sperchias' son Aneristus, the same man who took Halieis, a Tirynthian colony, with a merchant ship and an armed crew – this, to me at least, is clear evidence of divine intervention. What happened was that these two men were sent by the Spartans on a mission to Asia and were betrayed by Sitalces son of Teres, the king of Thrace, and by Nymphodorus son of Pythes, a native of Abdera; they were made prisoners at Bisanthe on the Hellespont and taken to Attica, where they were put to death by the Athenians in company with Aristeas son of Adeimantus, of Corinth.[1] This, however, took place long after Xerxes' invasion of Greece, and I must get back to my story.

The purpose of Xerxes' expedition, which was directed nominally

1. Late in 430 B.C.; the latest event mentioned by Herodotus.

against Athens, was in fact the conquest of the whole of Greece. The various Greek communities had long been aware of this, but they viewed the coming danger with very different eyes. Some had already made their submission, and were consequently in good spirits, because they were sure of getting off lightly at the invaders' hands; others, who had refused to submit, were thrown into panic partly because there were not enough ships in Greece to meet the Persians with any chance of success, and partly because most of the Greeks were unwilling to fight and all too ready to accept Persian dominion. At this point I find myself compelled to express an opinion which I know most people will object to; nevertheless, as I believe it to be true, I will not suppress it. If the Athenians, through fear of the approaching danger, had abandoned their country, or if they had stayed there and submitted to Xerxes, there would have been no attempt to resist the Persians by sea; and, in the absence of a Greek fleet, it is easy to see what would have been the course of events on land. However many lines of fortification the Spartans had built across the Isthmus, they would have been deserted by their confederates; not that their allies would have wished to desert them, but they could not have helped doing so, because one by one they would have fallen victims to the Persian naval power. Thus the Spartans would have been left alone – to perform prodigies of valour and to die nobly. Or, on the other hand, it is possible that before things came to the ultimate test, the sight of the rest of Greece submitting to Persia might have driven them to make terms with Xerxes. In either case the Persian conquest of Greece would have been assured; for I cannot myself see what possible use there could have been in fortifying the Isthmus, if the Persians had command of the sea. In view of this, therefore, one is surely right in saying that Greece was saved by the Athenians. It was the Athenians who held the balance: whichever side they joined was sure to prevail. It was the Athenians, too, who, having chosen that Greece should live and preserve her freedom, roused to battle the other Greek states which had not yet submitted. It was the Athenians who – after God – drove back the Persian king. Not even the terrifying warnings of the oracle at Delphi could persuade them to abandon Greece; they stood firm and had the courage to meet the invader.

The Athenians had sent their envoys to Delphi really to ask an oracle, and as soon as the customary rites were performed and they had entered the shrine and taken their seats, the Priestess Aristonice uttered the following prophecy:

> *Why sit you, doomed ones? Fly to the world's end, leaving*
> *Home and the heights your city circles like a wheel.*
> *The head shall not remain in its place, nor the body,*
> *Nor the feet beneath, nor the hands, nor the parts between;*
> *But all is ruined, for fire and the headlong God of War*
> *Speeding in a Syrian chariot shall bring you low.*
> *Many a tower shall he destroy, not yours alone,*
> *And give to pitiless fire many shrines of gods,*
> *Which even now stand sweating, with fear quivering,*
> *While over the roof-tops black blood runs streaming*
> *In prophecy of woe that needs must come. But rise,*
> *Haste from the sanctuary and bow your hearts to grief.*

The Athenian envoys heard these words with dismay; indeed they were about to abandon themselves to despair at the dreadful fate which was prophesied, when Timon, the son of Androbulus and one of the most distinguished men in Delphi, suggested that they should take branches of olive in their hands and, in the guise of suppliants, approach the oracle a second time. The Athenians acted upon this suggestion. 'Lord Apollo,' they said, 'can you not, in consideration of these olive boughs which we have brought you, give us some better prophecy about our country? Otherwise we will never leave the holy place but stay here till we die.'

Thereupon the Prophetess uttered a second prophecy, which ran as follows:

Not wholly can Pallas win the heart of Olympian Zeus,
Though she prays him with many prayers and all her subtlety;
Yet will I speak to you this other word, as firm as adamant:
Though all else shall be taken within the bound of Cecrops
And the fastness of the holy mountain of Cithaeron,
Yet Zeus the all-seeing grants to Athene's prayer
That the wooden wall only shall not fall, but help you and your children.
But await not the host of horse and foot coming from Asia,
Nor be still, but turn your back and withdraw from the foe.
Truly a day will come when you will meet him face to face.

> *Divine Salamis, you will bring death to women's sons*
> *When the corn is scattered, or the harvest gathered in.*

This second answer seemed to be, as indeed it was, less menacing than the first; so the envoys wrote it down and returned to Athens. When it was made public upon their arrival in the city, and the attempt to explain it began, amongst the various opinions which were expressed there were two mutually exclusive interpretations. Some of the older men supposed that the prophecy meant that the Acropolis would escape destruction, on the grounds that the Acropolis was fenced in the old days with a thorn-hedge, and that this was the 'wooden wall' of the oracle; but others thought that by this expression the oracle meant the ships, and they urged in consequence that everything should be abandoned in favour of the immediate preparation of a fleet. There was, however, for those who believed 'wooden wall' to mean ships, one disturbing thing – namely, the last two lines of the Priestess' prophecy:

> *Divine Salamis, you will bring death to women's sons*
> *When the corn is scattered, or the harvest gathered in.*

This was a very awkward statement and caused profound disturbance amongst all who took the wooden wall to signify ships; for the professional interpreters understood the lines to mean that they would be beaten at Salamis in a fight at sea. There was, however, a man in Athens who had recently made a name for himself[1] – Themistocles called Neocles' son; he now came forward and declared that there was an important point in which the professional interpreters were mistaken. If, he maintained, the disaster referred to was to strike the Athenians, it would not have been expressed in such mild language. 'Hateful Salamis' would surely have been a more likely phrase than 'divine Salamis', if the inhabitants of the country were doomed to destruction there. On the contrary, the true interpretation was that the oracle referred not to the Athenians but to their enemies. The 'wooden wall' did, indeed, mean the ships; so he advised his countrymen to prepare at once to meet the invader at sea.

1. In reality, he had probably been elected to the chief magistracy (archonship) already in 493, when Dionysius of Halicarnassus names him to fix a date in Roman history. Hostile (Alcmeonid?) sources are no doubt responsible. Cf. p. 357 and n.

The Athenians found Themistocles' explanation of the oracle preferable to that of the professional interpreters, who had not only tried to dissuade them from preparing to fight at sea but had been against offering opposition of any sort. The only thing to do was, according to them, to abandon Attica altogether and seek a home elsewhere.

Once on a previous occasion Themistocles had succeeded in getting his views accepted, to the great benefit of his country. The Athenians had amassed a large sum of money from the produce of the mines at Laurium, which they proposed to share out amongst themselves at the rate of ten drachmas a man; Themistocles, however, persuaded them to give up this idea and, instead of distributing the money, to spend it on the construction of two hundred warships for use in the war with Aegina. The outbreak of this war at that moment saved Greece by forcing Athens to become a maritime power. In point of fact the two hundred ships were not employed for the purpose for which they were built, but were available for Greece in her hour of need. The Athenians also found it necessary to expand this existing fleet by laying down new ships, and they determined in debate after the discussion on the oracle, to take the god's advice and meet the invader at sea with all the force they possessed, and with any other Greeks who were willing to join them.

At a conference of the Greek states who were loyal to the general cause guarantees were exchanged, and the decision was reached that the first thing to be done was to patch up their own quarrels and stop any fighting which happened to be going on amongst members of the confederacy. There were a number of such disputes at the time, the most serious being the quarrel between Athens and Aegina. Having learnt that Xerxes and his army had reached Sardis, they next resolved to send spies into Asia to get information about the Persian forces; at the same time, in the hope of uniting, if it were possible, the whole Greek world and of bringing all the various communities to undertake joint action in face of the common danger, they decided to send an embassy to Argos to conclude an alliance, another to Gelon, the son of Dinomenes, in Sicily, and others, again, to Corcyra and Crete. Gelon was said to be very powerful – far more powerful than anyone else of Greek nationality.

These decisions were put into force at once. The private quarrels were made up, and three men sent off to Asia to collect information. They arrived in Sardis and found out all they could about the king's army, but were caught in the process, tortured by the Persian army commanders, and condemned to death. But when Xerxes was told that they were about to be executed, he disapproved of his generals' decision and sent men from his bodyguard with orders, if the three spies were still alive, to bring them before him. As the sentence had not yet been carried out, the spies were brought to the king, who, having satisfied himself about the reason for their presence in Sardis, instructed his guards to take them round and let them see the whole army, infantry and cavalry, and then, when they were satisfied that they had seen everything, to let them go without molestation to whatever country they pleased. After giving this order he explained the purpose of it by pointing out that, if the spies had been executed, the Greeks would not have been able to learn in good time how incalculably great the Persian strength was – and the killing of three men would not have done the enemy much harm; but if, on the other hand, the spies returned home, he was confident that their report on the magnitude of the Persian power would induce the Greeks to surrender their liberty before the actual invasion took place, so that there would be no need to go to the trouble of fighting a war at all. Xerxes had expressed a similar opinion on another occasion, when he was at Abydos and saw boats sailing down the Hellespont with cargoes of food from the Black Sea for Aegina and the Peloponnese. His counsellors, learning that they were enemy vessels, were prepared to seize them, and looked to the king for orders to do so. 'Where are they bound for?' Xerxes asked. 'To Persia's enemies, my lord,' came the answer, 'with a cargo of grain.' 'Well,' said the king, 'are we not bound ourselves for the same destination? And does not our equipment include grain amongst other things? I do not see that the men in those ships are doing us any harm in carrying our grain for us.' The three spies, then, after their tour of inspection, were allowed to return to Europe.

The Greeks who had united for resistance to Persia next dispatched their representatives to Argos. The Argives themselves explain their subsequent behaviour as follows: they were aware from the beginning of the Persian preparations against Greece, and knew very well that the Greeks would try to enlist their support in meeting the invasion; so they sent to Delphi for advice upon what action would, under the circumstances, be best for them to take. The reason for this step was the fact that six thousand of their men had recently been killed by the Spartans under Cleomenes, the son of Anaxandrides. The Priestess' answer to their question was this:

> Loathed by your neighbours, dear to the immortal gods,
> Hold your javelin within and sit upon your guard.
> Guard the head well, and the head will save the body.

This oracle had already been delivered, when the envoys arrived in Argos, and entered the council-chamber to deliver their message. The Argive answer was, that they were willing to do what they were asked upon two conditions: first they must obtain a thirty years' truce with Sparta, and, secondly, share with Sparta, on equal terms, the command of the confederate forces. By right Argos was entitled to the sole command; nevertheless they would be content with an equal division.

Such, according to them, was their government's answer, in spite of the fact that the oracle had forbidden them to join the confederacy. Moreover, though they shrank from disobeying the oracle, it was important to them to secure the thirty years' truce, to give their sons the chance of growing up during the period of peace; and if they failed to secure it, and were unlucky enough to suffer another defeat – this time at the hands of the Persians – it seemed only too likely that they would find themselves permanently subject to Sparta. The Spartan envoys replied to the demands of the Argive government by saying that they would refer the question of the truce to their own government at home; on the other matter, however, namely the army command, they already had their instructions, and their answer was that Sparta had two kings and Argos only one, and it was not possible to deprive either of the Spartan kings of his command; on the other hand, there was nothing to prevent the Argive ruler from expressing his views in conjunction with the two Spartans.

The Argives add that they found the Spartan attitude intolerably presumptuous, and, rather than give way to it, they preferred to submit to foreign domination; accordingly they gave notice to the envoys that they must be out of the country before sunset, or be treated as enemies.

So much for the Argive account of this transaction; there is, however, another story current in Greece, to the effect that Xerxes sent a man to Argos before his army started on its march. 'Men of Argos,' this person is supposed to have said upon his arrival, 'King Xerxes has a message for you. We Persians believe that we are descended from Perses, whose father was Danae's son Perseus, and whose mother was Andromeda the daughter of Cepheus. Thus we are of the same blood as yourselves, and it would not be right for us to make war upon the people from whom we have sprung, any more than it would be right for you to help others by opposing us. Rather you should hold aloof from the coming struggle and take no part in it. If things turn out as I hope they will, there is no people I shall hold in greater esteem than you.'

The story goes on to say that the Argives were much impressed by Xerxes' message; they made no promises for the moment, and put forward no demand for a share in the command of the army; later, however, when the Greeks were trying to obtain their support, they did make the claim, because they knew that the Spartans would refuse to grant it, and that they would thus have an excuse for taking no part in the war. There are people in Greece who say that this account is borne out by a remark made long afterwards by Artaxerxes. Callias, the son of Hipponicus, and a number of other Athenians were in Susa, the city of Memnon, on quite different business, and it so happened that their visit coincided with that of some representatives from Argos, who had been sent to ask Xerxes' son Artaxerxes if the friendly relations, which the Argives had established with his father, still held good, or if they were now considered by Persia as enemies. 'They do indeed hold good,' Artaxerxes is said to have replied; 'there is no city which I believe to be a better friend to me than Argos.'

For my own part I cannot positively state that Xerxes either did, or did not, send the messenger to Argos; nor can I guarantee the story of the Argives going to Susa and asking Artaxerxes about their relationship with Persia. I express no opinion on this matter other than that of the Argives themselves. One thing, however, I am very sure of: and that is, that if all mankind agreed to meet, and everyone brought his own faults along with him for the purpose of exchanging them for somebody else's, there is not a man who, after taking a good look at his neighbour's faults, would not be only too happy to return home with his own. My business is to record what people say, but I am by no means bound to believe it – and that may be taken to apply to this book as a whole. There is yet another story about the Argives: it was they, according to some, who invited the Persians to invade Greece, because their war with Sparta was going badly and they felt that anything would be better than their present sufferings.

Another embassy was sent by the confederates to Sicily, to confer with Gelon. One of the allied representatives was the Spartan Syagrus.

Gelon's ancestor, who first settled at Gela, came from the island of Telos, off Triopium, and when the settlement at Gela was made by Antiphemus and the Lindians of Rhodes, he took part in the expedition. In course of time his descendants became priests of the Earth Goddesses, an office which they continued to hold ever since Telines came into possession of it. How Telines got it makes a remarkable story: as a result of party struggles in Gela, a number of men had been compelled to leave the town and to seek refuge in Mactorium on the neighbouring hills. These people were reinstated by Telines, who accomplished the feat, not by armed force, but simply by virtue of the sacred symbols of the Earth Goddesses. How or whence he came by these things I do not know; but it was upon them, and them only, that he relied; and he brought back the exiles on condition that he and his descendants after him should hold the office of Priest. In view of what I have heard, it is very surprising that Telines should have been capable of such a feat. I have always imagined that it is by no means everybody who is equal to things like that, which usually call for both strength and courage; yet people in Sicily maintain that Telines was neither strong nor brave, but, on the contrary, a rather soft and effeminate person. In any case, that was how he obtained his office.

After the death of Cleander, the son of Pantares – he was murdered by Sabyllus after ruling Gela for seven years – power passed to his brother Hippocrates; and Gelon, the descendant of the priest Telines, was, with many others including Aenesidemus and Pataecus, a member of his bodyguard. Gelon was soon to be General of Cavalry, for he had served with very great distinction under Hippocrates in various battles and sieges against Callipolis, Naxos, Zancle, Leontini, Syracuse, and a number of native peoples besides. Of the towns here mentioned not one escaped subjection except Syracuse, which, after a defeat on the river Elorus, was saved by the intervention of Corinth and Corcyra, who negotiated a peace on the condition that Syracuse should cede Camarina to Hippocrates, a town that in old days belonged to it.

Hippocrates enjoyed absolute power at Gela for the same length of time as his brother Cleander, and died attacking Hybla during a campaign against the Siccls. His death gave Gelon his opportunity: masking his real purpose under the pretence of supporting Hippocrates' sons, Eucleides and Cleander, in their struggle against the people of Gela, who were now eager to throw off the yoke, he crushed the insurgents by force of arms, and then, robbing the two young men of the fruits of victory, seized power himself. He followed this successful stroke by making himself master of Syracuse. The Syracusan landowners had been expelled by the commons with the help of their slaves (known as Cyllyrii), and had fled for refuge to Casmene. Gelon brought them back to Syracuse and got possession of the town; for the commons made no resistance, but surrendered as soon as they saw him coming.

The acquisition of Syracuse made Gelon much less interested than before in Gela. He handed it over to his brother Hieron, and himself proceeded to strengthen Syracuse, which had now become the apple of his eye. At once Syracuse shot up and budded like a young tree; Gelon brought to it all the people of Camarina, which he had razed to the ground, and gave them citizen rights, and, in addition, more than half the population of Gela. The Sicilian Megara, too, had to make its contribution – the town had been at war with Gelon and had surrendered on terms; the men of substance, who had started the war, naturally expected death at Gelon's hands, but they were transferred instead to Syracuse and given citizen rights like the rest. The Megarian commons, who imagined they would be well treated because they had had no share of responsibility for the war, were also brought to Syracuse and then sold as slaves abroad. The Sicilian Euboea suffered similar treatment, the same distinction being made between the men of property and the commons. In both cases Gelon's motive was his belief that the masses are very disagreeable to live with. In these ways Gelon rose to despotic power and wielded very great influence.

And now the envoys from Greece arrived in Syracuse, approached Gelon, and spoke to the following effect: 'We have been sent by the Spartans and their allies to obtain your help against the foreigner. You are, of course, aware of what is coming to Greece; that a Persian is about to bridge the Hellespont and to march against us out of Asia with all the armies of the east at his back, and that his true purpose, which he veils under the pretence of an attack on Athens, is the subjugation of the whole of Greece. Your power is great; as lord of Sicily you possess no inconsiderable portion of the Greek world; we ask you, therefore, to help us, and to add your strength to ours in our struggle to maintain our country's liberty. Greece united will be strong and a match for the invader; but if some of us betray and others stand aside, and only a minority is sound, then there is reason to fear that all Greece may fall. Do not imagine that if the Persians defeat us in battle they will not afterwards visit *you*. They will – so be on your guard in time. By supporting us you will be defending yourself. It usually happens that well-laid plans have a prosperous issue.'

Gelon's answer to this speech was made with passionate vehemence. 'What,' he cried, 'have you the face to come here and urge me with your selfish arguments to help you resist a foreign invader? Have you forgotten that I, too, was once at war with a foreign power – the Carthaginians – and that I applied to you for help? Yes, and I begged you to avenge upon the men of Egesta their murder of Dorieus the son of Anaxandrides, and offered to help free the ports which have been the source of such profit and advantage to you. But what was your answer? You refused to come either to help me or to avenge Dorieus' death – and for all you cared, this whole country might now be subject to foreign rule. Well – luck, as it happens, has come my way; the wheel has come full circle and now it is you who are in danger – so you remember Gelon! Nevertheless, though you treated me with contempt, I will not imitate your conduct. I am willing to help you by a contribution of 200 ships of war, 20,000 heavy-armed infantry, 2000 cavalry, 2000 archers, 2000 slingers, and 2000 light horsemen; and I undertake to provision the entire Greek army for as long as the war may last. My offer, however, is subject to one condition – that the supreme command of the Greek forces against the Persians shall be mine. On any other terms I will neither come myself nor send troops.'

This was too much for Syagrus, and he burst out: 'Agamemnon, son of Pelops, would groan in his grave if he heard that Sparta had been robbed of her command by Gelon and his Syracusans! Let us hear no more of our giving you command. If you wish to help Greece, you must understand that it will be under Spartan leadership. If you dislike the idea of a subordinate position, then you need not help.'

Gelon, seeing from what Syagrus said that he was unlikely to accept his terms, made his last proposal. 'My Spartan friend,' he said, 'reproaches have a way of making a man angry; nevertheless in spite of your insults I will answer you with courtesy. Surely, if you maintain so eagerly your right to the command, it is only reasonable that I should urge my own claim more strongly still, as I have a much bigger fleet and an army many times the size of yours. However, since my proposal is so painful to you, I will make some concession: suppose you command the army, and I the navy. Or, if you prefer to command at sea, I am willing to take over the land forces. You must either be content with this, or do without the powerful support I am able to give you.'

The Athenian envoy gave Syagrus no time to reply to this, but as soon as Gelon had made his offer, 'King of Syracuse,' he cried, 'Greece did not send us to ask for a commander but for an army. But clearly you are unwilling to send troops unless you have command – the one thing you are set upon getting. Now when you asked for the supreme command of all the Greek forces, we were content to hold our tongues, because we knew that our colleague from Sparta would be quite capable of answering for us both; but things are different now that, having failed in your original claim, you ask to command at sea. Even if Sparta allowed this, we should not. Command of the fleet, provided Sparta herself does not want it, belongs to us. We do not object to Sparta having it if she wishes, but we refuse to give it up to anybody else. What would be the use of our having built up the finest navy in Greece if we surrendered the command of it to the Syracusans? Are we not Athenians – the most ancient of all Greek peoples, the only nation never to have left the soil from which it sprang? Did not the poet Homer say that we sent to Troy the best man for ordering and marshalling an army? Surely, then, we need not be ashamed of speaking as we do.'

'My friend,' Gelon replied, 'it looks as if you have the commanders – but will not have any men for them to command. Since, therefore, you claim everything and yield nothing, you had better go home as quickly as you can and tell Greece that the spring of the year, the fairest of the four seasons, is lost to her.'

That was the end of the Greek negotiations with Gelon, and the envoys set out for home.

Gelon himself was afraid that Greece would be unable to survive the Persian invasion; at the same time, as lord of Sicily, he could not bring himself to go to the Peloponnese and submit to taking orders from Spartans. Accordingly he chose a different course. As soon as news came that Xerxes was over the Hellespont, he sent three galleys under the charge of Cadmus, the son of Scythes, a native of Cos, with instructions to go to Delphi, where, equipped with a large sum of money and plenty of friendly words, he was to wait and see how the war would go; then, if the Persians won, he was to give the money to Xerxes together with earth and water of Gelon's dominions. If the Greeks won, he was to bring the money back again.

Some time before this Cadmus had inherited the position of absolute master of Cos from his father, who had established his power there on firm foundations; yet of his own free will, without threat of violence from any quarter, he had, simply from his sense of justice, abdicated his power and handed it over to the people. He then left home for Sicily, where he took the town of Zancle with[1] the Samians – or Messene, as it was afterwards called – and lived there. This was

---

1. Some manuscripts here read 'with' and some 'from'. For the events, cf. p. 396, above; but Cadmus' exact part in them (or after) is not clear.

how Cadmus came to Sicily, and was the reason why Gelon, having had evidence already of his sense of honour, chose him for the mission to Delphi. And now yet another honest action, perhaps the most remarkable of all, was to be added to the former ones: having in his hands the large sum of money which Gelon had entrusted to him, with every opportunity of keeping it, he preferred not to; and after the Greek victory, and the departure of Xerxes, he returned to Sicily with the money intact.

There is a story in Sicily that Gelon would have sent help to Greece in spite of the necessity of serving under Spartan commanders had it not been for the action of Terillus, the son of Crinippus and ruler of Himera. Driven from his home by Aenesidemus' son Theron, the master of Agrigentum, he brought into Sicily just about this time an army 300,000 strong, from Carthage, Libya, Iberia, Liguria, Helisycia, Sardinia, and Corsica – under the command of Hamilcar, the son of Hanno and king of Carthage. Terillus had induced Hamilcar to bring over this force partly by the friendship which existed between them, but more particularly through the warm support of Anaxilaus of Rhegium, the son of Cretines; for Anaxilaus, who was married to Terillus' daughter Cydippe, and wished to be of service to his father-in-law, gave Hamilcar his own children as hostages in order to persuade him to undertake the expedition. Under these circumstances, as it was impossible for Gelon to give military aid to Greece, he sent the money to Delphi. The Sicilians also maintain that the victory of Gelon and Theron over Hamilcar of Carthage took place on the same day as the Greek victory over Persia at Salamis. Hamilcar was Carthaginian on his father's side only, for his mother came from Syracuse; he won the throne of Carthage by right of merit, and it is said that during the battle, when things were beginning to go against him, he vanished. Gelon afterwards searched for him everywhere, but there was no trace of him, alive or dead. The tradition in Carthage – and it may well be true – is that all the time the battle lasted, which was from dawn to late in the evening, Hamilcar remained in camp trying to obtain a favourable omen from sacrifices, burning whole carcasses on an immense fire; and at last, seeing, as he poured the wine upon the sacrificed victims, that his army was giving way, he leapt into the flames and was burnt to nothing. But whatever explanation we adopt of his disappearance, the fact remains that the Carthaginians offer sacrifice to him, and monuments were erected to him in all their colonies in addition to the one – the most splendid of all – in Carthage itself. So ended the campaign in Sicily.

The envoys who went to Sicily called also at Corcyra and put their request for help in the same words as they used to Gelon. The immediate result was a promise from the Corcyraeans to send a fleet in support of the alliance. It was impossible, they said, to stand aside and see Greece overwhelmed; they must help her to the utmost of their power, because if she fell not a day would pass before they themselves were reduced to slavery. This answer sounded promising enough, but when the time came to act upon it, the Corcyraeans changed their minds; and having put into commission a fleet of sixty warships, they dawdled about before getting to sea, and then sailed only as far as the Peloponnese, where they hung round in the neighbourhood of Pylos and Taenarum, waiting, like Gelon, to see the result of the fighting. They thought it most unlikely that the Greeks would win; the Persians, in their opinion, would gain a complete victory and make themselves masters of all Greece. Their conduct was deliberately designed to enable them to say, in this event, to Xerxes that, though they might have answered the Greek appeal for aid by sending a fleet second in strength only to that of Athens, they had refused to do so, not wishing to oppose him or to take any action which he would not like. They hoped, no doubt, that this would get them better treatment than the other Greek states – and so, indeed, it would have done, I admit. They also had an excuse ready to offer to the Greeks – and used it when the time came and they were reproached for their failure to send assistance. The excuse was that they had fitted out sixty ships, but had been prevented by prevailing north-easters from getting round Cape Malea: this explained their absence from the battle of Salamis – an absence in no way due to disloyalty or cowardice.

The Cretans, on the arrival of the Greek envoys with their appeal, sent to Delphi to inquire jointly whether or not it would be to their advantage to make common cause with Greece. 'Foolish men,' the oracle replied, 'do you not still resent all the tears which Minos in his anger caused you to weep after you helped Menelaus? Was he not angry because they did not help you to avenge his death at Camicus, whereas you did help them to avenge the rape by a foreign prince of a woman from Sparta?' When the Cretans heard that answer, they refrained from joining the alliance.

The story goes that Minos went to Sicania – or Sicily, as it is now called – in search of Daedalus, and there met a violent death. In course of time all the Cretans except the people of Polichna and Praesus, encouraged by omens from heaven, went with a large fleet to Sicania, where for five years they besieged Camicus – a town which in my day belonged to Agrigentum. Unable to take the place, or to continue the siege because of lack of provisions, they finally gave up and went away. In the course of their voyage they were caught by a violent storm off Iapygia and driven ashore, and, as their vessels were smashed up and they had no apparent means of getting back to Crete, they built for themselves the town of Hyria. Here they stayed, and instead of Cretans, became the mainland Iapygians of Messapia. From Hyria they founded the other towns which the people of Tarentum, long after, suffered such severe loss in attempting to overthrow; indeed, on that occasion there was the worst slaughter in Greek history; not only the Tarentines were involved but the people of Rhegium as well, for they were compelled by Micythus the son of Choerus to support Tarentum and lost three thousand men. The losses of Tarentum were too many to count. Micythus had been a household servant of Anaxilaus and was left by him in charge of Rhegium. It was he who settled in Tegea in Arcadia after his expulsion from Rhegium and made the offering of all those well-known statues at Olympia. However, I must leave this digression about Rhegium and Tarentum and get back to my story.

According to the tradition in Praesus, men of various nationality, but especially Greeks, came to settle in Crete after it was depopulated by the expedition to Sicily; then in the third generation after the death of Minos came the Trojan war, in which the Cretans proved themselves by no means the most despicable champions of Menelaus; their reward for this service on their return home was famine and plague for both men and cattle, so that for the second time Crete was denuded of its population. Thus it happens that the present Cretans, together with the remnant of the former population, are the third people to live in the island. It was these events of which the Delphic Priestess reminded the Cretans in her answer to their question, and thereby prevented them from joining the Greek confederacy in spite of their readiness to do so.

The Thessalians did not submit to Persia until they were compelled, for they showed plainly enough that the intrigues of the Aleuadae were not to their liking. No sooner had the news reached them of the imminent crossing of the Persian army into Europe than they sent representatives to the Isthmus, where delegates from all Greek towns loyal to the common cause were assembled. On their arrival the Thessalian delegates addressed the assembly in these terms: 'Fellow countrymen, in order to save Thessaly and the whole of Greece, it is necessary to defend the passage past Mt Olympus. We are ready to assist you in the defence of this vital pass, and you, for your part, must send a strong force. If you fail to do so, we give you fair warning that we shall come to terms with Persia. We are in an exposed position, and cannot be expected, alone and unassisted, to give our lives merely to save the rest of you. If you are unwilling to send us aid, you cannot compel us to fight your battle for you; for sheer inability is stronger than any compulsion. We shall try to devise some means of saving ourselves.'

The Greek answer was to determine to send an army by sea to Thessaly, to defend the pass. The troops assembled and, after passing through the Euripus, came to Alus in Achaea, where they left the ships and proceeded to Thessaly on foot. Here they occupied Tempe, the pass which leads from lower Macedonia into Thessaly along the Peneus, between Mt Olympus and Mt Ossa. It was here that some 10,000 Greek heavy infantry, reinforced by the Thessalian cavalry, took up their position. The Spartans were commanded by Euanetus son of Carenus, who had been chosen for the post from the Polemarchs, though he was not of the royal blood; the Athenians were commanded by Themistocles, son of Neocles. But the army had not been in Tempe many days when a message arrived from Alexander, the son of Amyntas, in Macedonia advising the Greek troops to withdraw, and not stay in the pass to be trampled underfoot, adding an indication of the strength of the Persian army and fleet. The advice seemed to be sound, and was clearly offered by the

Macedonian in a friendly spirit, so the Greeks took it. I think myself that what persuaded them to go was the alarm they felt upon learning that there was another way into Thessaly through upper Macedonia and Perrhaebia, near Gonnus – the pass, in fact, by which Xerxes' army actually did come in.[1]

The Greeks, then, re-embarked and returned to the Isthmus. Such were the circumstances of the expedition to Thessaly – it took place while Xerxes was at Abydos, just before he crossed the strait from Asia into Europe. The result of it was that the Thessalians, finding themselves without support, no longer hesitated but whole-heartedly worked in the Persian interest, so that in the course of the war they proved of the greatest use to Xerxes.

The Greeks on their return to the Isthmus then discussed, in consideration of the warning they had received from Alexander, where they should make a stand. The proposal which found most favour was to guard the pass of Thermopylae, on the grounds that it was narrower than the pass into Thessaly and at the same time nearer home. They knew nothing as yet about the mountain track by means of which the men who fell at Thermopylae were taken in the rear, and only learnt of its existence from the people of Trachis after their arrival.

The decision, then, was to hold the pass in order to prevent the Persians from entering Greece, and at the same time to send the fleet to Artemisium on the coast of Histiaea; for these two places being close together, communication would be easy. The topography is as follows. Artemisium is where the sea south of Thrace contracts into a narrow channel between the island of Sciathos and the mainland of Magnesia; pass through this channel and you come to the strip of coast called Artemisium. It is a part of Euboea, and contains a temple of Artemis. The pass through Trachis into Greece is, at Thermopylae, fifty feet wide; elsewhere, both east and west of Thermopylae, it is still narrower; at Alpeni to the eastward, it is only a single waggon track, and to the westward near Anthela on the river Phoenix it is about the same. To the south-west – inland – there is no way through, passage being barred by a lofty and precipitous ascent, running up to

1. The country north and west of Olympus is, in fact, not rugged; only the forest, then, had to be cut through.

Mt Oeta, while on the other side of the roadway is the sea, full of banks and shoals. There are hot springs in the pass – known locally as the Basins – with an altar over them dedicated to Heracles. A wall was once built across this passage, and there used long ago to be a gateway in it; both were constructed by the Phocians in fear of an invasion from Thessaly, at the period when the Thessalians came from Thesprotia to settle in the country of Aeolis, which they still occupy. The new settlers tried to overrun Phocis, and the Phocians raised the wall as a protective measure, and at the same time turned the water from the hot springs over the pass, to cut up the ground into gullies, resorting to every device to keep the Thessalians out. The wall had been built a very long time ago and most of it had fallen into ruin through age; now, however, it was decided to rebuild it, and to use it to help stop the Persians from getting through into Greece. Quite close to the road is a village called Alpeni, from which the Greeks counted upon drawing supplies.

These, then, were the places which the Greeks thought would best suit their purpose; careful consideration of all the circumstances, and the realization that the Persians would be unable, in the narrow pass, to use their cavalry or take advantage of their numbers, determined them to make their stand at this point against the invader; so when news came that the enemy was in Pieria, they broke up from the Isthmus and proceeded to their new positions, some on foot to Thermopylae, others by sea to Artemisium.

Meanwhile, as the Greek troops hurried to their stations, the people of Delphi, in great alarm for their own safety and for Greece, applied to their oracle for advice. 'Pray to the winds,' was the answer; 'for they will be good allies to Greece.' The first thing the Delphians did upon receiving this oracular counsel was to report it to all the Greek states who were determined to fight for their freedom; and, by thus communicating the divine message at a time when Greece was in the grip of fear at the prospect of invasion, they earned everlasting gratitude. Subsequently they consecrated an altar to the winds at Thyia – a place named after Cephisus' daughter, who has a shrine there – and offered sacrifice upon it to the winds in supplication. In memory of this oracle the Delphians still, to this day, pray to the winds for favour.

Xerxes' fleet now left Therma, and ten of the fastest ships set a course direct for Sciathos, where three Greek vessels, one from Troezen, one from Aegina, and one from Attica, were on the look-out. At the first glimpse of the enemy all three fled. The Persians gave chase; the ship from Troezen, under the command of Prexinus, fell into their hands at once, and her captors, picking out the best-looking of the fighting men on board, took him up forward and cut his throat, thinking, no doubt, that the sacrifice of their first handsome Greek prisoner would benefit their cause. The unfortunate man's name was Leon – and possibly his name had something to do with his fate. The trireme from Aegina, commanded by Asonides, gave the Persians some trouble. One of the soldiers on board – Pytheas, the son of Ischenous – distinguished himself that day; for after the ship was taken, he continued to resist until he was nearly cut to pieces. At last he fell, but, as there was still breath in his body, the Persian troops, anxious to do all they could to save the life of so brave a man, dressed his wounds with myrrh and bound them up with linen bandages. On returning to their base, they exhibited their prisoner admiringly to everybody there, and treated him with much kindness. The other prisoners from this ship were treated merely as slaves.

Two of the three Greek vessels thus fell into Persian hands; the third, commanded by the Athenian Phormos, went ashore, while trying to escape, at the mouth of the Peneus. Here she was taken, though the men in her got away; for the instant the vessel grounded the Athenians aboard leapt out and made their way back to Athens through Thessaly.

News of what had happened was flashed to the Greeks at Artemisium by fire-signal from Sciathos. In the panic which ensued they left their station and moved to Chalcis, intending to guard the Euripus, and leaving look-outs on the high ground of Euboea. Three of the ten Persian ships ran aground on the Ant, a sunken reef between Sciathos and Magnesia; in consequence of this the Persians marked the reef with a stone beacon, after which, the danger being removed, the whole fleet set sail from Therma, eleven days after Xerxes had marched from the town with his army. The Ant lies right in the fairway; Pammon, a native of Scyros, took the Persians to it when they erected their beacon. A day's voyage brought the Persian fleet to

Sepias in Magnesia and the strip of coast between Cape Sepias and the town of Casthanea.

The Persian fleet got as far as Sepias, and the army as far as Thermopylae, without loss. I find by calculation that their numbers up to this stage were as follows: first there was the fleet of 1207 ships belonging to the various nations which sailed from Asia, with its original complement of 241,000 men – allowing 200 to each ship. Each of these vessels carried, apart from native soldiers – or marines – and in addition to the crew, thirty fighting men who were either Persians, Medes, or Sacae, making an additional 36,210. Add to these the crews of the penteconters (50-oared galleys), carrying roughly 80 men apiece; there were, as I have already said, 3000 penteconters, so this will make another 240,000. This was the naval force brought by Xerxes from Asia, and the total number of men aboard comes to 517,610.

As to the army, the infantry was 1,700,000 strong and the cavalry 80,000. Then there were the Arabian camel corps and the Libyan charioteers, which I reckon as a further 20,000. The grand total, therefore, of land and sea forces brought over from Asia was 2,317,610, excluding army servants and the men in the food transports. To this, moreover, must be added the troops which were collected as Xerxes passed through Europe. Here I must be content with a rough estimate. The Greeks of Thrace and of the islands off the coast furnished, I should say, 120 ships: this would make 24,000 men. The strength of the infantry furnished by the Thracians, Paeonians, Eordi, Bottiaei, Chalcidians, Brygi, Pierians, Macedonians, Perrhoebians, Enionians, Dolopes, Magnetes, Achaeans, and the coastal settlements of Thrace, I would put at 300,000. So by adding these to the original force from Asia we get a total of 2,641,610 fighting men. Lastly, it is my belief that the army servants and camp followers, the crews of the provision boats and of other craft which sailed with the expedition were not less, but more, numerous than the actual fighting troops; however I will reckon them as neither more nor fewer, but as equal, and thus arrive at my final estimate, which is, that Xerxes, the son of Darius, reached Sepias and Thermopylae at the head of an army consisting, in all, of 5,283,320 men.

So much for the actual army and its attendants; as for eunuchs, female cooks, and soldiers' women, no one could attempt an estimate of their number, any more than of the various pack-animals and Indian dogs which followed the army. They were far too numerous to count. I am not surprised that with so many people and so many beasts the rivers sometimes failed to provide enough water; what does surprise me is that the food never gave out, for I reckon that if no more than a quart of meal was the daily ration for one man, the total daily consumption would have amounted to 110,340 bushels – and this without counting what was consumed by the women, eunuchs, pack-animals, and dogs. Amongst all these immense numbers there was not a man who, for stature and noble bearing, was more worthy than Xerxes to wield so vast a power.

The Persian fleet, as I have mentioned, made the Magnesian coast between Casthanea and Cape Sepias, and on its arrival the leading ships made fast to the land, while the remainder, as there was not much room on the short stretch of beach, came to anchor and lay off-shore in lines, eight deep. In this position they remained during the night; but at dawn next day the weather, which was clear and calm, suddenly changed, and the fleet was caught in a heavy blow from the east – a 'Hellespontian', as the people there call it – which raised a confused sea like a pot on the boil. Those who realized in time that the blow was coming, and all who happened to be lying in a convenient position, managed to beach their vessels and to get them clear of the water before they were damaged, and thus saved their own lives as well; but the ships which were caught offshore were driven some on to the place called the Ovens at the foot of Mt Pelion, others on to the beach itself; a number were driven on to Sepias, and others, again, were forced ashore off the towns of Meliboea and Casthanea. The storm was very violent and there was no chance of riding it out.

There is a story that the Athenians had called upon Boreas to help them, in consequence of another oracle, by which they were advised to 'ask the assistance of their son-in-law.' Boreas, according to Greek legend, married a woman of Attica, Erechtheus' daughter Orithyia, and in consequence of this marriage the Athenians (so the tale goes) supposed Boreas to be their son-in-law; so when they observed from their station at Chalcis in Euboea that it was coming on to blow – or possibly even sooner – they offered sacrifice to Boreas and Orithyia and begged them to come to their aid and to repeat the former disaster at Athos by once again destroying the Persian fleet. I cannot say if this was really the reason why the fleet was caught at anchor by the north-easter, but the Athenians are quite positive about it: Boreas, they maintain, had helped them before, and it was Boreas who was responsible for what occurred on this occasion too. On their return home they built him a shrine by the river Ilissus.

Four hundred ships, at the lowest estimate, are said to have been lost in this disaster, and the loss of life and of treasure was beyond reckoning. It proved, however, to be a very good thing indeed for a certain Magnesian named Ameinocles, the son of Cretines, who owned land in the neighbourhood of Sepias; for he subsequently picked up a large number of gold and silver drinking-cups which were washed ashore, and found Persian treasure-chests containing more gold, beyond counting. This made him a very rich man, though in other respects he proved less fortunate; for he met with a distressing disaster in the murder of his son.

The number of merchant vessels and other craft lost in the storm was too great to reckon. Indeed, such was the magnitude of the disaster that the Persian naval commanders, fearing that the Thessalians might take advantage of their desperate plight to attack them, protected themselves by building a high barricade out of the wreckage. The storm lasted three days, after which the Magi brought it to an end by sacrificial offerings, and by putting spells on the wind, and by further offerings to Thetis and the sea-nymphs – or, of course, it may be that the wind just dropped naturally. The reason why the Magi sacrificed to Thetis was that they had learnt from the Ionians that she was supposed to have been carried off from here by Peleus, and that all the headland of Sepias was sacred to her and the other daughters of Nereus. In any case, on the fourth day the weather was fine again.

On the second day of the storm the look-out men on the Euboean hills came hurrying to the Greeks and described in detail the destruction of the Persian ships. On hearing the news, they offered prayers of thanksgiving and libations of wine to Poseidon their saviour, and made all speed to return to their station at Artemisium, in the expectation that only a few ships would be left to oppose them. For the second time, therefore, they lay off Artemisium. From that day to this they have always addressed Poseidon by the title of Saviour.

Meanwhile, after the wind had dropped and the sea had gone down, the Persians got the ships they had hauled ashore into the water again, and proceeded along the coast round the southern point of Magnesia straight into the bay which leads to Pagasae. There is a place in this bay where it is said that Heracles, at the start of the voyage of the *Argo* to fetch the Golden Fleece from Aea (Colchis), was put ashore by Jason and his companions to get water, and was left behind. The place got the name of Aphetae – 'putting forth' – because it was the intention of the Argonauts to make it their point of departure after watering the ship. It was here that Xerxes' fleet brought up.

Fifteen of the Persian ships were far behind in getting under way, and the men aboard, happening to catch sight of the Greek ships at Artemisium, mistook them for their own, and on making towards them fell into the enemies' hands. These vessels were under the command of Sandoces, the son of Thamasius and governor of Cyme in Aeolis. Sandoces, who was one of the royal judges, had been arrested by Darius some time before and crucified, on a charge of perverting justice for money. But while he was actually on the cross, Darius came to the conclusion that his services to the royal house outweighed his offences, and realizing in consequence that he had acted with more promptitude than wisdom, caused him to be taken down. Thus he escaped with his life from King Darius, but this time, when he fell foul of the Greek navy, he was not destined to escape again; for as soon as the Greeks saw his squadron approaching they realized his mistake, put to sea, and captured it without difficulty. Amongst the prisoners in one of the ships was Aridolis, the master of Alabanda in Caria; in another was Penthylus, the son of Demonous, the Paphian commander, who had brought twelve ships from Paphos. Eleven of them were lost at Sepias in the storm, and he was taken as he sailed to Artemisium in the only one which survived. The Greeks questioned these two prisoners on all they wished to know about Xerxes' forces, and then sent them away in chains to the Isthmus of Corinth.

Meanwhile the Persian fleet, with the exception of the fifteen ships under Sandoces' command, arrived safely at Aphetae. Two days previously Xerxes with the army had passed through Thessaly and Achaea and entered the country of the Malians. While he was in Thessaly he had held races between the native horses and his own, because he had heard that the horses of Thessaly were the best in Greece. The Greek mares were, however, soundly beaten. Of the Thessalian rivers, the only one which failed to supply enough water for the troops was the Onochonus; but in Achaea even the biggest – the Apidanus – scarcely sufficed.

At Halos in Achaea Xerxes' guides, wishing to give him all the information they could, told him the local legend about the Laphystian Zeus. The story is that Athamas, the son of Aeolus, plotted with Ino the death of Phrixus; subsequently the Achaeans in obedience to an oracle laid a penalty upon the descendants of Phrixus and his son Cytissorus: this was that the eldest of the family should be forbidden to enter the Council Chamber – or People's House, as the Achaeans call it – and that they themselves should keep watch to see that the ban was observed. If one of them does enter the Chamber, he can never get out again except to be offered as a sacrifice. They went on to relate that many of them, when recognized entering the Chamber and threatened with death in this war, escape in terror to some other country, and perhaps return long afterwards. They further described to Xerxes the ritual of the sacrifice, how the man was always made to wear a wreath, and was led to his death in a solemn procession. The reason why the descendants of Cytissorus and Phrixus are forced to endure this treatment is that when the Achaeans were about to kill Aeolus' son Athamas as a sin-offering, or scapegoat, on behalf of their country, Cytissorus came from Aea in Colchis and rescued him, thus calling down the wrath of God upon his descendants.

In consequence of this story Xerxes kept clear of the sacred ground and issued orders to his army to do the same; he showed respect also to the house and precinct of the family of Athamas.

From Thessaly and Achaea Xerxes went on into Malis, following the coast of a bay in which there is a daily rise and fall of tide. The country round this bay is flat – broad in one part, very narrow in another; all round is a chain of lofty and trackless mountains, called the Cliffs of Trachis, which enclose the whole territory of Malis. As one comes from Achaea, the first town on the bay is Anticyra, near to which is the mouth of the Spercheius, a river which comes down from the country of the Enianes. Some three and a half miles further on there is another river, the Dyras, which, according to the legend, burst from the ground to help Heracles when he was burning;[1] then, at about the same distance, is a third stream, the Melas, and rather more than half a mile beyond that is the town of Trachis. At Trachis the space between the hills and the sea is more extensive than anywhere else, the area of the plain being over 5,000 acres.[2] South of Trachis there is a cleft in the ring of hills; through it the river Asopus issues, and comes down to the foot of the hills. Further south another small stream, the Phoenix, runs down from the hills and joins the Asopus. It is at the Phoenix that the plain is narrowest, there being room here only for a single cart-track. From the Phoenix to Thermopylae is about two miles, and between them lies the village of Anthela, which the Asopus passes just before it reaches the sea. Round Anthela the ground is more open; there is a temple there dedicated to Demeter of the Amphictyons, as well as seats for the deputies of the Amphictyonic league, and a shrine of Amphictyon himself.

The position, then, was that Xerxes was lying with his force at Trachis in Malian territory, while the Greeks occupied the pass known locally as Pylae – though Thermopylae is the common Greek name. Such were the respective positions of the two armies, one being in control of all the country from Trachis northward, the other of the whole mainland to the south. The Greek force which here awaited the coming of Xerxes was made up of the following contingents: 300 heavy-armed infantry from Sparta, 500 from Tegea, 500 from Mantinea, 120 from Orchomenus in Arcadia, 1000 from the rest of Arcadia; from Corinth there were 400, from Phlius 200, and from Mycenae 80. In addition to these troops from the Peloponnese, there were the Boeotian contingents of 700 from Thespiae and 400 from Thebes. The Locrians of Opus and the Phocians had also obeyed the

1. In the shirt of Nessus.
2. The text here says 'over 400 miles across', which is obviously a mistake. – Translator's note.

call to arms, the former sending all the men they had, the latter one thousand. The other Greeks had induced these two towns to send troops by a message to the effect that they themselves were merely an advance force, and that the main body of the confederate army was daily expected; the sea, moreover, was strongly held by the fleet of Athens and Aegina and the other naval forces. Thus there was no cause for alarm – for, after all, it was not a god who threatened Greece, but a man, and there neither was nor ever would be a man who was not born with a good chance of misfortune – and the greater the man, the greater the misfortune. The present enemy was no exception; he too was human, and was sure to be disappointed of his great expectations.

The appeal succeeded, and Opus and Phocis sent their troops to Trachis. The contingents of the various states were under their own officers, but the most respected was Leonidas the Spartan, who was in command of the whole army. Leonidas traced his descent directly back to Heracles, through Anaxandrides and Leon (his father and grandfather), Anaxander, Eurycrates, Polydorus, Alcamenes, Teleches, Archelaus, Agesilaus, Doryssus, Labotas, Echestratus, Agis, Eurysthenes, Aristodemus, Aristomachus, Cleodaeus – and so to Hyllus, who was Heracles' son. He had come to be king of Sparta quite unexpectedly, for as he had two elder brothers, Cleomenes and Dorieus, he had no thought of himself succeeding to the throne. Dorieus, however, was killed in Sicily, and when Cleomenes also died without an heir, Leonidas found himself next in the succession. He was older than Cleombrotus, Anaxandrides' youngest son, and was, moreover, married to Cleomenes' daughter. The three hundred men whom he brought on this occasion to Thermopylae were chosen by himself, all fathers of living sons. He also took with him the Thebans I mentioned, under the command of Leontiades, the son of Eurymachus. The reason why he made a special point of taking troops from Thebes, and from Thebes only, was that the Thebans were strongly suspected of Persian sympathies, so he called upon them to play their part in the war in order to see if they would answer the call, or openly refuse to join the confederacy. They did send troops, but their secret sympathy was nevertheless with the enemy. Leonidas and his three hundred were sent by Sparta in advance of the main army, in order that the sight of them might encourage the other confederates to fight and prevent them from going over to the enemy, as they were quite capable of doing if they knew that Sparta was hanging back; the intention was, when the Carneia was over (for it was that festival which prevented the Spartans from taking the field in the ordinary way), to leave a garrison in the city and march with all the troops at their disposal. The other allied states proposed to act similarly; for the Olympic festival happened to fall just at this same period. None of them ever expected the battle at Thermopylae to be decided so soon – which was the reason why they sent only advance parties there.

The Persian army was now close to the pass, and the Greeks, suddenly doubting their power to resist, held a conference to consider the advisability of retreat. It was proposed by the Peloponnesians generally that the army should fall back upon the Peloponnese and hold the Isthmus; but when the Phocians and Locrians expressed their indignation at this suggestion, Leonidas gave his voice for staying where they were and sending, at the same time, an appeal for reinforcements to the various states of the confederacy, as their numbers were inadequate to cope with the Persians.

During the conference Xerxes sent a man on horseback to ascertain the strength of the Greek force and to observe what the troops were doing. He had heard before he left Thessaly that a small force was concentrated here, led by the Lacedaemonians under Leonidas of the house of Heracles. The Persian rider approached the camp and took a thorough survey of all he could see – which was not, however, the whole Greek army; for the men on the further side of the wall which, after its reconstruction, was now guarded, were out of sight. He did, none the less, carefully observe the troops who were stationed on the outside of the wall. At that moment these happened to be the Spartans, and some of them were stripped for exercise, while others were combing their hair. The Persian spy watched them in astonishment; nevertheless he made sure of their numbers, and of everything else he needed to know, as accurately as he could, and then rode quietly off. No one attempted to catch him, or took the least notice of him.

Back in his own camp he told Xerxes what he had seen. Xerxes was bewildered; the truth, namely that the Spartans were preparing themselves to die and deal death with all their strength, was beyond his comprehension, and what they were doing seemed to him merely absurd. Accordingly he sent for Demaratus, the son of Ariston, who had come with the army, and questioned him about the spy's report, in the hope of finding out what the behaviour of the Spartans might mean. 'Once before,' Demaratus said, 'when we began our march against Greece, you heard me speak of these men. I told you then how I saw this enterprise would turn out, and you laughed at me. I strive for nothing, my lord, more earnestly than to observe the truth in your presence; so hear me once more. These men have come to fight us for possession of the pass, and for that struggle they are preparing. It is the common practice of the Spartans to pay careful attention to their hair when they are about to risk their lives. But I assure you that if you can defeat these men and the rest of the Spartans who are still at home, there is no other people in the world who will dare to stand firm or lift a hand against you. You have now to deal with the finest kingdom in Greece, and with the bravest men.'

Xerxes, unable to believe what Demaratus said, asked further how it was possible that so small a force could fight with his army. 'My lord,' Demaratus replied, 'treat me as a liar, if what I have foretold does not take place.' But still Xerxes was unconvinced.

For four days Xerxes waited, in constant expectation that the Greeks would make good their escape; then, on the fifth, when still they had made no move and their continued presence seemed mere impudent and reckless folly, he was seized with rage and sent forward the Medes and Cissians with orders to take them alive and bring them into his presence. The Medes charged, and in the struggle which ensued many fell; but others took their places, and in spite of terrible losses refused to be beaten off. They made it plain enough to anyone, and not least to the king himself, that he had in his army many men, indeed, but few soldiers. All day the battle continued; the Medes, after their rough handling, were at length withdrawn and their place was taken by Hydarnes and his picked Persian troops – the King's Immortals – who advanced to the attack in full confidence of bringing the business to a quick and easy end. But, once engaged, they were no more successful than the Medes had been; all went as before, the two armies fighting in a confined space, the Persians using shorter spears than the Greeks and having no advantage from their numbers.

On the Spartan side it was a memorable fight; they were men who understood war pitted against an inexperienced enemy, and amongst the feints they employed was to turn their backs on a body and pretend to be retreating in confusion, whereupon the enemy would pursue them with a great clatter and roar; but the Spartans, just as the Persians were on them, would wheel and face them and inflict in the new struggle innumerable casualties. The Spartans had their losses too, but not many. At last the Persians, finding that their assaults upon the pass, whether by divisions or by any other way they could think of, were all useless, broke off the engagement and withdrew. Xerxes was watching the battle from where he sat; and it is said that in the course of the attacks three times, in terror for his army, he leapt to his feet.

Next day the fighting began again, but with no better success for the Persians, who renewed their onslaught in the hope that the Greeks, being so few in number, might be badly enough disabled by wounds to prevent further resistance. But the Greeks never slackened; their troops were ordered in divisions corresponding to the states from which they came, and each division took its turn in the line except the Phocian, which had been posted to guard the track over the mountains. So when the Persians found that things were no better for them than on the previous day, they once more withdrew.

How to deal with the situation Xerxes had no idea; but just then, a man from Malis, Ephialtes, the son of Eurydemus, came, in hope of a rich reward, to tell the king about the track which led over the hills to Thermopylae – and thus he was to prove the death of the Greeks who held the pass.

Later on, Ephialtes, in fear of the Spartans, fled to Thessaly, and in his absence a price was put upon his head by the Amphictyons assembled at Pylae. Some time afterwards he returned to Anticyra, where he was killed by Athenades of Trachis. Athenades killed him not for his treachery but for another reason, which I will explain further on;[1] but the Spartans honoured him none the less on that account. According to another story, it was Onetes, the son of

1. The last of Herodotus' three unfulfilled promises.

Phanagoras of Carystus, and Corydallus of Anticyra who spoke to Xerxes and showed the Persians the way round by the mountain track. This is entirely unconvincing, my first criterion being the fact that the Amphictyons, presumably after careful inquiry, set a price not upon Onetes and Corydallus but upon Ephialtes of Trachis, and my second, that there is no doubt that the accusation of treachery was the reason for Ephialtes' flight. Certainly Onetes, even though he was not a native of Malis, might have known about the track, if he had spent much time in the neighbourhood – but it was Ephialtes, and no one else, who showed the Persians the way, and I leave his name on record as the guilty one.

Xerxes found Ephialtes' offer most satisfactory. He was delighted with it, and promptly sent off Hydarnes with the troops under his command. They left camp about the time the lamps are lit.

The track was originally discovered by the Malians of the neighbourhood; they afterwards used it to help the Thessalians, taking them over it to attack Phocis at the time when the Phocians were protected from invasion by the wall which they had built across the pass. So long, then, have its sinister uses been known to the Malians! The track begins at the Asopus, the stream which flows through the narrow gorge, and, running along the ridge of the mountain – which, like the track itself, is called Anopaea – ends at Alpenos, the first Locrian settlement as one comes from Malis, near the rock known as Black-Buttocks' Stone and the seats of the Cercopes. Just here is the narrowest part of the pass.

This, then, was the mountain track which the Persians took, after crossing the Asopus. They marched throughout the night, with the mountains of Leta on their right hand and those of Trachis on their left. By early dawn they were at the summit of the ridge, near the spot where the Phocians, as I mentioned before, stood on guard with a thousand men, to watch the track and protect their country. The Phocians had volunteered for this service to Leonidas, the lower road being held as already described.

The ascent of the Persians had been concealed by the oak-woods which cover all these hills, and it was only when they were up that the Phocians became aware of their approach; for there was no wind, and the marching feet made a loud swishing and rustling in the fallen leaves. Leaping to their feet, the Phocians were in the act of arming themselves when the enemy was upon them. The Persians were surprised at the sight of troops preparing to resist; they had expected no opposition – yet here was a body of men barring their way. Hydarnes asked Ephialtes who they were, for his first uncomfortable thought was that they might be Spartans; but on learning the truth he prepared to engage them. The Persian arrows flew thick and fast, and the Phocians, supposing themselves to be the main object of the attack, hurriedly withdrew to the highest point of the mountain, where they made ready to face destruction. But the Persians with Ephialtes and Hydarnes paid no further attention to them, but passed on along the descending track with all possible speed.

The Greeks at Thermopylae had their first warning of the death that was coming with the dawn from the seer Megistias, who read their doom in the victims of sacrifice; deserters, too, came in during the night with news of the Persian flank movement, and lastly, just as day was breaking, the look-out men came running from the hills. In council of war their opinions were divided, some urging that they must not abandon their post, others the opposite. The result was that the army split: some dispersed, contingents returning to their various cities, while others made ready to stand by Leonidas. It is said that Leonidas himself dismissed them, to spare their lives, but thought it unbecoming for the Spartans under his command to desert the post which they had originally come to guard. I myself am inclined to think that he dismissed them when he realized that they had no heart for the fight and were unwilling to take their share of the danger; at the same time honour forbade that he himself should go. And indeed by remaining at his post he left a great name behind him, and Sparta did not lose her prosperity, as might otherwise have happened; for right at the outset of the war the Spartans had been told by the Delphic oracle that either their city must be laid waste by the foreigner or a Spartan king be killed. The prophecy was in hexameter verse and ran as follows:

> Hear your fate, O dwellers in Sparta of the wide spaces;
> Either your famed, great town must be sacked by Perseus' sons,
> Or, if that be not, the whole land of Lacedaemon
> Shall mourn the death of a king of the house of Heracles,

For not the strength of lions or of bulls shall hold him,
Strength against strength; for he has the power of Zeus,
And will not be checked till one of these two he has consumed.

I believe it was the thought of this oracle, combined with his wish to lay up for the Spartans a treasure of fame in which no other city should share, that made Leonidas dismiss those troops; I do not think that they deserted, or went off without orders, because of a difference of opinion. Moreover, I am strongly supported in this view by the case of the seer Megistias, who was with the army – an Acarnanian, said to be of the clan of Melampus – who foretold the coming doom from his inspection of the sacrificial victims. He quite plainly received orders from Leonidas to quit Thermopylae, to save him from sharing the army's fate. He refused to go, but he sent his only son, who was serving with the forces.

Thus it was that the confederate troops, by Leonidas' orders, abandoned their posts and left the pass, all except the Thespians and the Thebans who remained with the Spartans. The Thebans were detained by Leonidas as hostages very much against their will; but the Thespians of their own accord refused to desert Leonidas and his men, and stayed, and died with them. They were under the command of Demophilus the son of Diadromes.

In the morning Xerxes poured a libation to the rising sun, and then waited till it was well up[1] before he began to move forward. This was accorting to Ephialtes' instructions, for the way down from the ridge is much shorter and more direct than the long and circuitous ascent. As the Persian army advanced to the assault, the Greeks under Leonidas, knowing that they were going to their deaths, went out into the wider part of the pass much further than they had done before; in the previous days' fighting they had been holding the wall and making sorties from behind it into the narrow neck, but now they fought outside the narrows. Many of the invaders fell; behind them the company commanders plied their whips indiscriminately, driving the men on. Many fell into the sea and were drowned, and still more were trampled to death by their friends. No one could count the number of the dead. The Greeks, who knew that the enemy

1. Literally, 'until the time when the forum is filled'.

were on their way round by the mountain track and that death was inevitable, put forth all their strength and fought with fury and desperation. By this time most of their spears were broken, and they were killing Persians with their swords.

In the course of that fight Leonidas fell, having fought most gallantly, and many distinguished Spartans with him – their names I have learned, as those of men who deserve to be remembered; indeed, I have learned the names of all the three hundred. Amongst the Persian dead, too, were many men of high distinction, including two brothers of Xerxes, Habrocomes and Hyperanthes, sons of Darius by Artanes' daughter Phratagune. Artanes, the son of Hystaspes and grandson of Arsames, was Darius' brother; as Phratagune was his only child, his giving her to Darius was equivalent to giving him his entire estate.

There was a bitter struggle over the body of Leonidas; four times the Greeks drove the enemy off, and at last by their valour rescued it. So it went on, until the troops with Ephialtes were close at hand; and then, when the Greeks knew that they had come, the character of the fighting changed. They withdrew again into the narrow neck of the pass, behind the wall, and took up a position in a single compact body – all except the Thebans – on the little hill at the entrance to the pass, where the stone lion in memory of Leonidas stands to-day. Here they resisted to the last, with their swords, if they had them, and, if not, with their hands and teeth, until the Persians, coming on from the front over the ruins of the wall and closing in from behind, finally overwhelmed them with missile weapons.

Of all the Spartans and Thespians who fought so valiantly the most signal proof of courage was given by the Spartan Dieneces. It is said that before the battle he was told by a native of Trachis that, when the Persians shot their arrows, there were so many of them that they hid the sun. Dieneces, however, quite unmoved by the thought of the strength of the Persian army, merely remarked: 'This is pleasant news that the stranger from Trachis brings us: if the Persians hide the sun, we shall have our battle in the shade.' He is said to have left on record other sayings, too, of a similar kind, by which he will be remembered. After Dieneces the greatest distinction was won by two Spartan brothers, Alpheus and Maron, the sons of Orsiphantus; and of the Thespians the man to gain the highest glory was a certain Dithyrambus, the son of Harmatides.

The dead were buried where they fell, and with them the men who had been killed before those dismissed by Leonidas left the pass. Over them is this inscription, in honour of the whole force:

> Four thousand here from Pelops' land
> Against three million once did stand.

The Spartans have a special epitaph; it runs:

> Go tell the Spartans, you who read:
> We took their orders, and are dead.

For the seer Megistias there is the following:

> Here lies Megistias, who died
> When the Mede passed Spercheius' tide.
> A prophet; yet he scorned to save
> Himself, but shared the Spartans' grave.

The columns with the epitaphs inscribed on them were erected in honour of the dead by the Amphictyons – though the epitaph upon the seer Megistias was the work of Simonides, the son of Leoprepes, who put it there for friendship's sake.

Two of the three hundred Spartans, Eurytus and Aristodemus, are said to have been suffering from acute inflammation of the eyes, on account of which they were dismissed by Leonidas before the battle and went to Alpeni to recuperate. These two men might have agreed together to return in safety to Sparta; or, if they did not wish to do so, they might have shared the fate of their friends. But, unable to agree which course to take, they quarrelled, and Eurytus had no sooner heard that the Persians had made their way round by the mountain track than he called for his armour, put it on, and ordered his servant to lead him to the scene of the battle. The servant obeyed, and then took to his heels, and Eurytus, plunging into the thick of things, was killed. Aristodemus, on the other hand, finding that his heart failed him, stayed behind at Alpeni. Now if only Aristodemus had been involved – if he alone had returned sick to Sparta – or if they had both gone back together, I do not think that the Spartans would have been angry; but as one was killed and the other took advantage of the excuse, which was open to both of them, to save his skin, they could hardly help being very angry indeed with Aristodemus.

There is another explanation of how Aristodemus got back alive to Sparta: according to this, he was sent from camp with a message, and though he might have returned in time to take part in the fighting, he deliberately loitered on the way and so saved himself, while the man who accompanied him on the errand joined in the battle and was killed. In any case, he was met upon his return with reproach and disgrace; no Spartan would give him a light to kindle his fire, or speak to him, and he was nicknamed the Trembler. However, he afterwards made amends for everything at the battle of Plataea.

There is also a story that one more of the three hundred – Pantites – survived. He had been sent with a message into Thessaly, and on his return to Sparta found himself in such disgrace that he hanged himself.

The Thebans under Leontiades remained for a time with the army and were compelled to make some show of resistance to the enemy; but as soon as they saw that things were going in favour of Persia, they took the opportunity of Leonidas' hurried retreat to the little hill, where his last stand was made, to detach themselves from his force; they then approached the enemy with outstretched hands, crying out that in their zeal for the Persian interest they had been amongst the first to give earth and water to the king, and had no share in the responsibility for the injury done him, because they had come to Thermopylae against their will. It was all too true – and, when it was backed up by the evidence of the Thessalians, it saved their lives. Nevertheless, their luck did not hold in every respect; for a few were killed by the Persians on their first approach, and all the rest were branded by Xerxes' orders with the royal mark, beginning with Leontiades their commander. Leontiades' son Eurymachus was afterwards killed by the Plataeans when he was leading a force of four hundred Theban troops at the capture of Plataea.

Such, then, is the story of the Greeks' struggle at Thermopylae. Xerxes, when the battle was over, summoned Demaratus to ask him some questions. 'Demaratus,' he began, 'you are a good man – the truth of your words proves it. Everything has turned out as you said it would. Now tell me – how many more Lacedaemonians are there? And how many of them are as good soldiers as these were? Or are they all as good?' 'Sire,' Demaratus answered, 'there are a great many men and many towns in Lacedaemon; but what you really want to know I will now tell you: there is in that country a town called Sparta, which contains about eight thousand men. All these are the equals of those who fought in this battle. The other men in Lacedaemon are not their equals – but good soldiers none the less.'

'Demaratus,' said Xerxes, 'tell me what you think would be the easiest way of defeating these people. You were once their king, so you must be well acquainted with all the ins and outs of their policy.'

'Sire,' replied Demaratus, 'if you are really serious in asking my advice, I am bound to tell you what I consider the best plan. Suppose you send three hundred ships from the fleet to Lacedaemon. Off the coast there is an island called Cythera – Chilon, the wisest man who ever lived amongst us, once said that it would be better for the Spartans if it were sunk beneath the sea, for he always expected that it would provide such just an opportunity for a hostile force as what I am now suggesting. It was not, of course, your attack that he foresaw – it was the prospect of any attack from any quarter that alarmed him. This, then, is my proposal: let your ships make Cythera their base, and from it spread terror over Lacedaemon. With a war of their own, on their own doorstep, as it were, you need not fear that they will help the other Greeks while your army is engaged in conquering them. Thus the rest of Greece will be crushed first and Lacedaemon will be left alone and helpless. On the other hand, if you decide against this plan, you may expect more trouble; for there is a narrow isthmus in the Peloponnese, and in it you will find all the troops from that part of Greece who have formed a league to resist you, and you will have to face bloodier battles than any you have yet witnessed. But if you take my advice, the Isthmus and the Peloponnesian towns will fall into your hands without a blow.'

Achaemenes, Xerxes' brother and commander of the fleet, who happened to be present and was afraid Xerxes might be persuaded to adopt Demaratus' proposal, spoke in answer: 'My lord,' he said, 'I see that you are allowing yourself to be influenced by a man who envies your success, and is probably a traitor to you. He is a typical

Greek, and this is just how they love to behave – envying anyone else's good fortune and hating any power greater than their own. In our present circumstances, when we have already had four hundred ships wrecked, if you detach another three hundred from the fleet for a voyage round the Peloponnese, the enemy will be a match for us. Keep the fleet together, and they will never dare risk an engagement – the disparity in numbers will see to that; moreover, if fleet and army keep in touch and advance together, each can support the other; separate them, and you will be no more use to the fleet than the fleet to you. Only lay your own plans soundly, and you can afford not to worry about the enemy, or to keep wondering what they will do, how many they are, or where they will elect to make a stand. They are quite capable of managing their own affairs, just as we are of managing ours. If the Spartans risk another battle with us, they will certainly not repair the injury they have already received.'

'Achaemenes,' Xerxes replied, 'I think you are right, and I will take your advice. Nevertheless, though Demaratus' judgement is not so good as yours, he told me in good faith what he thought best for me. I will not accept your suggestion that he is secretly hostile to my cause; I have evidence of his loyalty in what he has said on previous occasions, and, apart from that, there is the well-known fact that a man often hates his next-door neighbour and is jealous of his success, and when asked for advice will not tell him what he really thinks will help him most – unless, indeed, he is a man of exceptional virtue, such as one seldom finds. But the relationship between men of different countries is very different from that between men of the same town; a man is full of sympathy for the good fortune of a foreign friend, and will always give him the best advice he can. Demaratus is a foreigner and my guest; I should be obliged, therefore, if everyone would refrain from maligning him in future.'

After this conversation Xerxes went over the battlefield to see the bodies, and having been told that Leonidas was king of Sparta and commander of the Spartan force, ordered his head to be cut off and fixed on a stake. This is in my opinion the strongest evidence – though there is plenty more – that King Xerxes, while Leonidas was still alive, felt fiercer anger against him than against any other man; had that not been so, he would never have committed this outrage upon his body; for normally the Persians, more than any other nation I know of, honour men who distinguish themselves in war. However, Xerxes' order was carried out.

I will now return to a point in my story where I omitted to mention something. The Spartans were the first to get the news that Xerxes was preparing an expedition against Greece; thereupon they sent to the Delphic oracle and received the answer of which I spoke a little while ago. The way they received the news was very remarkable: Demaratus, the son of Ariston, who was an exile in Persia, was not, I imagine – and as is only natural to suppose – well disposed towards the Spartans; so it is open to question whether what he did was inspired by benevolence or by malicious pleasure. Anyway, as soon as news reached him at Susa that Xerxes had decided upon the invasion of Greece, he felt that he must pass on the information to Sparta. As the danger of discovery was great, there was only one way in which he could contrive to get the message through: this was by scraping the wax off a pair of wooden folding tablets, writing on the wood underneath what Xerxes intended to do, and then covering the message over with wax again. In this way the tablets, being apparently blank, would cause no trouble with the guards along the road. When the message reached its destination, no one was able to guess the secret until, as I understand, Cleomenes' daughter Gorgo, who was the wife of Leonidas, divined it and told the others that, if they scraped the wax off, they would find something written on the wood underneath. This was done; the message was revealed and read, and afterwards passed on to the other Greeks. That, at any rate, is the story of what happened.

BOOK EIGHT

THE following is the roll of the Greek naval force: 127 ships from Athens – partly manned by the Plataeans, whose courage and patriotism led them to undertake this service in spite of their ignorance of everything to do with the sea; 40 from Corinth, 20 from Megara, 20 more from Athens manned by crews from Chalcis, 18 from Aegina, 12 from Sicyon, 10 from Sparta, 8 from Epidaurus, 7 from Eretria, 5 from Troezen, 2 from Styra, and 2 – together with two fifty-oared galleys – from Ceos. Lastly, the Locrians of Opus joined with seven fifty-oared galleys.

These, then, were the states which sent ships to Artemisium, and I have given the number which each contributed. The total strength of the fleet, excluding the small galleys, was thus 271 ships of war. The general officer in command, Eurybiades, the son of Eurycleides, was provided by Sparta; for the other members of the confederacy had stipulated for a Lacedaemonian commander, declaring that rather than serve under an Athenian they would break up the intended expedition altogether. From the first, even before Sicily was asked to join the alliance, there had been talk of the advisability of giving Athens command of the fleet; but the proposal had not been well received by the allied states, and the Athenians waived their claim in the interest of national survival, knowing that a quarrel about the command would certainly mean the destruction of Greece. They were, indeed, perfectly right; for the evil of internal strife is worse than united war in the same proportion as war itself is worse than peace. It was their realization of the danger attendant upon lack of unity which made them waive their claim, and they continued to do so as long as Greece desperately needed their help. This was made plain enough by their subsequent action; for when the Persians had been driven from Greece and the war had been carried to Persian territory, the Athenians made the insufferable behaviour of Pausanias their excuse for depriving the Lacedaemonians of the command.

When the Greeks on their arrival at Artemisium found a large Persian fleet lying at Aphetae and all the neighbourhood full of troops, it was evident to them that things had gone very differently with the Persians from what they had expected. They were seized by panic, and began to consider abandoning Artemisium and making their escape into the inner parts of Greece. This greatly alarmed the Euboeans, who no sooner realized what they had in mind than they begged Eurybiades to stay at any rate long enough to allow them to move their children and servants to a place of safety. Eurybiades refused, whereupon they went to Themistocles, the Athenian commander, and by a bribe of thirty talents induced him so to arrange matters that the Greek fleet should stay and fight on the coast of Euboea. The method Themistocles adopted to attain this object was to pass on to Eurybiades, as if it were a personal present from himself, a sixth part of the sum he had received from the Euboeans. This was enough to secure Eurybiades' consent; of the other commanders, however, there was still one who hesitated – Adeimantus son of Ocytus, the Corinthian, who declared that he would withdraw his ships from Artemisium. To him, therefore, Themistocles now addressed himself. 'Never,' he cried with an oath, 'shall you leave us in the lurch! I will give you more for staying with us than the Persian king would ever send you if you deserted us'; and without further delay he sent aboard Adeimantus' ship three talents of silver. So Adeimantus and Eurybiades yielded to bribery and the Euboeans' wishes were gratified; Themistocles, too, made something out of the transaction, for he kept the rest of the money himself. Nobody knew he had it, and the two men who had received their share imagined that it came from Athens especially for the purpose. These were the circumstances which led to the Greeks engaging the Persians on the Euboean coast, and I will now describe the battle itself.

The Persians reached Aphetae early in the afternoon, and saw for themselves what they had previously heard reported – namely that a small Greek force was concentrated at Artemisium. At once they were eager to engage, in the hope of capturing the Greek ships. It did not, however, seem advisable to advance, in the first instance, openly to the attack; for the Greeks, seeing them coming, might try to escape, and then, when darkness overtook them, they would be sure to get clear away. This would not do, as the Persians were determined that not even a fire-signaller (as they put it) must be allowed to escape alive. Laying their plans accordingly, they detached a squadron of 200 ships with orders to sail outside Sciathus, in order to escape enemy observation, and then to turn southward round Euboea and into the Euripus by way of Caphareus and Geraestus; in this way they hoped to catch the Greeks in a trap, one squadron taking them in the rear and blocking their retreat, the rest of the fleet pressing upon them from in front. With this purpose in view the two hundred ships were dispatched, while the main body waited – for they did not intend to attack on that day, or until they knew by signal that the squadron coming up the Euripus had arrived. Meanwhile a review of the main fleet was held at Aphetae, and while it was going on an interesting event occurred Serving with the Persian force there was a man named Scyllias, a native of Scione and the most accomplished diver of his day, who after the wreck of the Persian ships at Pelion had saved a great deal of valuable property for his masters – besides getting a good deal for himself. This man had apparently been thinking for some time past of deserting to the Greeks, but no opportunity had occurred until then. I cannot say for certain how it was that he managed to reach the Greeks, and the commonly accepted account is, at the least, doubtful; for, according to this, he dived under water at Aphetae and did not come up until he reached Artemisium – a distance of about ten miles. There are other somewhat tall stories, besides this, told about Scyllias – and also a few true ones; as to the one I have just related, my personal opinion is that he came to Artemisium in a boat. In any case, come he did; and on his arrival he lost no time in giving an account to the Greek commanders of all the circumstances of the disaster to the Persian fleet in the storm, and also told them about the squadron which was on its way round Euboea.

The Greek commanders at once proceeded to discuss the situation which this piece of intelligence produced; and after a long debate it was decided to stay where they were until after midnight, and then put to sea to meet the Persians who were coming up the Euripus. However, as time went on and they met with no opposition, they waited till the evening of the following day and then attacked the main enemy fleet, with the intention of testing Persian seamanship and tactics.

When the officers and men of Xerxes' fleet saw the Greeks moving to the attack with such a small force, they thought they were mad and at once got under way themselves, in confident expectation of making an easy capture; nor, indeed, was the expectation unreasonable, in view of the disparity in numbers – the Greek ships being few, and their own many times as numerous, as well as faster. Thus assured of their superiority, they developed a movement to surround the enemy. Those of the Ionians who had been forced to serve with the Persian fleet in spite of their real sympathy with the Greek cause, were much distressed at the sight of the gradual encirclement of the Greeks, and convinced, in view of their apparent weakness, that not a man amongst them would escape alive; those, on the other hand, who welcomed the situation, entered into competition with each other to be the first to win a reward from Xerxes for the capture of an Athenian ship – for throughout the Persian fleet it was the Athenians who were most talked of.

At the first signal for action the Greek squadron formed into a close circle – bows outward, sterns to the centre; then, at the second signal, with little room to manoeuvre and lying, as they were, bows-on to the enemy, they set to work, and succeeded in capturing thirty Persian ships. Amongst the prisoners was Philaon, the son of Chersis and brother of Gorgus the king of Salamis, and a person of repute in the enemy force. The first Greek to take a prize was the Athenian Lycomedes son of Aeschraeus. He was decorated for valour after the battle.

After this success, when darkness put an end to the fighting, the Greeks returned to Artemisium, and the Persians – who had had a considerable shock – to Aphetae. The only Greek in the Persian force to desert and join his countrymen during the action was Antidorus, the Lemnian; the Athenians afterwards showed their appreciation by giving him a grant of land in Salamis.

After dark – the season was midsummer – there was a very violent rainstorm, which lasted all night, accompanied by much thunder from the direction of Pelion. Dead bodies and bits of wreckage, drifting up to Aphetae, fell athwart the bows of the ships which lay there, and fouled the oar-blades of any that were under way; this, and the noise of the thunderstorm, caused a panic amongst the Persian troops, who began to think their last hour was come: they had, indeed, had much to put up with – for almost before they could draw breath again after the storm at Pelion, which wrecked so many of their ships, they were faced with a hard fight at sea, and now, on top of that, they were exposed to floods of rain, the rushing of swollen streams into the sea, and a tremendous thunderstorm.

For the Persians at Aphetae it was a bad enough night, but it was far worse for the squadron which had been ordered to sail round Euboea, for they were at sea when the storm caught them. Their fate was miserable: just as they were off the Hollows of Euboea the wind and rain began, and every ship, overpowered and forced to run blind before it, piled up on the rocks. Heaven was indeed doing everything possible to reduce the superiority of the Persian fleet and bring it down to the size of the Greek. So much for the disaster off the Hollows.

The Persians at Aphetae were very glad to see the dawn next morning, and did not feel like taking any further risks; it was enough for them, badly shaken as they were, to let the ships lie and attempt nothing for the present. Meanwhile the Greeks received a reinforcement of fifty-three ships from Athens; the arrival of this fresh squadron, together with the news of the loss in the storm of the whole Persian force which was sailing round Euboea, was a great encouragement, and the Greeks, on the strength of it, waiting till the same time as on the previous day, once again put to sea and attacked some Cilician vessels; these they destroyed and then, at the approach of darkness, they returned to Artemisium.

The Persian commanders were humiliated at receiving such rough treatment from so small a fleet; they were beginning, moreover, to be alarmed at the thought of what Xerxes might do to them; so on the third day they took the initiative, and, without waiting for the Greeks to move, made their preparations and put to sea round about midday. It so happened that these battles at sea took place on the same days as the battles at Thermopylae, and in each case the object was similar – to defend the passage into the heart of Greece: the fleet was fighting for the Euripus just as the army with Leonidas was fighting for the pass. So the Greek cry was to stop the enemy from getting through, while the Persians aimed at destroying the defending forces in order to clear the passage.

Xerxes' fleet now moved forward in good order to the attack, while the Greeks at Artemisium quietly awaited their approach. Then the Persians adopted a crescent formation and came on with the intention of surrounding their enemy, whereupon the Greeks advanced to meet them, and the fight began. In this engagement the two fleets were evenly matched – the Persian, by its mere size, proving its own greatest enemy, as constant confusion was caused by the ships fouling one another. None the less they made a brave fight of it, to avoid the disgrace of defeat by so small an enemy force. The Greek losses both in ships and men were heavy, those of the Persians much heavier. Finally the action was broken off with such negative results as I have described. On the Persian side it was the Egyptians who came out of it with the best record, their most notable achievement being the capture of five Greek ships together with their crews; of the Greeks the most conspicuous were the Athenians – and in particular Cleinias, the son of Alcibiades, who was serving in his own ship manned by two hundred men, all at his own personal expense.

Both sides were glad when they parted and made all speed back to their moorings. The Greeks, once they were clear of the fighting, did, indeed, manage to possess themselves of the floating bodies and to salve the wreckage; nevertheless they had been so roughly handled – especially the Athenians, half of whose ships were damaged – that they determined to quit their station and withdraw further south. At this point it occurred to Themistocles that if the Ionian and Carian contingents could be detached from the Persian force, the Greeks would be able to deal successfully with the rest; accordingly he called his officers to a conference on the beach, to which the people of Euboea were already driving their sheep. Here he told them that he thought he had a plan, which might succeed in depriving Xerxes' fleet of its finest units. For the moment he gave no further details of

what the plan was, but merely advised them, in view of the circumstances, to slaughter as many of the Euboean sheep as they pleased,
as it was better that their own troops should have them than the
enemy. He further suggested that every officer should order his men
to light fires as usual; as for the withdrawal from Artemisium, he
made himself responsible for choosing the proper moment and for
seeing that they got home safely. These proposals proved acceptable;
so the commanders at once had fires lighted, and the men set to on the
cattle.

I should add here that the Euboeans had paid no attention to the
oracle of Bacis, supposing it to have no significance; they had taken
no precautions against the threat of war, either by removing property
from the island or by getting in stores, and consequently found
themselves in a highly dangerous position. The oracle was as follows:

When one of foreign speech casts a papyrus yoke upon the sea,
Bethink you to keep the bleating goats far from Euboea.

This warning they ignored; and the result was great suffering, both
then and later, in the troubles which were daily expected.

While the Greeks were thus occupied, their observer arrived from
Trachis. The Greeks had employed two, to keep communication
between the fleet and the army: at Artemisium Polyas, a native of
Anticyra, kept a boat ready to report to the army at Thermopylae
any reverse which might be suffered by the fleet, while the Athenian
Abronichus, the son of Lysides, did similar duty with Leonidas, and
had a thirty-oared galley always available to report to Artemisium,
if the army got into any trouble. It was this Abronichus who now
arrived with the news of the fate of Leonidas and his men. The effect
was immediate; the Greeks put off their withdrawal not a minute
longer, but got under way at once, one after another, the Corinthians
leading, the Athenians bringing up the rear.

Themistocles took the fastest ships and called on the way at all
the places where drinking water was to be found, and cut notices
on the rocks near by for the Ionians to read – as they did when they
moved up on the following day. 'Men of Ionia' – his message ran –
'it is wrong that you should make war upon your fathers and help to
bring Greeks into subjection. The best thing you can do is to join our

side; if this is impossible, you might at least remain neutral, and ask the Carians to do the same. If you are unable to do either, but are held by a force so strong that it puts desertion out of the question, there is still another course open to you: in the next battle, remember that you and we are of the same blood, that our quarrel with Persia arose originally on your account – and fight badly.'

In leaving this message Themistocles probably had two possibilities in mind: in the first place, it might, if the kings did not get to know of it, induce the Ionians to come over to the Greeks, and, secondly, if it were reported to Xerxes and made the ground of an accusation against the Ionians, they would be distrusted and not allowed, in consequence, to take part in engagements at sea.

Immediately after this a native of Histiaea sailed to Aphetae with the news of the Greek withdrawal from Artemisium. The Persians refused to believe it; they put the man under guard and sent off a party of some fast ships to see for themselves. Then, assured that the news was true, they moved at sunrise with the whole fleet to Artemisium, where they stayed until midday, before going on to Histiaea. They took this town, and overran all the coastal villages of Ellopia, a district belonging to Histiaea. While they were here, a messenger arrived from the king. Before sending him, Xerxes had arranged that of the twenty thousand men in the Persian army who had been killed at Thermopylae, all except about a thousand should be buried in trenches and covered over with earth and leaves, to prevent their being seen by anyone from the fleet. The remaining thousand were left exposed. On reaching Histiaea the messenger had the whole force assembled and delivered his message. 'Friends and fellow-soldiers,' he said, 'the king grants leave for anyone who wants it, to go and see with his own eyes how he fights against the madmen who thought they could beat him.' The announcement was no sooner made than so many people wanted to avail themselves of the king's offer that the supply of boats ran out. All who could, crossed the water and toured the battlefield to see the bodies; some of the corpses were, of course, those of helots, but the sightseers imagined that they were all Spartans and Thespians; however, Xerxes' ludicrous attempt to conceal the number of his own dead deceived nobody.

On the day after this, which had been spent in sight-seeing, the seamen rejoined their ships at Histiaea and the army with Xerxes set forward on its march. A few Arcadian deserters came in – men who had nothing to live on and wanted employment; they were taken to Xerxes and questioned about what the Greeks were doing. One Persian conducted the interrogation on behalf of them all, and he was told in reply that the Greeks were celebrating the Olympic festival, where they were watching athletic contests and chariot-races. When he asked what the prize was for which they contended, the Arcadians mentioned the wreath of olive-leaves which it is our custom to give. This drew from Tritantaechmes, the son of Artabanus, a very sound remark – though it made Xerxes call him a coward; for when he learned that the prize was not money but a wreath, he could not help crying out in front of everybody, 'Good heavens, Mardonius, what kind of men are these that you have brought us to fight against – men who compete with one another for no material reward, but only for honour!'

Meanwhile, immediately after the disaster at Thermopylae, the Thessalians sent a representative to Phocis. They had always been on bad terms with the Phocians, but especially so since the last blow they had received from them. Not many years before the Persian invasion they and their allies in full force had invaded Phocis and been defeated with serious losses. The Phocians were blocked up in Parnassus, and their subsequent success was due to a clever piece of work by an Elean named Tellias, who was serving with the Phocians as their diviner; what he did was to pick six hundred good men, cover their bodies and weapons all over with whitewash, and send them on a night attack against the enemy, with instructions to kill everyone they saw who was not whitened like themselves. The Thessalian sentries were the first to see them, and took them for some sort of appalling apparition; then the panic spread to the rest of the troops, who were so badly scared that the Phocians killed four thousand of them, and got possession of their bodies and shields. Half the shields were sent as an offering to the temple at Abae, the other half to Delphi, while from a tenth part of the plunder were made the great statues which stand around the tripod in front of the temple at Delphi, and also the similar figures at Abae.

In addition to breaking out from Parnassus and inflicting this signal defeat on the Thessalian infantry, the Phocians also did irreparable damage to the Thessalian cavalry during an attempted raid. They dug a deep trench across the pass near Hyampolis, put a number of big empty jars in it, and covered them over lightly with soil; then, making the surface smooth and level to conceal the trap, they awaited the attack. The Thessalians galloped up, expecting to sweep all before them, when their horses fell through into the jars and broke their legs. Thus the Thessalians had two reasons for resentment when they sent their representative to Phocis. Their message ran as follows: 'Men of Phocis, now at last you must admit your error, and own that you are not our equals. In the past, while it suited us to make one with the Greeks, we were always considered more important than you; and now our influence with the Persians is so great that a word from us would get you turned out of your country, and sold as slaves into the bargain. All the same, though we have you completely in our power, we are willing to let bygones be bygones: just pay us off with fifty talents, and we undertake to divert the danger which is threatening your country.'

Now the Phocians were the only people in this part of Greece who had not gone over to the Persians, and in my opinion their motive was simply and solely their hatred of Thessaly. If Thessaly had remained loyal, no doubt the Phocians would have deserted to Persia. As it was, when they heard what the Thessalian representative had to say, they refused to pay a penny and declared that they could join Persia just as easily as the Thessalians did, had they been inclined that way; nevertheless, they would never willingly prove traitors to Greece. This reply to their message made the Thessalians very angry, and they forthwith offered to act as guides to the Persian army.

From Trachis the army entered the narrow strip of Dorian territory, barely four miles wide, which lies between Malis and Phocis. In old days this region was called Dryopis, and was the original home of the Peloponnesian Dorians. The Persians did no damage to this part of Doris on their way through; the people in any case were friendly, and the Thessalians wished them to be spared. Passing from Doris into Phocis, they failed to catch the Phocians because they had already cleared out: some of them had gone up into the mountains – the height of Parnassus, called Tithorea, not far from Neon, has plenty of room for a large body of men, and a number of them had climbed up on to it and taken with them all they could move – while the majority had sought shelter with the Locrians of Ozolae and taken their property to Amphissa, the town which stands above the plain of Crisa. All Phocis was overrun; the Thessalians did not let the Persian army miss a bit of it, and everywhere they went there was devastation by fire and sword, and towns and temples were burnt. Along the valley of the Cephisus nothing was spared; Drymus, Charada, Erochus, Tethronium, Amphicaea, Neon, Pedies, Trites, Elateia, Hyampolis, Parapotamii – all these places were burnt to the ground, including Abae, where there was a temple of Apollo richly furnished with treasure and offerings of all kinds. There was an oracle there, as indeed there is to-day; the shrine belonging to it was plundered and burnt. A few Phocians were chased and caught near the mountains, and some women were raped successively by so many Persian soldiers that they died.

At Panopes, which they reached by way of Parapotamii, the army divided and one division, the stronger and more numerous, proceeded with Xerxes towards Athens, entering Boeotia near Orchomenus. All the Boeotians had gone over to the enemy, and their towns were protected by Macedonians, sent by Alexander, to make it clear to Xerxes that the people of Boeotia were friendly to him. The other division of the army made with their guides for the temple at Delphi, keeping Parnassus on their right. They, too, devastated all the parts of Phocis through which they passed, and burnt the towns of Panopes, Daulis, and Aeolidae. This division was detached from the main body of the army for the special purpose of plundering the temple at Delphi, and bringing its treasures to Xerxes; I have been told that he was better acquainted, from descriptions continually coming to his notice, with everything of importance there than with his own property at home, and especially with the precious objects which had been presented to the shrine by Croesus, the son of Alyattes.

The news of the approach of the Persians caused consternation at Delphi; and in their terror the people asked the God's advice as to whether they should bury the sacred treasures or get them out of the country. The God replied that they were not to be disturbed, for he was well able to guard his own. This being decided, the Delphians began to think about saving themselves; they sent their women and children across the water into Achaea, and most of the men took to the mountains in the summits of Parnassus, and stored their movable property in the Corycian cave, while a few of them made their escape to Amphissa in Locris. All abandoned the town except sixty men and the Priest of the oracle.

The Persians were now close at hand and within sight of the temple, when suddenly the Priest, whose name was Aceratus, saw weapons lying on the ground in front of the shrine – they were the sacred weapons which no human hand may touch, and they had been brought mysteriously out from their place within. He hastened to report this marvellous thing to the other Delphians who were still in the town. Meanwhile the enemy were drawing quickly nearer, and when they reached the temple of Athene Pronaea even stranger things happened to them than what I have just recorded. It is surprising enough that weapons of war should move of their own accord and appear upon the ground outside the shrine; but what occurred next is surely one of the most extraordinary things ever known – for just as the Persians came to the shrine of Athene Pronaea, thunderbolts fell on them from the sky, and two pinnacles of rock, torn from Parnassus, came crashing and rumbling down amongst them, killing a large number, while at the same time there was a battle-cry from inside the shrine. All these things happening together caused a panic amongst the Persian troops. They fled; and the Delphians, seeing them on the run, came down upon them and attacked them with great slaughter. All who escaped with their lives made straight for Boeotia. There is a story, I am told, amongst those who got away, that there was yet another miraculous occurrence: they saw, so they said, two gigantic soldiers – taller than ever a man was – pursuing them and cutting them down. According to the Delphians, these were Phylacus and Autonous, local heroes who have enclosed plots of ground near the temple, which are held sacred to them – that of Phylacus lies along the road above the temple of Pronaea, and that of Autonous is near the spring of Castalia under the peak called Hyampia.

The rocks which fell from Parnassus were still there in my time;[1] they lay in the enclosure round the shrine of Pronaea, where they embedded themselves after crashing through the Persian troops. So that was how these people took their departure from the Holy Place at Delphi.

The Greek fleet, having sailed from Artemisium, brought up, at the Athenians' request, at Salamis. The Athenians' object in urging the commanders to take up this position was to give themselves an opportunity of getting their women and children out of Attica, and also of discussing their next move – as their present circumstances, and the frustration of their hopes, most evidently demanded. They had expected that the full strength of the Peloponnesian army would concentrate in Boeotia to hold up the Persian advance, but now they found nothing of the sort; on the contrary, they learned that the Peloponnesians were concerned only with their own safety and were fortifying the Isthmus in order to protect the Peloponnese, while the rest of Greece, so far as they cared, might take its chance. It was this news which led to the request to the fleet to put in at Salamis.

While, therefore, the rest of the fleet lay at Salamis, the Athenians returned to their own harbours, and at once issued a proclamation that every one in the city and countryside should get his children and all the members of his household to safety as best he could. Most of them were sent to Troezen, but some to Aegina and some to Salamis. The removal of their families was pressed on with all possible speed, partly because they wished to take the warning which had been given them by the oracle, but more especially for an even stronger reason. The Athenians say that the Acropolis is guarded by a great snake, which lives in the temple; indeed they believed so literally in its existence that they put out regular rations for it to eat in the form of a honey-cake. Now in the past the honey-cake used always to be consumed, but on this occasion it was untouched. The temple Priestess told them of this, and in consequence, believing that the goddess herself had abandoned the Acropolis, they were all the more ready

1. They are still there in our time, below the road, one of them lying on top of the ruins of a sixth-century Doric temple or 'treasury'.

to evacuate the town. As soon as everything was removed, they re-joined the fleet on its station.

There were some other Greek ships which had been ordered to assemble at Pogon, the harbour of Troezen, and these, when news came through that the fleet from Artemisium had put into Salamis, left Troezen and joined it. Thus the fleet was larger than it had been at the battle of Artemisium, and made up of ships from more towns. It was still under the same commander, Eurybiades, the son of Eury-cleides – a Spartan but not of the royal blood; but the city which furnished by far the greatest number of ships, and the fastest, was Athens. The composition of the fleet was as follows: 16 ships from Lacedaemon, the same number from Corinth as at Artemisium, 15 from Sicyon, 10 from Epidaurus, 5 from Troezen, 3 from Hermione. The people of all these places except Hermione are of Dorian and Macedonian blood, and had last emigrated from Erineus, Pindus, and Dryopis. The people of Hermione are Dryopes, and were driven out by Heracles and the Malians from the country now called Doris.

The contingents mentioned above were from the Peloponnese; from outside the Peloponnese there were, first, the Athenians with 180 ships, half the whole fleet. These were manned by Athenians only, for the Plataeans did not serve with them at the battle of Sala-mis, because during the withdrawal from Artemisium, when the fleet was off Chalcis, they landed in Boeotia on the opposite shore and set about conveying their property and households to a place of safety, and were consequently left behind. When what is now called Greece was occupied by the Pelasgians, the Athenians, a Pelasgian people, were called Cranai. In the reign of Cecrops they acquired the name of Cecropidae. At the succession of Erechtheus they changed their name to Athenians; and when Ion, the son of Xuthus, became general of their armies, they took from him the title of Ionians.

From Megara there was the same number of ships as at Arte-misium; then there were 7 from Ambracia, and 3 from Leucas. The Ambraciots and Leucadians are Dorians from Corinth. Of the island states Aegina contributed 30 ships. The Aeginetans had others in commission, but these were employed in guarding their own island; their best thirty were the ones which fought at Salamis. The Aeginetans are Dorians from Epidaurus; the island used to be known as Oenone. Next was the squadron from Chalcis; this consisted of the same twenty ships which served at Artemisium; from Eretria there were the original 7. These two peoples are Ionians. Ceos (the Ceans are Ionians from Athens) sent the same number as before, and Naxos 4. The Naxian contingent, like those from the other islands, had been sent to join the Persians, but disobeyed orders and joined the Greeks at the instigation of Democritus, a man of distinction who was then in command of a trireme. The Naxians are Ionians of Athenian blood. Styra provided the same ships as at Artemisium, and Cythnus one trireme and a 50-oared galley. The Styreans and Cythnians are Dryopes. Seriphus, Siphnus, and Melos also took part – they were the only islands not to make their submission to Persia. All these states are situated on the hither side of the river Acheron and the country of the Thesprotians, who are neighbours of the people of Ambracia and Leucas – the two most distant places to contribute to the fleet. Beyond them, there was only one community – Croton – which helped Greece in her hour of danger; the Crotoniats sent one ship, under the command of Phayllus, a man who had won three victories at the Pythian games. The Crotoniats are of Achaean blood. All the contingents consisted of triremes, except the Melian, Siphnian, and Seriphian, which were 50-oared galleys. The Melians, who are of Lacedaemonian blood, sent two, the Siphnians and Seriphians, who are Ionians from Athens, one each. The total number of warships (excluding the light galleys) was 378.

When the commanders of the various contingents I have mentioned met at Salamis, a council of war was held, and Eurybiades called for suggestions, from anyone who wished to speak, on the most suitable place for engaging the enemy fleet in the territory still under their control – Attica was excluded, as it had already been given up. The general feeling of the council was in favour of sailing to the Isthmus and fighting in defence of the Peloponnese, on the grounds that if they were beaten at Salamis they would find themselves blocked up in an island, where no help could reach them, whereas if disaster overtook them at the Isthmus, they could find refuge amongst their own people. This was the view of the Peloponnesian officers. While the discussion was still going on, a man arrived from Athens with the news that the Persians had entered Attica and were firing the whole country. This was the work of the division of the army under Xerxes which had taken the route through Boeotia; they had burnt Thespia after the inhabitants had escaped to the Peloponnese, and Plataea too, and then entered Attica, where they were causing wholesale devastation. The Thebans had told them that Thespia and Plataea had refused to submit to Persian domination: hence their destruction. The march of the Persian army from the Hellespont to Attica had taken three months – and the actual crossing of the strait an additional one; it reached Attica during the magistracy of Calliades.

The Persians found Athens itself abandoned except for a few people in the temple of Athene Polias – temple stewards and needy folk, who had barricaded the Acropolis against the invaders with planks and timbers. It was partly their poverty which prevented them from seeking shelter in Salamis with the rest, and partly their belief that they had discovered the real meaning of the Priestess' oracle – that 'the wooden wall would not be taken'. The wooden wall, in their minds, was not the ships but the barricade, and that would save them.

The Persians occupied the hill which the Athenians call the Areopagus, opposite the Acropolis, and began the siege. The method they used was to shoot into the barricade arrows with burning tow attached to them. Their wooden wall had betrayed them, but still the Athenians, though in imminent and deadly peril, refused to give in or even to listen to the proposals which the Pisistratidae made to them for a truce. All their ingenuity was employed in the struggle to defend themselves; amongst other things, they rolled boulders down the slope upon the enemy as he tried to approach the gates, and for a long time Xerxes was baffled and unable to take them. But in the end the Persians solved their problem: a way of access to the Acropolis was found – for it was prophesied that all Athenian territory upon the continent of Greece must be overrun by the Persians. There is a place in front of the Acropolis, behind the way up to the gates, where the ascent is so steep that no guard was set, because it was not thought possible that any man would be able to climb it;

here, by the shrine of Cecrops' daughter Aglaurus, some soldiers managed to scramble up the precipitous face of the cliff. When the Athenians saw them on the summit, some leapt from the wall to their death, others sought sanctuary in the inner shrine of the temple; but the Persians who had got up first made straight for the gates, flung them open and slaughtered those in sanctuary. Having left not one of them alive, they stripped the temple of its treasures and burnt everything on the Acropolis. Xerxes, now absolute master of Athens, despatched a rider to Susa with news for Artabanus of his success.

On the following day he summoned to his presence the Athenian exiles who were serving with the Persian forces, and ordered them to go up into the Acropolis and offer sacrifice there according to Athenian usage; possibly some dream or other had suggested this course to him, or perhaps his conscience was uneasy for the burning of the temple. The Athenian exiles did as they were bidden. I mention these details for a particular reason: on the Acropolis there is a spot which is sacred to Erechtheus - the 'earth-born', and within it is an olive-tree and a spring of salt water. According to the local legend they were put there by Poseidon and Athene, when they contended for possession of the land, as tokens of their claims to it. Now this olive was destroyed by fire together with the rest of the sanctuary; nevertheless on the very next day, when the Athenians, who were ordered by the king to offer the sacrifice, went up to that sacred place, they saw that a new shoot eighteen inches long had sprung from the stump. They told the king of this.

Meanwhile at Salamis the effect of the news of what had happened to the Acropolis at Athens was so disturbing, that some of the naval commanders did not even wait for the subject under discussion to be decided, but hurried on board and began hoisting sail for immediate flight. Some, however, stayed; and by these a resolution was passed to fight in defence of the Isthmus.

During the night, when the various commanders had returned on board after the break-up of the conference, an Athenian named Mnesiphilus made his way to Themistocles' ship and asked him what plan it had been decided to adopt. On learning that they had resolved to sail to the Isthmus and to fight there in defence of the Peloponnese, 'No, no,' he exclaimed; 'once the fleet leaves Salamis, it will no longer be one country that you'll be fighting for. Everyone will go home, and neither Eurybiades nor anybody else will be able to prevent the total dissolution of our forces. The plan is absurd and will be the ruin of Greece. Now listen to me: try, if you possibly can, to upset the decision of the conference – it may be that you will be able to persuade Eurybiades to change his mind and remain at Salamis.'

Themistocles highly approved of this suggestion, and without saying a word he went to the ship of the commander-in-chief and told him that he had something of public importance to discuss. Eurybiades invited him aboard and gave him permission to speak his mind, whereupon Themistocles, taking a seat beside him, repeated Mnesiphilus' arguments as if they were his own, with plenty of new ones added, until he convinced him, by the sheer urgency of his appeal, that the only thing to do was to go ashore and call the officers to another conference. The conference met, and then, before Eurybiades even had time to announce its purpose, Themistocles, unable to restrain his eagerness, broke into a passionate speech. He was interrupted by Adeimantus, the son of Ocytus, commander of the Corinthian contingent. 'Themistocles,' he observed, 'in the races, the man who starts before the signal is whipped.' 'Yes,' was Themistocles' retort, 'but those who start too late win no prizes.' It was a mild retort – for the moment. To Eurybiades he used none of his previous arguments about the danger of the force breaking up if they left Salamis; for it would have been unbecoming to accuse any of the confederates actually to their faces. The line he took this time was quite different. 'It is now in your power', he said, 'to save Greece, if you take my advice and engage the enemy's fleet here in Salamis, instead of withdrawing to the Isthmus as these other people suggest. Let me put the two plans before you, and you can weigh them up and see which is the better. Take the Isthmus first: if you fight there, it will have to be in the open sea, and that will be greatly to our disadvantage, with our smaller numbers and slower ships. Moreover, even if everything else goes well, you will lose Salamis, Megara, and Aegina. Again, if the enemy fleet comes south, the army will follow it; so you will yourself be responsible for drawing it to the Peloponnese, thus putting the whole of Greece in peril.

'Now for my plan: it will bring, if you adopt it, the following advantages: first, we shall be fighting in narrow waters, and there, with our inferior numbers, we shall win, provided things go as we may reasonably expect. Fighting in a confined space favours us but the open sea favours the enemy. Secondly, Salamis, where we have put our women and children, will be preserved; and thirdly – for you the most important point of all – you will be fighting in defence of the Peloponnese by remaining here just as much as by withdrawing to the Isthmus – nor, if you have the sense to follow my advice, will you draw the Persian army to the Peloponnese. If we beat them at sea, as I expect we shall, they will not advance to attack you on the Isthmus, or come any further than Attica; they will retreat in disorder, and we shall gain by the preservation of Megara, Aegina, and Salamis – where an oracle has already foretold our victory. Let a man lay his plans with due regard to common sense, and he will usually succeed; otherwise he will find that God is unlikely to favour human designs.'

During his speech Themistocles was again attacked by the Corinthian Adeimantus, who told him to hold his tongue because he was a man without a country, and tried to prevent Eurybiades from putting any question to the vote at the instance of a mere refugee. Let Themistocles, he cried, provide himself with a country before he offered his advice. The point of the jibe was, of course, the fact that Athens had fallen and was in Persian hands. This time Themistocles' retort was by no means mild; he heartily abused both Adeimantus and the Corinthians, and made it quite plain that so long as Athens had two hundred warships in commission, she had both a city and a country much stronger than theirs – for there was not a single Greek state capable of repelling them, should they choose to attack.

With this he turned to Eurybiades again, and, speaking more vehemently than ever, 'As for you,' he cried, 'if you stay here and play the man – well and good; go, and you'll be the ruin of Greece. In this war everything depends upon the fleet. I beg you to take my advice; if you refuse, we will immediately put our families aboard and sail for Siris in Italy – it has long been ours, and the oracles have foretold that Athenians must live there some day. Where will you be without the Athenian fleet? When you have lost it you will remember my words.'

This was enough to make Eurybiades change his mind; and no doubt his chief motive was apprehension of losing Athenian support, if he withdrew to the Isthmus; for without the Athenian contingent his strength would not have been adequate to offer battle. So he took the decision to stay where they were and fight it out at Salamis.

After these verbal skirmishes, when Eurybiades had made up his mind, they prepared to fight where they were. Day broke; just as the sun rose the shock of an earthquake was felt both on land and at sea, and the Greeks resolved to offer prayers to the gods and to call upon the Sons of Aeacus to fight at their side. As they resolved, so they did: they prayed to all the gods, and called upon Ajax and Telamon there in Salamis, and sent a ship to Aegina for Aeacus himself and his other Sons.

There is a story which used to be told by Dicaeus, the son of Theocydes, an Athenian exile who had some repute among the Persians. After the evacuation of Attica, when the Persian troops were devastating the countryside, he happened to be in the plain of Thria with Demaratus the Spartan. They saw a cloud of dust, such as might have been raised by an army of thirty thousand men on the march, coming from the direction of Eleusis, and were wondering what troops they could be, when they suddenly heard the sound of voices. Dicaeus thought he recognized the *Iacchus* song, which is sung at the Dionysiac mysteries, but Demaratus, who was unfamiliar with the religious ceremonial of Eleusis, asked his companion whose voices they were. 'Sir,' Dicaeus answered, 'without any doubt some dreadful disaster is about to happen to the king's army. There is not a man left in Attica; so the voice we heard must clearly be a divine voice, coming from Eleusis to bring help to the Athenians and their friends. If it descends upon the Peloponnese, there will be danger for the king and for his army; if it moves towards the ships at Salamis, Xerxes may well lose his fleet. Every year the Athenians celebrate a festival in honour of the Mother and the Maid, and anyone who wishes, from Athens or elsewhere, may be initiated in the mysteries; the sound you heard was the Iacchus song which is always sung at that festival.'

'Do not breathe a word of this to anybody,' said Demaratus. 'If it should reach the ears of the king, you would lose your head, and neither I nor anyone else in the world could save you. So hold your tongue – the gods will see to the king's army.'

While Demaratus was speaking, the cloud of dust, from which the mysterious voice had issued, rose high into the air and drifted away towards Salamis, where the Greek fleet was stationed. By this the two men knew that the naval power of Xerxes was destined to be destroyed. Such was Dicaeus' story, and he used to appeal to Demaratus and others to witness the truth of it.

Meanwhile the Persian sailors had returned from Trachis to Histiaea after their sight-seeing tour of the battlefield, and three days later the fleet set sail. The ships passed through the Euripus, and in another three days arrived off Phaleron. In my judgement the Persian forces both by land and sea were just as strong at the time of their entry into Attica as they had been at Sepias and Thermopylae; for as an offset to the losses suffered in the storm, at Thermopylae, and at Artemisium, I reckon the reinforcements which had subsequently joined them. These were the Malians, Dorians, and Locrians, the Boeotians in full force except the Thespians and Plataeans; and in addition to these the Carystians, Andrians, Tenians, and all the other island peoples except the five whom I mentioned above. The further Xerxes advanced into Greece, the more peoples followed him.

All these troops came as far as Attica except the Parians, who stayed behind in Cythnus to watch the course of the war; and the rest of the fleet arrived, as I have said, at Phaleron. Here Xerxes paid it a personal visit, because he wished to talk to the commanding officers and hear their opinions; so when he had seated himself, the rulers of states and commanders of squadrons were summoned to appear before him, and took their seats according to the precedence which the king had assigned them – the lord of Sidon first, the lord of Tyre second, and so on in their order. Then, as they sat there in order of rank, Xerxes sent Mardonius to ask the opinion of each one about giving battle at sea. Mardonius accordingly went around putting his question, beginning with the lord of Sidon. The answers, with a single exception, were unanimously in favour of engaging the Greek fleet: the exception was Artemisia. 'Mardonius,' she said, 'tell the king for me that this is the answer I give – I, whose courage and achievements in the battles at Euboea were surpassed by none: say to him, "Master, my past services give me the right to advise you now upon the course which I believe to be most to your advantage. It is this: spare your ships and do not fight at sea, for the Greeks are as far superior to us in naval matters as men are to women. In any case, what pressing need have you to risk further actions at sea? Have you not taken Athens, the main objective of the war? Is not the rest of Greece in your power? There is no one now to resist you – those who did resist have fared as they deserved. Let me tell you how I think things will now go with the enemy; if only you are not in too great a hurry to fight at sea – if you keep the fleet on the coast where it now is – then, whether you stay here or advance into the Peloponnese, you will easily accomplish your purpose. The Greeks will not be able to hold out against you for long; you will soon cause their forces to disperse – they will soon break up and go home. I hear they have no supplies in the island where they now are; and the Peloponnesian contingents, at least, are not likely to be very easy in their minds if you march with the army towards their country – they will hardly like the idea of fighting in defence of Athens.

'"If, on the other hand, you rush into a naval action, my fear is that the defeat of your fleet may involve the army too. And there is one other point, my lord, to be considered: good masters, remember, usually have bad servants, and bad masters good ones. You, then, being the best master in the world, are ill served: these people who are supposed to be your allies – these Egyptians, Cyprians, Cilicians, Pamphylians – are a useless lot!"'

Artemisia's friends were dismayed when they heard this speech, and thought that Xerxes would punish her for trying to dissuade him from battle; but those who were jealous of her standing among the most influential persons in the forces were delighted at the prospect of her ruin. However, when the several answers to his question were reported to the king, he was highly pleased with Artemisia's; he had always considered her an admirable person, but now he esteemed her more than ever. Nevertheless his orders were that the advice of the majority should be followed, for he believed that in the battles off Euboea his men had shirked their duty because he was not himself present – whereas this time he had made arrangements to watch the fight with his own eyes.

The command was now given to put to sea, and the ships proceeded towards Salamis, where they took up their respective stations at leisure. It was late in the evening, with not enough light left to attack at once; so they prepared to go into action next day.

The Greeks were in a state of acute alarm, especially those from the Peloponnese: for there they were, waiting at Salamis to fight for Athenian territory, and certain, in the event of defeat, to be caught and blocked up in an island, while their own country was left without defence, and the Persian army that very night was on the march for the Peloponnese.

Nevertheless everything that ingenuity could contrive had been done to prevent the Persian army from forcing the Isthmus. On the news of the destruction of Leonidas' force at Thermopylae, troops from all the states hurried to the Isthmus, where they took up their position under Cleombrotus, the son of Anaxandrides and brother of Leonidas. Their first act was to break up and block the Scironian Way; then, in accordance with a decision taken in council, they began work on a wall across the Isthmus. As there were many thousands there and every man turned to, the work went fast. Stones, bricks timbers, sand-baskets – all were used in the building, and the labour went on continuously night and day. The peoples which joined in this work in full force were the following: Sparta, all the Arcadians, Elis, Corinth, Sicyon, Epidaurus, Phlius, Troezen, and Hermione: all these, in their overriding fear for the safety of Greece, helped in the work; but the other Peloponnesian communities (though the Olympic and Carneian festivals were now over) remained indifferent.

In the Peloponnese there are seven distinct peoples: two of them, the Arcadians and Cynurians, are indigenous; one, the Achaeans, have always been in the Peloponnese, though they moved from their original territory; the four others – Dorians, Aetolians, Dryopes, and Lemnians – are immigrants. The Dorian communities are numerous and well known; the Aetolians have only one, Elis; Hermione and Asine, near Cardamyle in Laconia, belong to the Dryopes, and all the Paroreatae are Lemnian. The indigenous Cynurians appear to be the only Ionians in this part of Greece, though they too have become Dorianized during the long time that they have been subject to Argos. Of these seven peoples all the communities except the ones

I mentioned remained neutral in the war – which, to put it bluntly, is as good as saying that they were on the Persian side.

The Greeks at the Isthmus, convinced that all they possessed was now at stake and not expecting any notable success at sea, continued to grapple with their task of fortification. The news of how they were employed nevertheless caused great concern at Salamis; for it brought home to everyone there not so much his own peril as the imminent threat to the Peloponnese. At first there was whispered criticism of the incredible folly of Eurybiades; then the smothered feeling broke out into open resentment, and another meeting was held. All the old ground was gone over again, one side urging that it was useless to stay and fight for a country which was already in enemy hands, and that the fleet should sail and risk an action in defence of the Peloponnese, while the Athenians, Aeginetans, and Megarians still maintained that they should stay and fight at Salamis.

At this point Themistocles, feeling that he would be outvoted by the Peloponnesians, slipped quietly away from the meeting and sent a man over in a boat to the Persian fleet, with instructions upon what to say when he got there. The man – Sicinnus – was one of Themistocles' slaves and used to attend upon his sons; afterwards, when the Thespians were enrolling new citizens, Themistocles established him at Thespia and made him a rich man. Following his instructions, then, Sicinnus made his way to the Persian commanders and said: 'I am the bearer of a secret communication from the Athenian commander, who is a well-wisher to your king and hopes for a Persian victory. He has told me to report to you that the Greeks are afraid and are planning to slip away. Only prevent them from slipping through your fingers, and you have at this moment an opportunity of unparalleled success. They are at daggers drawn with each other, and will offer no opposition – on the contrary, you will see the pro-Persians amongst them fighting the rest.'

His message delivered, Sicinnus lost no time in getting away. The Persians believed what he had told them, and proceeded to put ashore a large force on the islet of Psyttaleia, between Salamis and the coast; then, about midnight, they moved their western wing in an encircling movement upon Salamis, while at the same time the ships off Ceos and Cynosura also advanced and blocked the whole channel as far as Munychia. The object of these movements was – ironically – that the Greeks might be cut off in Salamis and there give the Persians their revenge for the battles of Artemisium. The troops were landed on Psyttaleia because it lay right in the path of the impending action, and once the fighting began, many men and damaged vessels would be carried on to it, and could be saved or destroyed according as they were friends or enemies. These tactical moves were carried out in silence, to prevent the enemy from being aware of what was going on; they occupied the whole night, so that none of the men had time for sleep.

Now I cannot deny that there is truth in prophecies, and I have no wish to discredit them when they are expressed in unambiguous language. Consider the following:

> When they shall span the sea with ships from Cynosura
> To the holy shore of Artemis of the golden sword,
> Wild with hope at the ruin of shining Athens,
> Then shall bright Justice quench Excess, the child of Pride,
> Dreadful and furious, thinking to swallow up all things.
> Bronze shall mingle with bronze, and Ares with blood
> Incarnadine the sea; and all-seeing Zeus
> And gracious Victory shall bring to Greece the day of freedom.

With that utterance of Bacis in mind, absolutely clear as it is, I do not venture to say anything against prophecies, nor will I listen to criticism from others.

The Greek commanders at Salamis were still at loggerheads. They did not yet know that the enemy ships had blocked their escape at both ends of the channel, but supposed them to occupy the same position as they had seen them in during the day. However, while the dispute was still at its height, Aristides came over in a boat from Aegina. This man, an Athenian and the son of Lysimachus, had been banished from Athens by popular vote, but the more I have learned of his character, the more I have come to believe that he was the best and most honourable man that Athens ever produced. Arrived at Salamis, Aristides went to where the conference was being held and, standing outside, called for Themistocles. Themistocles was no friend of his; indeed he was his most determined enemy; but Aristides was willing, in view of the magnitude of the danger which threatened them, to forget old quarrels in his desire to communicate with him. He was already aware of the anxiety of the Peloponnesian commanders to withdraw to the Isthmus; as soon, therefore, as Themistocles came out of the conference in answer to his call, he said: 'At this moment, more than ever before, you and I should be rivals, to see which of us can do most good to our country. First, let me tell you that the Peloponnesians may talk as much or as little as they please about withdrawing from Salamis – it will make not the least difference. What I tell you, I have seen with my own eyes: they *cannot* now get out of here, however much the Corinthians or Eurybiades himself may wish to do so, because our fleet is surrounded. So go in and tell them that!'

'Good news and good advice,' Themistocles answered; 'what I most wanted has happened – and you bring me the evidence of your own eyes that it is true. It was I who was responsible for this move of the enemy; for as our men would not fight here of their own free will, it was necessary to make them, whether they wanted to do so or not. But take them the good news yourself; if I tell them, they will think I have invented it and will not believe me. Please, then, go in and make the report yourself. If they believe you, well and good; if they do not, it's no odds; for if we are surrounded, as you say we are, escape is no longer possible.'

Aristides accordingly went in and made his report, saying he had come from Aegina and had been hard put to it to slip through the blockading enemy fleet, as the entire Greek force was surrounded. He advised them, therefore, to prepare at once to repel an attack. That said, he left the conference, whereupon another dispute broke out, because most of the commanders still refused to believe in the report. But while they still doubted, a Tenian warship, commanded by Panaetius, the son of Sosimenes, deserted from the Persians and came in with a full account. For this service the name of the Tenians was afterwards inscribed on the tripod at Delphi amongst the other states who helped to defeat the invader. With this ship which came over to them at Salamis, and the Lemnian one which previously joined them at Artemisium, the Greek fleet was brought up to the round number of 380. Up till then it had fallen short of that figure by two.

Forced to accept the Tenians' report, the Greeks now at last pre-pared for action. At dawn the fighting men were assembled and Themistocles was chosen to address them. The whole burden of what he said was a comparison of all that was best and worst in life and fortunes, and an exhortation to the men to choose the better. Then, having rounded off his speech, he gave the order for embarka-tion. The order was obeyed and, just as the men were going aboard, the ship which had been sent to Aegina to fetch the Sons of Aeacus, rejoined the fleet.

The whole fleet now got under way, and in a moment the Persians were on them. The Greeks checked their way and began to back astern; and they were on the point of running aground when Ameinias of Pallene, in command of an Athenian ship, drove ahead and rammed an enemy vessel. Seeing the two ships foul of one another and locked together, the rest of the Greek fleet hurried to Ameinias' assistance, and the general action began. Such is the Athenian account of how the battle started; the Aeginetans claim that the first to go into action was the ship which fetched the Sons of Aeacus from Aegina. There is also a popular belief that the phantom shape of a woman appeared and, in a voice which could be heard by every man in the fleet, contemptuously cried out: 'Fools, how much further do you propose to go astern?'

The Athenian squadron found itself facing the Phoenicians, who formed the Persian left wing on the western, Eleusis, end of the line; the Lacedaemonians faced the ships of Ionia, which were stationed on the Piraeus, or eastern, end. A few of the Ionians remembered Themistocles' appeal and deliberately held back in the course of the fighting but most not at all. I could if I wished give a long list of officers in the enemy fleet who captured Greek ships, but the only ones I will mention are Theomestor, the son of Andro-damas, and Phylacus, the son of Histiaeus, both of them Samians. My reason for naming these two is that Theomestor in reward for this service was invested by the Persians with the lordship of Samos, and Phylacus was enrolled in the catalogue of the King's Benefactors and presented with a large estate. The Persian word for King's Benefactors is *orosangae*.

These two officers, as I say, had some success; but the greater part

of the Persian fleet suffered severely in the battle, the Athenians and
Aeginetans accounting for a great many of their ships. Since the Greek
fleet worked together as a whole, while the Persians had lost formation and were no longer fighting on any plan, that was what was
bound to happen. None the less they fought well that day – far better
than in the actions off Euboea. Every man of them did his best for
fear of Xerxes, feeling that the king's eye was on him.

I cannot give precise details of the part played in this battle by the
various Greek or foreign contingents in the Persian fleet; I must,
however, mention Artemisia, on account of an exploit which still
further increased her reputation with Xerxes. After the Persian fleet
had lost all semblance of order, Artemisia was chased by an Athenian
trireme. As her ship happened to be closest to the enemy and there
were other friendly ships just ahead of her, escape was impossible.
In this awkward situation she hit on a plan which turned out greatly
to her advantage: with the Athenian close on her tail she drove ahead
with all possible speed and rammed one of her friends – a ship of
Calynda, with Damasithymus, the Calyndian king, on board. I
cannot say if she did this deliberately because of some quarrel she
had had with this man while the fleet was in the Hellespont, or if it
was just chance that that particular vessel was in her way; but in any
case she rammed and sank her, and was lucky enough, as a result, to
reap a double benefit. For the captain of the Athenian trireme, on
seeing her ram an enemy, naturally supposed that her ship was a
Greek one, or else a deserter which was fighting on the Greek side;
so he abandoned the chase and turned to attack elsewhere. That,
then, was one piece of luck – that she escaped with her life; the other
was that, by this very act she raised herself higher than ever in
Xerxes' esteem. For the story goes that Xerxes, who was watching
the battle, observed the incident, and that one of the bystanders
remarked: 'Do you see, my lord, how well Artemisia is fighting?
She has sunk an enemy ship.' Xerxes asked if they were sure it was
really Artemisia, and was told that there was no doubt whatever –
they knew her ensign well, and of course supposed that it was an
enemy ship that had been sunk. She was, indeed, lucky in every way
– not least in the fact that there were no survivors from the Calyndian
ship to accuse her. Xerxes' comment on what was told him is said to

have been: 'My men have turned into women, my women into men.'

Amongst the killed in this struggle was Ariabignes, the son of Darius and Xerxes' brother, and many other well-known men from Persia, Media, and the confederate nations. There were also Greek casualties, but not many; for most of the Greeks could swim, and those who lost their ships, provided they were not killed in the actual fighting, swam over to Salamis. Most of the enemy, on the other hand, being unable to swim, were drowned. The greatest destruction took place when the ships which had been first engaged turned tail; for those astern fell foul of them in their attempt to press forward and do some service before the eyes of the king. In the confusion which resulted, some Phoenicians who had lost their ships came to Xerxes and tried to make out that the loss was due to the treachery of the Ionians. But the upshot was that it was they themselves, and not the Ionian captains, who were executed for misbehaviour. While they were speaking, a ship of Samothrace rammed an Athenian; the Athenian was going down, when an Aeginetan vessel bore down upon the Samothracian and sank her, but the Samothracian crew, who were armed with javelins, cleared the deck of the attacking vessel, leapt aboard, and captured her. This exploit saved the Ionians; for when Xerxes saw an Ionian ship do such a fine piece of work, he turned to the Phoenicians and, ready as he was in his extreme vexation to find fault with anyone, ordered their heads to be cut off, to stop them from casting cowardly aspersions upon their betters.

Xerxes watched the course of the battle from the base of Mt Aegaleos, across the strait from Salamis; whenever he saw one of his officers behaving with distinction, he would find out his name, and his secretaries wrote it down, together with his city and parentage.

The Persian Ariaramnes, who was a friend of the Ionians and was present during the battle, also had a share in bringing about the punishment of the Phoenicians.

When the Persian rout began and they were trying to get back to Phalerum, the Aeginetan squadron, which was waiting to catch them in the narrows, did memorable service. The enemy was in hopeless confusion; such ships as offered resistance or tried to escape were cut to pieces by the Athenians, while the Aeginetans caught those which attempted to get clear, so that any ship which escaped the one enemy promptly fell amongst the other. It happened at this stage that Themistocles, chasing an enemy vessel, ran close by the ship which was commanded by Polycritus, the son of Crius,[1] the Aeginetan. Polycritus had just rammed a Sidonian, the very ship which captured the Aeginetan guard-vessel off Sciathus – the one, it will be remembered, which had Pytheas on board, the man the Persians kept with them out of admiration for his gallantry in refusing to surrender in spite of his appalling wounds. When the ship was taken with him and the Persian crew on board, he got safe home to Aegina. When Polycritus noticed the Athenian ship, and recognized the admiral's flag, he shouted to Themistocles and asked him in a tone of ironic reproach if he still thought that the people of Aegina were Persia's friends.

Such of the Persian ships as escaped destruction made their way back to Phalerum and brought up there under the protection of the army.

The most distinguished service at Salamis is admitted to have been that of Aegina; and next after Aegina was Athens. The greatest individual distinction was won by Polycritus of Aegina, and the two Athenians, Eumenes of Anagyrus and Ameinias of Pallene. It was Ameinias who gave chase to Artemisia, and if he had known that Artemisia was on board, he would never have abandoned the chase until he had either taken her or been taken himself; for the Athenians resented the fact that a woman should appear in arms against them, and the ships' captains had received special orders about her, with the offer of a reward of 10,000 drachmae for anyone who captured her alive. However, as I said, she escaped; some others, too, got away with their ships, and these now lay at Phalerum.

The Athenians have a story that right at the beginning of the action the Corinthian commander Adeimantus got sail on his ship and fled in panic. Seeing the commander making off, the rest of the squadron followed; but when they were off that part of the coast of Salamis where the temple of Athene Sciras stands, they were met by a strange boat. It was all very mysterious, because nobody, apparently, had sent it, and the Corinthians, when it met them, knew nothing of how things were going with the rest of the fleet. From

1. No doubt the Crius mentioned on pp. 404, 413.

what happened next they were forced to the conclusion that the hand of God was in the matter; for when the boat was close to them, the people on board called out: 'Adeimantus, while you are playing the traitor by running away with your squadron, the prayers of Greece are being answered, and she is victorious over her enemies.' Adeimantus would not believe what they said, so they told him that he might take them with him as hostages, and kill them if the Greeks were not found to have won the battle. On this, he and the rest of the squadron put about, and rejoined the fleet after the action was over. This, as I said, is an Athenian story, and the Corinthians do not admit the truth of it: on the contrary, they believe that their ships played a most distinguished part in the battle – and the rest of Greece gives evidence in their favour.

During the confused struggle a valuable service was performed by the Athenian Aristides, son of Lysimachus, whose high character I remarked upon a little while back. He took a number of the Athenian heavy infantry, who were posted along the coast of Salamis, across to Psyttaleia, where they killed every one of the Persian soldiers who had been landed there.

After the battle the Greeks towed over to Salamis all the disabled vessels which were adrift in the neighbourhood, and then prepared for a renewal of the fight, fully expecting that Xerxes would use his remaining ships to make another attack. Many of the disabled vessels and other wreckage were carried by the westerly wind to a part of the Attic coast called Colias, and in this way it came about that not only the prophecies of Bacis and Musaeus about this battle were fulfilled, but also another prophecy which had been uttered many years previously by an Athenian soothsayer named Lysistratus: the words of this one were, 'The Colian women shall cook their food with oars.' The Greeks had forgotten about it at the time, but it was to happen, all the same, after Xerxes was gone.

Xerxes, when he realized the extent of the disaster, was afraid that the Greeks, either on their own initiative or at the suggestion of the Ionians, might sail to the Hellespont and break the bridges here. If this happened, he would be cut off in Europe and in danger of destruction. Accordingly, he laid his plans for escape; but at the same time, in order to conceal his purpose both from the Greeks and from his own troops, he began to construct a causeway across the water towards Salamis, lashing together a number of Phoenician merchant-men to serve at once for bridge and breakwater. He also made other preparations, as if he intended to fight again at sea. The sight of this activity made everybody confident that he was prepared to remain in Greece and carry on the war with all possible vigour; there was, however, one exception – Mardonius, who thoroughly understood how his master's mind worked and was in no way deceived. At the same time Xerxes dispatched a courier to Persia with the news of his defeat.

There is nothing in the world which travels faster than these Persian couriers. The whole idea is a Persian invention, and works like this: riders are stationed along the road, equal in number to the number of days the journey takes – a man and a horse for each day. Nothing stops these couriers from covering their allotted stage in the quickest possible time – neither snow, rain, heat, nor darkness. The first, at the end of his stage, passes the dispatch to the second, the second to the third, and so on along the line, as in the Greek torch-race which is held in honour of Hephaestus. The Persian word for this form of post is *angarium*.

Xerxes' first dispatch telling of the capture of Athens caused such rejoicing in Susa amongst the Persians who had not accompanied the expedition, that they strewed the roads with myrtle-boughs, burned incense, and gave themselves up to every sort of pleasure and merrymaking; the second, however, coming on top of it, soon put a stop to all this, and such was the distress in the city that there was not a man who did not tear his clothes and weep and wail in unap-peasable grief, laying the blame for the disaster upon Mardonius. Nor was it distress for the loss of the ships which caused these demon-strations; it was fear for the personal safety of the king. The demon-strations, moreover, continued without a break until Xerxes himself came home.

Mardonius could see that Xerxes took the defeat at Salamis very hard, and guessed that he had determined to get out of Athens. In these circumstances, reckoning that he was sure to be punished for having persuaded the king to undertake the expedition, he felt it would be better to renew the struggle in order either to bring Greece into subjection or, failing that, to die nobly in a great cause – though he expected the former alternative. Accordingly, he approached Xerxes with a proposal. 'My lord,' he said, 'I beg you not to take recent events too deeply to heart. What are a few planks and timbers? The decisive struggle will not depend upon them, but upon men and horses. Not one of all these people who now imagine that their work is done, will dare leave his ship in order to oppose you, nor will the mainland Greeks – those who have done so already have paid the price. I suggest, therefore, an immediate attack upon the Peloponnese. Or wait a while, if you prefer. In any case do not lose heart; for the Greeks cannot possibly escape ultimate subjection. They will be brought to account for the injuries they have done you, now and in the past. That is your best policy; nevertheless I have another plan to offer, should you be determined to withdraw the army from Greece. My lord, do not give the Greeks the chance to laugh at us. None of the reverses we have suffered have been due to us – you cannot say that we Persians have on any occasion fought like cowards. Why should we care if the Egyptians and Phoenicians and Cyprians and Cilicians have disgraced themselves? Persia is not involved in their disgrace. No; it is not we who are responsible for what has occurred. Listen, then, to what I have to propose; if you have made up your mind not to stay here, then go home together with the greater part of the army, and I will make it my duty, with 300,000 picked troops, to deliver Greece to you in chains.'

The proposal was welcome to Xerxes in his dejection; he was highly delighted, and told Mardonius that he would consider the two alternatives and let him know which he preferred to adopt. Accordingly he summoned a conference, and during the debate it occurred to him that it would be just as well to send for Artemisia to take part in the discussion, as she on a previous occasion had been the only one to give him sound advice. When she presented herself, Xerxes dismissed his Persian advisers, and all the guards, and addressed her in these words:

'Mardonius urges me to stay in Greece and attack the Peloponnese. According to him, my army and my Persian troops, who have not been responsible for any of our recent disasters, are anxious to prove their worth. His advice, therefore, is, either that I should undertake this campaign, or allow him to choose 300,000 men from the army and lead the expedition himself, while I return home with the remainder of my troops. With that force he promises to deliver Greece into my hands. You gave me good advice when you tried to dissuade me from risking the battle we have just fought at sea; so I would ask you to advise me now. Which of these two courses should I be wise to follow?'

'My lord,' Artemisia answered, 'it is not easy to give you the best advice; nevertheless, circumstances being as they are, I think that you should yourself quit this country and leave Mardonius behind with the force he asks for, if that is what he wants, and if he has really undertaken to do as he has said. If his design prospers and success attends his arms, it will be *your* work, master – for your slaves performed it. And even if things go wrong with him, it will be no great matter, so long as you yourself are safe and no danger threatens anything that concerns your house. While you and yours survive, the Greeks will have to run many a painful race for their lives and land; but who cares if Mardonius comes to grief? He is only your slave, and the Greeks will have but a poor triumph if they kill him. As for yourself, you will be going home with the object of your campaign accomplished – for you have burnt Athens.'

Artemisia's advice was most agreeable to Xerxes, for it was the expression of his own thoughts. Personally, I do not think he would have stayed in Greece, had all his counsellors, men and women alike, urged him to do so – he was much too badly frightened. As it was, he complimented Artemisia and sent her off to Ephesus with his sons – some of his bastards which had accompanied him on the expedition.

To look after these children he also sent Hermotimus, his chief eunuch. Hermotimus came originally from Pedasus, and I have never heard of a case where a man has taken a more fearful revenge for an injury than he did. He was put up for sale as a prisoner of war and bought by a Chian called Panionius, a man who made his living by the abominable trade of castrating any good-looking boys he could get hold of, and taking them to Sardis or Ephesus, where he sold them at a high price – for it is a fact that in eastern countries eunuchs are valued as being specially trustworthy in every way.

Amongst the many boys whom Panionius, in the course of his trade, had served in this way, was Hermotimus. Nevertheless, he was not without his share of luck; for he was taken from Sardis and sent with a number of other things as a present to the king, and in the course of time came to be valued by Xerxes more highly than any other of his eunuchs. At the time when Xerxes was at Sardis at the start of his march to Athens, Hermotimus had gone on business to Atarneus, a port of Mysia which belongs to Chios. Here he happened to meet Panionius. He at once recognized him, and in a long and apparently friendly conversation told him of all the happy results of their previous relationship, and promised to do as much for him in return, if only he would bring his family to Sardis and settle there. Panionius was delighted, and brought his wife and children accordingly. Then, having got him and his whole household into his power, Hermotimus said: 'No man ever earned his living by a viler trade than you. What harm had I, or anyone connected with me, ever done to you or yours, that you should have made me a nothing instead of a man? Doubtless you hoped to hide your beastly practices from the eyes of God; but God is just, and for your vile crime has delivered you into my power, so that you cannot now complain of the vengeance I am about to take.'

Then, having told him what he thought of him, he sent for Panionius' sons – four in number – and forced him to castrate them with his own hand. That done, the boys were compelled to do the same to their father. So Hermotimus had his revenge.

Xerxes, having entrusted Artemisia with the duty of conducting his bastard sons to Ephesus, sent for Mardonius and told him to pick the troops he wanted, and to take care to make his deeds answer to his words. That day nothing further was done; but the same night the king gave his orders, and the fleet slipped away from Phalerum, the commander of every vessel making the best speed he could across to the Hellespont, in order to guard the bridges for Xerxes' use on his return. Off Zoster, where some little rocky headlands run out from the coast, the Persians mistook the rocks for enemy ships and gave them a very wide berth; however, they realized their mistake after a time, and continued the voyage in company.

At dawn the following day the Greeks, seeing that the Persian army had not moved, thought that the fleet would still be lying at Phalerum; so they prepared to defend themselves in expectation of another attack by sea. But the moment they learnt that the fleet was gone, they resolved to give chase, and did actually sail in pursuit as far as Andros, but without getting a sight of any enemy ships. At Andros they brought up and held a conference, at which Themistocles proposed that they should carry on through the islands direct for the Hellespont, and break the bridges. Eurybiades, however, objected, on the ground that to destroy the bridges would be to do Greece the worst possible service. If, he argued, Xerxes were cut off from home and forced to stay in Greece, he would hardly be likely to remain inactive. Inactivity would ruin all his chances of success and rob him of any opportunity of getting home again, and his troops would starve; whereas if he took the offensive and acted with vigour, the whole of Europe might gradually go over to him; for the various towns and peoples would, one by one, either be beaten in the field or agree to submit; moreover, the annual harvests would allow his troops to live off the country. Therefore, as Xerxes evidently intended, in consequence of his defeat at Salamis, not to remain in Greece, he should be allowed to make his escape back to his own country; and then, Eurybiades concluded, the war could be transferred to Asia.

Eurybiades was supported in his view by the other Peloponnesian commanders, whereupon Themistocles, finding the majority against him, suddenly shifted his ground and addressed himself to the Athenians – who of all the confederates were the most vexed at the enemy's escape, and were anxious to go on to the Hellespont alone, if the others refused to accompany them. 'From my own experience,' Themistocles began, 'and still more from what others have told me, I know very well that people who are beaten and cornered will often hit out again and make amends for their previous failure to play the man. Now we've had the luck to save ourselves and our country by the repulse of this great force, which seemed, like a cloud, to darken the sea. That force is now in flight – let it go. Indeed it was not we who performed this exploit; it was God and our divine protectors, who were jealous that one man in his godless pride should be king of Asia and of Europe too – a man who does not know the difference between sacred and profane, who burns and destroys the statues of the gods, and dared to lash the sea with whips and bind it with fetters. At the moment, all is well with us; so let us stay where we are, in our own country, and look after ourselves and our families. The Persians are gone – flung out, once for all; so repair your houses, every one of you, and attend to the sowing of your land. We can sail for the Hellespont and Ionia next spring.'

Themistocles' idea in saying this was to lay the foundation for a future claim upon Xerxes, in order to have somewhere to turn to in the event – which did in fact occur – of his getting into trouble with the Athenians. But whatever his ulterior motives, the Athenians were ready to take his advice; they had always thought him clever, and now that he had proved beyond a doubt both clever and successful, they were willing to follow his lead in everything.

Once he had persuaded them to accept his proposal, Themistocles lost no time in getting a message through to Xerxes. The men he chose for this purpose were all people he could trust to keep his instructions secret, even under torture. One of them, as on a previous occasion, was his servant Sicinnus. The party crossed to Attica, and then, while the others waited by the boat, Sicinnus went to find Xerxes, and deliver his message. 'I have come,' he said, 'on behalf of Themistocles, son of Neocles and commander of the Athenian fleet, the most brilliant leader of the confederacy. I am to inform you that Themistocles of Athens, in his desire to serve your interests, has stopped the Greeks from pursuing your navy and destroying the bridges on the Hellespont, which is what they wished to do. You may now, therefore, march your army home without danger of inter-ference.'

The message delivered, the men returned to Andros; and the Greeks, now that it was decided neither to continue the chase nor to sail to the Hellespont to break the bridges, invested the city with the intention of taking it. The Andrians were the first of the islanders to refuse Themistocles' demand for money; he had put it to them that they would be unable to avoid paying, because the Athenians had the support of two powerful deities, one called Persuasion and the other Compulsion, and the Andrians had replied that Athens was lucky to have two such useful gods, who were obviously responsible

for her wealth and greatness; unfortunately, however, they themselves, in their small and inadequate land, had two utterly useless
deities, who refused to leave the island and insisted on staying; and
their names were Poverty and Inability. With the support of these,
no money would be forthcoming; for however strong Athens was,
she could never turn Andros' 'can't' into 'can'. This answer, and the
refusal to pay, were the reasons for the siege.

Meanwhile Themistocles, always greedy for money, sent demands
to the other islands; he employed the same messengers as he had sent
to Xerxes, and backed his demand by the threat that, if they did not
pay what he asked, he would bring the Greek fleet and blockade
them into surrender. By these means he succeeded in collecting large
sums from the people of Carystos and Paros, who took fright and
paid up when they heard that Andros was already invested because
of her support of Persia, and that Themistocles had the highest
reputation of the Greek commanders. I cannot say whether or not
any of the other islanders gave Themistocles money – though they
probably did. The Carystians got no benefit from their compliance;
the Parians, however, having thus propitiated Themistocles, escaped
a visit from the fleet. Thus it was that Themistocles extorted money
from the islanders, while he lay at Andros. The other commanders
knew nothing of these proceedings.

A few days after the battle of Salamis, Xerxes' army began its withdrawal, marching into Boeotia by the same route as it had taken
during its advance. Mardonius wished to accompany the king for
part of his way home, and, as it was not then the campaiging
season, he judged that it would be better to winter in Thessaly and
make his attempt upon the Peloponnese the following spring. On
his arrival there he chose the troops which were to serve under his
command: these were, first, the Persian regiment of Immortals, all
except their commander, Hydarnes, who was unwilling to leave
the king; next, the Persian spearmen and the picked cavalry squadron,
a thousand strong; and, lastly, the Medes, Sacae, Bactrians, and
Indians, both horse and foot. These contingents he took over complete; from the other nationalities he picked a few men here and
there, being guided in his choice either by their appearance or by

his knowledge that they had distinguished themselves, until he had a total number, including the cavalry, of 300,000 men. The Persians with their necklaces and armlets provided the largest contingent; next were the Medes – though the Medes were not actually inferior in number, but only in quality.

While Xerxes was in Thessaly and Mardonius was selecting the troops for his army, the Lacedaemonians received a message from the oracle at Delphi, urging them to demand reparation from Xerxes for the killing of Leonidas, and to accept whatever he offered them. The Spartans at once sent a representative, who was in time to catch the Persian army before it left Thessaly. The man obtained an interview with Xerxes, and said: 'My lord King of the Medes, the Lacedaemonians and the house of Heracles in Sparta demand satisfaction for blood, because you killed their king while he was fighting in defence of Greece.' Xerxes laughed, and for a time did not answer; then, pointing to Mardonius who happened to be standing by him, 'They will get', he said, 'all the satisfaction they deserve from Mardonius here.' The messenger accepted this for an answer and went home.

Xerxes now left Mardonius in Thessaly and made his way by forced marches to the Hellespont. He reached the crossing in forty-five days, but with hardly a fraction of his army intact. During the march the troops lived off the country as best they could, eating grass where they found no grain, and stripping the bark and leaves off trees of all sorts, cultivated or wild, to stay their hunger. They left nothing anywhere, so hard were they put to it for supplies. Plague and dysentery attacked them; many died, and others who fell sick were left behind in the various towns along the route, with instructions for their care and keep – some in Thessaly, others at Siris in Paeonia, others in Macedon. It was at Siris that Xerxes, during the march to Greece, had left the sacred chariot of Zeus, and now he failed to recover it because the Paeonians had given it to the Thracians and, when Xerxes demanded it, pretended that the mares had been stolen at pasture by the up-country Thracians, who live near the source of the Strymon. Here, too, a Thracian chieftain, the king of Crestonia and the Bisaltae, did a peculiarly horrible deed: he refused to submit to Xerxes and fled inland into the hills of Mt Rhodope, and had also forbidden his sons to serve in the expedition against Greece. They, however, all joined up in the Persian army – either because they cared little about their father's orders, or simply from a desire to see the war. All six of them came back safe, and their father, to punish their disobedience, gouged their eyes out. So that was the pay *they* got.

The Persians having passed through Thrace reached the passage over the Hellespont and lost no time in getting across to Abydos. They crossed, however, in ships, as they found the bridges no longer in position, but shattered by storms. Food was more plentiful at Abydos than what they had had on the march, with the result that the men over-ate themselves, and this, combined with the change of water, caused many deaths in what remained of the army. The remnant proceeded with Xerxes to Sardis.

There is another account, different from the preceding, according to which Xerxes, on his retreat from Athens, travelled by land only as far as Eion on the Strymon; here he turned the army over to Hydarnes for the march to the Hellespont, and himself crossed to Asia in a Phoenician ship. During the passage, they were caught by a strong wind, blowing from the mouth of the Strymon, accompanied by a heavy sea; in the worsening weather the ship, her deck covered with a crowd of Persians who were accompanying the king, was in considerable danger; and Xerxes in sudden fright called out to the ship's master to ask if there was any way of getting out of it alive. 'None whatever, my lord,' the man replied, 'unless we can rid ourselves of this crowd on deck.' Upon this Xerxes is supposed to have said: 'Gentlemen, now is the moment for each one of you to prove his concern for the king; for my safety, it seems, is in your hands.' The Persian noblemen bowed low, and then, without more ado, jumped overboard; and the ship, lightened of her load, came safely to her port on the Asian coast. The moment Xerxes had gone ashore he presented the master with a gold crown as a reward for saving the king's life, and then, to punish him for causing the death of a number of Persians, cut off his head. Personally, I do not find this second account of Xerxes' return at all convincing – especially as regards what happened to the Persians. If the ship's master had really said to Xerxes what he is supposed to have said, surely not one in ten thousand would doubt that Xerxes would have made the people on deck go down below – after all, they were Persian noblemen – and would then have flung overboard an equivalent number of rowers – who were mere Phoenicians. No; the truth is, as I said before, that he returned to Asia by road with the army. Moreover, this is corroborated by the fact that Xerxes is known to have passed through Abdera on his journey back, and to have made a pact of friendship with the people there, and to have given them a golden scimitar and a gold-embroidered headband. The men of Abdera also say (though I do not believe them) that during Xerxes' retreat from Athens their town was the first place where he felt safe enough to undo his girdle. Now Abdera is nearer the Hellespont than Eion is, or the Strymon, where according to the other account Xerxes boarded a ship.

The Greeks, meanwhile, failed to take Andros and turned their attention to Carystos. They devastated its land, and then returned to Salamis. Their first act on reaching Salamis was to choose from the plunder taken in the battle the 'first fruits' to be offered in token of gratitude to the gods; these consisted of various objects, but most notably of three Phoenician warships, one to be dedicated at the Isthmus (where it was still to be seen in my own day), another at Sunium, and another, as an offering to Ajax, in Salamis itself. They then turned to the division of the plunder, and sent to Delphi the 'first fruits' set apart for the purpose; from these was made the statue, eighteen feet high, which has the beak of a ship in its hand, and stands beside the gold statue of Alexander of Macedon.

After the dispatch of the thank-offerings to Delphi, the Greeks asked the god, in the name of the country generally, if he felt he had received his full share and was satisfied. His answer was that he was satisfied with what everyone had given, except the Aeginetans: from them he demanded his due from their prize of valour won at Salamis. In consequence of this the Aeginetans dedicated the three gold stars on a bronze mast – now to be seen in the corner near the bowl which was dedicated by Croesus.

When the plunder had been distributed, the Greeks sailed to the Isthmus, where a prize of valour was to be awarded to the man who was judged best to deserve it by his conduct throughout the campaign. The commanders met at the altar of Poseidon to cast their votes for first and second place; and, as they all thought that they had fought more bravely than anybody else, every one of them put his own name at the top – though the majority agreed in putting Themistocles second. Consequently nobody got more than one vote for first place, while Themistocles easily headed the poll for the second. Mutual jealousy thus prevented a decision, and the various commanders sailed off home without making an award; in spite of this, however, Themistocles' name was on everyone's lips, and he acquired the reputation of being by far the most able man in the country.

Immediately after this, having failed to win from the men who fought at Salamis the mark of honour to which he was entitled, he went to Lacedaemon hoping for honour there. He was given a splendid welcome, and treated with the highest respect. The actual prize of valour – a wreath of olive – was, indeed, given to Eurybiades, but a similar wreath was granted to Themistocles as well, for his ability and skill. He was also presented with a chariot, the finest in Sparta, and received high praise. On his departure he was escorted as far as the borders of Tegea by the picked troop of three hundred Spartans called the Knights. Themistocles was the only person we know of who ever received the honour of an escort from the Spartans. Back in Athens he came in for a deal of abuse from a certain Timodemus of Aphidna, whose hatred of Themistocles was his only claim to distinction. Mad with jealousy, he reviled him for going to Sparta, and maintained that he had earned his honours there not by his own merit but merely by the fame of Athens. The continual repetition of this taunt at last drew from Themistocles a reply: 'I'll tell you what,' he said; 'I should never have been honoured as I was if I had been born a Belbinite – and you wouldn't, Athenian though you are!'

Artabazus, the son of Pharnaces, who was already a famous man in the Persian army and was further to increase his reputation as a result of the battle of Plataea, acted as escort to Xerxes, with 60,000 of Mardonius' picked troops, as far as the crossing over the Hellespont. Once the king was in Asia, Artabazus set out on his march back; realizing on his arrival in the neighbourhood of Pallene that Mardonius was wintering in Thessaly and Macedonia, and being as yet in no hurry to rejoin the rest of the army, he considered it his duty, as he found Potidaea in a state of revolt, to bring the town into subjection. The people of Potidaea, like the other inhabitants of the Pallene peninsula, had openly thrown off the Persian yoke as soon as Xerxes passed them on his march to the eastward and they knew of the flight of the Persian fleet from Salamis.

Artabazus, therefore, began the siege, and at the same time invested Olynthus in expectation of a similar revolt – Olynthus was at that time occupied by the Bottiaei, who had been expelled by the Macedonians from the country round the gulf of Therma. The town soon fell; Artabazus butchered the inhabitants and threw their bodies into a lake, turning over the town itself to the control of Critobulus of Torone and the Chalcidians – which was how these people got possession of Olynthus. Artabazus then turned all his attention to Potidaea. While he was vigorously pressing the siege, Timoxenus, commander of the troops from Scione, agreed with him to betray the town. How the thing began, I cannot say, for no account has reached us; but the final stage of the plot was as follows. Whenever Timoxenus and Artabazus wished to communicate with one another, they wrote the message on a strip of paper, which they rolled round the grooved end of an arrow; the feathers were then put on over the paper, and the arrow was shot to some predetermined place. Timoxenus' treachery was finally discovered when Artabazus, on one occasion, missed his aim, and the arrow, instead of falling in the spot agreed upon, struck a Potidaean in the shoulder. As usually happens in war, a crowd collected round the wounded man; the arrow was pulled out, the paper discovered and taken to the commanding officers – those of Potidaea itself and of the other peninsular towns which were supporting her. The letter was read, and the officers, finding who the culprit was, nevertheless resolved to bring no charge of treachery against him, in order to spare the people of Scione from being branded for ever afterwards with the name of traitors.

Three months later, while the siege was still in progress, there was an exceptionally low tide which lasted a long time. The sight of the shallow water suggested to the Persians the possibility of getting through it and across into Pallene. But when they were two-fifths of the way over, they were caught by the succeeding flood, which was of corresponding height – indeed, according to the people thereabouts, higher than it had been before, though big tides are not uncommon there. All the men who could not swim were drowned, and those who could were killed by the Potidaeans, who went out after them in boats. This excessive tide and the consequent disaster to the Persians are put down by the people of Potidaea to the fact that the men who met their deaths were the same ones as had previously desecrated the shrine of Poseidon, and the statue of him which stands just outside the town. Personally, I think their explanation is the true one. After this incident Artabazus withdrew with the remainder of his men and rejoined Mardonius in Thessaly.

The surviving ships of Xerxes' fleet, having made good their escape from Salamis to Asia, had ferried the king and the army across the strait from the Chersonese to Abydos, and then laid up for the winter at Cyme. At the first gleam of spring the following year the fleet mustered at Samos – where, indeed, some of the ships had wintered. Most of the fighting troops serving on board were Persians or Medes; and the command was taken over by Mardontes, the son of Bagaeus, and Artaÿntes, the son of Artachaees, together with one other – Ithamitres, Artaÿntes' nephew, who had been chosen for the position by his uncle. In view of the serious blow they had suffered, they went no further west, nor did anyone attempt to force them to do so – but remained in Samos to guard against a possible Ionian revolt. Their fleet, including the Ionian contingent, numbered 300 ships of war. It never entered their thoughts that the Greeks would undertake an expedition to Ionia; it was much more likely, in the Persian view, that they would be content to defend their own country, especially as they had not pursued the Persian fleet during its flight from Salamis but had so readily given up the chase. The fact is that, so far as naval operations were concerned, the Persians had completely lost heart, though they still believed that Mardonius and his army were sure of an easy victory. Accordingly they kept the fleet at Samos, laying plans for any possible means of harassing the enemy, and at the same time waiting for news of Mardonius.

The coming of spring and the presence of Mardonius in Thessaly roused the Greeks to action again. Before the army mustered, the fleet, 110 strong, proceeded to Aegina under the supreme command of Leotychides. Leotychides belonged to the younger branch of the Spartan royal house, and traced his descent back to Heracles through Menares, Agesilaus, Hippocratides, Leotychides, Anaxilaus, Archidamus, Anaxandrides, Theopompus, Nicander, Charilaus, Eunomus, Polydectes, Prytanis, Euryphon, Procles, Aristodemus, Aristomachus, Cleodaeus, and Hyllus – who was Heracles' son. All these except the two first named had been kings of Sparta.[1] The Athenian squadron was commanded by Xanthippus, the son of Ariphron.

After the arrival of the fleet at Aegina, representatives from Ionia – amongst them Herodotus, the son of Basileides – came to the Greek headquarters with a request for aid. They were the same men as had visited Sparta not long before to ask the Spartans to liberate Ionia. Originally there were seven of them, and they had formed a conspiracy to murder Strattis, the master of Chios; but the plot was betrayed by one of their number, and the remaining six left the island and went to Sparta; and after that, as I have said, they came on to Aegina with a request to the Greeks to undertake an expedition to Ionia. However, it was only with great difficulty that they persuaded them to advance as far as Delos, for the Greeks had little experience of what lay beyond, and imagined it to be full of Persian troops and of every sort of danger. As for Samos, it seemed to them as far away as the Pillars of Heracles. The result was that while the Persians were too badly scared to risk sailing west of Samos, the Greeks, in spite of the earnest solicitation of the Chians, did not dare to sail east of Delos. Their mutual fears stood sentry over the intervening area.

While Mardonius was wintering in Thessaly, he instructed a man named Mys, a Carian from the town of Euromus, to make the round of all the oracles which it was possible for him to consult. What precisely he hoped to learn from the oracles when he gave this order, I cannot say, for there is no record; but presumably he sent for infor-

---

1. Some editors substitute 'first seven', in order to square the account with the history of Sparta in Pausanias' guide-book (not an unimpeachable authority), III, 1. Since the mss. of Herodotus read 'two', and a descendant whose ancestors had not been kings for seven generations would hardly be next in line for succession, this alteration appears wanton.

mation and advice on the business he had at the moment in hand, and not for any other purpose.

It is known that Mys visited Lebadeia, where he paid a man to enter the cave of Trophonius, and the oracle at Abae in Phocis; he also visited Thebes, where he consulted the oracle of Apollo Ismenius (in whose temple oracles are sought by sacrifices, as at Olympia), and also paid somebody to pass the night in the temple of Amphiaraus. The person he persuaded to do this was not a Theban; for Thebans are forbidden to consult this oracle, because Amphiaraus, through the mouth of the Priestess, once gave them the exclusive choice of two alternatives – whether, that is, they would prefer to have him as a prophet to foretell the future, or as a friend to help them in war: and they chose the latter. And that is why no Theban may pass the night in his shrine.

One thing which the Thebans say happened at this time seems to me very remarkable: Mys, the man from Euromus, visited during his tour of the oracles the precinct of Apollo Ptoiüs; the temple, which is called Ptoiüm, belongs to Thebes and is situated very near Acraephia, on the hill overlooking Lake Copais. Mys entered the shrine accompanied by three men from Thebes, who had been officially appointed to take down whatever answer the god might give. The prophet through whom the god spoke at once delivered his oracles – in a foreign language. The three Thebans were astonished at hearing a strange tongue instead of Greek, and did not know what to do about it; Mys, however, snatched the tablet they had brought to write the oracle on, and, declaring that the god's response had been delivered in Carian, wrote it down himself and hurried back to Thessaly. Mardonius read whatever it was the oracle said, and then sent Alexander, the son of Amyntas, to Athens with a message. He chose Alexander, who was a Macedonian, for two reasons: first, because he was connected with the Persians by marriage – Bubares, a Persian, had married Alexander's sister Gygaea; they had a son who stayed in Asia, named Amyntas after his maternal grandfather, who enjoyed by the king's gift the revenues of the important Phrygian town of Alabanda; secondly, because he was well aware that Alexander's friendship with Athens was an official relationship, and was backed by deeds. Mardonius therefore thought that by sending him he would be most likely to bring Athens over to the Persian interest; he knew that the Athenians were a numerous and gallant people, and had been chiefly responsible for the defeat of the Persian navy, and expected that if only he could form an alliance with them, he would have no difficulty in getting the mastery of the sea – an expectation which was perfectly justified – while he was already confident of his superiority on land. In this way he reckoned that the defeat of Greece would be within his grasp. For all I know, the Athenian alliance had been what the oracles advised, and it was in obedience to them that he sent Alexander on his mission.

This Alexander was descended, in the seventh generation, from Perdiccas, who won the lordship of the Macedonians in the following way. Three brothers, Gauanes, Aeropus, and Perdiccas, descendants of Temenus, had been expelled from Argos and had taken refuge in Illyria. Thence they crossed into upper Macedonia and went to the town of Lebaea, where they hired themselves out to do menial work for the king, one tending the horses, another the oxen, and the youngest, Perdiccas, the sheep and goats. In the old days it was not only the common folk who were poor; even the reigning houses were of slender means, and in Lebaea the king's wife cooked the food. Now it happened that every time she baked, the loaf intended for the boy Perdiccas swelled to double its proper size. She said nothing for a while, but when it went on happening every time, she told her husband. At once it occurred to the king that it was a warning from heaven of some important event, so he sent for the three servants and ordered them to leave the country. The young men, in reply, said they had a right to their wages, and would go as soon as they were paid. The sun was shining through the smoke-hole in the roof of the house, and the king, when he heard wages mentioned, was inspired to his ruin, crying out: 'I give you the wages you deserve – there they are!' – and pointed to the sun. The two elder brothers, Gauanes and Aeropus, were struck dumb; but the boy, who had a knife in his hand, scratched a line with the point of it round the patch of sunlight on the floor, and said: 'King, we accept what you offer us.' Then three times he made as if to collect the sunlight into the folds of his tunic, and left the town together with his brothers.

When they were gone, somebody who was in attendance upon the king mentioned what a significant thing the boy had done; and suggested that the youngest of the three knew what he was doing in accepting the offered wage. The king was angry and ordered men to ride in pursuit of the brothers and kill them.

In this part of the country there is a river to which the descendants of these three men offer sacrifice as their saviour – for when they had crossed it, it suddenly rose so high that their pursuers were unable to get over. Once safe on the other side, the brothers went on to another part of Macedonia and settled near the place called the Gardens of Midas, where roses grow wild – wonderful blooms, with sixty petals apiece, and sweeter smelling than any others in the world. According to local legend it was in these gardens that Silenus[1] was caught. Above them rises Mt Bermium, the heights of which are so cold that none can climb them, and it was from the slopes of these mountains that the brothers conquered, first, the land in the immediate neighbourhood, and afterwards the rest of Macedonia.

From the Perdiccas of this story Alexander was descended: he was the son of Amyntas, Amyntas of Alcetas; the father of Alcetas was Aeropus; of Aeropus, Philippus; of Philippus, Argaeus; and of Argaeus, Perdiccas – who first won the sovereign power.

On his arrival at Athens as Mardonius' ambassador, Alexander spoke in the following terms: 'Men of Athens, this is from Mardonius: I have received a message from the king, which says: "I am willing to forget all the injuries which Athens has done me. So, Mardonius, first give the Athenians back their land; and secondly, let them take whatever other territory they wish, and have self-government. If they are willing to come to terms with me, you are also to rebuild the temples which I burnt." Those are the King's orders which I have to carry out, unless you yourselves put obstacles in the way. Why then – I ask you – are you so mad as to take arms against the king? You can never defeat him, and you cannot hold out for ever. You have seen his army, its size, and what it can do; you know, too, how powerful a force I have under me now. Even should you

1. A reminiscence of comic drama? Silenus, the immortal though ever drunken companion of Dionysus, was captured by Midas (later confused with historical kings of Phrygia), who was rewarded with a wish-fulfilment for treating him kindly; he chose the 'golden touch' and nearly died of it.

beat us – and, if you have any sense, you cannot hope to do so – another force many times as powerful will come against you. So stop trying to be a match for the king, at the cost of the loss of your country and continual peril of your lives. Come to terms with him instead – you have the finest possible opportunity of doing so, now that Xerxes is inclined that way. Make an alliance with us, with every usual guarantee against aggression, and so keep your freedom."

'So much for what Mardonius instructed me to say to you. Now let me speak for myself. There is no need to mention my goodwill towards you – that you already know well enough; I merely add my earnest entreaties that you will do as Mardonius asks. It is clear to me that you will not be able to maintain your struggle with Xerxes for ever – had I thought you could, I should never have come to Athens on this mission. But the fact is, Xerxes' power is super-human, and his arm is long. If, then, you do not at once conclude a peace, now that such excellent terms are offered, I tremble for your future, when I think how of all the confederate states you lie most directly in the path of danger. You alone will continue to suffer, since your country will be a sort of no-man's-land. Do, therefore, agree; for surely it is no small thing that the Great King should single you out from all the people of Greece, and be willing to forgive the past and to become your friend.'

In Sparta the news of Alexander's visit to try to bring about an alliance between Persia and Athens caused consternation. The Spartans, remembering the prophecy that the Dorians would one day be expelled from the Peloponnese by the Persians and Athenians, and greatly fearing that the alliance might be concluded, at once decided to send representatives to Athens. It so happened that Alexander and the Spartan envoys had their audience at the same time; for the Athenians had dragged out their business with Alexander, realizing that the Spartans would hear that someone had arrived in Athens to represent Persia in peace negotiations, and would then send representatives of their own without delay. So they did this on purpose, so that the Spartans might be present when they declared their views.

Accordingly, when Alexander had finished his speech, the Spartan envoys spoke in their turn: 'The Spartans have sent us here to beg you not to endanger Greece by a departure from your previous policy, and to listen to no proposals from Persia. For any of the Greeks to do such a thing would be inconsistent with decency and honour; for you it would be far worse, for many reasons. It was you, in the first place, who started this war – our wishes were not considered. It began by being a war for your territories only – now all Greece is involved. Again, it would be an intolerable thing that the Athenians, who in the past have been known so often as liberators, should now be the cause of bringing slavery upon Greece. We do, however, sympathize with you in your hardships – the loss of two successive harvests and the ruin of your homes and property over so long a time; and in compensation we offer, in the name of Sparta and her allies, to provide support for all the women and other non-combatant members of your households, for as long as the war lasts.

'Do not let Alexander's smooth-sounding version of Mardonius' proposals seduce you; he does only what one might expect of him – a despot himself, of course he collaborates with a despot. But such conduct is not for you – at least, not if you are wise; for surely you know that in foreigners there is neither truth nor honour.'

The Athenians then gave Alexander their answer. 'We know', it ran, 'as well as you do that the Persian strength is many times greater than our own: that, at least, is a fact which you need not rub in. Nevertheless, such is our love of freedom, that we will defend ourselves in whatever way we can. As for making terms with Persia, it is useless to persuade us; for we shall never consent. And now tell Mardonius, that so long as the sun keeps his present course in the sky, we Athenians will never make peace with Xerxes. On the contrary, we shall oppose him unremittingly, putting our trust in the help of the gods and heroes whom he despised, whose temples and statues he destroyed with fire. Never come to us again with a proposal like this, and never think you are doing us good service when you urge us to a course which is outrageous – for it would be a pity if you were the victim of an unfortunate incident in Athens, when you are our friend and benefactor.'

So much for the Athenians' answer to Alexander. To the Spartan envoys they said: 'No doubt it was natural that the Lacedaemonians should dread the possibility of our making terms with Persia; none the less it shows a poor estimate of the spirit of Athens. There is not so much gold in the world nor land so fair that we would take it for pay to join the common enemy and bring Greece into subjection. There are many compelling reasons against our doing so, even if we wished: the first and greatest is the burning of the temples and images of our gods – now ashes and rubble. It is our bounden duty to avenge this desecration with all our might – not to clasp the hand that wrought it. Again, there is the Greek nation – the community of blood and language, temples and ritual; our common way of life; if Athens were to betray all this, it would not be well done. We would have you know, therefore, if you did not know it already, that so long as a single Athenian remains alive we will make no peace with Xerxes. We are deeply moved, however, by your kindness and thoughtfulness, and the offer you made to provide for our families in this time of distress. Nothing could be more generous; nevertheless we prefer to carry on as best we can, without being a burden to you. That being our resolve, get your army into the field with the least possible delay; for unless we are much mistaken, it will not be long before the enemy invades Attica – he will do it the instant he gets the news that we refuse his requests. Now, therefore, before he can appear in Attica, it is time for us to meet him in Boeotia.'

Athens had given her answer; and the Spartan envoys left for home.

BOOK NINE

WHEN Alexander returned with the Athenians' answer, Mardonius left Thessaly and marched with all speed for Athens, levying troops on the way from all the places through which he passed. The leading families of Thessaly continued to maintain their previous attitude; indeed they urged the Persians to the attack more vigorously than ever. Thorax of Larissa even escorted Xerxes in his retreat, and now openly encouraged Mardonius in his assault upon Greece.

In Boeotia an attempt was made by the Thebans to persuade him to halt. There was no better place, they said, to encamp, and their advice was that he should proceed no further, but, with Boeotia as his base, take measures for the conquest of Greece without striking a blow. If the former confederacy of Greek states continued to hold together, the whole world would have a hard task to defeat them; 'But if', the Thebans added, 'you do as we suggest, you will put an end to all their schemes with no trouble at all. Send money to the leading men in the various towns – by doing that you will destroy the unity of the country, after which you will easily be able, with the help of those who take your part, to crush those who still oppose you.'

Mardonius did not act upon this suggestion. His whole heart was set upon taking Athens again – partly, no doubt, through mere obstinacy, and partly because he proposed to signal his capture of the town to the king in Sardis by a chain of beacons through the islands. When he reached Attica, once again there were no Athenians to be found; for nearly all of them, as he learnt, were either with the fleet or at Salamis. So he captured a deserted town – ten months after its previous capture by Xerxes.

From Athens Mardonius sent Murychides, a Hellespontine Greek, to Salamis with instructions to repeat to the Athenians the proposals already made to them by Alexander. Not that he was unaware of their feelings towards him; he knew well enough that they were far from friendly; but he made his second approach in the hope that the occupation of the whole of Attica by his troops might have gone some way towards breaking their spirit. So Murychides was dispatched on his errand, and delivered Mardonius' message to the Athenian council in Salamis. One of the councillors, a man named Lycidas, expressed the opinion that the best course would be to admit the proposals which Murychides brought, and to submit them for approval to the general assembly of the people. This was his expressed opinion – whether he had been bribed by Mardonius to express it or really thought so. In any case the Athenians, both those in the council and those outside, were so enraged when they heard it that they surrounded Lycidas and stoned him to death. Murychides they allowed to depart unharmed. With all the uproar in Salamis over Lycidas, the Athenian women soon found out what had happened; whereupon, without a word from the men, they got together, and, each one egging on her neighbour and taking her along with the crowd, flocked to Lycidas' house and stoned his wife and children.

The circumstances in which the Athenians had crossed into Salamis were these: so long as they expected an army from the Peloponnese to come to their assistance, they remained in Attica; but when they found that their Peloponnesian allies kept hanging about and were unwilling to move, and word came that the Persians were advancing and had actually got as far as Boeotia, they waited no longer, but crossed to Salamis with all their movable property, and at the same time sent a message to Lacedaemon to reproach the Spartans for allowing the enemy to invade Attica instead of marching with them to meet him in Boeotia, and to remind them, besides, of the offers they had received from Persia in the event of their deserting the Greek confederacy – not to mention the obvious fact that, if they got no help from Sparta, they would have to find some means of helping themselves.

The truth was, that just then it was the time of the Hyacinthia in Sparta; the people were on holiday and thought it most important to give the God his due. It also happened that the wall they were building across the Isthmus was almost finished and about to have the battlements put on.

The Athenian messengers, accompanied by representatives from Megara and Plataea, reached Sparta and came before the Ephors. This is what they said: 'The Athenians have sent us to tell you that the Persian king has offered both to restore our country to us, and at the same time, not only to make an alliance with us on fair and equal terms, openly and honestly, but also to give us any other territory we like to annex. We, however, from our reverence of the God whom all Greece worships, and our revulsion from the very thought of treachery, peremptorily refused the offer, in spite of the fact that we ourselves have been basely betrayed by our own confederates, and are well aware that we should gain more by an agreement with Persia than by prolonging the war. None the less, we shall never willingly make terms with the enemy. Thus we, at any rate, pay our debts to Greece with no counterfeit coin; but you, who were in terror lest we should make peace with Persia – now that you know our spirit without doubt, and that we shall never be traitors to Greece – and now, too, that your fortification of the Isthmus is almost complete – take no account of Athens. You agreed with us to oppose the invader in Boeotia, but you broke your word and allowed him to invade Attica. This conduct on your part has roused the anger of Athens; it was unworthy of the hour and of yourselves. However, your immediate duty is to accede to our present request: put your army in the field, that you and we together may meet Mardonius in Attica. Now that Boeotia is lost to us, the best place to engage him, within our own territory, is the plain of Thria.'

The Ephors undertook to give their answer on the following day; but when it came, they made a further postponement till the day after, and then till the day after that; in fact they kept putting it off from one day to the next for nearly a fortnight. Meanwhile the Peloponnesians in a body were working hard at the wall across the Isthmus, which was now nearing completion. Why was it that, when Alexander visited Athens, the Spartans were desperately anxious lest the Athenians should go over to Persia, whereas now they did not seem to care a jot? The only explanation I can give is, that the fortifications of the Isthmus were now complete, and they therefore felt that Athenian help was no longer necessary. At the time of Alexander's visit, the wall was not complete – they were still working at it, in great fear of the Persians.

At last, however, the Spartans did give their answer, and did put their army in the field. This was how it happened: on the eve of the day fixed for the final audience of the Athenian delegation, a Tegean named Chileus, a man with more influence in Sparta than anyone else who was not a native, asked the Ephors exactly what the Athenians had said, and having heard, he said: 'As I see it, gentlemen, if the Athenians desert us and make an alliance with Persia, then, however strongly the Isthmus is fortified, the postern gates are wide open for the Persian invasion of the Peloponnese. So you had better listen to them before they change their minds and adopt a policy which will ruin Greece.'

The Ephors took the warning to heart, and without a word to the delegates, immediately, before daybreak, dispatched a force of 5,000 Spartan troops, each man attended by seven helots, with Pausanias, son of Cleombrotus, in command.

The chief power in Sparta belonged by right at this time to Leonidas' son Pleistarchus; but he was still a minor, and Pausanias was his guardian and cousin. Cleombrotus, Pausanias' father and son of Anaxandrides, was no longer alive, but had died soon after he brought back the troops who had been building the fortifications at the Isthmus – he had brought them home because the sun was darkened in the sky during the course of a sacrifice he was offering, in the hope of favourable omens for a battle.[1] Pausanias appointed Euryanax, son of Dorieus and a member of the same family as himself, to share the command.

Next day the ambassadors, quite unaware that Pausanias and his troops were on the march, presented themselves before the Ephors for the last time, fully determined to leave Sparta and return to their respective homes. 'Then stay here if you want to,' they exclaimed; 'keep your Hyacinthia and amuse yourselves – and betray your friends. But we warn you: the Athenians will resent this injustice and, for lack of other allies, will make such an arrangement with the Persians as they can. That being done, it is plain that we shall be Xerxes'

1. The eclipse was probably that of the previous autumn, 2 October 480.

friends and shall fight, in consequence, against whatever country the Persians choose to lead us. The effect of that upon yourselves you will then be able to appreciate.'

At this the Ephors replied that they would take their oath that the army was already at Orestheium, on its march against the 'strangers'. ('Strangers' was the word they used for foreigners.) The delegates, at a loss, asked what they meant, and were told the truth. They were surprised, and hurried off after them. With them went 5,000 picked Lacedaemonian troops drawn from the outlying towns.

The Argives, who had previously agreed with Mardonius to prevent Spartan troops from taking the field, no sooner learned that Pausanias' army had left Sparta than they dispatched the best runner they could find with a message to Attica. There he presented himself to Mardonius, and said; 'I have been sent by the Argives to tell you that the fighting force of Lacedaemon is on the march, and that the Argives have been powerless to stop it. You must take measures accordingly.' The runner then left for home, and Mardonius, having heard his report, no longer felt inclined to remain in Attica. Up till then he had held on there because he wanted to find out which way the Athenians would go, and in the hope that they would come to terms he had refrained throughout his stay from doing damage of any kind to crops or property. Now, however, that he had failed to win them over, and the whole position was clear, he withdrew from the district before Pausanias' force reached the Isthmus. Before he went, he burnt Athens and reduced to complete ruin anything that remained standing – walls, houses, temples, and all. His reason for abandoning Attica was that it was bad country for cavalry; moreover, had he been beaten in an engagement, his only way of retreat would have been by a narrow defile, which would have been held by a very small force. His plan, therefore, was to retire on Thebes, where he could fight in good cavalry country and near a friendly town.

He was already on the road when news reached him that another Spartan force, 1,000 strong, had arrived at Megara in advance of Pausanias. Considering this news, and wishing, if possible, to destroy them first, he wheeled about and made for Megara, while his cavalry, pushing on ahead, overran all the surrounding country. This was the most westerly point in Europe that was reached by this Persian army.

More news now came that the Greek forces had concentrated in strength at the Isthmus, and Mardonius, in consequence, began his withdrawal by way of Decelea. The chief magistrates of the Boeotians had sent for men from the valley of the Asopus, and they acted as guides to the army, bringing it first to Sphendale and then on to Tangra, where it halted for a night. Next day Mardonius made for Scolus, and so found himself in Theban territory. In spite of the fact that the Thebans were on his side, he cut down all the trees in the neighbourhood – not as an act of hostility to Thebes, but simply for his own military needs, for he wished to construct a palisade to protect his troops and to have somewhere to retreat to in the event of the battle going against him. The position he occupied was along the Asopus, from Erythrae, past Hysiae, to the territory of Plataea; the palisade did not cover all this ground, but was approximately ten furlongs square.

While the Persian troops were working on the palisade, a Theban named Attaginus, the son of Phrynon, invited Mardonius and fifty other distinguished Persians to a banquet, for which he had made elaborate preparations. The invitation was accepted and the banquet was held in Thebes. What I am about to relate, I heard from Thersander, a man greatly respected in his native town Orchomenus. Thersander told me that he himself had an invitation from Attaginus, and that there were, besides the Persians, fifty Thebans. At table, the two nationalities, Greek and Persian, were not kept separate, but on each couch there sat a Persian and a Theban, side by side. During the drinking which followed the banquet, the Persian who shared Thersander's couch asked him, in Greek, what town he came from. 'Orchomenus,' was the answer. 'Since you and I', the Persian said, 'have eaten together at the same table and poured a libation from the same cup, I should like to leave you something by which you may remember the soundness of my judgement; thus you will be forewarned and be able to take proper measures for your own safety. You see these Persians at their dinner – and the army we left in camp over there by the river? In a short time from now you will see but a few of all these men left alive.' The Persian, as he spoke, wept copiously, and Thersander, greatly surprised at what he had said, answered: 'Are not Mardonius and the other high Persian officers under him the proper people to be told a thing like that?' 'My friend,' rejoined the other, 'what God has ordained no man can by any means prevent. Many of us know that what I have said is true; yet, because we cannot do otherwise, we continue to take orders from our commander. No one would believe us, however true our warning. The worst pain a man can have is to know much and be impotent to act.'

This tale, as I have said, I heard from Thersander of Orchomeus; he also told me that he repeated it soon after to various people before the battle of Plataea.

While Mardonius was in Boeotia, all the Greeks in that part of the country who had gone over to Persia sent troops to join his army, and also took part in his attack on Athens – all, that is, except the Phocians. The Phocians had, indeed, warmly embraced the Persian interest, but under compulsion and not of their free choice. A few days after Mardonius' arrival at Thebes, he was joined by a force of Phocian infantry, a thousand strong, under the command of Harmocydes, one of their most distinguished men. On their arrival, Mardonius sent them an order to take up a position in open ground, apart from the rest of the army. The order was no sooner obeyed than the Persian cavalry made their appearance in full force. On this, a rumour went round the Greek contingents serving with the Persians that Mardonius meant to attack the Phocians and shoot them down. The same idea ran through the Phocians, too. Their commander Harmocydes then urged them to fight. 'Fellow-countrymen,' he cried, 'you can't fail to see that these fellows have deliberately planned to murder us – no doubt because of some lie the Thessalians have told about us. Come then; show what you are made of, every one of you. It is better to die actively defending ourselves than just to give up and be butchered – that disgrace, at least, we can avoid. Let us show them that the men they have plotted to murder are Greeks – and they themselves mere foreign trash.'

The Persian cavalry then surrounded them, and began to close in with weapons poised, as though to make an end of them. A few spears were actually let fly; but the Phocians stood firm, drawing close together and packing their ranks tight, whereupon the Persians wheeled about and retired. Possibly the Thessalians had asked them to commit this crime, but, on seeing their victims prepared to defend themselves, they were afraid of being roughly handled and withdrew, according to Mardonius' orders; it may be, on the other hand, that Mardonius merely wanted to test their courage. I cannot say for certain which explanation is the true one. In any case, after the cavalry had retired, Mardonius sent a message to the Phocians, telling them not to be alarmed: 'You have proved yourselves brave men,' he said, 'quite contrary to the report I had of you. Your duty now is to play a zealous part in the war. As for benefits, you will not outdo either me or the king.' That was the end of this incident.

The Lacedaemonians halted at the Isthmus on their arrival there, and the other Peloponnesians who chose to do their duty – some of them only when they saw the Spartans on the march – felt ashamed to stay behind and take no part in the expedition. Accordingly, after getting favourable omens from the sacrifice, the combined forces of the Peloponnese left the Isthmus and advanced to Eleusis. Here they again offered sacrifice, and again getting good omens continued their advance, having now been joined by the Athenians, who had crossed to the mainland from Salamis. At Erythrae in Boeotia they learnt that the enemy had taken up his position on the Asopus, and, in view of this, themselves occupied the lower slopes of Cithaeron.

When the Greek forces showed no intention of leaving the high ground, Mardonius sent his cavalry to attack them in force, under command of the distinguished Persian officer Masistius – or Macistius, as the Greeks call him – who rode a Nisaean horse with a bridle of gold and other splendid trappings. The cavalry advanced to the attack in successive squadrons, and at each assault inflicted heavy losses on the Greeks, taunting them and calling them women. It so happened that the point in the Greek line which was most open and vulnerable to a cavalry charge was held by the Megarians, who found themselves hard pressed by the repeated attacks. Accordingly they sent a message to the allied commanders. 'Friends and fellow-soldiers,' the message ran, 'without assistance we are unable to hold the Persian cavalry or to maintain our original position. Up to the present, in spite of severe losses, we have continued to resist with firmness and courage; but now, unless you send other troops to relieve us, we warn you that we shall have to quit our post.'

Pausanias, on recept of the message, called for volunteers to relieve

the Megarians, but nobody was willing to go except the Athenians –
three hundred of them, picked men, commanded by Olympiodorus,
the son of Lampon. This, then, was the force which consented to act
as relief; taking the archers to accompany them, they marched to
their post at the point of danger on behalf of all the other Greek
troops present at Erythrae. For some time the battle continued, until,
during the successive attacks of the Persian squadrons, Masistius'
horse, which was in advance of the rest, was shot in the flank, and the
pain of the wound made him rear and throw his rider. No sooner was
Masistius down than the Athenians were upon him. They seized his
horse and finally – though not without difficulty – killed Masistius
himself, who fought hard for his life. The reason why they could not
kill him at once was the armour he wore – a corslet of golden scales
under his scarlet tunic. No blow upon the corslet had any effect, until
at last a soldier saw how it was and struck him in the eye, and he fell
dead. This occurred without the knowledge of the rest of the squadron, who had not observed either their commander's fall or his death;
for he fell just as they had wheeled about and retired for another
charge. It was only when they drew rein again that they missed him –
for there was no one to give the commands. Without a moment's
delay, now that they realized what had happened, word was passed
from man to man, and the entire force rode in again in the hope, at
least, of recovering the body. Seeing a mass attack now coming, the
Athenians called out to the rest of the army for support, and while the
infantry was on the way to their assistance, a sharp struggle took place
round Masistius' body. Before the reinforcements arrived, the three
hundred Athenians, fighting alone, had much the worst of it and
were forced to surrender the body; but once they were joined by the
other troops in full force, the enemy cavalry were no longer able to
hold their ground. They failed to keep possession of the body, and
lost, in the attempt, a number of their men besides. They then retired
a quarter of a mile or so, to take stock of their situation, and finally
decided, having lost their commander, to report to Mardonius. On
their arrival at headquarters with the news, Mardonius and the whole
army showed the deepest distress at Masistius' death – a man more
highly thought of, both by the king and by his subjects, than anyone
else in the Persian army except Mardonius himself; they shaved their

heads, cut the manes of their horses and mules, and abandoned themselves to such cries of grief that the whole of Boeotia was loud with
the noise of them.

While the Persians, in this typical fashion, were paying their respects to the dead Masistius, the Greeks, having both held and repulsed the cavalry charge, were much encouraged. They put Masistius' body on a cart and paraded it along the lines. It was certainly
worth looking at, for Masistius was a tall and splendidly handsome
man – this was why they did it – and men broke their ranks to get a
sight of Masistius.

The Greeks now determined to leave the high ground and move
down to Plataea, a much more convenient position than the country
round Erythrae, especially as it was better supplied with water. The
best thing, therefore, seemed to be to shift camp and take up a new
position, in their proper detachments, near the spring called Gargaphia in Plataean territory. The march began, and, proceeding
along the lower slopes of Cithaeron, past Hysiae, the army reached
the territory of Plataea, and the contingents of the several confeder-
ated towns halted close to the spring and the sacred enclosure of
Androcrates, in flat country rising here and there in low hills. Here,
in the process of assigning to each contingent its position in the line,
a hot dispute arose between the troops from Tegea and those from
Athens. Both claimed the right to hold one of the wings, and both
supported the claim by adducing instances of distinguished service
either in their previous history or during recent events. 'Hitherto',
the Tegeans urged, 'we have always by universal consent been given
the privilege of holding this position in every campaign undertaken
jointly by the Peloponnesians both in recent and in former times –
ever since, indeed, the Heracleidae made their attempt to force their
way back into the Peloponnese after the death of Eurystheus. Let us
remind you how, on that occasion, we won the privilege: the story
goes that when, in company with the Achaeans and Ionians who then
occupied the Peloponnese, we marched to the Isthmus to take our
stand against the invaders, Hyllus made a proclamation to the effect
that there was no need for the two armies to risk their lives in a general
engagement; it would suffice, he suggested, if a champion chosen
from the Peloponnesian army met him in single combat upon agreed

conditions. The Peloponnesians accepted the proposal and engaged upon oath that, if Hyllus were victorious, the Heracleidae should be allowed to resume the ancient rights of their family, and that if he were vanquished, they should withdraw their army and make no further attempt upon the Peloponnese for a hundred years.

'The man chosen to represent the confederate armies was our own commander and king, Echemus, the son of Aeropus, and grandson of Phegeus. He volunteered for the service, engaged Hyllus in single combat, and killed him; and it was in recognition of this act that we were granted important privileges amongst the Peloponnesians of that time; we enjoy them still, and the greatest of them is the privilege of leading one of the wings in any campaign undertaken jointly by Peloponnesian troops. Naturally, we do not set ourselves up against you, the Spartan contingent; we willingly grant you the right of choosing whichever wing you prefer; but we do claim the privilege of commanding the other one, according to precedent.

'Even apart from the greatest exploit we have mentioned, our title to the position of honour is better than that of the Athenians – witness, for instance, the many glorious fights we have fought with Sparta herself, not to mention other towns. To us, therefore, belongs this privilege, not to them. They can point to no exploits of their own, either in modern or in ancient times, comparable to ours.'

The Athenian answer was as follows. 'We are well aware that we are assembled here to fight the invader, not to make speeches. Nevertheless, as the Tegeans have started a competition in talking of the brave actions we have respectively performed during the long course of our history, we can hardly refrain from indicating the grounds upon which we, as a people who have always distinguished themselves, claim precedence over the Arcadians as our proper heritage. In the first place, when the Heracleidae, whose chieftain the Tegeans claim to have killed at the Isthmus, were refused shelter by all the Greeks to whom they applied in the hope of escaping slavery under the Mycenaeans, we alone received them, and with their help brought down the tyrannical rule of Eurystheus by a victorious campaign against the masters of the Peloponnese. Again, when the dead Argives were left unburied after their attack upon Thebes with Polyneices, we marched against the Cadmeans, recovered the bodies, and gave them burial within our own territory at Eleusis. Another memorable exploit of ours was against the Amazons from the river Thermodon, on the occasion of their inroad into Attica; and in the troubles at Troy our men were by no means the least distinguished. However, there is not much point in recalling all this ancient history; for people who were brave once might easily have deteriorated to-day, just as people who in old times were nothing to speak of might by now have improved. So let us leave ancient history out of it, and come to the present. Suppose, then, that we had never done anything but fight at Marathon – in point of fact we have done much besides: more than any other people of Greece – but just suppose; then Marathon alone would be enough to qualify us not only for the privilege we are claiming but for others too; for in that fight we stood alone against Persia – we dared a mighty enterprise and came out of it alive – we defeated forty-six nations! Do we not, for this act alone, deserve the place of honour on the wing?

'Nevertheless, at a time like this, it is unseemly to quarrel about who shall hold which place in the line; we are ready to take our orders from you Spartans, and to hold whatever part of the line, against whatever enemy contingent, you consider most useful. Whatever that position may be, we shall endeavour to fight like men. Give us our orders; we shall obey.'

At this answer there was a shout from every man in the Lacedaemonian army that the Athenians were the better men and better deserved the position of honour than the Arcadians. So the Athenians got it – at the Tegeans' expense.

In addition to the Greek troops who had first arrived in the neighbourhood of Plataea, other reinforcements had subsequently joined; and after the incident mentioned above the various contingents moved into line. The order was as follows: on the right wing were 10,000 Lacedaemonians, of whom the 5,000 from Sparta were attended by 35,000 light-armed helots – seven to a man. Next to themselves the Spartans stationed the Tegeans – 1,500 heavy infantry – as a tribute of respect to their worth. Next came the 5,000 Corinthians – who had obtained leave from Pausanias to have the 300 men from Potidaea in Pallene at their side. Then there were 600 from Orchomenus in Arcadia, 3,000 from Sicyon, and 800 from Epidaurus; after these, 1,000 from Troezen, 200 from Lepreum, 400 from Mycenae and Tiryns, 1,000 from Phlius, and 300 from Hermion; next, 600 from Eretria and Styra, 400 from Chalcis, 500 from Ambracia, 800 from Leucas and Anactorium, and 200 Paleans from Cephallenia; then 500 from Aegina, 3,000 from Megara, and 600 from Plataea. Last or first came the Athenians, 8,000 strong, on the left wing of the army, with Aristides, the son of Lysimachus, in command. All these troops, except the seven helots who attended each of the Spartans, were heavy-armed infantry, and their total strength amounted to 38,700 men. In addition to the heavy infantry there were light-armed auxiliaries: the 35,000 helots in attendance, as already mentioned, upon the Spartans, all of them fighting men, and 34,500 others, belonging to the other towns both in Lacedaemon and elsewhere – at the rate, that is, of one auxiliary to every man-at-arms. The total number of auxiliaries was thus 69,500, making the aggregate strength of the Greek army at Plataea 110,000 – all but 1,800, a deficiency which was made up by the Thespians, whose surviving men (1,800 precisely) had joined the Greek force. They were not, however, fully armed.

So much for the strength and organization of the Greek army when it took up its position on the Asopus. Mardonius' men, when they had finished mourning for Masistius, also moved up to the river upon learning that the Greeks were at Plataea, and were posted in the following order. Facing the Lacedaemonians Mardonius stationed his Persians, who, as they greatly outnumbered the Lacedaemonians, were drawn up in greater depth than usual and extended far enough to cover the Tegeans as well. Mardonius saw to it that the best of them faced the Lacedaemonians, the weaker ones being on their flank to cover the Tegeans. This precaution was taken at the suggestion, and by the advice, of the Thebans. On the right of the Persians were the Medes, covering the Greek contingents from Corinth, Potidaea, Orchomenus, and Sicyon; then the Bactrians, covering the Greeks from Epidaurus, Troezen, Lepreum, Tiryns, Mycenae, and Phlius; then the Indians, covering the men from Hermion, Eretria, Styra, and Chalcis; then the Sacae, covering the Ambraciots, Anactorians, Leucadians, Paleans, and Aeginetans; and, finally, on the right of the Sacae, and facing the Athenians, Plataeans, and Megarians, were posted the contingents from Boeotia, Locris, Malis, and Thessaly, together with the Phocians, 1,000 strong. Not all the Phocians had gone over to Persia; a certain number of them, from their base amongst the hills of Parnassus, did good service to the Greek cause by raiding and harrying Mardonius' army and the Greeks who were serving with it. Mardonius also posted on his right wing, facing the troops from Athens, the Macedonians and certain contingents from Thessaly.

I have named here the most efficient and important of the various national contingents which Mardonius put into the line on this occasion; his army also contained a sprinkling of troops of other nationalities – Phrygians, Mysians, Thracians, Paeonians, and so on, as well as Ethiopians and Egyptians. These last belonged to the caste called Hermotybians and Calasirians – the only fighting men in Egypt. Their weapon is the sword. They had previously served with the fleet, but Mardonius brought them ashore before leaving Phalerum; there were no Egyptian troops in the land force which Xerxes brought to Athens.

The foreign troops in Mardonius' army numbered, as I have already shown, 300,000; the number of Greeks who were serving under him nobody knows, for they were never counted. My own guess is that there were about 50,000 of them. All the above-mentioned troops which were put into the line were infantrymen; the cavalry formed a separate unit.

When Mardonius' dispositions were complete, with the national contingents all in their respective places in the line, both armies, on the following day, proceeded to offer sacrifice. The man who officiated for the Greeks was Tisamenus, the son of Antiochus, who was serving with the army in the capacity of diviner. He came originally from Elis and belonged to the Clytiad family of the Iamidae, but the Lacedaemonians had adopted him as one of themselves, under the following circumstances. Having no children, he had gone to Delphi to consult the oracle on the subject, and the Priestess, in her reply, told him that he was destined to win the 'five greatest contests'. Failing to understand the meaning of this prophecy, he went into training for athletics under the impression that that was the kind of 'contest' he was to win, and actually came within a single event of winning the Olympic pentathlon against Hieronymus of Andros. The Lacedaemonians, however, realized that the word 'contests' in the oracle referred not to athletics but to war, and attempted to induce him, by the offer of a wage, to become joint leader with their Heraclid kings in the conduct of their wars. Tisamenus saw that the Spartans were extremely anxious to get his support, and consequently raised his price, indicating that he would do as they asked only if they made him a Spartan citizen with full civic rights. Otherwise he would have nothing to do with the proposal. The first effect upon the Spartans of Tisamenus' demand was indignation, and they stopped asking for his services; but later on, under the terrible threat of the Persian invasion, they again sought him out and agreed to his terms. Tisamenus, however, seeing that they had come round, declared that he was no longer satisfied with the original conditions, but must have his brother Hagias, too, made a citizen of Sparta with the same rights as himself. In making this demand Tisamenus was following the example of Melampus – if one can compare a demand for citizenship with a demand for a throne. For Melampus, it will be remembered, when he was fetched by the Argives from Pylos and offered a fee to restore their women, who had all gone mad, to sanity, claimed half the kingdom as payment for the service. The Argives thought the demand a monstrous one, and left him; but later, when more of their women caught the disease, they brought themselves to consent, and went back to Melampus to promise what he asked. Thereupon Melampus, seeing they had come round to his terms, reached out for a bit more, and refused to perform the service they wanted unless they gave, in addition, one-third of the kingdom to his brother Bias. The Argives, who were in a very awkward position, had to consent to this too. It was just the same with the Spartans – they needed Tisamenus badly, and consequently gave him everything he asked for. The result was that this man from Elis, having become a citizen of Sparta, helped the Spartans, in his capacity as diviner, to win five 'contests' of the greatest importance. (Tisamenus and his brother were the only two foreigners ever to be made Spartan citizens.) They were the following: first, the battle of Plataea, which I am about to describe; second, the fight at Tegea against the Tegeans and Argives; third, at Dipaees against the combined forces of Arcadia, excluding Mantinea; fourth, against the Messenians at Ithome; and, last, against the Athenians and Argives at Tanagra.

This Tisamenus, then, brought by the Spartans, was acting as diviner for the Greek forces at Plataea. The omens turned out to be favourable to the Greeks, provided that they fought a defensive action, but unfavourable should they cross the Asopus and attack. For Mardonius the omens were similar – good for defence, bad if he yielded to his eagerness to attack. Mardonius too made use of the Greek ritual to get his omens; his diviner was Hegesistratus of Elis, the best-known member of the clan of the Telliadae, and a man who had had a remarkable history. He had once been arrested by the Spartans on a charge of doing them a number of injuries of a very serious nature. Flung into prison and condemned to death, Hegesistratus, realizing, in his desperate situation, not only that his life was at stake but also that he would be tortured before his execution, dared a deed which one cannot find words adequate to praise. He was lying with one foot in the stocks – which were made of wood reinforced with iron – and somehow managed to get hold of a knife, which was smuggled into the prison. No sooner was the knife in his hand than he contrived the means to escape – and how he did it was the bravest thing I have ever heard of: he cut a bit off his foot, having nicely judged how much to leave in order to pull it free. Then, as the prison was guarded, he worked a hole through the wall and escaped to Tegea, travelling at night and lying up during the day in the woods. The Lacedaemonians went out in force to try to find him, but he got clear and reached Tegea on the third night. They were astonished at the man's toughness when they saw half his foot lying by the stocks and were unable to find him.

In this way Hegesistratus escaped his captors and made his way successfully to Tegea, which was not at that time on good terms with Sparta. When his wound healed he got himself a wooden foot made, and openly avowed his enmity to the Spartans. This, however, was destined ultimately to bring him into trouble; for at a later period – after Plataea – while he was performing his duties as diviner in Zacynthus, the Spartans caught him and put him to death. On the occasion of which I am speaking, he was with Mardonius on the Asopus; he was by no means poorly paid, and he performed his duties with great zest – partly out of hatred for the Spartans, partly for the sake of the money.

All this time the Greek forces were increasing by a continual influx of men; and in view of this, added to the fact that both for the Persians and for their Greek allies (who were served by their own diviner Hippomachus of Leucas) the omens were unfavourable for attack, a Theban named Timagenides, the son of Herpys, advised Mardonius to watch the passes of Cithaeron, as he would be able to cut off a great many of the men who every day were streaming through them to join the Greek army. The proposal was made when the two armies had already been eight days in position, facing one another. Mardonius saw that it was a good one, and that evening sent his cavalry to the pass over Cithaeron which leads to Plataea – the pass, that is, which is known locally as Three Heads, though the Athenians call it Oak Heads. The movement was not without success; a train of five hundred mules bringing food from the Peloponnese for the army was caught, together with the men in charge, just as it was coming down from the hills. The Persian cavalrymen showed no mercy; they killed beasts and men indiscriminately, and drove the remnant, when they were sick of slaughter, back to Mardonius within their own lines.

Two more days went by, and no further action took place. Neither side was willing to begin the general engagement. The Persians provoked the Greek forces to attack by advancing right up to the river, but neither of them ventured actually to cross. Nevertheless Mardonius' cavalry harassed the Greeks continually: this was due to the Thebans – Persia's firm friends; their hearts were in the war, and again and again they led the cavalry to within striking distance, when the Persians and Medes took over, and proceeded to show what stuff they were made of.

During those ten days nothing happened beyond what I have mentioned. The armies faced one another and no move was made, and all the time the Greek forces were rapidly increasing. At last, on the eleventh day, Mardonius, irked by the protracted inactivity, entered into conference with Artabazus, the son of Pharnaces – a Persian of the very highest reputation with Xerxes. In the discussion which followed Artabazus urged that the best thing to do would be to abandon their present position at once, and to withdraw the entire army within the fortifications of Thebes, where they had stored abundant supplies, including fodder for the animals. They had with them a great deal of gold, both coined and uncoined, besides plenty of silver and plate; and they could easily achieve their purpose, without making any active move, simply by sending lavish presents out of this treasure to the Greeks – especially to those of them who were most influential in the various towns. This would very soon bring them to give up their liberty. It would be a mistake, on the other hand, to risk another battle. This opinion coincided with that of the Thebans – for they reckoned that Artabazus was a man of more than average foresight.

Mardonius expressed himself in much more uncompromising terms, and did not agree at all. In his view, the right policy, as the Persian army was far stronger than the Greek, was to force an engagement at once, and not allow the enemy forces to increase any further; as for Hegesistratus and his sacrifices, it would be best to ignore them – certainly not to try to force their meaning – and to engage in battle in the good old Persian way. The proposal was carried without opposition – for it was Mardonius, not Artabazus, who held from Xerxes the command of the army. He then sent for his divisional commanders and the Greek officers who were serving under him, and asked if they knew of any prophecy which foretold the destruction of Persian troops in Greece. Nobody said a word: perhaps some of them were unaware of the prophecies, while others, who knew them well enough, felt it was safer not to mention them. Mardonius accordingly said: 'Either you know of no such prophecy, or are afraid to speak of it. Well, I *do* know of one, and I will tell it to you. It says that the Persians will come to Greece, sack the temple at Delphi, and then perish to a man. Very well then: knowing that, we will keep away from the temple and make no attempt to plunder it – and thus avoid destruction. All of you, therefore, who wish your country well, may rejoice at this, and be very sure that we shall defeat the Greeks.' Thereupon he issued his orders to prepare for battle on the following day.

I happen to know that the oracle, which Mardonius applied to the Persians, actually referred to the Illyrians and the army of the

Encheles; there are, however, some verses of Bacis which did, in fact, refer to this battle:

> By Thermodon and Asopus, where the grass grows soft,
> Shall be gathering of Greeks and the sound of strange tongues;
> And there beyond lot and portion many Medes shall fall,
> Armed with the bow, when the day of doom comes.

These verses, and other similar ones of Musaeus, I know referred to the Persians. The Thermodon flows between Tanagra and Glisas.

After Mardonius had asked his question about the oracles and spoken the words of encouragement which I mentioned, darkness fell and the watches were set. Some hours passed; and as soon as silence had descended on the two armies and the men all seemed to be asleep, Alexander, the son of Amyntas, the king and commander of the Macedonians, rode up to the Athenian guard-posts and asked permission to have a word with the officers in command. Most of the pickets stayed at their posts, but a few of them hurried off and informed their officers that a man on horseback had arrived from the Persian army: he would say nothing, except that he wanted to speak to the officers in charge, whose names he mentioned. The Athenians at once accompanied the guards back to their post, and Alexander delivered his message. 'Men of Athens,' he said, 'I trust to your honour for what I am about to tell you: keep it a secret from everybody except Pausanias or you will ruin me. I should not be here at all if I had not at heart the common welfare of Greece – I am myself a Greek by descent, and have no wish to see Greece exchange her freedom for slavery. Listen, then: Mardonius and his army cannot get satisfactory omens from their sacrifices – but for this, you would have been fighting long before now. Mardonius has decided, however, to ignore the omens and to attack at dawn – in anxiety to prevent still further reinforcements from reaching you, as I guess. Be ready for him, therefore. If, on the contrary, he should postpone his attack, my advice to you is to hold on where you are: for he has only a few days' supplies left.

'In the event of your bringing this war to a successful conclusion, you must remember me, and do something for my freedom: for the sake of Greece I have taken a great risk, in my desire to acquaint you with what Mardonius intends, and thus to save you from a surprise attack. I am Alexander of Macedon.'

This said, Alexander rode back to the camp and resumed the position assigned to him, while the Athenian commanders hurried to Pausanias, on the right wing of the Greek army, and told him what they had just heard. Pausanias was much alarmed. 'As we are to be in action at dawn,' he said, 'you Athenians had better take position opposite the Persians, while we deal with the Boeotians and the other Greeks now opposite you. Marathon gave you experience of Persian tactics – unlike us, who know nothing about them whatever. No Spartan here has ever been in action against Persian troops – but we are all familiar enough with the soldiers of Boeotia and Thessaly. So get moving at once, and come and take over the right wing. We will take your place on the left.'

'It occurred to us,' the Athenians replied, 'long ago – ever since we saw that your section would have to face the Persian thrust – to make the very suggestion which you have now been the first to put forward; but we were afraid of offending you. Now, however, that you have mentioned it yourselves, we willingly accept, and will do what you ask.'

The matter being settled to the satisfaction of both parties, at the first signs of dawn the Athenian and Spartan contingents changed places. But the Boeotians detected the movement and reported to Mardonius, who immediately shifted his Persian troops to the other wing, so as still to face the Spartans. Pausanias, seeing that his own movement had not escaped observation, then marched his men back again to the right wing – and, as before, Mardonius followed suit, so that Persians and Spartans were once again facing one another in their original positions. Mardonius then sent a herald to the Spartan lines. 'Men of Lacedaemon,' the message ran, 'everybody about here seems to think you are very brave. Everyone admires you for never retreating in battle and for never quitting your post: you stick to it, so they say, until death – either your enemy's or your own. But it turns out that all this is nonsense: for here you are, running away and deserting your post before the battle has even begun or a single blow been struck, and giving the place of danger to the Athenians, while you yourselves face men who are merely our slaves. This is by no

means what brave men would do; indeed, we have been sadly mistaken about you. Your reputation led us to expect that you would
send us a challenge, in your eagerness to match yourselves with none
but Persian troops. We should have accepted the challenge, had you
sent it; but you did not. We find you, instead, slinking away from us.
Well, as you have sent no challenge, we will send one ourselves: why
should we not fight with equal numbers on both sides, with you
(who are supposed to be the most valiant) as the champions of Greece,
and ourselves as the champions of Asia? Then, if it seems a good thing
that the rest should fight too, they can do so after we have finished;
otherwise, let us settle it between us, and let the victor be considered
to have won the battle for the whole army.'

The herald waited for a time after delivering this challenge; then,
as nobody gave him an answer, he returned to Mardonius and told
him what had happened. Mardonius was overjoyed and, in all the
excitement of his empty victory, ordered his cavalry to attack. The
Persian cavalry, being armed with the bow, were not easy to come
to grips with; so when they moved forward, they harried all the
Greek line with their arrows and javelins; they also choked up and
spoilt the spring of Gargaphia, from which all the Greek troops got
their water. Actually, only the Lacedaemonians were near the spring,
the rest of the army being some distance away, in their various positions, but all close to the river Asopus; nevertheless they, too, had
been forced to resort to the spring for water, because the enemy
cavalry, with their missile weapons, prevented them getting it from
the river. In these circumstances, their men being continually harassed
by the Persian cavalry and cut off from their water, the commanders
of the various Greek contingents went in a body to Pausanias on the
right wing, to discuss these and other difficulties with him. Lack of
water, though bad enough, was by no means the only cause of distress; food, too, had run short, and the servants who had been sent to
bring supplies from the Peloponnese had been stopped by parties of
Persian cavalry and had failed to rejoin. In the course of the discussion
it was agreed that, if the Persians let the day pass without bringing on
a general engagement, they should shift their position to the Island –
a tract of ground in front of Plataea, rather more than a mile from the
Asopus and Gargaphia, where they then were. This place is a sort of

'island on land': there is a river which splits into two channels near its source on Cithaeron, and in the plain below the channels are about three furlongs apart, before they unite again further on. The name of the river is Oeroe, and it is known locally as 'daughter of Asopus'. Two reasons led them to choose the Island for their new position: first, they would have an abundant supply of water; and, secondly, the enemy cavalry would be unable to hurt them. The plan was to make the move during the night, at the second watch, to prevent the enemy from observing them as they marched out, and thus to escape trouble from his cavalry on the way. It was further agreed that upon reaching the tract of land 'islanded' by the two channels of the Oeroe as it flows down from Cithaeron, they should detach, during the same night, one half of the army and send it as far as the hills of Cithaeron, to relieve the food convoys which were cut off there.[1]

Having made these decisions, they continued throughout the day, without a moment's respite, to suffer harassment from the enemy cavalry; but towards evening the attacks ceased, and after dark, at the time agreed upon for departure, the greater part of the Greek forces moved off. However, they had no intention of making for the Island, according to plan: on the contrary, once they were on the move, they fled to Plataea, only too thankful to escape the Persian cavalry. Here they came to a halt in front of the temple of Hera, which stands outside the town, at a distance of about two and a half miles from Gargaphia.

When Pausanias saw the troops moving from their original position, he gave orders to the Lacedaemonians to strike camp and follow them, in the belief that those who had already started were making for the agreed position. Pausanias' officers were ready to obey the order, with one exception – Amompharetus, the son of Poliades and commander of the Pitanate regiment. This officer refused to run away from the 'strangers' and thus deliberately to dishonour his country, and (as he had not been present at the conference) expressed his astonishment at the sight of this unexpected move. Pausanias and Euryanax were highly indignant at this refusal to obey orders; none the less they felt it would be even worse, just because of Amompharetus' obstinacy, to leave the Pitanate regiment to its fate; for both he and his men would almost certainly be killed, if the rest of the army carried out their agreement and abandoned them. Accordingly the order to move was countermanded, and Pausanias and Euryanax made every endeavour to convince Amompharetus that he was mistaken. The Athenians, meanwhile, being well aware of the Spartan habit of saying one thing and meaning something else, did not move from the position they occupied, until the withdrawal began; then they sent a man on horseback to find out if the Spartans themselves had any intention of going, or not, and to ask Pausanias for instructions. The messenger found the Lacedaemonians still in their old position, and their officers at loggerheads; for Euryanax and Pausanias had failed in their efforts to persuade Amompharetus not to endanger the lives of his men by staying behind while the others withdrew, and they had begun to quarrel just at the moment when the Athenian messenger arrived. Still arguing violently, Amompharetus picked up a rock in both hands, and, laying it at Pausanias' feet cried: 'Here's my voting-pebble – and I cast my vote against running away from the strangers!'[1] Pausanias said he was a fool and had taken leave of his senses; then, when the Athenian messenger put his question, he told him to report the state of affairs in the Spartan lines, adding a request that the Athenians should move over in their direction and, in the movement, conform to the Spartan lead. So the messenger returned, and the Spartans continued to wrangle until dawn next morning.

With the coming of daylight Pausanias, thinking – quite rightly, as the event proved – that Amompharetus would not stay behind if all the other Lacedaemonian troops withdrew, at last gave the order for retreat, and marched off all his men, except the Pitanates, along the line of the hills, the Tegean contingent accompanying them. The Athenians followed in good order, but by a different route; for while the Spartans kept to the higher ground and the foothills of Cithaeron for fear of attack by the Persian cavalry, the Athenians took the lower road across level country.

Amompharetus did not at first believe that Pausanias would actually go so far as to leave him behind, and for that reason urged the necessity of holding their position; but when Pausanias' men had already got some distance on their way, he could no longer have any

1. An evident canard; for the Spartan assembly did not vote with pebbles.

doubt about it: he was left behind in good earnest. Accordingly, he gave his regiment orders to march, and followed, at a leisurely pace, the rest of the Spartan troops, who halted about half a mile off to wait for him, near the river Moloïs and a place called Argiopium, where there is a temple dedicated to Demeter of Eleusis. Their reason for waiting was to give them a chance of going back to the assistance of Amompharetus and his men in the event of his deciding, after all, not to abandon his position. No sooner had Amompharetus rejoined the main body than the cavalry attacks began again: the Persian horse, meaning to continue their old harassing tactics, had found the enemy gone from the position they had occupied during the last few days, and had ridden in pursuit. Now, having overtaken the retreating columns, they renewed their attacks with vigour.

When Mardonius learned that the Greeks had slipped away under cover of darkness, and saw with his own eyes that not a man remained in the position they had previously held, he sent for Thorax of Larissa and his two brothers, Eurypylus and Thrasidaeus. 'Well, gentlemen,' he exclaimed, 'what will you say, now that you see that place deserted? You, who are neighbours of the Lacedaemonians, used to tell me that they were grand fighters, and never ran away! Only yesterday you saw them try to get out of their place in the line, and now it is plain to all of us that last night they simply took to their heels and fled. Once they found it necessary to fight against troops which are, in actual fact, first-rate, they showed clearly enough that there's nothing in them, and that their reputation was gained merely amongst Greeks – who have nothing in them either. Now *you* I can excuse for praising these men: you know nothing about the Persians – and you did know one or two things the Spartans have done; but I was much more surprised at Artabazus, that *he* should be frightened of the Lacedaemonians, and allow his fear to suggest to him the shameful policy of a general retreat within the fortifications of Thebes, where we should stand a siege. I shall take care that the king is informed of that proposal of his – but that can wait; our immediate task is not to let the Greeks escape us by what they have done: they must be pursued till they are caught and punished for all the injuries they have inflicted upon us.'

So saying, Mardonius gave the order to advance. His men crossed the Asopus and followed at the double in the track of the Greek forces, who, it was supposed, were in full flight. Actually, it was the Spartans and Tegeans only that Mardonius was after, for the Athenians, who had marched by a different route across the level ground, were hidden from sight by the intervening hills.

When the officers of the other divisions of Mardonius' army saw the Persian contingent start in pursuit, they immediately ordered the standards to be raised, and all the troops under their command joined in the chase as fast as their legs would carry them. Without any attempt to maintain formation they swept forward, yelling and shouting, never doubting that they would make short work of the fugitives. Pausanias, when the enemy cavalry fell upon him, sent a rider to the Athenians with an appeal for help. 'Men of Athens,' the message ran, 'the great struggle is now upon us – the struggle which will determine the liberty or enslavement of Greece; but our friends fled last night from the field of battle and have betrayed us both. Now, therefore, our duty is plain: we must defend ourselves and protect each other as best we can. Had it been you who were first attacked by the Persian horse, we should have been bound to come to your assistance, together with the Tegeans who are, like us, loyal to the cause of Greece; but as we, not you, are bearing the whole weight of the attack, it is your duty to support those who are hardest pressed. If you are in any difficulty which prevents you from coming to our aid, then send us your archers, and we shall be grateful. We acknowledge that throughout this war your zeal has been equalled by none; you will not, then, refuse this request.'

On receipt of this message the Athenians started to the relief of the Spartans, to whom they were anxious to give all the help they could; but they were no sooner on the move than they were attacked by the Greek troops under Persian command, who held the position facing them. The attack was a heavy one, and made it impossible for them to carry out their purpose, so that the Lacedaemonians and Tegeans, whom nothing could induce to leave their side, were left to fight alone – the former 50,000 strong, including the light-armed auxiliaries, the latter 3000.

Once more, as they were about to engage with Mardonius and his men, they performed the ritual of sacrifice. The omens were not favourable; and meanwhile many of their men were killed, and many more wounded, for the Persians had made a barricade of their wicker shields and from the protection of it were shooting arrows in such numbers that the Spartan troops were in serious distress; this, added to the unfavourable results of the sacrifice, at last caused Pausanias to turn his eyes to the temple of Hera and to call upon the goddess for her aid, praying her not to allow the Greeks to be robbed of their hope of victory. Then, while the words were still upon his lips, the Tegeans sprang forward to lead the attack, and a moment later the sacrificial victims promised success. At this, the Spartans, too, at last moved forward against the enemy, who stopped shooting their arrows and prepared to meet them face to face.

First there was a struggle at the barricade of shields; then, the barricade down, there was a bitter and protracted fight, hand to hand, close by the temple of Demeter, for the Persians would lay hold of the Spartan spears and break them; in courage and strength they were as good as their adversaries, but they were deficient in armour, untrained, and greatly inferior in skill. Sometimes singly, sometimes in groups of ten men – perhaps fewer, perhaps more – they fell upon the Spartan line and were cut down. They pressed hardest at the point where Mardonius fought in person – riding his white charger, and surrounded by his thousand Persian troops, the flower of the army. While Mardonius was alive, they continued to resist and to defend themselves, and struck down many of the Lacedaemonians; but after his death, and the destruction of his personal guard – the finest of the Persian troops – the remainder yielded to the Lacedaemonians and took to flight. The chief cause of their discomfiture was their lack of armour, fighting without it against heavily armed infantry.

Thus the prophecy of the oracle was fulfilled, and Mardonius rendered satisfaction to the Spartans for the killing of Leonidas; and thus, too, Pausanias, son of Cleombrotus and grandson of Anaxandrides, won the most splendid victory which history records. Mardonius was killed by Arimnestus, a distinguished Spartan, who some time after the Persian wars met his own death, together with the three hundred men under his command, at Stenyclerus fighting against the entire forces of the Messenians.

Once their resistance was broken by the Lacedaemonians, the

Persian troops fled in disorder and took refuge in the wooden fort which they had erected in Theban territory. It is a wonder to me how it should have happened that, though the battle was fought close to the holy precinct of Demeter, not a single Persian soldier was found dead upon the sacred soil, or ever appears to have set foot upon it, while round about the temple, on unconsecrated ground, the greatest number were killed. My own view is – if one may have views at all about these mysteries – that the Goddess herself would not let them in, because they had burnt her sanctuary at Eleusis.

Artabazus, the son of Pharnaces, had disapproved from the first of Xerxes' action in leaving Mardonius behind in Greece, and had done his best, though without success, to dissuade Mardonius from an engagement; consequently having from the first disliked Mardonius' strategy, this is what he did. He had under his command a considerable force of some 40,000 men; well aware, as he was, of what the issue was likely to be, he gave orders to this force, as soon as the fighting began, to advance in good order and to follow his lead at whatever pace he might set them. At first he made as if to lead his men into battle; but he had not advanced very far before he saw the Persians already in flight, whereupon he no longer kept to his order of march, but suddenly wheeled about and beat a retreat – not to the barricade, or to Thebes, but direct to Phocis, in his desire to reach the Hellespont with the least possible delay.

Most of the Greek troops on the king's side made little or no attempt to distinguish themselves. This, however, was not true of the Boeotians, who had a long struggle with the Athenians; for the Thebans who had gone over to the enemy, far from deliberately shirking duty, fought so hard that three hundred of their best and bravest men were killed. When they, too, were overpowered, they fled to Thebes, and did not accompany the defeated Persians or the mixed crowd of confederate troops, who made their escape without striking a blow or doing any service whatever. It is perfectly obvious that everything depended upon the Persians: the rest of Mardonius' army took to their heels simply because they saw the Persians in retreat, and before they had even come to grips with the enemy. The only section of Mardonius' army which was not hopelessly routed was the cavalry – especially the Boeotian cavalry: this force did good service to the fugitives, keeping all the time in close contact with the enemy and acting as a screen between their friends and the pursuing Greeks.

During the panic rout of the enemy, while the victors were still pursuing the fugitives with great slaughter, news of the battle and of Pausanias' success reached the Greeks who were stationed near the temple of Hera and had taken no part in the fighting. The moment they heard the turn events had taken, they rushed forward in a mob, the Corinthians and their division by the upper routes across the foot-hills of Cithaeron, straight for the temple of Demeter, the Megarians, Phliasians and others by the level route through the plain. These last had nearly got into touch with the enemy when they were seen by the Theban cavalry under Asopodorus son of Timander, who, taking advantage of their complete lack of order and discipline, promptly attacked, killing six hundred of them and driving the remainder in headlong flight into the hills – an inglorious end. Mardonius' men – Persians and all – who took refuge behind their wooden palisade, managed to get up into the bastions before the Lacedaemonians were on them, and at once did what they could to strengthen their de-fences. When the Lacedaemonians arrived, a struggle of some vigour began, but, as they have never mastered the art of attacking defen-sive works, the Persians kept them out and had much the better of it, until the Athenians reached the scene of action. Then, with the arrival of the Athenians, the fight for the palisade was long and violent, until at last, by courage and perseverance, they forced their way up and made a breach, through which the rest of the army poured. First in were the Tegeans; and it was they who plundered Mardonius' tent, taking from it, amongst much else, the manger used by his horses – a remarkable piece of work, all in bronze. They placed this manger as an offering in the temple of Athene Alea, whereas everything else they took was brought into the common stock of plunder taken by the Greeks generally. Once the palisade was down, the Persians no longer kept together as an organized force; soldierly virtues were all forgotten; chaos prevailed and, huddled in thousands within that confined space, all of them were half dead with fright. To the Greeks they were such an easy prey that of the 300,000 men (excluding the 40,000 who fled with Artabazus) not 3000 survived. The Spartan losses in the battle amounted to 91 killed; the Tegeans lost 16, the Athenians 52.

Of the enemy's infantry, the Persian contingent fought best; of the cavalry, the Sacae; and of individuals Mardonius himself is said to have been as good as any. On the Greek side, the troops from Tegea and Athens were conspicuous in the fighting, but both were surpassed by the Lacedaemonians: the only evidence I can offer to support this statement (for all three were victorious in their own section of the line) is the fact that the Lacedaemonians had the hardest task. They were matched against the best troops of the enemy – and beat them. Much the greatest courage was shown, in my opinion, by Aristodemus – the man who had suffered the disgrace of being the sole survivor of the Three Hundred at Thermopylae. After him, the greatest personal distinction was won by the three Spartans, Posidonius, Philocyon, and Amompharetus. However, when, after the battle, the question of who had most distinguished himself was discussed, the Spartans present decided that Aristodemus had, indeed, fought magnificently, but that he had done so merely to retrieve his lost honour, rushing forward with the fury of a madman in his desire to be killed before his comrades' eyes; Posidonius, on the contrary, without any wish to be killed, had fought bravely, and was on that account the better man. It may, of course, have been envy which made them say this; in any case, the men I mentioned all received public honours except Aristodemus – Aristodemus got nothing, because he deliberately courted death for the reason already explained. These, then, were the men who beyond others made names for themselves at Plataea; Callicrates, on the other hand, was killed before the real action began – Callicrates, the handsomest man in the Greek army, Lacedaemonians and everyone else included. He was sitting in his place, while Pausanias was offering sacrifice, and was hit in the side by an arrow. As the two armies engaged, he was carried out of the line, and died hard. 'It is no sorrow to me', he said to Arimnestus the Plataean, 'to die for my country; what grieves me is, that I have not used my arm or done anything worthy of myself, such as I longed to do.'

The Athenian who is said most to have distinguished himself was Sophanes, the son of Eutychides, from the village of Decelea – once upon a time the scene of an action which, the Athenians say, has been useful to them ever since. Long ago, when the sons of Tyndareus invaded Attica with a large army to recover Helen, and, unable to find her hiding-place, were laying the village in ruin, the men of Decelea (or perhaps Decelus himself), in resentment at Theseus' high-handed conduct, and alarm for the safety of the whole Athenian territory, revealed the whole thing to the invaders and guided them to Aphidnae, which Titacus, a native of the place, betrayed into their hands. In return for this service, Sparta has ever since given the Deceleans the freedom of their city and special seats at public functions – so that during the war, many years after these events between Athens and Sparta, the Spartans in their raids on Attica always left Decelea unharmed. This, then, was the village to which Sophanes belonged. Of his prowess at Plataea two accounts are given: according to one, he carried an iron anchor made fast to the belt of his corslet with a bronze chain; with this he would anchor himself whenever he got near the enemy, to prevent their attacks from shifting him; then, when the enemy retreated, he would up-anchor and chase them. According to the other account, which differs from the former one, he did not have an actual iron anchor attached to his corslet, but merely bore the device of an anchor on his shield, which he kept continually spinning round and round. Another famous exploit of Sophanes was during the Athenian siege of Aegina, when he killed Eurybates the Argive, a winner of the pentathlon, in single combat.[1] His ultimate fate was to meet his death in a battle with the Edoni for the gold mines at Datum, where he did good service as joint commander of the Athenians with Leagrus, the son of Glaucon.

After the rout at Plataea, a woman, who had made her escape from the Persians, came into the Greek lines. She was a captive of the Persian Pharandates, the son of Teaspis; and when she realized that the Persian army was done for and that the Greeks were winning the day, she dressed herself and her maids in the finest things she possessed, loaded herself with gold ornaments, and, getting down from her covered waggon, made her way to the Spartans while the work of slaughter was still in progress. She soon recognized Pausanias; for not only was she already acquainted, from what she had often heard,

1. Repeated from VI, 92 (p. 421).

with his name and country, but she could also see for herself that he was directing all the operations. 'O King of Sparta,' she cried, clasping his knees in supplication, 'save me, I beg you, from the slavery which awaits the prisoner of war! For one service I am already in your debt – the killing of these men, who reverence neither gods nor angels. I am a native of Cos, and the daughter of Hegetorides and granddaughter of Antagoras. That Persian took me by force and made me his concubine.'

'You need not be afraid,' Pausanias replied; 'as a suppliant you are safe – and still more so, if you are indeed the daughter of Hegetorides of Cos, for he is bound to me by closer ties of friendship than anyone else in those parts.' With these words he put her in charge of the Spartan magistrates who happened to be on the spot, and afterwards sent her, at her own wish, to Aegina.

Immediately after this woman's visit, the troops from Mantinea arrived upon the scene – too late. Such was their indignation and distress when they found that all was over, that they declared they deserved to be punished. Somebody told them about the Persian force which had made its escape with Artabazus, and they were all for going in pursuit of it to Thessaly; but the Spartans refused to allow them, so they returned home and passed sentence of exile upon their army leaders. Next the troops from Elis arrived – and they, too, had to go home again in disappointment, which they marked in the same way as the Mantineans, by banishing their officers.

Serving with the Aeginetans at Plataea there was a man named Lampon. His father was Pytheas, and he was a person of the highest distinction in his native town. This man went to see Pausanias, and urged upon him a really shocking proposal. 'Son of Cleombrotus,' he said, 'the service you have already rendered is noble beyond all expectation. God has granted you the privilege of saving Greece and of winning for yourself the greatest name in history. Now, to crown all, there is one thing more that you should do, both to increase your own reputation and to make foreigners think twice in future before they offer insult and injury to the Greeks. When Leonidas was killed at Thermopylae, Xerxes and Mardonius had his head cut off and stuck on a pike: have your revenge, then; render like for like, and you will win the praise not only of every man in Sparta, but of every man in

Greece. Impale Mardonius' body, and Leonidas, your father's brother, will be avenged.'

Lampon really thought that this would be an acceptable suggestion; Pausanias, however, replied: 'I thank you, my Aeginetan friend, for your goodwill and concern for me; but, in regard to your judgement, you have failed to hit the mark. First, you exalt me and my country to the skies by your praise of my success; and then you would bring it all to nothing by advising me to insult a dead body, and by saying that my good name would be increased if I were to do a barbarous thing fitter for savages than Greeks – and even then we think it repulsive. No, indeed; in this matter I hope I shall never please the Aeginetans, or anyone else who approves such beastliness. It is enough for me to please the Spartans, by reverence and decency in both word and deed. As for Leonidas, whom you wish me to avenge, he is, I maintain, abundantly avenged already – surely the countless lives here taken are a sufficient price not for Leonidas only, but for all the others, too, who fell at Thermopylae. Never come to me with such a proposal again, and be grateful that you are allowed to go unpunished.' When he heard that, Lampon retired.

Pausanias now issued an order that everything of value which had fallen into their hands as a result of the battle should be collected by the helots, and that nobody else should touch it. The helots accordingly went through the whole camp. Treasure was there in plenty – tents full of gold and silver furniture; couches overlaid with the same precious metals; bowls, goblets, and cups, all of gold; and waggons loaded with sacks full of gold and silver basins. From the bodies of the dead they stripped anklets and chains and golden-hilted scimitars, not to mention richly embroidered clothes which, amongst so much of greater value, seemed of no account. Everything which the helots could not conceal – and that was a great deal – they declared to their superiors; but there was a great deal, too, which they stole and sold afterwards to the Aeginetans, who, by buying the gold at the price of brass (which the helots supposed it to be), laid the foundation of their future wealth.

When all the stuff had been collected, a tenth was set apart for the God at Delphi, and from this was made the gold tripod which stands next the altar on the three-headed bronze snake:[1] portions were also assigned to the Gods at Olympia and the Isthmus, and from these were made, in the first case, a bronze Zeus, fifteen feet high, and, in the second, a bronze Poseidon, nine and a half feet high. The rest of the booty – the Persians' women, pack-animals, gold, silver, and so on – was divided amongst the troops, every man receiving his due. There is no record of any special awards for distinguished service in the battle, but I imagine that they must have been made. Pausanias himself was granted ten of everything – women, horses, camels, and everything else.

It is said that Xerxes on his retreat from Greece left his tent with Mardonius. When Pausanias saw it, with its embroidered hangings and gorgeous decorations in silver and gold, he summoned Mardonius' bakers and cooks and told them to prepare a meal of the same sort as they were accustomed to prepare for their former master. The order was obeyed; and when Pausanias saw gold and silver couches all beautifully draped, and gold and silver tables, and everything prepared for the feast with great magnificence, he could hardly believe his eyes for the good things set before him, and, just for a joke, ordered his own servants to get ready an ordinary Spartan dinner. The difference between the two meals was indeed remarkable, and, when both were ready, Pausanias laughed and sent for the Greek commanding officers. When they arrived, he invited them to take a look at the two tables, saying, 'Gentlemen, I asked you here in order to show you the folly of the Persians, who, living in this style, came to Greece to rob us of our poverty.'

Long after these events many people in Plataea found coffers full of gold, silver, and other valuables. Another interesting thing also came to light: when the flesh had fallen away from the bodies of the Persian dead, and the Plataeans were collecting the skeletons, a skull was found with no join in it – the bone being seamless and continuous; a jaw, too, was picked up, which had all the teeth, front and back, joined together in a continuous line of bone; also the skeleton of a man of seven and a half feet high.

1. The Serpent Column, removed under the Christian empire to Constantinople and, headless and half buried, still to be seen there in the Hippodrome (At-Meidan).

The body of Mardonius disappeared the day after the battle; but I cannot say with certainty who it was that took it away. I have heard of many people of all sorts who are said to have buried him, and I know that many have received substantial rewards from his son Artontes for doing so; none the less, I am unable to satisfy myself which of them it really was that removed the body and buried it. One story has it that it was a man from Ephesus named Dionyso- phanes. In any case it appears that he *was* buried somehow.

After the distribution of the booty the Greeks proceeded to bury their own dead, those from each contingent in a separate grave. The Lacedaemonians made three graves – one for the priests,[1] amongst whom were Posidonius, Amompharetus, Philocyon, and Callitraces; another for the rest of the Spartans; and a third for the helots. The Tegeans buried all their dead in a common grave; so did the Athen- ians, and the Megarians and Phleiasians buried together those who had been killed by the cavalry.

Unlike these tombs, which were real ones containing the bodies of the dead, all the other funeral mounds which are to be seen at Plataea were, so far as my information goes, erected merely for show:[2] they are empty, and were put up to impress posterity by the various states who were ashamed of having taken no part in the battle. There is one tomb there, bearing the name of the Aeginetans, which I am told was constructed at their request ten years after the battle by Cleades, the son of Autodicus, and representative of Aeginetan interests in Plataea.

After the burial of the dead, a conference was held at which it was decided to attack Thebes and demand the surrender of all those who had gone over to the Persians, especially the two teachers, Tima- genides and Attaginus. In the event of a refusal, it was determined to continue the siege of the town until it fell. Accordingly, on the eleventh day after the battle, the siege of Thebes was begun, and the

1. These, like the priests of ancient Rome (such as Julius Caesar), would be chosen from among aristocratic families. Some editors change the manuscript reading *irées* (priests) to *irénes* (young soldiers), a word which a later dictionary alleges to occur in Herodotus, but not found in our mss. Since Amompharetus was commanding one of the five Spartan regiments, and Sparta was not renowned for quick promotion of the young, this is most unlikely. More probably the lexicographer had a wrong reading.

2. See Introduction, p. 36.

demand for the surrender of the traitors sent in. The demand was refused, and the besieging forces proceeded to assault the walls and devastate the surrounding country. For twenty days the devastation continued, and then Timagenides made a proposal to his fellow-townsmen. 'The Greeks,' he said, 'are determined not to raise the siege until either the town is taken or you hand us over. Very well, then: Boeotia must not suffer any longer just because of us. If what they really want is money, and the demand for the surrender of our persons is only a pretext, then let us give them money out of the public funds – for it was with public approval that we joined the Persians; if, on the contrary, it is we whom they want, we will give ourselves up to answer their charges.' The suggestion seemed to meet the case admirably, so the Thebans at once sent a message to Pausanias to the effect that they were willing to hand the men over. The terms were no sooner agreed upon than Attaginus made his escape from the town; his sons, however, were seized and taken to Pausanias, who refused to condemn them, on the ground that mere boys could not be held responsible for treachery. The other men whom the Thebans surrendered expected to get a chance to defend themselves and hoped, in that case, to secure acquittal by bribery; but Pausanias, who had a pretty good idea of what was in their minds, had no sooner laid hands on them than he dismissed the whole confederate army, and took the the men to Corinth, where he had them executed. So much for events at Plataea and Thebes.

Artabazus, the son of Pharnaces, who had made his escape from Plataea, was already some distance on his way. In Thessaly he was hospitably received, and questions were asked him about the rest of the Persian army, for no news of Plataea had yet come in. Artabazus was well aware that, if he told the truth, both he and his men would be in imminent danger, as everyone who learned of the course events had taken would be sure to attack them. Accordingly, as he had already done in the case of the Phocians, he gave nothing away in his answer to the Thessalians' question. 'As you can see,' he said, 'I am on my way, in a great hurry, to Thrace, whither I have orders to take this detachment on a special mission. Mardonius and his men are close on my heels, and may be expected at any moment; when he comes, mind you entertain him with the same friendliness as you have shown to me – you will never have cause to regret it.' He then continued his march straight for Thrace, by the inland route through Thessaly and Macedonia – for he was, in point of fact, in a very great hurry indeed. He reached Byzantium, but not without severe losses; for many of his men were cut down on the way by the Thracians, and many succumbed to hunger and exhaustion. From Byzantium he crossed the water by boat, and so reached Asia.

It so happened that the Persians suffered a further defeat at Mycale in Ionia on the same day as their defeat at Plataea. While the Greek fleet under Leotychides the Spartan was lying at Delos, three men arrived from Samos with a message; they were Lampon, the son of Thrasycles, Athenagoras, the son of Archestratides, and Hegesistratus, the son of Aristagoras, and had been sent by the Samians without the knowledge either of the Persians or of Theomestor, the son of Androdamas, whom the Persians had set up as despot. They came to the commanders, and Hegesistratus appealed to them with all sorts of arguments, declaring that the mere sight of a Greek naval force would be enough to make the Ionians revolt, and that the Persians would offer no resistance to it – or, if they did, that they would provide the Greeks with as rich a prize as they were ever likely to get. Then, in the name of all that Greece held sacred, he urged them to save the Ionians, men of the same blood as themselves, from slavery, and expel the foreigner. 'It will be easy enough,' he said. 'The Persian ships are unhandy and no match for yours. Moreover, if you suspect us of treachery, we are willing to offer ourselves as hostages and to sail with you.' As the stranger from Samos continued to press his appeal with the greatest importunity, Leotychides – either by chance, or because he really hoped that the answer might prove an omen of success – asked wha t his name was. 'Hegesistratus,'[1] the man replied; whereupon Leotychides cut short anything else he might have had in mind to say, and cried: 'My Samian friend, I accept the omen! And now, before you and your two companions sail away, give us a pledge that the people of Samos will grant us their wholehearted support.' No sooner were the words spoken than the oath was administered; the Samians took it at once, and a spoken compact

1. i.e. 'Leader of the Host'.

of mutual support was made. Two of the strangers then left; the third, Hegesistratus, was ordered to sail with the Greek fleet, as Leotychides thought that his name – 'Leader of the Host' – would be a good omen.

The Greeks stayed where they were for the rest of that day, and on the following offered the usual sacrifice, with good results. Their diviner was Deiphonus, the son of Euenius of Apollonia in the Ionian gulf. Euenius' story was an odd one, and I will here relate it. In Apollonia there is a flock of sheep sacred to the sun; during the day-time these sheep graze along the banks of the river which rises on Mt Lacmon, and, after running through Apollonian territory, joins the sea by the harbour of Oricus; at night, however, they are looked after by men specially chosen from the wealthiest and most distinguished families – each man having one year's spell of duty. The people of Apollonia value these sheep very highly because of an oracle they once received concerning them. The place where they are penned for the night is a cave, a long way from the town, and here it was that Euenius, who had been chosen for the task, was keeping watch. One night he fell asleep on duty, and some wolves got in and killed about sixty of the sheep. When, on waking, he saw what had happened, Euenius kept silent and told nobody about it, intending to buy some more to make good the losses; but the people of the town got to know of the disaster, and at once brought the culprit to trial and condemned him to have his eyes put out for sleeping at his post. The sentence was carried out, and immediately afterwards the sacred ewes had no more lambs, and the land ceased to produce the normal harvests. The oracles both at Dodona and Delphi were consulted upon the reason for this calamity, and the answer in each case was that it was due to the fact that Euenius, the guardian of the sacred sheep, had been unjustly deprived of his sight: it was the gods themselves who had set the wolves on the sheep, and they would continue to punish the people of Apollonia for the wrong they had done Euenius, until they made him such amends as he himself might choose; and when this was done, they, too, would give him something, for the possession of which many men would call him blessed. The people of the town did not make this oracle generally known, but instructed certain men to carry out the arrangements with Euenius, which they did in the following way. They went up to him as he was sitting on a bench, and, taking their seats beside him, entered into conversation on various topics, leading up to an expression of sympathy for his misfortune. Having thus drawn him on, they asked him what he would choose by way of reparation, should the townspeople undertake to offer it. Euenius, who knew nothing of the oracle, replied that if he were given So-and-so's land (naming the men whom he knew to possess the two best estates in the community), and a certain house, which he also knew was the finest in the town, he would consider that adequate reparation had been made, and would bear no further resentment. 'Euenius,' came the answer, 'the citizens of Apollonia will grant what you ask, in compensation for the loss of your eyes, according to the advice of the oracle.' On learning the whole story, Euenius was angry at what he considered to be the deception which had been practised on him. The townspeople, however, bought the house and the two estates from their owners, and gave them to him; and immediately afterwards he received an implanted power of divination, so that he became a famous man.

The son of this Euenius was Deiphonus, who was brought by the Corinthians to act as diviner for the fleet. I have also heard a different story, according to which Deiphonus was not Euenius' son at all, but merely assumed the name and got work in various parts of Greece on the strength of it.

Once the ritual of sacrifice seemed to portend success, the Greek fleet got under way from Delos and sailed for Samos. Here the ships brought up near Calami, off the temple of Hera which stands there, and preparations were made for action. The Persians, however, learning of their approach, dismissed their Phoenician contingent and themselves made off towards the Asiatic coast; for they had decided after discussing the matter that, as they were no match for the Greek fleet, they had better not risk an engagement. Accordingly they sailed to Mycale on the mainland, where they could have the protection of their own troops which, at Xerxes' orders, had been detached from the main army to guard Ionia. This force was 60,000 strong, and commanded by Tigranes, the tallest and best-looking man in the Persian army. Their plan was to beach their vessels under the protection of these troops, and to construct a defensive rampart round them, within which they could themselves take refuge, should occasion arise.

With this purpose in mind they set sail, and after passing the temple of the Eumenides arrived at Gaeson and Scolopoeis in Mycale, where there is a temple sacred to Demeter of Eleusis; the temple was built by Philistus, the son of Pasicles, when he accompanied Neileus, the son of Codrus, on the expedition for the founding of Miletus. Here they beached the ships and threw up a wall of stone and timber round them, cutting down fruit-trees in the neighbourhood and adding an outer ring of sharpened stakes, so that all was ready to stand a siege.

The Greeks were much vexed when they discovered that the Persians had given them the slip and cleared out for the mainland, and could not at once decide whether to return home or sail for the Hellespont. Finally, however, they decided to do neither, but to make for the Asiatic coast. All gear – boarding-gangways and so on – necessary for a naval engagement was put in readiness, and the fleet sailed for Mycale. No enemy vessel was to be seen coming out to meet them as they approached the Persian position; on the contrary, they saw that all his ships had been hauled ashore within the protection of the palisade, and that a strong infantry force was drawn up along the beach. In these circumstances Leotychides took his ship as close in-shore as he could, and, as he passed along, got a crier to shout the following appeal to the Ionians who were serving with the enemy: 'Men of Ionia, listen, if you can hear me, to what I have to say. The Persians, in any case, won't understand a word of it. When the battle begins, let each man of you first remember Freedom – and secondly our password, *Hera*. Anyone who can't hear me should be told what I say by those who can.' In this he had the same intention as Themistocles had at Artemisium. Either the Persians would not know what he had said and the Ionians would be persuaded to leave them, or if his words were reported to the Persians they would mistrust their Greek subjects.

Immediately after this appeal the Greeks ran their ships ashore and the troops took up positions on the beach. The first act of the Persians, when they saw the Greeks preparing to fight, was to disarm the Samians, whom they suspected of sympathy with the Greek cause; for it was a fact that when certain Athenians, caught in Attica by Xerxes' men, had been brought over in Persian ships as prisoners, the Samians had released them and sent them back to Athens with provision for their journey. This – the fact of their having rescued five hundred of Xerxes' enemies – was the chief cause of their being suspect. Next, the Persian command ordered the Milesians to guard the passes which lead up to the heights of Mycale – ostensibly because the Milesians were familiar with that part of the country, but actually to get them well out of the way. Then, having taken these precautions against the Ionians who they thought might cause trouble if they got the chance, they proceeded to make their own dispositions – a defensive line protected by a barrier of interlocking shields.

The Greeks, on their side, moved forward against the enemy as soon as their preparations were complete. During the advance, a herald's staff was found on the edge of the beach, close to the water, and at the same time a rumour flew through the ranks that the Greeks had beaten Mardonius in Boeotia. Many things make it plain to me that the hand of God is active in human affairs – for how else could it be, when the Persian defeat at Mycale was about to take place on the same day as his defeat at Plataea, that a rumour of that kind should reach the Greek army, giving every man greater courage for the coming battle and a fiercer determination to risk his life for his country? It was another odd coincidence that both battles should have been fought near a precinct of Demeter of Eleusis – for, as I have already mentioned, the fighting at Plataea was in the immediate neighbourhood of Demeter's temple; and the same thing was to happen at Mycale. Moreover, the rumour that Pausanias' men had already been victorious at Plataea was perfectly correct; for Plataea was fought early in the day, but the action at Mycale did not take place until evening: and the fact of this concurrence of dates – the same day of the same month – was proved when they reckoned back a short time afterwards. Before the report of Plataea reached them, there was profound misgiving amongst the troops, not so much on their own account as for the fate of Greece at the hands of Mardonius; but once the good news came, they moved to the assault with better heart and quicker pace. And so it was that both sides were eager to come to grips, knowing that the stake for which they were fighting was control of the Hellespont and the Aegean islands.

Now the Athenians, with the troops next to them, approximately as far as the centre, had to advance along the beach and across flat ground, but the route of the Lacedaemonians and those next them lay up a watercourse and over high hills. Consequently the Athenians were already engaged, while the Lacedaemonians were still on their way round. The Persians, so long as their line of shields remained intact, successfully repelled all attacks and had by no means the worst of things; soon, however, the Athenians and their neighbours in line, wanting the credit for the day's work for themselves rather than for the Spartans, passed along the word and made great effort – and from that moment it was a very different matter. They burst through the line of shields and fell upon the enemy in a mass assault. For a time, indeed, the assault was held, but in the end the Persians were forced to retreat within the protection of their barricade. The Athenians (this was their order in line) and men of Corinth, Sicyon, and Troezen, forced their way inside on the heels of the enemy. That was the end; for once the barricade had fallen, the enemy made no further serious resistance; all of them turned and fled, except only the Persians, who, in scattered groups, continued to fight against the Greeks who were still pouring in through the breach in the barricade.

Of the Persian high officers two, Artaÿntes and Ithamitres, who were in command of the fleet, escaped; Mardontes and the army commander Tigranes were killed fighting. The Lacedaemonians arrived with the rest of their division while the Persian troops were still holding out, and took their share in what remained of the fighting. The Greek losses were also considerable, especially amongst the Sicyonians, whose commander Perilaus was killed. The Samians who were serving with the Persians and had been disarmed, seeing right from the start that the result of the battle was in doubt, did all they could to help the Greeks, and the other Ionians, following the Samian lead, deserted their Persian masters and attacked them. The Milesians, as I have said, had received orders to watch the hill-tracks as a precautionary measure to enable them to act as guides to the safety of the hills, in the event of any disaster to the Persians such as in fact occurred. They had also, it will be remembered, been assigned this task for another reason – namely to prevent them from causing trouble in the Persian army; in any case, what they actually did was the exact opposite of their orders; for when the Persians were trying to escape, they led them the wrong way, by tracks which brought them back amongst the enemy, and finally joined in the slaughter and proved their bitterest enemies. Thus this day saw the second Ionian revolt from Persian domination.

The Athenian troops distinguished themselves more than any others in this battle, and the most conspicuous amongst them was Hermolycus, the son of Euthynus, a champion all-in wrestler. Some years later, when Athens was at war with Carystus, he was killed in action at Cyrnus, in Carystian territory, and was buried on Geraestus. After the Athenians, the greatest distinction was won by the men from Corinth, Troezen, and Sicyon.

When most of the enemy forces had been cut to pieces, either in the battle or during the rout, the Greeks burnt the Persian ships and the fort, having first removed everything of value, including a number of money-chests, to a place of safety on the beach. They then sailed for Samos, and on their arrival there held a council upon the future of Ionia. The idea was to remove the Ionians and resettle them in some part of Greece which was under their own control, and to abandon Ionia itself to the Persians. They did not think it was possible to be for ever on the watch in order to protect Ionia, and at the same time there was little hope, failing such perpetual vigilance, of the Ionians escaping Persian vengeance for their revolt. It was accordingly proposed by the Peloponnesian leaders to turn out the Greeks who had supported Persia and settle the Ionians in their commercial centres; the Athenians, however, strongly disapproved; for they had no wish to see Ionia depopulated, quite apart from their feeling that Peloponnesians had no right to discuss the future of Athenian colonists. They expressed their disapproval with great vigour, and the Peloponnesians gave way. Thus they brought into the confederacy the Samians, Chians, Lesbians, and other island peoples who had fought for Greece against the foreigner; oaths were sworn, and all these communities bound themselves to be loyal to the common cause. This done, the fleet sailed for the Hellespont with the purpose of destroying the bridges, which, it was supposed, were still in position.

The small remnant of the Persian force which had escaped destruction and taken refuge in the hills of Mycale, now made its way to Sardis. During the march Darius' son Masistes, who by chance had witnessed the disaster, had words with Artaÿntes, the general. He abused him roundly, and, to crown all, told him his leadership was worse than a woman's, and that there was no punishment too bad for the hurt he had done to the king's house. To call a man 'worse than a woman' is, of course, the greatest insult one can offer a Persian; so Artaÿntes, after listening for a while, drew his scimitar in rage and would have killed Masistes but for the prompt action of a certain Xenagoras. This man – he was a Halicarnassian and the son of Praxilaus – was standing behind Artaÿntes and, seeing him about to rush forward, caught him round the middle and dashed him to the ground, thus giving time to Masistes' bodyguard to get into a position to defend him. This action won Xenagoras the favour not only of Masistes himself but also of Xerxes, whose brother he had saved; and he was rewarded for it by a gift from Xerxes of the governorship of the whole province of Cilicia. Nothing else of interest occurred during the march. The army ultimately reached Sardis, where the king had been ever since his retreat from Athens after the defeat at Salamis.

During his stay at Sardis Xerxes fell in love with Masistes' wife, who was also there. He sent her various messages, but without success, and at the same time was unwilling to resort to compulsion out of respect for his brother Masistes. The woman was well aware of this, and no doubt her knowledge that Xerxes would not dare to force her, helped her to hold out against him. Xerxes, therefore, gave up his other ways of approach, and arranged a marriage between a daughter of Masistes and this woman and his own son Darius, under the impression that by this means he would be more likely to get her. The betrothal took place with all the usual ceremonies, and Xerxes left Sardis for Susa. At Susa he received the girl – whose name was Artaÿnte – into his own house as his son's bride, with the result that he forgot the mother and transferred his affections to the daughter – now the wife of Darius. This time his passion was successful. But as time went on the connection came to light in the following way: Xerxes' wife Amestris gave him a long robe, of many colours and very beautiful, which she had woven with her own hands. Much pleased, he put it on, and, still wearing it, went to visit Artaÿnte – who pleased him no less, with the result that he told her to ask for anything she fancied as a reward for her favours, and he would assuredly grant it. Artaÿnte, who must have been doomed to come to a bad end, together with all her house, asked in reply if the king really meant to give her whatever she demanded, and Xerxes, never suspecting what the request would be, pledged his word to do so. Thereupon she boldly demanded the robe. Xerxes did everything he could think of to get out of giving it, simply because he was afraid of Amestris, who already guessed what was going on and would now, he feared, find her suspicions confirmed. He offered her cities, gold in unlimited quantity, an army – a thoroughly Persian gift – under her sole command; but all in vain – nothing would do but the robe. So he gave it her, and she, in great delight, put it on, and gloried in wearing it.

When Amestris found out, as she soon did, that Artaÿnte had the robe, it was not against her that her anger was directed. On the contary, she thought that the girl's mother, Masistes' wife, was the person responsible for the whole trouble, and consequently plotted her destruction. She waited for the day when her husband the king gave his Royal Supper – a ceremony which occurs once a year, on the king's birthday. The Persian word for the supper is *tycta*, a word equivalent, in our language, to *perfect*; it is the one occasion in the year when the king anoints his head and gives presents to the Persians. Then, when the day for the supper came, she asked Xerxes for her present – Masistes' wife. Xerxes, who understood the reason for her request, was horrified, not only at the thought of handing over his brother's wife, but also because he knew she was innocent. But Amestris persisted – and, moreover, the law of the Supper demanded that no one, on that day, might be refused his request; so at last, much against his will, Xerxes was forced to consent. Then, having told his wife to do with the woman what she pleased, he sent for his brother. 'Masistes,' he said, 'you are my brother and Darius' son; in addition to that, you are a good man. Do not live any longer with your present wife – I will give you my own daughter instead. Marry her: part with your present wife – I do not approve of your keeping her.'

'My lord,' replied Masistes in astonishment, 'this is indeed a strange proposal! What is the use in your telling me to get rid of a wife who is the mother of grown-up sons and daughters – one of whom you married to your own son – and who is, moreover, everything I could wish for, and to marry your daughter instead? No, sire; I will do neither of these things, proud though I am that you should think me worthy of your daughter. Do not, I beg, force this request upon me; but let me live with my wife in peace. You will find another man as good as I am for your daughter.'

Xerxes was angry at this reply. 'Very well, then,' he cried, 'I will tell you, Masistes, what you have done for yourself: I no longer offer you the chance of marrying my daughter – nor will you live another day with that wife of yours. Thus may you learn to accept a proffered gift.'

'Master,' said Masistes, 'you have not killed me yet!' And without another word he left the room.

Meantime, while Xerxes was talking to his brother, Amestris sent for the soldiers of the royal bodyguard and had Masistes' wife horribly mutilated. Her breasts, nose, ears, and lips were cut off and thrown to the dogs; then her tongue was torn out and, in this dreadful condition, she was sent home. Masistes, who knew as yet nothing of what had happened, but suspected mischief of some sort, hurried to his house; and when he saw his wife's fearful injuries, at once he took counsel with his sons and with them and certain other friends set off for Bactria, with the intention of stirring up revolt in the province and of so doing serious harm to the king. He would, I think, undoubtedly have succeeded had he had time to reach the Bactrians and Sacae; for he was greatly beloved by both, and was, moreover, governor of Bactria. But Xerxes discovered his purpose and sent an armed force in pursuit, which caught him on the road and killed him together with his sons and all the men under his command. So ends the story of Xerxes' love and the death of Masistes.

The Greeks who sailed for the Hellespont from Mycale after being delayed for a time by foul winds at Lectum, reached Abydos and found, contrary to expectation, that the bridges had already been broken up – to destroy them had, indeed, been the chief purpose of their coming. In these circumstances Leotychides and his Peloponnesians thought that the best thing to do was to return to Greece, but the Athenians under their commander Xanthippus determined to stay where they were and make an attempt upon the Chersonese. Accordingly, after the departure of the Peloponnesians, they crossed thither from Abydos and laid siege to Sestos. This town was the most strongly fortified place in the district, and as soon as the news got about that the Greek fleet had arrived in the Hellespont, men from neighbouring towns came into it for refuge; amongst them was the Persian Oeobazus, who came from Cardia, where he had stored the cables used in the construction of the bridges. The town was held by its own native Aeolians, but there were Persians in it too, and a large number of their allies and dependants. The governor of the district for Xerxes was one Artaÿctes – a terrible fellow, as clever as he was corrupt. By a pretty piece of knavery, during Xerxes' march to Athens, he had got possession of the treasures of Protesilaus, son of Iphiclus, which were at Elaeus in the Chersonese, where the tomb of that hero stands, surrounded by a plot of sacred ground. There was much here of great value, gold and silver cups, bronze, rich garments, and other things which had been offered at the tomb, and Artaÿctes stole it all. Actually, he tricked Xerxes into giving it to him, by saying: 'Master, there is the house of a Greek here who made war on your country and met the death which he deserved. Give me his house – it will be a lesson to men hereafter not to do as he did.' It was only to be expected that these words should easily persuade Xerxes to give him the 'house' – for he had no suspicion of what was really in Artaÿctes' mind. Artaÿctes was right, in a certain sense, in saying that Protesilaus made war on the king's country; for the Persians consider that the whole of Asia belongs to them, and to their reigning king. So the request was granted, and Artaÿctes removed the treasures to Sestos and turned over the sacred enclosure to agriculture – and, what is more, whenever he visited Elaeus on subsequent occasions he used to keep his harem in the sanctuary.

So now Artaÿctes was blocked up in Sestos by the Athenians. He was not prepared for a siege and had not expected the arrival of a Greek army, which consequently caught him unawares. As the siege dragged on into the autumn, the Athenians, impatient at their long absence from home and their failure to take the place, pressed their officers to abandon the enterprise, but they refused to do so until either the town fell or they were recalled by the government in

Athens. So the troops had to put up with their hardships. Inside the town, the besieged were already reduced to the direst extremity – even to boiling and eating the leather straps of their beds. When these, too, gave out, the Persians, with Artaÿctes and Oeobazus, made their escape under cover of darkness, letting themselves down from the wall at the back of the town, where the enemy lines were weakest; and on the following day the men of the Chersonese signalled to the Athenians from the bastions to let them know what had happened, and opened the gates. The greater part of the Athenian force thereupon went in pursuit of the fugitives, while the remainder took possession of the town.

Oeobazus managed to reach Thrace; but there he was caught by the Apsinthian Thracians who offered him, as their manner is, as a sacrifice to Pleistorus, a local deity. The men with him were killed in another way. Those who accompanied Artaÿctes left the town later, and their small party was overtaken by their pursuers not far from Aegospotami. They made a stout fight of it, but all of them, in the end, were either killed or taken prisoner. The prisoners were tied up and taken back to Sestos, Artaÿctes and his son amongst them. There is a story current in the Chersonese that one of the prisoners' guards was roasting salt fish when the fish began to jump and struggle on the coals, as if they had been freshly caught. Everyone came crowding round to see this extraordinary sight; but Artaÿctes called the sentry who was cooking the fish and told him not to be alarmed. 'This prodigy,' he said, 'has no reference to you, my Athenian friend. It applies to me: Protesilaus of Elaeus is telling me that though he is as dead as dried fish, he yet has power from the gods to punish the man who wrongs him. Look now; I am willing to pay him a hundred talents in compensation for the treasure I took from the shrine, and I will pay the Athenians two hundred, on condition that they spare my life and the life of my son.'

Such was Artaÿctes' offer; but Xanthippus, the Athenian commander, refused to accept it. The people of Elaeus wanted their revenge for Protesilaus, and urged his death; moreover Xanthippus' own feelings were in sympathy with them. So they took him to the spit of land where Xerxes' bridge had been – or, as some say, to the hill above the town of Madytus – and there they nailed him to a plank and hung him up. His son was stoned to death before his eyes. This done, the fleet set sail for Greece with all sorts of stuff on board, including the cables of the bridges, which the Athenians proposed to dedicate as an offering in their temples. And that was all that happened during the course of the year.

This Artaÿctes who suffered death by crucifixion had an ancestor named Artembares; and he it was who made the Persians a proposal, which they readily accepted and passed on to Cyrus. 'Since,' they said, 'God has given empire to the Persians, and among individuals to you, Cyrus, by your conquest of Astyages, let us leave this small and barren country of ours and take possession of a better. There are plenty to choose from – some near, some further off; if we take one of them, we shall be admired more than ever. It is the natural thing for a sovereign people to do; and when will there be a better opportunity than now, when we are masters of many nations and all Asia?'

Cyrus did not think much of this suggestion; he replied that they might act upon it if they pleased, but added the warning that, if they did so, they must prepare themselves to rule no longer, but to be ruled by others. 'Soft countries,' he said, 'breed soft men. It is not the property of any one soil to produce fine fruits and good soldiers too.' The Persians had to admit that this was true and that Cyrus was wiser than they; so they left him, and chose rather to live in a rugged land and rule than to cultivate rich plains and be subject to others.

THE END

MAPS

Greece
and Western Asia Minor

THRACE

Hebrus R.

Bosphorus

Byzantium

Abdera   Doriscus

Calchedon

THASOS

PROPONTIS

SAMOTHRACE

MELAS

Sestos

IMBROS   Abydos

ATHOS   CHERSONESE

Hellespont   MYSIA

LEMNOS

AEGEAN

LESBOS   Atarneus

LYDIA

Phocaea

SCYROS   Hermus R.

Sardis

CHIOS   Smyrna

SEA

EUBOEA   R. Cayster

Ephesus

CEOS   ANDROS   SAMOS   Priene   CARIA

MYCALE

R. Maeander

DELOS   Miletus

PAROS   Halicarnassus

NAXOS

COS   LYCIA

MELOS

THERA   RHODES

CARPATHUS

CRETE   Miles

0   100

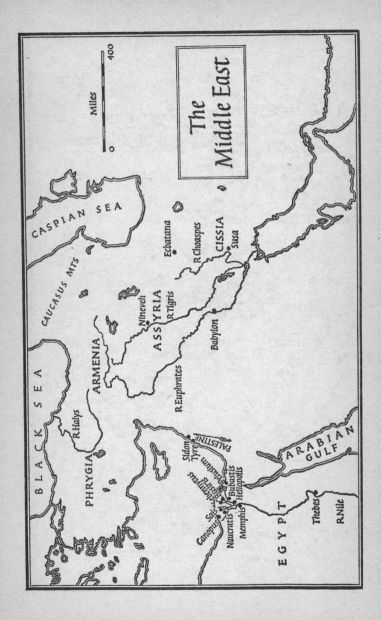

The Middle East

Miles
0   400

CASPIAN SEA

CAUCASUS MTS

BLACK SEA

R.Halys

ARMENIA

PHRYGIA

ASSYRIA

Nineveh
R.Tigris

Babylon

R.Euphrates

Ecbatana
R.Choaspes

CISSIA
Susa

Sidon
Tyre
PALESTINE
Pelusium
Canopus
Bubastis
Heliopolis
Sais
Busiris
Naucratis
Memphis
Canopus

ARABIAN GULF

EGYPT

Thebes
R.Nile

INDEX

INDEX

THE PENGUIN CLASSICS

Some recent and forthcoming volumes

MORE ABOUT PENGUINS
AND PELICANS

Penguinews, which appears every month, contains details of all the new books issued by Penguins as they are published. From time to time it is supplemented by *Penguins in Print*, which is our complete list of almost 5,000 titles.

A specimen copy of *Penguinews* will be sent to you free on request. Please write to Dept EP, Penguin Books Ltd, Harmondsworth, Middlesex, for your copy.

In the U.S.A.: For a complete list of books available from Penguins in the United States write to Dept CS, Penguin Books, 625 Madison Avenue, New York, New York 10022.

In Canada: For a complete list of books available from Penguins in Canada write to Penguin Books Canada Ltd, 41 Steelcase Road West, Markham, Ontario.